SPIDER'S WEB

SPIDER'S WEB

The Secret History of How the White House Illegally Armed Iraq

ALAN FRIEDMAN

BANTAM BOOKS
NEW YORK · TORONTO · LONDON · SYDNEY · AUCKLAND

SPIDER'S WEB
A Bantam Book/December 1993

The excerpt from "Gerontion" is reprinted by
permission of Faber and Faber Ltd. and
Harcourt Brace & Company Inc. from
Collected Poems 1909–1962 by T. S. Eliot.

Library of Congress Cataloging-in-Publication Data

Friedman, Alan, 1956–
Spider's web : the secret history of how the White House illegally
armed Iraq / by Alan Friedman.
p.   cm.
Includes index.
ISBN 0-553-09650-8
1. United States—Foreign relations—Iraq.   2. Iraq—Foreign
relations—United States.   3. Military assistance. American—Iraq.
I.   Title.
E183.8.I57F75   1993
327.730567—dc20   93-36578
                                                   CIP

Published simultaneously in the United States and Canada

Bantam Books are published by Bantam Books, a division of Bantam
Doubleday Dell Publishing Group, Inc. Its trademark, consisting of the
words "Bantam Books" and the portrayal of a rooster, is Registered in
U.S. Patent and Trademark Office and in other countries. Marca Regis-
trada. Bantam Books, 1540 Broadway, New York, New York 10036.

PRINTED IN THE UNITED STATES OF AMERICA
BVG   0 9 8 7 6 5 4 3 2 1

For Dizzi

After such knowledge, what forgiveness? Think now
History has many cunning passages, contrived corridors
And issues, deceives with whispering ambitions,
Guides us by vanities. Think now
She gives when our attention is distracted
And what she gives, gives with such supple confusions
That the giving famishes the craving. Gives too late
What's not believed in, or if still believed,
In memory only, reconsidered passion. Gives too soon
Into weak hands, what's thought can be dispensed with
Till the refusal propagates a fear. Think
Neither fear nor courage saves us. Unnatural vices
Are fathered by our heroism. Virtues
Are forced upon us by our impudent crimes.
These tears are shaken from the wrath-bearing tree.

—T. S. ELIOT, "Gerontion"

CONTENTS

AUTHOR'S NOTE

I tried to interview George Bush for this book, but I was informed that the former president is "out of the interview business." James Baker communicated to me through his public relations spokesperson, Margaret Tutwiler, that he had no comment for this book. Other former Reagan and Bush administration officials were more cooperative, although many would speak only if they were promised that their names would not appear in print. The same was true in London, where some very senior former government officials, including a cabinet minister, did not wish to be quoted on the record. In Rome, numerous extremely helpful sources in government and banking knew and at times personally experienced the story but preferred not to be named. I thank the dozens of sources in these three countries, named and unnamed, who believed enough in the importance of getting this story out to cooperate with information, comments, and documents.

Among those I can name, the single most important is John Fielding, the major collaborator on this book who has also become a good friend. I first met John, a senior producer at ABC News, in 1991 when we worked together on a joint ABC *Nightline/Financial Times* investigation of U.S. policies toward Iraq. During the preparation and writing of this book, John's tireless reporting, especially from Britain, proved invaluable, as did his camaraderie, his many suggestions, and his passionate encouragement for this project.

The other person without whom *Spider's Web* would not exist is Emanuela Minnai, an extraordinarily talented friend and colleague from Milan. Her creative input and collaboration in discussing the shape of various chapters and her valuable editing suggestions quite literally made it possible to get the job done.

This book, which has involved research in three countries and hundreds of interviews, has also been made possible by an investigative team that worked very hard, under great pressure, and over long periods of time. In Pennsylvania, Tom Flannery of the *Lancaster Intelligencer Journal,* who broke the story of James Guerin and his arms operation, helped mightily to make sense of this dark chapter in the history of the CIA. Tom has put himself on the line numerous times in the pursuit of this story, and he merits both the awards he has already won for his work on Guerin, and more. In London, Richard Donkin's reporting on the background of Britain's arms-to-Iraq scandal was superb and so was his devotion to this story; he is a truly fine investigative journalist. Susan Baumel's reporting in Washington filled in important gaps, and her fact-checking later in the project was meticulous. In New York, Rachel Ehrenfeld's assistance and advice were also much appreciated.

The project also benefited from the material support and encouragement provided by the Arca Foundation, where Janet Shenk and Smith Bagley showed nonpartisan enthusiasm. So did Tom Blanton, the director of the National Security Archive, and his team of first-rate researchers and staff, who helped make the book possible. Several anonymous donors also contributed generously to the completion of our work.

Special appreciation is due Robert Morgenthau, the Manhattan District Attorney, who provided friendship and counsel. His integrity and commitment to the cause of justice have long made him a model of public service.

At ABC, the support of Ted Koppel and Tom Bettag proved critical, as did the collegial assistance of *Nightline* colleagues such as Tara Sonenshine, Jay LaMonica, Gordon Platt, and Jay Weiss. Part of what we learned is also due to the excellent work put in during the joint ABC/FT investigation by ABC colleagues Scott Willis, Peter Demchuk, and Marilyn Fletcher. The research efforts of Madeline Cohen and her team were much appreciated.

Thanks are also due to Richard Lambert, the editor of the *Financial Times*, who permitted me to take several months of leave to complete the project, to Martin Dickson and Rivka Nachoma of the New York bureau, who provided encouragement and put up with a great deal of hassle; and to Lionel Barber, my friend and colleague who helped greatly in the early reporting of this story.

Others who contributed to the book either with advice or moral support include Doug Frantz, Jimmy Burns, Bob Fink, William Gowen, Tom Moran, Jim and Bonnie Crown, Roberto Lasagna, Massimo Riva, John Barry, Joe Trento, Adel Darwish, Ellen Samrock, Ferruccio

Petracco, and Otto Teitler, who sacrificed his summer house to ensure the book's success.

A special category of friends who read early drafts of the manuscript, helped with logistics, and made life more bearable deserve special thanks. They are Jonathan Ehrlich, Michael Tracey, Mitch Foushee, Mark Moskin, Phoebe Tait, Gareth Harris, Laura Incardona, and Chiara Clementi. The affection and understanding of my sister Anita, and of our parents Charles and Lilli Friedman, was a wonderful constant that helped to keep me going.

Ann Harris, my editor at Bantam Books in New York, deserves extra-special thanks; she displayed the devotion, grace, determination, and professionalism of an editor who truly cared about the final product. I am also grateful to Ann's assistant, Ilene Block, who kept us all going.

Bantam's president and publisher, Irwyn Applebaum, showed that even in this day of mass markets and mega-corporations, a senior publishing executive is allowed to believe in doing the right thing, in getting the story out. Stuart Applebaum, Bantam's publicity vice president, helped get that story out, quite literally and quite exceptionally. Lauren Field and Victor Kovner proved that lawyers can be editorially sensitive as well as demanding. Thanks also to Janet Biehl for her superb assistance.

In London, Matthew Evans and Susanne McDadd of Faber and Faber kept the faith for many months and showed what a truly independent publisher can achieve.

In Milan, it is a pleasure to be publishing my third volume with Mario Spagnol and Lorenzo Pellizzari of Longanesi, both of whom are now like family.

Finally, for the faith he had in this book and this author, a very great word of thanks to Ed Victor, whose energies and talents go well beyond those normally associated with a literary agent.

A brief word is in order about two of the characters who appear in the first part of this book. Robert Johnson and Richard Smith are not the real names of the American operatives who were involved in the arming of Iraq; their names and the name of their company have been changed to protect their identities. This book aims to take the wraps off a decade of deceit, but there is no desire to expose intelligence community sources gratuitously.

Alan Friedman
New York City, September 1993

PROLOGUE

On a sultry Rome night in early September 1989, a large chauffeur-driven car sped down the Via Veneto, taking the curves on the wide and sloping boulevard so quickly that it would almost certainly have knocked down a score of tourists had this been daytime. It was, however, nearly three o'clock in the morning, and the streets of the city were deserted as the dark blue Alfa Romeo pulled silently past the gates of the American embassy. The car braked to a halt a few feet away, not far from the imposing gray marble headquarters of Italy's biggest bank, a great stone monument typical of 1930s Mussolini architecture.

Only one door was unlocked. A nervous and bespectacled bank executive, the sweat stains beneath his armpits running down his white shirt to his belt, bounded out of the car. He told the driver to wait, and in a flash he was inside the bank, waving to the night watchman. He inserted a metal key into the elevator control panel. Moments later, he stepped out on the second floor and made his way to a specially secured chamber. There, in a cavernous and high-ceilinged room, five lower-level bankers were gathered before a disc-reading computer. Only one of them was authorized to know and use the specially encrypted software program. The team, working around the clock, was busy analyzing data that included 130,000 pages of secret bank and government documents from the United States. So far, nobody knew what to make of the mysterious loan documents, letters, and telexes.

The nervous banker handed his top deputy a piece of paper with names of a handful of U.S. and British companies scrawled across it. "Check the computer for these!" he barked, without explaining why. The aide punched in the names and watched as the eight hundred-megabyte machine silently delivered a series of documents on the laser printer. The banker stared at the pages. He felt a peculiar dryness in his mouth and gave an involuntary shiver. "Holy Mother of Mary!" he muttered as his staff looked on in amazement. And then: "We must wake up the chairman, maybe the prime minister. We can all go to jail for this. The police and the secret services will take us away in the morning. This is Iraq's nuclear missile we have been funding. *Oh Maria! Oh Maria!*"

The traumatized banker calmed down eventually, but the institution he worked for—the Banca Nazionale del Lavoro—did not recover so quickly. The bank suffered losses of more than one billion dollars and was trapped at the center of an international scandal that would eventually lead investigators to question the secret policies and actions of Presidents Ronald Reagan and George Bush, Prime Minister Margaret Thatcher, and leading members of Italy's political class. The role of Western intelligence services such as the CIA and Britain's MI6 would figure in the story, as would a small body of clandestine foot soldiers who were used by their government patrons to assist members of an elaborate Iraqi arms procurement network that scoured the world searching for the technology to help Saddam Hussein toward his dream of turning Iraq into a nuclear power. Some of this technology, financed by the Italian bank through an obscure branch office in downtown Atlanta, Georgia, would end up being used to manufacture the very weapons that Saddam turned on the half-million allied troops who were sent to do battle in Operation Desert Storm. The official policy of the government of the United States, from the White House down, was to avoid the transfer of any goods that could bolster Saddam's war machine. The reality was decidedly different.

On the day in January 1981 when the Reagan administration took office, America was still gripped by the nightmare of the U.S. hostages trapped in Tehran; they were released literally at the moment that Jimmy Carter handed over the reins of government to Ronald Reagan. This hostage-taking by Ayatollah Khomeini's militants left deep scars on the national psyche, and followed two other collectively experienced events that had shaken America's confidence, the defeat in Vietnam and the agony of the Watergate affair. Khomeini and his fiery fundamentalism were anathema to Washington, which had previously put its faith—in the form of money and arms—in the Shah of Iran, the perennial strongman who had long served as the protector of American interests in the Persian Gulf region. Those interests, whether couched in political or strategic terms, began and ended with oil. And that is where Iraq's strongman, Saddam Hussein, entered the picture.

The philosophy of the Reagan White House was that although Saddam might be an odious figure, he was one who could prove acceptable as America's new regional policeman. He was also convenient, being a sworn rival of Iran and in control of vast oil reserves, and being a cynical deal-maker who welcomed American business, unhampered as he was by either religious fanaticism or political ideology. What is more, ever since September 1980 Saddam had been locked in a bloody war against Khomeini, a war that suited Washington's interests both in containing Islamic fundamentalism and in insuring that neither side was strong enough to exert hegemony over the Gulf. The war also made Saddam more desirous of Western military and financial help. Before then, Moscow had been his principal benefactor; thus, Washington reasoned, American assistance could have the additional benefit of drawing him away from the Soviet Union.

As the Iran-Iraq war dragged on for eight long years, the White House spent a disproportionate amount of time plotting strategies, both overt and covert, that would bolster Saddam. By the late 1980s, Iraq had become a vehicle for the White House, and soon the prime vehicle, for furthering U.S. economic and political interests in the Persian Gulf. The State Department put this in forthright terms in August 1988, in a secret memo on American concerns in the region that was sent to its embassies from Washington: "The U.S. has vital interests in the Persian Gulf. Access to oil at reasonable rates and blunting Soviet advances are strategic requirements. Trade, finance and development policies as well as the political orientation of each of the Gulf states is important to us . . . Iraq is our only improving market."

Thus had oil, money, and political power been mixed into a Molotov cocktail of Western policy toward Baghdad. In Washington throughout the decade, few policy-makers had more pro-Iraqi views than George Bush and James Baker. So convinced were they that American business interests would benefit from a close government relationship with Iraq that they turned a blind eye to the perils of treating Saddam Hussein as a friend. They believed that neither the public nor Congress could be trusted with the truth of America's deepening involvement with Saddam. They were the ones who knew what was best for America, they understood the politics of oil, and they believed Saddam could in some way be turned around, sweetened, made into a more reasonable junior partner. Bush and Baker were among the architects of a series of secret policies that committed American taxpayer dollars to assisting Saddam and allowed the reckless export of U.S. technology to some of the Iraqi dictator's most cherished and lethal weapons projects.

This deeply mistaken vision ultimately led to Saddam's near success at building an atomic weapon, and then to his conviction that Washington would not react if he invaded Kuwait. More than anyone else, Bush and Baker must bear responsibility for paving the road to Operation Desert Storm, a war they justified as necessary in order to wipe out the very nuclear weapons capacity the U.S. had helped foster in Iraq. There was also grand rhetoric about preserving the sovereignty of Kuwait, but the bottom line was once again Washington's determination to guarantee itself access to oil. Even as Bush basked in the glory of leading Operation Desert Storm, he was presiding over a systematic cover-up in order to avoid being embarrassed politically. The Bush administration's attempts to hide the truth about American policy was a more insidious threat to the proper functioning of democratic government than any weapon Saddam could have employed.

In the eight years before Bush took office in 1989, he had supported the Reagan administration's public posture of neutrality in the Gulf region even as it became involved in a remarkable series of clandestine operations that violated laws and stoked the flames of the war between Iran and Iraq. The same gap between public proclamations and secret policies existed in London and Rome, which increasingly coordinated their actions with Washington.

Operation Desert Storm cost the lives of twenty-six Americans and tens of thousands of Iraqis. It should also be remembered that the killing machine that these covert policies helped to build contributed to the death of one million people in the Iran-Iraq war, which ended two years before Saddam invaded Kuwait.

What were the forces that shaped the White House's persisting embrace of Saddam, a dictator whom George Bush would eventually compare to Adolf Hitler? How and why did Washington and its NATO allies in London and Rome nurture a frequently illicit rapport with Saddam, and how did they seek to cover up their past dealings with the Iraqi leader after he was finally driven from Kuwait in February 1991? The answers to these questions go far beyond Iraq, and they are both significant and disturbing.

If, as seems the case, leading political figures such as George Bush, James Baker, and Ronald Reagan condoned and fostered much of the financing, intelligence-sharing, and technology exports that built Saddam into so formidable a military threat that it took a war to tame him, then the American government was guilty of far greater duplicity than has been generally recognized. The secret history of how the White House, together with allies in Europe, brushed aside laws and officially stated policies to aid Saddam throughout the 1980s has implications more serious than would be the case if, as Bush has claimed, these were mere policy blunders. The truth is that the 1980s were a decade of deceit both at the White House and at Downing Street, a period during which accountability to Congress or Parliament was almost completely ignored and the abuse of power became the rule rather than the exception.

The evidence now gathered tells a sorry tale of that abuse of power by some of America's highest-level government officials and of the frequent disregard for established laws and constitutional procedures. The story needs telling because the 1980s were a period during which many of the most unsavory of these actions were considered to be business as usual. Only by understanding what happened will it be possible to learn the lessons that may prevent such actions in the future.

The discovery made by that nervous banker in Rome one night in September 1989 was more portentous than he could ever have imagined, and for a long time it seemed that the truth might remain under wraps. It is impossible, however, to keep some matters secret forever.

BOOK ONE

SPINNING THE WEB, 1981–1989

Misrule, you see, has caused the world to be malevolent.
DANTE, *Purgatorio*

ONE

The Tilt Takes Off

In the late afternoon of Sunday, June 7, 1981, a squadron of eight Israeli F-16 jets took off from an air base in the eastern Sinai and headed across the northern fringes of Saudi Arabia. Their secret flight plan soon brought them into Iraqi air space. Flying low, in less than an hour the pilots spotted their target: a nuclear reactor site located just twelve miles southeast of Baghdad. While six twin-engine interceptor jets provided protective cover, the F-16s dropped two two-thousand-pound bombs that punched holes into Saddam Hussein's most cherished nuclear project, the Osirak reactor. Then they unloaded ten additional bombs. The roof collapsed instantly, as did both the reactor's walls and its core, which contained twenty-six pounds of weapons-grade uranium, enough to fashion a crude nuclear weapon.

The preemptive strike shocked many, but it was the result of Israel's deep frustration at its apparent inability to get the Reagan administration to focus on the Iraqi nuclear project. The raid was based on a timetable that accorded with Iraq's own plans for Osirak; according to the Israelis, the reactor was scheduled to begin functioning by early July. For months they had been warning top aides to President Ronald Reagan that it posed a serious threat, but few in Washington wanted to hear about it. Most of Reagan's aides assumed the Israelis were simply exaggerating the extent of the Iraqi dictator's progress. Yet it was hardly a secret that Saddam was aiming to develop nuclear weapons. He had already shelled out $3 billion, purchasing much of the equipment from the French. Indeed, Saddam had even given an interview to a Lebanese journalist in 1975 in which he called his dealings with France "the first concrete step toward the production of the Arab atomic weapon."

Although Saddam had been obtaining most of his arms from the Soviet Union since the early 1970s, the top-of-the-line equipment he really craved was Western. So he had begun cultivating the Europeans, especially the French, and in September 1975 he found himself flying into Paris for a champagne reception offered by Prime Minister Jacques Chirac. It was not long before France, which saw billions of francs' worth of business just over the horizon, began selling Saddam missiles, helicopters, defense electronics, and ultimately the materials and technology he needed to construct a nuclear reactor. So obvious was his intended use of this technology that the French press even allowed itself some grim humor, referring to the Iraqi reactor as "O'Chirac." After he approved the Osirak deal and other weapons transactions for Baghdad, he became known in certain French business circles as "Mr. Iraq."

Within hours of the raid, aides to CIA director William Casey briefed him on it, and America's KH-11 "Big Bird" photoreconnaissance satellite was diverted from its normal orbit over the Soviet Union and China in order to assess the damage. The next day, President Reagan convened a meeting in the Oval Office to decide how the United States should respond. Among those assembled were Vice President George Bush, Reagan's chief of staff James Baker, Defense Secretary Caspar Weinberger, and Secretary of State Alexander Haig. What transpired during that Oval Office meeting has never been made public. According to Haig, it was far more than a mere discussion of what should be said in public about the Israeli action; it was effectively a high-level debate about how the Reagan administration should behave toward Saddam Hussein. George Bush and James Baker, both of whom would play a primary role in shaping Washington's policy toward Baghdad throughout the 1980s, helped to steer the debate.

"Reagan went around the room and asked each of us to give our opinion on the Osirak raid. I remember Bush and then Baker making it very clear that they thought Israel needed to be punished," Haig, who quickly found himself outflanked, later recalled. "Weinberger was also angry with the Israelis. When I was asked my opinion, I said we should be grateful and thank the Israelis for taking care of a potential nuclear problem down the road. My position was thank God they did it."

Pentagon officials were told right after the meeting that Weinberger was furious and wanted to punish Israel. Indeed, after the meeting, he persuaded President Reagan to delay the scheduled delivery of four F-16s that Israel had bought—ironically, the very same type of aircraft that had been used in the bombing of Osirak. Haig was not even informed of the decision, which was announced two days later, and he complained bitterly to President Reagan when he found out. The reality, however, difficult as it was for Haig to accept, was that Weinberger was part of the Reagan inner circle, and he was not.

The Pentagon chief perceived Iraq as America's secret ally in the struggle against the Ayatollah Khomeini's regime in Iran and the dangers posed by the possible spread of Islamic fundamentalism throughout the Persian Gulf. Weinberger, Bush, and Baker couched the threat in terms of national security, but what that really meant was giving support to Iraq to prevent Iran from challenging the security of navigation for oil tankers and American access to Middle East oil. Weinberger was a consistently strong advocate of strengthening U.S. ties with the Arab world and especially with Iraq.

In fact, from the early days of the Reagan administration, which took office just four months after the bloody war between the two countries began, a political battle was being fought inside the White House between the faction seeking to prop up Saddam and the one seeking reconciliation with Iran. U.S. policy toward the Persian Gulf was the prisoner of this internal policy strife, which the president did little to control. As one former White House official recalled: "There was substantially no leadership. Reagan was sleeping through it all."

Within days of the Oval Office meeting, Haig found himself losing still another policy battle. He discovered that Jeane Kirkpatrick, the U.S. ambassador to the United Nations, was secretly cooperating with Iraqi foreign minister Saadun Hamadi and Saleh Omar al-Ali, then Iraq's UN ambassador, in crafting a resolution that would condemn Israel. As the UN discussions went on, Haig found himself increasingly undercut by Kirkpatrick. A National Security Council official in the White House told her to sign the resolution, and she did so on June 19, 1981.

Haig hit the ceiling. The day after Kirkpatrick voted to condemn Israel at the United Nations, he stepped off a plane in Los Angeles and was driven to the Beverly Wilshire Hotel, where the president was staying that day. The meeting between them was anything but convivial. Reagan instructed Haig not to cross Kirkpatrick—a curious instruction since Haig, as secretary of state, was senior to the UN ambassador. Replying to this censure, Haig said that Kirkpatrick should take orders from her boss and "not from some flack in the White House." It made no difference. Pro-Iraqi sentiment abounded there. Alexander Haig's position was turning out to be very much a minority view.

In Baghdad a few weeks later, a very satisfied Saddam Hussein announced that he planned to treat the head of the U.S. interests section in the Belgian embassy as a de facto American ambassador. Although Iraq had broken diplomatic relations with the United States after the 1967 Arab-Israeli war, Saddam liked the Reagan administration's apparently flexible attitude.

During the week of September 17, 1981, Haig was forced to set aside his personal misgivings toward the Iraqi regime and listen patiently to the words of Ambassador Saleh at the United Nations. The occasion was an encounter during the annual meeting of the General Assembly. In a private conference room far from the delegates' lounge, where pinstriped diplomats sat sipping drinks and chatting away, Haig and Saleh engaged in a more weighty discussion.

Ambassador Saleh cut a proper diplomatic figure in his dark suit and his quiet demeanor. Yet the State Department's files on him painted quite another picture. Saleh, like Saddam Hussein, was a citizen of the Iraqi village of Tikrit. In 1969, as corpses were twisting on makeshift gallows in Baghdad, Saleh had harangued the crowds and praised the regime's public hanging of fourteen people for espionage, eleven of them Jews. At the time, the incident had aroused worldwide anger and revulsion. Western critics had dusted off various expressions of outrage. Soon after the hangings, however, Saleh had been appointed minister of culture and information in one of the most brutal regimes in the Middle East. As Saddam had consolidated his hold on power, so had Saleh risen. He had become Saddam's chief propagandist.

Now, in the quiet of the private room at the United Nations, Saleh was probing the U.S. secretary of state about the degree to which the Reagan administration was prepared to assist Iraq in its war against Iran. Even before the Reagan team took office in early 1981, Iraq had been working in Washington and New York to leverage the Khomeini threat into a new deal between itself and the United States. The most prominent target was the newly elected vice president, and the man assigned to flatter George Bush was Saddam's deputy foreign minister, Ismat Kittani. Kittani, a career diplomat who had worked in the United Nations for the best part of twenty-five years before joining Saddam's cabinet, had been a good friend of Bush from the days when both men represented their countries at the United Nations. The day after the 1980 election, Kittani had flown to America, bringing personal congratulations to the Reagan-Bush team, and in a gesture of striking extravagance he nearly buried his friend George Bush in flowers.

As soon as Reagan took office, Iraqi diplomats and procurement agents forwarded a variety of informal requests for military aid to their contacts in the Pentagon, the Republican party, and to American businessmen with political connections. Now the administration had been in office for eight months, and Saleh felt it was an appropriate time to assess the relationship between Washington and Baghdad, not least because Kittani had been elected president of the General Assembly only a few days earlier.

Saleh reminded Haig that, at the request of Ambassador Kirkpatrick, he had cooled the Iraqi diplomatic offensive against Israel that he had orchestrated during the summer in the wake of the Osirak raid. Since then, signals had reached him from other Arab diplomats still engaged in the war of words against the Israelis, suggesting that U.S. policy toward Iraq was about to be modified. Did Haig have any good news?

Some years later, Saleh recalled that the answer had been in the affirmative. The U.S. government was taking very seriously Iraq's request for help in its military struggle against the fundamentalism of Ayatollah Khomeini. In fact, the Iraqi ambassador already knew more than he let on during his meeting with Haig. He was aware, for example, that from its earliest days and in conditions of utmost secrecy, the Reagan administration had wasted little time in befriending his country. In particular, Saleh knew that American military observers had been sent to Iraq and were being housed at the Ministry of Defense in Baghdad.

As Saleh later recalled the conversation, Haig concluded his message by acknowledging the threat Baghdad was facing from the Khomeini regime, armed as it was with U.S. weaponry left over from the days when the shah had been a major buyer of American arms. The United States understood that it was essential to restore a balance in the region. Appropriate measures would be taken, Saleh remembered Haig telling him.

Though Haig would later recall the meeting with Saleh, he denied making any promises and maintained that "the Iraqis didn't get any help from me." In fact, after leaving the Reagan administration in 1983, he became angry when he learned of the extensive clandestine help that had been provided to Iraq—behind his back—by President Reagan's director of central intelligence, William Casey.

The meeting between Saleh and Haig ended cordially enough, and in an optimistic mood the Iraqi ambassador made his way uptown from the UN building to his town house on Manhattan's Upper East Side.

* * *

THE NEXT DAY, the telephone rang in a small suite of nondescript offices at the American Steel Export Company on Madison Avenue. Word of the meeting between Haig and Saleh had already reached an Iraqi procurement agent living on Long Island. He conveyed the news to a friend at American Steel, implying that if Washington were more willing to help Iraq, this could soon translate into business—and profits.

American Steel Export had nothing to do with steel. The name was a holdover from the days when it had been an export arm of Bethlehem Steel, but the company was now one of countless medium-size businesses with a Manhattan address. Import-export was its business, seventy or eighty different types of products were its stock in trade, and the Middle East was its market. Chemical additives, specialty oils, Maytag washing machines, bulk flour, medical equipment, electronics—American Steel dealt in all of them.

It was providing Larry Hickey, the company president, with a good life. Home was an apartment on Sutton Place, just off the East River, and his fellow executives were a decent bunch. Like him, they tended to have a military background, an appetite for travel, and a proper respect for a company almost a hundred years old. As was usual with former military men, they kept in touch with old acquaintances inside and outside the Pentagon. For months they had been hearing through the grapevine that the Iraqis were in the market for U.S. arms. The phone call from the Iraqi on Long Island confirmed this, and that fit nicely with a sensitive matter already in hand. Six months earlier, in March 1981, an Iraqi military officer from Baghdad named Lieutenant Abu Ali had arrived at American Steel with an introduction from an Iraqi businessman in New York. He was shopping for a highly sophisticated security system.

To the men who ran American Steel, there had been something about Lieutenant Abu Ali on that first visit that didn't quite fit, and one didn't have to wear khaki to be able to figure out what it was. To begin with, what was a mere lieutenant doing trying to buy a $12 million security system? What kind of lieutenant had two bodyguards and a driver for his black Mercedes? Why was the lieutenant's interpreter—the Iraq-born chairman of a New York chemical company—being so deferential, even toadying? Just as odd was the mere presence of an Iraqi military man on a shopping trip in the United States. Since 1979, Iraq had been on the State Department's list of states identified as sponsors of terrorism. What was an army officer from a country certified by the U.S. government as a terrorist state doing in America, when there weren't even any diplomatic relations?

Similar thoughts may have crossed the minds of certain New York

City police officers at the time. A special group had been detailed to beef up protection at Ambassador Saleh's private residence, where Lieutenant Abu Ali was staying. The ambassador's town house, although spacious, was bursting at the seams. There were twenty-one bodyguards who had been flown in from Baghdad, and during the day an additional security detail of seven Americans provided by the State Department. The reason for the security lay in the identity of the guest of honor, who was Sajida Khairallah, Saddam Hussein's wife. With her personal entourage, the number of people staying at Saleh's town house for two weeks came to thirty. Madame Saddam Hussein, Lieutenant Abu Ali, and the rest of their group had arrived in New York on a private Iraqi government-owned Boeing 747.

While Madame Saddam Hussein visited Bloomingdale's and the couture houses, the mysterious lieutenant carried a shopping list of a somewhat different order. Half a dozen bombproof cars, bulletproof vests, security and communications equipment, and electronic components figured prominently among his requirements.

It was the search to fill part of that shopping list that had brought the lieutenant to American Steel. The attempt to provide the equipment on this and subsequent Iraqi shopping lists would change forever the life of a young Jordanian-born employee of American Steel named Fred Haobsh.

In March 1981, Haobsh's horizons barely extended beyond his daily commute from his wife, child, and home in Ridgewood, New Jersey, to the chores of Middle East regional manager at American Steel in Manhattan. If the truth were known, he was fed up with selling auto parts and Maytag washing machines to clients in the Middle East. He was thus more than intrigued to learn from an Iraqi friend in New York that the real name of the visiting Lieutenant Abu Ali was Hussein Kamel, the son-in-law of Saddam Hussein. After Saddam Hussein himself, Hussein Kamel was regarded as the most powerful man in Iraq. His ostensible rank of lieutenant now provided him with cover for his true role as head of Saddam's weapons-procurement program. It was Hussein Kamel who spearheaded Saddam's clandestine drive to obtain Western technology and equipment for Iraq's nuclear, chemical, and biological weapons projects. Furthermore, he was about to add to his responsibilities the command of Saddam's elite Republican Guard. Ruthless and brilliant, he was a man to be reckoned with. The word was that Saddam trusted Hussein Kamel more than his own son.

On that spring day in 1981 when Hussein Kamel visited the offices of American Steel in the guise of a lieutenant, Fred Haobsh was in the office.

Conventionally dressed, a premature touch of gray in his hair, he looked the perfect executive assistant to the conservative officials of American Steel as they welcomed the Iraqi officer. Haobsh took no part in the discussions beyond pleasantries, but since he spoke fluent Arabic, he understood every word that passed between the mysterious lieutenant, his translator, his driver, and his bodyguards. He understood in particular that the security system that Iraq wanted to buy was on the cutting edge of American electronics technology, and he knew enough about export regulations to realize immediately that somebody outside of American Steel was going to have to sign off on this.

When Larry Hickey assigned him the job of putting the bid together, Haobsh raised the export-licensing question with him. Expansively, Hickey indicated that there would be no problem, no problem at all. And as it happened, the deal did not work out, so the licensing question was moot.

A few weeks later, in April 1981, a phone call came in from the New York-based Iraqi who had acted as translator for Lieutenant Abu Ali during his visit to American Steel. On behalf of the lieutenant, the businessman relayed an invitation to Larry Hickey to come to Baghdad for a business discussion. The call raised the same suspicions in Haobsh's mind that he had felt about Abu Ali during his visit, but he had little time for reflection. Hickey made an immediate decision to go to Baghdad, and since he spoke no Arabic, he asked Haobsh to accompany him.

It fell to Haobsh to deal with what, at first glance, seemed to be a set of insuperable practical problems, starting with tickets and visas. Because there were no diplomatic relations between the United States and Iraq, there was no embassy, no consulate, and no airline in America that flew to Baghdad. But Fred Haobsh would discover, as he took his first, unwitting steps toward his new and dangerous existence, visas and formal diplomatic barriers were matters of no consequence in the world of clandestine operations. On Hickey's instructions, Haobsh found himself within hours in the Upper East Side home of Ambassador Saleh. Sitting at his elegant desk, the ambassador penned a note in Arabic to the consular officer in the Iraqi interests section of the Indian embassy in Washington, instructing the officer to provide Hickey and Haobsh with visas and first-class tickets to Jordan via Paris. He handed the note to Haobsh, who read it. One phrase struck him immediately. The visa and ticket authority was being signed by the ambassador "upon the instructions of Lieutenant Abu Ali." Bon voyage, said a smiling Saleh Omar al-Ali.

*   *   *

HAOBSH'S TRIP TO BAGHDAD in April 1981 was full of urgency, tension, and for want of a better word, adventure. Just to get to Iraq had required lying to his colleagues at American Steel about his true destination and dodging perfectly normal questions from his wife. Then, to avoid suspicion when he returned to the United States, he had to make sure his passport wasn't stamped in Baghdad. That part was fairly simple, but in the middle of it all, he never answered his own question to himself: Why was he doing this when he wasn't even sure what the mission was about? If Hickey knew, he certainly hadn't told Haobsh. Still, it was a dangerous and exciting feeling, and Fred Haobsh had felt only a moment's guilt in savoring it.

On the Iraqi Airways flight from Amman to Baghdad, the airplane was completely blacked out. The cabin lights were turned off, the window shades were drawn, and somewhere off each wing, Iraqi fighter jets flew escort. Upon arrival in Baghdad, brass from the army, the air force, and the Republican Guard were waiting for them in the VIP lounge. A three-Mercedes convoy laden with armed guards sped Haobsh and Hickey from the airport to the Melia Al-Mansour Hotel, into a suite that belonged on a movie set. No bills were presented. The words "Guest of the Palace" were murmured by the attentive hotel staff. Fred Haobsh was now a guest of the Iraqi government.

Given the luxurious surroundings at his hotel, Haobsh did not feel that he was in the capital of a nation at war until he looked out the window and saw that Baghdad was blacked out. Inside, however, there were the five bodyguards, the flowers, the constant champagne—or was his preference Scotch? For a thirty-five-year-old who had previously been consigning Maytag washing machines around the Middle East, it was giddy stuff, a far cry from Ridgewood, New Jersey, and the dreary commute into midtown Manhattan.

Twenty years ago, as a high school student in Jordan, Fred Haobsh had visited Baghdad on a tour organized by the Ba'ath party of Iraq. He could still recall the fourteen-hour journey from a village near Amman in a battered old bus. He had gone out to the ancient biblical site of Babylon and seen all the sights, but what stayed with him after the trip were images of a capital remaking itself. There was a big-city energy to Baghdad, a buzz that made the Jordanian capital feel parochial by comparison.

By 1981, Haobsh had come a long way. His boss, Larry Hickey, had taken an immediate liking to the young Jordanian when they first met in the restaurant of a hotel in Riyadh in 1979. Hickey had been on one of his Middle East sales swings for American Steel; Haobsh was a struggling

journalist in his early thirties. Hickey liked the young Jordanian's enterprising spirit enough to offer him a sales job if he ever moved to the
United States. Aside from Arabic, Haobsh spoke excellent English,
French, and Farsi, and he had other potential besides. He was extremely
well connected in Jordan, and he was of Circassian stock.

Ever since the Ottoman Turks forced them to migrate from the
Caucasus in the nineteenth century to what ultimately became Jordan,
Circassians had exercised power in that country out of all proportion to
their tiny number. Haobsh's father, now retired, had been the governor of
Jordan's second-largest city. Other family members and relatives were
spread throughout the government and especially the military, a tradi-
tional locus of Circassian power. The family connections ran right up to
the royal palace, where the king's own guards were exclusively Circassian.
So when Haobsh knocked on Hickey's door at American Steel in New
York in 1980, he was more than welcome.

When he and Hickey finally met with Hussein Kamel in Baghdad,
who was no longer disguised as Lieutenant Abu Ali, the session was not
exactly what Haobsh had expected of American Steel. Hickey asked
Haobsh to take the lead, largely because Hickey spoke no Arabic. The
Iraqi had come to the point immediately. The palace regretted that Ameri-
can Steel had not gotten the contract to supply the security system that
Hussein Kamel needed. Now, however, he had a new list with other items.
What could American Steel deliver?

Haobsh remembered the mixture of terror and awe he felt when he
looked at the list. To begin with, the cost would be staggering—at a guess,
it would run over a billion dollars. Then, of course, there would be the
commissions, totaling millions and millions of dollars. It was all down
there in black and white—a complete arsenal, from radar through tanks
to aircraft, helicopters, battlefield missiles, and spare parts—the list went
on and on. In more ways than one, Fred Haobsh was out of his depth. He
barely knew one end of a tank from the other. But he was sure that to fill
this wish list would be one hundred percent illegal. His instincts were
correct. Under the 1976 Arms Export Control Act, American exports
with military potential required approval from the State Department.
Since Iraq had been certified as a sponsor of terrorism, approval of such
arms shipments was highly unlikely. Further, to prevent weapons transfers
to Iraq and Iran, President Jimmy Carter had imposed a ban on arms sales
soon after the two countries went to war in September 1980.

Haobsh also did not know that while he and Hickey were being
asked by Saddam's son-in-law to come up with American arms, Morris

Draper, a State Department envoy, had been visiting Saadun Hamadi, Iraq's foreign minister, in Baghdad on the initiative of the United States to explore the possibility of reestablishing diplomatic relations with Iraq. Though the Reagan administration's gambit was rebuffed, it had come about in part because of the increasingly pro-Iraq sentiment at the White House, and in part because U.S. allies such as Jordan and Saudi Arabia were advising the administration to get closer to Saddam.

The meeting between Haobsh, Hickey, and Hussein Kamel lasted less than an hour, and Haobsh emerged from it depressed; it was clear that all Iraq wanted was American weaponry. Hickey, on the other hand, had taken a surprisingly relaxed position about the whole thing, which Haobsh found difficult to comprehend. American Steel wasn't in the arms business—how could Hickey have responded to Hussein Kamel that, in essence, he would see what he could do?

Haobsh did not obtain even a partial answer to that question until much later in the year. During the summer after the trip he heard little about the $1 billion Iraqi shopping list, and for several months he was assigned back to his normal task of selling Maytag washing machines and other industrial and consumer goods in the Middle East. Hickey seemed to bring him into the more mysterious world of arms-dealing only when he required either his Arabic language skills or his Middle East contacts. In the autumn, to be sure, a friend of Hickey's did take Haobsh on a couple of quick trips to Brazil, where a deal was made with a factory in Rio de Janeiro to supply Iraq with armaments, from 75-mm. antiaircraft shells right through to 105-mm. and 155-mm. ammunition for howitzers and major artillery pieces. But since the transfer of arms to Iraq from a South American country was of no legal consequence as far as an American citizen was concerned, that experience did not worry Haobsh.

By the beginning of December 1981, however, Haobsh was beginning to learn a good deal that did worry him. The way some of Hickey's friends treated official, publicly stated American policies and laws governing the sale of arms to Iraq astonished him. It made him nervous—he didn't relish the idea of going to jail—but Hickey's friends, all well connected to the U.S. military, tried to reassure him. When it came to arms deals, they explained, governments tended to know precisely what was going on. Very few middlemen in the arms trade actually went to jail. If anything, they went to Geneva, Monte Carlo, or Paris, perhaps to visit their properties. In time-honored fashion, they brought buyer and seller together, took their cut, and moved on.

Haobsh still didn't believe it could be that easy until December 2, when he met Robert Johnson and Richard Smith. Once again, Hickey made the introduction, this time one that would plunge Haobsh into the world of covert operations.

FROM THE OUTSIDE, the offices of Johnson Consultants, worldwide marketing consultants in northern Virginia, were no different from a thousand others in the five-mile wall of glass facing Washington across the Potomac. The principals, Richard Smith, chief operating officer, and Robert Johnson, president, fit easily into the community whose lifeblood is government business, public or private.

In much of this neighborhood, stretching south from Langley to Falls Church, the brass plates and gold lettering that confront visitors hint at high-tech operations with an international flavor whose purpose is not immediately clear. The impression conveyed, enhanced by the rosewood desks and rented art, is of importance, connections, significance. The government has offices here too, quiet little operations and subdivisions of departments dealing in the sensitive and secret that don't appear in any directories or phone books. This is the neighborhood of plausible deniability, the home of the cut-out—an innocuous corporate entity whose actual function the government prefers to keep under wraps.

In neighborhood parlance, Johnson and Smith were longtime Agency people—not on the staff of the Central Intelligence Agency but, like hundreds of others in the loose-knit fraternity, placed under contract from time to time to perform operational assignments either personally or through one of their handful of nebulous-sounding corporations. By and large, the Agency contractors who use their companies as fronts for the government do not perform the glamorous assignments so colorfully chronicled by novelists and filmmakers. Their tasks tend to be humdrum and can range from making and maintaining contacts to acquiring and passing on information. At times, these contractors must also organize the transportation of goods in politically sensitive areas, in which the hand of government is not to be detected. Rarely do such companies and their owners know, or have the need to know, the larger picture in which the task they are carrying out plays a part. The work is unpredictable, irregular, and not always very lucrative. Months or years may go by between calls from the Agency requesting assistance. For their own differing reasons, therefore, it is necessary for both the Agency and the contractor that the latter maintain an entirely legitimate business as well.

Nineteen eighty-one, however, was an unusual year. It marked the end of what many Agency people regarded as an unnecessarily self-righteous but thankfully short period in which the Carter administration had naively cut to a minimum the use of covert operations as an arm of government policy. The shrinking of the Agency's operational—as opposed to analytical—staff numbers, which Carter's CIA director, Admiral Stansfield Turner, had carried out in the late 1970s, had been matched by a decline in the use of front companies for covert Agency purposes. But with the arrival of the Reagan administration, the installation of former CIA director George Bush as vice president, and the appointment of William Casey, one of the very architects of America's postwar intelligence apparatus, as CIA director, the mood in the Agency heartland of suburban Virginia had become decidedly upbeat. Furthermore, a war of extraordinary ferocity was being conducted in the Persian Gulf—a region of crucial strategic importance to the United States. If ever there was a scenario in which intelligence operatives of all types could play a vital role in assisting the national interest, this was it. The victims of Admiral Turner's changes at the CIA, their skills undiminished, stood ready to do their part, as did dozens of contractors and providers of other services.

There was another unusual aspect to that year. Before the Reagan administration was six months old, the intelligence network was humming with the word that the U.S. government wanted both sides to lose the Iran-Iraq war, and the prospect was laden with moneymaking possibilities. Given the public pronouncements of neutrality by the new administration, direct involvement of the CIA or any other government agency was officially out of the question, quite apart from the fact that severe penalties in law precluded any unauthorized military trade with Iraq. Nevertheless, while Iraq might officially be a pariah state, to counter Iran's offensives the White House seemed quietly to let it be known that Iraq needed help with whatever armaments could be provided in the so-called gray market, and as soon as possible.

At American Steel in New York City, Larry Hickey had already picked up on this rumor by the time Hussein Kamel paid him the visit in March. And after Hickey and Haobsh returned from Baghdad in April with Hussein Kamel's weapons wish list, it was only a question of time before the two men found themselves working Hickey's contacts in the Department of Defense and the intelligence community.

On December 2, 1981, not long after his deal-making in Rio, Fred Haobsh walked with Hickey into the fourth-floor office suite of Johnson

Consultants in Virginia. Haobsh, who had been told little about the firm by Hickey, was expecting the usual chat with a couple of executives who had contacts in the right quarters. He would come away stunned.

The offices themselves were what he expected—well-appointed with mahogany furniture, spacious, and sunny. The carpets were deep, and the artwork on the walls could best be categorized as inoffensive modern. Apart from a secretary, there seemed to be no other staff. Both principals were present. Richard Smith, the older of the two, was probably in his late fifties, and like the executives at American Steel, he carried himself with a military bearing. During the course of the meeting he was oddly silent. The man whom Hickey had come to see was Robert Johnson.

It took Haobsh no time at all to understand that he was sitting opposite a player of substance. Johnson's comportment implied army, but his manner of speaking implied government. Indeed, to the knowledge-able it would suggest intelligence services. He never said more than he needed to, and he tended to listen far more than he spoke. The only thing striking about him was his piercing blue eyes. Johnson had many friends in the Pentagon and at the Joint Special Operations Command (JSOC) at Fort Bragg, North Carolina. Bragg was the home of the legendary Delta Force, of the Navy SEALs and the Green Berets.

Johnson also had excellent connections with military suppliers and represented a number of companies that made bomb fuses, artillery pieces, and other items that form the stock in trade of an arms merchant. According to Pentagon officials and intelligence agents, Johnson was also on very friendly terms with Robert Gates, the CIA man who was now rising steadily at Langley as William Casey's protégé. He was clearly someone who could count on friendships and contacts even at the higher levels of government.

Despite his activities thus far, Haobsh was unprepared for this meet-ing in Virginia. He had still barely cut his teeth in the arms business—putting together a deal in which a South American company would sell weapons to Iraq was of little consequence. But the Iran-Iraq war was making a lot of people rich in a lot of countries, and few paid attention to the unanimous resolutions of the UN Security Council that called upon all states to exercise the utmost restraint in selling anything that could lead to a further escalation of the conflict. In the United States, however, the law was far more binding. One simply did not export arms to Iraq without formal approval. That was why Haobsh couldn't believe what happened next in the little office suite in Virginia. Robert Johnson sat back in his chair on that winter afternoon and scrutinized Hussein Kamel's billion-dollar shopping list. He ran through the items with his partner: the missiles, the defense electronics, the tanks, the helicopters, and more. No problem, said Johnson.

Haobsh continued to associate with Johnson and Smith in the months that followed. In early 1982, he began to suspect that his value to them was less as a colleague than as a legman, one who spoke Arabic and knew his way around the Middle East. Still, "after a few meetings they loosened up a bit," said Haobsh years later, recalling the way he had been drawn further into the plan to fill the billion-dollar shopping list. Johnson and Smith finally told Haobsh they were ex-CIA. They also introduced him to their lawyer, another former Agency man. In fact, the lawyer had been a longtime operator in the smoke-and-mirrors world of government special operations. Haobsh's most vivid recollection of the lawyer was the way he constantly reminded them that the word *Iraq* should not be used, even in conversation. The word *Jordan* should be substituted, "even though we all knew where the goods were going."

"The only problem these guys seemed to have was getting phony end-user certificates from somewhere to cover the deliveries to Iraq," Haobsh recalled. "Jordan was the obvious place, but that meant all kinds of diplomatic maneuvering, and it was the Iraqis' responsibility to set this up. Because I had family in Jordan, they kept asking me to put pressure on anyone I could in Jordan to try and move things along."

Johnson and Smith were not the only people interested in using Jordan as a transshipment point to supply weaponry to Iraq. "That 1981–82 period was pretty grim for Iraq, and we were worried about the imbalance in the war with Iran," recalled a former member of the Reagan cabinet. By 1982, the Jordanian military was diverting U.S.-made helicopters to Iraq, even though American export laws expressly prohibited the third-party transfer of U.S.-made weapons without approval from Washington. But the Reagan administration, by now convinced that Baghdad needed help, looked the other way when such transfers occurred.

Thus the appeal of Jordan as a fake end-user of U.S. arms actually destined for Iraq was no different at the political level than it was for covert operators like Johnson, Smith, and their new recruit, Fred Haobsh. By chance, while on a visit to Johnson in Virginia one day in late March 1982, Haobsh recognized a figure walking across the office parking lot. It was General Ahmad Jweiber, a family friend from his years in Jordan who at the time was the Jordanian military attaché in Washington. The Jordanian diplomat was soon befriended by Johnson, who laid plans to ship some of the latest-model Cobra helicopters to Amman, intended for Baghdad.

Haobsh's unease about his new colleagues grew when he saw the way they could arrange to ship these Cobras to Iraq by way of Jordan, even though the Jordanian air force had only recently been denied those same Cobras and had had to settle for a less-advanced model. He learned from Jweiber that the prices being quoted for the more advanced models were less than what Jordan had paid for the inferior models it had bought directly from the American government. "That is what really convinced me that Johnson and his people were government," Haobsh reflected later. "Most arms dealers would double or treble the price for top-of-the-line equipment. In this case they were pretty much giving it away. And they also agreed not to take payment until after the matériel had been delivered and tested. That again was not the way normal arms dealers work."

But by the spring of 1982, despite his growing doubts, Haobsh found himself too deeply involved with Johnson and Smith to back away. He had left the staff of American Steel and was now working on a free-lance basis both for his old boss and for Johnson Consultants. It was under these circumstances that he agreed to make another trip to Baghdad, to deliver the news that the Iraqi shopping list was about to be filled.

Back at the Melia Al-Mansour Hotel in early April, the effects of the Iran-Iraq war were far more obvious to Haobsh than they had been a year ago. Shortages were beginning to bite deep, and it seemed that every other doorway in Baghdad was draped in black. The hotel manager had taken Haobsh aside in a quiet moment and wept. His two sons had already been killed in the war, and while overseeing the delivery of every extravagance to his hotel guests, he himself had barely enough to live on. Nevertheless, he said as he regained his composure, he was better off than most people he knew.

On both sides of the border the television pictures were running red with the carnage, accompanied by martial music and forecasts of ultimate victory, but there was no denying that Iraq was in trouble. The Iranians were relentlessly pushing the Iraqi forces back. Iraq had spent a billion dollars a month on the war. The death toll on both sides had already reached 100,000. In the dining room of the hotel, though the hour was late, Haobsh saw military figures from half a dozen Western countries dotted around the tables. Most of those not in uniform looked as if they should have been. For more than a year now their home countries had been paying sonorous lip service to the UN resolutions against shipping war matériel to either Iran or Iraq, but there was no way these men were observers. They were here to sell. The picture had been pretty much the same in the chief of staff's waiting room at air force headquarters on his last trip, where uniformed British, French, Soviet, and Czech military officers were awaiting their turn at bat.

The United States also had taken a step toward helping Iraq. On February 26, 1982, the Reagan administration told Congress that it had dropped Iraq from the list of nations that supported acts of international terrorism. Before coming to Baghdad, Haobsh had read about the move and the complaints from senators about Congress not being properly consulted ahead of time. The State Department had made it clear that taking Iraq off the list of terrorist nations did not mean the United States was lifting its ban on arms shipments to Iraq. Little was said, however, about the significant hidden value of the change in Iraq's status: Baghdad would now be eligible for American government loan guarantees. The decision in Washington was more important than people like Fred Haobsh could have realized. To covert operators like Johnson and Smith, it was a signal that they now had political cover to go ahead with their plans to provide U.S. equipment to Iraq, albeit by way of unofficial channels. They would have much less need of bit players like Fred Haobsh.

Just now, in his Baghdad hotel suite, Haobsh was bothered by a more pedestrian concern: He disliked waiting around. Twenty-four hours after he had arrived in town, he had still not heard from the presidential palace. It was frustrating to sit there with good news for Hussein Kamel and not be able to deliver it. Not until his third day did the call finally come from the reception desk: The visitors were on their way up.

Hussein Kamel, dressed in civilian clothes, welcomed Haobsh to Baghdad and apologized for the delay in meeting him. Then he introduced the military figure at his side, Lieutenant General Shenshel, the army chief of staff, and without delay the three men were driven with military escort to Hussein Kamel's office in the presidential compound. For the next two hours Haobsh set out his good news in detail. It had taken most of a year to put this deal together, he said, but finally, with the help of nongovernment contractors with CIA backgrounds, it would be possible to fill the shopping list. Once friendly officials in Jordan agreed, shipments would come into Amman for onward transit to Baghdad. Training on the American equipment would be arranged through Jordan. As long as they carried Jordanian passports, Iraqi pilots might even be trained within the United States—that was a matter still to be dealt with. Haobsh would come to Baghdad as often as necessary while details of the entire package were being finalized.

The men finished their Turkish coffee and embraced. Then, as Haobsh turned to leave, Hussein Kamel drew him aside and explained that there was somebody he needed to meet. The two men stepped out into the sunshine and walked together across the compound to the palace, passed through two antechambers, and arrived in a large but rather undistinguished room. Seated behind a dark wooden desk was Saddam Hussein. He rose immediately and walked across to Haobsh, and they embraced in greeting. There was no small talk. In formal language, Saddam expressed his thanks for the work Haobsh had done on behalf of Iraq, then gestured to an aide, who approached Haobsh and pressed a small suede pouch into his hand. The audience was over within three minutes.

Back in his hotel suite Haobsh reached into his pocket and pulled out the brown suede pouch. He opened a little flap that had been tucked beneath a leather band and carefully withdrew a finely crafted fob watch three inches across, made of solid gold. He clicked the gold cover open. Occupying most of the enameled face of the watch was the image, in head-and-shoulders portrait, of Saddam Hussein.

WHEN HE GOT BACK to the United States, Haobsh reported to Johnson and Smith, who continued to reassure him that everything would go smoothly. In fact, they dispatched him on two more trips to Baghdad, and when Haobsh complained to Johnson that customs agents in New York were questioning him about the many passport stamps marked Amman, Johnson easily resolved the problem. On the way home from his next trip, Haobsh telephoned Johnson from Paris, and when he arrived at Kennedy Airport, there were no more difficulties with customs.

For many months now, Johnson had given very little away to Haobsh about the invisible source of support that made it possible for him to travel back and forth to Baghdad and to organize the sale of U.S. arms to Iraq with the help of Jordanian end-user certificates. The question had been left hanging, and by the summer of 1982 Haobsh wanted an answer. Nobody he had met in this enterprise foresaw jail time in their crystal ball, Haobsh said to Johnson. So who was behind all this?

Johnson vaguely mentioned the White House and the CIA, but he did not name the expediters. Only after Haobsh pressed him on several more occasions did he eventually get some names. The first one mentioned was William Casey, who had been to visit the Saudis and had relayed back to Washington their urgent advocacy of arming Iraq quickly and heavily. Then there was Robert Gates, Casey's deputy director for intelligence. Another name was Judge William Clark, the national security adviser to President Reagan. Casey died in 1987, but a former cabinet member who worked with him recalled "a lot of such activity and some hurry-up requests for arms from Casey." Gates has repeatedly denied he was involved in any covert operations to arm Iraq, and William Clark has said he has "no recollection" of any involvement either.

As for Robert Johnson, he was extraordinarily concerned about being named in public, but he was willing to confirm that his marching orders came "directly from the White House."

T W O

The Covert Ethic

I n January 1982, the West Wing of the White House was not a very happy place in which to work. The atmosphere was thick with acrimony, back-stabbing among presidential aides, and an unseemly controversy that centered upon Richard Allen, President Reagan's national security adviser. Allen had just been forced to resign after less than a year on the job. To the outside world his sudden departure was the result of an embarrassing scandal over his acceptance of three watches from a Japanese interpreter and a thousand dollars from Japanese journalists, all of whom he had helped by getting them an interview with Nancy Reagan.

Insiders later told a different tale, one that basically chronicled the intense ambition of James Baker, the former campaign manager to George Bush who had maneuvered his way into the job of chief of staff to President Reagan. At the time, the White House made it clear that Baker, who had pushed the investigation of Allen, had also recommended firing him because he was a "political liability." To at least one former cabinet member, however, "Baker was angling for the national security adviser's job and was quite happy to see Allen bite the dust." But to replace Allen Reagan turned not to Baker but to his friend and confidant William Clark, the man who had accompanied the Reagans on their odyssey from the state house in Sacramento to the mansion on Pennsylvania Avenue. In December 1981, Clark, then serving as deputy secretary of state, was named to take over the National Security Council (NSC) from Allen.

Clark insisted at the time that his deputy national security adviser be Robert C. "Bud" McFarlane, a retired Marine Corps colonel who had gotten his first taste of the big time as an NSC staffer under Henry

Kissinger, back in the Nixon administration. McFarlane had a penchant for secret missions, engendered by having tagged along on several of them in the Middle East with Kissinger. He also proved highly adept at bureaucratic gamesmanship, especially in getting things done through back channels. This love of secrecy and clandestine operations would ultimately lead to McFarlane's adventurism in U.S. dealings with Iran and later to his pleading guilty to four criminal misdemeanor charges for his role in the Iran-Contra scandal. In early 1982, however, he was a newly appointed and rising star at the White House. When he became deputy national security adviser, McFarlane wanted a Middle East specialist at his side whom he could trust. The person he chose, who had worked for him at State, was a high-flying twenty-six-year-old named Howard Teicher.

Although the bearded and youthful Teicher was assigned at first to the Near East and South Asia directorate of the NSC, he was essentially Bud McFarlane's right-hand man. His job would expand in time, and soon he would be the key White House person who was monitoring arms deals in the Middle East. Teicher already had experience in the boiler room of policy-making, both at State and during a prior two-year stint at the Pentagon. He had finished his graduate studies at the School of Advanced International Studies (SAIS), an elite branch of the Johns Hopkins University that used to be nicknamed "the CIA Training School" by its students. This was unfair, since SAIS's tiny number of graduates fanned out into top jobs in many areas: diplomacy, banking, business, journalism, and Congress. Each year, only a few would actually go to work for the CIA. At SAIS, Teicher had kept very much to himself. At the White House he found himself in conversation with everyone, including President Reagan and Vice President Bush. Like others with a very high security clearance at the NSC, Teicher got to read the most sensitive intelligence reports, cable traffic, and cabinet- and presidential-level memos. It was heady stuff for so young a man, and fascinating as well.

Teicher had had a special interest in Saddam Hussein from the start of his career. Back in 1979, while he was working as an analyst in the Office of the Secretary of Defense, he had written a fifty-page paper predicting that Saddam would invade Iran, seek to annex oil-rich provinces from Tehran, and eventually even try to renew Iraq's historical claims to Kuwait. So obsessed with Saddam and Iraq did Teicher become that colleagues at the Pentagon jokingly nicknamed him Teicher al-Tikriti; the reference was to the Tikriti clan from which Saddam came. But Harold Brown, the secretary of defense under Jimmy Carter, brushed aside Teicher's dire warnings, scribbling at the margin of the report, "I disagree. Iraq has changed. It has moderated its behavior." This did not persuade Teicher to change his view of the Iraqi threat; if anything, he grew more convinced of it when he joined the Reagan White House.

In 1982 and 1983, when monitoring arms transactions in the Middle East was part of his job, Teicher began to notice some strange things. From time to time he read cables referring to U.S. arms shipments that had found their way through third countries to Iraq. He knew that such transfers were illegal. He also learned something from colleagues that surprised him: U.S. military equipment was being sent to Iraq on the order of the White House, including ammunition, spare parts, defense electronics, and computers. When Teicher asked what was going on, the answers he was given struck him as very odd indeed. He was told that certain officials at the White House simply picked up the telephone and "cleared" the deployment of a plane with a classified cargo. Teicher inquired how this could happen. He was informed that there were "channels" that the White House used to carry out such policies. "I asked my colleagues how we were getting the stuff to Iraq," he remembered, "and I was told that there are people out there who do it for us." Although it seemed incredible to him that officials at the White House could be assisting in the clandestine transfer of U.S. matériel to Iraq, Teicher was told not to bother himself about it.

Teicher was a stubborn man, however, and as he continued to serve in the Reagan White House, he took notes, watched, listened, and argued his case against helping Iraq. He was intrigued and angered that senior U.S. officials would take it upon themselves to authorize people outside the government to transfer arms to Iraq. He asked friends both at the White House and in the intelligence community who these people were. That was how he learned the names of Robert Johnson and Richard Smith.

Johnson, recalled Teicher, "was one of the channels used by the White House. His name came up when I asked my colleagues how we were getting the stuff to Iraq." What about Smith, the other former CIA operative involved in the transactions? "Yeah," said Teicher, "they were a couple of the guys. These were former government operatives who were trying to leverage their government past into current business. You have to understand something, though. These off-the-shelf operations in the Middle East occurred with great regularity. Yes, they were illegal. But people think the Irangate affair was something strange. It wasn't. It was just the one that went public. It was not at all abnormal."

To hear a former White House official discussing outright illegalities so forthrightly is an unusual experience. Would he go further? How did it work? Teicher took every question he was asked in stride. "The government found third parties and private channels for our shipments. I call this our 'dirty policy.' This was all consistent with covert operations at the time. False fronts were used a lot." But under U.S. law that kind of activity—in the White House or anywhere else in the government— surely had to have a secret presidential authorization, a piece of paper known as a presidential finding, that allowed U.S. arms export laws to be broken only in the name of national security. Were there any presidential findings for these shipments to Iraq? "No," said Teicher matter-of-factly. "It was all done off the books." So that would make it what kind of operation? "That," said Teicher, "would make it illegal."

Who in the White House helped to facilitate covert shipments? Who knew? "Two of the most active people," said Teicher, "were Judge Clark and William Casey." While Clark denies this, Casey certainly helped coordinate the secret arms transfers with officials of the government of Saudi Arabia. "Casey would tell people at the White House to make it happen, and they would get it done. Casey would travel to Saudi Arabia a lot. He went every two or three months to coordinate. Not many people know this, but Casey had an office in the Old Executive Office Building, right next to the White House. Casey didn't even spend that much time at CIA headquarters in Virginia. He was frequently at the White House, and he would meet with Reagan all the time."

The other person Casey confided in, recalled Teicher, was George Bush. "Bush knew about the covert operations, and Casey felt he could trust him, with his intelligence orientation and all that." Teicher also remembered Bush making his position explicit in meetings at the White House: "I attended meetings where Bush made clear he wanted to help Iraq. His door was always open to the Iraqis. If they wanted a meeting with Bush, they would get it."

In February 1982, Casey's belief in the importance of helping Iraq led not only to secret arms transfers to Baghdad but to the critical decision to remove Iraq's name from the list of countries sponsoring international terrorism. Casey was convinced that only Saddam Hussein could effectively prevent Tehran from dominating Persian Gulf oil resources, and he was a man who was more interested in ends than in the means used to achieve them. "Casey was very fearful that Iran would come out on top in the war being fought in the Persian Gulf," recalled Alexander Haig. "I wouldn't have helped either Iraq or Iran, but Casey had a position that I called active neutrality." Haig, Teicher, and others in the administration who tended to be concerned about the underlying threat that Saddam posed to Israel, a strategic American ally, were shocked when they found out that Iraq had been taken off the terrorism list.

Secretary of State Haig was especially upset at the fact that the decision had been made at the White House, even though the State Department was responsible for the list. "I was not consulted," he complained. Casey had gone around everyone's backs in pressing for the change in Iraq's status, ignoring information about Saddam that was available to the CIA and the White House. "We knew very well that Abu Nidal was based in Baghdad," Teicher recalled. "We knew of Iraq's support for his and other terrorist organizations. The decision to take Iraq off the terrorist list was Casey's, and Clark's." Clark, when asked about the way the decision had been made, said it "could very well be" that Casey approached him, but he could not recollect this.

The removal of Iraq from the list set the tone for Washington's covert policies toward Baghdad. Casey's "active neutrality" fostered a quiet pro-Iraqi bias not only in the White House but in many other parts of the government, reinforced by the entreaties of U.S. allies in the Arab world such as Jordan, Saudi Arabia, and Egypt.

Casey and his White House colleagues perceived King Hussein of Jordan as a willing middleman for arms shipments to Iraq. When White House officials decided they wanted to get arms to Baghdad, they didn't have to ask the Jordanian monarch for help; rather, they had to restrain his repeated efforts to get every kind of armament conceivable to Saddam, his friend, protector, and chief oil supplier. They were well aware of the king's interests; the CIA's station chief in Amman sent several messages back to headquarters on the subject, and Casey himself met with the king during his frequent missions to the area as CIA director. According to a former American military officer who had personal dealings in Jordan, King Hussein had been advocating assistance for Saddam from the minute the Reagan administration took office.

In many ways the king was like a poker player with a permanently rotten hand; he had to make do with a small country that lacked oil resources, a rebellious Palestinian population that would rather he were not in power, a dependence on the United States for arms, and a reliance on Saddam as his big brother in the Persian Gulf. In such a situation the poker player's best tactic is either to bluff or fold his hand and look to a friend to cover his losses. In March 1982, American intelligence reports to Washington suggested that Baghdad was in serious trouble militarily, so King Hussein began playing on the White House's panicky reaction to the possibility of Iraq's defeat at the hands of Iran, and simultaneously he bent down to kiss the hand of Saddam.

To Casey's way of thinking, Jordan was the perfect front for covert U.S. operations, whether they involved intelligence-sharing or arms. Jordan bordered Iraq, and its port of Aqaba gave it an ideal harbor for shipments that would arrive by way of the Red Sea and later travel overland to Baghdad. Its weak and cowardly monarchy, which could not or would not control a corrupt officialdom that featured dozens of would-be arms dealers, shippers, hangers-on, and middlemen, made it the ideal staging ground for these activities. By this time, people like Fred Haobsh, Robert Johnson, and a string of other covert operators were already receiving winks and nods from the White House. The fact that there was a longstanding CIA presence in the little kingdom was even better. All this made it their preferred route for clandestine shipments to Iraq.

In June 1982, a White House meeting was called to discuss the Iran-Iraq war. The prevailing view was that if Washington wanted to prevent an Iranian victory, it would have to share some of its more sensitive intelligence photography with Saddam. Some officials resisted the idea of providing a Soviet client state with this information, but William Casey ultimately persuaded the president to make it happen.

A few weeks later, the first U.S. satellite photographs were passed to Baghdad. What was kept deeply secret—and has remained so until now—was that it was no spy, no courier, no special agent, but rather King Hussein himself who was used by Washington to hand-carry and present the intelligence data to Baghdad to ensure that it wasn't lost or stolen.

Then, as the covert intelligence-sharing became more frequent, arrangements were made for an Iraqi liaison to travel along the dusty road from Baghdad to Amman in order to pick up the material. At times, thanks to the White House's secret backing for the intelligence-sharing, U.S. intelligence officers were actually sent to Baghdad to help interpret the satellite information. As the White House took an increasingly active role in secretly helping Saddam direct his armed forces, the United States even built an expensive high-tech annex in Baghdad to provide a direct down-link receiver for the satellite intelligence and better processing of the information.

By early 1983, Saddam Hussein had received enough positive signals from Washington to make him think the prospects for a closer relationship were real. In February of that year, when Iraqi envoy Saadun Hamadi met in Washington for the first time with George Shultz, Haig's successor as secretary of state, he worked hard to build on the rapport he had already established with Jeane Kirkpatrick. Baghdad, the urbane Hamadi argued to Shultz, could be as reliable a partner in the Persian Gulf as Saudi Arabia.

Also among those arguing on Saddam's behalf were a number of U.S. diplomats, including William Eagleton, head of the U.S. interests section in Baghdad. In an October 1983 cable to Washington Eagleton suggested that the United States "selectively lift restrictions on third-party transfers of U.S.-licensed military equipment to Iraq." The official response was that this bright idea would not work because of legal restrictions and because it would certainly trigger opposition if Congress were informed. Several months later, Shultz sent a cable to Eagleton in which he reiterated that it was against U.S. policy to permit third-country transfers of U.S. arms to Iraq. Yet, Shultz wrote, "under present circumstances in which Iraq is clearly on the defensive and Iran is in little danger of defeat, we are not actively opposing non-U.S. controlled exports of arms to Iraq which do not contribute to widening the war. Our interest is in maintaining a strategic balance between the belligerents in the interest of regional stability." The truth, however, was that while official correspondence between diplomats in Baghdad and the State Department stuck to the letter of U.S. law, covert shipments of U.S. arms were already being sent through Jordan, Egypt, and even Kuwait.

EAGLETON CONTINUED TO LOBBY Washington for more cooperation with Baghdad, recommending that the United States take the initiative to restore diplomatic relations with Iraq. In November 1983, Saddam's deputies informed Eagleton that if an American envoy were now to visit Baghdad, he would be welcome to discuss the prospect of exactly such a resumption. In Washington this idea fit logically with the views of Casey, Reagan, Bush, and others who were willing to avert their glance from Saddam's more outlandish behavior in the interests of protecting U.S. security interests in the Gulf. Thus, on December 17, 1983, President Reagan's special Middle East envoy, Donald Rumsfeld, flew into Baghdad bearing a handwritten letter to Saddam. In it Reagan offered to renew diplomatic relations and to expand military and business ties with Baghdad. Teicher, who traveled to Baghdad with Rumsfeld, said that it was this letter that paved the way for the U.S. tilt to Iraq: "Here was the U.S. government coming hat-in-hand to Saddam Hussein and saying, 'We respect you, we respect you. How can we help you? Let us help you.' " Saddam listened politely and then told Rumsfeld that America should try to stop the flow of arms to Iran. The United States did even more: It began offering U.S. government–backed loan guarantees to Iraq.

Among the vehicles chosen for this back-door aid was the Export-Import Bank, known in Washington as the Eximbank. The Eximbank is actually a U.S. government agency that helps American exporters by guaranteeing to cover their loans if foreign customers default. In the spring of 1984 pressure was put on Eximbank to provide $500 million in American taxpayer-backed loan guarantees for an Iraqi project: the new Aqaba pipeline. The pipeline was to carry one million barrels of crude oil each day from northwestern Iraq to the Jordanian port of Aqaba, thus diverting the oil away from the Persian Gulf war zone and carrying it to the Red Sea. Because of its distance from the fighting and from the Strait of Hormuz, which Iran was threatening to close, the pipeline would make it harder for Tehran to disrupt oil sales critical to Saddam Hussein.

The contractor on the project was the Bechtel Corporation, a multibillion-dollar-a-year California company that had worked for many years in the Persian Gulf. Bechtel, which provided employment to Caspar Weinberger and George Shultz when they were not in government, was the biggest engineering and construction firm in the United States, with interests in 135 countries; in fact, Shultz had left Bechtel to become secretary of state. The company was virtually an unofficial expediter of U.S. policy, so close to Washington's thinking were its executives.

Saddam had given the green light for the project, but he had one reservation. In order to reach Aqaba, the pipeline would pass through Jordanian territory only a few miles from the border with Israel, making it an easy target. What Saddam wanted was a U.S.-brokered political guarantee that Israel would not attack the pipeline. At a meeting in Baghdad in February 1984, Foreign Minister Tariq Aziz told Richard Murphy, the ardently pro-Iraqi assistant secretary of state, that Saddam was insisting on "direct U.S. involvement" in the project; if this were not forthcoming, then Washington could "just forget it." There was also a problem back in Washington: Eximbank was opposed to extending any U.S. credits to Iraq because it feared that the cash-strapped country would be unable to repay the loans it guaranteed. Help was clearly needed. It was at this stage that Vice President George Bush was asked to lend a hand.

On June 12, 1984, Shultz's executive secretary at the State Department sent a confidential memorandum to Donald Gregg, the former CIA man who was Bush's national security adviser. The memorandum came with two attachments: a background paper on the status of the proposed Iraqi oil pipeline, and suggested talking points for Bush to use in calling the chairman of Eximbank to urge financing for the project. The background paper explained that the pipeline project was worth $1 billion, that Iraq and Jordan had asked Bechtel to maximize U.S. official and private participation by June 25, that the project was "a major test of U.S. intentions" toward Iraq, and that Eximbank support was of crucial importance. "A call by the Vice President would be particularly useful in confirming the Administration's support," the background paper concluded.

Bush had already embraced covert military aid for Iraq, and now he would labor to push through financial assistance. The call to Eximbank was made easier for him by the friendship he and its chairman, William Draper, had shared since their days together at Yale. Bush's talking points spelled out that the United States was seeking "means to bolster Iraq's ability and resolve to withstand Iranian attacks." But the bottom line was that neither Iraq nor Iran should be dominant in the Persian Gulf. According to the script, Bush was to say to Draper: "We believe that victory by either side would have a serious destabilizing effect on the region."

Bush reviewed the memorandum and its attachments and placed the call to Draper. On June 25, just a few days later and after months of refusal, Eximbank suddenly reversed itself and announced it was offering more than $500 million of financing for the Aqaba pipeline.

Washington's relations with the Iraqi dictator, both at the covert and at the official level, were becoming warmer. Saddam might still have a reputation as an international outlaw, but the White House had decided where its interests lay. It was thus natural that the U.S. courtship should be consummated in a resumption of full diplomatic ties. On November 26, 1984, the day relations were formally restored, Ronald Reagan welcomed Foreign Minister Tariq Aziz to the White House as a sign of friendship. That evening, Aziz was the guest of honor at a lavish banquet at the Washington residence of the Iraqi ambassador. At the State Department, an office was established for the specific purpose of managing U.S. policy while the Iran-Iraq war raged in the Gulf. In the spring of 1985, an American businessman was told by a State Department official that relations with Iraq were good—so good, in fact, that Aziz had been able to obtain a meeting with Shultz on twenty-four hours' notice.

Baghdad was now a formal partner of Washington, and Saddam was extracting as much as he could in the way of benefits from the Reagan administration. His fortunes in the continuing war against Khomeini's

Iran kept changing, but the same thing could be said of the rival factions at the White House; some continued to assist Iraq, while others were party to a new and secret policy toward Iran. The idea of opening up lines of communication to the so-called moderates in Khomeini's regime resulted in a series of covert operations that were in odd contradiction to the steady support that Washington was providing to Baghdad. Casey and his White House allies plotted secret arms sales to Tehran, partly in order to seek the release of American hostages held in Beirut by Iranian-supported terrorists and partly to counteract the perceived threat of Soviet influence in Iran. By 1986, the White House was steeped in a covert ethic. The off-the-books operations involving the diversion of profits from arms transfers to Iran, in contravention of the law prohibiting aid to Nicaragua, were eventually exposed and became known to the public as the Iran-Contra affair. The equally egregious and simultaneous covert aid to Iraq, however, remained secret.

ON JULY 23, 1986, a group of senior officials from the NSC, the Pentagon, the State Department, and the CIA met at the White House to discuss American support for Iraq. One of their tasks was to decide on a request from the American embassy in Baghdad to move U.S. weaponry from Jordan to Iraq, which would be against the Arms Export Control Act. After the meeting, Richard Murphy sent a cable to the American ambassador in Baghdad stating: "As for the possibility of Iraq's 'borrowing' U.S.-supplied Jordanian equipment, there are legal restrictions on any action of that sort, besides the difficult policy questions which you have pointed out. Then, too, any such transfer has to be notified to the Congress and thus made public. In addition, the experts here believe that the equipment in question would not have a significant impact on the war effort."

This particular request was rejected, but the White House meeting that July explored other ways to help Saddam. Iran had launched a major military offensive against Iraq earlier that year, and the war now seemed to be approaching a stalemate. The CIA was worried that Saddam was not making effective use of the secret intelligence data it was sending him. He seemed reluctant to respond to Iranian attacks with aerial bombings because he was trying to conserve his resources. The White House meeting, according to Murphy's cable, "reviewed the military situation, discussed in detail the Iraqi conduct of the war, explored possible further . . . efforts by us, and looked at U.S.-Iraq relations . . ." Murphy also wrote that the idea of sending a senior U.S. emissary to talk with Saddam Hussein was still under discussion.

The most important decision taken at that White House meeting was to employ once again the talents of George Bush, who was about to make a trip to various countries in the Middle East, including Jordan and Egypt. Bush was to provide strategic battlefield advice to Saddam through intermediaries who were heads of state. "We have encouraged the Vice President to suggest to both King Hussein and President Mubarak that they sustain their efforts to convey our shared views to Saddam regarding Iraq's use of its air resources," Murphy wrote. (See Appendix B, pages 310–311.) "If Saddam does what he says he would do with the Air Force, that would be a major plus." Saddam might have been highly amused, or even flattered, if he had known that the secret cable was entitled "U.S. Government support for Iraq during the war." This was no longer a tilt— it was becoming a bear hug.

On Monday, August 4, 1986, George Bush was in Cairo, nearing the end of an eleven-day swing through the Middle East. He had been shuttling across the region on Air Force Two. When he set off on his trip, the White House was asked if the vice president had a policy goal in mind. Since Bush and James Baker had begun gearing up for Bush's presidential campaign to succeed Ronald Reagan, the answer was no, "nothing but politics." This was somewhat disingenuous. Although there were a dozen campaign-style photo opportunities during the trip and television crews filmed Bush meeting Israelis and visiting the Egyptian pyramids, no cameras were allowed into his two-hour private meeting with Hosni Mubarak. While Bush was in Cairo officially to continue the search for a Middle East peace, to strengthen diplomatic relations, and to spread good cheer, he had more than good cheer in mind for Mubarak. Bush had been briefed to talk to the Egyptian president about how Saddam could best bomb the Iranians. According to a member of the senior-level group that prepared the brief, the vice president carried out the request that had been made of him after the White House meeting in late July: He asked Mubarak to tell Saddam to make better use of his air force against Iranian troops.

For his part, Mubarak needed little persuading. The Egyptian president was a pragmatic man with a chameleonlike ability to survive. To the Americans he was a reasonable partner, a leader with whom one could do business. To Saddam Hussein, he was a friend and a weapons source. It didn't matter that Saddam had led the Arab world in condemning the Camp David Accords between Israel and Egypt; there were other realities for Mubarak, such as his need for oil and money and political allies in the Middle East. Indeed, during the 1980s Mubarak sold some $3.5 billion worth of missiles and arms to Iraq, only to find Saddam later refusing to pay for them. In 1984, he also agreed with his colleagues in the Egyptian government to work with Iraq on a secret nuclear-capable ballistic missile program for Iraq that was named the Condor II project (or as it was called in Cairo, BME, for Ballistic Missile Egypt). By the time of his meeting with Bush in 1986, Mubarak had turned Egypt into a channel for a wide range of NATO-based missile technologies that front companies in Europe were smuggling to Baghdad. Among Mubarak's government cronies at the time of the Condor II project were Abu Ghazala, the defense minister, and Boutros Boutros-Ghali, the minister of state for foreign affairs.

In short, Mubarak's pro-Iraqi credentials were not in doubt; nor was his willingness to act on occasion as a conduit for the covert transfer of U.S. weapons technology to Baghdad. "We knew Mubarak was a middle-man for arms sales to Iraq, for the Condor missile and other stuff," recalled Teicher. "He was actually *our* covert agent."

After Bush delivered his secret message about the need for Saddam to use more air power, Mubarak acted as expected. The Iraqi air force suddenly intensified its raids against Iran, stepping up its bombing in September 1986 and inflicting significant damage on Iranian oil fields and shipping facilities along the Gulf. Saddam gained in the short run, but his escalation triggered an Iranian response that led both sides to target civilian centers over the next two years, contributing mightily to the resulting bloodbath.

At the same time that Bush and Mubarak were meeting, Prince Bandar bin Sultan, the Saudi ambassador to Washington, was making an unusual confession. Bandar acknowledged to the State Department that Saudi Arabia had transferred to Iraq hundreds of U.S.-made two-thousand-pound MK-84 bombs, known as "dumb bombs" because they are not guided by any special electronics. The MK-84 is nonetheless a highly lethal weapon, and in 1986 a number of them were used by Iraq against Iranian soldiers. Shultz, who did not share the relaxed attitude toward Iraq that was prevalent at the White House, cabled the American embassy in Riyadh, demanding more details about the transfer. He reminded the embassy that whatever the explanation for the shipment to Iraq, the U.S. government was still required by law "to report promptly repeat promptly to Congress" such a transfer.

As it happened, the public heard nothing about the transfer, although a U.S. government official who had had dealings with Iraq said that Washington had informally blessed the covert military aid for Iraq. Years later, James Baker would go before a congressional committee and explain away the Saudi transfer as "inadvertent." Washington, said Baker, did receive reports "that Saudi Arabia transferred to Iraq some U.S.-origin equipment." He was careful to add, however, that "I don't personally know the circumstances of that transfer."

Yet Baker's explanation did not sit well with an American intelligence agent who had been personally involved in the region. "Saudi Arabia was a proxy for Washington," the agent later recalled, "and shipped plenty of arms and money to Saddam as part of U.S. covert operations." One diplomat close to the Saudis said there was "no way in the world that Saudi Arabia would transfer one bullet out of its inventory without getting U.S. government approval." At the time, in fact, Washington was already playing a far more direct role in Baghdad, and on the ground.

THREE

The Secret War

By 1986, Robert Johnson was spending an inordinate amount of time facilitating covert shipments to Iraq. The job was growing burdensome. He had to liaise with messengers from the U.S. government, supervise the foot soldiers who executed the details of his deals, and coordinate frequent trips to Europe and the Middle East. There were some missions, moreover, that he simply could not leave to others.

One of those missions came in early November of that year. His contacts in the intelligence community reported that the White House was worried by how poorly Saddam Hussein was faring in his war against Iran and thought it necessary to get more military supplies into Baghdad. While for Johnson it was just another of what he called his "technical operations," the aim this time was to transport Soviet-made ground-to-ground 122-mm. missiles, which was an odd thing for an American operative to be doing. "The reason," he later explained, "was that the Iraqis had Soviet-made equipment, and it was cheaper to get them what they needed from the Eastern bloc than to provide entirely new systems from America. They were having financial problems anyway, and we were trying to supplant their dependence on the Soviets. So we ended up getting them some of the equipment through gray channels that they used to get directly from Moscow." Since the Reagan administration had decided to provide covert assistance to Baghdad but couldn't achieve its objective through official routes, the task of handling the shipments fell to operatives like Johnson.

On this trip he headed to Bern, Switzerland, where he met a CIA contractor who operated his own specially fitted Boeing 707 cargo jet, in which the two men flew on to Bucharest. There, a Romanian arms broker who had worked for years with American intelligence had the missiles ready for loading. They had been purchased on Eastern Europe's thriving black market for Soviet-made arms. The missiles were designed for use in multiple launchers and were eight feet long, so it took some time to get them packed aboard the 707. Then the operatives took off for Iraq. "I didn't like the flight or having to deal with the Iraqis," recalled Johnson. "We landed in Baghdad at night, and the air force guys came up to the plane. We gave them bottles of Scotch whisky, copies of *Penthouse* magazine, and cartons of cigarettes so they would unload the stuff quickly. We carried $18,000 in cash, the amount needed to pay for refueling, in a bowling bag. Then we were put up at a government hotel. It was tricky because our own U.S. intelligence officers in the embassy didn't know the details of what we were doing. We were supposed to keep the entire operation to ourselves."

This kind of work had occupied Johnson for more than five years by then, and he was weary of personally handling missions; he was no longer a young man. As a former CIA operative who was senior enough to contract work to others, he didn't like going out in the field himself anymore. But there were a number of extra flights that winter, and in 1987 at least one a week into Baghdad. He made the exhausting trip only a few more times before deciding he had had enough.

He was not the only American who found himself in Baghdad for confidential purposes. Some were American military personnel whom the Reagan administration had secretly begun to station in the Iraqi capital for intelligence-sharing in the early 1980s; at the White House, they were known as "liaison officers" or "observers." At first they came in teams of four or five, from the Defense Intelligence Agency (DIA) in Washington and from the Joint Special Operations Command headquarters at Fort Bragg, North Carolina; but over time, their numbers began to swell.

Other Americans in Baghdad were visiting arms merchants, and the most prominent among them was Sarkis Soghanalian, a Miami-based former CIA contractor who brokered tens of billions of dollars' worth of military hardware for Iraq during the 1980s, reporting many of his transactions to officials in Washington. Soghanalian, who resembled an Arab Sidney Greenstreet, was close to the Iraqi leadership and to intelligence officers and others in the Reagan administration. In many respects he was the living embodiment of plausible deniability, serving as a key conduit for CIA and other U.S. government operations. When Vice President Bush secretly sent his chief of staff to Panama to meet Manuel Noriega, Soghanalian supplied the aircraft from a nongovernment carrier in Miami. Soghanalian claimed that Vice President Bush was among those senior American officials who knew of his arms sales to Iraq; another was William Eagleton, the head of the U.S. interests section, who welcomed the arms dealer to Baghdad and described him to a journalist as a "friend of the U.S. government."

Back in 1983, that friendship had led DIA officials to consider an offer from Soghanalian to procure a Soviet-made Hind helicopter from Iraq in exchange for American permission to sell to Baghdad U.S.-made helicopters equipped with missile launchers. The offer was refused, however, when in a secret memo General Richard Stilwell, a deputy undersecretary of defense, advised against the deal because Soghanalian was already facing criminal charges. "I believe the potential for causing embarrassment to the U.S. government is too great," wrote Stilwell, "if it became known that the U.S. had used the services of such a notorious individual to arrange an arms deal with Iraq." (See Appendix B, page 307.)

But although Soghanalian might have been notorious, he was useful. A year later, in Baghdad, he helped broker the sale of forty-five Bell helicopters to Iraq. This time the Reagan administration approved the deal, despite fears that the helicopters would probably be used by the Iraqi military. He even flew CIA contractors to Baghdad aboard his private jet; their job was to help install some of the equipment that would transmit U.S. satellite photographs to the Iraqis.

In the mid-1980s, Soghanalian also brought military officers to Baghdad on his plane, and since he had a personal relationship with Iraqi defense officials, including Adnan Khairallah, the defense minister, he arranged quiet introductions between the U.S. officers and Iraqi battlefield strategists. Joseph Trento, a documentary filmmaker who accompanied Soghanalian on one trip to Baghdad, was surprised to learn that in addition to the officers Soghanalian transported, an American general had come to Baghdad, arriving on an Alitalia flight by way of Rome "to do business, to discuss arms." In 1984, Trento stayed in Baghdad for a month, and while he was there he was summoned to meet with William Eagleton, who told him that Soghanalian's relationship with the Iraqi defense minister "helps us." During the visit Eagleton showed Trento a map that highlighted suspected Iraqi poison gas-manufacturing facilities. "Aren't you uncomfortable about the poison gas and about this being a haven for terrorists?" Trento asked Eagleton, adding that it seemed odd that Washington would countenance the arms shipments Soghanalian was bringing in. "Yes," Eagleton answered, "I am very uncomfortable. These are not nice people, but you have to do what you have to do."

The American military commitment that had begun with intelligence-sharing expanded rapidly and surreptitiously throughout the Iran-Iraq war. A former White House official explained that "by 1987, our people were actually providing tactical military advice to the Iraqis in the battlefield, and sometimes they would find themselves over the Iranian border, alongside Iraqi troops." A military officer who was sent to the war zone remembered the Iraqis being relaxed about his presence and grateful for it: "Access to the battlefield was allowed not just to Americans, but to military personnel from other nations such as Britain and France. There was great interest on our part in strategy and order of battle, and we wanted to know about the competence of Iraqi officers. They wanted any advice we could give. We were under instructions to give them everything they wanted in the way of information." The officer, like his colleagues, carried a sidearm only, for self-defense, and he did his best to avoid the heaviest fighting on the front lines. The only problem was that it became impossible at times to know where that line was. "As a result," he said, "I guess some of us from America ended up inside Iranian territory from time to time."

There was another problem with the deployment of U.S. military personnel on the ground in the Iran-Iraq war: It took the Reagan administration to the very fringes of the law. The War Powers Act requires that Congress be notified whenever American soldiers are deployed in a military conflict, or even involved in imminent hostilities, whether they number in the dozens or the thousands. Calling the soldiers in Iraq "observers" made aides to President Reagan feel more comfortable, but some White House officials, already jittery about the breaking Iran-Contra affair, worried that they were becoming involved in yet another off-the-books operation. These worries were compounded when the same NSC staff members who were using the services of facilitators like Robert Johnson and Richard Smith and their operatives decided, along with William Casey, to ship U.S. military supplies to Iraq directly from American military bases in Europe. Once again, U.S. military officers were called upon to perform tasks that were not only politically controversial and secret but illegal because they were not being reported to Congress.

NATO stockpiles in Europe were the source of these shipments, according to a former NSC official. The U.S. base most utilized was the sprawling Rhein-Main compound at Frankfurt, the largest combined cargo and passenger terminal in the air force and home of a squadron that flew in support of Defense Department and European airlift require-ments. Rhein-Main was convenient because it shared runways with Ger-many's largest civilian airport, the busiest on the continent. "The chain of command was secret but incredibly simple," said a former Special Opera-tions officer from Fort Bragg who was sent to Frankfurt to organize the clandestine transfers. "A call would be made by someone at the National Security Council to a midlevel officer at the Pentagon. We would then hear about the request at Bragg, and we would go over to Frankfurt and into the warehouses on base, where we would arrange the flight manifests. There was so much surplus equipment there that if you came over with confidential orders and dealt with the right supply people, they would move the stuff over to the civilian side of Rhein-Main. Then an Iraqi Airways cargo jet would land and the pallets would be loaded up by the local airport workers without any American personnel in sight."

The matériel involved was always very carefully selected and was determined chiefly by judging which critical supplies the Iraqis could not manufacture themselves or purchase with ease. These determinations were made in Washington after consultations with U.S. military personnel on the ground in Iraq. "The kinds of things we handled out of Frankfurt included spare parts mainly, such as fuses for artillery pieces. You could get hundreds of thousands of fuses into just a few packing pallets," recalled the Fort Bragg officer. "We also sent chopper parts, specialty fuels, and graphite lubricants, and a few black box items, meaning high-tech electronics and other sensitive bits and pieces."

In January 1987, as the war entered its seventh year and the com-bined death toll neared one million people, Iran began yet another major offensive. This time, it pushed deep into Iraqi territory. Saddam Hussein needed help—but he also required reassurance from Washington about its intentions, since revelations in the Iran-Contra scandal were now detailing the U.S. covert military aid that had been going to his enemy Iran. From Baghdad's point of view, Washington was either ambivalent or duplicitous. Thanks to the rival pro-Iraq and pro-Iran factions inside the government, the United States had indeed sent out very confusing signals. Nonetheless, the secret shipments to Iran paled when compared with the support given Saddam, and William Casey led the drive to placate Iraq. He had already met with Tariq Aziz at the United Nations to make sure Iraq was happy with the flow of intelligence it was receiving, and he encouraged Aziz to go ahead with more attacks on Iranian economic targets.

Then neutral ships in the Persian Gulf began coming under attack from both Iran and Iraq. Those of oil-rich Kuwait were of particular concern to the administration. Kuwaiti leaders wanted their oil tankers protected by either Moscow or Washington, and in March 1987 top U.S. officials, including Caspar Weinberger, George Shultz, and Admiral William Crowe, the chairman of the Joint Chiefs of Staff, decided to defend Kuwaiti vessels that were navigating the Gulf. Two months later, on May 17, pro-Iraqi officials such as Weinberger suffered an instant case of political whiplash when a U.S. frigate, the *Stark,* was attacked by an Iraqi warplane and thirty-seven Americans on board were killed. The episode was quickly dismissed as an error, and Baghdad apologized and offered to compensate the families of the crewmen who had died. Nonetheless, the *Stark* incident underscored the increasingly risky state of affairs in the Gulf, and it was followed by a formal announcement from President Reagan that the United States would reflag Kuwait oil tankers so that the U.S. Navy could escort them.

On Capitol Hill, the reflagging announcement drew protests, and some in Congress demanded that if the United States were to become militarily active in such a dangerous venture, then the War Powers Act ought to be invoked. The White House rejected the idea, and the State Department's Richard Murphy argued that the entire reflagging operation was merely a defensive action based on the need to protect the freedom of navigation and the flow of oil. Yet Murphy also gave a not-so-subtle hint of the administration's intentions by warning Iran, not Iraq, that any attack on American naval forces in the region could result in U.S. involvement in the war in the Gulf. The reflagging exercise, he said, was part of a comprehensive strategy.

Murphy did not describe that strategy in detail, but it soon became known, on a need-to-know basis, to lower-level operatives at the CIA, at Fort Bragg, and in the U.S. Navy. "The real plans were for a secret war, with the U.S. on the side of Iraq, against Iran, on a daily basis," said retired Lieutenant Colonel Roger Charles, who was serving in the Office of the Secretary of Defense at the time and who later conducted an extensive investigation of American clandestine operations in the Persian Gulf. Using military terminology, Colonel Charles called it "a mixture of black and white operations at the same time." The black operations were covert, aimed at provoking Iran; the white operations were public, aimed at defending navigation rights in the Gulf.

In June 1987, although senators of both parties had warned that the United States was in danger of being drawn into armed conflict with Iran, President Reagan ordered warships into the Gulf. The White House pronounced the threat to American personnel as "low to moderate." Simultaneously, but hidden from public view, the administration sent a team of high-ranking officers to Baghdad, including an admiral, to begin sharing strategic information with Iraq about movements in the Gulf. In U.S. military circles, the purported reason for these visits was to improve understanding and avoid a repeat of the *Stark* incident. The reality was that it was a black operation, in which cryptographic radios were provided to Iraqi pilots, allowing them to communicate with American petty officers stationed on ships in the Gulf. "What happened," said a retired military officer, "was that as the Iraqis flew their airplanes down the Gulf, they would talk to our officers. As the relationship grew on a daily basis, the petty officers would give them the bearings and range of tankers that were trading with Iran, thus helping the Iraqis to choose their targets."

The reflagging of Kuwaiti tankers began on July 18; three days later, American naval ships started the escort operation. Some of the navy's biggest warships, designed for the open sea, were now on patrol in the constricted and unpredictable war zone of the Persian Gulf. The first disaster was not long in coming. On July 24, the 400,000-ton *Bridgeton,* a Kuwaiti supertanker, struck a mine as it moved through a major shipping channel. The explosion was so powerful, as Admiral Crowe would later write, that the captain and some crew members were literally bounced up in the air, but although the ship's hull was torn open, there were no casualties. In Washington, the *Bridgeton* accident set off political mines; several dozen members of Congress announced that they planned to file a suit in federal court against President Reagan's Persian Gulf policies in order to force the president to comply with the War Powers Act. The lawsuit was ultimately dismissed, but George Shultz was already busy taking evasive action. Frank Carlucci, the national security adviser, had sent Shultz a memo asking him to take charge of efforts at the United Nations to end the war. "There is no support in Congress for our Gulf policy," Carlucci wrote to Shultz, "so we need to draw attention away from the reflagging idea." Shultz went to New York and joined decisively in a discussion at the Security Council, which voted unanimously to approve a resolution calling for a cease-fire.

The summer of 1987 was dominated by diplomatic efforts to bring about peace and by a mounting number of military incidents involving the United States and Iran. A navy fighter jet fired missiles at an Iranian aircraft, an American supertanker operated by Texaco hit a mine, and several navy men were killed when their helicopters and jets crashed into the sea. At the same time, Washington was conducting black operations with the help of a CIA mission code-named Eager Glacier. Only fragments of this story have been made public up to now. It is known that the CIA sent spy planes and helicopters over Iranian bases starting in July 1987. In fact, the CIA's intelligence-gathering operation soon turned military. The CIA utilized the assistance of an American oil service company that transported its workers on helicopters from the Saudi air base of Dhahran to oil platforms in the Persian Gulf. During the day, Agency operatives flew in the company's civilian helicopters; at night, they used their own aircraft to patrol, and eventually they engaged in secret bombing runs. The Agency aircraft flew over Iranian territory, and late in the summer of 1987, having located a factory in which mines were being manufactured, they blew up a warehouse full of mines.

The CIA's clandestine activities in the Gulf were followed by a more public incident. On Monday, September 21, 1987, a Special Operations helicopter equipped with night-vision equipment spotted the *Iran Ajr*, an Iranian minelaying ship, swooped down, and fired rockets and a barrage from its machine guns. The shots riddled the entire side of the ship, shattering windows and piercing the bulkheads, stairwells, and oil barrels. Three Iranian sailors were killed instantly, and twenty-six were captured, including four who were wounded. The crew members were held briefly and then repatriated.

In Washington, President Reagan defended the helicopter attack, claiming it was authorized by law. But what he did not say was that many of the military actions in the Gulf were being discussed on an almost daily basis by a special committee comprised of senior officials from the White House, the State Department, the Pentagon, and the CIA on a secure telephone conference line. By agreement, the truly black operations were handled by lower-level officials in the Pentagon and the CIA on a highly compartmentalized basis. That way, Reagan's political appointees could plausibly deny any awareness of the details.

The helicopter that shot at the *Iran Ajr* was a Hughes AH6 attack helicopter from the U.S. Army's Delta Task Force 160, a special unit that had traveled to the Gulf all the way from Fort Campbell, Kentucky. These helicopters, nicknamed Sea Bats, were stationed on a U.S. barge the size of a football field that was anchored in the middle of the Gulf. In February 1988, the pilots from Fort Campbell were joined by colleagues from Fort Bragg, who manned a second barge and flew small, heavily armed OH-58D helicopters made by Bell Helicopter. Fifteen of these helicopters, called Little Birds by their pilots, had been specially modified at

Bell's facilities in Fort Worth, Texas, to spectacular effect. "These things looked extremely sinister," recalled a Special Forces officer who was stationed on the barge. "They were all black and bristling with antennas and had a huge round sight module about two feet in diameter stuck on a mast above the rotor blades. That contained radar and cameras. The impression you got, just looking at one of these things on the ground, was of a giant insect staring at you before you die."

The Sea Bats and the Little Birds flew missions night and day, conducting reconnaissance and at times firing on Iranian minelayers. Some of their successes were made public, but when one helicopter crashed, the accident was kept secret. "A Marine buddy of mine saw the helicopter afterward," said a former Pentagon official. "It had been hit by our own ordnance. The operation was so secret that the families of the two crew members who died were told the men had been killed in a car crash."

Also kept secret were the navy's black operations. Lieutenant Colonel Charles learned that in 1988 a couple of Mark III patrol boats were lowered by cranes from a barge and sent off on a decoy mission aimed at luring Iranian gunboats away from territorial waters and provoking an incident. "They took off at night and rigged up false running lights so that from a distance it would appear there was a merchant ship, which the Iranians would want to inspect. Deceptive radio traffic was also used in that instance."

"I talked to Marines from Fort Bragg who were given these black missions, and they weren't confused about what they were doing," he added. "They said they were at war, that their daily actions included combat activities against Iran. The truth, which the government has never told, is that in 1987 and 1988 there were two operations going on in the Persian Gulf. One tracked with President Reagan's policy declarations, that we were there to defend international waterways and Kuwaiti tankers, and the other was a black operation, designed to provoke the Iranians."

Admiral Crowe, who had gone before the House Armed Services Committee and denied a press report suggesting that Congress had been misled about any covert operations, decided in his memoirs to address the definition of American actions in the Gulf. He wrote that the administration had argued in Congress that the Gulf operation was not subject to the War Powers Act. "The argument was somewhat dubious, but nevertheless that was our story and we were sticking to it," wrote Crowe. Years later, after he had left government, Frank Carlucci was asked if it was fair to say that America had been fighting an undeclared war. "Oh, yes, I don't think there's any question that—well, war—you get into semantic issues here. The military would call it more an engagement or a firefight. . . . We were having problems with the War Powers Act, so I hesitate to use the term war, but there's no question it was a conflict."

FOUR

The Chilean Connection

Half a world away from the Persian Gulf, the remote Chilean harbor town of Iquique was booming in 1986. Iquique, located on the Pacific coast some eleven hundred miles north of Santiago, was benefiting from the opening of a nearby free-trade zone and a new airport. At least once a month, an empty Iraqi cargo aircraft landed on the runway, taxied to the edge of the field, and safely out of sight of passengers boarding regular flights, picked up shipments produced in an anonymous-looking industrial plant situated nearby. Visitors to Iquique, which was once no more than a collection of shanties at the base of a barren headland, had no idea the town had become the home of a manufacturing facility that was supplying some of the deadliest weapons in Saddam Hussein's arsenal, cluster bombs.

Most of the people of Iquique, including the laborers in the factory, did not know the final destination of the weapons until early 1986, when the community was shattered by an explosion that killed twenty-nine of the seven hundred workers at the cluster bomb plant. The local Roman Catholic bishop was appalled. He condemned the plant as "social sin" and warned that "these are the same bombs that are killing people in Iran and Iraq, and now they have been turned on our brethren."

Cluster bombs, originally invented in the United States to halt tank columns, dispense a particularly gruesome form of death by very simple means. A cluster bomb is simply a container packed with hundreds of small bomblets. Each bomblet is no more than twelve inches long and weighs less than two pounds. As the bomb drops, it rotates, a small charge opens the casing, and the spinning bomb distributes the bomblets in an elliptical pattern of spaced clusters that spread devastation over a wide area. Known in the trade as "area denial ordnance," cluster bombs are effectively aerial mincing machines—they shred everything in their path. The U.S. Air Force first used them as antipersonnel weapons in the Vietnam War; when dropped properly, a single bomb has the capacity to kill or maim anyone in an area the size of ten football fields. Some of the bombs that were being made in Chile were timed to explode hours after they had been dropped, causing further casualties among troops and rescuers who had assumed they were now safe. Although technically considered conventional weapons, cluster bombs can wreak almost as much mass destruction on the battlefield as unconventional arms such as chemical weapons.

Saddam's military planners in Baghdad found cluster bombs highly effective in killing the huge numbers of Iranians who poured into battle in human waves. For Carlos Cardoen, the owner of the plant in Iquique as well as other arms factories scattered around Chile, they had proved to be a very lucrative business. Not only was Iraq eagerly buying as many bombs as he could produce; he paid no taxes or duties in the Iquique free-trade zone, and his own costs were extremely low. His workers received the equivalent of ninety dollars a month, often for a twelve-hour day, and the average output of the factory was one thousand bombs a month. Thanks to all this, Cardoen was able to price his cluster bombs at as little as $7,000 each, or $19,000 less than his competitors in Europe, and still prosper.

Cardoen was both an enterprising businessman and a quick study, especially adept at making use of political contacts. The son of a middle-class family of Belgian extraction, he had grown up in rural surroundings in the Santa Cruz region of central Chile. Both at technical school in Chile and then in the 1960s on a scholarship to the University of Utah, his chosen discipline was metallurgy. He came home to Chile equipped with an engineering doctorate from Utah, and by the 1970s, he was managing a company that supplied explosives to the mining industry. In 1977 he founded his own business, Industrias Cardoen, expecting to continue working in the mining sector.

In February 1976, the United States had imposed an arms embargo on Chile because of congressional anger at the persistent human rights abuses and political assassinations in Santiago under the junta headed by President Augusto Pinochet, and President Jimmy Carter continued the embargo when he took office in 1977. The U.S. government was beginning to see the Chilean government as a pariah regime almost as troublesome as South Africa.

This marked a shift in Washington's turbulent relations with Santiago. Early in the 1970s the Nixon administration had orchestrated an attempt to overthrow the Socialist government of Salvador Allende. When Pinochet seized power in 1973 in a military coup that left Allende dead in his blazing palace, the finger of suspicion pointed to Washington. That suspicion was heightened in 1976 when Orlando Letelier, Allende's former ambassador to the United States, was blown to pieces by a car bomb in downtown Washington and little was done to pursue the case until Carter took over the White House.

As Pinochet's death squads used terror to eradicate all traces of the leftist ideals that had originally brought Allende to the presidency through the ballot box, the symbol of Chile's suffering became the soccer stadium, the holding pen where thousands were hauled for questioning and beatings following the dreaded midnight knock on the door. Thousands of people were said to have "disappeared," a term meaning they had been murdered or exiled by the Chilean secret police.

In 1978, when a territorial dispute with Argentina made a war seem imminent, the military junta headed by Pinochet launched a desperate appeal for local businessmen to manufacture whatever arms they could. The U.S. embargo had cut off access to American arms, but as had also happened in South Africa when it was hit by sanctions, the embargo forced Chile to develop a domestic industry. For Carlos Cardoen, it was the opportunity of a lifetime. Senior officers in Chile's air force approached him with a request for bombs. General Fernando Matthei, its commander, said that in 1978 Cardoen had never even seen one. "But we showed him one," said Matthei, and fifteen days later Cardoen returned with a sample fashioned by his engineers. It was the start of his intimate business relationship with the Chilean military. "I'll have to build Jimmy Carter a statue," Cardoen later declared. "If it hadn't been for the U.S. embargo we would never have invested in arms production here."

In addition to aerial bombs, Cardoen began making armored vehicles under Swiss license, as well as antitank mines and hand grenades, and in 1981, when his achievements in the world of arms-manufacturing were still modest, he began to develop his first prototype of a cluster bomb. The financing came from low-interest government loans, but the source of the technology—which Chile did not possess—was kept a mystery. Cardoen completed a prototype the next year, but he still lacked the international contacts that would generate sales. That began to change on July 13, 1982. On that day a business associate of Cardoen's in Miami encountered Nasser Beydoun, a Lebanese-born former cigarette salesman who was then exporting food and other goods to the Middle East, and in the course of their discussion mentioned the hard time Cardoen was having breaking into the right military circles in Iraq. Beydoun was a natural door-opener. Almost immediately, he was asked to represent Cardoen in Iraq, and a few months later he found himself sitting in Cardoen's Santiago office and signing a commission agreement worth about five hundred dollars for every cluster bomb he could sell. If Beydoun pulled off a big deal, he and Cardoen could both become rich. In 1991, when Beydoun found himself suing Cardoen to collect $30 million in unpaid commissions, he would recall their first meeting: "The sky was the limit when we started. According to him, heaven is opened by a golden key. He called me his golden key, rightfully really."

Thanks to Beydoun, Cardoen won his first contract with Iraq in March 1983 for a trial order of three thousand cluster bombs. He had written to Beydoun with a message for Baghdad: "We are pleased to inform you that Industrias Cardoen is willing to take its share [sic] in helping Iraq in this time of need. We can provide you with our cluster bombs at the lowest possible price." Baghdad didn't know it, but it had made its deal on the basis of a brochure that Cardoen's graphics people had rushed together. When the news that Iraq had accepted the deal and was placing an order was telexed back from Baghdad to his Santiago office, Cardoen didn't know whether to laugh or cry. He was still unable to produce bombs in any kind of volume. As he confessed to Beydoun, he still had to "iron out the bugs" in the bomb's mechanism.

He did. Cardoen hastily set up shop in Iquique, and in early 1984 the first shipment, worth $21 million, was delivered to Iraq. More sales followed, and within a year he was to visit Saddam Hussein in Baghdad. So important did Iraq become to Cardoen that it soon represented about three-quarters of his annual arms-export revenues of $100 million a year.

Later that year, as business with Baghdad increased, Cardoen's representatives began shopping for complete factories in the United States that they could dismantle and ship to Chile. They were looking for ammunition and bomb factories with all the associated equipment in place, and courtesy of the U.S. military, a couple of interesting possibilities were made available. One was an abandoned factory in New Orleans that had been used to manufacture 105-mm. heavy mortar shells back in the days of the Vietnam War; the other was a disused plant in Los Angeles that had made general-purpose bombs ranging in size from 250 to 1,000 pounds. There were, of course, certain constraints attached to both, since it was against U.S. law to ship anything with military applications to Chile. The factories were to be sold on the condition that they were demilitarized—that is, their weapons-making capacity had to be removed. Straightening out this crucial difficulty took some effort.

Lieutenant Colonel Carlos Rickertson, a retired American air force officer who represented Cardoen in Washington at the time, recalled there was "a great deal of trouble with U.S. Customs," and the sale of the two munitions factories was held up for nearly a year. Eventually, however, they were reclassified by U.S. officials as "scrap metal." After some further hassles with suspicious customs men who couldn't figure out why all these presses and drills to make shells had been officially designated scrap metal when they were in such good working order, the factories were finally shipped to Chile.

In 1985 two American diplomats from the embassy in Santiago flew up to Iquique on one of Cardoen's factory tours. There they were proudly shown the new operation, which was already turning out a range of general-purpose bombs. In the presence of Cardoen and surrounded by all the noise and bustle of a war machine at work, it seemed churlish for the diplomats to point out that nobody had bothered to remove the labels from the tools that clearly stated that they had come from the United States. "I saw them myself," recalled Rickertson. "It should have been quite evident to them that this was U.S. equipment because the placards on the bomb-making presses identified them."

As his business with Baghdad increased, Cardoen began to find himself in the company of American officials from the embassy in Santiago more often. At first, there were the usual military attachés of lower rank, who came to arms fairs and other public forums where his burgeoning empire was becoming more publicly visible. But before long he found himself with military guests of an altogether different rank—people like General Henry D. Canterbury, deputy commander-in-chief of U.S. Southern Command, responsible for all air force command matters in Latin America. To Cardoen, being with the general was the kind of ultimate endorsement, a bestowal of legitimacy, that he memorialized in his growing library of photograph albums. Here was General Canterbury examining a fuse, General Canterbury examining a gun, General Canterbury in conversation with Cardoen. Over time there were photos of Cardoen with other new-found military and diplomatic friends as well: in March 1986, General Robert Reed, assistant vice-chief of staff of the U.S. Air Force; also in

March 1986, General Ramon Vega, chief of staff of the Chilean air force; and in 1990, Charles Gillespie, the U.S. ambassador to Chile, strolling past a Cardoen exhibit headed "Technology Transfer."

Cardoen was a tireless promoter of himself and his fast-growing company. He accumulated stacks of photographs and hours of videotape showing himself with military men from America; he would be dressed in his immaculate tan silk suits, and they in crisp khakis, highlighted by quantities of gold braid and medals. Cardoen would also pose by himself in front of a helicopter here, an artillery piece there, and occasionally he would be seen peering somewhat incongruously from behind the controls of his latest armored vehicle. From time to time, in the background of these photographs would appear examples of the major source of his prosperity: white-painted cylindrical objects about seven feet long and thirty inches in diameter, carefully lit and set on stands for the officers to examine and assess with the help of colored brochures. These were Cardoen's very own cluster bombs, the most desired item in his weapons catalog.

There were, however, a few faces relevant to the Cardoen success story who were extremely camera-shy, for reasons having to do with their own personal security and also as a matter of policy—the secret policy of those at the very top of the Reagan administration. Among those figures was Robert Johnson. "I knew Cardoen quite well. We did business together," he said years later, pulling out one of the Chilean's brochures. The cluster bomb technology that Cardoen was selling to Baghdad had come from the United States, according to Johnson: "It was easy to get technical specifications down to Santiago. They could be carried as blueprints or drawings in a suitcase."

Colonel Rickertson, who knew Cardoen's cluster bombs as well as those used by the U.S. Air Force, said the Chilean model was "almost a duplicate." There was a good reason for this. The same people who worked for William Casey on other arms shipments for Iraq were directing the smuggling of American cluster bomb technology to Cardoen by covert operatives.

"I remember seeing cable traffic at the National Security Council in 1984, discussing concerns that were being raised by the Defense Department about shipments of cluster bomb technology to Chile for Iraq," said former White House official Howard Teicher. "The Pentagon wanted to stop the shipments, but nobody else really minded. I argued with people all the time about this, but Casey wanted this to happen, and he kept saying the Iraqis were undermanned."

Few U.S. military technologies were as sensitive as cluster bombs. The use of the weapon was sufficiently controversial that the Reagan administration had expressed public anger at Israel in June 1982 after Israel acknowledged it had employed cluster bombs against Syrian armor and infantrymen in Lebanon. In 1978 the United States had forced Israel to give explicit assurances that it would limit its use of U.S.-made cluster bombs, and the 1982 incident was viewed as a breach of that agreement. Yet the administration's determination to help Iraq had become so great that Cardoen was now receiving the technology itself, unofficially and in direct violation of the arms embargo on Chile.

Cardoen, claimed a former CIA contractor, was considered by the intelligence community in Washington to be of great use to the U.S. government. "He was an all-purpose asset, designed to be one of those offshore stockpilers of military equipment who could be used by the CIA to ship arms to the Afghan rebels, to the boys in Angola, or anywhere the U.S. needed some help, except the war matériel wouldn't be seen to be coming directly from America. So Cardoen became extremely useful," the contractor recalled.

By 1986, Robert Gates, the deputy director of intelligence in the CIA, was taking a personal interest in the flow of arms from Chile to Iraq. Iraq was not unknown to him. Gates had already been involved in overseeing the preparation of American intelligence data that was being shared with the Iraqi military. That sharing had been authorized by the National Security Council, but in the summer of 1986 Gates exceeded that brief by approving the provision of intelligence to Iraq that went beyond the scope of the White House guidelines. Not until October, several months after the fact, was there formal authority for what was being provided to Baghdad, and under U.S. law what Gates did could be construed as a covert action that should have been reported to congressional oversight committees.

Gates later admitted his personal involvement, although he argued that "we were not trying to influence Iraqi behavior, but to enhance their ability to pursue the war." He went on to say, "I believed at the time that the activities were fully consistent with the understanding and practices of the law then in effect," while acknowledging that in hindsight the clandestine aid for Iraq could be seen as a "significant intelligence activity."

Except among people such as William Casey, George Bush, and a few other old hands in the national security establishment, Robert Gates had never been very popular in Washington. The Kansas-born CIA officer had spent five years—1974 to 1979—assigned to the National Security Council. In 1981, Casey assured him a bright future by tapping him to be his executive assistant. Only one year later he showed his continuing confidence in Gates by catapulting him over dozens of other candidates into the job of deputy director of intelligence, a senior CIA position with responsibility for collecting and analyzing all intelligence.

Casey felt safe with his disciple, and especially with Gates's willingness to bend the rules when necessary. The fact that the two men shared the same views on critical issues such as the Soviet threat and the need to assist Iraq also pleased Casey. But on the surface, tutor and pupil could hardly have been less alike. Casey, an operations man to his bootstraps who would devour spy novels for light relief, cut a figure as a cunning but agreeable old rogue, with a silent contempt for the processes of law and accountability. The boyish-looking Gates was more of a conventional bureaucrat, ambitious and ready and willing to serve. He had spent the bulk of his career as an analyst on the paper-pushing side of the Agency. For almost two decades—ever since 1966, when the CIA had recruited him while he was still in college—he had carefully made the right career moves. When he emerged at Casey's side in 1981, he was noted for little beyond a politically appropriate hard-line approach in his analytical studies of the Soviet Union, his field of expertise, and a talent for making important friends within the national security apparatus.

In fact, however, there were other aspects to Robert Gates. Inside the Agency, as in most organizations through which a particular individual can rise with great rapidity, his appointment as deputy director of intelligence generated some resentment and a good deal of grumbling. Malicious gossip circulated around Langley in 1982 when Gates went to Fort Peary, the Agency's training ground outside Washington, to learn to shoot a sidearm. "There was no reason on earth for a senior CIA official to learn how to shoot," recalled one intelligence officer. "He just liked it."

But other officers explained this as an example of the desire of some CIA people from the analytical side to emulate their counterparts on the more glamorous operational side. And indeed, as Casey's right-hand man, Gates did do more than sit at his desk in Langley and analyze the paper flow relating to the secret arming of Iraq.

"Gates got things done," said an intelligence officer who worked with him on the covert tilt to Iraq. "He liked to pick up the telephone and call people. He did not shy away from doing things. He was not just a faceless administrator. He was truly involved in the details, without micromanaging, if you see what I mean." There were occasions in the mid-1980s when Gates decided to travel to the Middle East or to implement policy personally by meeting with members of the gray network of operatives who supplied arms to Baghdad. Historically, the handful of top jobs at the CIA were filled by people who had spent more time in conference rooms than in the field. Besides, travel involved risk—whether it was the risk of being recognized or the risk of attack—no matter how elaborate the security. But Gates was an exception to the rule, his former colleague recalled: "One of the less well-known traditions, at least since Casey, was that the top CIA men go out and get their hands a bit dirty. These guys get bored just sitting behind the desk all the time."

The manner in which Robert Gates got his hands dirty was to oversee the transfer of American cluster bomb technology to Carlos Cardoen, first in 1982 and again later, when more technical information was required to improve the weapons. Over at the National Security Council, Howard Teicher knew that Gates was involved: "Sure. He was tight with Casey and with the White House. He was one of those who helped get things done." The CIA has denied in blunt terms that Gates facilitated or oversaw any illegal shipments of U.S. military technology to Iraq by way of Chile or any other third country during the 1980s. But in the summer of 1986, Robert Johnson was visiting Cardoen in the large and comfortable house Cardoen owned near Miami. They had been discussing details concerning the outfitting of Mirage aircraft with cluster bombs, and as Johnson prepared to leave, stepping across the white-tiled entrance hall, a new visitor appeared at the door. It was Robert Gates, arriving for his own meeting with Cardoen. Why would Gates meet with Cardoen? Though Johnson was clearly uncomfortable discussing the meeting, he later summed up the situation matter-of-factly: "Gates is a great patriot, a very loyal man, and he knows how to get things done. He and Cardoen had a series of meetings in 1986 and 1987. We needed an offshore supplier, and the Chileans were very cooperative. That is a place where money talks. Cardoen could move quickly, and we needed to keep the balance in the Iran-Iraq war. This was a policy decision. Therefore the White House had to get something done. Where would they turn? Langley. But Gates was not given specific instructions on how to do it. He was just told to get it done. Cardoen was already well known. We could rely on him. For Gates to meet Cardoen was like a blessing from Washington—he was giving his imprimatur. He didn't have to get into details."

The CIA took a very careful position on the matter of a meeting between Gates and Cardoen. It issued statements denying that Gates had been involved in a covert CIA operation that supplied Iraq with U.S. arms and weapons technology. It denied that the CIA had ever had a relation-ship of any type with Cardoen. But it never specifically denied that the two men had met. That task was left to the White House, which issued a statement in July 1991 saying, "The whole story is unfounded. There never were any sales, overt or covert, to Iraq or Iran through a third country. Mr. Gates never met with Carlos Cardoen."

Nonetheless, another U.S. government agency's computer records do make mention of the encounter between the two in Florida, and a knowledgeable American intelligence agent explained that there were actually two reasons for the meeting: "First, Cardoen knew what was moving to Iraq at the time, and that was useful information, very useful. Second, it was purely a matter of coordination of the shipments. Coor-dination of what we wanted Saddam to have."

Although the meeting was carried out in secrecy, Gates left a trail that would gradually be pieced together later. Almost inevitably, word of his involvement with Cardoen leaked out to some of Cardoen's own top-level employees in Santiago. As one former executive confided: "If I start to make trouble, I will have trouble not only here in Chile, but outside. I know about these things, and many other meetings with the Americans. There were meetings with Gates, and other meetings in the States and in Europe." Indeed, the report of Gates liaising with Cardoen was an open secret as far away as London, the city to which Iraq's former UN ambas-sador Saleh Omar al-Ali had moved after leaving his diplomatic post in 1983. "I received the information informally about Gates when I was in Baghdad in the early 1980s," he would later recall. "It was one of those things that I wasn't supposed to know, even though I was ambassador," he said with a smile.

CARDOEN OBTAINED MORE from the American government than cluster bomb technology and private encouragement from senior officials for his trade with Iraq. He also was allowed to import large quantities of the metal zirconium from the United States, more than thirty tons in 1984, thirty-seven tons the following year, and over seventy-five tons by 1987. Zirconium is a vital ingredient in the bomblets inside a cluster bomb canister because it enhances the incendiary effect when they explode. In 1985 a Commerce Department bureaucrat handling the export licenses raised concerns about the size of the shipments, but he was told that if there were any problems, the American ambassador to Chile at the time, James Theberge, would be willing to help. The export licenses were approved. In the spring of 1987 another Commerce Department official also noted the substantially increased quantity of zirconium being sent to Santiago, and he too wondered why Cardoen required so much of the metal for his civilian mining activities. He was informed that the American embassy in Santiago would conduct a postshipment check. Was the zirconium actually being used for mining? The cable that the embassy in Santiago sent back to Commerce failed to answer the question directly; instead, conveying information that was not news to anyone by then, it reported that "Cardoen is best known as the producer of cluster bombs. Approximately 68 percent of his total production is exported to Iraq." The American embassy then saw fit to end its cable to Commerce in a reassuring manner: "Banking and trade sources report that Cardoen Industries has an excellent financial reputation and that it complies well with financial obligations. Although Cardoen is involved in the sale of armaments and has made his fortune from it, he is considered to be a responsible recipient of U.S. products."

The definition of a responsible recipient may be a matter for interpretation, but in 1987 there was no doubt about Cardoen's wealth. He had sold nearly $500 million worth of cluster bombs to Iraq by then, and he was now operating from a well-appointed office suite at the top of Chile's tallest building, the twenty-nine-story Santa Maria Tower in Santiago. On the wall in his office there were only two photographs: one of General Pinochet, and the other of Cardoen offering a handshake to Saddam Hussein.

Cardoen had good reason to be grateful both to Saddam, the best client a cluster bomb maker could dream of, and to Pinochet, whose drive to develop Chile's arms industry had launched him into prosperity. He also had a good friend in Ambassador Theberge, who made numerous visits to Cardoen's factories during his time in Santiago from 1982 until October 1985, and who knew of Cardoen's Iraqi dealings in great detail. Indeed, when Theberge left his diplomatic post, Cardoen offered him a part-time job in Washington, working for a subsidiary of Cardoen's armaments company. Theberge represented Cardoen in Washington until early 1987, at the same time that he held a second part-time job. In January 1986, William Casey had recruited Cardoen's new associate to be a member of the CIA's Senior Review Panel, which consisted of experienced former intelligence, military, and foreign affairs specialists who advised the CIA director. For the next year Theberge was thus a paid employee of *both* the CIA and Carlos Cardoen. It was a comfortable closing of the circle.

FIVE

The Tools of the Trade

Being the Reagan administration's unofficially approved vehicle for supplying cluster bombs to Saddam Hussein was a profitable venture for Carlos Cardoen, but he wanted still more. It was in pursuit of that objective that he checked into a hotel on the outskirts of Montreal on the afternoon of November 14, 1984. That evening a Learjet touched down, four American businessmen stepped out, rented a car, and drove to the hotel where Cardoen was staying. There, over dinner, Cardoen and the Americans began a discussion in which billions of dollars were at stake. They had come to Canada, neutral territory, to decide among themselves how to carve up the world's cluster bomb market.

The conversation was intense. Cardoen did most of the talking and chiefly addressed his remarks to the most senior of the Americans, a quiet, bespectacled man named James Guerin. After dinner they repaired to Cardoen's room for further negotiations. On the table as their talks proceeded was a list of 109 nations, divided into three columns. The A column would be Guerin territory, the B column would be Cardoen territory, and the C column would "constitute targets of opportunity" for both men. In all territories the two would cooperate by parceling out work on the cluster bomb components to each other's companies. The deal would cover a period of three years.

It was one of those moments in which the atmosphere fairly crackled with the sense of possibilities. In the huge potential market that ran from Australia to Zimbabwe on the agreement, there were endless riches to be made from the thousands upon thousands of lethal bombs the two men would manufacture. Even more promising, their cluster bombs were cheaper than those of the handful of European manufacturers against whom they would now compete jointly. Guerin's U.S. government-model clusters sold for nearly three times the price of Cardoen's, at $20,000, but the Europeans wanted $26,000 for their version. The prospects were intoxicating. The deal was made.

Guerin and his team left the hotel very late that evening, and on the flight back to the United States, one of the deputies asked him about Cardoen. "He had nothing but accolades for Cardoen," recalled Tom Jasin, Guerin's marketing manager. "He said they had this longstanding relationship, and he praised the way Cardoen had started up his company in Chile and how he had prospered." Jasin then asked Guerin if the carving-up that had just been agreed to wasn't against some antitrust law. "Tom, you've got to get your head screwed on right," Guerin answered. "This is perfectly legal, it's international business, the world."

James Guerin liked to think in global terms, and manufacturing defense products was his chosen route to success. Born in Morristown, New Jersey, the son of a local farmer, he had studied agriculture at Rutgers College before switching to electrical engineering and taking a graduate degree at the University of Arizona. After a stint in the navy during the Korean War, Guerin landed a job in 1960 at the Lockheed Missile and Space Corporation in Sunnyvale, California. For nine years he worked as a Lockheed manager, learning about the world of defense contracts, working in the Polaris missile program, and running a 280 strong engineering department. In 1969, he crossed the country to go to work as a manager for Hamilton Watch, one of the great names in the town of Lancaster, Pennsylvania. The company had decided to diversify by launching a military electronics division and had won an army contract to make field radios. Guerin was brought in to manage sixteen hundred employees in the new division, but he did not fare well. A former personnel officer at Hamilton dismissed him as socially inept, professionally "mediocre," and altogether "not very impressive." To his employees at Hamilton, Guerin had sketched a bright future for the division, complete with a company aircraft; but it floundered financially, and Hamilton finally shut it down.

In 1971, frustrated and eager to make his own way, Guerin left Hamilton and set up his own electronics firm, first in the cellar of his Lancaster home and then in a converted chicken coop near his back yard. He gave his company a grand name, International Signal and Control, but its beginnings were inauspicious. "Oh, the smell some days!" he remembered later, reminiscing about the stench of manure that wafted in from the surrounding farmyard.

Guerin had a light touch in those very early days. When potential customers came to call, he would introduce them to a horse named Sam, who wore a sign that read "production control manager." But he was serious in his determination to make ISC into a great company, and by concentrating on what he knew best, military communications equip-ment, he was soon able to move into a one-story office building in Lancaster. He hired a staff that numbered twenty people, and he experi-mented in the manufacture of a bewildering hodgepodge of consumer electronics, such as video games, computers, electric insect killers, and radio parts. Money was almost always a problem, since Guerin had expanded his business interests far beyond his means. "He was hanging on by his teeth for a while," recalled a former employee. "What he really wanted was to get into the defense business. He used his Pentagon connections from his Lockheed and Hamilton days."

Guerin filled the ranks of ISC with former military and intelligence officers, talking all the time of the multinational colossus he planned to create. In his relentless drive to make money and attach some importance to his life, he was willing to call in favors wherever he could. He was also prepared to break the law. In 1975, he began selling defense goods to South Africa, in violation of the longstanding UN arms embargo that had been imposed because of the country's regime of apartheid. The United States was observing the embargo at the time, but this did not matter to Guerin. One day in 1975, he called an aide to his office and told him he wanted to procure a variety of electronic components and arrange their shipment to South Africa. By hook or by crook, International Signal and Control was finally going to live up to its name by achieving sales outside the United States. The South Africans, Guerin told his aide, were "fed up" dealing with European distributors of defense electronics; ISC would now take the lead.

What he did not tell his employee was the reason he felt able to go about breaking American export laws so cavalierly. That year, James Guerin struck a deal with the government of the United States; he had entered the world of espionage and found a way to ship goods to South Africa.

In 1975, working closely with Admiral Bobby Ray Inman, then the director of naval intelligence, Guerin became a trusted covert operator for the Ford administration. The United States wanted to spy on Soviet ships off South Africa's coast, and the plan was to have Guerin ship advanced electronic sensors, optics, and related goods to South Africa in an intelligence venture that would supply the listening posts at the Simontown naval station, off the Cape of Good Hope, with what it needed. Despite the official U.S. policy of seeking to isolate Pretoria, the leaders of both countries shared a fervent anti-Soviet sentiment. Business between the two could thus be rationalized in terms of the need to fight the cold war. In exchange for the electronics technology, Pretoria agreed to share the information it had on Soviet ships and submarines with Washington.

Admiral Inman was the most prominent intelligence official to work with Guerin on the clandestine operation, which was code-named Project X. "ISC had the South African connection," Inman later confirmed. But Guerin's institutional partner in the covert operation was the National Security Agency (NSA), the secretive American electronic surveillance agency.

In order to facilitate ISC's shipments to South Africa while concealing the hand of the American government in the operation, the NSA helped Guerin set up a front company called Gamma Systems Associates. Gamma was not really a company at all; it was just the address of an office located in the Jamaica, Queens, section of New York City, near Kennedy International Airport, used mainly to generate shipping records. In the jargon of the intelligence world, Gamma was a mail and phone drop, a destination through which ISC could send equipment before the goods were shipped out from New York aboard airliners bound for South Africa.

Guerin set up a specially walled-off area at ISC's headquarters in Lancaster that did nothing but liaise with intelligence contacts in Washington, procure goods for Gamma, and arrange for their delivery to the address near Kennedy airport. No one was allowed to enter the restricted zone without authorization from Guerin, and those given such authorization had to tap a special code into a lock on the door. Former colleagues recalled that as Project X developed between 1975 and 1977, Guerin seemed to relish the intrigue almost as much as the profits derived from his sales to South Africa. While to his neighbors in Lancaster, Guerin seemed the perfect family man, singing in his local church choir and always generous when it came to civic causes, he was actually becoming something of a Jekyll and Hyde figure. The select group of ISC executives who were party to Project X watched his ego grow by the day, along with his penchant for the twilight world of spies.

In 1977, when President Jimmy Carter took office and decided he did not want the United States to have any further intelligence relations with South Africa, his administration ordered the cancellation of Project X. By then, however, Guerin had made enough new contacts in the project to launch himself and ISC in the defense sector, and he won several lucrative contracts from the Pentagon. In fact, his very first connection, Admiral Inman, would eventually accept a part-time paid assignment from ISC.

By 1982, having moved from being director of naval intelligence to director of the National Security Agency and then to the CIA, where he was deputy director under William Casey, Inman retired from his last senior position in U.S. intelligence. In that job he had run the Agency's day-to-day operations and coordinated the preparation of national intelligence estimates for the White House; after Casey, Inman had become the CIA's best-known representative on Capitol Hill. Now he went into the private sector, starting up his own defense electronics research and development business in Austin, Texas. "I get bored managing the status quo," he later observed.

Inman's private sector relationship with ISC began as a result of a shrewd financial move Guerin made in 1982. He wanted to raise capital to expand ISC by selling stock to the public, but he did not want to subject himself to the extensive disclosure requirements imposed by the Securities and Exchange Commission. His solution was to float the company on the London Stock Exchange, whose disclosure rules were far less rigorous than those in the United States. In September of that year Guerin launched an aggressive fund-raising campaign in the City of London, and his timing was propitious. Although he disclosed next to nothing other than that ISC was a go-go defense electronics company with exceedingly bright prospects in the areas of security, communications, and electronic warfare systems, capital was readily available. At the time, investors in London were enthusiastic and surprisingly undiscriminating about small North American companies. A number of dubious oil exploration businesses from Calgary and Houston had already come to Britain in 1982, announcing lavish plans and bearing away millions of pounds by selling shares at inflated prices. Guerin did exactly the same thing. He persuaded market analysts in London that he was a sure-fire winner and sold $56 million worth of stock in a matter of weeks. "The London financial community," Guerin said at the time, "looks at foreign trade in a more mature way than the U.S., and understands the need for confidentiality."

The London share flotation provided Guerin with the capital he needed to pay back some debts and grow ISC, but it also meant he had to conform to a U.S. law that required any American defense contractor that was fully or partly owned outside the United States to form a special "proxy" board of independent directors. The idea was to create a buffer between U.S. companies and foreign investors that would prevent the leakage of classified information in Pentagon contracts. Bobby Ray Inman was obviously an ideal candidate for ISC's board, and he had the added virtue of already knowing something about the firm. The Pentagon approved him and two others—retired General John Guthrie and former Assistant Secretary of Defense Barry Shillito—for appointment to the ISC proxy board without reservation. The board was responsible for dozens of contracts, but beginning in 1983, none was as important as the company's manufacture of cluster bombs for the Department of Defense.

That summer, Guerin paid $43 million to buy Marquardt, a California-based armaments-maker that had the primary contract with the Pentagon to supply the Rockeye cluster bomb. The Rockeye, a five-hundred-pound weapon that was considered the most efficient cluster bomb in the world, guaranteed Guerin a steady flow of income from the U.S. government. It also gave him the chance to contemplate conquering the world market. He combined Marquardt's operations with ISC in logical fashion: Marquardt made the canisters, and ISC produced the electronic fuses that timed the release of each cluster of bomblets. The bombs were assembled at a plant on a navy weapons depot site near Indianapolis.

It was Guerin's takeover of the cluster bomb maker that led him to step up cooperation with Carlos Cardoen. By 1984, the two men had forged an unholy alliance in a number of areas. Two ISC technicians were sent down to Santiago to assist Cardoen in repairing a radio system that emitted the coded electronic messages that detonated explosives used by the Chilean air force. Other cooperative ventures would follow, including negotiations for ISC to sell production-line capability and components to a Cardoen subsidiary in Spain that would manufacture fuses for use in Eastern Bloc artillery rounds.

Cardoen, however, was receiving more than help from Guerin's technicians and ISC's goodwill. In 1984, in flagrant violation of the U.S. embargo on Chile, Cardoen received design specifications of ISC's Rockeye that markedly improved the performance of the cluster bombs he was selling to Iraq. Nasser Beydoun was among those who knew of the secret transfer of ISC cluster bomb technology. But neither James Guerin nor Carlos Cardoen was personally involved; they knew how to keep their hands clean. The cluster bomb technology was transported from ISC to Cardoen by a covert operative who was himself working for a front company indirectly owned by the CIA. Law enforcement officials have spent years trying to trace this technology transfer, but they have remained unable to make any arrests. The carve-up of the world cluster bomb market, meanwhile—the one meant to enrich both Cardoen and Guerin—eventually crumbled. Guerin continued selling cluster bombs to the U.S. government and he enjoyed some modest sales abroad, but it developed that he and Cardoen were not meant for each other after all.

YET SEVERAL SENIOR OFFICERS of the CIA, while careful to maintain as much distance as possible from the gray network of foot soldiers who aided Baghdad, found there was something irresistible about James Guerin and his business in Lancaster. The feeling was mutual. The common ground between Guerin and the Agency was the continuing interest both had in South Africa. "The Carter administration is supposed to have shut down Project X," a former executive recalled. "Well, we kept right on going, and with the cooperation of the CIA." Richard Moose, the assistant secretary of state for African affairs during the Carter administration, was among those skeptical of the Agency's behavior. Moose was the man who had written the 1977 presidential order banning any further intelligence cooperation with Pretoria. Despite that ban, Moose said, the CIA "felt their interests were best served by a collaborative relationship" with South Africa. "I didn't trust our own agencies any more than I trusted the South Africans. . . . Responsible officials of the Agency sat in my office and lied to me about what they were doing," said Moose.

In 1984, Moose's worst fears were borne out. Although intelligence cooperation with South Africa had now been banned for nearly seven years, one of the Agency's most senior Africa experts developed a new rapport with Guerin and his fellow ISC executives. Clyde Ivy, an electrical engineer and missile expert who worked for Guerin, had spent the latter part of the 1970s consulting with Armscor, the South African government-owned arms company. Ivy, who lived in modest surroundings in suburban Lancaster when he was not in Pretoria, had offered South Africa his professional expertise to design a number of its ballistic missiles. In the summer of 1984 he was running an educational computer business for Guerin in South Africa. During a visit back to Lancaster he reported to Guerin that he had seen some very sensitive nuclear weapons programs in South Africa. Guerin picked up the telephone and called an official at the CIA's Africa division. The next morning, a team of four CIA officers showed up at ISC, proceeded to debrief Ivy, and because he traveled back and forth to South Africa, asked him to stay in touch.

Thereafter, before each trip Ivy would dial a special number in Washington, and a contact would come on the line, sometimes making a special request for information. Upon his return he would get a call from the Agency, and a debriefing session in Lancaster would be arranged. Ivy reported to his CIA handlers about military progress in South Africa; Guerin told him that it was fine to export military goods to South Africa using Gamma, since the front company near Kennedy airport that had been established during Project X still existed.

Over the next four years, Gamma became busier than it had ever been in the old days. Guerin's staff at ISC would procure equipment and ship it up to Gamma in New York. A truck would drive from Lancaster to Kennedy airport every Friday and load up a South African Airways 747 cargo jet. The planes that went to South Africa in this way were packed with some of the most sophisticated testing equipment needed for missile systems. It included telemetry tracking antennae that could monitor signals from missiles in midflight, along with gyroscopes needed to guide the missiles. There were photo-imaging systems that are used in conjunction with high-speed cameras to photograph and measure the targeting accuracy of missiles, and advanced radar-controlled antiaircraft equipment. Not a single item had the proper export license, and it was highly unlikely that the sale of such sensitive goods would have been approved by the State Department. Yet Guerin kept the shipments flowing, and the sales totaled more than $15 million a year. "I discussed some such exports on occasion with some of the CIA agents," Ivy later wrote in a sworn affidavit. "During the six years of my meetings and discussions with the CIA, none of the agents suggested that any of our exports or shipments were illegal, and the CIA encouraged the continuation of our relationship and contacts with South Africa."

As one customs agent put it, the CIA "let all that shit go and did nothing to stop it." More disturbing still, Armscor was turning around and selling much of the equipment that had been sent from Guerin's company to Baghdad. "It went into the Condor II missile that Iraq was developing to carry a nuclear warhead. It went into their antiaircraft defenses. And who knows where else it went?" said the customs man, who, like former Assistant Secretary Moose, did not trust some of his fellow government employees.

Moose suspected that CIA officers made sure that "longstanding contacts they had would continue, transactions and export licenses that had been facilitated would continue. People who believe they are above the law will make those kinds of arrangements." But the CIA was not supposed to be above the law. In fact, it has a statutory obligation to inform law enforcement agencies of any illegality discovered in the United States. There was a certain irony in the recollection of a Senate Intelligence Committee staffer years later that "Robert Gates told us in closed hearings that the ISC case showed that CIA should be more careful about informing law enforcement agencies of these things."

Langley's blithe attitude gained it some intelligence from ISC executives on South Africa's weapons programs, and it certainly kept the South Africans happy. More ominously, it kept James Guerin's Lancaster operation going and offered him time and money to organize further transactions with South Africa, including some that would directly benefit both his friend Carlos Cardoen and the government of Iraq. In one peculiarly triangular relationship, ISC in 1986 began making use of the Gamma channel to sell South Africa PS-115 power supplies, tiny high-tech batteries that are inserted into proximity fuses. A proximity fuse is the component that causes a bomb or artillery round to explode above the ground, thus ensuring that the blast will spread over a bigger area and cause more damage. ISC started by filling an order for ten thousand power supplies in July 1986; they were shipped to Fuchs Electronics, a private South African company that acted as a middleman between Carlos Cardoen and the Iraqi procurement network headed by Hussein Kamel. Cardoen had a contract with the Iraqis to build a proximity fuse factory near Baghdad, but until it was completed he had to acquire the power supplies from the United States. Fuchs acted as a subcontractor to Cardoen, buying a total of 330,000 power supplies from ISC and shipping them on to Baghdad. In 1987, Clyde Ivy informed his CIA debriefers that the South Africans were working with Cardoen and sending the power supplies to Iraq. Yet the Agency took no action to halt the ISC shipments, which ended up being installed inside 155-mm. shells that would be fired from Iraqi guns.

Busy as he was with all this, James Guerin still took time to burnish his image in Lancaster. If there was anything incongruous about running an international arms operation out of a city in the heart of the Amish countryside, Guerin didn't dwell on it. His one concession to his surroundings was to tell his employees not to speak about cluster bombs or other weapons. "We keep it quiet. We don't want the community to know," he explained to one new recruit.

Guerin preferred to be seen in the company of prominent locals or, when the occasion arose, with celebrities. Alexander Haig was one of those whose name Guerin sought to exploit, both for personal gratification and in the interests of ISC business. In November 1984, he was introduced to Haig and persuaded him to become a consultant to ISC. Over the next two years the former secretary of state would earn $150,000 in consulting fees, mainly for his help in trying to open up new international markets for the company, but he visited Lancaster only rarely. He was there once on December 12, 1984, and he returned exactly two years later for a reception at Guerin's home that was designed to build political support for Haig's presidential candidacy. Guerin had suggested the fund-raiser—as always, he was covering his bets, just in case Haig ever did make it to the White House. Haig was not impressed by him. "I always thought Jim Guerin was a weirdo," he later recalled.

AT THE TIME of the fund-raiser, James Guerin was preoccupied with yet another secret operation, although this one was financial rather than military. Despite his shipments to South Africa, business elsewhere was not going well; ISC's stock price was flagging, and the company needed cash. The problem was not new, and to resolve it Guerin had long before embarked on a strategy that was every bit as illegal as his weapons sales. In order to mask the weakness of his company's accounts, he had created a complex web of phantom contracts, phony customer lists, and overseas bank accounts filled with slush funds. He invented the names of these customers, forged purchase orders, receipts, and shipping papers, and, taking a leaf from his experience with covert operations, had set up front companies in Switzerland, Panama, and the United States to "document" payments that didn't exist. By 1986, he had laundered more than $700 million through this network, taking some of the money for personal use but sending most of it through a continuous international loop that made each payment look like a new one when, in fact, he was simply recycling the same cash from account to account.

In November 1986, with his legitimate business under pressure, Guerin had to prevent the loop from unraveling. He decided to sell part or all of his company—if he could find the right buyer. Since he had enjoyed a warm reception in London when he sold stock there in 1982, Guerin set off once again for the British capital. He approached Sir Derek Alun-Jones, the chairman of Ferranti, one of Britain's biggest defense electronics groups. Would Ferranti be interested in acquiring ISC? The answer, based on ISC's poor stock price and its dependence on a limited number of customers, was a polite no thank you. Guerin had little intention of giving up, however, and the following summer he returned to

London and asked Ferranti to reconsider. This time Alun-Jones, who presided over a company that was having trouble expanding into new markets, was persuaded. He instructed his staff to conduct a thorough investigation of ISC, and he asked auditors from the firm of Peat Marwick to evaluate the financial health of Guerin's company.

On Tuesday, September 8, 1987, the board of Ferranti received an internal report on the merits of the proposed takeover. The directors were told that on one missile project, involving components from South Africa, Guerin had made use of a British company "specifically to avoid any U.S. embarrassment and/or U.S. export license limitations." The report also noted that Guerin kept certain unnamed Washington contacts informed of his activities, and "where a specific license is needed it has been obtained." Then there was Gamma, another ISC program about which "Washington is fully aware." Also flagged for the Ferranti board was a program to supply naval communications equipment to Iraq by way of an Italian subsidiary of ISC that faced a possible loss of $11.5 million. Finally, the report warned, political risks "exist on a scale unusual in Ferranti markets." In particular, there was the problem that while ISC "keep very close relations with Washington, one must recognize that some of this is in the covert policy area and ISC could be left on a limb." (See Appendix B, page 316.) In London, Guerin's company had only limited "clearance" from the Defence Ministry and would require more in order to do business with countries such as Iraq, Chile, South Africa, and others.

Altogether, it could be read at best as a most tepid endorsement of the merger plan, although not nearly as negative as a separate analysis that was prepared shortly afterward for a family trust by the merchant banking firm of Lazard Frères; this warned that buying ISC could be a "significant drain" on Ferranti's cash resources.

The financial pitfalls of closing the deal seemed apparent, and ISC's secrecy made it almost impossible for Ferranti to assess certain arms contracts, but Guerin had told Alun-Jones that the company had won a huge missile contract with the government of Pakistan that was worth more than $500 million. So Alun-Jones supported the agreement, and in November 1987 Ferranti paid $670 million to buy ISC, issuing stock instead of cash and naming Guerin deputy chairman of the British group.

At the age of fifty-six, James Guerin had achieved his El Dorado. His long march to wealth and power in Lancaster, Pennsylvania, had taken eighteen years, but it was to last only that many months. In June 1989, a former business partner publicly accused Guerin of masterminding a huge fraud, claiming he had inflated the value of ISC prior to its takeover by Ferranti. All of Guerin's secret financial transactions now came tumbling forth. At the heart of the fraud was a conspiracy hatched by Guerin to create the impression for Ferranti's benefit that ISC had promising contracts, such as the Pakistani missile deal, when in fact neither that contract nor others totaling $1.1 billion existed.

When the fraud was discovered, it threatened Ferranti's very existence; the company had to write off more than half of the $670 million it had paid for ISC, and its share price crashed in London. In the United States a lengthy federal investigation showed that since the early 1980s Guerin had been going well beyond faking sales in order to pad the size of ISC's revenues. There was a pathological cast to the way in which he misled banks, investors, and auditors about a number of contracts while he devoted his real energies to illegal arms sales to countries such as South Africa, and through South Africa, to Iraq. He even received some help from Carlos Cardoen, who had permitted Guerin to stage a phony inventory inspection for auditors in Santiago. While the CIA had looked the other way on the weapons front, Guerin had falsified almost every facet of ISC's finances.

Of all the tools of deception he had employed, none was more effective than the front company, the phone and mail drop that could be used not merely for weapons shipments, but also to receive and transmit false invoices. James Guerin had been given this tool as a covert operator for the U.S. government. Now it brought him a criminal indictment, and Ferranti the consequences of a corporate scandal that rocked the City of London.

SIX

On Her Majesty's Secret Service

Five days out of Glasgow the driving became progressively rougher. The going across Europe had been pretty good. Half a dozen currencies and the usual selection of girlie magazines had cut through the hassle at the East European border crossings. Now the problem was the geography and the elements. The unrelenting mountainous terrain in southeast Turkey challenged the seventeen-truck convoy as it wound its way toward the northern border with Iraq. These were great rigs, modified by the Ford truck division at Langley, a few miles from London's Heathrow Airport. They could carry up to forty-two tons and had sixteen gears that could take you pretty much anywhere, from a day-long ninety-mile-an-hour cruise on an Autobahn to a tricky drive on a desert piste irregularly marked by rusted oil drums—or as had happened before, through an ugly-looking roadblock between you and the West.

So far so good. The transit paperwork was all in order. And the bandits on the Turkish border with Iraq, who would normally expect a bribe or else they'd be at your throat, had understood they had better not so much as wave at this particular shipment. What was really making this trip such a bitch was the fact that at least half of the trucks had been specially winterized to plow their way from Britain through the Soviet Union as far east as Siberia. You could spend a couple of endless black nights in the sleeper cab without freezing to death, no matter where you broke down in the frozen wastes. But it was ninety degrees already, there was a clear run from here to the top of the thermometer, and Frank Machon and his tight-lipped crew of drivers already felt set to die in the heat. "Trans-Siberia Spedition," read the huge black panels on the truck sides in English and Cyrillic lettering. That simply confirmed that these guys were crazy.

The call to Frank Machon in October 1982 had come from Whitehall, the Ministry of Defence. It was the usual MI5 intelligence officer on the phone. He announced Machon's destination: It would be Basra. Frank paused. Basra—that was in southern Iraq. So Her Majesty's government had cleared a special delivery all the way down there? Yes, a ministry-approved trucker was needed to get the wellhead pumps to Basra, and the manufacturer had already been given Machon's name. Still, it was almost three thousand miles from Glasgow to Basra—that added up to an eight-day nonstop drive. The Ministry of Defence man was bland, even casual. He was sure Machon could handle the mission. For a thousand pounds a day, they'd learn to live with it, thought Machon.

Machon knew where to find his recruits. Young men looking for driving jobs would come down to his warehouse directly from the Pollokshaws Road employment office, a couple of miles away toward Glasgow city center. They'd have short haircuts, not an ounce of fat on them, and they'd be carrying one of those small cards the employment office clerk handed them for consideration by the prospective employer. Name, education, previous job, if any. Area of special skills. And then in the right-hand corner at the bottom of the card there would be a small pen mark, placed there for the particular attention of Frank Machon. He'd look up from behind the Formica-topped desk in his office, stub out his cigarette in one of those hollow ashtrays that conceal too many dead butts, and know that he was looking at an ex-military man, with certain special skills to be evaluated during the course of the interview.

Sixteen of those young men were behind him now, as the convoy rolled onto the paved highway toward Mosul and Baghdad, then south to Basra. Each truck carried two wellhead pumps, twenty-one tons apiece, and the destination was the Basra oil field. What made this assignment particularly tricky was the fact that the oil field had been seized by the Iranians, and the front line lay between the city of Basra and the oil field itself. Seventeen truckloads, thirty-four pumps in all, had to be delivered. Machon had run enough strange Ministry of Defence loads to enough strange places to know not to waste time trying to figure this one out. That was the deal. And now he was driving down through Iraq on a perilous journey, crossing battle lines to make another delivery.

"Outside Basra we picked up an Iraqi tank escort," recalled Machon. "Nothing special, just one or two tanks that led us up toward the front, then stopped and waved us past. We had no way of telling how far we had to go from there. So we turned our headlights on and drove like hell toward the oil field. Nobody shot at us."

It was neither the first nor the last lesson he would learn about the broad chasm between appearance and reality in the business of war. For almost a decade before the Basra assignment, Machon and his trucking company had run all over Eastern Europe and the Soviet Union for the British government, hauling politically dangerous cargo. Empty crates containing accommodation for people being moved across borders. Food, printing equipment, and paper for the Polish strikers in Gdansk. Other material he couldn't talk about, all of it liable to land him in an Eastern Bloc jail or in a ditch with a bullet in the head.

On some assignments his truck would be rigged with fiber optic lenses that fed into a hand-built camera concealed in the truck's pancake air filter directly behind the cab. Bridges and airports, railroad junctions and depots—he had photographed them all for British intelligence. He'd crashed through border crossings using the reinforced snowplow on the front of his truck. He'd been shot at. Just on suspicion, he'd been beaten up by East European policemen, to the point where he could hardly walk. One time, he was so badly injured that he was forced to spend two weeks in a safe house in Poland before recovering enough to get out of there, but by the grace of God he and the truck had been clean on the occasions when the cops turned nasty. He had never pressed the innocuous button among the dozens of others on the dash, the one that would have signaled to London by satellite that he was in trouble and would have activated resident British agents in Eastern Europe to try and help.

Now, ten years after that October 1982 phone call with the instructions for Basra, those dangerous times passing in and out of the Eastern Bloc felt like the good old days to Machon. Days when serving Her Majesty's government had been a clear-cut business. The Soviet Union had been the enemy, it had to be fought in a number of different ways, and he was happy to play his part and take the risks that went along with it. In a sense, this kind of endeavor ran in the family. Machon's father had been in British military intelligence. Both father and son held their government in high esteem. Then the world had turned. Machon had found himself drawn into the much murkier area of the Middle East, and British dealings with Iraq during the Iran-Iraq war. There were none of the clear policy markers along the way that he was accustomed to, but his faith in the fundamental values publicly articulated by the British government sustained him. What he would discover about Britain and Iraq in the late

1980s would shatter that faith and leave him bitter and betrayed. It would come to obsess him and wreck his life.

Machon lit a cigarette and told his story. He was wearing dirty black slippers because shoes had hurt him too much ever since his motorcycle accident as a kid. He had been crushed against the big bike's exhaust pipe and burned his feet so badly that teams of doctors said he wouldn't walk again. They had been wrong on that one. In fact, most people who didn't take a little time had a way of getting Frank Machon wrong, underestimating his brains, his streak of Victorian morality, and for want of a better way of putting it, his flat-out Scottishness. He had a kind of gritty independence, inseparably entwined with grim tenacity in pursuit of what he believed in, no matter what the price. Those character traits are of great value in the intelligence business. But when the time came for him to be thrown overboard into the sea of deniability, half-truths, and innuendo that concealed British policy toward Iraq during the 1980s, those same traits—combined with his sense of betrayal, his knowledge, and his contacts—made Frank Machon a political nuisance. He already knew too much, and he knew exactly how and where to unearth more.

When Machon finally went public in 1992 with his allegations about what he perceived to have been the illegal arming of Iraq, the Whitehall response was predictable. They had never heard of this guy—a trucker or something from Glasgow? Glasgow—north of the border, and so far removed from the values of Whitehall that it was pretty much off the map. It was the kind of place timorous ancient cartographers used to leave blank, save for the warning "here be dragons." Then the disinformation boys got to work on the media, and in doing so, they got Frank Machon wrong again. Government officials attempted to steer Fleet Street investigative journalists away from Machon, claiming he was just another wacko with a farfetched story. But Machon did not take kindly to being branded a CIA agent, unpatriotic, a nut case, or any of the other smears that accompany the disowning of a recalcitrant former intelligence asset. He became more determined than ever to publicize what he regarded as government duplicity, wrongdoing, and cover-up.

Frank Machon, of Polmadie Storage and Packing Limited, Glasgow, is five-seven and thin as a rail. The joints on his fingers are too big for his hands, and his nose is too big for his face. Beneath his grimy overalls, his navy-issue sweater has chafed a mark around his neck where his shirt would be if he wore one. If he has a suit at all, it's hanging somewhere waiting for the next funeral or similar occasion. His brutal accent was scraped off the walls of Glasgow's meanest tenements. On top, most of his black hair has gone. Nighttimes like this one, after too many hours of talking and cigarette smoke, his eyes are weary and defeated. For a man of forty-seven, he looks awful.

Outside on the dreary trading estate, a thin, chill drizzle rakes a half-century's worth of industrial detritus. It's freezing in this warehouse where he's sitting, but the place is immaculate. It is old and solid, about two hundred feet long, forty feet high, and sixty feet wide. The adjoining warehouse is the same: solid construction, from those prosperous and muscular days when Glasgow's engineers and shipbuilders set the standard for everyone everywhere, days when this was a gun factory. Now everything from freezer display cases to portable power plants to military goods is stored here. Most of the material is boxed in huge wooden crates bearing multilingual stencils, arrows, and cautions. Running the length of the warehouse up in the ceiling are the red-painted gantry cranes and hoists that move the stuff around. Occupying most of the space in this particular warehouse are five plastic-hulled shallow-draft troop landing craft that were never delivered to Iran because of the shah's departure in 1979. The Ministry of Defence has informed Machon they will take them away shortly; a new buyer has been found.

Inside the rolldown steel doors of the first warehouse is a locked, red-painted wooden cabin, the kind you see at construction sites full of engineers with hard hats and rolled-up plans. The cabin is furnished with a crude heater, a long folding table, two beat-up chairs, and a huge photocopier. The table is awash in paper. It looks as though somebody tore the lid off half a dozen old tea chests full of documents and pitched the contents onto the table, the chairs, the floor. The ashtrays are overflowing, the walls are bare, and the coffee in the cups is old and cold. Nobody has visited Machon's archive recently.

What bothered him more than anything was the duplicity of it all. Since 1988 he had been volunteering information to the government about Iraq in confidence, offering a paper trail of huge dimensions that took in half a dozen countries and suppliers with household names. He had copies of phony end-user certificates certifying that military goods were going to places they weren't. He had found out where they actually were going. He had copies of papers signed by British government officials authorizing all kinds of shipments that contravened the official stance of neutrality. He had handed in the paper, stacks of it. At a quarter to midnight on July 19, 1988, he was given a receipt for the dossier from the Strathclyde Police, which covers the greater Glasgow area—and nothing had happened.

Well, one thing had happened. He had received a phone call one morning shortly afterward from an anonymous but friendly police officer, who clearly knew what he was talking about. The message was simple. The investigation that had been started when Machon turned over the documentation had come to a full stop after exactly a week. The orders to do this had come from London. The police officer hung up.

So Her Majesty's government didn't want to know. Furthermore, it now had all his paperwork. But Frank Machon had kept copies in that red wooden cabin inside his warehouse, and more copies stashed elsewhere in Europe. He wasn't about to quit, and he was becoming angry. For more than a year he persisted, writing letters to local and national politicians and pressing local law-enforcement authorities to take up his cause. In November 1989, a middle-aged man showed up at the warehouse. He said he was from customs, but Machon figured he might be intelligence. Anyway, it made no difference—by now, they were all the enemy. The man stood across the desk in Machon's second-floor office, looking out past the plastic plants, through the grubby blinds, and down over the interior of the warehouse, and he wondered out loud why Machon kept gnawing away at this tale of his. Machon just didn't seem to understand: The government was grateful for the information he had accumulated and passed along, but it was time to leave the whole matter behind. This was a question of national security.

Then the man's demeanor changed. Quietly, he mentioned that Machon should watch out for the safety of his eight-year-old daughter. It was one of those lines from a bad TV movie, and for Machon it didn't play. Not at all. With his crass ploy, the man lit a fire in Machon that smolders yet. There had always been a certain clarity of purpose in Machon's existence, and if any of the Faceless Ones ever thought about it, they would likely have categorized him—in governmentspeak—as a blunt instrument of the expendable variety: about as diplomatic as a crowbar, but loyal, extremely loyal, with a clear idea of right and wrong, a man who would risk his life in the cold war to further the values of democracy as espoused by Her Majesty's government. They got that part right. Now he was having to listen to this shit from the same bunch of people who had been relying upon him all these years.

"Ye canna keep watching the kids all the time," the man had said. "Ye'd not have the time to work, would ye?"

Pop.

Machon busted him on the jaw quick as that, and the man in the Marks & Spencer suit went over backward against the trash basket, spilling coffee and old cigarette butts onto the cheap yellow carpeting. Seconds later, Machon's unsmiling young men from down in the warehouse were up the stairs two at a time, and they threw Her Majesty's representative out into the street. Frank Machon had had it with Her Majesty's government.

THERE HAD BEEN A TIME—it seemed light-years ago—when names like James Guerin in Pennsylvania and Carlos Cardoen in Chile had meant nothing to Frank Machon. But when he signed up his trucking company as a licensed explosives carrier for Allivane International Limited in March 1988, he learned a great deal about them very quickly. Machon first heard from his contacts in the Ministry of Defence that Allivane had a large contract to fill, the supply of complete 155-mm. artillery ammunition rounds to Saudi Arabia. Allivane subcontracted everything but the fuse assembly and the propellant charges and made them at a factory on the outskirts of Glasgow; what was needed was somebody who could truck explosives from the local ammunitions depot to the production plant. Machon got the job, and soon he began to realize there was something very wrong about Allivane. For starters, the company's managing director, Gerard Heneaghan, spoke mysteriously to Machon about missing funds and missing company documents. Heneaghan also seemed to have exceedingly poor relations with Allivane's chairman, Terry Byrne. Then there was the nature of Allivane's work in the defense sector: Machon was used to security measures, but Allivane's secrecy seemed obsessive. Even Heneaghan told Machon he knew little about certain contracts.

Both Heneaghan and Byrne were former employees of James Guerin. In 1982, after three years at ISC, where he had been responsible for marketing weapons systems in Europe and the Middle East, Byrne had founded Allivane with Guerin's encouragement. At the outset, the company did not manufacture anything—it was a contract procurer of arms. Guerin kept up his ties to Byrne, even maintaining him on the ISC payroll as a consultant for the first two years of Allivane's existence. Heneaghan had worked on NATO military aircraft and weapons systems for Ferranti in the 1970s, and from 1982 to 1987 he had looked after the sale of weapons technology to the Middle East at ISC Technologies Limited, the London arm of Guerin's group.

By the time Machon went to work for Allivane, it was suffering heavy losses and having trouble paying its bills. That was one thing Allivane had in common with ISC in 1988; the other was that both enjoyed a relationship with Carlos Cardoen. Arms-dealing was a cutthroat business, but at the same time there existed in the upper reaches of the trade a kind of fraternity to which a few big players belonged, the kind of operators whose business embraced both government defense contracts and commercial arms sales, and whose continuing success and prominence depended upon a certain patronage dispensed by individuals at the higher levels of government. Cardoen and Guerin were just such people.

In the spring of 1988, Machon's suspicions about the company grew when he walked into an office at Allivane and saw what looked like plans for a missile plastered on a wall. "The plans had been sent to Allivane by Carlos Cardoen, and they concerned a component we were supposed to supply to Iraq's Condor missile program," a former Allivane executive later admitted.

Except for a very restricted segment of the international arms community, for a long time nobody had ever heard of Allivane. But in 1988, Allivane had become quite well known, and even notorious, both at the Pentagon and at the Ministry of Defence in London. "Allivane? Somebody was looking after them. They were untouchable. And they were linked to Jim Guerin," said one Pentagon official, recalling his own frustration at being unable to stop a string of strange arms shipments to Iraq in the 1980s. "Allivane was a facilitator, used in covert weapons shipments to Iraq, and at times to Iran as well," explained an American intelligence officer.

Allivane's London offices in Horseferry Road were conveniently just around the corner from the Ministry of Defence. According to a former Allivane executive, senior officials at the Defence Ministry were briefed "all the time about everything we were doing, including our arms shipments to Iran." Indeed, Allivane did not discriminate between the two combatants in the Iran-Iraq war. Back in 1983, it had signed up as a subcontractor for Luchaire, a French company that was selling the popular 155-mm. shell to Iran. The Luchaire sales, based on false end-user certificates, were approved at cabinet level in Paris and contradicted France's officially stated policy of neutrality. When they became public, they caused a political fracas. For Allivane, participating in Luchaire's Iranian sales was nothing more than an early step into the gray network of those companies selling to both sides in the war, with either implicit or direct government approval.

Within months of going to work for the company in 1988, Machon was hearing from Allivane executives about secret dealings with Iraq, specifically that Saudi Arabia was not the real end-user of the 155-mm. shells being assembled in Glasgow; the weapons were actually destined for Baghdad. The more he learned, the more Frank Machon felt he wanted to expose Allivane's secret arms sales. When Allivane failed to pay him for work he had done, his determination to get the story out grew stronger.

He remembers speaking about Allivane on several occasions with the British defense minister, an affable Scot named George Younger who later was given a peerage and became Lord Younger, the present chairman of the Royal Bank of Scotland. The two had known each other since the 1970s, when Lord Younger was an aspiring Scottish politician and Machon a helpful constituent. Back in 1983, when plain old George Younger was serving as Margaret Thatcher's secretary of state for Scotland, the Scottish Development Agency had even helped set up the fledgling Allivane with £147,000 of government-provided grants.

In May 1988, Frank said he picked up the telephone and called Lord Younger in London. He wanted to warn the defense minister of a bizarre plot. It seemed that a group of Allivane employees were thinking of blowing up one of their explosives trucks in order to collect the insurance. The explosives onboard were to be used in Allivane's manufacture of shells for Saudi Arabia, according to the export license issued by Britain's Department of Trade and Industry.

Today Lord Younger denies any detailed knowledge of Allivane, or of having heard much about it during briefings at the Defence Ministry. But Younger cannot completely deny knowing of Allivane. In the spring of 1988, when Allivane was having financial problems, he even authorized his deputies to intervene directly to make sure that arms to Saudi Arabia were shipped on time by the company. Years later, he would have difficulty recollecting this. "I may well have done that. I can't personally recall doing it . . . but I'm not saying in any way it's not true. It probably is," he said, embarrassed.

Lord Younger would have been even more embarrassed if he had seen what was on the wall of Frank Machon's scruffy little office in Glasgow. There, on the cheap plywood wall behind Frank's desk, hangs a framed certificate expressing Lord Younger's personal appreciation of Frank's crime prevention efforts. "Secretary of State's Crime Prevention Committee. This certificate is presented to Frank Machon in recognition of outstanding assistance given to the police and the community," reads the inscription, followed by the signature of George Younger, secretary of state for Scotland. Not far away, sitting atop a tin file cabinet, is a black-and-white eight-by-ten-inch photograph of a beaming Lord Younger shaking hands with an awkward-looking Frank Machon as the certificate is presented. Not many clandestine operatives for the British or American government have photographs of themselves and such prominent political friends on display.

IN THE WORLD of arms-dealing, government, and espionage, Allivane was perhaps best known as one of the world's largest producers and suppliers of American-designed fuses. At first glance, since both Britain and the United States had embargoed the sale of munitions to Iran and Iraq, it was difficult to see where Allivane found such a large volume of business and how such an upstart company could obtain such a large piece of the action in such a short period of time. The answer, as Frank Machon discovered in 1988, was that Allivane *was* doing business with Iraq, thanks in part to the good offices of Dr. Gerald Bull, the errant Canadian rocket scientist.

Bull was thought to be an evil genius who would work with any government, any intelligence service, in order to fulfill his lifelong obsession with building the world's largest gun—a huge cannon that could fire a projectile hundreds of miles. His search for the money and political backing he required to build this "supergun" had taken him from the Pentagon to the Caribbean to South Africa and ultimately to Baghdad, where he was welcomed. The pursuit of his dream, however, would later cost him his life.

In the summer of 1988, while Machon was working at Allivane, he came into possession of some curious drawings that he didn't really understand but that he believed would be of interest to Her Majesty's government. They showed, in its projected final form, an assembly of twenty-six steel segments that appeared to form an extremely long barrel. Machon didn't know it then, but he was looking at the plans for Bull's supergun, which Iraq had just commissioned. In 1988, Bull, working through his Brussels-based Space Research Corporation, was just beginning to set up a clandestine network of component suppliers for the supergun in Britain and across Europe. Bull was also the brains behind some of the most advanced artillery shells in the world, including his own specially modified long-range 155-mm. shell. Bull turned to Allivane to help the Iraqis set up a production line to manufacture fuses for these shells, an understandable choice since Allivane by now had a reputation

for being willing to sell to proscribed countries. An eighteen-page copy of
the plan agreed upon by Bull and Allivane was replete with references to
detonators, fuses, and artillery projectiles.

Allivane had no problem doing the deal, even though it was strictly
against London's restrictive official guidelines covering arms sales to Iran
or Iraq. The issue of how the government would treat arms sales to Iraq
had in fact been resolved long before. Back in January 1981, before the
men who surrounded Ronald Reagan had given the nod to American
clandestine operatives who would get arms to Iraq, the British government, headed by Margaret Thatcher, had made a similar decision.
Thatcher's plan took shape during a meeting of the cabinet's Overseas and
Defence Committee a mere four months after the start of hostilities
between Iran and Iraq. With Thatcher in the chair, the committee discussed how to "exploit Iraq's potentialities as a promising market for the
sale of defence equipment." The war between Iran and Iraq might be
bloody, but the mercantile spirit dominated the secret proceedings. The
cabinet committee agreed that the sale of "lethal items should be interpreted in the narrowest possible sense and the obligations of neutrality as
flexibly as possible."

"We never had any problems cooperating on the Iraqi fuse facility we
negotiated with Dr. Bull. We informed the Defence Ministry of exactly
what we were doing. Somebody up there in the government loved us," a
former Allivane manager later recalled. "We learned about Allivane very
early on," said an American intelligence officer. "It must have been about
1983. Before that, most covert policies on Iraq were formed independently. Gradually Washington and London became aware of each other's
operations and began coordinating."

Had the intelligence operatives in either country been seriously
interested in staunching the flow of weapons to Iraq, it would have taken
only a little effort to make the journey to suburban Wayne, New Jersey,
some twenty miles across the Hudson from New York City. For a small
company there named Rexon was the source of the fuses that Allivane
bought and then sent to Jordan, for onward shipment to Iraq and use in
artillery shells.

Over the course of six years the Allivane executives had no problem
getting as many as 25,000 fuses a month from Rexon. It didn't take much
more than a phone call from Scotland to New Jersey to get things moving.
"Allivane bought the fuse parts from Rexon through an intermediary, then
shipped them to us in Glasgow," said a former Allivane executive. "There
was no problem with export licenses from the U.S. because they were

going to the U.K.—a friendly country, right? Then we would bounce the fuses from the States on to Jordan and Iraq. It was like clockwork."

Gerald Bull valued the fuses made by Rexon as much as the men from Allivane did. On February 6, 1990, the New Jersey company was contacted by a branch of Lloyds Bank in Birmingham, England, and informed that the Central Bank of Iraq had just opened a $2.9 million credit that was being transferred through the Space Research Corporation to Rexon. Bull had ordered the Rexon fuses on Iraq's behalf, and Rexon was legally protected by the U.S. government when it filled the order since the fuses were sent from the United States to Jordan with approval from the State Department. They ended up in Iraq.

In March 1990, Gerald Bull was assassinated in Brussels. One year later, an embarrassed State Department official took a second look at the paperwork that had given Rexon the green light to ship the fuses to "the Al-Fao State Establishment, c/o Jordan Armed Forces." In a plaintive note to another division within the State Department, the Office of Defense Trade Controls asked, "Can you conclusively identify the Al-Fao State Establishment? With what country or countries might it be connected?" The answer, when it came, was to the point: "We suspect that this organization has been involved in Iraq's military development programs—possibly including nonconventional weapons—for many years." The U.S. Customs Service had the same suspicion. "I have followed Allivane and Rexon and Bull for three years," said a senior customs investigator, "and I can tell you that none of this could have been done without government approval."

In Britain, Allivane had shut down by the time the last fuses reached Iraq. And Frank Machon found himself hitting a brick wall. He had been owed £68,000 by Allivane and was unable to obtain payment. When he could not get his money, he had one more reason to feel crushed. His solution was to go public, to tell the world about Allivane's covert shipments, about the shells for Saudi Arabia that really went to Iraq. He wanted the attention of Parliament, of Margaret Thatcher, of anyone in Her Majesty's government. But Margaret Thatcher was not interested in hearing about Saudi deals unless they were large and profitable for Britain. The British government had no interest in embarrassing Saudi Arabia, the prize customer for British armaments and everything military.

In fact, the shipment of shells to Saudi Arabia that had so enraged Machon was tiny compared with an immense deal that Thatcher herself had signed personally. In 1985, after extensive negotiations with the Saudis over a period of years, she had concluded the agreement, worth

around £20 billion to British manufacturers, called the Al Yamama deal—
after the Riyadh palace of King Fahd. It was the biggest arms transaction
in British history. The money from it was scheduled to pour into Britain
for years to come. Given the overwhelming political significance of the Al
Yamama agreement and the importance of British trade relations with the
Saudi kingdom, Machon's suggestions that any shells made by Allivane
for Saudi Arabia had subsequently been transferred to Iraq could prove a
distinct embarrassment if they became public.

In fact, controversy had already surrounded the Al Yamama contract
when it was rumored that various middlemen had played a pivotal role in
the accord. Both the British and Saudi governments vociferously denied
that any unofficial agents had been involved, and that included a suggestion about Mark Thatcher, the prime minister's son. His name was
dragged into the controversy in late 1992, when Howard Teicher went on
British television and claimed: "I read of Mark Thatcher's involvement in
arms deals in diplomatic dispatches from U.S. embassies in Europe and
Saudi Arabia." Teicher's suggestion that Mark Thatcher had played a role
was also swiftly denied.

Quite apart from these charges, the Al Yamama contract itself underwent unusual scrutiny in London. In 1989, Britain's National Audit Office
began a three-year inquiry into how the Ministry of Defence had accounted for billions of pounds in contract payments that it had passed on
from the Saudi government to British arms suppliers involved in the deal.
The Public Accounts Committee of the House of Commons also probed
suspicions about alleged payoffs to middlemen in Britain. But in 1992 the
parliamentary committee agreed to suppress the confidential findings of
the National Audit Office, even though only Robert Sheldon, the committee's chairman, had read them. No evidence of fraud or corruption had
been found, the report apparently said. Yet one reason given by Sheldon
for not releasing the report was the "highly sensitive" situation regarding
jobs in the defense industry.

Thus the veil of secrecy surrounding *any* British arms deal with Saudi
Arabia—be it Al Yamama or the separate Allivane sale of artillery shells—
remained intact. For a long time the Allivane story and Machon's allegations of the arms diversion to Iraq would stay as hidden as the details of
his own missions on Her Majesty's Secret Service. Britain's covert role in
the arming of Iraq was to be treated as a state secret for several years more.

SEVEN

From Rome to Atlanta

At exactly 11:30 on the morning of Tuesday, March 5, 1985, the door of the Oval Office swung open, and President Ronald Reagan strode across the room to welcome two of the toughest politicians ever to emerge from the corrupt caldron of Italian politics. Prime Minister Bettino Craxi, the bald and abrasive Socialist leader who would later come under criminal investigation in a massive bribery scandal, stuck out his hand and exchanged pleasantries with the American president. The better-known foreign minister, Giulio Andreotti, the Christian Democratic godfather of Italian politics who eight years later would finish out his career under criminal investigation for alleged Mafia activities including a murder, mumbled his greetings as well. Since neither Craxi nor Andreotti knew more than a smattering of English, both men relied on the interpreting skills of Ambassador Rinaldo Petrignani, a cheerful and punctilious diplomat who had been on duty in Washington since 1980.

The White House meeting proceeded at a leisurely pace and spilled over into a working luncheon, as befits a summit between the heads of a NATO member government and that of the United States. During the two-hour discussion the subject of Reagan's beloved Star Wars antimissile project came up in a substantial way; Italian hopes of winning research contracts were high on Craxi and Andreotti's agenda. Following their meeting, Craxi would give qualified support for Star Wars research, although it would be nothing like the ringing endorsement that had come from Margaret Thatcher when she was at Reagan's side two weeks before. Still, Craxi knew that Fiat, Italy's biggest industrial empire, was keen to get a piece of the Star Wars research pie, so in his public remarks later on he was careful to state that both the Italians and the Americans would draw benefits from Star Wars—an apparent reference to Washington's willingness to offer some contracts to its European allies.

The lunchtime conversations included the normal discussions about East-West relations and U.S.-Soviet arms control efforts. A word or two was spent on the situation in Nicaragua. There was a delicate verbal minuet about Libya and its controversial Colonel Qaddafi, with whom the Italians had close economic ties. Reagan addressed the Italians on the state of relations between Israel and the PLO. As lunch progressed, there was a brief chat about Egypt and Syria. Finally, the leaders engaged in a round of mutual admiration at the way the governments of Italy and the United States had been working together against terrorism, drug-trafficking, and organized crime.

The one item that did not appear in the subsequent press notices and briefings by "senior officials," however, was the discussion of Saddam Hussein and Iraq's conduct of its five-year war against Iran. That week, although Saddam was already using Carlos Cardoen's U.S.-designed cluster bombs and had just begun a new round of air attacks on civilian population centers, Iran was preparing to launch a new offensive that would lead to more than twenty thousand deaths in a single battle. The White House had been receiving intelligence reports on the war and was busy with its covert shipments, but it recognized that certain things just could not be done because of U.S. laws on arms exports. As a senior diplomat present at the White House meeting later recalled it, "Craxi, Andreotti, and Reagan discussed the danger of Iran overrunning Iraq, and both were very clear in saying they must do something." The Americans, in short, wanted some help from Rome.

In 1993, a tired and discredited seventy-four-year-old Giulio Andreotti finally acknowledged what had transpired at that White House meeting. He sat in his lonely office in Rome reminiscing, complaining of sleepless nights, and sputtering his denials of mounting allegations that he had colluded with the Sicilian Mafia. But when asked to recall that Oval Office discussion with Reagan, the old fox of Italian politics came alert. Had there been a request from Reagan to help supply arms to Iraq? "Yes, that is true," replied Andreotti, glancing out the window at the sun-baked streets of the Italian capital.

The normally secretive Andreotti, as Machiavellian a politician as Italy has ever produced, seemed almost eager to talk about White House meetings of days gone by. Old glory—anything was better than the daily battering he had to face from the Italian press in the spring of 1993. After a career in politics that had spanned half a century and made him prime minister of Italy seven times, the Mafia accusations were proving to be Andreotti's Waterloo. It was the first time Italian magistrates had dared to probe the allegedly sinister relations between the Cosa Nostra and top politicians in Rome. Until now, Andreotti had been Mr. Untouchable; he had, in fact, survived no fewer than forty investigations since the 1950s. Questions about Bush and Iraq and covert assistance to Saddam that Rome provided at the request of the White House might even have been a relief. He seemed too bitter, too tired, and ultimately too cynical to be concerned about whether his remarks would expose intrigues that led back to Ronald Reagan and George Bush. There was no question that it had all seemed so normal at the time. The Italians had always served Washington's interests, and Rome had been the favored staging ground for CIA operations in the Middle East throughout the cold war. "Ask me anything," said Andreotti.

George Bush, he observed, had earned his everlasting admiration as a man of experience and diplomacy who had run the CIA and who knew his way around the upper echelons of power. The new president, Clinton, seemed a bit "young." And Reagan? Oh, there were tales to tell about that fellow. Like the time in 1984 when Andreotti had visited Qaddafi, the Libyan dictator who was a longstanding friend, and the Mad Colonel of Tripoli had given him a copy of his Green Book with a special dedication just for the president of the United States. "I gave it to Reagan a few days later, in Los Angeles, in a meeting we had toward the end of the Summer Olympics," he recollected with relish.

The question of Iraq was brought up again, in particular the issue of what Ronald Reagan and George Bush might have done or not done in their dealings with Saddam. What was Andreotti's position during that White House meeting when the U.S. president had asked for help? "My position with them was always to tell them that it was an error to place their faith in Iraq as though it were a democratic power, while all the others were considered devils. And in particular, later on, I told them that after the Iran-Iraq war ended [in 1988], they had no need to continue arming Iraq. And I remember that Iraq had been armed to the teeth by Egypt, by everyone, by America."

Here was the old maestro of Mediterranean diplomacy again—here was the Andreotti who had served as a channel for Washington, for Reagan, for Bush. Why did he think the Americans had gone on arming Iraq like that? "Because they had a foreign policy that was far too simplistic.

They thought in terms of good and evil, but the reality is that things are rarely so clearly divided. Let me explain better. Even back in the days of Carter, when the United States didn't have relations with Iraq and I was convinced that Washington should have relations in view of their role in the world, even then I tried to explain the Arab mind to the Americans. I told the president, and I wrote him a letter too, that for an Islamic person to be polygamous is not unusual. They can have four wives, for example. So forget it when it comes to foreign policy. The important thing is to be present—otherwise, you'll push them too much in one direction, and they'll go in the other."

The Italians had already pushed in the direction of Baghdad, and they had done so in order to serve mercantile interests as much as foreign policy goals. Italy had had warm relations with Saddam and had actively competed with France to serve as his premier supplier of Western weaponry and technology. Back in the 1970s, the Italians had even contributed to the Iraqi nuclear project at Osirak. In 1977, there had been an infamous $50 million contract to deliver four laboratories to the Iraqi Atomic Energy Commission, including a fuel-fabrication laboratory and a laboratory to test nuclear fuel-processing equipment that would be used for plutonium extraction. This technology was a vital ingredient in helping Saddam further his nuclear weapons ambitions. A year later, the Italians trained more than one hundred Iraqi technicians and scientists who were working on the atomic project.

If the White House had been perturbed by this and other assistance for Iraq, it didn't show. In 1980 it had come as no surprise to Washington that the Italian government had signed a $2.65 billion contract with Saddam to provide him with a small, ready-made auxiliary navy. The megadeal included four Lupo-class frigates, six Assad-class corvettes, munitions, support craft, and even a floating dock, to be manufactured at an Italian state-owned shipyard near Genoa and then delivered directly to Iraq. Francesco Cossiga, who was serving as prime minister at the time, hailed both the deal and Saddam Hussein, whom he called "a symbol of peace and stability."

One of the banks called in to help finance the Iraqi naval order was a sprawling government-owned institution that had been set up in 1913, ostensibly for the benefit of the Italian working man. By 1980, however, the bank, which was called Banca Nazionale del Lavoro (BNL), or the National Labor Bank, had gained a very different reputation. Its roots had become thoroughly tangled in the dank undergrowth of Italian politics, and it was known at the time to be one of the most corrupt and manipulated of the state banks. All manner of crooked bag-carriers and fixers found themselves "recommended" by their political patrons for easy jobs at BNL.

The bank was owned by the Italian Treasury. Its top management, including executives who were occasionally politicians rather than bankers, was appointed on the advice of government leaders such as Craxi and Andreotti. Indeed, there was even a tradition at BNL that the chairman was a member of Craxi's Italian Socialist party and the director-general came from Andreotti's Christian Democratic party.

After the Iraqi naval deal was signed, however, BNL faced two major embarrassments. First, the Italian government collapsed after cabinet members were exposed as belonging to the Mafia-like Masonic lodge known as the P-2 Freemasons. The lodge, a sinister organization that plotted coups, robberies, and a variety of financial and political intrigues, was run by a friend of Andreotti's; BNL was quickly shown to have among its upper echelons a veritable nest of P-2 operatives, including Alberto Ferrari, the bank's director-general, and four of its top ten executives. As former BNL chairman Nerio Nesi has recalled, "being the chairman of BNL is difficult if you don't have good relations with the director-general. But if the director-general is a member of the P-2, then life is almost impossible." Dubbed "the bank of the P-2," BNL was, by all accounts, a genuinely rotten bank.

The second embarrassment related to Iran. From 1983 to 1985, BNL had participated in the illegal financing of arms to Iran through Luchaire, the French company that employed among its subcontractors Allivane of Britain. The Luchaire-Iran arms case would haunt BNL throughout the 1980s and lead eventually to indictments against the bank's officials.

In 1984, Italy's state-owned Agusta helicopter manufacturer sold $164 million worth of helicopters to Iraq. The order was for military helicopters fitted out for antisubmarine warfare, but Rome had needed permission from Washington because the choppers were sold by Agusta Bell, which made them under license from Bell Textron in the United States. Andreotti, when asked in 1993 about the sale of Agusta helicopters to Iraq, sat stiffly at his desk in Rome and confirmed with a terse "*sì*" that they had indeed been sold as part of a top-level understanding between President Reagan and Prime Minister Craxi to try to assist Saddam. "Certainly the policy we were all following at the time was a policy of great support for Iraq," said Andreotti.

Washington's view of Rome's support was benevolent, to say the least. At one point in 1987 the Italians complained to the American embassy in

Baghdad that they were under pressure from Saddam to deliver the ready-made navy BNL had helped finance in 1980. From the Iraqi capital, Ambassador David Newton cabled back to Secretary of State George Shultz that Washington should make plain to the Italians "that while we do not sell weapons to either side in the Gulf conflict, we have no policy of seeking to limit weapons sales to Iraq." "I met with Andreotti six or seven times and am aware of Italy's help during the tilt years. We did ask him for help," recalled a senior White House official at the time.

As for BNL and Iraq, throughout the 1980s U.S. intelligence services tracked the increasingly cozy relationship between the Italian bank and Saddam's minions. The information was not hard to come by; the American embassy in Rome was located literally right next to BNL's headquarters on the elegant Via Veneto, and American diplomats had warm relations with the bank's executives. If something special was required from the Italian prime minister's office or the infamous SISMI, the intelligence unit whose agents were frequently available to do free-lance work, there was no problem. A top aide to Craxi would later explain that "the Italian intelligence and security services have long been notoriously subservient to the Rome CIA office and the American embassy." Long indeed; during the cold war Andreotti had worked in close collaboration with James Jesus Angleton, the fabled CIA counterintelligence chief. Rome was well wired by U.S. intelligence; it was a most user-friendly place as far as the CIA was concerned.

For reporting purposes, the CIA's task was augmented by officers from the Defense Intelligence Agency (DIA), the Pentagon's intelligence unit, and in fact some of the better reporting Washington received from Rome concerning arms flows came from the DIA. In one confidential DIA report, for example, agents in Rome reported back to Washington that a BNL branch in the north of Italy had been used by Iraq to pay for the shipment to Baghdad of nine million antipersonnel mines worth a total of $225 million. In 1981, Saddam's procurement officers had approached both BNL and the Italian government when Iraq was seeking the mines and the financing. Later in the decade, the requests would go directly from the Iraqi Defense Ministry to the Italian embassy in Baghdad—government to government, just like the frigates deal. And once again Italy would lend a hand while Washington kept track of events.

The mines that Iraq asked for—and received—were a particularly nasty brand of circular plastic explosive device that measured less than two inches in diameter. They could be scattered from helicopters or simply dropped on the surface of the desert. They would ignite when stepped upon, instantly blowing the feet or legs off the helpless victim, soldier or civilian. In the spring of 1991, after the end of Operation Desert Storm, the lethal little mines remained a serious hazard for U.S. and allied troops stationed near the southern border of Iraq. Two years after that, they were still finding victims—this time the long-suffering Kurds of northern Iraq. Nearly every day people would be blown apart as they trod on them. The source of the mines was quickly identified by international relief workers. They had come from a company that was 50 percent owned by Fiat, the group controlled by Gianni Agnelli. The seventy-two-year-old Agnelli, who is still known today as the uncrowned king of Italy, is not technically speaking an aristocrat. But he had a blue-blooded friend named Count Ferdinando Borletti, whom he put on the Fiat board in the 1980s when Fiat bought half of a company in the northern Italian city of Brescia. The count's company was called Valsella, and it made the mines that were shipped to Iraq.

Years later, employees of another Fiat subsidiary would be found by the secret services to have shipped parts for Saddam Hussein's Condor II nuclear missile project, the one Saddam was working on with the help of Hosni Mubarak and his Egyptian cronies. Fiat sidestepped these accusations by claiming its employees had acted on their own and without Agnelli's knowledge.

In the case of the Iraqi mines, Fiat offered a different kind of denial, saying that yes, it owned half of Valsella, but no, it didn't have any "management control" over the company. What it did have was two of its top executives sitting on the four-man Valsella board of directors. When asked if it was possible that Fiat owned 50 percent of the mine-making company and had two of its senior executives on the board, yet still knew nothing of the clandestine shipments, Fiat said yes it was possible, and declined to respond further.

The Iraqi mines story went far beyond Fiat, though, and most of it has remained secret until now. BNL executives in Rome have always denied that the bank played any role in the mines shipments. So have Italian politicians. In fact, the paper trail shows that both BNL and Italian politicians were involved, including aides working for Foreign Minister Giulio Andreotti himself. In one of the more byzantine capers ever to emerge from Rome, millions of the deadly mines were shipped to Iraq by way of a front company in Singapore. The mine sales required ministerial approval. Advisers to Andreotti, as well as aides to the ministers of defense, finance, foreign trade, and intelligence agencies, sat through several meetings and approved shipping the mines, even though they knew they were going to Baghdad, not to Singapore, as the fake end-user certificates claimed.

By 1993, when Andreotti sat down for the interview in Rome, he had some difficulty remembering details of the mines. Government documents show quite explicitly that the interministerial committee approved the shipments to Singapore. Could he recall that? "On this Valsella matter, I don't know. Surely it was an earlier meeting," said Andreotti. But there were several meetings about the mines at the time when you were foreign minister. "I think so," added a weary Andreotti, "but remember, in general we were inspired by the policy of the NATO alliance in these matters."

BNL could not remember full details of its financing of the Iraqi mines. But a review of the bank's archives revealed that yes, Baghdad had asked BNL to open letters of credit totaling $155 million for the mine exports. These financial guarantees were never used by Iraq, said a senior BNL executive, so BNL had never financed any mine sales to Iraq. Unfortunately, the bank's archive search was not complete. BNL did play its part in the Iraqi mines story, and what is more, it did so with the vital assistance of a gray network company. It was not Guerin's Gamma nor any of Cardoen's partners this time, but the company did have its CIA and British intelligence links.

The company was called Casalee, and Casalee records make it totally clear that BNL did lend a hand with the Iraqi mines, through Singapore. An obscure tobacco trading business based in the European tax haven of Luxembourg, Casalee acted as the intermediary in the mines deal. Throughout the 1980s, in fact, Casalee was accused of involvement in a variety of mysterious arms deals around the world, of which the Iraqi mines deal was only one. Although the company has denied any involvement in arms deals, Western intelligence officials have confirmed that Casalee worked with U.S. and British agencies.

Casalee's man in the Middle East was an enterprising Italian called Mario Fallani. "He flew in and out of Baghdad, he did multimillion-dollar arms deals, and he worked with spies from every nation. Fallani was a real-life James Bond," claimed one admiring Swiss investigator. Fallani would eventually blow the whistle on the Italian government ministers who had approved the falsified end-user certificates that made believe the mines were going to Singapore. After all, how many antipersonnel mines can Singapore use? Nine million is more than three times the country's population.

Fallani knew exactly what he was talking about when he spilled the beans in an Italian court. He was in a position to know; secret documents bearing his name tell the tale. On May 29, 1984, Fallani sent a letter to Valsella back in Italy informing the company's managing director that the contracts had been signed and the Iraqi Defense Ministry had consulted with the Italian embassy in Baghdad. In September of the following year, he wrote to the mine-maker saying that delays in the shipments were causing "grave difficulties" in the prosecution of Saddam's war.

In October 1985, Mario Girotti, a BNL banker then in Singapore, sent a telex to a middleman involved in the mines deal. In that telex Girotti announced that the money was available for the mines shipment and a BNL credit had been "opened in your favor by [the] Central Bank of Iraq—Baghdad, military accounts." Girotti even offered discounts on further transactions. By February 1986, the mines had been delivered to Baghdad, BNL had provided the money, and the Iraqis were already defaulting on their payments to BNL. It seems that a certain Colonel Ibrahim in the military accounts department of the Iraqi Central Bank was a bit slow when it came to paying. (See Appendix B, pages 312–313.)

THE IRAQI CENTRAL BANK'S TARDINESS in making payments on the antipersonnel mines may have stemmed from the way Saddam's war against Iran was draining his treasury's coffers. But whatever attitude Baghdad held toward BNL's Singapore office, it projected nothing but effusive goodwill toward an equally remote outpost in the BNL world empire: the bank's small but industrious branch in Atlanta, Georgia. This was because BNL Atlanta had become a kind of private banking operation for Saddam Hussein, and its increasingly ambitious branch manager, Christopher Drogoul, had become Iraq's favorite American.

Drogoul had been hired by BNL in December 1981, at the age of thirty-two. At the time, his career prospects were not particularly bright; he was earning $31,000 a year as an account manager in the Atlanta branch of Barclays Bank. Back in 1974, he had joined the New York office of the British bank as a trainee operations clerk and four years later transferred to Atlanta. Life at Barclays made for a morose existence; he had made careless errors in lending that raised questions about his competence, and in truth he was really hoping to move back to New York. It was not too late for him to change careers, or at least employers. In fact, his boss at Barclays was prepared to help Drogoul leave the bank, and in October 1981, during a cocktail party at Atlanta's World Trade Club, he introduced him to an Italian banker named Giuseppe Vincenzino. Drogoul felt at home among

Europeans; his father was French, and he even spoke a little Italian thanks to a summer course he had attended at the University of Rome in his student days. He made a good impression on Vincenzino, who in March 1980 had opened a tiny representative office in Atlanta for BNL. Drogoul did not know much about BNL, but the two men chatted for a long time and liked each other.

Although Drogoul's professional banking experience was modest, he was personable in a quietly reassuring way, and he cut a handsome figure with his strawberry blond hair, lanky physique, and nonchalant manner. He had a way of appearing both vulnerable and easygoing at the same time, which made people want to help him and enabled him to persuade strangers such as Vincenzino that he was a man who would make a good team player. Drogoul's natural charm came from the French influences in his family. The passive side of his character resulted from a fairly gray childhood in Jersey City, where he was born; he had not been much of a student, and when he was just eight years old, his family life had been disrupted when his father went off with a younger woman. Pierre Drogoul remained a presence in his son's life, albeit from a distance, but he was disappointed at the way young Christopher tended to drift about in a haze of indecision. Pierre had wanted him to go to Columbia Law School. "I know you don't like lawyers," he told his son, "but just do it for three years. Get your stupid degree. You don't have to use it. You can get a master's degree from the Sorbonne, become an international lawyer, travel, and write your own ticket."

Instead, Drogoul flirted with the idea of going to film school and ended up earning a philosophy degree at Temple University in Philadelphia. When he accepted the entry-level job at Barclays, his prime responsibility had been to process refund claims for customers who had lost their travelers checks. Even when he began to handle company accounts at Barclays in Atlanta, his experience was found to be so slight that he was sent off to Dallas for a one-week training course in the summer of 1981 to learn about corporate lending. He found the course ghastly and came away feeling he had learned little. Yet over the years Drogoul had always managed to appear brighter than his professional standing would suggest; he was inspired by a powerful ambition to prove himself to his father by achieving material success, and he traded on a self-mocking irony and an astounding skill at soothing those he met.

After another, more formal meeting with Vincenzino, the Italian banker offered Drogoul a job at a salary of $42,000. That would be quite a jump for Drogoul; the only hitch was that the position was as a junior lending officer. Apparently the Italians wanted to drum up some business in the Sunbelt, and Atlanta was the place they had chosen. The money would certainly be very good. But bank lending again? Drogoul pondered his decision, asked a number of people about BNL, and ultimately decided he could not turn down the salary. At the beginning of 1982, he reported for duty at BNL's offices on the twentieth floor of the Peachtree Center South Tower, in the heart of a bustling and booming Atlanta.

Drogoul was an immediate hit with his colleagues—there were only a few of them—but the work itself was hardly glamorous. In his first year at BNL he helped convert the representative office into a regular branch of the Italian bank. This was not very challenging; it was really a question of meeting and greeting prospective clients and trying to make contacts at endless rounds of luncheons and cocktail parties. Drogoul was also told to develop corporate and trade finance business with companies in places such as West Virginia, Mississippi, Kentucky, Georgia, and Alabama. He didn't actually do much for the bank that first year, but Vincenzino nonetheless seemed pleased with his new recruit.

As for Vincenzino, there was something about him and the BNL operation that Drogoul could not quite figure. The office that BNL had established in Atlanta didn't have much business; Vincenzino had told him that it was still just getting started. Yet it seemed to Drogoul that generating business—ostensibly the bank's goal—was in fact rather a low priority. And Vincenzino seemed to serve mainly as a representative rather than as a financial man. He said that earlier in his career he had worked for ten years at the American consulate in Palermo. That accorded with Drogoul's impression of Vincenzino as more of a diplomat or a government official than a banker. From what Drogoul could make out, he seemed to be well connected; his acquaintances included Andrew Young, the mayor of Atlanta, and the governor of Georgia. Vincenzino also informed Drogoul that he knew a very important friend of Ronald Reagan's—a certain Maxwell Rabb, the millionaire Republican who was then the American ambassador in Rome. Vincenzino certainly seemed to have connections, thought Drogoul, but few of them had to do with banking.

That was how Drogoul's relationship with BNL began: with Vincenzino bragging, and the Atlanta operation achieving almost nothing in terms of business. Ultimately, however, working for BNL would land Drogoul in big trouble. Nearly ten years after he was hired at BNL's Atlanta branch, Christopher Drogoul would become the central figure in the American political scandal known as "Iraqgate."

There was, of course, no hint of this in late 1982; in fact, Vincenzino told his superiors that Drogoul was an outstanding employee who had the ability to become the deputy branch manager in Atlanta and potential that BNL could use anywhere in its sprawling network. This was high praise, but the reality was that the branch itself had still not really moved beyond the formation stage and had fewer than a dozen employees. The truth was that Vincenzino was unhappy with his present deputy and wanted a replacement. He recommended Drogoul for a promotion, and in early 1983 he succeeded in getting him named a vice-president and deputy manager. That meant a salary of $60,000. Life began to go well for Christopher Drogoul; the promotion allowed him to contemplate new horizons, and it eased the pain of the recent ending of his marriage. He found reason to be optimistic again, and in 1983 he rekindled his friend-ship with Lynn Washam, a former colleague from his days at Barclays Bank. Before the end of the year their romance had turned to marriage; they would have four children.

Vincenzino seemed to have grand plans for his protégé. He even tried to direct his private life, attempting to imbue his deputy with the same social-climbing skills for which he himself was known. In 1983 he introduced Drogoul to Priscilla Rabb, daughter of the ambassador to Rome whose name he had dropped in the past. Priscilla Rabb, who would later rise to a senior position working for Lawrence Eagleburger, the deputy secretary of state, was herself a junior banker in Atlanta at the time, in the local office of First Chicago Bank. She later recalled meeting Drogoul at dinner parties in the Vincenzino home, but she perceived none of his charm. In the company of his boss, she said, Drogoul struck her as "a lackey, like a bag-carrier for Vincenzino, like a guy who ran errands." The BNL branch itself seemed like "an amateur operation. There were just a handful of people there, five or six if that. One wondered why they were there at all." As for Vincenzino, he was pleasant enough, "a little guy with a moustache who reminded me of the guy you see on those Italian expresso machines."

IN 1983, just as Drogoul was settling into his job as deputy manager of the BNL Atlanta branch, policy issues were being discussed both at BNL headquarters in Rome and at the State Department in Washington that would greatly affect his future. The bank's deliberations concerned Iraq, an important client for BNL in Italy.

Executives in Rome were fretting because in 1982 Baghdad had begun to make huge withdrawals from the bank, and nearly $1 billion in Iraqi money was being siphoned out. This came at a time when the bank was trying to rid itself of the stain of the P-2 Freemasons scandal. It was engaged simultaneously in reordering its finances, and at a time like that, $1 billion in deposits was a lot to lose.

Saddam, for his part, was having money problems. Iraq's crude oil production, which accounted for 99 percent of its currency-earning exports, had dropped to only a third the level of 1980, when Saddam had first deployed his shock troops against Iran. Oil earnings had tumbled from nearly $28 billion a year in 1980 to what would be only $8 billion in 1983. Saddam was no longer able to pay foreign contractors.

In Washington, the State Department was monitoring Baghdad's finances as the war escalated. Officials were increasingly worried by the success of the ground attacks Iran had launched. They were bringing the war directly into Iraqi territory, food shortages were growing worse in Baghdad, and administration officials feared that Saddam Hussein might soon be overthrown, opening the way to the Ayatollah Khomeini's brand of Islamic fundamentalism. Pro-Iraqi sentiment in the White House was such that keeping the otherwise odious Saddam in power was now an acceptable, if unpublicized, American policy goal.

Secretary of State George Shultz was kept up to date on Saddam's predicament. In March 1983, he learned that Iraq's financial position was worsening steadily; in fact, there was likely to be a shortfall of as much as ten billion dollars for the year. As a result, even though diplomatic relations did not exist between Washington and Baghdad, Saddam's representatives were pressing U.S. officials to extend financial aid in the form of credits, loans, and technical cooperation. Washington was willing to help.

Shultz's staff presented him with a range of options that might enable such assistance. One option was that the State Department could press the Export-Import Bank to provide loan guarantees for U.S. companies selling to Iraq, thus making certain that the American exporters would not lose money even if Iraq failed to pay. Eximbank, however, was not welcoming the few inquiries it had received from U.S. exporters because the law governing the bank required "a reasonable assurance of payment," and that would be hard for Iraq to provide. Equally problematic was the legal requirement that specifically prohibited Eximbank from funding any government that harbored terrorists. Although Iraq had been taken off the Reagan administration's list of nations backing terrorism the previous year, Shultz's people were not so sure that Baghdad had truly

reformed. Might not a request for Eximbank help from the Iraqi government trigger a new review of Saddam's links to terrorists? Pressing Eximbank, Shultz was told, would mean that "the question of whether Iraq
was harboring terrorists would have to be decided."

A better idea than Eximbank financing for Saddam, said Shultz's
advisers, would be to make use of an obscure U.S. government loan-
guarantee program that had been set up at the Department of Agriculture
to help American farmers increase their foreign sales. The program was
known by the acronym CCC, which stood for the Commodity Credit
Corporation. An export arm of the Agriculture Department, the CCC
system was first conceived in the 1970s, when officials at Agriculture were
looking for ways to help American farmers develop new export markets.
It worked on the same principle as the Eximbank guarantees: the government promised exporters of U.S. agricultural products that their bank
loans would be covered in the event that the foreign buyer failed to pay.
What that actually meant in this case was that if Iraq, the buyer, didn't pay
for the exported products, the CCC would cover the loss and the American taxpayer would end up footing the bill.

The Iraqis had never been offered the CCC loan guarantees in the
past. The reasons had not simply been commercial; relations between
Washington and Baghdad had hardly warranted such favorable treatment. But in early 1983, with pro-Iraqi sentiment spreading inside the
Reagan administration, both the United States and Iraq were seeking to
normalize their relationship; the CCC credits could not only provide
material aid but serve as a sign of good faith. In February a senior-level
group of Reagan administration officials quietly approved the first $230
million of CCC loan guarantees to cover the shipment to Iraq of American
wheat, barley, eggs, rice, and feed grains. Washington still didn't have
formal diplomatic relations with Baghdad, but George Shultz went ahead
and asked the senior U.S. diplomat in Baghdad, William Eagleton, to tell
Saddam's aides the good news. Before the year was out, the Reagan
administration had allocated Iraq a total of nearly $400 million worth of
the guarantees, enabling hundreds of exporters to take advantage of the
program.

Christopher Drogoul would soon learn to love the CCC program,
and when BNL Atlanta became involved in it, he made lots of money from
the commissions on the easy loans. But the bank that first got involved in
financing farm exports to Iraq with U.S. government backing was not
BNL but Morgan Guaranty Trust, the blue-blooded Wall Street institution. In the view of most money men, the Morgan bank is not only

America's richest and most solid financial institution; it is so close to bank regulators that it is often seen as a kind of semiofficial organization. It is not unheard of for Morgan to be asked, very discreetly, to lend a hand to other banks in times of weakness. All in all, it was not surprising that when the Reagan administration decided to use the CCC program to assist Iraq, it was Morgan that played a leading role in initially providing CCC-backed loans. Thanks to Morgan's participation, the U.S. policy of supporting Saddam with food exports got off to a galloping start.

By 1984, the amount of taxpayer-backed credits approved in Washington had jumped to nearly $650 million. Not everyone agreed that this was such a good idea. Indeed, the Department of the Treasury, one of the agencies involved in deciding how much Iraq would receive in loan guarantees each year, continued to worry that Baghdad was a poor risk. Yet the State Department pressed for ever larger amounts to be authorized for food exports to Iraq and ultimately, Treasury lost the interagency battle on political rather than economic grounds. Disappointed Treasury officials were careful to make sure their colleagues elsewhere in the government knew they were unwilling to support any further increases in the program until the economic situation in Iraq improved.

Nonetheless, Iraq, as Ambassador Maxwell Rabb would later recall, "was popular at the time. It was popular to be with Iraq. We were suspicious of Saddam, but we didn't hate him." That sentiment prevailed throughout NATO. It did not appear to trouble either London or Rome that Baghdad was having to reschedule its debt repayments with many creditors, including Western governments. The Italian government was doing more than its part—government ministers there approved a hefty $500 million in new export guarantees for Iraq. In London, Margaret Thatcher's ministers made £300 million of guaranteed financing available to Saddam.

London had business and strategic interests to foster and was not deterred by Saddam's behavior toward his own people in February 1984, when he used poison gas against the Kurds in the north. Equally undeterred were Rome and Washington. In fact, Washington not only turned a blind eye; it went a step further and sold him two thousand heavy trucks. Though Secretary of State Shultz would not okay a blanket permission for militarily useful exports to Iraq, he did approve the truck sale, worth $224 million, even though officials at the Pentagon were concerned that Saddam would almost certainly make military use of them in his war against the ayatollah. This was made plain in a memo sent to Shultz through the office of then-Undersecretary of State for Political Affairs Lawrence

Eagleburger. It warned him that if the United States relaxed its formal controls on the sale of militarily useful goods to Iraq, this could add to the growing perception "that we are tilting toward Iraq." More explicitly, Shultz was informed that such a move "could be perceived as permitting at least some arms sales to Iraq." The secretary of state was not deterred.

DOWN IN ATLANTA, Christopher Drogoul was busy clambering up the career ladder at BNL. In the spring of 1984, when his mentor Vincenzino transferred from Atlanta to Chicago, a replacement was needed in a hurry. Despite BNL rules that branch managers be Italian citizens, an exception was made and Drogoul found himself catapulted into the top job. He was now the manager, though of a branch that had not made any money since its inception.

As Drogoul's career soared, so did Saddam's appetite for money and arms. In 1984, the Iraqi leader redoubled his arms-procurement efforts around the world. Not only was he fighting a war, he badly wanted fresh funds to finance his nuclear ambitions. But first he needed more basic equipment. By late November 1984, when Washington reestablished its diplomatic relations with Baghdad, a variety of American-expedited efforts to assist Saddam were well under way. Intelligence information and satellite photographs were regularly going to Baghdad. Past and present CIA contractors, such as Sarkis Soghanalian, were plying their arms trade—and reporting back to the Reagan administration on what was being sent to Iraq. With the full knowledge of the CIA, the Iraqi leader was obtaining U.S. equipment and technology through Carlos Cardoen of Chile. From Lancaster, Pennsylvania, the indefatigable James Guerin was busy selling military goods to South Africa that would go to Saddam; his activities were also being monitored by the CIA. Even some of the big U.S. grain traders were briefing the CIA on their Iraqi activities.

Christopher Drogoul knew nothing of these Western government and intelligence service operations to help Iraq, but he was about to be drawn into them. It was unwitting at first. In late 1984, after nearly thirty-six months on the job at BNL Atlanta, he received his first invitation to do business with Baghdad. The fateful offer came from one of America's biggest grain traders, Continental Grain. The company had heard that Drogoul's Atlanta branch was involved in making loans with CCC backing, although he had made none for Iraq at this stage. "Continental Grain called to inquire whether we might be interested in handling a $13 million transaction to Iraq involving a shipment of wheat and flour," Drogoul remembered. "We had never done business with Iraq before, so I called Rome and asked them for permission. They said 'Iraq? No problem. Go ahead.' So we did."

Thanks to the Continental Grain deal, Drogoul saw a new world opening up for him, a world of easy transactions backed by U.S. government loan guarantees. Everyone was so friendly, so solicitous. Grain companies like Continental, Cargill, and Louis Dreyfus seemed to beat a path to his office on Peachtree Street, once they had heard about BNL's willingness to lend. It was a small community, and word traveled fast.

And then there were the Iraqis themselves. Drogoul was put in touch with them by a business associate at Continental Grain; he did not realize at the time how significant the introduction would be. A meeting was set up in New York, at the Sheraton Hotel. Drogoul traveled up from Atlanta in the company of his deputy, a Bronx-born loan technician named Paul Von Wedel. The two made an offbeat pair; Drogoul was calm and somewhat continental, while Von Wedel's demeanor more closely resembled that of a raucous used-car salesman. At the Sheraton they received a warm welcome from Sadik Taha, the politically powerful director-general for loans at the Central Bank of Iraq who doubled as a front man for Saddam's arms-procurement network. The match between the rather junior bankers from Atlanta and the worldly-wise Iraqi was decidedly uneven. When an offshore company needed to be set up or financed, or when Hussein Kamel or others responsible for Iraqi weapons procurement needed to make discreet bank transfers involving large sums, Taha was the man they called upon. He was, according to various accounts, accorded privileges that few of Saddam's brass received, whether that meant first-class international travel or signatory rights to disburse hundreds of millions of dollars at the stroke of a pen. Taha was trusted, and he enjoyed having that trust.

Drogoul would see a lot of Sadik Taha over the next few years; indeed, their lives would become intertwined. Right now, however, all he knew was that the friendly Iraqi central banker was suggesting that BNL Atlanta take on at least $100 million of the lending under the U.S. government's farm export program. It was hard to see the down side of such a transaction. BNL would earn on the deal—although comparatively little, since Drogoul, in his frenzy to succeed, had agreed to slash the interest he was charging down to just one-sixteenth over the commercial lending rate. The loans were backed by Uncle Sam, which would cover 98 percent of the bank's risk in case of default. And Mr. Taha seemed keen to foster a relationship with Drogoul. So Drogoul proposed the loan package to

BNL's North American headquarters office in New York, which checked with Rome. The answer came back swiftly, in the affirmative. In early 1985, the first $100 million BNL Atlanta line of credit was agreed. Drogoul's dealings with Iraq were up and running in the most straightforward way.

After his first meeting with the Iraqi central banker, Drogoul found his fortunes improving rapidly at BNL. Word spread among colleagues in the bank's foreign department back in Rome that he was the man to see for CCC-backed loans to Iraq. He arranged CCC-backed deals for exports to various other countries, too, including Algeria, Turkey, and even the Soviet Union. He began to travel extensively. He started to meet senior executives at the big commodity-trading companies. And based on his conversations with Sadik Taha, he realized "that it was very important to the U.S. government that the Iraqis be satisfied. Moreover the Iraqis told us directly that the relationship they had with the CCC program was part of the backbone of their financial system during the war years. They relied on it."

Drogoul still understood only a few of the implications of the CCC program, but he certainly saw the opportunities it could afford him. He started making frequent trips to the nation's capital to meet visiting Iraqis. Whenever Sadik Taha and his colleagues came to the United States, Drogoul headed their list of appointments, along with State Department and Agriculture Department officials. These were festive occasions, thanks to the fact that BNL Atlanta was steadily increasing its Iraqi-related loans; sometimes his bank paid for the hotel rooms, but more often U.S. wheat growers, the growing army of brokers who served as middlemen, or the Iraqis themselves picked up the tab. The loan-signing ceremonies were often conducted in the privacy of Taha's hotel room in an atmosphere of much joviality.

On one such occasion two years after the first loan, Drogoul and a colleague flew from Atlanta to Washington and went to the Vista Hotel. By now, Drogoul had learned the cosmopolitan ways of international banking and bought gifts of solid gold Parker pens to be used for the signings. Friends who were watching his progress observed that he now cut quite a figure. The astute Iraqis liked this pleasant American, and they played on his relative naïveté when it came to international banking. At the hotel Taha welcomed Drogoul and his colleague, poured generous glasses of Chivas Regal, and after the loan papers were signed pulled out an array of gifts from Baghdad, among them several antiques and a handmade oriental rug in which was woven the face of a Babylonian warrior. Then he took everybody to a lavish dinner at Trader Vic's that ended with a choice of fine cigars. Life had become very good for the men from BNL Atlanta.

By the end of 1985, Drogoul had been seduced by the ease with which he could hand out loans to the Iraqis and still be covered by U.S. government guarantees. In December of that year he made a quantum leap in his Iraqi dealings and signed a $556 million line of credit for Baghdad backed by the CCC program. The only problem was that BNL Rome had never authorized him to lend sums beyond $100 million, even if they were CCC-backed. He was now committed to a huge new loan that was not allowed by his bank's headquarters. Not until four months after the fact, on April 18, 1986, did Drogoul finally ask a colleague at BNL Atlanta to telex Rome for approval. The answer, three days later, was no.

The reason for Rome's refusal had to do with a separate issue that was souring relations between the governments of Italy and Iraq. Baghdad had finally paid a substantial part of the $2.6 billion it owed for the fleet of Italian naval vessels it had commissioned back in 1980, but Italy was now refusing to deliver the ships from Genoa to the Persian Gulf, lest they fall prey to bombardment in the raging war. As a result, Baghdad suspended its debt repayments to Italy. That meant that Italian banks, especially government-owned banks such as BNL, were not making any new loans to Iraq.

With more than half a billion dollars of loans on their books that were not approved by Rome, Drogoul and his colleagues in Atlanta were in a very tight spot. His initial solution was to try to get other banks to take over some of the loans, but there were few takers. Was there any other way out? The method Drogoul chose marked the beginning of a secret operation that continued for years and eventually piled one hidden Iraqi loan on top of another; BNL Atlanta engaged in a legally questionable practice that they called "skipping." Beginning in April 1986, when they made their monthly reports to their superiors at BNL in New York and Rome, they would simply remove the total $600 million of loan exposure they had accumulated. The next day they would put the loans back on the books, and when the next report was due, they would hide them again.

No matter how well Drogoul thought he was concealing his Iraqi loans, the truth was that his CCC lending had become something of an open secret at the head office in Rome. On June 17, 1986, senior executives there prepared an internal report that warned of problems in the Atlanta branch. The report, which was forwarded to BNL's North

American regional headquarters in New York, was quite explicit in stating that the records of the Atlanta branch failed to show a total of more than $406 million worth of CCC-backed loans. That was a fairly serious finding, and it meant that no matter how successful Drogoul imagined his "skipping" to be, traces of his lending were turning up in the branch's accounts anyway.

Incredible as it might seem, however, Rome did not censure Drogoul for the gaping hole in his balance sheet. The head office, with $100 billion of assets to manage, was still in the process of restructuring its entire operation and was in far too much disarray to devote time and energy to criticizing Atlanta. Drogoul's offense might have been egregious, but as a former BNL Rome executive later recalled, "We were in a state of near anarchy. The Bank of Italy had just finished a lengthy inspection of our domestic operations, and we were under fire for a host of sins." The Bank of Italy had indeed delivered a blistering attack; it had found BNL to be deficient in its internal controls, its efficiency, its management structure, and in just about every area of its business.

In fact, far from being criticized, Drogoul found himself being lauded. In August 1986, the head office in Rome singled him out for high praise. BNL Atlanta's results, a one-million-dollar net profit for the first six months of 1986, were described as brilliant. Although the razor-thin interest rates Drogoul was charging Baghdad could not have produced earnings like this, there was enough non-Iraqi business to carry the branch. "Atlanta," a former top manager at the Rome headquarters recalled, "was the only foreign branch in our world network that was even turning a profit. That's how Drogoul came to be loved so well in Rome."

Indeed colleagues in Rome who knew of Drogoul's Iraqi dealings became intensely jealous of the man from Atlanta. Word even spread around the foreign division at BNL headquarters on the Via Veneto that Baghdad was the place to be, business-wise. "If you don't work with Iraq, you won't get ahead around here," Drogoul's Italian colleagues repeated to one another like a mantra.

The following year, it was a further relief to Drogoul—and an eye-opener—when Giacomo Pedde took him aside during a BNL managers' meeting in Italy and jokingly called him "Mr. CCC." Although Pedde denied this, Drogoul later recalled that the director-general even congratulated him on his Iraqi lending, telling him that the "business is very important to us at this time." Pedde would later appear shocked to hear of the extent of Drogoul's Iraqi lending, but the message Drogoul remembered receiving from Rome was that "Iraq had a special relationship with Italy and the United States." As long as Iraq repaid its CCC loans, Rome was not going to fret, and with the loans covered almost in full by the U.S. government, even a default did not pose much of a financial threat.

Thus encouraged, Christopher Drogoul was becoming a man who hated to decline any transaction. As far as he was concerned, this was only the beginning.

EIGHT

The Money Machine

Christopher Drogoul began to sense how important he had become to his Iraqi clients when at the invitation of the ubiquitous Sadik Taha he made his first visit to Baghdad in March 1986. The purpose of the invitation was to discuss further business—U.S. government loan-guarantee business—but the Iraqis did not restrict the visit to this. His hosts smothered Drogoul with hospitality, housing him at the luxurious Al-Rasheed Hotel, and Taha personally escorted him around town, though under normal circumstances the Iraqi central banker was far too senior to perform such a task. Drogoul, however, was a very special visitor, having recently given Baghdad that very large, exceedingly low-interest loan, a loan that would constitute nearly the entire U.S. government CCC allocation to Iraq for 1986.

As he toured Baghdad, the martial music he heard everywhere and the number of walking wounded and uniformed Iraqis he saw in the streets made Drogoul realize for the first time that he might be engaged in something more than normal banking business. "I recognized that this was a war zone, and given that it was a war zone, people had to know what we were doing," he later said. The veil of secrecy he thought he had drawn over his Iraqi loans was looking thinner by the moment.

BNL headquarters was aware of it. "There were people in Rome who knew he was making the trip. Chris had approval from BNL's international division," recalled Paul Von Wedel. And when Drogoul returned to the Al-Rasheed from his touring with Mr. Taha, he had ample reason to think his activities were known to the U.S. government as well. "There was a string of messages, three or four of them, from the U.S. embassy in

Baghdad. The caller was the U.S. agriculture attaché, Larry Panasuk," Drogoul remembered. When he tried to return Panasuk's calls, however, Drogoul couldn't get through. Panasuk, now at the American embassy in Ankara, remembered leaving the messages. "I tried to get in contact with him because I used to be asked a lot about the banks that were financing Iraqi business. The U.S. exporters told me Drogoul was in town and doing business, so I tried to reach him." In fact, he made similar efforts when Drogoul came to Baghdad on subsequent trips, but the two men never succeeded in connecting.

In early 1987, Taha came to Washington for another round of loan discussions with Drogoul. Iraq needed money. The war had escalated yet again, Saddam was sending his air force jets in waves over enemy territory, and they were dropping bombs from the sky in "war of the cities" attacks on Tehran and elsewhere. The casualties in the month following Christmas were enormous, and the Iraqi morgues near Basra were pro cessing more than a thousand bodies on the bloodiest days.

In a hotel room in Washington, Drogoul listened to Taha's complaints about his health—he had serious heart disease—and to his financial requests. He promised the Iraqi yet *another* $644 million of loans. This time, in addition to the customary CCC-backed loans from BNL Atlanta, Drogoul even threw in as part of the package $25 million dollars of unsecured loans to pay for freight charges on the agricultural shipments. Not a single penny of these loans was reported either to BNL or to U.S. bank regulators, as required by law. But Paul Von Wedel recalled that after Drogoul began making them, BNL Atlanta received encouragement from U.S. government officials and was told the CCC would guarantee ocean freight from the United States to Jordan as well as the land freight charges for the transshipment to Baghdad. "It was unprecedented," he said. "The U.S. government had never done anything like this before. And the CCC encouraged us to please stay in the program because other banks had pulled out."

Back in Atlanta, Drogoul and his staff of a dozen people were working overtime just to keep up with the telex traffic and Iraqi loan documentation. It was at this stage that the shifting of large Iraqi loans right off the official books began to escalate in a serious way. Until now, it had been sufficient to engage in "skipping" them off the branch's accounts when it came time to file the monthly reports. But a new device was invented in the Atlanta branch, and most of the employees became party to the scheme. "We went from not showing the loans one day to not showing them on any day," Drogoul later remembered. The entire Iraqi loan portfolio was shifted onto a parallel set of accounts that the staff nicknamed "the gray books." The actual loan documentation was kept on a ledger in a box that could be moved about with ease. It became standard practice to remove the records of gray book transactions from the branch when auditors came to visit.

The gray book operations may have been clandestine, but they fit very nicely with the U.S. government's policy of backing Iraq. BNL Atlanta played an increasingly important role in lending to exporters of industrial goods through Eximbank guarantees and to exporters of farm commodities through the CCC program. As the size of the CCC program grew, so did the Atlanta branch's loans. By the end of the 1980s, Washington had approved a total of $5 billion of the loan guarantees for Iraq, making Saddam one of the biggest recipients of official U.S. largesse. BNL Atlanta financed some $1.89 billion of these loans, many of them in secret. Drogoul was thus providing more than a third of the entire lending for farm exports to Baghdad that was covered by U.S. government guarantees. Moreover, to those in the U.S. government who needed to know, Drogoul's Iraqi loans were not really a secret. In fact, the details of the Iraqi financing that he provided went straight to Washington, since the exporters informed government officials of each deal BNL Atlanta funded. BNL's name appeared in thousands of transactions that were reported, filed, and stored at the Department of Agriculture.

Washington administered the CCC program so sloppily that the Agriculture Department didn't always know whether the goods shipped had actually arrived at their destinations. Since Iraq is almost entirely landlocked, most of the shipments had to go to the Jordanian port of Aqaba and then be sent overland. American intelligence officials who were tracking the use of Jordan as a part of Saddam's military procurement network say that grain or flour might arrive in Aqaba and then be bartered away in exchange for arms. Since Jordan had frequently served as a staging ground for clandestine military aid to Iraq, those intelligence officials at the DIA or CIA who learned of the grain-for-weapons swaps filed their reports almost matter-of-factly. The reports were treated on a need-to-know basis upon arrival in Washington and not widely circulated. Had they been passed on to Agriculture Department officials at the time, the information might have caused a halt in the CCC program for Iraq.

Sometimes one of Drogoul's own BNL colleagues in Italy would actually be asked to arrange a quiet swap of U.S. grain for Soviet-made weapons. "It was done through places like Czechoslovakia," a former BNL executive in Italy explained. "My colleagues in the bank knew what we were doing. So did the Italian secret services. We ran into them as we did the deals. They were watching us." In Washington, a top Pentagon official summed up the situation by saying he had not known what was happening until years after the fact, but had then become satisfied that there was "no doubt about the swap." It was for Soviet arms, he said, and the beneficiary was Iraq.

The BNL farm export loans also threw off millions of dollars in pure cash because the prices charged for the commodities were sometimes more than double the normal market price. By padding the cost of shipments, Iraqi agents were able to skim large sums that could then be used to purchase weaponry. "There is no doubt that they used the guarantees to mobilize more money," an Israeli intelligence official who had tracked the Iraqi procurement network later told *U.S. News & World Report.* "They did it a lot of ways. You have to see this as a sort of symphony, not as a single instrument." Paul Dickerson, the senior Agriculture Department official who investigated BNL and Iraq's use of CCC-backed loans, claimed that he had never personally found the program being abused for arms procurement, yet Dickerson had to admit that "money is fungible, and the money we made available meant that the Iraqis could obviously spend more on defense."

By 1986, when Drogoul first went to Baghdad, the defense of Iraq had become a cherished objective not only for many American government officials but also for serving diplomats in Iraq. Once Drogoul— supposedly operating in secrecy—actually met then-ambassador David Newton, whom he ran into at a Baghdad luncheon given by the Iraqi grain board. Newton was no slouch when it came to urging the Reagan administration to provide more help for Saddam. In May 1986, when he was on a visit to Washington, Newton went to see the new chairman of Eximbank, John Bohn, who had replaced George Bush's old Yale colleague, William Draper. Bohn, like his predecessor at the bank, was not inclined to help Baghdad with U.S. taxpayer–backed guarantees. The $200 million program that Vice President Bush had pressed Draper to approve in 1984 had been suspended in March 1986, two months before Newton's call on Bohn, when Iraq was unable to keep up with payments.

"The ambassador was quite downtrodden considering both the status of the war as well as the economy," said an internal memorandum on Newton's visit. Given the dismal state of Baghdad's finances, Eximbank's enthusiasm for doing any new business with Iraq varied "from zero to not much," the memo concluded.

Others in the Reagan administration were also pressing Iraq's cause at Eximbank, and few were more active than Assistant Secretary of State Richard Murphy. In November 1986, when Murphy lobbied an Eximbank board member, the venue chosen for the pitch was the home of Iraq's ambassador, Nizar Hamdoon. Hamdoon was among the most effective of the diplomats representing Saddam's regime in the United States. As an ardent lobbyist for Baghdad, he moved effortlessly in and out of Washington's media and political circles and barnstormed around the country, making speeches that played upon the American hatred and fear of Khomeini's Iran.

Hamdoon and Murphy were joined in their efforts by Robert Abboud, a high-flying banker who was chairman of the influential U.S.-Iraqi Business Forum and who made it his business to praise the Iraq of Saddam Hussein. Abboud's efforts on behalf of U.S. business interests in Iraq had played a large part in encouraging administration officials to believe that assisting Saddam was an economic as well as a strategic interest of the United States. Since the Business Forum included a number of Fortune 500 companies, such as Exxon, Bechtel, Texaco, Lockheed, General Motors, and AT&T, it was no ordinary trade association; it carried impressive political as well as financial clout.

Despite Hamdoon's hospitality and the efforts of Abboud and Murphy to press the Eximbank board member for loan credits to Iraq, this particular effort did not succeed. It was time for an even heavier hitter to enter the game.

At the end of February 1987, Vice President George Bush, in a repeat of what he had done in 1984, picked up his telephone and asked the chairman of Eximbank to assist Iraq. The call was prompted by a scheduled meeting, just days away, between Bush and Nizar Hamdoon, and it was preceded by a State Department memorandum suggesting a script for the Hamdoon meeting that was delivered to Bush's office on February 26. It told Bush that the State Department had received advance warning that Hamdoon was planning to raise the issue of Eximbank guarantees; State recommended "strongly" that before meeting Hamdoon, Bush telephone bank chairman John Bohn. The idea was for Bush to "emphasize to Bohn the advantages for U.S. regional policy of resuming short-term credit insurance for Iraq." (See Appendix B, pages 314–315.) That done, Bush was told, "you could review the results of your call to Bohn during your conversation with Hamdoon."

It was a fairly neat two-step, and Bush carried it off with flair. He was, as White House officials had noted many times, a quick study when it came to memorizing his talking points. He placed the call to the Eximbank chief, and when he welcomed Hamdoon to his office on March 2, he was able to give the Iraqi diplomat better news than he might have hoped for: word that he had personally telephoned the chairman of Eximbank and urged him to drop his objections to providing new loan guarantees for Iraq. The call worked. Although staff-level employees at Eximbank continued to object, a few weeks after Bush's intervention some $200 million of new Eximbank loan credits to Iraq were approved.

Bush had had other good news for Hamdoon as well: Some U.S. export licenses that would allow Saddam to buy some militarily very sensitive American technology had just been approved by the government. These licenses, including one that would allow American technology to be shipped directly to Iraq's Space and Astronomical Research Center, had been held up at the Pentagon by a zealous official in charge of reviewing defense technology exports. The official had been convinced that one of the licenses would give Saddam the kind of advanced equipment that could be used to relay satellite information to ground stations and thereby watch Iranian troop movements or perform other aerial spying. The State Department briefing memo to Bush had said that the long delays in granting such licenses—even if they were going into Iraq's space research center—appeared to be "capricious." The Pentagon's objection was overridden. Now there would be no further problem.

CHRISTOPHER DROGOUL was among those who would take advantage of Eximbank's decision to reverse itself. BNL Atlanta used Eximbank guarantees as it had used the CCC program, although on a smaller scale; Drogoul managed to process $47 million of Eximbank-backed loans for Iraq, a trifling sum compared with the CCC credits but nonetheless a substantial part of the Eximbank program.

The subordination of Eximbank's credit policy toward Iraq to the American government's foreign policy was mirrored in Italy. Both Bettino Craxi and Giulio Andreotti were firm believers in keeping faith with the Arab world and in helping Saddam Hussein, and this policy was naturally reflected in the government's biggest bank, BNL. On December 9, 1986, a Rome-based BNL banker named Teodoro Monaco told his superiors that there was "a strong political sentiment" in favor of providing Italian government guarantees for loans to Iraq. Loans like these were normally backed by Sace, the Italian equivalent of Eximbank. But in 1986, Sace had canceled its guarantees for a ten-million-dollar line of credit that BNL Rome had been planning to extend for Fiat group exports to Iraq. Fiat reacted by sending a strongly worded telex to Monaco, complaining that it was embarrassed, was losing credibility with the Iraqis, and demanding that BNL "find a solution." When Fiat spoke, Rome usually listened, and Monaco discussed with Fiat the setting up of a meeting with Sace.

Separately, in an internal memorandum to BNL executives in December 1986, Monaco noted that given the government's policy of assisting Iraq, Sace had asked BNL to "renounce" any attempt to press Baghdad for back payments of outstanding loans. He also reported that Iraqi bankers were asking BNL to provide fresh loans. And fresh loans are precisely what the Rome government promised to Iraq. In March 1987, seventeen senior officials of the Italian and Iraqi governments met for two days to discuss bank lending for Baghdad. The Italians assured the Iraqis that new export facilities could soon be made available and that Baghdad could take another couple of years before it had to begin paying back some of the loans it already owed. That in itself was a generous position; with the Iran-Iraq war still raging, there were few in the international financial community who remained willing to make any new funds available to Baghdad.

Drogoul and BNL Atlanta were one of the exceptions. On February 17, 1988, he and Paul Von Wedel flew to Baghdad on Royal Jordanian Airlines, via New York, Amsterdam, and Amman. Although it was 1:30 A.M. when they arrived, the reliable Mr. Taha was there to meet them. He whisked them through customs into a VIP lounge of Saddam International Airport, then to the Al-Rasheed Hotel. On the way Taha queried Drogoul about "the agreements." What agreements? Von Wedel wondered, before learning they stemmed from a promise Drogoul had made to offer the Iraqis a loan very different from the normal U.S.-guaranteed farm credits.

This time Drogoul was proposing to give Baghdad a five-year loan worth $200 million, and it would be unsecured. No longer would BNL Atlanta simply piggyback on the CCC program, confident that it could not lose on an Iraqi loan. Now Drogoul was talking of lending to Iraq's so-called industrial "reconstruction" projects, including a dam project on the Tigris. This was an entirely new dimension; it implied a high degree of risk over a fairly long period of time, for a country still fighting a war.

The three men spent the next day discussing details of the loan, and when evening came and the work was still not completed, Taha took the two BNL bankers out to dinner at a traditional Baghdad restaurant. There, Von Wedel recalled in a personal memoir, they watched a performance by dancing girls who were there not as entertainment but to observe an Iraqi tradition in which wives honor their husbands by performing a ritual dance for them in public. The $200 million loan agreement was concluded the next morning, at a rate of interest that was only a half-percent above the standard London interbank rate. This rate was ludicrously low; any other bank willing to engage in such risky lending to Iraq at that time would have charged a rate of two or three percent.

The loan agreed to was extraordinarily favorable to the Iraqis. It was effectively an open line of credit that would allow them to tap into BNL's coffers. All Baghdad had to do was agree to buy products or technology from a U.S. or European company, then telex or telephone Atlanta with instructions on where to make payment. This agreement called for a celebration, and Taha treated Drogoul and Von Wedel to a sightseeing tour at Babylon. Watching boys on donkeys and their flocks of sheep meandering through fields of tall grass near the ancient ruins, neither man could know that the agreement they had just concluded was the first in a series of loans that Iraq would use for some of Saddam's most nefarious weapons projects.

It was also the start of Drogoul's vertiginous descent into the Iraqi arms-procurement network. Indeed, the amount of money he was making available to Iraq dwarfed BNL Atlanta's authorized limit for making unsecured loans, a mere one million dollars.

The trip to Baghdad had not been authorized by Luigi Sardelli, Drogoul's boss at BNL's North American regional office in New York; he was on vacation at the time. But while Drogoul and Von Wedel were at the Al-Rasheed, they ran into a colleague from BNL's head office in Rome. "We walked into the hotel and went to the front desk to get our room keys. And I heard a familiar voice behind me calling out, 'Chrees, what are you doing here?' It was Ted Monaco."

Monaco didn't seem disturbed to see Drogoul in Baghdad and would later say that Drogoul's work for Iraq was well known to all and sundry at BNL, "and he had every reason in the world to be there." He and Drogoul strolled over to the huge elephant-skin sofas at the left of the Al-Rasheed lobby, and there Monaco introduced him to other BNL colleagues. They were visiting Baghdad to restructure a $50 million Iraqi debt from a BNL trading subsidiary in Milan. Also on hand was the commercial attaché of the Italian embassy in Baghdad.

Drogoul recalled that Monaco asked him the reason for his visit. "I told him I was in Baghdad on business, to work on commercial loans for

Iraq that would be part of the country's re-industrialization program. Monaco said he was trying to do the same thing and asked me to keep him advised."

Monaco later insisted he had not heard about the $200 million in loans during this encounter with Drogoul, but the Italian banker did remember an even more important exchange between the two. The well-connected Drogoul offered to introduce Monaco to a senior Iraqi Central Bank official. This meeting resulted in Iraq's opening two large accounts at BNL's London branch.

Over the next fourteen months, Drogoul would reach the $2.1 billion mark by making three more large unsecured loans to Iraq, for $300 million, $500 million, and then, in April 1989, $1.1 billion—all of them, as in the past, kept off the official books and in the branch's gray books. In order to obtain the funds, his assistants in Atlanta would borrow from dozens of other banks in the wholesale money markets. Nearly the entire staff of the Atlanta branch got involved. Because the Iraqi loans would not be repaid for years and because the money BNL Atlanta borrowed from the other banks was usually very short term—sometimes only thirty days—it became a constant struggle to roll over the short loans in order to finance the longer-term commitments. One of Drogoul's deputies likened the process to "running a bank in the closet."

Although Drogoul kept the Iraqi loans on gray books, that did not mean they were unknown to the government. From its headquarters in a Maryland suburb just outside of Washington, the National Security Agency (NSA), the ultrasecretive U.S. intelligence service that specializes in electronic surveillance and code-breaking, was monitoring the thousands of telexes that were passing almost daily between BNL Atlanta and Baghdad. The NSA also tracked money flows. One of Drogoul's clients, a shipper of industrial equipment to Iraq who came to Atlanta on a regular basis and asked questions about BNL's Iraqi loans, even acknowledged to Drogoul that he was a former NSA official.

Norman Bailey, a former White House official who had helped invent a program to track illegal money-laundering in the mid-1980s when he was at the National Security Council, has said flat out that he is convinced that the BNL-Iraq transactions were being intercepted by the NSA. It was, Bailey said, "inconceivable" that intercepts of telex traffic between Baghdad and Atlanta were not then reported to high-level officials of the Reagan administration and, after George Bush took office as president in January 1989, of the Bush administration.

"The only explanation I can think of is that the authorities knew all about it and approved it. They were using this as a channel for the financing of certain activities," said Bailey. Another U.S. official with direct knowledge of the NSA's surveillance was quoted as saying that there was "voluminous" information on Drogoul's loans to Iraq, including information on the low rates of interest that the Iraqi government was paying on the loans. An American intelligence officer who spent years monitoring Iraq's procurement network was blunter still: "The U.S. government was well aware of [these loans]. BNL was being used as a U.S. conduit. The Iraqis would talk to the American embassy in Baghdad and be told to which U.S. suppliers they should go."

In Rome, BNL has consistently denied it knew anything of the 1988 loan or the others that were unsecured. What several of Drogoul's former Italian colleagues recall is that his biggest protector was Giacomo Pedde, the Sardinian who in 1987 became the bank's director-general. Pedde, a long-serving Christian Democrat, was known by insiders less for his banking expertise than for the fact that he was a close friend of President Francesco Cossiga, who is also a Sardinian and became Italy's head of state. "The other thing about Pedde," a former BNL executive remembered, "was that he loved intrigue and would frequently brag to us about his friends in the intelligence services."

According to Drogoul, Pedde knew about the $200 million Iraqi loan that he signed during that Baghdad trip in February 1988. Upon his return to Rome headquarters, Monaco had told several colleagues, including Pedde, of his chance meeting with Drogoul. Pedde later denied any knowledge of the $200 million loan or of Monaco's meeting with Drogoul. "I inherited Drogoul along with a very messy and disorganized bank," claimed Pedde. Amid that mess, the fact that BNL Atlanta's manager was conducting business in Baghdad hadn't seemed strange to anyone. Nor had BNL Atlanta's growing business with Iraq surprised people in U.S. financial circles. As one senior executive at a big New York bank recalled, "There was only one bank lending in a big way to Iraq in the 1988–89 period, and that was Banca Nazionale del Lavoro, the Italian bank. But nobody in New York understood why BNL was lending Iraq all this money through its branch in Atlanta."

THERE WAS, however, one man who understood a great deal about what Drogoul was doing, and who played a critical role in the growth of BNL lending to Iraq while keeping on good terms with diplomats at the American embassy in Baghdad and with administrators of the U.S. farm credits program in Washington. His name was Wafai Dajani, and he was a mysterious Jordanian intermediary who presented himself to the outside world as an ordinary businessman.

To those who shipped U.S. goods to Baghdad, Dajani was known as a commodity trader whose companies handled more U.S.-Iraqi trade than anyone else in the world. This was in part because Dajani was close to the Iraqi government and also because he and his partners exercised effective control over the Jordanian port of Aqaba, the critical transshipment point for cargo that arrived for transport overland to Baghdad.

During the 1980s, Dajani's companies unloaded, stored, often packaged or repackaged, and then trucked nearly 80 percent of all the U.S. agricultural commodities that were destined for Iraq and financed with U.S. government loan guarantees. Since the total goods shipped to Iraq with CCC backing amounted to $5 billion, Dajani alone was responsible for handling about $4 billion worth. Dajani's firms handled more than one million tons of U.S. wheat and 350,000 tons of U.S. rice a year. For a number of Dajani's deals, involving exports of American commodities to Iraq by way of Jordan, Drogoul provided the loan finance.

In the 1980s, Wafai Dajani exerted a powerful influence over Christopher Drogoul. Their relationship dated back to 1985, when one of the big grain traders, Louis Dreyfus, had sought financing from BNL Atlanta for a joint venture it had formed to ship goods to Iraq in a fifty-fifty partnership with a big Norwegian shipping concern called Gearbulk. That same year, one of Dajani's companies, Amman Resources, joined with Gearbulk to start a company that kept a 60,000-ton ship, the *Tanga*, as a floating Iraqi silo in the port of Aqaba. The ship, which was fitted out with special vacuum hoses, would funnel grain from other ocean-going vessels and bag it. The bags were then loaded onto a fleet of eighteen hundred trucks that traveled the dusty and war-torn road from Amman to Baghdad.

At the beginning Dajani frequently served as an intermediary between the Iraqis and BNL Atlanta. He brokered many of the grain sales and other commodity exports that were financed by Drogoul and guaranteed under the CCC program. Many of the CCC guarantees were used for loans Drogoul made to Amman Resources. Among his transactions with BNL Atlanta, Dajani persuaded Drogoul to finance Comet Rice, a U.S. rice shipper selling from Texas to Baghdad. Then Dajani persuaded the State Department's Agency for International Development (AID) to lend four million dollars for a Comet rice-bagging plant in the port of Aqaba. The destination of the rice was Iraq, and thanks to Dajani's connections, it ended up being funded with backing from the CCC program.

A retiring man in his fifties, Dajani came from a Palestinian family that had moved to Amman after Israel was founded in 1948. In the 1970s, the Dajani clan became extraordinarily prominent in Jordan, so much so that a brother of Wafai's served as minister of the interior. Wafai Dajani himself would upstage his brother, becoming one of King Hussein's closest personal friends. His easy familiarity with America came from having studied under a State Department scholarship at the University of Iowa.

By the 1980s, Dajani was operating from his various offices in downtown Amman, in an elegant London town house a few blocks from Kensington Palace, and in the fashionable Georgetown section of Washington. His relationship with Drogoul made him even wealthier than he already was; his dealings with officials in Saddam's government prospered along the way.

Among Dajani's closest contacts in Iraq was Sadik Taha. Together, Dajani and Taha advised Drogoul and sometimes steered him; Drogoul, for his part, became increasingly dependent on them. On one occasion, he even asked Dajani to be the intermediary in conveying a confidential telex to Taha for his review before it was sent to Taha's boss. "Please excuse me for imposing upon you once again, but may I ask you to very discreetly pass this fax to Mr. Taha for his review and comments. Thanks again, Chris," read the fax from Drogoul to Dajani. Taha scribbled his corrections, and Dajani refaxed the draft back to Atlanta.

Dajani had enormous influence over Drogoul, but he also served other purposes in the spider's web that was being spun from Atlanta and Washington to Amman and Baghdad. In the U.S. Congress he was alleged to have acted as a broker for Saddam's arms-procurement agents. "I couldn't be involved in arms. I am too big and easy to watch," said Wafai Dajani when he was accused of helping to ship howitzers, ammunition, and small arms to Iraq in 1992. At that same time, when American politicians were worrying whether Iraq had obtained militarily useful equipment through kickbacks paid on exports funded by U.S. government loan guarantees, Dajani took the relaxed view of a businessman knowledgeable in the ways of the Middle East. "If you wanted the business, you had to provide after-sales services," he explained. "Otherwise you would get no business." Dajani denied each allegation that came from Congress: No, he had never used his facilities at Aqaba as a staging ground to barter grain for weapons. No, his firms were not involved in Iraqi weapons programs. No, he had never done anything wrong. Yet *U.S. News & World Report* reported in 1992 that it was Dajani who had helped set up meetings between Drogoul and members of Iraq's military technology-procurement network in the United States, Europe, Jordan, and Iraq, noting that despite his denials, U.S. intelligence files on Dajani linked him directly to the transfer of arms to Baghdad. According to one American intelligence agent, Dajani was also "the intermediary for German, Italian, and French companies that were selling into Iraq's nuclear and missile programs. He was everywhere, he dealt with everybody," said the agent.

Paul Von Wedel had a different view of Drogoul's Jordanian mentor: "We knew that Dajani was doing work for the CIA, for The Company. He told us in Washington during one of his visits." An American intelligence officer put it slightly differently: "Well, Dajani wouldn't have signed on any dotted line with the Agency. That would have been death. He would have been used by the Agency." Did Dajani's name ring a bell with Howard Teicher? "Yes, it does. Dajani was involved in our dirty policy. He performed services for the CIA and was involved in the CCC program." Dajani himself denied working with the CIA, just as he had denied involvement in the Iraqi arms network. "I don't work for anybody. I work for myself," he said.

THE GOODS that Iraq wished to purchase with the $2.1 billion in loans that BNL Atlanta extended in 1988 and 1989 were not the kind that would be eligible for purchase with CCC loan guarantees. There was no question of the loans funding food exports. Many of the exports Iraq bought were officially termed "industrial products and technology," but a number of them were put to final use as components of Saddam's war machine. "It doesn't matter whether it's machine tools or computers. The one thing they have in common is high technology. It all clearly has an arms linkage," explained a British government official who had watched BNL's loans assisting exports to Iraq.

More than $1 billion of the BNL loans were to be coordinated with the government ministry in Baghdad that handled military procurement, including conventional weapons, missiles, cluster bombs, and the ballistic missile, nuclear, and chemical weapons projects. This ministry was called MIMI, an acronym for the Ministry of Industry and Military Industrialization, and it was run by Saddam's son-in-law, the powerful Hussein Kamel, who in 1989 welcomed Chris Drogoul to Baghdad, offering him pomegranate juice and his gratitude for all that BNL was doing.

Saddam was eager to use the money from BNL to finance his lifelong ambition of seeing Iraq achieve the status of a nuclear power. Washington, Rome, London, and other NATO governments knew very explicitly that this was the Iraqi leader's ultimate goal. "We have been tracking every aspect of Iraq's military procurement effort since the autumn of 1984. It is not a pretty picture," said one of the British government's top advisers on nuclear policy in the autumn of 1989. But cabinet ministers and government heads throughout Europe and the United States rarely turned their attention to the minutiae of arms-procurement networks, and powerful business lobbies wanted to sell to Iraq; there were profits at stake, and it could easily be argued that not every piece of equipment would find its way into a nuclear weapons plant. The result of both private-sector greed and gross government negligence was that Saddam was able to obtain much of what he sought. In both the Reagan and Bush administrations this dangerous attitude represented a notably cynical brand of "business as usual."

Between February 1988 and July 1989, BNL Atlanta made good on its unsecured loans to Baghdad by processing more than twenty-five hundred separate letters of credit for companies in the United States and Europe that exported equipment and technologies to Iraq. Some of Drogoul's loans went straight to front companies in Switzerland that were sending sensitive NATO-based equipment and technologies to Baghdad for the Condor II missile project, Saddam's high-priority ballistic missile that was at the top of the State Department's list of dangerous nuclear proliferation risks. In late 1988, a BNL Atlanta letter of credit was agreed for exports to an Iraqi entity called Project 395. This was Baghdad's code name for the entire Iraqi missile program. Other BNL Atlanta loans went directly to Iraq's Technical Corps for Special Projects, the state agency that ran the Condor II and other missile projects.

Not all the loans that helped Iraq's nuclear projects were clearly labeled as such. On April 8, 1989, BNL Atlanta provided a $5.4 million credit to finance the shipment of what was described as "300 tons of yarn" by Entrade, a Turkish-owned New York commodity exporter that had benefited from CCC-backed loans and had become one of Drogoul's best clients. The destination of the Entrade yarn was listed clearly on a telex sent to Drogoul from Baghdad: the Iraq Atomic Energy Commission. (See Appendix B, page 317.) Either yarn had become the newest ingredient in atomic research, or Baghdad was being circumspect about the nature of the actual goods it was buying.

Among those who received BNL money were a number of companies that formed part of Iraq's weapons-procurement network, including Iraqi front companies in London such as the Technology and Development Group (TDG) and TMG Engineering. Both were owned by the Al-Arabi Trading Company of Baghdad, the master procurement vehicle that was itself controlled by Hussein Kamel. TDG had a partnership with Dr. Gerald Bull's Space Research Corporation, and it financed purchases for Bull thanks to loans from BNL Atlanta. In late 1987, TMG had bought an obscure machine tools business in the city of Coventry and renamed it Matrix Churchill. In short order, Matrix Churchill began supplying Iraq with advanced and computer-driven cutting lathes that went into Iraqi armaments factories. Drogoul first met Matrix's Iraqi owners—who doubled as members of Baghdad's procurement network—in the company of Sadik Taha in London in October 1988. That same year, Matrix signed contracts to supply machinery to Iraq's Nasser Enterprise for Mechanical Industries, another of Baghdad's procurement and weapons-development state companies. BNL Atlanta provided a letter of credit to Matrix on May 23, 1989, to finance the shipment to Nasser of goods that were described elliptically as "hot forging dies project." (See Appendix B, page 318.) In fact, the project involved artillery shells and other weapons.

Drogoul's loans funded many genuinely dangerous projects, such as improving the range of Saddam's Soviet-made Scud missiles and providing thermal imaging night-vision components that would allow Iraqi troops to see their enemy in the dark. This sophisticated military technology, manufactured by the Hughes Aircraft Company of Santa Barbara, California, was shipped by a Belgian company that received nearly $28 million of Atlanta credits. In effect, Drogoul provided finance to any American or European exporter who was directed to him by the Iraqis.

After his friend Sadik Taha underwent a heart transplant operation in early 1989 and was replaced at the Central Bank, Drogoul finally saw with his own eyes the military use that Baghdad had made of his bank's money. His new Iraqi counterparts proved entirely different; they were no-nonsense military procurement men who worked directly for Hussein Kamel. In the spring of 1989, on his last trip to Baghdad, a visit was arranged for Drogoul and Von Wedel to the Nasser industrial complex in the company of TDG executives. There Drogoul viewed a bomb plant and a machine tool production plant filled with Matrix Churchill equipment. Thanks to BNL Atlanta's loans, Matrix Churchill had provided equipment that went straight into Iraq's nuclear missile project; its computer-controlled lathes helped shape the very missile casings. No longer could there be any doubt about what Baghdad was doing with the Atlanta loans.

It also became clear to Drogoul that this dangerous game involved the world of espionage as well as arms. During one of their increasingly frequent weekend visits to meet Matrix Churchill executives in London in the winter of 1988–89, Paul Von Wedel told him he thought they were being followed by intelligence agents. Drogoul immediately asked the Iraqis about this: Was it possible the CIA knew what was going on? Were American intelligence officers aware of what they were doing? Drogoul's Iraqi contact shrugged nonchalantly and informed the banker from Atlanta that there was no problem. "There is nothing to worry about. We are working together. We have been working together for years with the Americans."

If Baghdad's nuclear weapons ambitions were acknowledged by London and Washington at the same time they were officially condemned by them, the same was true of Iraqi chemical weapons development. The Iraqis would frequently order BNL to provide funds to finance a huge petrochemicals complex called PC2, located about seventy kilometers south of Baghdad, near the natural gas feeder lines that came from the southern oil fields. PC2 was to be the pride of the Iraqi military establishment because it had the support of contractors from the United States, Japan, Italy, France, and Britain. More significant, as Western intelligence agents knew, although PC2 would manufacture normal petrochemicals upon completion, like many of Saddam's disguised operations, it would be dual-use. This meant it would be able to generate chemical compounds needed to make mustard gas and nerve gas as well. The head of Iraq's chemicals industry, Lieutenant General Amer Hamoudi al Saadi, was proud of PC2. Al Saadi was himself a dual operative—his other job was as the head of Saddam's ballistic missile and chemical weapons programs, reporting to Hussein Kamel and his father-in-law, Saddam Hussein.

The general contractor on PC2 was the Bechtel Corporation, a familiar name when it came to Iraqi business. Bechtel was the company that had been ready to handle the Aqaba pipeline project back in 1984, the project for which George Bush had lobbied Eximbank so hard. The pipeline project had never worked out, but in the summer of 1988 Iraq asked Bechtel's London office to manage the entire PC2 petrochemicals project. The U.S. embassy in Baghdad was pleased for Bechtel, as was the Department of Commerce in Washington, which encouraged Bechtel to go ahead. Managers at Bechtel thought nothing of the request from Baghdad that they accept payment through letters of credit issued by BNL Atlanta. They also gave little thought to the fact that the plant's principal product—ethylene oxide—was a chemical that is easily converted to thiodiglycol, which is used to make mustard gas.

Only when Secretary of State George Shultz left the Reagan administration in early 1989 and returned to the Bechtel board of directors did the company focus on the possibility that it was going to build a plant that Saddam could use to manufacture chemical weapons. Shultz, who had been president of Bechtel before going to the State Department in 1982, had plenty of clout at the California company. When he found out about the PC2 project and asked questions, he was initially given assurances that it had nothing to do with chemical weapons. "But I thought about it a little more, and I gave my advice they should get out," he recalled.

Shultz's advice was ignored for several months, even though he realized "these things could be converted pretty easily." Finally, at a board meeting, Shultz pressed his case. He insisted to his fellow directors that "something is going to go very wrong in Iraq and blow up, and if Bechtel is there, it will get blown up too." This time Bechtel listened, and it pulled out of PC2.

The same kind of dual-use shipments occurred many times over, but few companies wanted to contemplate the ultimate use of their technology if the profits were sufficiently attractive. And the Atlanta branch on Peachtree Street kept generating letters of credit. A few weeks after taking care of Bechtel's bills, Drogoul's staff was forwarding to Eximbank an application for U.S. government loan guarantees in a transaction involving Dow Chemical. This time it was a shipment of pesticides for Iraq. An employee at Eximbank examined the request, then told his superiors that the compound was highly toxic to humans. "It behaves like a nerve gas. Death ultimately results from asphyxiation." Yet, added the Eximbank analyst, the Dow product was not on the State Department's munitions list, and there was no reason to deny the application. Almost as an afterthought—or perhaps to protect himself—the memo writer added a final note: "I cannot categorically state that these materials cannot be used as chemical warfare agents, nor that they cannot be converted to such." Dow Chemical, according to a former senior BNL executive, did not get Eximbank's blessing for this transaction, but it did obtain loans from BNL Atlanta for a series of other exports to Iraq.

BNL Atlanta, meanwhile, was doing more than just financing Saddam's conventional, nuclear, and chemical weapons projects. In the time-honored tradition in which BNL performed services on behalf of the Italian government, Drogoul's branch was also being used for military transfers from the United States to Italy. From 1984 onward, the Italian government, through both the Defense Ministry and the Foreign Currency Office, designated the Atlanta branch as the official vehicle for a number of military procurement transactions. Between 1986 and 1988, BNL Atlanta credits were requested, signed, and disbursed for the transfer from U.S. Air Force bases of satellite-tracking equipment and a thousand target-detectors for Sidewinder missiles. The Sidewinder is the most widely used air-to-air missile in the NATO arsenal. It is deployed by a variety of combat aircraft and helicopters and is top-of-the-range technology. The Ministry of Defense in Rome instructed the Italian embassy in Washington to use BNL Atlanta in order to finance the Sidewinder component shipments. U.S. investigators were later told that the Sidewinder parts were to be transshipped to Iraq rather than remain in the stated destination of Italy. In Rome, this triggered investigations years later.

Drogoul's Iraqi loans, hidden in gray books or not, were actually something of an open secret in parts of the banking community. BNL Atlanta even had its clearing account at Morgan Guaranty Trust in New York; Morgan regularly channeled payments between BNL and the Central Bank of Iraq. The account had been originally opened by Giuseppe Vincenzino back in 1984; five years later, no fewer than four Morgan employees were handling BNL Atlanta, and Morgan processed a total of $1.7 billion worth of Drogoul's Iraqi business in just seventeen months. Morgan would later argue, reasonably, that this was no reason to become suspicious, since in its handling of fund transfers for a wide range of institutions, it cleared sums many times larger than this each day. But within the BNL network in North America, the Atlanta branch was the only office that used Morgan to transfer funds.

Drogoul's office became so loaded with Iraqi business that, as it had in 1986, it once again began trying to share out loans with other banks. When customers came in to seek finance for exports to Iraq, Drogoul would occasionally send them to the Gulf International Bank in New York, an Arab-owned bank in which Baghdad itself was a minority shareholder. He also asked the National Bank for Cooperatives in distant Colorado to take a piece of Iraq's CCC business. Word was spreading, and very quickly, that BNL Atlanta was the Grand Central Station of U.S.-Iraqi banking traffic.

The Federal Reserve Board in Washington and other U.S. banking authorities appeared to be completely in the dark about BNL Atlanta, despite its extraordinary level of activity, its sharing out of loans around America, and its constant tapping of the wholesale money market for funds to lend to Iraq. Patrick Clawsen, a former Iraq specialist at the International Monetary Fund, shook his head in disbelief when he was later informed of the supposedly secret operation being run by Drogoul: "If some bank starts on a regular basis tapping the interbank market for nearly $2 billion over seventeen months and sending the money to Iraq, don't you think the Federal Reserve or other banks would hear about it?"

Other bankers involved in international business certainly did. Indeed, Drogoul became something of a legend, the kind of enterprising banker who makes news. Even while he was in Baghdad in 1988, a widely read newsletter—the *Middle East Economic Digest*—published word of his Iraqi dealings and the backing he had received from the U.S. Department of Agriculture. The newsletter also detailed problems such as the low level of interest being charged by BNL and the fact that other banks were unwilling to join it as partners in lending to Baghdad, leaving the bank "highly exposed to Iraqi risk."

In the autumn of 1988, Drogoul's money machine for Iraq was still running smoothly, but other parts of his Atlanta branch were malfunctioning. Luigi Sardelli of the North American regional office, who disliked Drogoul, noted that there had been no inspection of Atlanta for more than a year. He dispatched internal auditors from New York, and almost immediately they found irregularities in the way the books were kept. In September, Louis Messere, the chief auditor, telephoned New York and reported that "the situation is really very bad." In his written report Messere concluded that BNL Atlanta was in a disastrous state, suffering from administrative disorder; letters of credit were not being recorded on a timely basis, cash advances for travel by Drogoul had not been put into expense reports, loans had been made without proper documentation, and the quality of the staff was judged to be poor. A summary of the draft report was handed to a visitor from BNL's Rome headquarters in October 1988.

In December a final and scorchingly critical version was sent to Rome. Nothing happened, so BNL New York sent a duplicate copy to Rome in early 1989. It was six months more before executives at the Via Veneto headquarters even saw the report. Still no action was taken. Drogoul seemed untouchable. He even wrote to Rome and accused the auditors of "New York myopic arrogance." Sardelli was furious and later claimed that Pedde was protecting Drogoul, a charge that Pedde later denied. As far as Drogoul was concerned, the auditor's report might never have been written.

While this scathing yet ineffective auditor's report was being prepared for Rome, Drogoul was dining with U.S. government officials and visiting Iraqis in Washington. At a convivial dinner held in a Lebanese restaurant that autumn, Drogoul heard a Department of Agriculture official urge the Iraqis to sign up for more CCC-backed loans before the November 1988 presidential election. If Michael Dukakis were to defeat George Bush, the Iraqis were warned, "the Democrats will cut you off."

In December 1988, Christopher Drogoul was ready to celebrate seven exciting and frenetic years with the Banca Nazionale del Lavoro. For the past four of those years he had been immersed in the world of Iraqi business, realizing only gradually that the results of his work were not like those of other bankers in Atlanta. He had admirers such as Pedde in Rome and enemies such as Sardelli in New York. He had friends in Baghdad and in Washington, and he had learned something about the seemingly intertwined worlds of covert action, politics, and diplomacy.

But not everything was rosy. Of some annoyance that December was the fact that for several weeks he had been exchanging telexes with Teodoro Monaco and other BNL executives in Rome on the subject of lending to Iraq. In yet another indication that Rome was aware Drogoul was doing business with Baghdad, Drogoul was told with firmness that he should make sure there was some cash collateral to back up a pending Iraqi loan from Atlanta. A few weeks later, Monaco did more than advise Drogoul on how to construct a proper loan for Iraq; he contacted him with a business proposition for Atlanta to finance an Italian export to Iraq. Monaco had received an inquiry from a company called Danieli that wanted BNL loans to help finance the shipment of parts for an Iraqi steel plant. He informed the Central Bank of Iraq that Atlanta would handle the transaction; the Danieli deal was channeled to Atlanta, and Drogoul duly provided the necessary paperwork.

In July 1989, Rome headquarters offered Drogoul an even stronger reason to think it knew of and approved his Iraqi dealings; the bank's third-ranking executive, Davide Croff, approved a $50 million line of credit from Atlanta to the Central Bank of Iraq. Drogoul had first sent the request to Rome on December 20, 1988, making clear the proceeds of the credit would be used by American companies that were trading with Baghdad. He provided all the details and arguments in favor of the deal, and he made sure the telex went to senior officers in Rome headquarters.

The loan request sat in BNL's Via Veneto offices for six months. "Our efficiency was not what you could call the greatest," admitted a senior executive in Rome. Not until June 1989 was the loan request finally presented to Croff, who asked his deputies to run a check on the state of

BNL's business with Iraq and, in particular, whether there might be any negative repercussions for the bank if the loan did not go through. In reply, Croff was told that the Atlanta branch had "good relations" with Baghdad, thanks to its previous work with U.S. companies and the backing of loan guarantees from Washington. There was no obstacle to Rome approving Atlanta's request and the bank saw no impropriety in doing so. On July 14, Croff and his colleagues signed the approval form and told Drogoul his transaction with Iraq was fine. Atlanta had asked, and in due course Rome had signed. It was as simple as that.

Unbeknownst to Drogoul, however, a problem far more serious than whether Rome approved an Iraqi deal was in the making back in Atlanta. At the end of June two women on his staff—Mela Maggi, who ran the money desk, and Jean Ivey, an assistant vice-president who helped keep the gray books—quietly decided to hire lawyers and blow the whistle on the entire Iraqi loan saga. Maggi, a rotund, dark-haired woman who quite literally kept the entire Iraqi loan operation going by raising funds from other banks, was known inside the BNL branch for her volatile personality. She was a workaholic who would not stop her fund-raising efforts even when driving and made calls from the cellular telephone installed in her white Cadillac. Ivey, a soft-spoken blonde, was an old friend of Drogoul's and had followed him to BNL from Barclays Bank in the early 1980s.

Why these two junior BNL Atlanta officers decided to become informants has never been clear. William Hinshaw, a former special agent in charge of the FBI's Atlanta office, later recalled hearing speculation that they had been forced to tell all because of pressure from Mossad, the Israeli intelligence service. That the Israelis might wish to bring a halt to loans that were fueling Saddam's nuclear weapons projects is plausible, but it is hard to imagine they would have got to Maggi and Ivey. "It was strange, real strange," remembered Hinshaw. In any event, lawyers for the two women obtained immunity from prosecution, and on July 29, 1989, Maggi and Ivey provided local prosecutors and officials from the Federal Reserve with a mind-boggling story of what they and Drogoul had been up to for the past five years. A team of law enforcement agents from Atlanta, New York, and Washington was assembled toward the end of July and laid careful plans to close in on BNL Atlanta.

As far as Christopher Drogoul was aware, everything was going well that summer. Everyone at BNL Atlanta was a little fatigued by the workload, but vacation time was just around the corner. At the beginning of August, Drogoul and his family were themselves traveling from

Atlanta to Paris, en route to his father's country home in the south of France. The prospect of good food, good weather, and a much-needed rest made them all cheerful. It would not last long; the vacation in France was about to be interrupted by a most upsetting development. When Christopher Drogoul returned to the United States, his life would never be the same.

THE BOSS WAS AWAY on vacation, and it was a hot and humid Friday afternoon in Atlanta on that fourth of August 1989 when the sixteen employees of BNL Atlanta began to wind down for the coming weekend. In only ten more minutes it would be five o'clock.

Suddenly, the double doors of BNL's twentieth-floor suite of offices on Peachtree Street swung open, and more than two dozen federal agents fanned out before the startled receptionist, flashing their badges. "FBI. Everyone stay where they are. We have a search warrant."

The branch's employees were ordered into the conference room and told to turn over their purses and wallets. The agents raced from room to room, gathering up files and boxes. Every file cabinet was thrown open, every desk drawer emptied of its contents, every scrap of paper collected. Some of the agents placed themselves in front of personal computers, racing over the keyboard, searching directories, and making sure they obtained every floppy disk in sight. In the conference room the employees waited as the drama unfolded. They were not told the reason for the raid. Eventually they were given back their purses and wallets, but only after they had been thoroughly searched. The document seizure took hours, while the employees sat huddled in little groups, staring aimlessly at one another, speculating among themselves as to what was going on. If anyone wished to go to the toilet, an FBI escort was required. Not until ten o'clock that night were the employees allowed to leave the building, and then only after records of their identities and addresses had been provided to the agents and meticulously recorded.

Within minutes of the start of the FBI raid in Atlanta, another group of agents, accompanied by bank inspectors from the Federal Reserve, made their way through the New York offices of BNL's North American headquarters building on Fifty-first Street between Fifth and Sixth avenues, in the heart of the Rockefeller Center complex. The newly appointed head of BNL's American operations, a timid banker named Pietro Lombardi, whose command of the English language was modest at best, welcomed the federal agents without protest. The search of BNL New

York was every bit as thorough as the exercise in Atlanta. The same process occurred at BNL branches in Chicago, Los Angeles, and Miami.

Late that Friday evening in Rome, while these blitzes were under way, the bank's chairman and chief executive emerged from their car and passed below the huge palm trees that grace the headquarters of the Bank of Italy on the Via Nazionale. Giacomo Pedde, the Christian Democratic director-general, and Nerio Nesi, a balding Socialist from Turin who had a greater penchant for party politics and international travel than for his responsibilities as the chairman of BNL, entered a private elevator to the right of the gray-cobblestoned courtyard and stared at each other in a state of bewilderment. They had been ordered to come here by the central bank, on a Friday night in early August, for an unspecified purpose. What on earth was going on? The elevator doors slid open on the second floor of the central bank. Although it was past 10:30, the bank's dark-suited receptionists were expecting the pair and escorted them immediately down a long, high-ceilinged marble corridor to the office of Lamberto Dini, director-general of the Italian central bank.

Dini, an erudite bank regulator with more experience of the United States than anyone else in the Italian government, greeted Nesi and Pedde in his usual way; he was polite yet brief. Bringing the long fingers of his hands together above the bridge of his nose, Dini almost looked like a clergyman in prayer. With the BNL executives seated before him, Pedde in an armchair, and Nesi on the black leather couch in Dini's office, the central banker began to speak.

As he described the FBI raid at the Atlanta branch to them, Pedde fell back in his chair, his face turning pale and distorted by panic and shock. Dini was relentless as he informed his guests of the gravity of the situation. Loans that had no backing and that totaled at least $2 billion—about the same as the bank's entire capital base—appeared to have been extended by BNL Atlanta to a most unreliable customer: the government of Iraq.

At this very moment, Dini explained, federal agents were raiding all of BNL's offices in the United States, including New York and Atlanta. Meanwhile, the New York Federal Reserve Bank was worried that a leak of news of the situation at BNL could trigger a liquidity crisis in the banking system, as other banks called in their loans to the Italian bank. By now, Pedde was in a state of collapse; he was literally speechless. Nesi, who had a quizzical look on his face, did his best to carry on the rest of the conversation. He was instructed by Dini to arrange the immediate trans-fer of emergency funds to New York in order to prepare for a possible collapse in BNL's money-market financing from other banks in the event the Atlanta raid leaked. Dini also ordered Nesi to send a group of managers to the United States that weekend in order to take control of Atlanta and the other branches.

When Nesi and Pedde finally left the Bank of Italy, it was midnight. An hour later, Pedde told Nesi he felt ill and would be leaving Rome for his native Sardinia, to take his annual vacation as scheduled. Throughout the weekend Nesi was left alone inside the great Mussolini-era headquarters of BNL on the Via Veneto. After a frantic round of telephone calls, he managed to track down other senior officials of the bank, most of them already on vacation.

On that fateful Friday evening, Christopher Drogoul was in Paris with his wife, Lynn, and the children. They were two days into their August vacation, staying at a small hotel on the Left Bank and preparing to travel on to Drogoul's father's country house in the Dordogne region in the south. The Drogouls went to sleep that night with no idea of what was transpiring in Atlanta, New York, or Rome.

At five o'clock in the morning, the telephone rang in Drogoul's hotel room. It was his father, Pierre, who had just received a call from Atlanta from Paul Von Wedel, who had taken the previous day off from BNL, but not from the FBI. Not finding him at Peachtree Street, the federal agents had gone to Von Wedel's home in suburban Atlanta that evening and subjected him to nearly four hours of tough questioning. After they left, Von Wedel was visited by a female colleague whom the FBI had just released. Together they had telephoned Pierre Drogoul's house in France, expecting Chris and the family to be there. Once Pierre reached his son at the hotel in Paris, Chris Drogoul called his colleagues back in Atlanta. He listened to their report of the raid and told them he would return to Atlanta immediately, stopping off only to confer with senior managers at the BNL regional headquarters in New York.

The next morning, and until he left for New York on Sunday, from the moment Chris Drogoul and his wife stepped out of their Paris hotel and onto the street, they were followed. "We had five people tracking us at one point. They went wherever we went," he recalled. Whoever was following Drogoul must have noticed that he made a very quick trip from Paris to London and back again that Saturday, August 5. In London he conferred with a handful of Iraqi contacts, including his old friend Sadik Taha, who was still convalescing in the wake of his heart transplant operation earlier in the year. Then he flew back to Paris and on Sunday made the transatlantic journey.

On Monday morning, Drogoul walked into BNL's New York office and had a long conversation with Pietro Lombardi. Also present at the session were BNL's New York lawyers. The meeting was cordial enough; Drogoul was questioned about the Iraqi loans; about the gray books, some of which Maggi had given to prosecutors even before the FBI raid; and the nature of his relations with Baghdad. But he was not dismissed by his superior. Instead, he was told not to worry; in fact, BNL's corporate lawyer even offered legal counsel for Drogoul in Atlanta. He accepted the offer, which was quickly organized, and returned to Atlanta.

At 9:15 the next morning, Gerald Corrigan, president of the Federal Reserve Bank of New York, placed a telephone call to Lewis Preston, who headed Morgan Guaranty Trust. Corrigan, a bluff and red-faced Irishman who had spent most of his career in the Federal Reserve System, had taken a direct hand in the BNL Atlanta case. As the U.S. bank regulator with the main responsibility for both Wall Street and international financial affairs, Corrigan was used to handling crises. In fact, he reveled in taking command when the financial system appeared to be threatened, as he had in October 1987, when the New York Stock Exchange suffered its worst plunge since the Depression. The previous week, it had been Corrigan who first contacted Lamberto Dini at the Bank of Italy to tell him of the Atlanta problem. Now he was calling his friend at Morgan Guaranty, having learned that at least $1 billion of BNL Atlanta's Iraqi money had been channeled through Morgan's New York clearing system.

"We have a trickly little problem that we need help with," Corrigan informed Preston. He sketched out the Atlanta loans and then told Preston "they were undertaken largely, if not exclusively, through an account at Morgan.... This is part of a criminal investigation." (See Appendix B, page 319.) Corrigan made clear that his inspectors would have to go through Morgan's books. He added that there was a question in his mind about the ease with which the operation had run over a fairly long period of time. While the amounts had started at relatively modest levels, they had built up to a "pretty goddamn" good size.

While the Fed's Corrigan and Morgan's Preston were talking, Drogoul was briefing BNL lawyers in Atlanta on the Iraqi loans. He was suspended from BNL, then fired, then subjected to what would become an endless round of questioning by local and federal law enforcement officials. In Rome, Nesi was laboring behind the scenes, trying to put out the fire as best he could. So far, the press had no inkling of the unfolding crisis, and BNL asked U.S. officials to avoid making any public statements.

By the middle of the month, as word of the raids spread in Italian banking and political circles, BNL finally released a distinctly anodyne statement that said its Atlanta branch was under investigation for "procedurally improper practices" related to the financing of exports to Iraq. No mention of military purchases by Iraq was made; in fact, BNL categorically denied that arms sales were involved. The bank also refused to speak of either the companies that had benefited or the actual sums involved. Its aim was secrecy, not disclosure.

BOOK TWO

THE WEB UNDONE, 1989–1993

Whole sight; or all the rest is desolation.
JOHN FOWLES, *Daniel Martin*

NINE

BushBaker and Saddam

Not surprisingly, James Baker was deeply concerned about the BNL affair. Although the Italian bank did its best to keep a lid on the dimensions of the problem, word quickly leaked to the media that Drogoul's Iraqi loans had been used to finance the Condor II missile and related nuclear weapons projects. The growing scandal was beginning to have a serious impact on relations between Washington and Baghdad. The secretary of state kept abreast of developments after Drogoul returned to Atlanta and a task force of officials from nearly a dozen federal, state, and local agencies descended on the little bank branch in Georgia. Gale McKenzie, the assistant U.S. attorney in Atlanta who was leading the BNL task force, noted in her daily logs that Baker was "most interested" in BNL and was receiving "frequent briefings."

The BNL-Iraqi loans case became public late in the summer of 1989—a particularly awkward time for the White House. President Bush and Secretary Baker were just putting the finishing touches on a set of secret policies that would intensify U.S.-Iraqi relations as never before. If BNL became too much of a problem, it could threaten the new policy that was now being drafted. The president and the secretary of state, as one congressional staffer put it, "had firmly decided to establish a pro-Iraqi policy, and the BNL scandal threatened to expose Iraq again as an outlaw regime. There were mounds of evidence already, but here was something on U.S. soil. It made government agencies nervous."

The BNL task force in Atlanta that Baker and Bush were hearing about during the summer and autumn of 1989 was not the best-organized team in the world, but its members eventually came across enough unexplained links among BNL-funded companies, Iraqi procurement agents, and the U.S. government to make them wonder whether there wasn't more to the story than merely a bank fraud. They eventually wrote to ask Washington to explain "what knowledge and role, if any, the Central Intelligence Agency had or played in BNL dealings with foreign governments in general and Iraq more specifically." Help was needed on this question because "experience has demonstrated that CIA knowledge and participation can seriously impact a decision to prosecute." Their question went unanswered.

Actually, the CIA had monitored relations between BNL and Iraq for years. It had first reported on BNL's role in helping finance the sale of Italian frigates to Iraq in the early 1980s. "BNL's work with the Iraqis was known about for a long time. The CIA knew about it, and so did the Defense Intelligence Agency," said a U.S. intelligence official involved in monitoring the arms trade in the Middle East.

In mid-September the Pentagon's DIA filed a report in which it mused that "the BNL mechanism was but a part of a larger NATO strategy to ensure an Iraqi victory in its war with Iran." Later that month, the CIA obtained information clearly linking BNL Atlanta and the Iraqi procurement network. That kind of information did not go down well with the men who wanted to step up relations with Saddam, their chosen pillar of stability in the oil-rich Persian Gulf. Neither did a classified CIA report that James Baker and other top officials received in September, describing Saddam's efforts to buy nuclear weapons technology around the world.

On September 21, the U.S. Customs Service reported its suspicion that BNL Atlanta had provided loans to American companies for the illegal export to Iraq of missile technology for the nuclear-capable Condor II project. The Pentagon, the Federal Reserve, and prosecutors in Atlanta were also communicating their fears about the suspected use of BNL funds for the Condor II project at the same time. Indeed, Baker had been reminded six months earlier, in explicit terms, of how hard Iraq was working to develop its missiles and chemical and biological weapons— and both he and Bush were well aware that the Iraqi arsenal was growing fast.

For the past eight years the two men had lobbied, cajoled, and politicked their way through the executive and legislative branches on behalf of a consistently lenient approach to Saddam. Now George Bush was in the White House, and he and Baker at last had the authority to codify their views and work to force them through. No intelligence reports or unfolding bank scandal was going to alter that.

Members of Bush's transition team had advised the president-elect that it was time to set a new direction for U.S. policy toward Iraq. The war with Iran had ended at last, a policy review explained. It was now up to the new administration "to decide whether to treat Iraq as a distasteful dictatorship to be shunned where possible, or to recognize Iraq's present and potential power in the region and accord it relatively high priority. We strongly urge the latter view."

This secret policy review informed the leaders of the new administration that "the lessons of war may have changed Iraq from a radical state challenging the system to a more responsible, status-quo state working within the system, and promoting stability in the region." The phrase "may have changed" was used because the policy advisers who wrote the review recognized that Iraq's postwar intentions were still evolving. In its quest for military and political power, the review advised, Iraq was "aiming higher." Indeed, overnight success with the new policy was not likely: "Saddam Hussein will continue to eliminate those he regards as a threat, torture those he believes have secrets to reveal, and rule without any real concessions to democracy. He has announced a few cosmetic improvements, but few expect a humane regime will come to Iraq any time soon."

The policy advisers left Bush and Baker in no doubt about Iraq's "unlawful" use of chemical weapons and its "abominable" human rights record. They offered no argument to the fact that Saddam's military capabilities and aspirations made him "an alarming prospect to Israel— and to many in the U.S." The advisers informed Bush administration decision-makers that Hussein Kamel was pushing for more U.S.-Iraqi ties, "often through military channels," and that Iraq's military attaché in Washington had been active in trying to buy dual-use and high-tech items that Iraq needed.

Much would have to change before it would be "prudent" to sell weaponry to Baghdad, the advisers continued, but they concluded nonetheless that military exchanges should be encouraged, particularly those that would increase personal contacts, such as attendance by midlevel Iraqi officers at War College seminars on infantry strategy and some "higher level dialogue" as well. And while the risk of "diversion" of U.S. exports to Iraq's war machine was great, trade was described as the key to influencing Iraq. "We should begin a major effort to free up licensing requests" that were being blocked by the experts on defense technology in the Pentagon. Indeed, the policy review articulated a prime U.S. business interest that influenced both Bush and Baker in their thinking: Iraq's "vast oil reserves promising a lucrative market for U.S. goods." The review noted that U.S. oil imports from Iraq had skyrocketed after Iraq began offering American oil companies "large price incentives."

The idea, as one of the officials involved in preparing these views at Baker's State Department summarized it, was "to embrace Saddam in a cocoon of moderation."

While many saw evidence that Baghdad was no less a menace than before, Bush and Baker wanted to emphasize the positive. So on Monday, October 2, 1989, with all the necessary information available to him, President George Bush lifted a pen and with one stroke set in motion a secret presidential policy to help Saddam. He signed his name to a secret order that would become known by the acronym of NSD 26, for National Security Directive 26. (See Appendix B, pages 320–322.)

"When you look at NSD 26, you find out it was the Administration's sole desire and policy to aid and abet Saddam Hussein," said Congressman Sam Gejdenson, a Connecticut Democrat who became one of Bush's harshest critics. "The cop was put in the intersection, and he was waving the sellers on."

NSD 26 stated the BushBaker policy in unequivocal terms. Access to Persian Gulf oil and the security of key friendly states in the area were vital to the U.S. national interest. The United States would propose "economic and political incentives for Iraq" to moderate its behavior and to increase Washington's influence in Baghdad. Chief among these was the administration's plan to encourage American companies to get more involved in Iraq's oil industry.

There was little in either man's experience that should have led them to believe that befriending Saddam would produce such results. By the autumn of 1989, Iraq had been off the U.S. terrorist list for seven years, yet Baker had been told that terrorists such as Abu Abbas were still moving in and out of Baghdad. NSD 26 said explicitly that the United States would apply sanctions if Saddam used chemical and biological weapons or violated international rules on the development of nuclear weapons, yet just one year before, Bush had been among those in the Reagan administration who resisted congressional efforts to levy sanctions on Iraq that were intended to punish Saddam for gassing the Kurds in August 1988.

Nonetheless, in his directive Bush laid out a pro-Iraqi agenda that even decreed that the United States should consider various forms of military assistance to Iraq on a case-by-case basis. Within weeks, the Joint Chiefs of Staff had prepared a set of proposed U.S.-Iraqi military initiatives, ranging from military officer exchange programs to aerial reconnaissance training. From Baghdad, Ambassador April Glaspie recommended such steps because they would improve the dialogue with the Iraqi government.

The policy of enhancing Washington's relationship with Baghdad had been dictated directly from the Oval Office, and it was now official, though still classified a state secret. James Baker wasted no time at all in implementing it. On October 3, 1989, just one day after NSD 26 was signed, officials from the Departments of State, Agriculture, Commerce, and Treasury, the Federal Reserve, and other agencies gathered to discuss a new proposal to offer a $1 billion loan guarantee for Iraq, to be backed by the same CCC program that had figured so prominently in the BNL affair. They met in a committee that reported to the National Advisory Council (NAC), a cabinet-level group that called in actual cabinet members only when their lower-level surrogates could not resolve their differences. The council convened when U.S. government financial commitments needed to be weighed against foreign policy goals. Iraq was certainly such a case.

The State Department representative at the meeting was particularly forceful in arguing that the program should go forward, but others, such as officials at the Treasury Department, were fearful of giving Iraq more financial aid when evidence was mounting of its involvement in illegal behavior. In fact, on the same day that Bush had signed NSD 26, aides to Treasury Secretary Nicholas Brady were filing a memorandum warning that the CCC guarantees for Iraq "should not go forward at this time." The Treasury aides had heard there was "good reason to believe there are serious irregularities" in the CCC scheme for Iraq that were linked to the BNL affair.

Dozens of career bureaucrats and political-level officials in the Bush administration were now monitoring the BNL situation. Each new revelation about the scandal that leaked in the press—an Iraqi missile financed by BNL here, a suspected grain-for-arms deal there—put the secret U.S. policy on Iraq under greater threat. Trying to force the machinery of government to grant Saddam another $1 billion of taxpayer loan guarantees was becoming a serious challenge, even for the White House.

The Treasury officials who objected to Baker's push for this loan, as well as concerned colleagues at the Federal Reserve and the Office of Management and Budget, had all seen the reports that summer stating that Baghdad was not creditworthy and revealing that Saddam was now spending 42 percent of his $12 billion of annual oil revenues on military procurement. The Treasury representative at the NAC meeting was among the toughest opponents of Baker's plan. He noted that Baghdad was desperate for cash and was demanding that BNL's Rome headquarters still honor hundreds of millions of dollars' worth of fraudulent credits. And the prosecutors in Atlanta were convinced that the Iraqis were involved in the fraud. Treasury officials in Washington had learned from the Atlanta team of possible kickbacks and the financing of illicit military exports. It just made no sense to hand out more U.S. credits to Saddam.

Indeed, Baker's own aides were being told that lending to Iraq was not a good deal. One secret State Department cable to Baghdad disclosed that William Ryan, the acting Eximbank chairman, had called on Undersecretary Robert Kimmitt and told him Iraq was "overspending its resources to develop an unprofitable military-industrial complex that will not produce exports to service long-term debt. Iraq's attitude toward its foreign debt is special. Once the Iraqis suck you in, they only service the debt if you give them ever-increasing amounts of credit." At the October 3 meeting the Treasury's desk officer for Iraq echoed this view, saying that if the CCC approved another billion dollars for Iraq, it would be contributing to a "Ponzi-type" scheme, the term used to describe what happens when swindlers persuade investors to throw good money after bad.

Although Baker's representative at the October 3 NAC meeting pressed hard, he and others were aware that Washington was among the last Western governments still willing to trust Saddam when it came to money. Germany and France were reluctant to do any more for Saddam. Britain's government loan-guarantee program was open to Iraq only because Margaret Thatcher had made a political commitment to invest more each year. On the other side of the world, Japan had stopped further financial support. The Commerce Department official at the NAC meeting addressed the problem directly: The U.S. government would be "courting disaster" if it did not ban BNL from the loan-guarantee program.

The meeting was in clear danger of reaching a stalemate, so the officials engaged in the time-honored Washington tradition of settling on half a loaf—or in this case, a bit less. Only $400 million of CCC credits would be offered, and the BNL investigation would be watched for further developments.

Two days later, on Thursday, October 5, USDA officials met with a visiting Iraqi delegation that included among its ostensible farm and financial experts a friend of Christopher Drogoul's—an official from the military industrialization ministry in Baghdad that was busy supervising the development of nuclear weapons.

It was left to these Agriculture officials to break the bad news of the reduced loan guarantees. But while the Americans knew what they had to tell the Iraqi delegation, they could not have anticipated what the Iraqis would tell them. The Iraqis admitted that they had demanded and received bribes and kickbacks, except that they refused to call them by those names. Instead, they euphemistically referred to them as requests for "after-sales services." Yes, there had been trucks and trailers and cash involved, but this was a normal Iraqi business practice.

Midlevel officials in the Bush administration now heard the Iraqis acknowledge directly this clear violation of the U.S. law governing the CCC program, in which kickbacks were simply not allowed. According to the CCC program's rules, an admission like this should have led to the program's immediate suspension. Government loan guarantees were not supposed to be extended to anyone who engaged in criminal behavior. U.S.-Iraqi talks about the new loan were suspended.

JAMES BAKER WAS in an embarrassing position at that point because he was twenty-four hours away from a meeting at the State Department with Tariq Aziz, who was now holding two very influential portfolios: as Iraq's deputy prime minister and its foreign minister. Baker had been told by his briefers that Aziz might raise the issue of BNL and that he might already have heard that the billion-dollar Iraqi request for loan guarantees had been slashed by 60 percent. He had also been told about press coverage that focused on possible military uses of goods shipped to Baghdad with BNL financing. This could be a tough session.

At two o'clock on the afternoon of Friday, October 6, Baker warmly welcomed the Iraqi foreign minister to the State Department. Summoning his customary grace, Baker made small talk as he walked Aziz to the very end of the eighth floor and down a few steps into the Henry Clay Room, the stately sunken dining room reserved for private encounters with heads of state and other visiting dignitaries. The two men and their aides gathered around the long mahogany table. If this was going to be a difficult meeting, at least it was taking place in handsome surroundings.

Aziz had just flown to Washington from New York, where he had

met with UN Secretary General Javier Perez de Cuellar and then delivered a lengthy address to the General Assembly. Aziz had grown in
political stature since his previous encounters with the Reagan administration, and he was by far the most Westernized member of Saddam's
inner councils, a fluent English speaker who on foreign trips in the late
1980s increasingly gave the impression of being a jovial civilian. As
Baghdad sought to nurture its relations with the Bush administration,
Aziz was the man it chose to present the apparently acceptable face of the
Iraqi dictatorship. It was only back at the presidential palace in Baghdad
that Aziz would revert to form, donning his boots and fatigues, strapping
a pistol to his belt, and joining Saddam and his inner clique to plot
policies, wars, and weapons deals.

Baker made a point of explaining how he appreciated Aziz's willingness to find the time to come to Washington. His briefing memo had
warned him that Aziz liked to lecture and that it would be advisable to
lead off with a discussion of bilateral relations, so he stressed how much
the United States valued its relationship with Iraq and wanted to see it
strengthen and broaden. Aziz responded cordially, assuring Baker he
always conducted his meetings with American officials in a friendly and
open manner.

But once he had finished his introductory remarks, Aziz, while still
perfectly cordial, announced that speaking quite frankly, Iraq had not
seen "enough improvement" in its relationship with the United States
since the end of the war with Iran the year before. Indeed, it had received
a number of disturbing signals, such as a negative approach toward
Baghdad's efforts to develop its industrial and technological base, and the
very recent reports that "some American agencies" had been trying to
destabilize Iraq. Then he came to the main point. Iraq had received $1
billion of CCC credits a year ago, but he had just learned from the Iraqi
agricultural team now in Washington that the 1990 allocation was to be
only $400 million. Worse, the CCC program was being linked to the BNL
Atlanta scandal, in which Iraq had had no part. The government of Iraq
viewed this as a setback and was "very unhappy."

Baker tried to reassure Aziz that there were no efforts to destabilize
Iraq and that as far as technology was concerned, the two countries
should "work together on specific requests." As for the CCC credits, yes,
he was aware that a problem existed. But the $400 million was only an
interim allotment; the balance was being held pending further investigations into the BNL scandal.

Aziz argued that his government had not been involved in any illegal actions. If the bank had been willing to make the loans, then any customer would have said it was the bank and not the customer who had the problem. In fact, said Aziz, he had just met the Italian finance minister, and *he* had said Iraq was not involved in the BNL affair. If the Italian government was not taking action against Iraq, it seemed very strange that the U.S. government would. These American actions would "sour" relations with Baghdad.

Baker began to speak about the need to cooperate on the investigation, but Aziz pressed his point: If Iraqi officials were implicated, his government wanted to know "immediately." Iraq, after all, took pride in its ability to root out corruption. Meanwhile, it was urgent to resolve this matter quickly.

Baker assured Aziz he wanted to find a way to resolve it and promised that he would personally look into what could be done, but he said that Washington might need assurances from Baghdad that it would aid in the investigation. It had been a difficult meeting after all.

Nor was the meeting the end of the story. Even as Baker was escorting Tariq Aziz from the Henry Clay Room, his ambassador in Baghdad, April Glaspie, was being confronted by the same subject. Glaspie had been attending a diplomatic reception in Baghdad that Friday evening when she was collared by the Iraqi trade minister, who pressed her for news of the CCC credits and asked her to urge Washington not to make any announcement about the loan unless the amount was restored to the full $1 billion. Anything less would create "a global perception" that the U.S. government suspected Baghdad was in some way involved in the BNL scandal.

At this point the Iraqi finance minister joined them. He claimed that during his just-completed visit to Washington, he had called at the Federal Reserve, where Alan Greenspan, its chairman, had asserted he was aware of no links between Iraq and the BNL affair. It was unlikely that the chairman could have been so ill informed. By this time, Greenspan's Federal Reserve had received literally dozens of reports on Iraq and the BNL Atlanta case.

Glaspie promised both ministers that there was no U.S. intention "to infer Iraqi involvement in the BNL issue." But her reassurances were not enough. Two evenings later, on Sunday, October 8, Baker's Iraqi problem became worse. Aziz's deputy, Nizar Hamdoon, the undersecretary of foreign affairs who had been so friendly with George Bush throughout his stint as Saddam's envoy to Washington, ordered Glaspie's deputy, Joseph Wilson, over to the ministry. Hamdoon had a message for Washington that came from "the highest authorities in the Iraqi government"—the usual code word for Saddam himself. The government of Iraq was interested in strengthening bilateral relations with the United States, but it needed to stabilize commercial relations and make them more predictable. No announcement should be made on the current CCC negotiations unless an agreement on the full program was reached. Wilson reported the threat succinctly to Baker: "With his mailed fist still in his velvet glove, Hamdoon then pointed out that Iraq does have alternative sources of supply." (See Appendix B, pages 324–325.) He also reported that Hamdoon had raised the issue of favoring the United States when it came to repaying its debts. Implicit in Hamdoon's remarks, wrote Wilson, was that unless Washington agreed to an acceptable CCC program, Iraq would rethink both its dependence on U.S. suppliers of agricultural products and the priority treatment it accorded to U.S. creditors in the repayment of its debts.

Both Bush and Baker were now in a serious bind. Just days into their new Iraqi policy, they were facing not only protests from below, in the form of conscientious U.S. officials who suspected Iraq of criminal behavior, but protests from Saddam, who wanted his $1 billion of promised credits and wanted it now. But much as Baker wished to help Saddam, his own deputies continued to offer him more evidence of serious wrongdoing that involved BNL, the Iraqis, and the CCC program. A few days after Hamdoon's threat, Baker received a confidential report on the situation from Richard McCormack, his undersecretary for economic affairs. McCormack, a Reagan administration holdover who had previously worked for Senator Jesse Helms of North Carolina, didn't mince words. He informed Baker that several agencies—including the FBI, the Pentagon, Agriculture, and the Internal Revenue Service—were looking at allegations of "widespread and blatant" irregularities in the CCC program.

Among the concerns were the suspected diversion and transshipment of U.S. commodities to places other than Iraq, the reported use of CCC money for arms purchases, and the apparent overpricing of some commodities to double and triple wholesale prices. Any one of these would have made it illegal to approve a penny more from U.S. government coffers. "The unfolding BNL scandal," McCormack told Baker, "is directly involved with the Iraqi CCC program and cannot be separated from it."

Word of the suspected abuse of U.S. taxpayers' money was also being reported to administration officials by Gale McKenzie, the assistant U.S. attorney who headed the BNL task force in Atlanta. In 1989,

McKenzie was a junior prosecutor with no particular experience in international banking, diplomacy, the Middle East, military matters, or any of the other aspects involved in the Iraqi loans case. The daughter of a Georgia peach grower, McKenzie was known in Atlanta legal circles as an ambitious woman, and her peers in Atlanta sensed that the Drogoul case represented the chance of her lifetime to tackle something really big. While she would later find herself floundering in the investigation and stymied by interference from Washington, in that autumn of 1989 Gale McKenzie had understood very well certain fundamentals, like the nature of the crimes likely to have been committed in the Iraqi loans case.

On October 11, 1989, McKenzie was visited in Atlanta by two officials from the Department of Agriculture. There she told them of the criminal complicity of Iraqi government officials involved in the BNL loans and the CCC program, of the use of BNL funds to acquire equipment for nuclear missiles, and of kickbacks that involved the CCC program and that were continuing even after the United States had warned Iraq this was illegal. McKenzie had already explained to the Federal Reserve that the volume of U.S. farm products supposedly being shipped to Iraq was so inflated that in some cases there were contracts for seeds that exceeded the needs of the entire country.

The game was up now. On October 12, Clayton Yeutter, the secretary of agriculture, was briefed by his people, and the next day they informed the Iraqi delegation in Washington that even the $400 million of CCC credits was now uncertain. In fact, Yeutter had suspended the credits entirely. The visiting Iraqis reported the news back to Baghdad and were ordered to return home at once.

At 8:40 on the morning of October 13, aides participating in Baker's daily senior staff briefing conveyed Agriculture's decision to the secretary of state. The crimes were also explained to him. When he heard the news, Baker was not a happy man. His response was immediate. Withdrawing the $400 million of CCC credits for Iraq was a "step in the wrong direction," said the secretary of state. "Get it back onto the table!" he instructed his aides.

Baker could order his staff to figure out a way to resurrect a government program for Iraq that was now clearly riddled with suspected illegalities, but he could not stop another member of the State Department bureaucracy from giving him even worse news. Later that same day, a thirty-two-year-old Foreign Service officer named Frank Lemay returned from a briefing he had attended at the Agriculture Department. Lemay, a special assistant to Richard McCormack, had met with Agriculture

Department lawyers to hear about the status of the BNL case. When he came back to the State Department, he scribbled down what is known at State as a "memcon," or memorandum of conversation. The memorandum was classified as confidential and immediately sent to five of Baker's top people, including McCormack, Jock Covey, the acting assistant secretary for Near East affairs, and Abraham Sofaer, the State Department's legal adviser.

Lemay reported that ten separate BNL investigations were now under way, covering violations of U.S. banking laws, CCC abuses, and help for Iraq's nuclear weapons project. The investigations had reached "the explosion state," and colleagues at the Agriculture Department were saying the BNL affair could "blow the roof off the CCC." This was not what James Baker wanted to hear.

Lemay also reported that the Agriculture Department had briefed him on suspected corruption at the Ohio affiliate of Matrix Churchill, the Iraqi-owned machine tools company in Britain that was supplying "military hardware" to Baghdad with illegal BNL loans. The young Foreign Service officer didn't know it, but Matrix Churchill was a company Baker had already encountered.

A few months before the BNL raid, the unmistakable signature of "James A. Baker, III" had appeared on a State Department approval form that certified the worthiness of the Ohio-based Matrix Churchill to do business with Iraq. Baker had signed the approval form, which made Matrix eligible as a contractor in Baghdad, even though his State Department was sitting on intelligence reports that spelled out the company's role as an arm of Saddam's nuclear-weapons-procurement network.

The hapless Lemay, whose career would suffer precisely because of this memo, urged the top brass at State to "proceed carefully" with any CCC guarantees for Iraq. "If smoke indicates fire," he concluded, "we may be facing a four-alarm blaze in the near future." (See Appendix B, pages 326–327.)

"I guess I'm the guy who did the wrong thing at the wrong time," Lemay said later, after he began to feel his career at the State Department sinking into a Washington version of the gulag archipelago. "The issue was brought to the attention of all the big boys, and Baker was aware of all the assertions through the huge paper trail," a rather defensive State Department official recalled later. "We knew Saddam Hussein wasn't a saint and there was this bank thing in Atlanta, but we couldn't cut off a policy based on hunches and assertions."

Lemay's memo frightened some at State, but not Baker. He was going to try to carry out George Bush's order to aid Saddam, come what may. He had already told his staff to get the financial aid for Baghdad back on the table. Now he had to reassure Tariq Aziz again.

"Dear Mr. Minister," Baker wrote in a secret message to Aziz on October 21. "I appreciated the opportunity to meet you and I found our meeting extremely useful." (See Appendix B, pages 328–329.) He then conveyed a message from George Bush:

> The President has asked me to say to you, and through you to President Saddam Hussein, in the most direct way possible, that the United States is not involved in any effort to weaken or destabilize Iraq. Having looked into the matter, and discussed it with the President, I can tell you this with the highest authority. Such an action would be completely contrary to the President's policy, which is to work to strengthen the relationship between the United States and Iraq whenever possible.

Turning to the question of the CCC guarantees, Baker wrote as follows:

> Mr. Minister, you also asked me to look into the issue of CCC credit guarantees. I am doing so on an urgent basis and will give you a final response as soon as I can. An investigation is underway and in all candor there are some serious allegations that need to be examined further. I can assure you that our actions in connection with the CCC program are not in any way motivated by political considerations. The government of Iraq has set a high standard on issues of integrity of public officials and corruption and I am sure you will understand the determination of my government to be thorough. At the same time, I very much hope that it will be possible to resolve the problems which have arisen quickly and to continue with this important program. As you requested, I will continue to give this matter my personal attention.

On October 24, Ambassador Glaspie called on Aziz to deliver the letter. She watched him read it and then reported back from Baghdad that he was "clearly delighted with the Secretary's message." He assured her that Baghdad was "ready to cooperate with the United States in any matter needing cooperation." When Glaspie finished her meeting with Aziz, Hamdoon had taken her aside to say that "the ball is in Washington's court."

Nonetheless, Baker clearly still had his work cut out for him if he was going to push through U.S. government financing for Iraq in the face of a spreading criminal investigation. He decided to ask Abraham Sofaer, the State Department lawyer, to examine the legality of going ahead with the CCC credits for Iraq.

Sofaer, an American Jew of Iraqi descent, never felt as comfortable serving Baker as he had when he worked for George Shultz at State. He did not fit in with Baker's inner circle of wealthy Texans, many of whom had oil money in their families. But Sofaer followed orders. He checked into the BNL and CCC affair. "We had a CCC policy," Sofaer later remembered. "The CCC was a policy tool concerning Iraq. The Iraqis were paying us back with our own money. But they had very substantial oil reserves. When the thing came to me, I asked some questions. I asked if there was some reason they wouldn't pay us back, and I was told it was well within their means. I asked the Department of Justice if there was a possibility that senior Iraqi officials would be shown to have participated in any fraud. That could have been politically damaging to the president and the secretary of state. I was told that at the present time it was not considered likely that high Iraqi officials were involved. My job was to tell Baker what I learned. And there was no basis to interfere with the National Security Council directive the president had signed."

Baker was pleased with the memo he received from Sofaer on October 26. It reminded Baker, further, that since the 1988 cease-fire in the Iran-Iraq war, trade had become the central factor in the U.S.-Iraqi relationship. "Iraq is now our ninth largest customer for agricultural commodities, and the U.S. is Iraq's largest supplier of non-military goods." Having looked into the BNL affair and spoken directly with the U.S. attorney's office in Atlanta, Sofaer believed the investigation was largely focused on "widespread, systematic banking fraud by persons working for BNL or under consulting relationships with BNL." He did add, however, that "it may involve several high Iraqi officials, though this is unclear." In order to "wall off" the CCC program from the BNL investigation, "it is sufficient to exact Iraq's promise to cooperate in the investigation into past practices" and to cooperate in establishing future safeguards. Finally, Sofaer advised Baker that since Tariq Aziz had recently promised cooperation in the BNL case and there was no point in going back to the Iraqis with a partial program, it was best to go ahead with the original $1 billion. The credits could be made available in a series of smaller allocations, provided there was no further evidence of Iraqi wrongdoing. (See Appendix B, page 323.)

Baker was then handed talking points with which to lobby the secretary of agriculture so that the $1 billion could be pushed through on foreign policy grounds. He picked up his telephone, called Clayton Yeutter, and reassured him that "with safeguards I hope we can get this important program back on track quickly." He replaced the receiver much encouraged. He even scrawled a quote from Yeutter over his talking points: "I think we're seeing it the same way you guys are."

Once he had persuaded Yeutter, Baker made sure the entire weight of the State Department was thrown behind the Iraqi program. His deputy, Lawrence Eagleburger, made phone calls and sent letters to his counterparts at Treasury and the Office of Management and Budget, the two agencies most vigorously protesting the idea of promising Saddam any more U.S. credits.

The lobbying by Baker and Eagleburger seemed to do the trick. Yet when the National Advisory Committee met again on November 3, it still couldn't force through the one billion dollars. Treasury and the Federal Reserve had moved formally to block the decision and the only solution was to bump it up to the political level. A meeting was scheduled for Wednesday, November 8, and this time the decision-makers would be the second-ranking officials at each government department. At this stage, Baker's staff was joined in their efforts by aides to President Bush himself. It was a case of all hands on deck for Saddam.

AMONG THE MOST PROMINENT of those at the White House who had been tracking the BNL affair and reporting to George Bush was Stephen Danzansky, a congenial lawyer and a Washington insider. His experience in the White House had taken him from the Nixon administration to a stint on the National Security Council under Ronald Reagan to his present job as an assistant to President Bush and director of Cabinet Affairs. Danzansky got involved in any number of issues as a troubleshooter, as the president's eyes and ears. BNL was no different.

"We had a lot on BNL. We knew it didn't smell great. We knew the thing was stinking. I think we all understood this was not a happy situation," Danzansky later recalled. Throughout the autumn he had been receiving regular updates on the BNL scandal as well as keeping track of efforts to get the billion dollars of U.S. credits approved for Iraq. Officials at Agriculture told him how concerned they were about the kickbacks and other criminality in the BNL case. BNL, as Danzansky later put it, "was the one with spooks running around New York and Atlanta. We knew all about that one."

In the three weeks before the November 8 meeting to decide the

Iraqi matter at the political level, Danzansky participated in a string of meetings and conversations about the whole business. Working on behalf of the president, he made it his business to know about the scandal.

Two days before the November 8 meeting, both the White House and the State Department received a report that theoretically should have halted any efforts to provide Iraq with U.S. taxpayers' funds. The six-page report, entitled "Iraq-Italy: Repercussions of the BNL-Atlanta Scandal," came from the directorate of intelligence at the CIA. (See Appendix B, pages 330–335.) The CIA report was something of a mixed blessing for Bush and Baker. On the eve of their final push for the one billion dollars, the CIA named Matrix Churchill, the front company at the center of the BNL affair, as a member of Baghdad's "complex procurement network of holding companies." These companies were acquiring technology for Saddam's chemical, biological, nuclear, and ballistic missile programs, the CIA explained. The report also said Iraqi intelligence was "directly involved" in the activities of these holding companies. That didn't quite fit with Baker's hopes that the Iraqis would not be implicated in wrongdoing.

Yet the CIA report on November 6 also said that "the loss of BNL financing and, more important, any reduction in U.S. agricultural credit guarantees because of negative publicity about the scandal probably would damage U.S.-Iraqi commercial ties." The strain in U.S.-Iraqi political relations caused by the BNL scandal would be short-lived, the CIA concluded, "if Baghdad believes additional U.S. credits will be forthcoming after the dust of the investigation settles."

On November 7, one day after the CIA report was dispatched, another White House official who was tracking the BNL affair did an extraordinary thing. Jay Bybee, a lawyer in the office of C. Boyden Gray, the president's counsel, was a point man on BNL, getting detailed briefings from other government agencies and making sure he was contacted about any significant developments regarding Iraq. Just before the $1 billion of CCC credits for Iraq was to be decided once and for all, Bybee breached normal procedure and telephoned Gale McKenzie at the U.S. attorney's office in Atlanta to discuss the criminal investigation of BNL. It is highly inappropriate for the White House to contact a prosecutor directly for any reason; normally, a request is made to the Justice Department, which makes its own inquiries and reports back. Bybee later denied there was anything improper about the call, but notes indicate that McKenzie, having been called from the White House, "got [the] impression they are concerned about embarrassment level."

Bybee's boss, Boyden Gray, claimed the White House call was made because Bybee was doing "due diligence for us on the CCC question." Yet Gray, almost as close a confidant to George Bush as was James Baker, later admitted that Bybee ought not to have made the call. "He shouldn't have called Atlanta. He should have called somebody at the Department of Justice and had them check."

On November 8, 1989, when the National Advisory Council met to discuss the controversial $1 billion program for Iraq, James Baker placed his faith in Robert Kimmitt to represent him at the meeting. The session dragged on a long time, and toward the end John Robson, the deputy treasury secretary, noted that absent compelling agricultural export and foreign policy interests, the proposed program for Iraq would not go forward. But it did. Those present were political-level players, and concerns about BNL were soon brushed aside. Baker's man laid down the law by invoking the name of George Bush. To terminate the program in Iraq abruptly, declared Kimmitt, would "clearly run counter to the President's intention and would, furthermore, cause a deterioration in our relationship with the Iraqis." There might be "possible future revelations" in the BNL affair, but "overwhelming foreign policy considerations" called for support of the Iraqi credit. The trump card worked, and Baker's billion dollars of U.S. credits for Iraq was recovered. There was only one condition—that it be divided into two $500 million parts so that the second could be suspended if any wrongdoing by Iraq were uncovered. "Oh, yes," remembered a smiling Stephen Danzansky, who had sat in on the meeting as President Bush's representative, "there was State, doing its thing."

Kimmitt reported back to Baker immediately and suggested "that you break the good news to Foreign Minister Tariq Aziz." Baker did so in a letter that argued soothingly the manner in which "this decision by the Administration reflects the importance we attach to our relationship with Iraq."

James Baker had won his fight. The foreign policy vision that he and George Bush had shared for so many years was finally being implemented. But there was still more work to do.

TEN

See No Evil

N othing, it appeared, would stop Bush and Baker's policy of giving overwhelming and unequivocal support to Saddam Hussein. Warnings about Iraq's suspected criminal behavior in the BNL case and Baghdad's drive to develop unconventional weapons did not matter. The president had defined Washington's national interest in the Persian Gulf in National Security Directive 26, and by signing that document he had bet on Baghdad as the cornerstone of political stability in the region. When the CIA or other government officials came up with reasons to recoil from Saddam, Bush and Baker didn't want to know about them.

Only days after Saddam Hussein and Tariq Aziz extracted the promise of up to one billion dollars in U.S. loan guarantees came a new challenge for Washington. The administration had to decide what to do about American companies that wanted to deliver highly sensitive technology to Baghdad. NSD 26 had explicitly recommended promoting U.S. business ties with Iraq, and the welfare of corporate America was top priority. Not surprisingly, when difficult cases were considered, it was business that was likely to win the day.

On November 12, 1989, a high-level interagency committee headed by the State Department met to consider a handful of export-license requests. Among the commodities were goods, including computers and machine tools, that were ostensibly to be used for civilian purposes, but the addresses of the recipients were almost all military establishments.

The importance of the interagency committee, which brought together officials from the Defense, Commerce, State, and Energy departments, was belied by its nondescript bureaucratic name: the Subgroup on Nuclear Export Control, or SNEC. Although Commerce had chief responsibility for issuing export licenses, the State Department and the Pentagon were generally asked to offer their views on so-called dual-use items, or industrial equipment suspected of having a potential military use. In cases of exports that had possible nuclear applications, SNEC would be called in to settle disputes between different agencies over which sensitive technologies could be licensed for export. At the SNEC meeting on November 12, there were at least nine items on the agenda relating to Iraq that caused alarm bells to ring.

The SNEC officials faced a real dilemma in considering these export proposals, not least because they were trying to follow the guidelines of George Bush's still-secret policy on Iraq. "SNEC policy for some years has been not to approve exports for Iraq's nuclear program," wrote one participant in the meeting. (See Appendix B, page 336.) But "at the same time, U.S. policy as confirmed in NSD 26 has been to improve relations with Iraq, including trade, which means that exports of non-sensitive commodities to 'clean' end-users in Iraq should be encouraged." He added that the State Department's Near East affairs division had said exports of dual-use commodities "for conventional military use" could be approved.

In order to reach an informed decision, members of the committee asked for and received a detailed intelligence briefing on Iraq's nuclear program. What they learned only compounded their predicament.

They were told of "a presumption by the intelligence community and others that the Iraqi government is interested in acquiring a nuclear explosive capability." They were made aware of "evidence that Iraq is acquiring nuclear related equipment and materials without regard for immediate need" and that Iraqi front companies were engaged in nuclear-related procurement. And they were left in no doubt that the substantial quantities of equipment such as computers and machine tools that the Iraqi state enterprises listed as end-users had ordered could well go into military projects.

Those at the SNEC meeting took note of the warning before them and the probable use to which Iraq would put the U.S. products it had requested. The consequences of the decisions they were to make could not have been laid out more clearly. Yet after the meeting, most doubts were brushed aside by the State Department, the lead agency in the SNEC process. State described the intelligence information as "complicating factors" but was not particularly troubled by it. Within twenty-four hours of the intelligence briefing, State had already made up its mind. It recommended seven of the nine export applications for immediate approval.

The way the State Department got around the obvious danger that the exports would go into the Iraqi nuclear program was to recommend that each license carry a kind of health warning. Thus, the export of a special measuring device to an Iraqi front company engaged in weapons research was to be marked: "Approve subject to license conditions with no nuclear use and no retransfer without prior consent." A similar warning was affixed to a shipment of optical heads for cameras that went to the Daoud Research Center "for work on projectile behavior and terminal ballistics." The rationalization for sending such equipment directly to an Iraqi installation engaged in work on nuclear-capable missile development was the surmise that the speed of the equipment was appropriate for conventional artillery rounds but too slow for nuclear applications. But how could Washington ensure the conditions were complied with? It was utterly impossible, and the State Department knew it. With decisions like these in late 1989, the secretary of state had opened the door to a dictator with a well-documented appetite for money and an equally clear, even outspoken intention to build nuclear weapons.

"State had the policy responsibility for nonproliferation. The other agencies were simply not in the same league," recalled Bryan Siebert, a senior export-control official at the Department of Energy who specialized in spotting items that were headed for Saddam's nuclear weapons projects. During 1989, said Siebert, a number of sensitive exports to Iraq were approved by SNEC: "We sent a lot."

Indeed, even before the November 12 meeting a $140,000 shipment of sophisticated frequency synthesizers was already en route to Baghdad from Hewlett-Packard of California. "According to our information," read the caption on confidential Commerce Department records, "the end-user is involved in military matters." The end-user was the Salah al-Din establishment, one of Iraq's most prominent military electronics factories. In fact, the Bush administration knew that the Hewlett-Packard synthesizers would be used "in calibrating, adjusting and testing" an Iraqi surveillance radar system. A little more than a year later, during Operation Desert Storm, the same system would provide ground support for Iraqi missiles, helping Baghdad detect and shoot down U.S. planes.

It was not merely in SNEC that the State Department campaigned to speed up the shipment of sensitive technologies to Iraq. As far as James Baker's aides were concerned, SNEC was actually an *obstacle* to the promotion of U.S. exports. In early 1990, John Kelly, the assistant secretary of state with responsibility for the Middle East, complained in a memorandum that "our licensing procedures have been a drag on trade with Iraq." He even drafted a letter on the subject for Robert Kimmitt, to be sent to the Commerce Department. Difficult though it may be to believe, the letter said specifically that the examination of nuclear proliferation concerns by SNEC needed to be balanced "by other considerations, including our duty to support U.S. exporters who can right our trade imbalance with Iraq and the broader needs of the overall relationship."

President Bush's national security directive was thus casting a long shadow over policy-makers, and this created a dangerous ambiguity. Stopping Saddam's nuclear weapons development was a frequently stated U.S. policy goal, but NSD 26 made far more prominent mention of promoting trade. The result was that when decision-makers were uncertain about the ultimate use of an export product, they tended to lean toward approval.

"If we were selling nuclear equipment to Iraq, then we were incompetent and Commerce couldn't run an export control program," Abraham Sofaer, the former State Department legal adviser, later remarked. "It happened, of course, and it may well be that people in the State Department learned from CIA memos that Iraq was building a nuclear capability from our exports. I certainly didn't see any CIA memos, and I don't know what Baker knew. We did not have a close relationship."

"The U.S. granted scores of licenses," commented Gary Milhollin, a leading expert on Iraq's nuclear weapons program. "The government knew very well that Saddam was running a big missile and nuclear program and that the exports were almost certainly going to help both. But the State, Commerce, and Energy departments acted like the three little monkeys: 'See no evil, hear no evil, and speak no evil.' "

It had been that way, Milhollin recalled, from the beginning of the Bush administration. In February 1989, the month after it took office, for example, the Du Pont company of Delaware was cleared to supply nuclear-grade vacuum pump oil to the "State Organization for Oil Production," a state company involved in both civilian and military projects. UN inspectors would later discover that the Du Pont product "was used or intended for use in Iraqi efforts to establish a centrifuge production and operation capability." The nuclear-grade oil was vital to atomic bomb production because it lubricated the centrifuges that created the weapons-grade uranium that forms the core of the bomb.

Even before Bush took office, in December 1988, Saddam's opera-tives had come shopping to the Finnigan Corporation of California and received SNEC approval to buy $661,000 worth of computing equipment that Iraq used to measure the progress of uranium enrichment. The actual value of the shipments could be misleading; as far as Baghdad was concerned, items that were valuable for nuclear weapons research did not need to cost a lot—they just needed to be secured.

"ALLAH AKBAR, ALLAH AKBAR." God is great, God is great. The shouts of the assembled technicians crescendoed over the an-Anbar desert range 230 kilometers southwest of Baghdad on the morning of December 5, 1989, as a three-stage, eighty-foot-long rocket weighing forty-eight tons lifted off the launch pad and blasted through the high cloud cover into the upper atmosphere.

The missile, a bundle of modified Scud missiles that was given the name *al-Abid*, "The Worshipper," was supposed to deliver a warhead over a distance of more than a thousand miles. When word of the test launch reached Washington, it caused consternation in the White House and State Department. Admittedly this was just a test, but the prospect of Saddam Hussein having a missile with a range of a thousand miles sent tremors through every Middle Eastern capital.

The Bush administration kept its public reponse to Saddam's missile launch muted, but certain quarters of the Commerce Department well understood the significance of the event. While Secretary of Commerce Robert Mosbacher was very much part of Bush's pro-Saddam team, worries about Iraq's nuclear procurement had been growing among working-level officials within his department. They were the people who had to carry out the department's see-no-evil policy toward Saddam's requests for nuclear-related technology, a policy that had been firmly in place well before NSD 26 was signed in October. "When Saddam sent up his Roman candle, it became clear to me that we were going to have a problem with this country," said Dennis Kloske, Commerce's undersecre-tary for export administration. In fact, Kloske had already made up his mind about Iraq the preceding autumn, when he became alarmed at the amount of money Iraq was pouring into its weapons programs and the number of high-technology items it had obtained from the United States and elsewhere.

He raised his concerns during informal discussions with his counter-parts in other cabinet agencies but got little in the way of response. In

Baker's State Department, in particular, the preoccupation as always was less with the details of Saddam's weapons programs than with U.S. diplomatic relations toward Iraq; the overriding concern, it seemed, was to keep Saddam happy. Without the support of the State Department and the National Security Council, there was no chance of modifying the policy that was worrying people both at Commerce and at the Pentagon. "We were being left in a situation where we were going to be screwed," said an official in the Commerce Department. "We made it very clear to our counterparts that Commerce had a major problem with the desultory diplomatic initiatives toward Saddam that were not going anywhere," he added. "We made it very clear that we had to tighten up the controls—but we were met with indifference."

The same level of frustration existed at the Department of Energy, where Bryan Siebert had been waging a lonely and unsuccessful battle to get James Baker and National Security Adviser Brent Scowcroft to do something about the steady flow of U.S. exports that were materially assisting Iraq's nuclear weapons program.

Siebert had been monitoring Saddam's nuclear-procurement operations since 1987. Armed with data from both the CIA and the Energy Department's own intelligence sources, he concluded in February 1989 that Saddam was not ten years away from building an atomic bomb, as the government had generally assumed, but three—and perhaps even less if the flow of technology from the United States were not halted. Saddam was spending heavily, he was determined, and he was ingenious.

That spring, Siebert tried to bring the issue of how the United States was contributing to Saddam's nuclear program to the attention of Baker and Scowcroft. His strategy was to have Admiral James Watkins, the energy secretary, suggest to them that the National Security Council initiate a high-level review of Iraq's growing nuclear ambitions. If Baker agreed, it was Siebert's hope that he would be able to present his information to the National Security Council, thereby empowering the Department of Energy to take the lead in an interagency review of export controls regarding Iraq.

In late March 1989, Siebert began to pull together the telltale intelligence indications of Saddam's nuclear plans. He worked days, nights, and weekends sifting through data as he prepared to ask Admiral Watkins to approach Baker. But Siebert could not know that at this same time Baker was busy consolidating U.S. relations with Iraq, which had become Washington's second-biggest trading partner in the Arab world. In preparation for a March 24 meeting with Iraq's Nizar Hamdoon, Baker was told

of Baghdad's desire for "freer export licensing procedures for high tech."
Applications were often held up, his staff wrote him in a briefing memorandum, because of the Commerce and Defense departments' fears that
the U.S. exports could bolster Iraq's military capabilities.

Siebert decided to make his report to Admiral Watkins blunt and
brief. He had already learned the need to keep things simple when sitting
in meetings with President Bush or with Brent Scowcroft and his aides at
the NSC. "At White House meetings I would raise something complex
and Bob Gates [by now the deputy national security adviser] would say,
'God damn, we shouldn't have these types of complicated questions,' " he
later recalled.

On April 17, a nervous Bryan Siebert finally sounded his alarm. (See
Appendix B, page 337.) "Recent evidence," he wrote to Admiral Watkins,
"indicates that Iraq has a major effort under way to produce nuclear
weapons." Baghdad already had enough specifications to point "unambiguously" to detailed knowledge of how to produce nuclear materials.
Beyond that, it was "attempting to procure some items in the United
States" that included a component identical to one used in U.S. nuclear
weapons.

Siebert stated that if Iraq were able to obtain these goods in the
United States, "it would embarrass the U.S. government, as well as injure
U.S. nonproliferation objectives." In light of this risk, he recommended
that the secretary of energy contact both Baker and Scowcroft and warn
them of the problem.

There could be no misunderstanding what Siebert was saying. He
also had every reason to assume that his message would get through. After
all, only two months before, George Bush had proclaimed in his first State
of the Union message that "our diplomacy must work every day against
the proliferation of nuclear weapons." Siebert's memorandum was an
action call.

He felt relieved after he delivered it. "This thing had been getting
clearer every day," he later said. "If State took it up and it went to the
National Security Council, it would be tough to turn a blind eye."

But the State Department never even saw Siebert's warning, nor did
Admiral Watkins. The memo was dismissed as overly alarmist by Robert
Walsh, the deputy assistant secretary for intelligence, defense programs,
in the Department of Energy. Walsh, who attended White House meetings on such matters on a regular basis, felt "uncomfortable with a
Secretarial level initiative." He refused to go ahead with the recommendation, terming it "premature."

Siebert had been stopped, but he would not give up. On May 11, he wrote another memorandum, this one protesting that his evidence of the Iraqi bomb program was being ignored. "I would bet my job [that] Iraq is moving toward a nuclear weapons program and the time to try and stop it is now." The second memo had equally little effect on policy, but it eventually had personal consequences. In April 1991 Siebert was stripped of his senior responsibilities for technology policy and export control and left with lesser responsibilities as head of the Department of Energy section that handled the classification of documents.

Four months after Siebert's second memo—and three months before Saddam launched *al-Abid*, his first intermediate-range ballistic missile—Siebert and other officials who worried that the United States was helping Iraq's nuclear program were appalled when they discovered that the Department of Energy—in conjunction with nuclear weapons laboratories, the air force, and the navy—had invited two Iraqi nuclear scientists to visit Portland, Oregon, for a symposium on detonations. They had come from Saddam's Al Qaqaa establishment, where Iraqi technicians were researching the kind of missile technology that would help to deliver nuclear payloads. The Iraqis were only too pleased to attend the symposium, which was staged by the U.S. armed forces and the national laboratories such as Los Alamos and Lawrence Livermore. As a senior Energy Department official wrote later on, "In a nutshell, the conference was the place to be in September 1989 if you were a potential nuclear weapon proliferant."

A year after his memos, Siebert was still trying to get word to higher-ups, discussing proliferation concerns with colleagues from the State Department, and briefing the secretary of energy every time he got the chance. On two occasions he accompanied Admiral Watkins to cabinet meetings at the White House, where the subject under discussion was U.S. export controls.

As a nuclear expert, Siebert would sit in the second row of chairs in the cabinet room, behind President Bush, with a view of the cabinet members assembled around the table and portraits of former presidents on the opposite wall. He later remembered feeling his want of stature in the elevated presence of the decision-makers. But the absence of any real debate about export controls at the cabinet meetings astounded him. "Scowcroft would outline the purpose of the meeting for the benefit of the president, but then the atmosphere was like a high-level funeral," he recalled. "This was not a gathering of cabinet members who wanted to talk and politic around. It was more like a board of directors composed of good old boys. John Sununu [the chief of staff] did much of the talking, and he was quite a bully. He dominated the cabinet, and Bush let him get away with it."

Robert Gates, who attended the meetings, had warned Siebert that the difficulty in kicking an export-control decision up to the cabinet level was that most people didn't understand the issues. But the ignorance displayed when it came to matters of technology shocked Siebert nonetheless. As the likes of Gates, Robert Mosbacher, Colin Powell, and Admiral Watkins looked on, Siebert heard Brent Scowcroft deliver a report to George Bush on a proposed transfer of fiber optic technology, only to be interrupted by a question from Bush: "What is fiber optic?"

"Ambivalence was thick in the room," Siebert recalled. "It was almost as if the cabinet members' discussion was scripted. Each one would stick to his department's line, and there were no meaningful discussions. The cabinet members looked at things like junior lieutenants, unable or unwilling to see the big picture."

Siebert's goal had been to get the White House to realize the danger posed by the casual approval of exports to Iraq. But the subject hardly ever came up. On one occasion Scowcroft laid out the issue of numerically controlled machine tools exports destined for a variety of countries, including Iraq. Sophisticated machine tools were a vital component in the manufacture of nuclear materials, and Iraq had been ordering them from, among other firms, the Ohio affiliate of Matrix Churchill, the BNL-funded and Iraqi-owned company based in Britain. But Matrix Churchill was not discussed at the cabinet meeting, even though the CIA had reported its activities to both the White House and the State Department in November 1989. Instead, "we were made aware of how American machine tool competitiveness was going to hell because of unfair practices by the Japanese," said Siebert. When the cabinet meeting was over, he added, "we walked out of the room and weren't even sure what had happened."

Siebert's experience was matched by that of others who had watched U.S. export policy toward Iraq evolve over the years. In many ways the Bush administration was simply continuing the decade-long tilt, regardless of the dramatic change in circumstances.

"During the Reagan administration exports were knowingly sent to Iraqi nuclear installations for a variety of reasons," a former White House official explained. "Some people didn't want to believe Saddam was going to get there. Others claimed that Saddam would never actually use a nuclear weapon. There were some very ugly debates about Saddam's intentions in the interagency groups." When it came to the White House position, however, there had been no argument. "Bush as vice president made it clear he wanted to help Iraq."

Siebert was by no means the only official feeling frustrated in the spring of 1990. An intelligence agent who had watched the mushrooming growth of Saddam's nuclear machine and who knew the extent to which the Bush administration export policy had nurtured it, put it succinctly: "It was policy. The White House knew what was happening and didn't really care."

THAT SPRING WAS a momentous period in U.S.-Iraqi relations—the beginning of the end. In keeping with the still-secret NSD 26, President Bush had decided to void the prohibition that Congress had imposed on any new financing for Iraq by the Eximbank. Ignoring Saddam's human rights violations, which had prompted the congressional ban, Bush reversed it with a stroke of his presidential pen. On January 17, 1990, he signed a waiver that determined that the prohibition was "not in the national interest of the United States." Thanks to this two-paragraph document, Saddam was once again eligible for U.S. taxpayer-backed loan guarantees, some $200 million worth.

But in spite of Bush's efforts to befriend Saddam Hussein, the Iraqi leader soon proved ungrateful. Within weeks of the waiver, the alarm bells began ringing louder than ever. In February, Saddam surprised both Washington and the Arab world by demanding that the United States end its military presence in the Persian Gulf. "If Arabs are not careful, they will see the Gulf governed by U.S. will," he declared. The statement, which came out of the blue, made little sense unless one understood the growing sense of paranoia inside the presidential palace in Baghdad.

Saddam, short of cash now that the BNL spigot had been turned off and the price of oil was too low to meet his economy's needs, was flexing his muscles again. Washington's response was to remain demure rather than risk his wrath. James Baker had learned from first-hand experience with Tariq Aziz just how upset the Iraqis were about the BNL affair and the prospect of their American loan guarantees being reduced. Money was of great importance to Saddam, especially when he was trying to maintain a national economy that included the world's fourth-largest standing army *and* to develop unconventional weapons at the same time. Suspicious as always, he was convinced that the Western media's interest in the BNL case and in his weapons program was part of a campaign of

government-inspired attacks. His son-in-law, Hussein Kamel, had repri-
manded the British ambassador in Baghdad over articles on BNL that
were appearing in *Financial Times* of London. Italian diplomats were also
called to account when their newspapers published articles about the
Iraqi loans scandal.

For the Bush administration, the truth was hard to face. There were
fresh indications that same February that Iraq was still abusing the loan-
guarantee program. "Possible indictments for violations of CCC regulations" were in the wind as a result of the investigation into BNL Atlanta,
noted Paul Dickerson, the CCC program's administrator, on February 23.
The question troubling Dickerson, as he wrote to his boss at the Department of Agriculture, was whether to publicly announce any more loan
guarantees. There were good reasons to go ahead with the announcement,
but there were also reasons not to. Among them was the prospect of
"considerable adverse Congressional reaction and press coverage." And
there was an even worse scenario to contemplate if "investigators would
find a direct link to financing Iraqi military expenditures, particularly the
Condor missile."

The problem of Iraq's demand for kickbacks could perhaps be
finessed somehow for public consumption, but the Condor was an entirely different matter. If there was one thing that would destroy Bush's
embrace of Saddam in a split second, it would be the revelation that the
United States had guaranteed for Saddam loans whose proceeds he might
have used to help build a nuclear-capable missile.

It didn't help matters when, on March 15, Saddam ordered the
hanging of Farzad Bazoft, an Iranian-born reporter for a British newspaper. Amid protests from Margaret Thatcher, Bazoft was accused of
being an Israeli spy and put to death in an exceedingly public display.
Later that month, relations between Saddam and his would-be supporters
in the U.S. and British governments were jolted again, this time by a
reminder of Iraq's nuclear intentions. To make matters worse, BNL was
also involved.

On March 28, 1990, customs officers at London's Heathrow Airport
intercepted a shipment of nuclear detonators en route from California to
Baghdad, closing a successful eighteen-month Anglo-American sting operation. Eight days later, the link between the nuclear triggers and BNL
was confirmed in a confidential memo addressed to Gerald Corrigan,
president of the New York Federal Reserve. "As you suspected, there is a
connection," wrote a member of his staff, adding it was "entirely possible
that BNL financed some of this material." (See Appendix B, page 338.)

The sting proved to have more symbolic than practical value, however, since a smiling Saddam Hussein appeared on Iraqi television shortly afterward holding a nuclear detonator in his hand. "We can make these in our own factories," he said to his cheering audience. That statement, true or false, gave added menace to an address he gave to senior Iraqi military officers at a decoration ceremony on April 2. Wearing a general's insignia, Saddam delivered a chilling speech that lasted more than an hour and would echo across the world.

"We don't need an atomic bomb because we have advanced chemical weapons," said Saddam. "Iraq's chemical weapons capability is matched only by the United States and the Soviet Union." His bloodcurdling speech ranged far and wide over real and imagined adversaries. "I swear to God we will let our fire eat half of Israel if it tries anything against Iraq," he proclaimed, and concluded ringingly: "May God's curse fall upon the big powers."

While world leaders searched for suitably outraged responses, George Bush seemed stunned. "I think these statements are very bad," he mused as he digested the news aboard Air Force One on his way from Washington to Indianapolis. "I'm asking Iraq very strongly to immediately reject the use of chemical weapons. I don't think it'll help the Middle East or Iraq's security; I would even say that it'll have the opposite effect."

Then Bush ended with the observation, "I suggest that such statements about chemical or biological weapons be forgotten." It was an extraordinary response, tinged with a mixture of regret and wishful thinking. It seemed as if Bush could not believe his ears. For almost ten years Washington had delivered to Saddam enormous amounts of agricultural credits and Eximbank guarantees, weapons and technology, sometimes covertly and sometimes quite openly. Now the Iraqi leader was making speeches like this. Surely he could not mean it.

The truth was, George Bush was beginning to find himself in a political straitjacket. Congress was already demanding sanctions on Iraq; several bills had been introduced. Various legislative proposals would cut off CCC and Eximbank aid programs, ban high-technology exports of computers and other equipment that might be used in making or operating weapons systems, and halt any loans from international financial institutions. Without even knowing of the existence of NSD 26, Congress was threatening to destroy the heart of Bush's secret policy.

While Saddam's threats to use chemical weapons against Israel were producing politically violent reactions on Capitol Hill, both George Bush and James Baker were sending private messages that sought to reassure Saddam. The President's first message was carried by Senator Robert Dole, the dour Republican minority leader from Kansas who led a Senate delegation to Iraq in a two-hour meeting with Saddam on Thursday, April 12. Dole did express U.S. concern at Saddam's publicly acknowledged development of unconventional weapons, but he also lent a sympathetic ear to the Iraqi's complaints that he was the victim of a smear campaign.

"He indicated to us that he feels very strongly that there's an American-British-Israeli campaign to tarnish the image of his government and his country," said Dole, upon emerging from the meeting in the northern Iraqi town of Mosul, which happened to be the site of several Iraqi missile projects. Senator Alan K. Simpson, a Republican from Wyoming, embraced Saddam's views, telling him, "I believe that your problems lie with the Western media, and not with the U.S. government. As long as you are isolated from the media, the press—and it is a haughty and pampered press—they all consider themselves political geniuses." Saddam also gave the senators the implausible promise that he was prepared to destroy all of Iraq's weapons of mass destruction. There was only one catch—Israel would have to do the same.

Dole told Saddam that if there were any smear campaign, it certainly didn't come from President Bush, who only twelve hours before had "assured me that he wanted better relations, and that the U.S. government wants better relations with Iraq." The senator, who represented a state that had exported large quantities of wheat to Iraq on the back of CCC credits, added his personal assurance that President Bush would oppose sanctions legislation in Congress.

On the same day that Dole was carrying a message from the president, James Baker sent a secret cable to the U.S. embassy in Baghdad, instructing Ambassador April Glaspie to meet with Saddam or his top aides. The cable noted that Iraqi actions in recent weeks and months had caused a sharp deterioration in U.S.-Iraqi relations. It requested that Glaspie spell out the administration's disapointment over Saddam's demand for a withdrawal of the American naval presence in the Gulf; that she question Baghdad's human rights record; and that she protest clandestine attempts by the Iraqi government to smuggle nuclear triggers from the United States. Baker also reminded Glaspie to register disapproval at Saddam's drive toward unconventional weapons and his threats against Israel earlier in the month.

But Baker softened the blow considerably by stipulating that the ambassador deliver an additional message: "We want one thing very clearly understood, however. As concerned as we are about Iraq's chemical, nuclear, and missile programs, we are not in any sense preparing the way for a preemptive military unilateral effort to eliminate these programs." Baker even reminded Saddam that back in 1981, when Israel had launched such a bombing raid against Iraq's Osirak nuclear plant, "we condemned the 1981 raid. And would do so again today. We are telling Israel so."

Two weeks later, George Bush tried an even more direct approach when he sent Saddam his own conciliatory message. While the rest of the world waited to see what the Iraqi dictator would do next, President Bush told him he hoped that ties between the United States and Iraq would contribute to the peace and stability of the Middle East.

But the tensions between Washington and Baghdad were real, and so were the differences among U.S. government agencies. Bureaucrats and political-level officials inside the Bush administration were already waging a form of guerrilla warfare over Iraqi policy. That same April, the Commerce Department began taking unilateral action to curtail trade with Iraq, while the Defense Department made it clear to colleagues at State that it would support initiatives to limit technology transfers to Baghdad. State officials who had been among the staunchest supporters of Saddam in the past, such as Robert Kimmitt, were now being warned by their aides that critics of the U.S.-Iraqi relationship at other agencies were ready to seize the moment and cripple the relationship for the foreseeable future.

Assistant Secretary John Kelly, one of the most pro-Iraqi officials at State, wrote to Kimmitt outlining the need "to regain control of policy toward Iraq." Kelly's memorandum was designed to brief Kimmitt before he and other senior officials assembled in the White House Situation Room for what was known as a deputies committee meeting, so called because it was composed of second-ranking officers from the cabinet departments. The committee was to meet on April 16, 1990, to decide whether the Bush administration should try to punish Iraq. It would be chaired by Robert Gates, the former CIA man who was now President Bush's deputy national security adviser.

Kelly laid out the problem succinctly for Kimmitt: "The dilemma we face is that the relationship is already paper-thin. We do nothing *for* Iraq." If a message of displeasure was to be sent to Baghdad, it could take the form of placing the CCC program on review and not releasing the second $500 million that Baker had pushed for in November 1989; or the government could withdraw the presidential waiver that George Bush had signed in January that allowed Eximbank to continue servicing Iraq. The latter move, read Kelly's memorandum, would have the virtue of "placating Congressional critics" and could even help head off sanctions legislation in Congress, which the Bush administration was already fighting. As for those who wanted tougher controls on exports to Iraq, State now agreed that it should not approve exports of technology if they were deemed likely to contribute to Iraq's nuclear or missile programs.

The deputies committee meeting at the White House on April 16, however, resolved nothing. "We had already labeled Iraq as a member of the 'Sleaze Bucket Four' countries that were pouring money into weapons of mass destruction, along with Syria, Libya, and Iran," said an official who attended the meeting. But when Dennis Kloske of Commerce suggested taking firm action to limit sensitive technology sales to the Persian Gulf, aides to Brent Scowcroft at the National Security Council objected to any measures "that singled out Iraq." Both State and the NSC were still insistent on maintaining good relations with Iraq despite Saddam's rising militance and his fiery speech two weeks before. As one disgruntled participant at the meeting recalled, the State Department allowed that it might consider some minor moves to remind Saddam that his behavior was losing him support in the White House, but there was no question of a radical policy shift. When Kloske pressed his case for action, "State effectively told him to get out of our face."

The deputies committee, whose deliberations were still secret, had in any case deferred making any decisions until May. Ten days after the meeting, when a House Foreign Affairs subcommittee questioned John Kelly about the Bush administration's Iraq policy, he had little to say that was new. He fielded questions for ninety minutes, but the real import of the hearing was the depth of congressional anger it revealed. Tom Lantos, a California Democrat, listened politely to Kelly and then lost his temper, branding the president's policies toward Saddam Hussein as "Alice in Wonderland." Kelly, he said, had catalogued a "chamber of horrors" and then expressed the hope that Saddam would change. Rhetoric like Saddam's had not been heard since Adolf Hitler. When was the Bush administration going to recognize that sanctions were appropriate?

Kelly protested that dealing with countries that do atrocious things was difficult, but the U.S. government believed "there is a potential for positive alteration in Iraq's behavior." When pressed about Saddam's unconventional weapons programs, however, Kelly acknowledged that the recent attempt to procure nuclear triggers "leads us to believe Iraq is actively pursuing a nuclear weapons capability." This, of course, was precisely what Bryan Siebert had been trying to tell James Baker and Brent Scowcroft more than a year before.

Scowcroft got a chance to do something about Iraq a month later. The NSC-sponsored deputies committee had prepared a list of policy options, which was forwarded to Scowcroft on May 16. The options ranged from political actions—such as ending U.S. intelligence-sharing with Baghdad, or reducing the size of the U.S. embassy staff—to more stringent economic measures, such as suspending CCC and Eximbank credits. The full panoply of options was to be considered at a one-hour meeting in the White House Situation Room on the afternoon of May 29. Yet once again, as Robert Gates wrapped up the White House meeting, little of substance had been agreed upon.

In money terms, the single most important option put to the May 29 meeting concerned barring Iraqi oil sales to the United States, which the NSC estimated totaled more than three billion dollars in 1990. A ban on the purchase of Iraqi crude would thus be a serious step indeed. Favoring this option was the argument that "oil provides the wherewithal for Iraq's efforts to develop its own non-conventional military production capacity." Against it was the reality that a ban on imports from Iraq might have an impact on American oil prices.

The significance of oil as a factor in the Bush administration's special relationship with Baghdad had never been a secret, but few people knew of the dramatic rise in U.S. consumption of Iraqi crude. The CIA calculated that from only 80,000 barrels a day in 1987, U.S. imports of Iraqi oil had jumped to 675,000 barrels in 1990, and the figures were increasing dramatically from month to month. By July 1990, the figure had leapt to 1.1 million barrels a day—more than a quarter of Iraq's total oil exports.

Oil revenues were even more important from Saddam's point of view. He was in urgent need of money for his arms buildup, and he was becoming impatient with low oil prices. For months, he had been at odds with other members of the Organization of Petroleum Exporting Countries (OPEC) and in particular with Kuwait. He openly accused his fellow OPEC members of exceeding agreed-upon quotas on oil production at a time when the market was glutted. So low was the price of oil that in March 1990 a special OPEC meeting had been convened in Vienna to reduce the level of production. Yet the price had still failed to climb.

To make Saddam's situation worse, his debts from the Iran-Iraq war were enormous. At an Arab summit meeting in Baghdad on May 28, he demanded forgiveness of all the debts he had accumulated with Saudi Arabia, Kuwait, and the other Gulf states during the course of the war, a total of $35 billion. Iraq, said its leader, "needed to return to its economic situation of 1980." That meant he wanted an additional ten billion dollars in cash to meet his most pressing needs.

Kuwait, which had a border dispute with Iraq that dated back to the 1930s, was not pleased to be accused of exceeding its quotas or to be pressed to cancel Iraq's repayment of debts. Saddam coveted Kuwait's oil wealth, as well as its large natural harbor and its 120 miles of Persian Gulf coastline. In response to Saddam, Kuwait's oil minister said at another OPEC meeting held in Jeddah on July 10, that Kuwait would respect production quotas only if other members did the same. "If we believe that the agreement is not being taken seriously, then obviously we will act to protect our national interests," he said.

As the summer progressed, Saddam became even more desperate for cash, and he increasingly saw the prospect of getting his hands on more oil-producing land as the solution to his problems. At a meeting of Arab foreign ministers in Tunis that July, Iraqi foreign minister Tariq Aziz accused Kuwait of stealing oil worth two billion dollars from the Iraqi sector of the Rumaillah oil field, which lay on a disputed border territory between the two countries. By the time the Tunis meeting broke up in disarray on July 17, Saddam Hussein's position had hardened. In a speech he gave that day to mark the anniversary of the Iraqi revolution, he boasted of his new weapons and hinted that he would take military action. Attacking the "agents of imperialism" for waging an economic guerrilla war, he railed that "their policy of keeping oil prices at a low level is a poisoned dagger planted in Iraq's back." Within hours of his speech, he moved the first Iraqi troops and equipment toward the border with Kuwait.

It would be two more weeks before Saddam's tanks rumbled into Kuwait City. In that period any number of warnings reached both his Arab neighbors and the Bush White House. This time Saddam meant business.

ELEVEN

And So to War . . .

To Margaret Thatcher, prime minister of Great Britain, the States-
man Award. To George Bush, president of the United States, the
Distinguished Leadership Award. These were among the prime
items on the order of business at the fortieth anniversary celebrations of
the Aspen Institute in Colorado. But by the evening of Thursday, August
2, 1990, when President Bush arrived in Aspen, there was very little to
celebrate.

Bush made the trip to Aspen, where an anxious Margaret Thatcher
was waiting, even though Saddam Hussein had sent two Republican
Guard armored divisions and eight hundred tanks over the border into
Kuwait only a few hours before. Both politicians would soon lead the
world in condemning Iraq's aggression, but in his initial pronouncement
Bush remained circumspect: "We are not ruling any options in, but we are
not ruling any options out." The British prime minister was equally
careful that weekend when asked for her reaction to the Iraqi invasion. "I
have a very good rule," she said. "First find the facts. It has stood me very
well in Parliament."

As the world's attention shifted between the unfolding drama in
Kuwait and the gathering in Colorado, both Bush and Thatcher worked
the telephones, conferring with other world leaders as their advisers
scrambled to come up with options to defuse the crisis.

Thatcher might have been surprised had she known that on July 28,
just days before, Bush had sent a message to Saddam, thereby exercising
an option that had been under consideration for more than two months.
The list of policy options on Iraq that the deputies committee had

furnished to Brent Scowcroft in May included the option of sending a presidential message to Saddam Hussein. The Iraqi leader, Scowcroft was informed, "likes the personal touch." In favor of such a move was the argument that "a carefully crafted message from the President could be effective if it hit hard on our key concerns, proliferation and regional tension, but also emphasized a continued desire for improved relations." On the other hand, however, such a message "could be construed here as being soft on Saddam."

Early on the morning of July 28, CIA director William Webster had gone to the White House to brief the president, carrying with him in a thick manila envelope satellite intelligence photographs that showed Iraqi troops transporting ammunition, fuel, and water to the northern border of Kuwait. The infrared photography that Webster put in front of Bush that morning confirmed that this was no routine exercise. Some 35,000 Iraqi troops had massed and were ready to move. Four tank divisions in the same area were being joined by fuel trucks and tank transporters, an ominous sign that they were prepared to travel long distances.

Bush did not want to overreact, no matter how detailed the intelligence information might be. Later that day, he went ahead and sent a cable to Saddam, saying he was concerned about the Iraqi leader's threats to use force. He did not mention Kuwait by name, however, preferring instead to reiterate the standard U.S. policy line: "Let me reassure you that my Administration continues to desire better relations with Iraq." The president's message, coming after years of equally friendly signals, gave Saddam little reason to be deflected from invading Kuwait. It was, as one State Department hand put it later, "another busted signal." Before Bush sent the cable, senior Defense Department officials had tried to stop it, fearing it was so weakly worded that it would send the wrong message to Saddam. "We were already seeing troops moving. We were getting worried, and we were putting up this piece of pap. It was just very weak. We should have been much more threatening," remembered Henry Rowen, assistant secretary of defense for international security affairs at the time. Rowen and others at the Pentagon, concerned that Ambassador April Glaspie had already been spineless in her dealings with Saddam and that a conciliatory message from Bush would be equally ineffectual, had done their best, but the president was not deterred.

Margaret Thatcher's position had been similarly encouraging to Baghdad until the spring of 1990. London's own tilt to Iraq had been as lopsided as Washington's during the Iran-Iraq war, and in its aftermath Downing Street had been an eager competitor in the race to keep Saddam happy and to enrich its own treasury's coffers in the bargain. While continuing publicly to espouse the British embargo on supplying arms to Baghdad after the war was over, Thatcher's ministers privately exulted at the moneymaking possibilities the Iraqi market presented.

Late in 1989, even as the British public was deluging the Foreign Office with thousands of letters urging action against Saddam for his use of chemical weapons against the Kurds, William Waldegrave, a senior Foreign Office official, had suggested to John Major, the foreign secretary, that he make a personal visit to Saddam in order to drum up business. There was no pussyfooting or brave rhetoric about bringing Saddam into the community of nations. This was purely a matter of commerce; Iraq was known among Major's staff as "the big prize." Waldegrave wrote in a memorandum in October 1989, "I doubt if there is any future market on such a scale anywhere where the UK is potentially so well placed. . . . We must not allow it to go to the French, Germans, Japanese, etc. The priority of Iraq should be very high." But time was of the essence. He argued that the arrest of Farzad Bazoft, the British journalist whom Iraq would hang as a spy a few months later, meant Major should go sooner rather than later. "A few more Bazofts or another bout of internal repression would make this more difficult," wrote Waldegrave.

So as the Iraqi army dug into Kuwait in the summer of 1990 and Thatcher joined Bush in rounding up world leaders against Saddam's aggressive move, both leaders had much to reflect upon. Neither Bush nor Thatcher was in any doubt when it came to assessing Saddam's capabilities and intentions. The part their governments had played in helping to build up the Iraqi dictator was another matter.

On the American side, the embrace of Saddam Hussein had begun with intelligence-sharing. Not long after the beginning of its war with Iran in 1980, Iraq had been secretly provided with details of Iranian troop movements and other information obtained from satellite surveillance. This had eventually escalated into more active cooperation in locating Iranian targets and even guiding Iraqi aircraft while they were airborne.

The intelligence flow to Iraq had continued after the war ended in 1988. The man who held direct responsibility for deciding what information Iraq would receive was Robert Gates. From the days when he had served as a top aide to William Casey in 1982, Gates had been involved in implementing White House strategy toward Iraq.

American intelligence-sharing had continued as Saddam adopted an increasingly belligerent posture in the spring of 1990. It had continued after Iraq had been caught trying to ship critical nuclear components from the United States to Baghdad through London in March. It had continued after Saddam threatened to burn half of Israel in early April. It had even continued after April 10, when British customs officers seized eight one-thousand-millimeter-diameter tubes on the docks of Teeside, en route to Iraq, where they were intended for Dr. Gerald Bull's science fiction-like supergun. Indeed, it was not until the end of May 1990, two months before Iraq invaded Kuwait, that the question of discontinuing the comfortable arrangement with Saddam had come up for discussion. Even then, it had been treated simply as a possible option at the White House meetings on Iraq that Gates chaired, and few people really wanted to discontinue it, so natural had it become.

An options paper that was prepared that May had laid out the arguments for and against continuing to supply Saddam with CIA data. In favor of doing so was the fact that such intelligence flows "still provide Iraq with limited information on Iranian military activity that would be missed." A reason given for not changing the policy was that "ending this contact would close off our very limited access to this important segment of the Iraqi establishment." It was this latter view that prevailed.

There were those in the intelligence community who felt that as a result of this well-established arrangement, Iraq had learned enough about American intelligence capabilities over the years to shelter its weapons from U.S. surveillance. They were right. To the embarrassment of the Western allies who came together in Operation Desert Storm, Saddam successfully concealed hundreds of Scud missiles before, during, and after his invasion of Kuwait.

On August 2, the day the invasion took place, James Baker was in the company of Soviet foreign minister Eduard Shevardnadze in the Siberian town of Irkutsk. He had planned to finish his talks with Shevardnadze and then spend a weekend in Mongolia, hunting in the Gobi Desert. Events in the Middle East overshadowed his trip, however, and forced him to return to Washington on Saturday, August 4. Before doing so, he managed to persuade Shevardnadze to issue a joint U.S.-Soviet statement condemning the invasion of Kuwait. This would be one of the few important contributions Baker would make in the Gulf crisis.

Upon his arrival in Washington, Baker discovered that Bush had been playing to his own strengths by dialing every world leader he could reach, with some success. Baker hardly had time to get over his jet lag before German chancellor Helmut Kohl reported to Bush that the European Community would join the United States in boycotting Iraqi oil. Even Japan, which was heavily dependent upon Iraqi oil imports, had agreed to the boycott. It was a highly personal triumph for Bush when the UN Security Council voted overwhelmingly on August 6 to condemn Iraq and imposed a worldwide embargo on trade with Iraq. Never in its history had the United Nations voted such sweeping sanctions.

James Baker, however much he might have discussed the UN move with Bush, had played only one part in the UN deliberations: calling Shevardnadze to liaise on the resolution. Most of the hard work had been done by Thomas Pickering, the American ambassador to the United Nations. Meanwhile, the president was turning increasingly to other senior officials, such as Dick Cheney, the defense secretary, who was dispatched to Saudi Arabia in order to map out logistics, and Brent Scowcroft, who was constantly at Bush's side.

Amid the crisis atmosphere in Washington, more than a few people were gossiping about the relative eclipse of James Baker and the collapse of America's Mideast policy. Even before calls for his resignation appeared in the media, other oft-repeated criticisms of Baker had resurfaced, in particular his reliance for advice upon an extremely small group whose professional acumen was exceeded by their political loyalty. Baker only made matters worse for himself by leaving Washington for his ranch near Jackson Hole, Wyoming, within two weeks of the invasion.

While Baker went fishing in August 1990, U.S. troops, ships, and warplanes were already en route to the sands of Saudi Arabia. Baker's critics saw this as a telling sign of the failed policy of which he had been the joint architect, and they said he was taking it hard. At the most critical moment in the history of U.S.-Iraqi relations, he had disappeared. "During most of the post-Cold War period Baker was clearly in the driver's seat, all the way to August 2nd," commented a senate committee aide. Thereafter, said the aide, "Baker and his people played a lesser role to Scowcroft, Cheney, and their staffs."

Some in Washington believed the Wyoming trip showed that Baker was uncomfortable with the military buildup that the Bush administration ordered in response to the invasion of Kuwait. This belief was dismissed as "ludicrous" by Margaret Tutwiler, Baker's loyal spokesperson. She noted that he was in constant touch with Washington and unquestionably had been entitled to take a break. Nonetheless, Baker found himself labeled "Mr. Invisible" in the Persian Gulf crisis. Wyoming almost seemed to be a form of purdah.

However much President Bush might now be depending on others, he did not forget his old friend. Six days after the invasion and before Baker left for Wyoming, the president signed an unusual document that had been drawn up by White House counsel Boyden Gray. It was a financial conflict-of-interest waiver that authorized Baker and ten other cabinet officers and officials—including Brent Scowcroft, Robert Mosbacher, and Robert Gates—to participate in "current United States policy-making, discussions, decisions, and actions in response to the Iraqi invasion of Kuwait."

Gray had asked the president to sign waivers for all those officials who had substantial oil, defense, or other business holdings that might be affected by the Persian Gulf crisis. A waiver was also issued for Gray himself. "I insisted we couldn't afford to take any chances," Gray recalled after the waivers became public two years later, to howls of protest from congressional Democrats. "We wanted to make sure that there wasn't the slightest question in terms of anyone asking questions and shouting 'Independent counsel! Independent counsel!' The goddamn press. They get it so goddamn wrong."

The three-page waiver, dated August 8 and presented in the form of a memorandum from the president to the attorney general, was couched in grandiloquent terms. (See Appendix B, pages 339–341.) "As you know, vital United States and world interests are at stake in the Middle East as a result of the Iraqi invasion of Kuwait," wrote Bush. "As Commander in Chief and the Nation's Chief Executive I am confronting decisions of immense import with lasting consequences for the nation and the world. . . . We now face a series of decisions, large and small, about policies and military measures required to defend United States interests and counter this act of blatant aggression." The president noted that he had been briefed on the financial interests of Baker and the others for whom he was issuing the waiver, and that in some instances "individuals have quite substantial financial interests in industries that may be affected . . . by the resolution of situations that may arise."

What was noteworthy about Bush's move on behalf of Baker was the absolute secrecy imposed by the White House. The waiver document was regarded as so sensitive that not even Baker himself was to be given a copy. "Because of the breadth and sensitivity of the waiver, the White House is currently unwilling to distribute copies to affected individuals," a State Department memorandum reported. Baker's potential conflict of interest, of course, concerned oil. The memorandum informing State of the waiver explained that it would "allow Secretary Baker to participate in all foreign policy questions related to the Kuwait crisis, even those directly involving oil production and prices." A quick glance at the holdings of Baker and his immediate family indicate why his might be an especially sensitive case. The information was filed by Baker in January 1989, right after his nomination as secretary of state. He and his family held interests in the major oil companies Amoco, Exxon, and Texaco, three other oil-related companies, and ten limited partnerships in oil wells or leases. (See Appendix B, page 342.)

THE PRESIDENT COULD WAIVE conflicts of interest with a stroke of the pen, but it was not so easy to wipe out Washington's assistance to Saddam Hussein, both official and covert. Weeks before the invasion of Kuwait, the CIA had warned the Bush administration of the old problem of arms shipments to Iraq that were transiting through Jordan.

This was a sticky issue for George Bush, especially because King Hussein of Jordan, who was walking a political high wire to keep on friendly terms with both Baghdad and Washington, was scheduled to visit the president in Maine. He flew to Kennebunkport on August 16, 1990, to meet with Bush at his vacation home. The media was informed before-hand that this would be an occasion for a stern lecture to Hussein. Jordan had refused to join Saudi Arabia, Kuwait, and Egypt in supporting the Western coalition Bush was assembling to force Saddam out of Kuwait. The king had limited himself to stating he would abide by the UN embargo against Iraq. It wasn't enough: Saudi Arabia acted to cut off $700 million in aid and oil sales to Jordan, and Washington put its $50 million a year in economic and military aid on hold as a result of congres-sional indignation at the king's stance.

It was clearly time for George Bush to persuade the monarch to get in line. As the two men stood before TV cameras outside the Bush home after their mid-August meeting, it did indeed look as if Hussein had been firmly dealt with.

Appearances were one thing, but the truth was that the underlying relationship between King Hussein and President Bush had barely changed. There was a good deal of harrumphing in public as the king insisted that he was abiding by the UN embargo, even as television pictures showed trucks on their way over the border from Jordan to Iraq and ships in Jordan's port of Aqaba unloading cargo also destined for Iraq. Behind the scenes in both Washington and London, though, not only was there sympathy for the king, there was awareness of the uncom-fortable fact that for almost a decade both Britain and the United States had used the Jordanian monarch and his generals as a conduit to arm Saddam Hussein covertly.

In the autumn of 1990, several weeks after King Hussein's visit to Kennebunkport, officials from Baker's State Department went to Capitol Hill to brief members of Congress on the issue of whether Jordan was still receiving U.S. military shipments. They assured the legislators that as of August 2, 1990, the day of the invasion of Kuwait, the State Department had stopped approving new arms exports to Jordan.

Shipping any arms to Jordan was a very serious matter in the autumn of 1990, yet the White House was receiving intelligence briefings that showed King Hussein still to be transferring U.S. military technology on to Baghdad. What is more, despite the assurances to Congress that military aid to Jordan had been cut off, the flow of weapons from the United States to Jordan in fact continued. Bush and Baker's policy on Jordan was cynical enough to ignore even Jordan's violations of the UN embargo after the invasion of Kuwait. Between August 2 and October 4, 1990, the State Department approved twelve new military equipment orders worth five million dollars, including items such as spare parts and components for TOW missiles, helicopter components for the AH-1S Cobra, 105-mm. cartridges for artillery shells, and conversion kits for the M-16 rifle.

King Hussein had always been considered a good friend to British leaders, and he had forged a relationship based on their mutual interests for many years. But the king's closeness to Saddam now left Margaret Thatcher in a quandary. In the past, when the king had asked for arms from Britain, Thatcher's top aides had been more than willing to assist, even if they suspected some of it might end up in Baghdad. In Britain during the late 1980s, that Jordan was fronting as an arms buyer for Iraq had become so well known in Whitehall that bureaucrats handling the paperwork had taken to calling Jordan "Jorq." It was by no means a new arrangement. The British intelligence services had known of Jordan's role as middleman as early as 1983, but as one of Thatcher's most senior cabinet ministers put it later, "We'd had a forty-year relationship with plucky little Jordan, and if they asked for some kit, well then, by and large we would let them have it."

Now that Saddam had marched into Kuwait, however, it was harder for Thatcher to take such a relaxed view. On August 31 the prime minister and the king spent two and a half difficult hours at Downing Street, in what were clearly tense and fractious discussions. The two leaders, said Thatcher's spokesmen, were "quite far apart." The British leader would have no truck with any Jordanian proposal to mediate between Iraq and the United Nations. Nor was she pleased at King Hussein's support for Saddam. "We did appreciate the difficulties he was having, being utterly dependent on Iraq for so much, but the king found himself in some very frosty discussions with the prime minister, very frosty indeed," recalled one former Downing Street aide.

But however frosty the encounter might have been, on September 14, 1990, more than six weeks after the invasion of Kuwait, Britain's Department of Trade and Industry was still continuing its business-as-usual approach to Jordan, approving the sale of large quantities of British artillery shells. These were shells, the British knew, that were liable to be diverted to Iraq. But for London, as for Washington, there was no simple way to shut off the channel between Amman and Baghdad. Nor was there enough political will to deal effectively with the continuing supply of Western arms to Jordan itself, whatever the consequences.

In fact, as hundreds of thousands of American troops were being airlifted into makeshift bases in the Saudi desert that autumn, Bush and Baker found they had a new political problem on their hands—the need to sell the Gulf buildup to the American people. Bush tried a dramatic approach. In mid-October he used the phrase "Hitler revisited" to describe the apparent atrocities that Saddam's forces were perpetrating in occupied Kuwait. That made the headlines, but the public remained skeptical about the escalating stand-off in the Persian Gulf; American lives might soon be on the line, and it was hard for most people to imagine shedding blood in defense of crude oil.

That was when James Baker made his gambit. Baker's greatest talent, said both his friends and his critics, had always been as a political operator, a pragmatic adviser and campaign manager for George Bush. Yet even that skill seemed to fail him during the fateful autumn of 1990. While the president was comparing Saddam to Adolf Hitler, Baker came up with a new reason for the United States to get involved in a possible war: He claimed Operation Desert Storm would help to protect American jobs.

"The economic lifeline of the industrial world runs from the Gulf and we cannot permit a dictator such as this to sit astride that economic lifeline," said Baker, referring to oil reserves. "To bring it down to the level of the average American citizen, let me say that means jobs. If you want to sum it up in one word, it's jobs." For the average American, however, the argument did not ring true. Nor did it play very well in the heartland. Jobs were of vital concern to Americans, but justifying a war against Saddam on these grounds was considered something of a stretch.

In mid-November, Bush found a more effective argument to deploy. Opinion polls in American newspapers indicated that preventing Iraq from acquiring atomic weapons was a more worthwhile goal for U.S.

policy than protecting oil and jobs or restoring the sovereignty of Kuwait, a sheikdom that was difficult to present as a paragon of democratic virtues. On November 22, during a visit to the Saudi desert to celebrate the Thanksgiving holiday with American troops, the president stressed a new justification for confronting Iraq. "Those who would measure the timetable for Saddam's atomic program in years may be seriously under-estimating the reality of the situation and the gravity of the threat," he said. "Every day that passes brings Saddam one step closer to realizing his goal of a nuclear weapons arsenal. And that's why, more and more, your mission is marked by a real sense of urgency."

On the public level, each day seemed to bring a new rhetorical flourish, a new exchange, in the phony war between George Bush and Saddam Hussein. Behind the scenes, the CIA and other intelligence services continued to gather what information they could, hoping to steal a march on their Iraqi adversaries. The irony for some operatives was that they were now being asked to spy on the very same people they had previously assisted in covert operations.

THAT WAS CERTAINLY true of Fred Haobsh. When his telephone rang in Dallas at the end of August, the former Maytag washing machine sales-man and supplier of arms to Iraq had not heard from his old contacts for years. Yet here was the local office of the CIA on the line, inquiring whether Haobsh would be prepared to return to his former home country of Jordan on an assignment. Given Jordan's intimate trading links with Iraq, he could collect valuable information for the Agency about Jordan's role in helping Saddam survive the UN trade embargo. Using his import-export company as a cover, he could also help the CIA identify what kinds of equipment Saddam was seeking.

Haobsh agreed without much hesitation, and he found himself once again on the kind of high-rolling odyssey that had shaped his life nine years earlier in Baghdad. This time, however, there was a significant difference. Instead of working on a commission for ex-CIA operatives with White House connections, he would be on the CIA payroll as a contractor. What that would mean in terms of his own safety, his com-pany's future, or his family's fortunes was not immediately clear to him. He did know that he had been finding his life in Dallas bleak and uninteresting and that Jordan was the place to be in the fall of 1990, at least if he wanted to take risks and savor once more the knife-edge uncertainties that some part of him still missed.

When Haobsh stepped off the Air France flight from Paris on September 30, Amman was chaotic. More than half a million refugees had arrived there from Kuwait and Iraq since the invasion, and a huge business was to be done simply in feeding them. But that was not Haobsh's concern. He checked into the Intercontinental Hotel and turned on the news. Soviet foreign minister Eduard Shevardnadze was announcing that Soviet troops were ready to participate in military operations against Iraq, even though not all Saddam's Soviet advisers had yet been repatriated.

Haobsh didn't realize the significance of the Iraqi whom he would meet in Amman. The instructions from his CIA handler had been to establish and cultivate contacts that might produce information on the Iraqi economy, sanction violations, weapons flows, and the like. On October 2, when he went to dine at the Intercontinental's restaurant, Haobsh hit the jackpot. A business friend introduced him to Anas Dohan, a man who ranked as one of the CIA's most-wanted sources of information on the true state of affairs in Baghdad.

Anas Malik Dohan was a well-traveled Iraqi who maintained homes in Baghdad, Amman, and London. He claimed an engineering degree from the University of Edinburgh, where he had met his first wife, and he combined the role of peripatetic international businessman with a more formal responsibility as deputy minister of industrialization in Saddam's government. The UN trade embargo made his job doubly important. He tried to secure whatever food and medical supplies he could despite the embargo. And most critical of all, he had to continue trying to procure the materials needed to sustain the most secret project in Iraq, Saddam's nuclear weapons program.

Haobsh and Dohan talked over a period of twenty-four hours, both at the Intercontinental and then at Dohan's Amman apartment. Their exchanges were stilted at first, but then Haobsh reached into an inside pocket of his suit and produced a talisman that would open a number of doors for him in his journey to the heart of Saddam's arms-procurement machine. It was the gold watch that Saddam had given him in thanks for his services in 1982. The conversation between Haobsh and Dohan began to flow more freely after that. On the first evening, the talk was of food, medicine, and humanitarian needs. By the next morning, October 3, when the men met again, their agenda had been greatly expanded. Dohan presented Haobsh with a shopping list that included chemical products, computers and components, communications equipment, machine tools, and even entire weapons systems. To Haobsh, it was an uncanny echo of the list he had received in Baghdad nine years earlier from Hussein

Kamel. But there were certain extra items this time, and although he didn't know for sure, to Haobsh they seemed to have nuclear overtones. Tungsten carbide cutting heads for computer-controlled lathes. Blocks of graphite of particular specifications and dimensions. Graphite—Haobsh knew it had many industrial applications, but Dohan mentioned it in connection with weapons-manufacturing at very high temperatures and insisted that the specifications be precise. As the conversation continued, so did the ironies. The man to whom Dohan said he reported was in fact Hussein Kamel himself, by now the minister of military industrialization, and the oil minister to boot. Back in the early 1980s, Haobsh had helped fill Hussein Kamel's shopping list. Now his mission was to prevent him from filling it. It was a strange world.

Dohan spelled out the details for Haobsh. Finding Jordanian front companies through which Haobsh could do business with Iraq would be no problem, said Dohan. Two hundred had been formed in Jordan since the invasion. Under instructions from his CIA handler to cultivate Iraqi contacts, Haobsh displayed vivid interest. "I told Mr. Dohan I would be happy to work and help the Iraqis in getting to them some of the products which they were looking for," he later recalled. Dohan asked for more details of what kind of products Haobsh could provide. Dohan said he had approval from Baghdad for some orders and was willing to open a bank account in Haobsh's name to deposit up to one million dollars to pay for some of the orders up front. Haobsh replied that the bank account would not be needed, that he preferred to deal strictly on the basis of individual orders. Dohan pressed him to visit Baghdad, but Haobsh was worried that he would have problems back in the United States if he traveled to Iraq. No problem, said Dohan; Haobsh's passport would not be stamped. Haobsh demurred, steering the conversation back to payment terms and shipping procedures. The port of Aqaba was one possible route, but Dohan also suggested that products be delivered to Italy or Turkey and then be trucked overland to Jordan, for transshipment on to Iraq.

When Dohan bade Haobsh farewell, the aircraft carrier USS *Independence* was steaming toward Iraq. Haobsh was relieved to leave Jordan. Twenty-four hours later, in a safe house across the Potomac from Washington, "Alan" and "Debbie" from the CIA and "Dan" from the Defense Intelligence Agency read his four-page report, debriefed him, and asked him to revisit Dohan as soon as possible. In the meantime, Haobsh was told to get in touch with Union Carbide and obtain a bid for the graphite that Dohan wanted. In the back of his mind, something began to trouble

Haobsh, just as it had when Dohan first mentioned graphite in Amman. Dohan had told him that the graphite was to be used "for casting purposes in weapons systems." Was the Agency actually going to have him deliver the graphite? he asked Debbie. "She told me yes," said Haobsh. "She also told me the Agency was well aware that American companies had been sending graphite to Saddam through Jordan after the UN sanctions. It did not seem to bother them."

As the downhill progress toward war quickened in the autumn of 1990, Haobsh made a second trip to Jordan for the Agency. British foreign secretary Douglas Hurd had just announced that the international community was willing to use force against Saddam, and Iraqi military commanders were ordered to prepare for a U.S. attack "within a few days." Haobsh arrived in Amman on October 27, just before President Bush announced he had "had it" with the mistreatment of American citizens in Kuwait, touching off another round of rumors that he was preparing the American public for war.

Despite the jittery times, however, Dohan was surprisingly upbeat when he met Haobsh again. He explained to Haobsh that he was moving his operations to Tunisia. War seemed to be just over the horizon, so he had set up new supply lines to Iraq through Tunisia, Algeria, and Morocco. What he needed were weapons of all kinds and spare parts for Iraq's air force, particularly brakes for its French Mirages. Haobsh said he would see what he could do. As before, Dohan emphasized that there would be no money problems. As if to illustrate the point, he detailed to Haobsh how Iraq had shipped gold bullion looted from Kuwait through Jordan to Europe, right under the nose of American warships.

Upon his return to Washington, Haobsh met Debbie and Dan and was again taken to a safe house for debriefing. "I was really worried when I left the meeting," he recalled later. "First of all, they weren't interested in the information about the gold, and that surprised me. I had details about a huge Saudi Arabian trading company that was acting as a front for Iraq, and they were not interested in that either." Haobsh gained the distinct impression that he was being used for a purpose very different from that which his handler had originally described. All these people seemed to want him to do, he concluded, "was to sell weapons to Iraq." After his next trip there would be no doubt in his mind.

BY THE END OF OCTOBER, secret plans had already been laid in Washington for the launch of an air war in January, with a ground war to follow after a month. After President Bush announced on November 8 that he was doubling the 200,000 troops already in Saudi Arabia, war seemed inevitable. The only question for the public was when it would begin. This prospect, in turn, raised the specter of Iraqi-sponsored terrorism in the American consciousness. After all, Iraq had once been on the State Department's blacklist of states sponsoring terrorism—before the Reagan administration quietly removed it in 1982—and it had been hastily put back on the list only after the invasion of Kuwait.

In June 1990, before the invasion of Kuwait, however, James Baker had received what he termed "disturbing reports that Iraqi officials had been in contact with members of the notorious Abu Nidal terrorist organization." On an official level, Baghdad had promised Washington years before that its policy was not to allow Abu Nidal to come to Iraq. In a message to April Glaspie on June 27, 1990, Baker wrote, "It is troubling therefore that we continue to hear reports that the Abu Nidal Organization has been allowed to open a new office in Iraq. As you well know, in our view the Abu Nidal Organization is among the most dangerous terrorist organizations in existence." (See Appendix B, pages 344–345.) Iraq might find itself back on the State Department's blacklist if the reports turned out to be accurate.

After the invasion, the matter of Abu Nidal's office in Baghdad became moot, since the UN embargo was more stringent than the sanctions that would have accompanied a new blacklisting by the State Department. Abu Nidal, however, was no less of a terrorist threat. The solution, devised by the Saudi government with the quiet blessing of Washington, was to neutralize him and his operations. This was done in a manner that was as simple as it was crude.

"Sometimes," noted a U.S. intelligence officer familiar with the plan, "you have to get your hands dirty." With Operation Desert Storm in the offing, an extraordinary deal was implemented. Fred Haobsh got wind of it during his travels on behalf of the CIA. Early in 1991, Saudi emissaries asked Abu Nidal to relocate himself personally to a safe haven in their kingdom. There he remained throughout Operation Desert Storm. A U.S. intelligence source later confirmed Haobsh's information, adding that in addition to a home and an office, Abu Nidal was provided with millions of dollars in cash to induce him to suspend his terrorist operations before and during the war. "The money came from the Saudis, but Washington knew what was going on. The Bush administration turned a blind eye. They didn't really want to know," said the intelligence officer.

This Abu Nidal episode was by no means the first time the Reagan or

Bush administration had allowed dealings with terrorists in pursuit of U.S. policy goals. In the mid-1980s, Washington had learned of Saddam's links to Abu Abbas, leader of the Palestinian terrorist group that hijacked the cruise ship *Achille Lauro* and coldly murdered a wheelchair-bound elderly American Jew before dumping him overboard. The State Department knew that shortly thereafter, Abu Abbas had been permitted to take refuge in Iraq. Under U.S. law, Saddam's provision of that safe haven for Abu Abbas should immediately have returned Iraq to the blacklist of states supporting terrorism, but that did not happen. Instead, in early 1986 Judge William Clark, by then back in the private sector, undertook a secret mission to Baghdad in order to deliver a warning directly to Saddam Hussein. If Saddam did not do something about the Iraqi training camps that both Abu Abbas and Abu Nidal were using, Iraq would be put back on the terrorist list. Saddam neither confirmed nor denied that he was once again harboring terrorists, but Iraq remained off the State Department's list and American covert assistance continued to flow to Saddam in the Iran-Iraq war.

Now, with only days to go before the United States began bombing Baghdad, the time was ripe for a discreet arrangement with Abu Nidal. The movement of the world's most dangerous terrorist from Iraq to Saudi Arabia was known about and countenanced.

AT ELEVEN O'CLOCK on the morning of January 9, 1991, in a conference room at Geneva's Intercontinental Hotel, James Baker and Tariq Aziz sat down opposite each other for what would be their final conversation. If their first encounter, in the Henry Clay Room of the State Department back in October 1989, had not been easy, this meeting would be far more difficult. The two men spent six and a half hours achieving nothing.

Early in the meeting Baker, on behalf of President Bush, had handed Tariq Aziz a letter addressed to Saddam Hussein. If Iraq fully complied with the many UN Security Council resolutions on the table, then Iraq would "gain the opportunity to rejoin the international community," wrote Bush. "More immediately, the Iraqi military establishment will escape destruction," Bush added, and he warned that if Iraq destroyed the Kuwaiti oil facilities, "you and your country will pay a terrible price."

Aziz responded to Baker in the clearest of terms: "I am sorry, I cannot receive this letter. The language in this letter is not compatible with language between heads of state." The letter lay on the table between the two men for the rest of the meeting. The die was now finally cast. At the separate press briefings each man held immediately after their meeting, Baker announced, "Regrettably, ladies and gentlemen, I heard nothing today that—in over six hours I heard nothing that suggested to me any Iraqi flexibility whatsoever on complying with United Nations Security Council Resolutions." Aziz was equally bleak: "The tone of [Secretary Baker's] language was diplomatic and polite. I reciprocated. But the substance was full of threats. And I told him, also in substance, we will not yield to threats."

General Norman Schwarzkopf, the Allied Forces Commander, was sitting alone in his office in Riyadh at the time, watching Baker and Aziz make their statements on TV. "I realized this was it: we were going to war," he thought to himself.

On the evening of January 16, Fred Haobsh was sitting in his living room in Dallas watching the about-to-be-famous CNN broadcast from Baghdad. He saw the clear sky over the Iraqi capital light up with antiaircraft fire like a Fourth of July fireworks display. Distorted through the eerie green hue of the TV camera's night-scope, liquid lines of tracer shells threaded up into the darkness, to the wailing accompaniment of constant air-raid sirens. The bombing of Baghdad had begun.

Cruise missiles and Stealth aircraft struck the three main air defense centers and central Baghdad itself, while three hundred more aircraft took out defense radars, communications links, and a wide range of major military targets. Millions of dollars' worth of the military equipment that the West had covertly supplied to Iraq, and billions more in high technology that Saddam Hussein had illicitly obtained, were now being bombed by his principal suppliers.

The cluster bomb factories that Carlos Cardoen had supplied and built were among the very first targets. Those had arrived in Iraq with CIA knowledge and blessings. The radar-guided antiaircraft systems that resembled fireworks over CNN as they assisted Baghdad's defenses had wound their way to the Iraqi capital from James Guerin's companies in Pennsylvania. The computers from Hewlett-Packard, the trucks from General Motors, the satellite down-links from California, and a thousand more U.S.-supplied components of Saddam's huge military machine were being methodically obliterated.

As dramatic as the bombing was, however, Fred Haobsh had other things on his mind. He was due to meet Saddam's procurement officer, Anas Dohan, in Tunis in less than two weeks. All the paperwork covering Dohan's order of graphite was in place—the letters and specifications from Union Carbide and the price quotations. All that remained was his pretrip briefing by Alan and Debbie, and an introduction to another CIA agent who would be making the trip with him, a man who called himself a commodities broker from Marietta, Georgia. The commodities broker would be introduced to Dohan as an associate of Haobsh's, and a well-connected one at that.

On January 28, Haobsh and his new CIA companion met Dohan in Tunis. The Iraqi seemed at first to be remarkably unworried by the war that was now under way. As the Hilton Hotel's television brought news of the 2,600 sorties that the allies had flown the previous day, Dohan belittled their efforts to destroy Saddam's mobile missiles. "He explained that Iraq had at least 150 Scud missiles and launchers left, while the allies had been saying there were only thirty-six," said Haobsh. The statement would turn out to be accurate.

The technical specifications and prices for the Union Carbide graphite were presented to Dohan, who examined the paper and promised to respond with an order shortly. During the course of the meetings, there was a constant flow of telephone calls to Dohan from the Iraqi embassy in Amman, but between interruptions it became clear that Dohan was prepared to pay heavily for Soviet-made shoulder-operated surface-to-air-missiles (SAMs). That was when Haobsh's CIA companion responded: He said there would be no problem. That was one of the "commodities" he knew all about.

Haobsh's inner alarm began to well up once more. "Here we were in the middle of Operation Desert Storm, with the TV on twenty-four hours a day, watching the war. And we were offering to sell Saddam's procurement officer a bunch of SAM missiles," Haobsh said. "I just didn't understand it, and I became frightened." Haobsh at first assumed his CIA colleague was willing to go along with Dohan's latest request because the missiles in question would be deliberately altered to be defective. But when the two men returned to Washington for their Agency debriefing on February 2, his fears mounted once more. Debbie was pleased with their progress. " 'Great,' she said, 'now we're going to sell Saddam some missiles,' " recalled Haobsh. Then she cut to the point: In fulfillment of Dohan's request, would Haobsh be prepared to sell him the SAMs? Despite his assumption that the CIA knew what it was doing and would never supply fully functioning missiles to Iraq, Haobsh nonetheless blanched at the idea.

"I knew I couldn't do it," he recalled. His CIA handlers tried to reassure him, but Haobsh was out of his depth and becoming increasingly nervous. "I asked if they could give me some kind of letter saying that I was acting on their behalf, in case I was prosecuted," said Haobsh. "But they said that was not possible. That's when I decided I wanted out."

From then on, Haobsh refused to travel anymore for the CIA. But the Agency emphasized how valuable his information had been and urged him not to quit; if he didn't want to travel, that was understandable, but he could not give up now. After all, he had immediate access at any time to Saddam's major procurement officer in the Middle East. So Haobsh continued fax contact from his Dallas office with Dohan in Tunis, and the CIA made the necessary arrangements to provide a sample batch of weapons.

Following instructions from his Dallas-based Agency contact, Haobsh faxed Dohan's office on February 4, 1991, offering him twenty-five SAM 7 and twenty-five SAM 16 shoulder-fired missiles of Soviet origin for delivery to Tunis within two weeks. The SAM 7 was a relatively primitive weapon, but the SAM 16 was a great deal more advanced and had been seen by the West only since 1987. It had a range of four miles and had already shot down some U.S. Marines' Harrier jump-jets during the course of Operation Desert Storm.

For reasons that were unclear at the time, Dohan took a long time in replying to the offer from Haobsh; in fact, he did not get back in touch until after the war had ended. When he contacted Haobsh on May 18, it was with a most curious fax. "Dear Fred," it began. "We have confirmed document that FBI is monitoring all our correspondences. Pls wait for the time being. We will come back to you when the matter is solved." Habosh had no idea how the FBI might have discovered his communications with Dohan, and he never heard from the Iraqi again.

By that time, Haobsh had formally cut his links with the Agency. No more cash payments came to him in envelopes from the CIA man in Dallas, and, he hoped, there would be no more bizarre and inexplicable scenarios like the one he had just been through. He didn't know if the CIA agents he had been dealing with were renegades out to make a fast buck or regular agents trying to sabotage and track Saddam's procurement network, and he never would. But soon it no longer mattered to him. Haobsh had sat out the rest of Operation Desert Storm in Texas, and "on February 28, the day after Desert Storm was over, I made up my mind," he said. "Never again would I have anything to do with the CIA."

PRESIDENT GEORGE BUSH had gone on national television on the evening of Wednesday, February 27, 1991, to tell the world that a cease-fire would go into effect in a matter of hours. The war against Saddam was now finished, although the Iraqi dictator remained in power. Around much of the world the president was feted as a hero. In the coming months there would be victory celebrations and ticker-tape parades across America, and funerals in both the United States and Iraq.

In Washington, however, there remained some unfinished business for the Bush administration. It concerned the troublesome BNL branch in Atlanta that had provided billions of dollars of Iraqi loans which helped arm Saddam Hussein. For many months now, the prosecutors in Atlanta had been ready to bring indictments, only to be stopped for one reason or another. The waiting was about to be over.

The next day, a number of journalists were called to the Department of Justice building in Washington. This was to be neither a military briefing nor a political event, but rather a press conference. The press conference, however, would raise many more questions than it would answer, and critics would later claim it was itself part of the Bush administration's attempt to cover up its prewar dealings with Iraq. The star was Richard Thornburgh, the attorney general of the United States.

TWELVE

Justice Delayed

T he war in the Persian Gulf had been over only for thirteen hours when the Bush administration began to cover up its prewar deal-ings with Saddam Hussein.

Shortly after one o'clock on the afternoon of Thursday, February 28, 1991, President Bush was telling reporters in the Oval Office that it was "an exciting day for all Americans." At the very same moment, a smiling Attorney General Dick Thornburgh greeted other reporters in the press room of the Department of Justice. The little room was packed and noisy because word had spread among the journalists that something "big" was coming, and it had to do with Iraq.

As they chattered away, the heat from the klieg lights that had been set up for the television network camera crews began causing visible discomfort for everyone, especially for Atlanta Assistant U.S. Attorney Gale McKenzie and a dozen other federal, state, and local law enforce-ment agents who stood in a row behind the attorney general.

The euphoria of America's apparent victory over Saddam Hussein made the journalists extremely convivial. A press aide to Thornburgh contributed to the carnival-like atmosphere when he handed out thick, stapled wads of paper that turned out to be a 347-count indictment and joked: "Here it is, folks, the Mother of all Indictments." There were waves of laughter as the indictments were distributed.

Thornburgh stood surveying the assembled crowd. A former gover-nor of Pennsylvania who had first served in the Ford administration's Justice Department in the wake of the Watergate scandal, he was a quintessential political survivor. He had become attorney general even before George Bush took office as president, having been named to the post in 1988 after Ronald Reagan's friend Ed Meese resigned in the wake of more than a year of controversy over alleged ethics violations.

The reporters chuckled again when it was announced that the attorney general was about to reveal the story behind "Operation Desert Fraud"; they settled down like students in a rowdy classroom as Thornburgh approached the microphone. Reading from a prepared text, he said a federal grand jury in Atlanta had just indicted ten persons for conspiracy, mail fraud, and wire fraud involving more than $4 billion in loans made to the government of Iraq by the Atlanta branch of an Italian government–owned bank. The bank was called Banca Nazionale del Lavoro. Four Iraqi officials and an Iraqi bank had also been charged in this "international white collar scam with dire global consequences."

The eighteen-month investigation, Thornburgh said, had unraveled a paper trail spanning three continents. "By utilizing modern technology such as computers, fax machines, and instant communication these defendants were able to silently pick the pockets of a major Italian bank of more than $4 billion . . . almost by the push of a button." U.S. authorities had also been deceived, he added, and possible violations of federal law in connection with the acquisition by Iraq of military armaments and other goods remained under investigation.

Thornburgh never mentioned the name of Christopher Drogoul, the former BNL branch manager; he left that task to Robert Mueller, the assistant attorney general in charge of the criminal division of the Justice Department. Mueller—who would spend the rest of the year denying repeated accusations that he was the man responsible for covering up U.S. government involvement in another banking scandal, the BCCI case—now accused Drogoul and his fellow defendants of defrauding BNL's Rome headquarters. Drogoul, he revealed, had been arrested that very morning in Atlanta.

The Iraqi loans had been made in violation of BNL, Italian, and U.S. lending limits, and the branch's books had been falsified along the way. Some of the loans, Mueller explained, were backed by U.S. government loan guarantees. Among the four Iraqi officials indicted was Sadik Taha, Drogoul's friend at the Central Bank. The others were Abdul Munim Rasheed, also of the Central Bank; Raja Hassan Ali, the director-general of the economic department at the Ministry of Industry and Military Industrialization; and Safa Al-Habobi, the director-general of one of the ministry's weapons plants and a director at several Iraqi front companies, including TDG and the British and U.S. branches of Matrix Churchill.

When the presentation was over, the reporters scrambled to ask questions. The very first one proved difficult for Thornburgh: How much of the money had gone to the Iraqi military machine, and how much of the guaranteed loans would the American taxpayer be stuck with? Thornburgh dodged the issue of military items, saying, "I can't answer the question with regard to where that investigation will lead." As for the pocketbook question: "With regard to the taxpayers, in one respect, again, that's—we can't answer that right now because these loans are due and owing, and in many respects the ultimate victim is going to be the bank." There were, however, "certain loan guarantee features that may cause some exposure to the U.S."

As he listened to the next questioner, Thornburgh squinted, scrawled some notes, then looked vaguely displeased. He was told that the *Financial Times* of London had obtained evidence showing that BNL money had gone into Iraqi missiles, chemical weapons, and other military projects, and that cabinet-level officials seemed to have been aware of this. If a British newspaper could obtain this information, presumably the Justice Department could as well. Why was the Bush administration not moving ahead with any indictments of those involved in using BNL loans to assist Iraq's weapons programs? And was the Justice Department investigating any past or present U.S. government officials for their partic- ipation in the BNL affair, including agents at the CIA? And what com- ment could the attorney general offer on documented evidence that a full year ago he himself had participated in delaying the BNL indictments?

The attorney general said he wouldn't discuss the military dimen- sion, which was still being pursued. He declared "without hesitancy" that there was no evidence of U.S. government officials being involved. As for his own role in delaying the indictments: "Well, I can certainly comment on the latter. I did not delay any of these indictments. This investigation has really been done . . . in a very expeditious manner. It's been about an eighteen-month investigation."

After this exchange, the reporters became progressively tougher on Thornburgh. Had the State Department played a role in the BNL investi- gation? None, replied Thornburgh, except that in matters concerning the "international arena" both the State Department and the National Secu- rity Council had been advised. Was there a White House decision that had had to be made about BNL? No, the White House had merely been kept abreast of where the investigation was going.

But how on earth could all the regulatory agencies in the United States and Italy, and the bank in Rome, have been in the dark about billions of dollars over several years? BNL, replied Thornburgh, was a victim rather than a participant. There had been "a very sophisticated and complicated scheme to conceal and cover up precisely what was being done, a scheme that was obviously very successful for a considerable period of time."

Then came another question that flustered Thornburgh. Hadn't a member of Congress from Texas named Henry Gonzalez, the chairman of the House Banking Committee, said just a week ago that a top-ranking administration official, whom he did not name, had knowledge that BNL credits had been used for military purchases? Thornburgh declined to respond. But Gonzalez, insisted the reporter, had claimed that he was having trouble with his own BNL investigation. "He claims that effectively you've been stiff-arming him. Is that true?" It was true, said Thornburgh, that Gonzalez did want to investigate, but the requests he had been making would have interfered materially with the Justice Department's own work.

At this point the reporters began to smell blood. Did Thornburgh have evidence of CIA knowledge of any of this BNL business? "Our business," the attorney general replied, "is to prosecute criminal cases, and that's as far as I can go in characterizing the nature of the investigation." But was there or was there not some awareness of the BNL loans? "We're not a general investigative agency; we're a law enforcement agency," Thornburgh said, becoming exasperated. There was, he repeated, no evidence that "anyone in the current government is involved."

Finally, a friendly face appeared, a reliable reporter whose daily bread was the Justice Department beat: "How are you going to get these people from Iraq to stand trial?" Thornburgh smiled broadly and with perfect timing he barked into the microphone: "Good question!" Laughter filled the room.

It was getting late. Thornburgh's press secretary said there was time for just a couple of questions more. The last one concerned the infamous Sadik Taha, the Iraqi Central Bank director. His death had been reported in the British press in June 1990, yet some U.S. investigators had said the death was faked in order to avoid his being implicated in the BNL affair. One law enforcement official said Taha had been spotted in Moscow four months after his supposed demise; others insisted he really was dead. Now he had been indicted. Was Taha alive or dead?

"Dead or alive," said Dick Thornburgh, laughing, "we've indicted him . . . and we always get our man, one way or the other!" And on that high note a relieved attorney general excused himself and strode briskly from the room.

There was quite a lot that Thornburgh did not say during his BNL press conference. He failed to mention that Gale McKenzie, the junior prosecutor in Atlanta, had been stymied on several occasions since her investigation had begun in the summer of 1989, sometimes by Washington and sometimes by her own mistakes. The first time indictments were said to be imminent, for example, had been in the autumn of 1989. At that point McKenzie was still investigating whether BNL's Rome head office was implicated in the Iraqi loan fraud. Yet she engaged in the rather unusual practice of meeting with BNL's own lawyer—who was representing a potential *defendant* in the case—to discuss the timing of indictments and Drogoul's statements.

For some time, investigators from the Federal Reserve Bank of New York had been less than impressed with McKenzie, whom they considered to be severely lacking in the kind of experience needed to handle the case. The Fed's own investigators were themselves among the ablest of the rather disparate BNL task force members who did not always work well together. One of McKenzie's closest collaborators was Arthur Wade, a Department of Agriculture investigator who had never before tackled an international financial scandal. The FBI men and women who had been drafted to assist could not fathom the details of the Iraqi loans saga. The IRS members of the task force were interested mainly in tax evasion by Drogoul and other BNL Atlanta employees. The Pentagon had sent members of the Defense Criminal Investigative Service to Atlanta, but their specialty was weapons, a vitally important aspect of the case that got short shrift in the final indictment. McKenzie herself had had to report to the U.S. attorney in Atlanta and to officials of the criminal and fraud divisions of the Justice Department in Washington. She had also had to contend with frequent requests for information and other interference from officials at the White House and the State and Agriculture departments.

McKenzie herself grew prickly at any criticism, and she did not hide her views. At six o'clock on the evening of September 11, 1989, at the U.S. attorney's office in Atlanta, McKenzie had met a group of investigators that included Thomas Baxter, an extremely talented lawyer-turned-investigator from the New York Fed. McKenzie told Baxter she was "irritated" at the New York Fed's suggestion that she was not doing enough on the case, though she did not say how this criticism had been communicated to her. A memorandum reflecting that meeting quoted

McKenzie as lecturing the Fed official that good criminal investigations took time, that all leads would be pursued, and that the Federal Reserve was getting all the information it wanted. Without explaining further, she then hinted that "things could be different." In early December 1989, a lawyer for the New York Fed wrote another memorandum that quoted McKenzie as predicting Drogoul would be indicted in January 1990. That did not happen, but by then Bob Mueller of the Justice Department was in regular contact with McKenzie, and one of Mueller's aides had gone to Atlanta to discuss the "national security" overtones of the situation. McKenzie, as her colleagues admitted, was swamped, both by the workload and by the varying requests for briefings that Washington kept sending her way.

Then there were the larger questions she had to wrestle with, such as whether Drogoul had acted alone, as a "lone wolf," and defrauded BNL Rome by making unauthorized Iraqi loans, or whether Rome had known and been a party to the fraud. Also to be resolved was the lurking matter of whether the U.S. government itself had been aware of the Iraqi loans or involved in them. These two issues would plague McKenzie and the Bush administration for the next two years.

At the end of January 1990, a CIA official made clear his view that "managers at BNL headquarters in Rome were involved in the scandal." It made abundant sense for McKenzie and members of her team to visit Rome to question the bank's executives. The trip was scheduled, as was another to interrogate witnesses in Istanbul—but neither was allowed to go forward. Who stopped them? On February 6, 1990, a senior lawyer at the New York Federal Reserve answered the question in a memorandum that was copied to Gerald Corrigan, president of the New York Fed. The memo said that "obviously the indictments that were expected to come down in January did not materialize. A planned trip to Italy by criminal investigators was put off because of BNL-asserted concerns regarding the Italian press. [See Appendix B, page 343.] A trip to Istanbul was put off at the request of Attorney General Thornburgh." It appeared that public criticism of the bank case involving BCCI had "motivated the Attorney General to have the BNL matter reviewed by main Justice." Thornburgh had thus taken control of the BNL case and done it a full twelve months before he announced the result of "Operation Desert Fraud."

The Iraqis, meanwhile, having promised James Baker their fullest cooperation, had yet to cooperate. Instead, as the Federal Reserve lawyer put it, Baghdad was "willing to sacrifice one individual to the vagaries of the United States criminal judicial system." On January 29, 1990, when

McKenzie sent her first "bare bones indictment" proposal to be reviewed by main Justice in Washington, it did not name a single Iraqi. When her superiors asked her to explain why this was the case, since she had previously indicated that Iraqis were indeed involved, the Atlanta prosecutor said she assumed that Iraqi officials could not be indicted because they were foreign government officials. Stunned by her ignorance, a Justice Department colleague told McKenzie "not to assume anything of that nature."

Now it was time for James Baker's State Department to get into the act. How would McKenzie and the Atlanta team take up Baghdad's offer to "cooperate" in the BNL investigation? McKenzie and Bob Mueller discussed the question in February 1990; it seemed the Agriculture Department was proposing that the Atlanta prosecutor travel to Baghdad along with a team of its inspectors who were still looking into the kickbacks and other abuses in the CCC program. But to let U.S. prosecutors run around Baghdad at a time when Baker was hoping to push through the second $500 million of the CCC credits he had secured in 1989 would be too much of a hot potato. On February 11, 1990, Baker's legal advisers told Agriculture officials and Boyden Gray, the president's lawyer, that McKenzie's questions for the Iraqis "should be as specific as possible" and should be cleared first in Washington. Then, after State had reviewed them, the questions could be submitted in writing to Baghdad in advance.

Gale McKenzie might have been inexperienced and under pressure from Washington, but she was not stupid: She balked at the idea of providing the Iraqis with a list of questions in advance. She also feared that if her team put tough questions to the Iraqis, they would simply deny any complicity in the BNL scheme and afterward assert they had "cooperated" with the American investigation, as Tariq Aziz had promised Baker. That, however, would allow the Iraqis to demand that Washington pay out the suspended second half of the CCC guarantees. The issue of this second $500 million installment hung over the Atlanta investigation like a cloud, and the politically loaded debate in Washington over what to do about it was one of the chief reasons McKenzie kept finding her investigation hampered in the spring of 1990. Instead of going to Baghdad, a revised plan was agreed upon; the State Department would invite Iraqi officials to come to the United States for questioning. Not surprisingly, it never happened.

In April 1990, McKenzie wrote a lengthy prosecution memorandum that called for the indictment of five BNL employees, two middlemen, and six Iraqis. It made brief mention of Wafai Dajani but suggested that any charges against him be deferred to an eventual second phase of her investigation. The same suggestion was made for Matrix Churchill, which McKenzie believed she could separate out from the first half of her probe.

Once again, the issue of Iraqi complicity in the BNL affair proved politically sensitive for the Bush administration. So inextricably was it bound to the question of whether to approve the second $500 million of CCC credits that senior officials at State and Agriculture were now spending time considering what normally would have been a wholly administrative decision. On April 17, Robert Kimmitt suggested to Baker that the United States halt the second $500 million—less because of BNL than as a signal to Saddam of the administration's growing displeasure at his behavior, especially in the area of nuclear proliferation.

That same week, a team of Agriculture inspectors was in Baghdad for what was supposed to be a major investigation of the CCC program; it was the trip that McKenzie had declined to join. They returned bubbling with enthusiasm at the level of Iraqi cooperation they had received. They dismissed the kickbacks as merely minor violations of the government credits program and claimed there was insufficient evidence of Iraqi complicity in the BNL case. Ambassador Glaspie sent a cheery cable back to Baker reporting that the discussions had been "very open and coopera-tive" and that the U.S. delegation had been shown copies of all documents it requested. "Concerning after-sales service issue," wrote Glaspie, using the polite term for kickbacks, a certain Farouk al-Obaidi, Iraq's deputy minister of trade, had promised to end the practice.

While in Baghdad, the Agriculture officials had found some time to socialize, and at a cocktail party they ran into Wafai Dajani. Dajani was as cooperative as the Iraqis, and he even informed the Agriculture officials that BNL's Rome headquarters had known about and authorized the loans to Baghdad that Christopher Drogoul had made. That was a helpful piece of information, and it was passed on to Gale McKenzie and her colleagues in Atlanta. In order to follow up, the Atlanta prosecutor's office placed a call a few months later to Dajani's Georgetown residence. The woman who answered Dajani's phone said the Jordanian business-man was not in the United States and was traveling overseas.

When McKenzie heard about the Agriculture delegation's draft re-port, she bristled. On May 7, she dashed off a memorandum urging Thornburgh's aides at Justice to inform Agriculture in writing of the Iraqi "criminal violations" that she had found. But Justice was busy trying to run the Atlanta investigation from Washington. By then, other BNL investigators, such as those at the New York Fed, no longer made any

bones about the mounting difficulties in the BNL case, which according
to one memo were "compounded by what is perceived as interference
from the Justice Department in Washington." McKenzie fired a second
shot at Thornburgh's staff later in May 1990, when she heard that Justice
planned to approve the Agriculture delegation's report on the Iraqi situation. It contained inaccurate information, she wrote in a memorandum,
and worse, it would put the Justice Department "in a position of misleading Congress."

In Atlanta, McKenzie had come across enough of the BNL paper
trail and had gathered enough testimony to become convinced of Iraqi
criminal behavior. But the White House was getting nervous about making public any decision whatsoever on Iraq or BNL or the CCC program.
It was fairly clear to many in the Bush administration that the Iraqis had
been stealing from a U.S. government program. Yet Brent Scowcroft, the
national security adviser to the president, continued to be reluctant to
alienate Baghdad. On May 18, 1990, Scowcroft telephoned Agriculture
secretary Clayton Yeutter and asked him "not to put out any press release
today saying we are terminating the program." A special review would
have to be held at the White House before any announcement could be
made about the U.S. credits for Saddam, he told Yuetter. Scowcroft and
his own deputy, Robert Gates, thereby bumped the issue up to White
House-level meetings. "We would be shooting ourselves in the foot," said
Scowcroft's men when the issue of canceling the second $500 million
came up at a meeting in the White House Situation Room convened on
May 29 to discuss U.S.-Iraqi programs and policy options.

In preparation for that meeting, Gale McKenzie, Arthur Wade, and
other Atlanta colleagues were brought to Washington and asked to provide a special briefing on the case. That morning, McKenzie met with
officials from State and a special guest—Nicholas Rostow, the White
House lawyer who served Scowcroft on the NSC. For a local prosecutor
to discuss the details of a criminal investigation with a White House
official, there had to be a very special reason. There was—and it concerned the politics of the Bush administration's relations with Baghdad.
Rostow's own memorandum of the meeting, which he promptly gave to
Robert Gates, quoted McKenzie as saying she planned to indict six Iraqi
officials in the BNL case; this was what she had already told Justice weeks
before. The meeting in the White House Situation Room took the issue
up that very day. It was chaired by Gates and attended by senior officials
from the CIA, State, Commerce, Defense, and Agriculture and by a
representative from the Joint Chiefs of Staff. When the issue of

McKenzie's findings came up, it was clear that the facts could no longer be ignored. The meeting decided simply to advise Baghdad that the United States would not go forward with the $500 million of remaining farm credits until the investigation in Atlanta was completed.

Further complicating the BNL investigation was the fact that Robert Barr, McKenzie's boss, was about to leave his job. Barr, a former CIA employee who had worked for George Bush when Bush served as CIA director in the mid-1970s, admitted later that in the BNL case considerations of foreign policy had become entwined with those of law enforcement. The State Department, he said, got involved early on, and the case soon became "complex both legally and because of foreign policy concerns." William Hinshaw, the FBI special agent on the BNL task force at the time, later recalled that in the spring of 1990, "we were ready to go with the indictment, but Washington was holding things up and I still have no idea why."

MEANWHILE, back at Thornburgh's Department of Justice, there were new fears about another problem. It seemed that Henry Gonzalez, the outspoken Democratic congressman from Texas, was gearing up to launch a full-scale BNL investigation. The House Banking Committee, which Gonzalez chaired, was asking a string of embarrassing questions about the White House's policy toward Iraq and its consequences in the BNL affair.

By September 1990, while George Bush was sending U.S. troops over to the Saudi desert to stanch Saddam, Gonzalez announced he would hold congressional hearings on the BNL affair. The timing was very awkward from the administration's point of view. It came just as the administration was engineering a speedy 180-degree shift in its Iraqi policy. Saddam was no longer the privileged friend of George Bush and James Baker; he was now the enemy. As part of the shift, President Bush signed an executive order freezing Iraqi assets in the United States. Yet when the Treasury official in charge of preparing the list of Iraqi companies whose assets were frozen was asked why certain known BNL-funded front companies had not been included, he demurred. "Can't talk about that. It's classified information," he replied.

There was, however, one prominent exception that he would discuss. U.S. Customs Service agents had been dispatched to Ohio to padlock the doors of Matrix Churchill, which was now publicly identified as an Iraqi front company, even if this was the same Matrix Churchill to which Baker had given his personal approval for exports to Baghdad a year before. The CIA had made the company's role in Saddam's arms network absolutely clear on many occasions and had been ignored—but that was last year. Now the Bush administration blasted Matrix Churchill for its role in "illegally acquiring critical weapons technology." As the White House was sounding the alarm about Saddam Hussein and the threat to Persian Gulf oil after Saddam invaded Kuwait, U.S. intelligence agents came forward to brief journalists as never before. Matrix Churchill, said one, "was brokering a whole host of things for the Iraqis, including the attempted purchase of entire turnkey factories and of fiber optics needed for their missile development sites."

The atmosphere in Washington had most definitely changed as America contemplated going to war, and the BNL affair now looked as though it could prove a major embarrassment for the Bush administration. Thus in September 1990, when Thornburgh learned that Henry Gonzalez was ready to hold hearings, he decided he had to move quickly to stop the BNL investigation. His staff prepared a briefing memo for the attorney general's telephone call to the stubborn Banking Committee chairman. "Our best attempt to thwart any further congressional inquiry by the House Banking Committee into this case is to have you contact Chairman Gonzalez directly," Thornburgh's legislative aide, Lee Rawls, wrote in that memo. But when the phone rang on September 25, 1990, Gonzalez declined to take Thornburgh's call. So a letter was drafted at the Justice Department. It went from Thornburgh to Gonzalez the next day.

"The purpose of this letter is to express my profound disappointment in your decision to ignore the strong objections of this Department in the Banca Nazionale del Lavoro matter," wrote Thornburgh. "I am similarly distressed by your refusal last evening to discuss the matter with me," he added. Thornburgh expressed powerful opposition to Gonzalez's plan to hold public hearings. He claimed the entire Atlanta investigation would be jeopardized. The most important reason he cited for stopping Congress was not, however, spelled out in great detail. "As you should be aware, this is a sensitive case with national security concerns," wrote Thornburgh. (See Appendix B, page 346.)

As if that weren't enough, Thornburgh's aides also had to contend with an extremely delicate situation in Atlanta. Congressional staffers working for Gonzalez were due to arrive from Washington to interview witnesses in the BNL affair. Gale McKenzie wanted to warn the witnesses not to speak with the staffers, but officials at Justice knew this was most certainly not the way to stop Gonzalez. A memo was hastily drafted by one of Thornburgh's top aides, suggesting that word be conveyed to McKenzie that under no circumstances should she advise, suggest, or imply to witnesses that they refuse to talk to anyone.

"If we have a valid reason to ask Congress to refrain from acting in a particular investigation, we tell the staff directly, and never try to block their investigation by chilling witnesses," the worried Justice Department official wrote. "If she [McKenzie] talks to those witnesses, the Congressional lead will be too hot for any but robots to handle." Then the Justice Department official added one line to the memo: "I thought that the U.S. Attorney's Office was under control now that Joe Whitley is in place?"

Joe Whitley, the man who was supposed to have McKenzie and the BNL team "under control," was a loyal friend of Thornburgh's. Thornburgh had chosen him to replace Robert Barr as the new U.S. attorney in Atlanta; he had been approved by President Bush and sworn in just three months before. Whitley became Gale McKenzie's boss, and the man who presumably would take charge of the BNL case, at a very interesting moment in the investigation; the more the Atlanta team examined the BNL case, the more some members were developing suspicions about the possible involvement of U.S. intelligence agents in the Iraqi loans saga. These suspicions were about to be set down in a formal request for a briefing at CIA headquarters in Langley, Virginia.

Whitley's own background was almost as interesting as the BNL case itself. In the summer of 1989 he had stepped down from his position as acting associate attorney general of the United States, the third-ranking job in Dick Thornburgh's Department of Justice, and moved back to his native Atlanta to become a partner in the law firm of Smith, Gambrell & Russell. Shortly after joining the firm, Whitley took on a most unusual corporate client with both British and American operations. The client was none other than Matrix Churchill.

As lawyer to the Iraqi-owned company, Whitley's task was twofold—to defend Matrix Churchill from any criminal charges McKenzie might bring, and to threaten BNL's Rome headquarters with a lawsuit in order to make sure the bank paid out money it had promised to Matrix Churchill as part of its funding of exporters shipping goods to Iraq. By December 1989, Whitley had written, signed, and formally lodged the legal action against BNL, demanding it make good on Drogoul's promises of credit to Matrix Churchill.

In April 1990, after consulting with the White House, Thornburgh named the thirty-nine-year-old Whitley to the job in Atlanta. He started on June 1. The U.S. attorney's office in Atlanta was investigating Matrix

Churchill at the same time, and on June 8 Whitley wrote a memorandum to McKenzie stating that "although it could be argued that there is no conflict of interest in my continued involvement, I believe it is appropriate to recuse myself and reevaluate this decision as the case progresses." Thus it made no sense when Thornburgh's deputy added that line to his memo on September 21, 1990: "I thought that the U.S. Attorney's office was under control now that Joe Whitley is in place?" By then, Whitley was supposed to be out of the case.

Reflecting on this development, Bob Mueller said later that "it would have been nice to know" about Whitley's work on behalf of Matrix Churchill. An aide to Mueller put it more bluntly to William Safire of *The New York Times:* "Whitley's recusal came as a shock to me and a shock to Bob Mueller. We were looking forward to a U.S. Attorney who could oversee this operation, and it was disappointing."

Whitley's decision to have nothing to do with the BNL case in the summer of 1990 seemed clear enough. But on February 15, 1991, Justice Department officials in Washington noted that details of the BNL indictment, now scheduled to be announced on February 28, might have to be "readdressed via Joe Whitley." Clearly, there was some confusion at Justice about Whitley's status.

THERE WAS ONE more item that Dick Thornburgh neglected to mention at his BNL press conference on February 28, 1991, and it concerned the pressure that James Baker's State Department had applied on behalf of both the Iraqi Central Bank and Wafai Dajani, the Jordanian middleman in the BNL affair.

In 1990, McKenzie and her team had prepared a list of six Iraqi officials who were suspected of complicity in the BNL affair; by February 1991, the Atlanta team's list of those to be indicted had been pared down to four Iraqis, plus Dajani. Also ready for indictment were Rafidain Bank, the state-owned Iraqi commercial bank, and the Central Bank of Iraq. At the last minute, Thornburgh had Mueller send the list of proposed indictments over to the State Department; that was the normal procedure in cases that could have implications for U.S. foreign policy. At that time Operation Desert Storm was still raging; indeed, General Schwarzkopf had begun his ground war. It was hard to imagine any objections State might have to indicting Iraqis at a time when Iraq was the enemy of the United States.

But there were objections. Baker's aides at State took a look at the proposed indictments and decided almost immediately that there were problems. "One guy was dead, this Taha, or at least we thought so," a senior aide to Baker later recalled. "As for the Central Bank of Iraq, we thought that would cause trouble because we might have to work with them after the war," he added.

Just days before President Bush ordered the cease-fire with Iraq, Baker's deputy Robert Kimmitt approved sending a memorandum on the list of proposed indictments to the Justice Department. Prepared by State Department aides, the memo said that the department formally objected to the indictment of the Central Bank of Iraq—even though Justice officials had argued that a criminal indictment would mean the United States could sequester $1.5 billion of Iraqi assets in the United States, which was about the same as the amount of money lost in the wake of the BNL Atlanta scandal. The indictment was a bad idea, said State, because the Iraqi Central Bank was a government agency that had sovereign immunity. State had even consulted with the British government, which agreed. The British "believe criminal immunity is absolute," the memo informed Justice. Moreover, there were "foreign policy implications." McKenzie would object to the quashing of the indictment, Baker's aides noted, but State's sense was that Justice "is prepared to acquiesce, as long as we and other agencies and departments object in writing and as long as someone (probably the State Department) is willing to carry the argument with Representative Gonzalez."

The issue of whether to indict the Iraqi Central Bank had been taken up by some of President Bush's top aides as well. Nicholas Rostow, the legal counsel at the National Security Council, was consulted, as was Robert Gates. "Don't indict them. Just destroy them," joked Gates.

The memorandum did not object in formal terms to the indictment of any individuals, and Baker's staff was relieved to see that, contrary to previous reports, Saddam's son-in-law "is not on the list." As for the mysterious Sadik Taha, the State Department took the view that he was "reliably reported to have died in London," but noted that "Justice says his death is unconfirmed." After Taha's body was reported to have been buried in Baghdad, "our former ambassador called on his widow and found her sincerely grief-stricken." So much for Mr. Taha.

Although Baker's legal advisers had not objected to the indictment of individuals, they did single out one man for special mention. He was Wafai Dajani, who had worked with Drogoul, Sadik Taha, the U.S.

embassy, and intelligence operatives from Washington. Baker's aides wrote a strange disclaimer about this prospective defendant in the memorandum: "Wafai Dajani is a Jordanian businessman, not a government official. His brother is a former Minister of the Interior, and Wafai himself is considered well connected to the King and to U.S. grain exporters. His indictment would be seen as a further U.S. attempt to 'punish' Jordan."

The reference to having already punished Jordan, as an angry Henry Gonzalez would later explain, was to the State Department's public expression of displeasure at the fact that Jordan had sided with Saddam Hussein and against the United States in Operation Desert Storm. By referring to Dajani's closeness to King Hussein, State implied that the indictment would be a personal affront to the king of Jordan. It also underscored the equivocal manner in which George Bush and James Baker handled their rapport with the king.

The communication from the State Department had its desired effect. The Justice Department scrambled to draft and redraft the BNL indictment. The first press release in February 1991 described a 516-count indictment against twelve defendants. Then it was rewritten as a 425-count indictment against eleven defendants. What Thornburgh finally unveiled on February 28, 1991, was a 347-count indictment against ten defendants.

Missing from the indictment were the Central Bank of Iraq and Wafai Dajani, whose status was reduced to that of an unindicted coconspirator, and an anonymous one at that. His name did not appear anywhere in the materials handed out at the Justice Department and would not emerge publicly for many months.

YEARS LATER, when a reflective Prime Minister Giulio Andreotti was asked about Rome's involvement in the scandal, he replied that "the really important question to ask is who in the bank knew." As the BNL case went forward in the wake of Operation Desert Storm and became a major political controversy in Washington, no single issue was more important than the Bush administration's repeated assertion that Rome was the *victim* and not a *participant* in the Iraqi loans affair.

What was really happening, however, was that the Italians were lobbying Washington in a hundred different ways to make sure that BNL, an Italian government entity, would not be indicted. As a close friend of Joe Whitley's in Atlanta remarked, "The folks representing BNL did a very good job of directing the U.S. government, and the prosecutors fell for it."

Right from the start of the BNL scandal, when George Bush and James Baker were continuing to press for U.S. financial and technology aid to Saddam in spite of evidence of Iraqi complicity, the issue of Rome's involvement was a sensitive matter. Italy was a NATO ally and had a talent for keeping on good terms with Washington.

Certain facts, however, pointed directly at Rome's involvement. As soon as the scandal erupted in the autumn of 1989, the State Department received a disturbing report from Joseph Wilson at the U.S. embassy in Baghdad. The confidential cable reported that an embassy source with "intimate ties" to the Italian embassy in Baghdad had informed Wilson that "the Italian embassy is under strong suspicion of complicity in the BNL financial scandal."

That diplomatic cable was one of many reports available to the White House and State Department on Rome's alleged role in the Iraqi loans saga. From September 1989 until Dick Thornburgh announced the BNL indictments in February 1991, at least six U.S. intelligence reports that were widely disseminated inside the Bush administration either suggested that BNL's Rome headquarters knew of the Atlanta loans to Iraq or stated it point-blank.

In Rome, after BNL's former chairman, Nerio Nesi, and director-general, Giacomo Pedde, were ousted in 1989, the new chairman, a close friend of former Prime Minister Bettino Craxi named Giampiero Cantoni, grew increasingly worried about the Atlanta investigation. Cantoni wanted to make sure BNL was not indicted; he believed in the theory of Drogoul having been a lone wolf. So did Guido Carli, the treasury minister who exercised formal control over the Italian government bank. On October 19, 1989, Cantoni strolled out of BNL headquarters on the Via Veneto, crossed the street, and walked into the American embassy. He went straight to the office of Peter Secchia, the Michigan lumber tycoon whom George Bush had named as his new ambassador to Rome.

Cantoni expressed his concerns about the BNL Atlanta case and suggested to the U.S. ambassador that the matter should be raised "to a political level." Secchia reported back to James Baker that the BNL chairman had indicated the bank's desire to cooperate fully with U.S. government authorities "while making it fairly clear they want to achieve some kind of damage control." (See Appendix B, page 347.) At the same time, Secchia noted, Treasury Minister Carli was trying to block an effort by the Italian Senate to open an investigation of the BNL affair.

The bank and the Italian government were thus taking parallel action. In effect, Rome had started its own cover-up. George Bush and

James Baker, although mainly preoccupied with their relations with Iraq, were kept up to date on how the Italians were reacting to the BNL matter. Less than three weeks after Cantoni had approached Secchia, the CIA informed the White House and State Department that the scandal had already become a major political embarrassment in Rome that could bring down the government. But the CIA also noted that Rome "appears pleased at the low-key manner in which Washington has reacted."

That may have been so, but members of the Rome bank's own task force on Atlanta, who spent long hours each day examining thousands of pages of telexes and loan records, were exhausted and frequently furious with Cantoni. "We kept getting demands to pay out millions of dollars that Drogoul had promised. One day it was Matrix Churchill. The next day it was General Motors or Mobil. We knew by then that many of the exports we were financing were going into Iraqi military projects, but the orders were to keep paying and keep quiet," complained one of the harried task force bankers at BNL Rome.

Then, for reasons that escaped the comprehension of these lower-level employees, the ubiquitous Wafai Dajani turned up in Rome and began discussing the Atlanta loans with senior BNL officials. "There was no doubt in our minds," a former BNL executive later recalled, "that when we met with Dajani he was representing the Iraqis." BNL officials such as Pierdomenico Gallo, the head of the Rome bank's task force on Atlanta, were brought into meetings with Dajani, but Gallo and his staff wanted to sue Baghdad for fraud rather than suffer through conversations with the Jordanian middleman. They were given little choice. The Italian government, in the person of Treasury minister Carli, had a different priority. "Carli considered Iraq to be a friend of Rome's because Iraq was a friend of Washington's. So we were ordered to follow the government policy even though the loans were bogus and the end-users were Iraqi military installations. It was terrible," complained one BNL man who eventually left the bank in disgust.

By the end of 1989, however, Dajani was no longer needed as an intermediary between Baghdad and BNL. A more direct line of communication had been established. Iraq was threatening to default on billions of dollars of debts it owed to a variety of Italian state-owned and private companies unless the Italian government ordered BNL to make good on all the Atlanta loan commitments. More than $500 million of such loans had still not been disbursed. Faced with this threat, the government decided it had to make a deal with Baghdad, even if that required the approval of Prime Minister Andreotti himself.

On the morning of December 6, 1989, Andreotti called in his treasury minister for a talk. Andreotti was extremely well briefed on the BNL affair and had in fact already received a top secret report from SISMI, the Italian military intelligence service, confirming that BNL money had financed Iraq's Condor II missile project using exports from around the world, including several Italian companies.

The prime minister, who wanted to maintain good relations with Baghdad, asked Carli to meet with the Iraqi finance minister, who was on a visit to Rome, and then brief BNL's top management on the decisions taken. That same evening, Carli sat down with the Iraqi minister, professed the continuing friendship between Rome and Baghdad, and listened politely as the Iraqi minister declared the Atlanta loans to be "totally legitimate." It was time for the remaining funds to be paid out, said the Iraqi. The meeting ended with both sides agreeing on the need for a political solution.

The next day, Carli informed the chairman of BNL of the meeting. For once, the normally bureaucratic machinery of Rome had functioned efficiently. A few days later, Carli went before the Italian parliament and announced that it was clear that Rome had been involved in a number of the BNL Atlanta transactions on behalf of Iraq. In Langley, Virginia, a CIA analyst following the BNL case read about the statement and filed a classified report confirming Carli's conclusion.

What Carli did not say to the parliament, however, was that a secret decision had been made in Rome to give the Iraqis the funds they were demanding. "We were obligated, in banking and legal terms," Andreotti would later claim.

The decision took only a few weeks to implement. On December 26, 1989, a delegation from BNL was sent to meet Iraqi officials in Tunis. "The meeting lasted two days, but it was the weirdest experience of my life," recalled a BNL executive who was part of the delegation. "An agreement had already been reached between our governments that would validate all the rotten loans made by Atlanta. We didn't like it, but we were told to pay out another $500 million of the money. So we sat there, virtually in silence, with the Iraqis for two days. The deal had already been done. There was little aside from details to negotiate."

"The most important element of the Tunis negotiations," wrote Paolo Di Vito, the BNL executive who was assigned to deal with both the political and the financial repercussions of the Atlanta scandal and who began keeping a daily diary that would ultimately run to hundreds of pages, "was the Iraqi decision to place the controversy with BNL clearly and unequivocally in the total picture of the complex Italo-Iraqi relation-ship."

The deal was formalized at an elaborate signing ceremony in Ge-neva early in 1990. It became known in Rome and Washington as the "Geneva accord." Baghdad had been dealt with, even if that had meant Rome's giving in to blackmail. Now the real problem was coming from Atlanta, where the criminal investigation led by Gale McKenzie was still under way.

CHAIRMAN CANTONI'S WORST fears about the American investigation indicting BNL seemed to be on the point of materializing. Early in January 1990, one of BNL's lawyers in Atlanta called Di Vito in Rome with some important news: McKenzie, it seemed, had told the lawyer that Drogoul planned to charge that BNL management had been aware of all the Atlanta branch activities.

Action was required by Rome, and fast. The bank made available a handful of executives from among its ranks and asked them to talk to McKenzie, who was finding it hard to get approval to travel to Rome. Then Di Vito himself went to Atlanta, and on the morning of February 8, 1990, he spent nearly four hours with McKenzie. After this meeting he was able to report back to Rome with some better news. Di Vito said in his report that he and McKenzie had discussed the case "with the principal aim of solidifying BNL's role as victim in the affair and to confute the expected charges against BNL from Drogoul's defenders."

But one month later, on March 6, Di Vito saw the pendulum swing-ing the wrong way again. Once again, BNL's lawyers in Atlanta were hearing that the bank itself might be charged with involvement in the scandal. Di Vito informed the chief executive of BNL that "the situation seems to be sliding from the original technical-legal context to a more markedly political one." That evening, while Di Vito was noting these observations in Rome, Prime Minister Giulio Andreotti was in Washing-ton with President Bush, attending a state dinner at the White House that included guests such as Frank Sinatra, Elizabeth Taylor, and Lee Iacocca. Earlier that day, as part of his visit to Washington, Andreotti had met with Attorney General Richard Thornburgh. The two had discussed a range of issues, and Thornburgh was more than ready for the Italian prime minis-ter when it came to the Iraqi loans controversy; his briefing papers had included a review of the status of the BNL investigation.

Whatever Andreotti and his American hosts may have actually discussed, however, it did not get BNL off the hook. A week after he left Washington, the most senior executives of BNL sat together at their Via Veneto headquarters bemoaning the fact that Thornburgh's deputies at Justice seemed unwilling to accept McKenzie's thesis that BNL Rome was an innocent victim in the affair. As a result, Di Vito wrote in his daily diary, steps would need to be taken to make the Italian government and the Foreign Ministry aware of the problem.

Life for Paolo Di Vito was now becoming a battle against time zones and stress. His previous employment—as a division executive at the Milan branch of Citibank until 1988—seemed a sinecure by comparison. His job at BNL—handling the Atlanta affair—meant that on any given day he was in touch with people in America, Europe, and Iraq. He darted from Baghdad to Rome and then on to Atlanta with utter disregard for jet lag. And every day he noted down the latest developments, so that BNL's top management could follow the events in the Atlanta affair. His highest priority, however, was finding a political solution that would stop BNL from being indicted in the United States.

On Friday, March 16, 1990, Di Vito briefed Raniero Vanni d'Archirafi, a senior aide to Italian foreign minister Gianni Di Michelis, on the BNL case and made plain "the consequent opportunity to intervene discreetly on a political level, through our ambassador in Washington, who is already abreast of the situation." Then Di Vito contacted Daniel Serwer, a top-ranking diplomat at the American embassy in Rome. He laid out the problem. The political campaign was now in full swing.

Vanni d'Archirafi reacted speedily to the BNL call for help. Within hours of the briefing, he was in touch with Rinaldo Petrignani, Italy's ambassador to the United States. Petrignani, who was on a visit to Rome, was called into Vanni's office. "What worries us is that the bank might be indicted. It would make a very bad impression," the ambassador was told.

The following Monday, before he returned to do battle in Washington, Ambassador Petrignani was summoned to another meeting by an even higher-ranking official: the chief of staff to the foreign minister. The ambassador was given three pages of notes on the BNL affair and told that the Italian government was worried that Drogoul might point the finger at the bank. "The foreign minister is personally concerned," said the chief of staff. "He cares about this very much."

So did Prime Minister Andreotti. "This is a bank that belongs to the Treasury Ministry," he explained later, when asked why Petrignani had been instructed to lobby the American government.

The Italian ambassador flew back to Washington on March 20, 1990, his mission clear. His government had told him to use his contacts in the Bush administration to make certain that BNL was not indicted. And Petrignani had plenty of contacts, having served as Italy's envoy to Washington for nearly a decade. Within twenty-four hours of his return, he had secured a meeting at the Department of Justice with three of Thornburgh's top aides—Robin Ross, chief of staff to the attorney general; Edward Dennis, head of the criminal division; and Mark Richard, a deputy assistant attorney general with special responsibility for the BNL case. Petrignani informed the Justice officials that for the United States to bring an indictment against BNL "would add insult to injury." The reply he received was reassuring. "Why worry now? There won't be any surprises," said Ross, adding that the Justice Department was tracking the case very closely.

The strategy "of taking advantage of access at political levels appears more promising," commented Paolo Di Vito, when he was briefed on the ambassador's meeting in Washington.

Petrignani kept the strategy going. On March 27 he attended a luncheon in the East Room of the White House, where he spotted Dick Thornburgh. He approached Thornburgh to raise the issue of BNL and told him he had just discussed the BNL case with Robin Ross and others at Justice. "The attorney general promised to treat the issue with absolute fairness," Petrignani said, recalling the conversation. Although Petrignani remembered the encounter clearly, Thornburgh did not, saying later that he had no "recollection" of the conversation.

At four o'clock that same afternoon, Petrignani carried his campaign to the State Department, where he met with Abraham Sofaer, the legal adviser to James Baker. The tone of that meeting, Di Vito informed Rome, "was decidedly more political." Sofaer told the Italian ambassador that BNL's lawyers should go directly to the Department of Justice to make their case. When Petrignani left the State Department, Sofaer informed Robert Kimmitt of "serious government of Italy concern over the possible federal indictment of the state-owned BNL."

Ambassador Petrignani then telephoned Chairman Cantoni in Rome to brief him on the efforts he had been making. Cantoni asked for help in finding some high-powered Washington lawyers.

On April 4, 1990, Di Vito flew to Washington, where he and Petrignani discussed a new legal strategy. At nine o'clock the next morning Petrignani accompanied Di Vito and a team of BNL lawyers from Rome and Atlanta to the law offices of Rogers & Wells, where they sat down with William Rogers, who had been Richard Nixon's first secretary of state.

Rogers said he would take the case, but he suggested that his firm be named as legal counsel to *both* BNL and the Italian government.

The no-holds-barred campaign waged by BNL and the Italian government would ultimately have its desired effect. At the end of May 1990, after two months of insistent lobbying, Di Vito received a call from Atlanta and was told that Gale McKenzie had just returned from Washington and informed BNL it was no longer a target of indictment. "We were all much more tranquil at that point," recalled a former Italian government official.

In Rome, however, Chairman Cantoni was not taking any chances. In July he collared Ambassador Secchia again, this time during a function in northern Italy. As Secchia reported to James Baker, Cantoni "expressed once more his concern over the ongoing investigation of the BNL-Atlanta branch's Iraqi loans." And then: "He made a pitch for the U.S. government to go slowly before making indictments."

The Italian strategy might have seemed potentially risky because of overkill, but it worked: The Bush administration did not indict BNL. The Italian Senate finally began its own investigation. Petrignani retired from the diplomatic service in 1991 and was offered a comfortable position in Washington. He went to work for Rogers & Wells, where he had the opportunity to be particularly helpful in advising the law firm's client, BNL.

When asked later if Rome had exerted improper pressure on the BNL case, Boyden Gray, President Bush's White House lawyer, said he didn't know. He was guarded in his response to the question. "If there was any pressure brought to bear not to press a prosecution," said Gray, "that is bad. That would be a proper subject for criminal investigation. The U.S. attorney in Atlanta wanted to expand the investigation and wanted to indict the Italians. The decision not to indict was made at the Department of Justice."

AT THE TIME when Thornburgh announced the BNL indictments in February 1991, the White House had good reason to be satisfied at its handling of Saddam Hussein. The war was over, and President Bush's approval ratings were higher than ever before. The Atlanta prosecutors had finished their job, and it looked to the outside world as though the main perpetrator was an obscure branch manager named Christopher Drogoul. The Central Bank of Iraq had escaped indictment, thanks to the intervention of the State Department. So had Wafai Dajani. So had Italy's state-owned bank. Those who questioned the U.S. government's handling of the scandal were told they did not possess the facts.

But the high spirits did not last; Thornburgh had been unable to resolve the chronic problem of Henry Gonzalez. Congressional Democrats, led by Gonzalez, were becoming increasingly vocal in their attempts to expose what they claimed was a secret White House policy on Iraq, a policy that was now being hidden through a cover-up of the Iraqi loans scandal. More than three weeks before the indictments were unveiled, Gonzalez had complained publicly of "substantial and formidable obstruction" of his BNL investigation by the Federal Reserve and the Justice Department. He had charged for the first time that U.S. intelligence had allowed the BNL loans to go ahead as part of Washington's tilt to Iraq.

Many in the White House had dismissed Gonzalez as a "flake" who would not be taken seriously. But on February 21, he made the second in a series of extraordinarily detailed statements about the BNL affair on the floor of the House of Representatives. He warned that "our boys" could face death or serious bodily harm in the Persian Gulf as a result of missiles or chemical weapons that had been funded and paid for by U.S. businesses and guaranteed by the American taxpayer.

He revealed that he had issued subpoenas for Federal Reserve documents and had been told by the Fed that the documents were being withheld at the request of the Justice Department. "We are obstructed blatantly, premeditatedly and coldly," charged Gonzalez, "and in defiance of the plain constitutional prerogative of the Congress to know."

That was a serious allegation. And Gonzalez was proving too specific and too well-documented to be dismissed as a flake for much longer. Other members of Congress and other committees were joining him in his demands for government documents. Chief among these was Sam Gejdenson, chairman of a House Foreign Affairs subcommittee whose investigation was going beyond the BNL affair and directly to suspicions that for the past decade the White House had played a role in providing arms to Iraq.

On the same day that Gonzalez spoke, Stephen Bryen, a former deputy undersecretary of defense for trade security policy, went before a House subcommittee and revealed that military items had been shipped to Iraq, even though "legitimate objections were made and clear-cut national security information provided, not only by the Defense Department, but by intelligence agencies." Bryen pointed his finger directly at the White House, disclosing that Brent Scowcroft's National Security

Council had pressed him in his official capacity to be "more forthcoming" and approve some of the riskier exports.

A few days later, the Bush administration released a list of $1.5 billion in technology and equipment that had been sold to Iraq, including items that might have helped Baghdad's nuclear missile projects. But one official, speaking only on the condition that he not be named, downplayed the importance of the list. "This is the post-mortem on Iraq. Everyone's going to be more careful in future," he said.

The new political strategy of conceding that mistakes had been made in the past did not work; instead, it only invited more probing by Congress. Embarrassing revelations about the Bush administration's dealings with Iraq kept on coming. One day a list of Iraqi front companies would be published, leading congressional and media investigators to discover that a number of the companies were BNL-funded. Another day, U.S. Customs agents would seize a helicopter in Texas and claim that Carlos Cardoen, the Chilean arms dealer, was modifying it on behalf of Iraq. Suddenly Cardoen, who had once served American covert aims so effectively, was being vilified by the Bush administration for his role in arming Iraq. But Dan Pettus, a Texas-based business partner of Cardoen's, went public, claiming that "the Commerce Department, the State Department, FBI and CIA and everybody in the U.S. government has known since 1988 that we were hired by Mr. Cardoen."

Stanching the campaign by the media and Congress was proving a difficult task for the Bush administration. In the press, William Safire of *The New York Times* led the charge by suggesting that Ambassador April Glaspie was being made a scapegoat by James Baker because "the Bush-Baker policy was appeasement of the dictator." Neither Bush nor Baker came to Glaspie's defense; instead, they allowed her to be pilloried for allegedly having been so weak and indecisive back in July 1990 that she had somehow single-handedly given Saddam the green light to invade Kuwait. In the jargon of tough Washington politics, Glaspie was being "hung out to dry."

The White House itself was receiving numerous congressional demands for documents concerning prewar U.S. dealings with Iraq. As these poured in from Capitol Hill, George Bush and his advisers grew concerned that the aura of victory in Operation Desert Storm was beginning to fade. In short, it was time to hold the line.

The president got conflicting advice from his closest associates. Brent Scowcroft argued strongly in favor of claiming executive privilege and not allowing any documents to be released. James Baker, as one White House official put it, "wanted to let the documents go and hope it would look like we had nothing to hide."

There were, however, some very sensitive interests at stake. The real story of how George Bush had made helping Iraq a paramount priority, both as vice president in the Reagan administration and as president from 1989 onward, still remained a state secret. NSD 26, with Bush's signature on it, was still classified, as were the minutes of top-level meetings in 1989 that had brushed aside evidence of criminal Iraqi behavior in order to hand Baghdad another $1 billion in loan guarantees.

The details of James Baker's dealings with Tariq Aziz were contained in still-classified cables at the State Department. So were thousands of pages of other documents that could, at a minimum, prove politically embarrassing. CIA reports on BNL, and State Department memos proving that Washington had kept Iraq off the terrorist list even though it knew Abu Nidal's group was operating in Baghdad, could even show that the Bush administration had followed neither its own policies nor the law. The CIA had a legal obligation to pass along evidence of wrongdoing to law enforcement agencies; if it had not done so in the BNL case, then the CIA had broken the law. Likewise, the State Department was obligated to name states that supported terrorism if it possessed such evidence; officials were not supposed to be able to simply forget they had seen the evidence and do nothing.

Action was needed, and it came from the White House in April 1991. But the solution that the NSC decided upon would make matters far worse. It would trigger still more accusations that the White House had acted to obstruct both justice and the Congress of the United States. That, however, was not the way the emergency action was perceived in April 1991, when Nicholas Rostow, the top legal adviser to Brent Scowcroft, set in motion a most unusual and elaborate mechanism.

THIRTEEN

The White House Steers the Cover-Up

O n the morning of Monday, April 8, 1991, a half-dozen government lawyers filed into a conference room on the third floor of the Old Executive Office Building, next to the White House. Seated around a long table, they listened to Nicholas Rostow, special assistant to President Bush and legal adviser to the National Security Council. The lawyers, from the Pentagon, the State and Commerce departments, were soon joined by presidential counsel Boyden Gray.

Gray remembered the session as the first of a dozen "fairly straightforward meetings" designed to coordinate a unified response to the multiple congressional requests for documents pertaining to the Bush administration's Iraqi policy prior to Saddam's August 1990 invasion of Kuwait. In fact, these meetings, set up by the White House, would later come to be seen as a secret task force whose brief was to *constrain* access to those documents.

By the time Gray, Rostow, and their associates left the third-floor conference room, there was little that was straightforward in what they had agreed to. The lawyers had been grappling with a tableful of congressional requests that included a letter to Brent Scowcroft seeking a copy of National Security Directive 26. This was a sensitive matter—a secret document that bore the signature of George Bush. "Stiff-arming," a State Department official who was present recorded in his notes of the meeting, "won't work." The best approach was to be "proactive," to take the offensive.

Later that day, on the letterhead of the National Security Council, Rostow wrote a memorandum setting down the results of the discussion.

After reviewing the requests for information on U.S. policy toward Iraq, the group had decided on a plan of action that would create multiple hurdles for any member of Congress who wished to obtain documents. (See Appendix B, page 350.) Step one was to try to block all requests for Iraq-related documents on the basis of executive privilege. The government lawyers were even given sample grounds for justifying such a move; among these samples were "deliberative process," "foreign relations," and the inevitable "national security." Next, Rostow reminded State, Defense, Treasury, Agriculture, Commerce, Justice, and the CIA to seek "alternatives to providing documents." Before any member of Congress was given access to documents, such a recommendation would have to be "circulated to this group for clearance." And finally, the Rostow group decided that even if access to documents were to be allowed, no document could be retained by a member of Congress; only notes could be taken, and these themselves were to be marked as classified documents.

The mechanisms decided upon that day would mark the start of the most robust assertion of White House prerogatives since the days of Richard Nixon. Rostow dispatched the memo to the participants in the meeting and scheduled a second meeting the very next day in order to discuss requests pertaining to "the BNL/CCC matters." There was more work to be done.

On April 9, when the Rostow group reconvened, it had plenty to talk about, and not merely the Iraqi loans scandal. Overnight, the White House had identified a new fire that needed dousing. While the small group of lawyers had been meeting the day before, an embarrassing problem had developed in a hearing room on Capitol Hill. George Bush's chief of staff John Sununu was furious as a result.

The Commerce Department's top export official, Undersecretary Dennis Kloske, had gone before a subcommittee chaired by Congressman Sam Gejdenson and disclosed that the White House had disregarded his strong recommendations to stop the flow of advanced equipment to Baghdad just weeks before the August 2, 1990, Iraqi invasion of Kuwait. Kloske revealed that he had made clear his fears about the sensitive and militarily useful shipments "at the very highest levels." He had pressed the matter at White House meetings chaired by Robert Gates of the NSC and attended by Robert Kimmitt, the undersecretary of state, and he blamed the State Department for its "adamant" opposition to halting the sales to Iraq. After Kloske finished speaking, Gejdenson announced that the State Department was refusing to allow Kimmitt to testify before Congress.

Reaction to Kloske's bombshell—the first time a senior Bush administration official had broken ranks over Iraq—came swiftly. Word leaked from the White House that Sununu had ordered Kloske to be fired. If Kloske was criticizing James Baker's State Department, said one source, "it criticizes the President. Sununu just doesn't put up with that sort of thing." Marlin Fitzwater, the president's spokesman, confirmed that Kloske was leaving the government, but when asked if Sununu had fired him, Fitzwater was vague: "I don't think he did, but I don't know." Gejdenson went on the warpath. He called a press conference and accused the State Department of a deliberate attempt to mislead Congress. "Firing a government official because he was willing to tell the truth to Congress," said Gejdenson, "is an outrage and represents a bastardization of the way our government is supposed to work." Kloske was not quite the martyr the congressman made him out to be, but he had certainly become a political liability.

The Kloske revelations only heightened the sense of urgency at the White House and at the meeting next door of Rostow and his colleagues. Full disclosure of the documents being demanded would not only show George Bush's role in building up Saddam Hussein; it would illustrate the escalating objections that officials such as Kloske had lodged.

"It was really a scary thing," recalled Stephen Rademaker, a protégé of Boyden Gray's who worked as a deputy to Rostow and participated in several of the Rostow meetings. "There were these hearings on the Hill, and so these witnesses would all point the finger."

As the heat was turned up in Congress, the pace of the Rostow meetings quickened. Several aspects of these sessions, which continued for nearly four months, were highly unusual. "It is normal for government agencies to coordinate these things on occasion, but I suppose it was fairly unusual for the top lawyers at CIA, Defense, Commerce, and State and all of us others to meet, physically, face-to-face, for a dozen discussions over a period of several months," admitted one participant.

A State Department official who attended the sessions recalled there having been a "bunker mentality." A White House aide who took part in them said "there was a really high level of discomfort about this process. People were already suggesting a cover-up. Everybody was nervous. There was a lot of hand-wringing, and at times it was quite pathetic. We sat around, and we couldn't figure out what to do. Rostow couldn't agree on anything. He just kept scheduling more meetings."

This was not the first time that Charles Nicholas Rostow had stared controversy in the face and taken action to loyally defend a president of the United States. Now forty-one, he had already dealt with accusations

on subjects ranging from George Bush's relations with Panama's Manuel
Noriega to Ronald Reagan's role in the Iran-Contra affair.

Rostow's pedigree was sterling. Like George Bush, he was a Yalie,
with a bachelor's, a doctorate in history, and a law degree from New
Haven. His father was not only a former dean of the Yale Law School, he
was the famous Eugene Rostow who had served as undersecretary of state
under President Lyndon Johnson and had then moved far to the right in
the 1970s as a founding member and chairman of the hard-line consor-
tium of anti-Soviet zealots known as the Committee on the Present
Danger. It was from the Committee's ranks that Ronald Reagan and
George Bush had drawn such 1980s luminaries as William Casey, Caspar
Weinberger, and George Shultz. The elder Rostow had himself served in
the Reagan administration, working on arms-control issues.

From his father, Nicholas Rostow inherited both a penchant for
fancy bow ties and a tendency to veer to the Republican right. In 1985, he
began to learn about the world of White House secrets from the inside
when he was hired as a counsel to the Tower Commission, the much-
criticized panel that investigated the Iran-Contra scandal and took its
name from its chief, Senator John Tower of Texas.

This job had given Rostow a special feel for the covert ethic; his
prime responsibility had been to keep a detailed chronology of the White
House's arms sales to Iran. He ended up as one of the principal writers of
the commission's report. Like better-known members of the Tower panel
such as Brent Scowcroft, the young Rostow was rewarded with a White
House job offer after the Iran-Contra report was completed. The job, in
1987, was as the chief lawyer on the National Security Council. This
position seemed to get Rostow into several imbroglios rather quickly.

Rostow proved his abilities as a protector of George Bush in 1988.
He triggered congressional complaints of "stonewalling" when he drafted
a White House order instructing the CIA, State Department, and Pentagon not to provide documents or information to an investigation that was
examining knowledge that George Bush was alleged to have had of
Manuel Noriega's drug-dealings when Bush was CIA director. Rostow's
technique was to order a review by government lawyers of the congressional demands and then cite "important statutory and constitutional
issues" that prevented any cooperation.

Six months later, in early 1989, Rostow was in trouble again. This
time he had to express his "regret" to a congressional investigation for
having tried to intimidate a secretary who was scheduled to testify about
the conduct of John Tower, by then President Bush's struggling nominee

as secretary of defense. John Dingell, the congressman investigating Tower, accused Rostow of seeking to interfere with a congressional witness. It was, said Dingell, "a serious matter."

In reply, Rostow conceded he should have used "a lighter touch" on the secretary. As he saw it, the issue was one of loyalty to George Bush. "You have to understand," he had told the frightened woman, "that Tower is the President's nominee." A month after the episode, President Bush promoted Rostow to the status of special assistant to the president for national security affairs, while making sure he would also maintain his position as the NSC counsel.

It was in that job that Rostow and his group held off congressional investigators into U.S. policy toward Baghdad for several months. Each time the group convened, Rostow would go around the room and ask each department representative to report on written requests, subpoenas, threats of subpoenas, and telephone calls it had received from Congress. After discussing tactics, the group would then advise Boyden Gray, Brent Scowcroft, and the various departments on how to answer the requests. It seemed routine enough, but handwritten notes of the meetings told a tale of increasing concern, anger, and involvement by the occupant of the Oval Office.

"Political vulnerability" was the heading under which an Agriculture Department lawyer grouped a laundry list of problems with handing over documents to the Congress. During the meeting of Rostow's group on April 9, 1991, the Agriculture official noted that information on the BNL affair or the CCC program for Iraq could show there had been "inadequate administrative controls." Worse, the documents could show that "largely, we were feeding the Iraqi army."

At another meeting, on April 15, a Justice Department official posed the problem in starker terms. The chief objectives were to protect the president's notes, to protect the "higher-level thinking process," and "to control the process."

By the end of April, the need to maintain control had increased tenfold. Sam Gejdenson, Henry Gonzalez, and a handful of other members of the House and Senate were now involved in full-scale investigations of the Bush administration's Iraqi policy. Thousands of pages of documents had been requested. The minutes of the November 8, 1989, meeting that pushed through CCC credits for Iraq had begun leaking to the media. The White House had still not complied with the congressional requests, and the Rostow group had still not come up with a definitive solution.

Rostow and his peers became even more alarmed when they examined a subpoena from Congressman Gejdenson to Secretary of Commerce Robert Mosbacher for documents related to Commerce's dealings with the National Security Council and NSC deliberations concerning technology shipments to Iraq. The notes from one Rostow meeting that spring included a discussion of the "criminal liability" that Mosbacher might face as a result of his not complying with the subpoena. Solutions were needed, but the notes from that Rostow meeting illustrate the way the lawyers were thrashing about: "The Sec[retary] w[ou]ld have to appear—or run risk of contempt—or app[ear] w/o doc[ument]s—still run risk of contempt . . . able to say Pres directed him to withhold . . . no crim liab[ility] . . . U.S. Atty will not prosec[ute] when official w[ith]holds at dir of Pres on EP gr[ou]nds—then could go through Hse, vote citation of contempt . . . Then try to enf[orce] crim[e]—" (See Appendix B, pages 348–349.)

In early June 1991, Boyden Gray began to play a more prominent role in the Rostow group deliberations. As close a soulmate to George Bush as anyone except James Baker, Gray was both an ideologue and a firm believer in protecting the president, come what may.

On June 5, Gray lectured the Rostow group, stressing the importance of maintaining the institutional prerogatives of the presidency through the use of executive privilege where appropriate. He suggested bringing in cabinet officials "to see the President so we all know where the bottom line is." While some agencies could try and "cut a sensible deal in the middle," Gray told the group it needed "to make sure all agencies are making the same cut." In short, more coordination was needed, and at the level of the president.

"Doesn't it look bad for us all to be meeting together?" asked one of the nervous government lawyers. "Listen," Gray shot back, "this is the Executive Branch." After that meeting, Wendell Willkie, the top lawyer at the Commerce Department, reported back that "Counsel to the President C. Boyden Gray indicated this week that it may be necessary to have Cabinet-level discussions with the President of executive privilege issues raised by the request" for Iraq-related documents. Gray was becoming impatient with the Rostow discussions.

"I remember one of the meetings was held in Boyden's office," recalled a participant. "He asked to see the documents we had selected so he and the attorney general could go straight to the president and say these were the documents we want to protect. But instead everybody sat around arguing in front of Boyden. After thirty minutes Boyden got up and walked out."

Before long, George Bush began to play a personal role in the efforts to keep Congress from learning of his Iraqi policies. The sheer inability of Rostow's group to sort out the problem seemed to warrant Oval Office attention. The notes that were kept at the Rostow meetings confirmed that the president was being consulted on a regular basis. "Protect. Pres has decided to.," read one of the minutes. Then the lines were crossed out and replaced by the words "B.S. will review EP," a reference to Brent Scowcroft and the question of executive privilege. On another occasion, Stephen Rademaker was quoted reporting that "S to talk to Pres this AM." Other notes described conversations between Scowcroft and President Bush about specific documents that were being withheld. At this point there was a "heated discussion," and the president was described as "very very mad."

One participant depicted a major problem that George Bush and Brent Scowcroft faced in their deliberations: James Baker was out of step on some of the issues the Rostow group was trying to deal with. Several of those who were directly involved in the work of the NSC, the State Department, and the Commerce Department in reviewing documents for the Rostow group recalled that Scowcroft was a powerful proponent of exerting executive privilege. Baker, whose strategy was to curry favor with select members of Congress such as Dante Fascell of the House Foreign Affairs Committee, opposed executive privilege on the grounds that it would raise more suspicions about the content of the documents being withheld. Baker found himself at loggerheads with Scowcroft on several occasions. "Baker did not want to get into a shoot-out with Congress. He was trying to cut a deal that permitted some access, but on the basis of eyes only for members of Congress. Baker and Brent and the president had a set-to about it."

Boyden Gray could remember President Bush only becoming "involved personally in one decision." But three other officials involved in the Rostow meetings recalled both Scowcroft and Bush as being the driving force behind the efforts to keep Congress from gaining access to the Iraq-related documents. None of these participants were willing to be quoted by name.

"I don't want to be the on-the-record source for this, so don't use my name," said one of them. "But I can tell you that the president was made aware on several occasions of all this, and he talked with Brent extensively about it."

"The president," said another, "was interested in the subject and he was concerned about it as he read all these stories about our Iraq policy in the papers. He was worried about it."

Baker, Scowcroft, and Bush were unable to resolve the matter for many months, while the White House did its best to hold the line through bureaucratic inertia and special pleading with its friends on Capitol Hill. The entire process itself was exhausting for those involved, and it was also very stressful. "When you're a lawyer at the White House," said a weary Stephen Rademaker, "everything that comes through the in-box is a potential hand grenade." Nonetheless, the Rostow meetings proved highly effective in slowing down congressional investigations, and many of the documents, including NSD 26, were withheld for another year.

BUT THE GRENADES eventually did explode. The following year, when Henry Gonzalez learned of the White House meetings, he went before Congress and christened them "the Rostow gang." It used to be, said an angry Gonzalez, "that cover-ups were sort of ad hoc events, a mad scramble to provide damage control for the moment. The Rostow gang advances the notion that cover-up mechanisms have become an integral cog in the machinery of this administration."

Gonzalez was not the only member of Congress who felt that way. Among the documents that the Rostow group was reviewing were Commerce Department papers that related to a longstanding investigation of U.S. exports to Iraq. The probe had first been launched in 1990 by Doug Barnard, a Georgia Democrat who suspected that Bush administration officials had tampered with records of export licenses to Iraq before sending them to Congress in October of that year. In the spring of 1991, Barnard, the chairman of a House subcommittee on commerce, consumer, and monetary affairs of the House Committee on Government Operations, was becoming increasingly irritated. His staff was being told to discuss his requests for documents with the National Security Council instead of the Commerce Department.

On June 4, 1991, the inspector general of the Department of Commerce reporting to Secretary of Commerce Robert Mosbacher revealed an unusual piece of news. He had found that Commerce officials had changed information on sixty-eight of the export records that were provided to Barnard's subcommittee the previous October, removing all references to the military end-use that Iraq would make of the goods it received. In particular, the designation "military truck" was changed, on licenses having a total value of more than $1 billion. The inspector general concluded that the changes were "unjustified and misleading."

Barnard and his staff did not see the inspector general's report until July 1991, and they would have been furious if they had known of an earlier memorandum on the subject from Dennis Kloske to Wendell Willkie, the general counsel at Commerce who was participating in the Rostow meetings. Kloske informed Willkie in his February 26, 1991, memo that Commerce had prepared the computer printout of Iraqi licenses to reflect "White House guidance not to provide information that was not directly responsive to the chairman's request." (See Appendix B, page 351.)

The Commerce documents were only some of the many the Rostow group had to review during the spring and summer of 1991. The idea of achieving some kind of damage control over the body of material that became known internally as the "Iraq papers" continued apace. The bunker mentality at the White House contrasted sharply with the image of a victorious world leader that George Bush was projecting to the general public.

On June 10, more than two million New Yorkers turned out to watch the victory parade for Operation Desert Storm. The air was filled with ticker tape and ribbons as Generals Norman Schwarzkopf and Colin Powell waved to the crowds from vintage convertibles, flanked by Secretary of Defense Dick Cheney and Mayor David Dinkins. But back at the White House the atmosphere was decidedly different. While Schwarzkopf basked, the president was reading an intelligence report indicating that a substantial portion of Saddam's nuclear and chemical weapons capability remained intact. The information showed that three months after the end of the war, Iraq was continuing its efforts to develop these weapons. Worse, only three of the seven Iraqi nuclear weapons sites had been properly identified and targeted during allied bombings.

The report was contained in the *National Intelligence Digest,* a top secret daily summary distributed to the president and selected senior officials. It quoted both photographic evidence and a top-level Iraqi nuclear physicist who had just defected by driving out to a Marine checkpoint in Iraq and turning himself in.

Moreover, CIA and Pentagon officials reported that arms were once again being shipped into Iraq by way of Jordan, mainly in specially hollowed-out oil tanker trucks. "Wafai Dajani and others close to King Hussein were back in business within weeks of the end of Desert Storm," said a U.S. intelligence agent who tracked the shipments. "Nothing changed. They just started up the old network again."

By the summer, the Bush presidency was already sliding into the political quagmire from which it would not recover. On the domestic front, the troubled economy showed no sign of recovery; in fact, unemployment was rising, the banking system was shaken by a crisis in the real estate market, and consumer confidence was fading. In foreign policy, Washington seemed impotent in the face of the coup attempt against Mikhail Gorbachev and then undecided over what to do about the rise of Boris Yeltsin. In Baghdad, Saddam Hussein was increasingly defiant of the West, while opposition Kurds in the north of Iraq complained they had been let down by the White House. With the passage of time, George Bush's victory over Saddam Hussein seemed less and less of an achievement.

As if there were not enough headaches for the president, more cries of cover-up over his Iraqi policies were emanating from Congress and the media. No longer content to examine the records of the president and his secretary of state, critics and investigators were starting to focus on Robert Gates, a lower-profile but controversial figure. On May 10, 1991, Bush had nominated him to be the new CIA director, and Gates came under fire almost immediately. It was the second time Gates had been named to the job, and to a chorus of criticism. The first was in February 1987, and the criticism concerned suspicions that he had played an improper role in the Iran-Contra affair; it had forced him to withdraw his nomination. Now Bush was trying to put him in charge of the CIA again.

What the outside world did not yet know was that Gates—who in early 1989 had transferred from the CIA, where he had been deputy director, to the White House as President Bush's deputy national security adviser—had played a prominent role in the pro-Iraqi policy. He had played a decisive role when it came to allowing U.S. dual-use exports to go to Iraqi nuclear installations. Nor did those outside the White House know that the name of Robert Gates featured prominently in a number of the documents that Rostow and his fellow lawyers were in the midst of holding back from Congress.

Suspicions and charges that Gates knew of illegal off-the-books diversions of profits to Nicaraguan Contra rebels derived from the White House's sale of missiles to Iran still lingered. But there were new and surprising accusations from former CIA colleagues that Gates had distorted the intelligence process to provide politically slanted reports to the White House. What is more, there were new allegations concerning Gates and America's tortuous relations with Saddam Hussein. Within two weeks of his nomination, the media revealed that while Gates was CIA deputy director in the late 1980s, the Agency had known about James Guerin's illegal shipments of ballistic missile technology and other equipment to South Africa and had done nothing to stop it. Many of these shipments, government officials now acknowledged, had then gone on to Baghdad. Since the CIA had a legal obligation to pass such information to law enforcement authorities, critics wondered how Gates could have allowed the shipments to continue.

Then it was revealed that in 1988, while Gates was serving as a top CIA official, the Agency had been warned repeatedly that one of the prime contractors who had helped Libya's Colonel Moammer Qaddafi build his chemical weapons plant at Rabta was at work on a potential chemical weapons factory in Boca Raton, Florida. The CIA took no action, even though cyanide produced at the plant was later shipped to Iraq.

Finally, on July 12, a major television network reported the alleged involvement of Gates in the approval of cluster bomb and other arms shipments to Iraq by Carlos Cardoen, the Chilean arms dealer. The White House was livid, and after denying the report, it used informal channels to make sure its anger was known to the network.

In fact, before the report aired, a former CIA operative and friend of Gates had warned the journalists that they risked opening "a real can of worms" with their probe of Gates, Cardoen, and the transfer of cluster bomb technology to Iraq. "You've got a number of government officials pretty rattled about this. You might get them in trouble," he said.

Other Iraq-related charges against Gates had been piling up for weeks, and they only heightened criticism of Bush's Iraqi policy, which left the president seething. On the afternoon of Friday, July 12, Bush lost his temper while chatting with reporters in the yard of his seaside home in Kennebunkport. Wagging his finger at the reporters, he railed against those politicians who had questioned the suitability of Gates to be CIA director. "They ought not to accept a rumor. They ought not to panic and run like a covey of quail because somebody has made an allegation against a man whose word I trust." His voice rising, Bush let his frustration get the better of him: "What have we come to in this country where a man has to prove his innocence against some fluid, movable charge? . . . I just don't think it's the American way to bring a good man down by rumor and insinuation."

The controversy continued through the rest of the summer and

David Boren, chairman of the Senate Select Committee on Intelligence, launched his own probe, but in the autumn Gates managed to win Senate confirmation anyway. By that time most of Washington was distracted by a more sensational fracas involving the president's nomination of Clarence Thomas to be a Supreme Court justice.

By year's end, although congressional inquiries into BNL and the Iraq papers continued, the White House was able to enjoy a brief respite from the issue. Most Americans were preoccupied with their pocket-books, the problem of recession, and to a lesser extent the search for a Democratic nominee to run against George Bush in the 1992 presidential election.

Little attention was paid, for example, when in early 1992 the name of a prominent Florida lawyer began circulating in Miami as President Bush's choice to become the new U.S. attorney there. The lawyer in question, a politically active Republican named Roberto Martinez, had a problem, and it brought shivers to those in law enforcement agencies who had followed the BNL case still pending in Atlanta. Martinez, the man the White House wanted as the chief prosecutor in Miami, was defending a certain Carlos Cardoen against charges that he had broken U.S. export laws and sold cluster bombs to Iraq. A civil suit had already been filed against Cardoen and it seemed only a matter of time before a grand jury would decide criminal indictments for violating U.S. arms export laws. The intensive investigation of Cardoen was being led by the U.S. attorney's office in Miami. Now Cardoen's chief defense attorney was being chosen to run the investigation and prosecution of Cardoen.

Like Joe Whitley in Atlanta, who had defended a BNL-funded Iraqi front company before he was named to head the office in charge of the BNL prosecution, Martinez had a quick solution. He dropped Cardoen as a client and promised to avoid any conflict of interest. His appointment went through without any problem.

The White House respite ended in the spring of 1992, when it found it had to pay more attention to the BNL affair, which was back in the news. In April, an Italian Senate investigation concluded that the governments in both Rome and Washington had probably been involved in Christopher Drogoul's Iraqi loans. The Italian senators called the BNL affair an "international political operation" to support Iraq, and the news traveled quickly across the Atlantic. Moreover, the Rostow group's strategy of going slow in its review of document requests was failing as congressional subpoenas poured in. The White House was politically a good deal weaker than it had been the year before, and Brent Scowcroft had failed in his efforts to impose the argument of executive privilege.

A select few documents had been provided to Gonzalez in August 1991, but only now were the more sensitive ones being released to Congress. As shocked staffers and their bosses started reading them, pieces of the broader story began to leak. Dennis Kane, the chief investigator for Gonzalez, recalled that when he first asked for NSD 26, Rostow "told me it would be a cold day in hell before Congress got NSD 26 or any of those documents." When a heavily edited version of NSD 26 was finally sent to Congress in May 1992, it provided critics with instant insight into why the Bush administration had set up Rostow's task force to limit the investigation of its pre-invasion policies. Henry Gonzalez was proving an indefatigable opponent. Almost every week he stood on the floor of the House of Representatives, often virtually alone in the chamber, reading his statements and on occasion placing secret documents into the *Congressional Record.* Not since the Pentagon Papers had so many classified materials been made available to the public.

Even so, the alarm Gonzalez was sounding attracted relatively little notice except among anguished aides to Brent Scowcroft, James Baker, and George Bush. A member of Baker's State Department staff later recalled that it was not really Gonzalez who troubled the secretary of state. It was William Safire, whose articles on Bush and Baker's handling of BNL and Iraq were appearing in *The New York Times* with almost as much frequency as Gonzalez's floor statements appeared in the *Congressional Record.* On May 18, 1992, Safire published an article entitled "Crimes of Iraqgate," in which he both coined the term and referred to "the Bush administration's fraudulent use of public funds, its sustained deception of Congress, and its obstruction of justice." The concept of Iraqgate was now formally in print, and it began dogging the Bush administration as never before.

While Safire was spelling out his suspicions, Gonzalez was revealing that the Bush administration had adopted a new and uncompromising stance. William Barr, who had taken over as attorney general in late 1991 after Thornburgh stepped down to wage an unsuccessful Senate race in Pennsylvania, informed Gonzalez that he was damaging "national security" and that the government would no longer provide him with *any* classified documents. Barr, a former CIA official who had worked for George Bush at the Agency in the 1970s and was fiercely loyal to the president, told Gonzalez that if more information was to be furnished, he would require an assurance that the congressman would no longer disclose any of the documents. This was the last straw for the Texas Democrat. Gonzalez retorted that none of the Iraq documents he had placed in the *Congressional Record* had compromised U.S. national security. Barr's threat to withhold documents, said Gonzalez, "has all the earmarks of a classic effort to obstruct a proper and legitimate investigation." As a result, Gonzalez disclosed that he would seek the appointment of a special prosecutor to investigate the Iraqgate affair.

Inside the White House, a new debate was joined: between those who wanted to launch a public counterattack and those who wanted to keep quiet and hope that Gonzalez would simply be viewed as a madman. Once again, James Baker and others in the administration were at loggerheads about what to do. "In the first few months of 1992, Baker tried to sit on the whole thing, even though many of us wanted to say something," said an unhappy former aide to President Bush. "Baker's stance allowed us to become a punching bag."

The debate was sharpened because Gonzalez was now demanding the testimony of top White House officials such as Brent Scowcroft, Boyden Gray, and Nicholas Rostow. The White House refused to let them appear, informing Gonzalez that it was "the long-standing practice of the Executive Branch to decline requests for testimony by members of the President's personal staff." Following the Rostow group guidelines for dealing with congressional requests on the subject of Iraq, Nicholas Calio, President Bush's aide for legislative affairs, then suggested somewhat obliquely to Gonzalez that the administration "work with you to develop an alternative, mutually acceptable mechanism" for making the White House officials available. Not surprisingly, Gonzalez saw this for what it was. "They just won't testify. They won't go public on Iraqgate," commented one of his aides.

ON MAY 21, 1992, the Bush administration finally decided it was time to make a public response to the Iraqgate charges. The man chosen to go before Gonzalez and his House Banking Committee was Lawrence Eagleburger, the deputy secretary of state and James Baker's point man on the Middle East.

Eagleburger knew what he was talking about when it came to Iraq. He had been personally involved in several significant and controversial decisions on Iraq that the Reagan and Bush administrations had made during the 1980s. As discussed earlier, in December 1983 Eagleburger had helped lobby Eximbank to provide loan guarantees for Baghdad in spite of the bank's worries about Iraq's previous support for terrorists. In October 1989, he had helped James Baker force through CCC loan guarantees for Iraq, in spite of Iraq's abuse of the government program. In February 1990, he sent Ambassador April Glaspie a cable describing the plan to provide written questions to Iraqi officials who were targets of the BNL investigation in Atlanta. In the spring of 1990, he participated in White House meetings that shaped the Bush administration's lenient approach to Saddam.

In addition, Lawrence Eagleburger was furious at Henry Gonzalez for singling him out for criticism in his floor statements, especially because the focus of the attacks concerned the BNL affair and Eagleburger's previous activities in the private sector. The criticism related to Eagleburger's term between 1984 and 1989 as president of Kissinger Associates, the New York-based international consulting firm founded by former Secretary of State Henry Kissinger.

While not accusing Eagleburger of illegality, Gonzalez had described what he termed "several interesting links" between the deputy secretary of state and companies involved with Iraq. The first was the fact that BNL had been a client of Kissinger Associates while Eagleburger served as its president. The second was that in 1986 Eagleburger, a former ambassador to Yugoslavia, had helped to establish LBS, a New York subsidiary of Ljubljanska Banka, a Yugoslav bank that had dealings with BNL Atlanta. Gonzalez quoted from a Federal Reserve inspection report revealing that between 1986 and 1989, while Eagleburger was a director of LBS, BNL fueled more than 20 percent of LBS's business in New York. Relations between LBS and BNL were indeed close. In 1987, LBS hired Renato Guadagnini, the former head of BNL's U.S. operations who had set up the Atlanta office in 1980, as a consultant.

Henry Kissinger had reacted with anger when Gonzalez disclosed his business links with BNL. BNL had been a client of Kissinger Associates, and Kissinger had served as a member of the bank's international advisory board. (See Appendix B, pages 352–353.) Kissinger had vehemently denied any knowledge of the improper Iraqi loans and claimed he had resigned from BNL in February 1991 precisely "because I don't want to be asked about this sort of question." Now it was Eagleburger's turn.

On the Thursday morning of May 21, 1992, at nine-twenty, Lawrence Eagleburger walked slowly into the Wright Patman Hearing Room, his trademark silver-handled black cane in hand, a gold watch dangling on a chain across his vest, and a couple of State Department aides trailing behind. Gonzalez arrived nine minutes later, and when he started speaking, it was clear that the chairman of the House Banking Committee was in a combative mood. It matched the scowl on Eagleburger's face.

"I would like to report a letter that was just hand-delivered to me in my office ten minutes ago from the White House," Gonzalez began, and announced that Stephen Danzansky, President Bush's former director of cabinet affairs, and Richard Haass, an aide to Brent Scowcroft, were not being permitted to testify as scheduled. Gonzalez read from the White House letter that said that "it is the long-standing practice of the Executive Branch to decline requests for testimony by members of the President's personal staff." Two chairs were therefore left unfilled at the witness table.

Eagleburger looked increasingly uncomfortable, then annoyed, as Gonzalez and his colleagues launched into their opening attacks. Charles Schumer, a New York congressman, termed Saddam Hussein "President Bush's Frankenstein" and said the Iraqi dictator had been created "in the White House laboratory with a collection of government programs, banks, and private companies." Joe Kennedy, Jr., the Massachusetts Democrat, blasted the White House for refusing to turn over any more Iraq documents on national security grounds. If there were legitimate concerns, "let them tell us," said Kennedy. He suggested that the White House was engaged in "the kind of Nixonian tactics we have seen in Watergate, of trying to undercut the truth being allowed to come forth because it is going to provide embarrassment."

Eagleburger shifted uneasily in his chair as he listened to the barrage of criticism. When he finally replied, at times angrily pounding the witness table, he defended the Bush administration's support of Iraq as prudent and modest. It was clear, he said, that the policy had not worked. "We tried to contain him. We did not succeed." Referring to the statements made by Gonzalez and others, Eagleburger was categorical: "Quite frankly, the selective disclosure—out of context—of classified documents has led—knowingly or otherwise—to distortions of the record, half-truths, and outright falsehoods, all combined into spurious conspiracy theories and charges of a cover-up."

Eagleburger then went on to deny that any investigation of BNL or the CCC had established any Iraqi abuse of the CCC program to purchase military weapons. When the State Department had pressed for one billion dollars of CCC credits in November 1989, it had not possessed any specific evidence of diversions, he claimed. Eagleburger used the further argument that only half of the billion dollars in promised credits had been extended to Iraq. He dismissed as merely speculative the memo that Frank Lemay had written to senior State Department officials warning of criminal behavior. The suggestion of a cover-up, he concluded, was simply not true. The State Department had already provided more than four thousand pages of documents "at a cost of over $100,000 in employee hours," said Eagleburger, and it was ready to turn over additional documents, but not until it received "appropriate assurances regarding the storage and protection of such materials."

Eagleburger then took time to deny that he himself had any ties to BNL: "Although the records at Kissinger Associates indicate that I may have attended one luncheon in 1986 at which two representatives of BNL Rome were present, I do not recall this luncheon nor any substantive meetings, conversations, or other contacts with anyone from BNL."

The interrogation of Eagleburger and the administration officials who followed him made for a brutal day; it did not end until nearly four o'clock. At one point, when Eagleburger argued that Iraq had been a creditworthy recipient of U.S. loan guarantees, Gonzalez shot back: "That statement, I respectfully submit, is patently untrue." When Eagleburger was asked which of the documents that had been released had compromised national security, he demurred: "I can't say. I haven't gone through the documents." Pressed on the push for CCC credits, Eagleburger said the program was "one of the few tools we had to try and influence Saddam to some moderation."

Finally, a very different question was put to him. Bernie Sanders, an independent congressman from Vermont, asked Eagleburger whether he was aware of any third-country transfer of U.S. military equipment to Iraq. Eagleburger started to reply, "No, I am not aware of anything . . . ," then stopped and turned around in his chair to listen to a whisper from an aide. Sanders asked the question again, this time referring specifically to a 1986 transfer of U.S. bombs from Saudi Arabia to Iraq. "I will have to get an answer for the record," Eagleburger answered, "but I am told, from behind here, this is all a classified issue, but that the Congress was notified at the time. Please let me get you an answer in writing that is accurate." The answer, when it was eventually supplied in writing, confirmed the Saudi transfer.

A week after Eagleburger's bruising session before the Banking Committee, an even more direct hit was scored against the White House, the CIA, and the State, Justice, and Treasury departments. Allan Mendelowitz, a senior official at the General Accounting Office (GAO), went before the committee and laid bare a record of obstruction of his own

independent investigation, which had been commissioned by the committee; he attributed the GAO's problems to the Rostow group. Mendelowitz, director of the International Trade and Finance Office of the
GAO, testified about his efforts to obtain information and documents
concerning the BNL Atlanta scandal and Iraq's abuse of the CCC program. He told the committee that under U.S. law, the GAO was supposed
to have access to executive agency records. "Generally, we do not encounter problems in accessing records in the course of most of our work," he
explained. However, "this was not the case in conducting our ongoing
review of Iraq's participation in the CCC's export credit guarantee programs and issues involving the Banca Nazionale del Lavoro." Mendelowitz attributed the lack of cooperation by the Bush administration to
"the procedures adopted by the Rostow group." The implementation of
these procedures, he added, "clearly was a White House initiative."

When the GAO asked the CIA for a briefing on BNL, for example,
"officials told us to obtain the information from the House Banking
Committee since it requested us to conduct our review." Mendelowitz
asked the CIA to reconsider its refusal since the GAO's policy was to
work independently of congressional committees. But he was fobbed off
with a vague promise that the matter would be reconsidered.

The State Department, he reported, claimed that it could show the
GAO only twenty-six cables and that everything else was subject to grand
jury secrecy rules because of the BNL case in Atlanta. But Mendelowitz
revealed that Gale McKenzie had said the opposite.

State referred Mendelowitz to Justice, but Justice said the question
was still "under consideration." And instead of gaining access to thousands of pages of Justice documents, the GAO was allowed to look at only
five documents, and it was not allowed to photocopy them or even take
proper notes. The Treasury Department refused to allow the GAO to
photocopy any of the minutes from the National Advisory Council meetings that had approved the Iraqi credits, and it said some of those minutes
were classified.

Taken together, Mendelowitz's revelations proved a significant counterpoint to Eagleburger's flat denial of every allegation that congressional
Democrats made about U.S. policy toward Iraq and the White House's
alleged cover-up.

Until these hearings late in May 1992, the issue of Iraqgate had been
something of a phony war, of interest principally to a few members of
Congress and the media. The Senate Intelligence Committee was quietly
moving forward with its own BNL probe, but nothing was publicly

known of it at the time. But in the weeks that followed the Eagleburger and Mendelowitz testimony, the scandal would grow into a full-blown national and even international controversy.

In the United States, the impetus to investigate and to publicize the revelations would come not only from congressional Democrats, who now accepted the advice of William Safire that they had "an election-year Watergate," but also from a hitherto obscure federal district court judge in Atlanta, who was just days away from presiding over a hearing involving one Christopher Drogoul. The revelations would not be restricted to the world of American politics—an entire decade of high-level intrigue involving Rome, London, and Baghdad as well as Washington would soon begin to unravel in an Atlanta courtroom. The hidden truth behind Iraqgate was about to emerge.

FOURTEEN

The Cover-Up Unravels

J udge Marvin Shoob had presided over some strange cases in his time
on the bench, but never had he seen anything like the saga of
Christopher Drogoul and the billions of dollars in Iraqi loans made
by the Atlanta branch of Italy's Banca Nazionale del Lavoro.

When the case was first assigned to him in early 1991, following
Attorney General Thornburgh's announcement of the BNL indictments,
it looked to Shoob like a routine bank fraud except for the large numbers
involved. But in the spring of 1992, as he was preparing for Drogoul's
trial, which was scheduled to begin in June, the judge began to wonder.
Gale McKenzie had asked him to set aside up to four months for the trial,
which would take it right through the summer. That would be a long trial
for a lowly branch manager whom the Justice Department insisted had
acted as a lone wolf, making the Iraqi loans without the knowledge of his
superiors in Rome.

For some time, Shoob had been growing more and more suspicious
about the BNL affair, first as he delved into reading the complicated
indictment, related banking documents, and press reports of the Gonzalez
hearings in preparation for the trial, and then in April, when McKenzie and
her team asked that Drogoul's bond be revoked and he be jailed. The
prosecutors were apparently concerned that Drogoul might flee the country. Shoob, a courtly, white-haired sixty-nine-year-old with a reputation as
one of the most even-tempered jurists in Georgia, agreed and sent Drogoul
to the federal penitentiary in Atlanta. But it was not just the risk of Drogoul
running away that had moved the judge. Shoob was aware that BNL
investigators in the Italian parliament were raising questions about the

possible involvement of intelligence services and the U.S. and Italian governments in the BNL affair. If there were others involved in the Iraqi loan scheme, reasoned the judge, "he might be better off in a safe place rather than where he is, on the outside."

Shoob became still more suspicious that spring, when Sheila Tyler, a lawyer from the Atlanta public defender's office, informed him that her client Drogoul was convinced that the Bush administration was so afraid of the case, it would never come to trial. "I had never heard of a case where the defendant says the government is afraid to go to trial," Shoob recalled.

Then, in May 1992, just weeks before the trial was set to start, Sheila Tyler informed Shoob that Drogoul had changed his mind and decided to plead guilty to all of the 347 charges against him. Faced with the prospect of 390 years in prison sentences and government demands that he provide $1.8 billion in restitution, that seemed an odd move. But Tyler explained that Drogoul wanted permission to make a statement in open court when he entered his guilty plea before Shoob. In that statement he would name those in Washington, Rome, and New York who were involved in the Iraqi loans affair. He would then place himself at the mercy of the court. "It is clear to me that my client was merely a small fish in a larger operation," said Tyler at the time. She added that the entire BNL-Iraqi loans effort had received covert U.S. government approval.

The guilty plea meant that a trial would not take place; instead, all that remained was a hearing to take the plea and to schedule another hearing to pronounce sentence. A plea hearing is the sort of court appearance that normally takes less than an hour; the prosecution lays out the crime, the defendant enters the plea, and the judge schedules a later hearing at which the defendant will be sentenced. If Drogoul wanted to make a statement at the plea hearing, that could take longer, but at least, thought Shoob, the truth would come out in his courtroom. He set the date of the plea hearing for June 2.

Less than a week before the court date, Shoob encountered Gale McKenzie on the street. He asked her if there was any possibility that Drogoul would not plead guilty to the full 347-count indictment and agree to a modified plea bargain. The prosecutor confirmed Tyler's statement that Drogoul was going to plead guilty to the entire indictment. On Friday, May 29, before the session scheduled for Tuesday, Tyler went to see the judge to say Drogoul had completed a five-hundred-page statement and wanted guarantees that he could read the full document in open court. "I said he could take as long as he liked," Shoob later recalled.

On the afternoon of Monday, June 1, 1992, the day before Drogoul was to make his statement in court, Shoob was shocked when the prosecutors informed him that a new deal had been made over the weekend, while McKenzie was out of town. The Justice Department had made a surprising offer to Drogoul—he could plead guilty to only sixty of the 347 charges against him and might then win a reduced sentence. The only requirement was that he agree to be debriefed extensively by government prosecutors for a period of several weeks. That meant that the plea hearing would go ahead, but his sentencing would have to wait until Drogoul had been fully debriefed.

A second strange occurrence on June 1 was the visit of a federal marshal to Judge Shoob's chambers on the nineteenth floor of the Russell Building in downtown Atlanta. The information he conveyed left the judge incredulous at first. The marshal told Judge Shoob that he was very concerned about Drogoul's safety and wanted to bring the former BNL branch manager to the courthouse that very evening, rather than wait until the next morning.

Shoob asked the marshal who might be threatening Drogoul. "Would you believe the CIA?" asked the marshal, to which the judge replied no, he would not. The two men agreed, however, on a compromise. Drogoul was to be awakened at five o'clock in the morning and brought by heavily armed guards from the Atlanta penitentiary to the Russell Building.

That night, the judge went home and told his wife, Janice, about the episode. The Shoobs went to bed with their floodlights still on. Only once before had Marvin Shoob ever experienced anything remotely like the drama of the BNL case, and that was in the early 1980s, when his home was vandalized after he ordered some of the Mariel Cubans who had been expelled by Fidel Castro to be released from a local prison. For Shoob, the issue had concerned basic human rights, but the Reagan administration had been furious because Attorney General Ed Meese wanted the Cubans detained or deported. Meese had contacted Shoob and said that "these people are all dangerous criminals," but the judge had replied that it was impossible to know if this was true of each and every one of them. Meese told Shoob that he had talked to President Reagan about the Cubans, "and we think it would be a good idea to just put them all on C-5 cargo aircraft and drop them over Cuba with parachutes." Shoob had not thought this was a very good idea and said so.

On June 2, when Christopher Drogoul appeared in Judge Shoob's packed courtroom looking tired and fragile in a rumpled dark blue suit, the judge did his best to maintain his reputation as a soft-spoken southern gentleman who was unflappable on the bench. His courtroom that morning had attracted an unusually international crowd of people, all of whom—lawyers, government officials, Italian diplomats, and journalists from around the world—were interested in either BNL or Iraq.

Shoob was already seething with anger because he felt he had been misled about the last-minute plea agreement. After the court had been convened, the judge was informed that in addition to the plea agreement, Drogoul had abandoned his plan to name names. The normally courteous judge lost his patience completely. He asked Drogoul if it was true that he never expected to come to trial "because there are so many substantial people involved." Drogoul replied that it was true. "I don't believe for a minute that you were able to do all of this on your own," said Shoob. "You're right," said Drogoul, and he confirmed before the court that he would not name any names just now.

Shoob was beside himself by then, and he told the court he would not allow the BNL case to be "sealed, stonewalled, or suppressed." Shoob then turned to Gale McKenzie and made a statement that would signal a turning point in the BNL affair: "I do not want to be in a position where I have to sentence Mr. Drogoul, where he takes the fall when there are other people involved who are equally culpable. . . . A special prosecutor ought to get into this entire matter, because I am not getting the information from Mr. Drogoul, and I am going to get a sanitized version at the time of the sentence. I will have no way of knowing what sort of disclosure he has made to the government and what is presented to me at the time of sentence."

When the judge mentioned the words *special prosecutor,* the little courtroom in Atlanta fell silent for a moment. Almost immediately afterward, people at the rear of the court whispered to each other; comparisons were made between Judge Shoob and the late Judge John Sirica, whose determination had helped unmask the Watergate scandal. That afternoon, Shoob went back to his chambers and talked privately with his law clerk and others about his deep suspicion that Drogoul was merely a convenient scapegoat, a victim of the Bush administration's attempt to hide its own knowledge and involvement in the Iraqi scandal.

That was precisely how an increasing number of Democrats in Congress were viewing the BNL case, which by now was understood to be at the heart of the broader scandal called Iraqgate. BNL, said congressional investigators as they pored through stacks of newly declassified White House documents, had been a financial mechanism, one of the biggest, in a decade-long effort to get aid to Saddam Hussein under the table.

At almost exactly the same time Judge Shoob was explaining the need for a special prosecutor in that Atlanta courtroom, members of Congress were saying the same thing in a very different venue. That morning, the House Judiciary Committee had convened its first hearing to examine whether a special prosecutor might be needed. The atmosphere was politically charged and highly partisan, yet Jack Brooks, the conservative Texas Democrat who chaired the committee, was a far more cautious man than Henry Gonzalez or others in Congress who were already convinced that the White House was seeking to cover up its embarrassing policies toward Iraq. Brooks listened attentively as his House colleagues argued for the appointment of a special prosecutor.

Doug Barnard, the Georgia Democrat whose subcommittee on commerce had investigated U.S. high-technology exports sent to Baghdad, appeared as a witness before the Judiciary Committee. He described how the Commerce Department had tampered with export licenses after discussing which documents to alter with the White House. "Wrongdoing has taken place," said Barnard, "and nothing has been done."

Vermont senator Patrick Leahy, whose Agriculture Committee had probed BNL and the CCC program for Iraq, accused the Bush administration of misleading Congress and said there was evidence that top officials might have violated criminal laws in carrying out and later justifying U.S. policy toward Iraq.

Gonzalez showed the Judiciary Committee "before and after" memos from Gale McKenzie to the Atlanta branch of the Federal Reserve on the BNL case in which entire paragraphs and pages had been blocked out by heavy black splotches. The original copies not only showed that the government had been ready to bring indictments as early as January 1990, but that a trip to Rome had been planned in order to speak with Italian executives who had been accused of complicity in the BNL Atlanta loans. One section that had been blacked out read: "The stop in Rome is necessary to speak with a number of BNL-Rome employees, officers, and directors at whom Christopher Drogoul and other key subjects have leveled charges of complicity in their BNL-Atlanta scheme. A Rome setting is required for immediate access to all relevant records which may assist in defeating these spurious claims by subjects of our criminal investigation." The trip, of course, had never taken place, having been put off by the Justice Department.

When the House Judiciary Committee finished its work that day, with Republicans accusing Democrats of trying to embarrass the White House in an election year, Brooks said he would put off any immediate decision on whether to seek a special prosecutor. But he allowed that the day's testimony had raised some troubling questions.

The handling of the BNL case thus became the single most prominent issue in the unfolding Iraqgate scandal. But there remained the uneasy sense among many in Congress that the White House was trying to hide something broader. In the days that followed, further revelations began to spill out, and with them came more denials of wrongdoing from the White House.

On June 8, less than a week after the Brooks committee met, it emerged that back in April, Admiral Bobby Ray Inman, a top intelligence adviser to President Bush, had written a letter to a judge in Philadelphia trying to win a lighter prison sentence for James Guerin, the arms-maker from Lancaster, Pennsylvania. Guerin had already been convicted of a $1 billion fraud and of illegally transferring military technology to South Africa and Iraq. But Inman, who had been CIA deputy director until 1982 and was now serving as the acting chairman of the president's foreign intelligence advisory board, called Guerin a patriot and revealed in the letter to the judge that he had worked secretly in the mid-1970s with intelligence agencies. That was the period when Bush had been CIA director. The fact that an intelligence official as prominent as Inman, albeit one who had once served on Guerin's proxy board, was willing to engage in special pleading for a convicted fraudster, raised further concern among Iraqgate investigators. (See Appendix B, page 354.)

The pressure was building on George Bush himself, especially after Brooks's Judiciary Committee sent a letter to the White House seeking the testimony of Boyden Gray, Nicholas Rostow, and Frank Lemay, the whistle-blower from the State Department who had tried to warn his superiors of the suspected use of U.S. government loan guarantees in Saddam's nuclear weapons arsenal in 1989. The General Accounting Office had already told Gonzalez's Banking Committee that its requests for the Iraq papers had been delayed and thwarted by the Rostow group. By inviting Gray and Rostow, officials with personal knowledge of how the White House had coordinated its response to congressional investigations, the Judiciary Committee seemed to be sending a message: The same committee that had led the congressional charge in the Watergate affair was now focusing on the possibility that the Bush administration had moved to cover up actions in order to limit political damage.

Iraqgate was beginning to follow the president wherever he went. In Rio de Janeiro on June 13 for the UN earth summit, a reporter asked Bush what he thought of the House Judiciary Committee's investigation. "I think it's purely political," said Bush, adding that as far as the administration was concerned, "we have had detailed testimony by Larry Eagleburger." He said he didn't know whether a special prosecutor would be named, but he offered his first formal defense against the cover-up charges: "We tried to bring Saddam Hussein into the family of nations. That policy was not successful."

The president's approach to the Iraqgate issue—the admission that in effect "mistakes were made"—swayed few members of the Judiciary Committee when it reconvened ten days later. Frank Lemay told the committee he had no regrets about sounding the alarm. But Brooks was more interested in the fact that the White House was refusing to allow Boyden Gray or Nicholas Rostow to testify. Obstruction of Congress, false statements, and perjury, said Brooks, reeling off some of the Iraqgate accusations, "are serious charges and should not be trivialized against what the Administration calls larger claims of foreign policy, executive privilege, and prosecutorial discretion."

The White House's efforts to keep congressional investigators at bay were set back twice more before the month of June was over. In testimony before the Judiciary Committee on June 23, the inspector general of the Commerce Department, whose report on the improper altering of export records of U.S. shipments to Iraq had been completed a month before, fingered Dennis Kloske as the man responsible for the changes. But Kloske, who had left the government after going public with his criticism of the very same exports to Iraq, claimed that White House officials had been aware of and even approved the preparation of the altered records before they were submitted to Congress.

Within days the testimony on Iraq that another senior Bush administration official gave to the House Banking Committee was contradicted by a subordinate. Richard Crowder, the Agriculture Department's undersecretary who had responsibility for CCC guarantees to Iraq, denied that the government knowingly supplied $1 billion of CCC credits even after it was faced with indications of Iraq's criminal abuse of the program. Crowder cited as proof a conversation he had had in early October 1989 with Arthur Wade, the junior Agriculture Department investigator who had been assigned to probe the BNL case in Atlanta. As Crowder recalled the conversation, he had asked Wade if the BNL investigators had uncovered any information in the case that suggested a reason for the United States not to proceed with more CCC credits for Iraq. "Mr. Wade said no." On June 30, however, Wade told Senate

Agriculture Committee investigators a different story: "I did not see Crowder and I did not meet Crowder. I never have."

Some pieces of the Iraqgate puzzle were starting to fit together, and the picture being assembled was disturbing. At the very least it was becoming clear that the Bush administration's dealings with Iraq had been a great deal more incestuous than the public had ever imagined. Then there was the Drogoul case in Atlanta, which remained in a state of suspended animation after Judge Shoob made clear that a special prosecutor was needed; the judge's views were being taken seriously by many in Washington, and not just by Democrats who were interested in election year politics. Even Elliot Richardson, the Republican who resigned as Richard Nixon's attorney general in protest at efforts to cover up the Watergate scandal, told friends he believed there was probably government wrongdoing in the Iraqgate saga. It didn't help the Bush administration's defense that an increasing number of officials, high and low, were running for cover, contradicting one another in public, or, like Lawrence Eagleburger, issuing angry and categorical denials of any improprieties. Nor did it look good that the White House had refused to allow Boyden Gray and others to be questioned. The president himself had demonstrated in his own public statements that the entire issue touched a raw nerve; he and his staff at the White House, Iraqgate investigators believed, were protesting far too much. They smelled a rat.

The president was finding that the subject continued to come up, even during a supposedly innocuous televised encounter with tourists in the Rose Garden on July 1. He reacted testily when asked about the BNL case and Frank Lemay's 1989 warning about the CCC program for Iraq. "You can talk about one State Department employee," Bush sputtered, then stopped himself. ". . . and if we'd have known it," he continued, "it wouldn't have happened." The president then denied flatly that his administration had helped Saddam's nuclear or chemical weapons capabilities. The problem was that fewer and fewer people believed him.

On the morning of Thursday, July 9, 1992, the House Judiciary Committee decided to act. Twenty Democrats signed a letter to Attorney General William Barr citing potentially criminal conduct by current and former high-ranking officials of the Executive Branch. The conduct in question related to suspected illegal activities designed to assist the regime of Saddam Hussein prior to the August 1990 invasion of Kuwait, and afterward to conceal information about the criminal activity.

"This is not an attempt to second-guess the administration's policy of tilting toward Iraq," said Jack Brooks. "We are concerned about the possibility that high government officials, in their zeal to carry out this policy and then to keep it from being exposed, may have broken the law."

The letter made clear that the committee suspected lawbreaking by officials in the White House and in other parts of the government. It asked for an independent prosecutor to look into charges of real crimes such as conspiracy to defraud the United States, obstruction of justice, falsification of records, perjury, and financial conflict of interest by high Executive Branch officials. In addition, the letter cited Judge Shoob's criticism of the sudden and unexpected plea-bargaining arrangement by the Justice Department with Drogoul as "mysterious and unseemly"; it also noted that the judge felt the case warranted the appointment of a special prosecutor.

Although Brooks would not say in public which government officials the committee suspected of breaking which laws, staff aides explained in private that the conspiracy allegations were based on the push by James Baker and other senior officials to give Iraq CCC credits in 1989. It would be against the law, they noted, to hand out U.S. government funds to Iraq or to any individual or state even thought to have engaged in criminal activities such as the misuse of BNL loans or soliciting kickbacks.

The obstruction of justice allegation was designed to include suspicions of White House, Justice Department, and State Department interference in the BNL case. The falsification of records charge referred to the Commerce Department's tampering with export licenses. The perjury suspicion concerned contradictory and possibly false statements about U.S. policy toward Iraq by administration witnesses in congressional hearings. The conflict of interest heading was intended to allow a special prosecutor to examine in detail the reasons why in August 1990 President Bush had granted waivers to Baker, Mosbacher, and other cabinet members involved in Iraqi policy.

The demand for a special prosecutor mentioned the possible diversion of government-financed loans for arms purchases. But the committee was most disturbed about the suspected mishandling and cover-up of investigations touching upon U.S. policy toward Iraq, starting with the BNL affair. Brooks laid out all the elements of the mosaic—the scope and timing of the BNL indictment, the recusal of Joe Whitley as U.S. attorney in Atlanta, the withholding of classified information from the Atlanta prosecutors, the eleventh-hour plea bargain deal in Atlanta, and the possible political interference of the White House in the case.

Nothing was more devastating than the revelation that same day that

Secretary of State James Baker and President George Bush. Throughout the
1980s their shared vision of the world shaped the dangerous American embrace
of Saddam Hussein.

Fred Haobsh. His odyssey as a foot soldier in America's covert arming of Iraq led him to the presidential palace in Baghdad. The gold fob watch with an enameled image of Saddam on its face is all he has left.

Nizar Hamdoon. Among the ablest of Saddam's diplomatic envoys to Washington in the 1980s, he cultivated a wide array of friends in high places.

Sarkis Soghanalian. The Miami-based arms dealer was both a CIA contractor and one of Saddam's biggest suppliers.

AP/Wide World Photos

President Bush poses with newly sworn-in director, Robert Gates, at CIA headquarters in Langley, Virginia, November 1991.

Lancaster Newspapers

James Guerin, the former
head of International
Signal and Control of
Lancaster, Pennsylvania.
He was convicted of financial fraud and illegal arms
exports, having worked
previously with U.S. intelligence agencies.

Carlos Cardoen is greeted by a grateful Saddam Hussein in Baghdad. The Chilean arms manufacturer provided nearly $500 million worth of deadly cluster bombs to Iraq, with the silent blessing of the United States.

SECURITY
YOU ARE ENTERING
A
RESTRICTED AREA
PASS HOLDERS ONLY

Frank Machon in his Glasgow warehouse. This tough-minded trucker waged a lonely battle to inform British authorities what he had learned about the covert channeling of munitions to Baghdad.

President Ronald Reagan and Italian prime minister Giulio Andreotti (*right*). The two leaders discussed the need to prevent the spread of Ayatollah Khomeini's Islamic fundamentalism, and both their governments assisted Iraq.

Giacomo Pedde, the director-general of Italy's Banca Nazionale del Lavoro until 1989. He presided over the day-to-day operations of the bank in Rome while its Atlanta branch was helping finance Saddam's nuclear and chemical weapons projects.

Giampiero Cantoni, who was named the new chairman of the government-owned BNL after the FBI raided the bank's Atlanta branch in 1989. Cantoni spent the next four years vehemently denying charges that his bank had been involved in the illicit Iraqi loans.

Christopher Drogoul, the former manager of BNL Atlanta whom the Bush administration accused of single-handedly masterminding $5 billion of loans to Iraq. *Right:* Drogoul in the Atlanta federal penitentiary in 1993. *Below:* In a relaxed moment at home in Atlanta in October 1989.

Attorney General Richard Thornburgh and President Bush. Thornburgh announced the indictment of Christopher Drogoul on February 28, 1991, the day after Operation Desert Storm ended.

The Rome headquarters of the Banca Nazionale del Lavoro, on the Via Veneto.

Giulio Andreotti meets with George Bush in the Oval Office. Both leaders denied there had been any impropriety in their relations with Iraq.

The late Guido Carli. As Italy's treasury minister in 1989, he ordered BNL executives to cut a deal with Iraq and make good on more than half a billion dollars of the improper loans that BNL's Atlanta branch had extended.

Iraqi foreign minister Tariq Aziz and U.S. secretary of state James Baker in an obligatory handshake during their abortive Geneva meeting on January 9, 1991.

White House counsel C. Boyden Gray, one of the president's closest confidants, confers with Bush. Gray later denied obstructing congressional investigations into Iraqgate.

Reuters/Bettmann

George Bush turns to the audience during a debate with Ross Perot and Bill Clinton in the 1992 presidential campaign. The Iraqgate scandal finally erupted when Perot forced Bush to address the issue on national television.

Reuters/Bettmann

President Bush and his Egyptian counterpart, Hosni Mubarak, meet in Cairo in November 1990 to discuss ways to counter Saddam Hussein. During much of the 1980s, Mubarak had pressed Washington to help get arms to Iraq.

British prime minister Margaret Thatcher and President Bush stroll together near Aspen, Colorado, on August 2, 1990, the day Saddam invaded Kuwait. Both leaders quickly jettisoned their pro-Iraqi stance and worked instead to defeat the Iraqi leader.

King Hussein of Jordan is greeted by President Bush at Kennebunkport on August 16, 1990, where he was rebuked for siding with Saddam. For a decade Jordan had served as a willing conduit for covert Western arms transfers to Iraq.

Paul Henderson, the former managing director of Matrix Churchill. The Iraqi-owned and British-based machine tool maker supplied Iraq with advanced manufacturing equipment for its war machine. Henderson worked for British intelligence, even as he supplied Iraq.

Financial Times

Photo News Service Old Bailey

Alan Clark, the former British junior trade minister. His surprise testimony led to the collapse of the trial of Paul Henderson and other former Matrix Churchill executives accused of deceiving the government about their exports to Iraq.

Representative Henry Gonzalez, the iconoclastic chairman of the House Banking Committee. He has spearheaded congressional efforts to investigate the Iraqgate scandal.

Frank Lemay. The young State Department official was punished after he sounded the alarm over Iraq's abuse of a U.S. taxpayer-backed program.

Attorney General William Barr (*right*), who refused to name an Iraqgate special prosecutor in October 1991, and retired judge Frederick Lacey, whose seven-week investigation for Barr was dismissed by critics as a whitewash.

AP/Wide World Photos

Janet Reno is named U.S. attorney general by President Bill Clinton. Her special assistant said Reno is committed to a full investigation of Iraqgate and is probing allegations of wrongdoing by senior Bush administration officials.

The Independent/John Voos

Lord Justice Scott, whose arms-to-Iraq inquiry threatens to rock the British political establishment.

Marvin Shoob, the federal district court judge in Atlanta who did not believe the Bush administration's version of the BNL affair. He became convinced there was a White House cover-up and has remained doggedly determined to see the truth emerge.

a lawyer in the office of Presidential Counsel Boyden Gray had telephoned Gale McKenzie in Atlanta to discuss a case as sensitive as the BNL affair. This was Jay Bybee, and he said that any notion that the White House had obstructed justice was "baloney." But he did not deny telling McKenzie of the White House's fear of being embarrassed "if we went ahead and guaranteed loans for Iraq at the same time the Justice Department was indicting Iraqi officials."

Over at the Justice Department, William Barr found himself in a difficult position. He was known to be a protégé and close friend of Boyden Gray, and both were vigorous opponents of the law on special prosecutors. Yet no attorney general of the United States had ever turned down a request from Congress to appoint a special prosecutor. William Barr became the first to do just that.

On August 10, Barr claimed that the only questions worthy of criminal investigation were the altering of Commerce Department records and the possibility that administration officials had deliberately misled Congress about Iraqi policy. The Justice Department could handle those investigations itself. Barr also decided there was "not a shred of evidence" that any official had acted improperly in the BNL case. Judge Shoob, he claimed, did not understand the case.

Barr's flat denial of the request came at the height of an intensely political summer in Washington. Bill Clinton had just been nominated to run against President Bush, and it was beginning to look like a close race. For his part, Clinton said he was "really troubled" by the attorney general's decision. Jack Brooks, fuming that Barr had rejected the demand for a special prosecutor in less than thirty days, even though he had the option under the law of making a preliminary determination to investigate further before deciding, spoke of "stonewalling, plain and simple."

The Bush administration's refusal to name a special prosecutor did not stop politicians from seeking the full story on Iraqgate. In fact, it had precisely the opposite effect. The House Banking Committee had already voted overwhelmingly to subpoena secret Iraq-related documents from the CIA and the National Security Agency. The Senate Intelligence Committee was reviewing what it assumed to be an "all-source chronology" on the BNL affair that had been furnished by Robert Gates, the CIA director.

Meanwhile, Christopher Drogoul spent the summer being questioned thirty-three times by the Atlanta prosecutors, who were preparing for a return to Judge Shoob's courtroom for the sentencing hearing on September 14. All that remained was for Drogoul to finally make his statement in court, ask for mercy from Judge Shoob, and then be sentenced. In August, however, his prospects changed notably when his sister contacted Bobby Lee Cooke, a prominent southern trial lawyer with a flair for publicity, who became interested enough to take the case without pay. The first thing Cooke did was to halt Drogoul's debriefing sessions with the government. He then employed a three-man legal defense team that scoured Washington, London, and Rome for information and documents on BNL.

AT HALF PAST NINE on the morning of Monday, September 14, the benches in Judge Shoob's austere Atlanta courtroom were once again packed with government officials, Italian diplomats, lawyers, and reporters. Gale McKenzie did less talking as the prosecution laid out its complicated case against Drogoul; this task was left mainly to Gerrilyn Brill, McKenzie's superviser. With officials of the Justice Department looking on, Brill argued that Drogoul had defrauded both the U.S. government and BNL's Rome headquarters. Although this was a sentencing hearing, which normally would have taken a few hours at most, the government prosecutors had asked Shoob for three days to present witnesses. They were taking no chances now that Cooke was on the case, since he appeared to have something up his sleeve. In the event, the sentencing hearing turned into a minitrial, but with a difference: at sentencing hearings the normal rules of evidence do not apply—even hearsay can be introduced as long as the judge is satisfied that the information is sufficiently reliable.

Brill sought almost immediately to preempt any talk of Iraqgate. "This is a sentencing hearing and not a political event," she proclaimed. The Atlanta team had investigated Drogoul's claims that higher-ups in Rome and in the U.S. government were involved in the scandal, she added, and had found no proof. She next implied that it would be of little consequence even if that were the case. "We are operating under the American system of justice. Knowing someone is committing a crime is not a crime. Negligence is not a crime," said Brill.

When it was Cooke's turn to respond, he began in grand style. " 'Nothing,' " he said, quoting Louis Brandeis, " 'can destroy a government more quickly than its failure to observe its own laws.' " Drogoul, said his lawyer, was certainly no angel, but the BNL case had been totally politicized in order to hide the blunders of top Bush administration officials.

"This case is the mother of all cover-ups," roared Cooke, and then, in a softer voice, proceeded to argue that his client had been manipulated for years. U.S. intelligence officials, said Cooke, had made regular visits to see Drogoul and were briefed on the Iraqi loans. Giacomo Pedde, the former director-general of BNL, was among the senior executives who knew of the Atlanta loans, Cooke claimed. A senior U.S. government official and the Iraqi ambassador had met Drogoul in 1988 and encouraged him to provide U.S.-backed loans.

Cooke's revelations came thick and fast, but it was in his questioning of Art Wade, the hapless Agriculture Department investigator, that the government's cover-up began to unravel. Wade admitted that he and other members of the BNL task force had never gone to Rome to interview bank executives and had relied instead on the bank to provide selected witnesses. He acknowledged he had no experience of international finance. When asked, he was unable to name a single member of the BNL board.

Cooke then questioned a previous lawyer for Drogoul who said he had hired a private investigator to look into the activities of a Virginia company funded by BNL for its sales of technology to Iraq, only to find that the company was also financed by the Central Intelligence Agency. Paul Von Wedel, Drogoul's old deputy, testified that the Virginia company's owner had told BNL bankers that he was a former employee of the National Security Agency and still supplied information to U.S. intelligence.

While the courtroom drama was going on in Atlanta, Henry Gonzalez took the highly unusual step of quoting from a classified CIA letter on the floor of the House of Representatives in Washington. The letter said that while most of the CIA's reports on Iraq and BNL did not add much that was new, there had been exceptions. Among these was one report that BNL financing had helped pay for the Condor II missile project, and another that confirmed that senior BNL officials in Rome "had been witting of BNL-Atlanta's activities."

The Gonzalez disclosure changed the focus of the entire Iraqgate scandal. How could the government charge Drogoul with defrauding Rome if the CIA had known about the involvement of BNL Rome officials—and had a legal obligation to provide such information to the Justice Department? The answer did not come immediately; instead, the CIA simply prepared a three-page document for the prosecutors in Atlanta, claiming its information on Rome's involvement came from publicly available sources.

Toward the end of September, as Drogoul's hearing entered its third week, there was more disquieting news. Judge Shoob summoned Cooke and the prosecutors for a bench conference one morning and revealed that three CIA reports he had read "definitely" showed that BNL's Rome headquarters were aware of the Atlanta loans. The reports, said Shoob, "undermine the government's position that this was a lone wolf type operation."

In Italy, meanwhile, two former BNL executives had informed the *Financial Times* of at least eight midlevel and senior BNL colleagues who were involved in the Atlanta loan affair. Both of the executives, who spoke only on condition that they not be named, had direct knowledge and involvement themselves. One of them explained how he had directed Iraqi business to Drogoul in Atlanta: "We knew there was an open line of credit to Iraq that was being run by our Atlanta branch. We were told that the highest levels of BNL wanted us to give privileged treatment to Iraq." The second former executive said he had been told not to worry too much about credit risk because a large portion of the loans was being guaranteed by the U.S. government. "There was also political cover in Rome for the bank," he added.

The chairman of BNL quickly issued a strong denial of any Rome involvement in either the loans or a cover-up. But the Justice Department's case began to crumble when Cooke revealed BNL documents in court detailing how the Italian government had pressured the Bush administration not to indict the state bank. Among them were the detailed diaries kept by Paolo Di Vito, in which the BNL executive had reported on the way the Italian ambassador to Washington had been ordered by his superiors in Rome to lobby the Justice Department that the bank not be indicted.

After Cooke revealed these documents on September 30, he informed the court that he wished to file a motion withdrawing Drogoul's plea bargain, changing his plea to innocent, and seeking a full-scale trial instead. Judge Shoob had already denied a similar motion on September 21, saying there had not been "fair and just reason," but now, after reading CIA reports that showed Rome's involvement and BNL reports that illustrated a lobbying effort by the Italian government to influence the indictments, he was prepared to change his mind. He didn't need to. The daily revelations that had been coming out of his courtroom since September 14 had so undermined the government's case that on October 1, Gale McKenzie, Gerrilyn Brill, and the other federal prosecutors threw in the towel. They told Judge Shoob they wanted to cancel their plea agreement with Drogoul and go to trial. For his part, Judge Shoob then said he simply did not believe the government's case anymore.

On October 5 he spelled out his conclusions in a fifteen-page court order that represented an extraordinarily bold ruling from the bench. "The court concludes," wrote Shoob, "that officials at BNL-Rome were aware of and approved Mr. Drogoul's activities." He cited classified reports from the CIA that showed in part "that a number of high-level BNL-Rome officials supported Mr. Drogoul's activities," and he described BNL Rome as "an extremely political organization operating more as an agency of the Italian government than as a bank."

Shoob also concluded that prosecutors had "failed to investigate seriously whether BNL-Rome knew of defendant Drogoul's activities," and he said this failure, coupled with or provoked by the involvement of other departments of the U.S. government, indicated "an effort to absolve BNL-Rome of complicity in the Atlanta branch loans to Iraq." He lambasted the telephone call from Jay Bybee in the White House to Gale McKenzie as "highly unusual and inappropriate" and added that the June 1992 plea bargain with Drogoul "effectively silenced Mr. Drogoul, who had announced his intention to make a full disclosure at the plea hearing."

It was an angry statement, and Shoob knew it. As a result, he reluctantly acceded to the government's request to remove himself from the trial on the grounds that he had already formed strong views about the case. But he saved his best for last, finishing the October 5 order with these words: "These are grave questions as to how the prosecutors made their decisions in this case—both as to the nature of the charges and whom to prosecute. It is apparent that decisions were made at the top levels of the United States Justice Department, State Department, Agriculture Department and within the intelligence community to shape this case and that information may have been withheld from local prosecutors seeking to investigate this case or used to steer the prosecution. Furthermore, the Attorney General's exceptional refusal to grant the Congressional request for an independent counsel in itself raises concerns for the Court about the government's impartiality in handling this case. Accordingly, this Court again strongly recommends that an independent prosecutor be named to investigate this matter."*

* * *

---

* The full text of this order will be found in Appendix A.

ONCE AGAIN THE WORDS of Judge Marvin Shoob echoed in Washington.
They galvanized the Democrats, now only weeks away from election day;
but more important, Shoob's order was a wake-up call for everyone who
cared about honesty in government. Something was clearly amiss when a
federal judge used language so strong, directly accusing the government
of serious malfeasance.

Members of the Senate Select Committee on Intelligence, which
quietly and away from the glare of publicity had been examining the Iraqi
loans case for months, were caught off guard by the Shoob statement. The
senators, led by David Boren, the committee chairman, had assumed that
Robert Gates had already supplied *all* the relevant CIA reports on BNL.
But Senator Boren soon learned from CIA officials who testified in a
hearing closed to the public that the CIA had deliberately misled the
Justice Department, Judge Shoob, the Atlanta prosecutors, and Congress.
The senator, a staunch supporter of both Gates and the CIA, was enraged
that critical CIA reports that undermined the government's BNL case had
been withheld from the committee.

On October 7, a day after Boren went public with the information,
Gates came up with a solution: The CIA would investigate itself to find out
why it had failed to report all it knew about the BNL scandal. As the Bush
administration grew increasingly embarrassed, a CIA spokesman played
down the unusual state of affairs, saying it was all "an honest mistake."

Forty-eight hours later, to make matters worse, Elizabeth Rindskopf,
the CIA's general counsel, changed the story again. She claimed that a
senior official at the Justice Department had pressured the CIA to put out
misleading information. That official had been Lawrence Urgenson, head
of the Justice Department's fraud section of the criminal division. Urgenson replied in anger: "If anybody swallows the notion that the general
counsel for the CIA was intimidated, I have a bridge in Brooklyn I want to
sell him. That is absurd, just plain absurd." Rindskopf, who had been a
leading member of the Rostow group in its deliberations over the Iraq
papers, insisted there had been no wrongdoing by the CIA. She did,
however, admit that information on BNL that the CIA released had been
"inartfully crafted," and she even made a promise: "We will never do it
again. We did not handle ourselves well."

The timing of this unusual slugfest between the CIA and the Justice
Department was not politically propitious for George Bush. The president was scheduled to hold his first televised debate with Bill Clinton on
Sunday evening, October 11. As White House political advisers set up a
weekend of mock debate in order to prepare Bush, a new cloud appeared

on the horizon. The FBI was asked by Justice to help investigate possible misconduct by senior administration officials at both the CIA and Justice. Senator Boren said on Saturday, October 10, that he had talked by telephone with William Sessions, the FBI director, who had assured him that because Justice Department officials might be targets of this politically sensitive probe, the FBI would conduct it independently. But the Justice Department promptly disputed this, saying *it* was in charge of the investigation and the FBI was merely a participant.

Just days after the FBI probe of the Iraqi affair was announced, word leaked from the Justice Department that the FBI director was himself facing a potential criminal inquiry concerning alleged abuse of his family's right to travel on government airplanes and other supposedly personal expenses Sessions had billed to the FBI. An exasperated Senator Boren said the timing of the accusations against Sessions "makes me wonder if an attempt is being made to pressure him not to conduct an independent investigation."

Sessions himself was suspicious about the timing of the leak. He later recalled that Boren had telephoned to express his concern about the conduct of both the CIA and the Department of Justice in the BNL affair. "I simply assured him that we would make a full, thorough, and independent investigation," said Sessions later. "I then called Attorney General Barr and told him I had indicated to the senator that we would conduct a full, thorough, and independent investigation of this matter. He said, 'You *what?*' and there was a pause in the conversation as I repeated that I told the senator we would conduct a full, thorough, and independent investigation of this matter. The conversation ended shortly thereafter. It was very brief after that."

"We conducted our investigation of the BNL matter in a factual way," Sessions remembered. "We had to know who knew what when, and who got what when very factually. I can't speculate about Iraqgate, but it seemed a very sore point with Barr. Now in hindsight I see that it was very sensitive and the action of leaking the investigation [of Sessions] was designed to deal with me. Certainly it was intentional. I don't know if Barr initiated the leak or someone else, but certainly it was done in order to inhibit me. You might say someone was firing a warning shot across the bow."

WITH THE CIA, the FBI, and the Justice Department now engaged in guerrilla warfare, and many in Congress complaining that they had been

misled by the White House on a number of Iraq-related matters, legislators in both the House and Senate renewed their demands that Attorney
General Barr name an independent prosecutor. Senator Howard Metzenbaum, a Democrat from Ohio and a member of the Senate Judiciary
Committee, told Barr that if BNL had financed a CIA front company, "we
would effectively be faced with a case of secret U.S. government involvement in arms sales to Iraq, as well as a possible cover-up." But it was the
intervention of Senator Boren, a well-known conservative, that proved
decisive. Boren wrote to Barr demanding "a truly independent investigation."

The attorney general responded with a half-measure. In the face of
such a political firestorm, he had to do something. Taking some form of
action mattered to the Congress, but more important, it mattered to the
White House, which was now worried that Iraqgate might affect the
presidential election just a few weeks away.

Nonetheless, Barr still could not bring himself to appoint an independent prosecutor. On October 16 he chose instead to pick his own
private investigator, a retired Republican judge from New Jersey named
Frederick Lacey. As a Department of Justice appointee, the hiring or
firing of Lacey was directly under Barr's control. In fact, Barr made use of
the same federal rule that had led to the appointment—and dismissal—of
Archibald Cox, who was ousted after challenging Richard Nixon during
the Watergate scandal. The rule, which predated the Ethics in Government Act, provided for the appointment of outside prosecutors to investigate accusations of wrongdoing by the Justice Department; but it allowed
the attorney general to fire the outside prosecutors. Ironically, it had been
President Nixon who in 1969 appointed Lacey as the U.S. attorney for
New Jersey, and then, a year later, to the bench as a federal district court
judge in the same state. Later, during the Reagan administration, Lacey sat
on the president's foreign intelligence surveillance court—the special
panel that grants requests for eavesdropping in national security investigations.

Barr set the tone for the Lacey investigation right from the start.
Standing at Lacey's side as he made the announcement, Barr said there
was "no reason to believe that any officials at the Department of Justice
have acted improperly or unprofessionally." He blamed the need even to
appoint Lacey on "media sensationalism." And while claiming he had not
discussed the matter with the White House, Barr did let slip that he had
telephoned Presidential Counsel Boyden Gray to tell him of his plans.

Many in Congress roundly condemned the appointment of Lacey.

Senator Boren pronounced it "unsatisfactory." Jack Brooks said Barr was covering up his responsibility to appoint an independent prosecutor "with the fig leaf of an investigator reporting to him personally, and not to the American public." While critics suggested that Barr was simply trying to stall the investigation until after the presidential election on November 3, Al Gore, the vice presidential candidate, went further and termed the whole affair worse than Watergate. "George Bush is presiding over a cover-up significantly larger than Watergate," charged Gore. "I'm not using the word impeachment," he said, adding nevertheless that "the Bush White House is having its attention diverted trying to manage this cover-up."

For his part, President Bush tried to avoid making any direct statements about Iraqgate. But in October, under pressure to discuss BNL and Iraqgate during a television interview, he made a most curious remark. "We were making agricultural loans. We were trying to bring the guy along. What happened was they had an illegal diversion of materials that would have helped them build a nuclear capability that we have substantially wiped out in the war." Having contradicted both himself and every senior government official who until then had denied that the White House knew of any illegal diversions into Saddam's nuclear weapons project, Bush then added a caveat: "To allege that we were building up his arms, or building up his nuclear power knowingly, is simply fallacious."

The cover-up was now unraveling in real time, on television and in the president's own words. Bush's White House advisers knew they had to act. Nicholas Rostow helped Brent Scowcroft draft an op-ed article for *The Washington Post* that would rebut the Iraqgate charges. In the article, Scowcroft contradicted what Bush had said just days before. Whereas Bush had acknowledged a diversion of materials to Iraq's weapons projects thanks to U.S. farm credits, Scowcroft said that no investigation had ever established "that Iraq misused credit guarantees to purchase weapons." And while it was true that $500 million of U.S. exports were shipped to Iraq between 1985 and 1990, most of these were for "low-level computers and heavy-duty trucks." Almost the same words were used by Lawrence Eagleburger, another Bush administration official wheeled into action, in an angry letter to *The New York Times* a few days later.

Bill Clinton, urged by his campaign strategists to focus on the economy, was content for the most part to leave comments on Iraqgate to Al Gore. But on the evening of Monday, October 19, in the last of the three televised presidential debates, Ross Perot forced the issue into the open.

"If you create Saddam Hussein over a ten-year period using billions of dollars of U.S. taxpayer money, step up to the plate and say it was a mistake," said Perot, adding the charge that Bush had given Saddam "the green light" to invade Kuwait. Bush defended his Iraqi policy, denied any green light had been given, and repeated his standard line about having tried to bring the Iraqi dictator into "the family of nations."

Clinton then said high-level officials had known Saddam was trying to develop weapons of mass destruction and had still pushed through aid to Iraq. Bush became furious. "There hasn't been one single scintilla of evidence" that any U.S. technology was used in Iraq's nuclear program, he insisted.

Within twenty-four hours, David Kay, the former chief of the UN inspection team in Iraq, contradicted the president. Kay said he had seen the U.S. technology with his own eyes. "The U.S. equipment was there and there is no disputing that. I simply don't see how the president can say that U.S. technology was not used in Iraq's nuclear program."

In a television interview the following week, Bush was pressed again on this claim. "Well, okay, let me clarify it. There was dual-use technology," he now said, adding that "maybe I overstated." Asked to comment on the cover-up charges over the BNL affair, Bush responded, "Wrong, wrong and wrong." He called Iraqgate a "Democratic frantic charge," but became testy again when he was reminded that the CIA had admitted misleading Congress. Was the CIA wrong? "May I say this? You've got an independent prosecutor looking at it. Let him make the determination," said Bush, referring to Frederick Lacey.

In fact, Lacey *had* made a preliminary determination three days before, on October 26. Following the law that required him to inform the attorney general whether there was enough substance in the case to go ahead with an investigation, Lacey had written to Barr saying he had found "sufficiently specific and credible" allegations to do just that. But October 26 was one week before election day, and the administration did not make public this highly sensitive piece of information. Instead, Lacey's preliminary findings were withheld until November 12, more than a week after George Bush had lost his battle to remain in the White House.

ON NOVEMBER 4, 1992, one day after Bill Clinton was elected president, events in Britain turned the Iraqgate affair into a transatlantic scandal.

The mood in London was glum, fostered by a lengthening economic slump that many blamed on Prime Minister John Major, a colorless

Conservative party politician who had taken over Number 10 Downing Street from Margaret Thatcher, now Baroness Thatcher, two years before.

Inside a courtroom behind the austere stone facade of the Old Bailey, Britain's most famous criminal court, a member of former Prime Minister Thatcher's government stepped up to the witness box. Alan Clark, a junior trade minister in the Thatcher government, was to be the star prosecution witness in the trial of three former executives of Matrix Churchill, the British machine tools company that had been bought in secret by agents of Iraq's arms procurement network. The company's executives, led by Paul Henderson, the former managing director, stood accused of violating Britain's export laws by lying about the military uses of the advanced equipment they had shipped to Iraq. The indictments had been brought in mid-February 1991, during Operation Desert Storm and just days before Dick Thornburgh announced the BNL charges in Washington. Like Drogoul in Atlanta, Paul Henderson and his fellow executives from Matrix Churchill had argued in court that they could not possibly have broken any laws because the British government had known what they were doing and approved of their activities.

There were other connections between the Matrix case in London and the BNL affair in Atlanta. Matrix had obtained BNL Atlanta financing that helped its Iraqi exports, and Henderson had recently received a secret offer of immunity from the Atlanta prosecutors, negotiated by Whitley's law partners and Gale McKenzie, in exchange for his testimony about BNL and the Iraqi procurement network. The immunity order would protect him from being charged in the United States.

In fact, Matrix Churchill was a name well known to senior officials of both the Bush administration and the government of Margaret Thatcher. In November 1989 the CIA had reported to the White House and the State Department that Matrix Churchill was part of "Iraq's complex procurement network of holding companies in Western Europe to acquire technology for its chemical, biological, nuclear and ballistic missile development programs." Then, following Saddam Hussein's invasion of Kuwait in 1990, the U.S. Treasury had publicly declared its American sister company in Ohio an Iraqi front and frozen its assets.

Matrix Churchill had shipped special lathes to Baghdad that were used to manufacture artillery shells. Its machine tools also ended up helping Baghdad to make mortars, fuses for howitzers, cluster bomb factory components, Scud missile parts, and gas centrifuge components for the development of nuclear weapons.

As in Atlanta, British government prosecutors in the Matrix Churchill case had initially tried to withhold intelligence reports and other documents relating to Iraq. In the autumn of 1992, four ministers in John Major's government signed papers to this effect, known as Public Interest Immunity Certificates. These ministers—Kenneth Clarke, the home secretary; Tristan Garel-Jones, a Foreign Office minister; Michael Heseltine, the secretary of state for trade and industry; and Malcolm Rifkind, the secretary of state for defense—were determined to keep secret the history of Britain's dealings with Iraq. (See Appendix C.) The certificates informed the court that it would not be "in the public interest" for secret government documents to be released during the trial. The problem, it seemed, was one of national security.

When Judge Brian Smedley asked to see the documents himself before pronouncing on their admissibility, they were brought to his room in safes. In addition to dozens of interdepartmental memos and letters, there were intelligence reports from the headquarters of both MI5 and MI6, the British intelligence services. Such was the secrecy surrounding these agencies and their relations to government that the guard remained outside the judge's room during an entire weekend as he studied the papers.

Like Judge Shoob in Atlanta, who did not see any threat to U.S. national security in disclosing information about Washington's past relations with the now-defeated government of Iraq, the British judge decided to permit at least some of the several hundred pages of paper to be seen by Henderson's lawyers. As a result of that decision, his lawyers, led by Geoffrey Robertson, an able barrister with a keen understanding of intelligence matters, were armed and ready. Well before it was time for Alan Clark to testify for the government, its case against the men from Matrix was being battered by courtroom revelations.

On October 13, the second day of the trial, the court heard that when Henderson had first been interviewed by Customs and Excise investigators, he had told them that officials at the Department of Trade and Industry had been prepared to "close their eyes" when granting export licenses to Matrix Churchill. Further, the British government was fully aware that some of the exports from Matrix often went to Baghdad by way of the Chilean arms dealer Carlos Cardoen, who had served as an intermediary. Henderson's own dealings with Cardoen, Iraq's biggest supplier of cluster bombs, fuses, and components for chemical weapons, were known in detail to British intelligence. Yet Matrix received British government loan guarantees to ship its equipment to Iraq by way of

Cardoen, a company that government records identified as "involved in chemical weapons manufacture." Evidence of the Matrix Churchill shipments to Iraq via Chile was first available back in 1987, but government ministers made a decision to let the exports go in order "to protect sources."

The London court was told that a Matrix executive had worked for MI6 while the company was selling to Iraq. An August 1989 British intelligence telegram released during the trial showed that the executive had reported back both on BNL and on Iraq's procurement network, which owned Matrix Churchill through a cascading series of front companies. The telegram also illustrated the closeness of the intelligence relationship between London and Washington, at one point suggesting "it would be useful if you could eventually get details from the Americans of other British and European companies involved in procurement."

On October 26, while Frederick Lacey in Washington was privately telling the Bush administration that he needed to go further with his Iraqgate probe, the jury in the London trial was hearing from a government official that the Matrix Churchill executive who had worked for MI6 was Paul Henderson. Eric Beston, an assistant secretary at the Department of Trade and Industry, also revealed that British ministers had approved Matrix exports while knowing they would go straight to Iraqi munitions production. One reason for allowing such dangerous cargo was the fear that breaking off the shipments would damage Henderson's cover as an intelligence-gatherer watching Iraq for Her Majesty's government. Was that really the reason? "That was one of the considerations," said the government witness.

There was another, less appealing justification for the British government's continuing to knowingly ship equipment into Iraq's weapons sites, and it was argued tortuously in a secret February 1989 report to senior Foreign Office officials. The report agonized about the likelihood that the Matrix exports could end up being used in Iraq's nuclear weapons project. "There is good reason to be skeptical about allowing any export which might help in the achievement of Iraq's nuclear objectives," noted the Foreign Office report, before arguing there was no reason to believe Matrix Churchill lathe equipment was "of specific interest" to the Iraqi nuclear program. Still, these same machines "are essential for the production of nuclear weapons." But, the report waffled, "they also have many other legitimate industrial uses." Simply withholding the Matrix Churchill lathes "would not therefore be an effective obstacle to the Iraqis' objectives." Neither, concluded the strange Foreign Office rationalization, "would it absolve Britain morally from any involvement in this network, since all non-licensable Matrix Churchill equipment would remain freely available to Iraq." (See Appendix B, pages 356–357.)

As the Matrix trial progressed, years of secret and cynical decisions by Margaret Thatcher's government were laid bare in the Old Bailey courtroom. On November 2 an officer from MI5 took the stand, seated behind a paper screen to protect his identity. He confirmed that Mark Gutteridge, a Matrix executive, had reported on Dr. Gerald Bull's Space Research Corporation. Geoffrey Robertson said Gutteridge first told MI5 about Bull and his supergun in May 1988. Secret documents showed that Matrix was being asked to provide machine tools for the supergun a year later, in October 1989. This was the same time that the Bush administration was approving its own export licenses that enabled Dr. Bull to send sophisticated U.S. technology to Iraq's supergun project. Gutteridge, it was later revealed in Paul Henderson's autobiography, had provided detailed reports on Iraq's procurement network as early as December 1987. The information provided by Gutteridge had been passed straight to the CIA.

On November 3, Paul Henderson's controller at MI6, whose secret name was Balsam, took the stand and, like his colleague from MI5, gave evidence anonymously, seated behind the screen. He revealed that Henderson had first worked for British intelligence in the early 1970s, providing information on commercial contracts behind the Iron Curtain. He had been "reactivated" as an agent for MI6 between 1985 and 1986 for the same purpose, spying on Iraq's military projects later in the 1980s.

"There are very few people who would take such risks and take them in their stride," said the MI6 officer, as prosecutors shook their heads in the knowledge that their defendant was now being *praised* by a government official. Henderson, said the MI6 agent, had even handed over blueprints for a projectile capable of being fired twelve hundred kilometers and said Matrix Churchill had been approached by the Iraqis to make machine tools for the project, believed to be Gerald Bull's supergun. And reports from Henderson's meetings with MI6 were sent to a "very high ministerial level."

It was becoming clearer each day to the jury that instead of violating Britain's arms export rules, the Matrix shipments of militarily useful goods to Iraq had been approved by the government. The real question was becoming a different one: Who in the government had approved such shipments, and how could *any* intelligence-gathering operation justify sending vital equipment straight into Saddam's war machine? The secret documents answered at least the first part of this question. They showed that Prime Minister Thatcher was herself kept informed about many of the sensitive exports. According to one memo, marked "Advice to Prime Minister," government officials discussed the suitability of selling engines for minelaying vessels.

There were thus some enormous question marks hanging over the trial when a somber-looking Alan Clark finally approached the witness box on November 4, 1992. Although he had been one of Thatcher's most ardent supporters, Clark was an unlikely politician. He was a man who enjoyed all the trappings of privilege. He lived in a castle in Kent, drove a Rolls-Royce Silver Ghost as well as a Porsche, and had private wealth that had brought him, among other things, 27,000 acres in the Scottish Highlands and an inclination to speak his mind, often at the wrong moment and in colorful terms. To Clark, teamwork and the diplomatic turn of phrase did not seem to come easily. As one former cabinet minister put it: "Alan is a charming fellow, but not a natural team player."

Before the trial began, Clark had told prosecutors he would implicate Henderson and the others by describing how they had lied to the Department of Trade and Industry about the intended use of Matrix equipment in Iraq. He had even denied press reports that suggested the government knew of the military end-use of Matrix exports to Iraq.

But on November 4, under persistent questioning from Geoffrey Robertson, Clark told a very different story. First he admitted that as late as 1989, London still perceived Iraq as "a very strong potential customer for defense sales." Then he said he had considered the government's guidelines on exports to Iraq to be "tiresome and intrusive." Finally, after hours of interrogation that had begun in a friendly manner and then taken on the flavor of an Oxford debate, Clark was asked whether it was true that he had met Paul Henderson in early 1988 and instructed the Matrix executive on how best to frame applications for export licenses so they would have a good chance of being granted. The answer was yes.

The former minister now found himself in a corner. He went on to admit that he had told Henderson the intended use of the Matrix machines should be couched in such a manner as "to emphasize their peaceful" rather than military aspects. So Clark did not want to let anyone know, at that stage, that the Matrix equipment was destined for munitions factories in Iraq? "No," replied Clark. And the emphasis on "peaceful" purposes was designed to keep the whole issue confidential? "I do not think it was principally a matter for public awareness," said Clark. "I think it was probably a matter for Whitehall cosmetics."

At this point the courtroom was mesmerized. Henderson allowed himself a quiet smile of satisfaction. With those last remarks, Clark had completely changed his story and destroyed the government's case. Here was a former government minister admitting under oath that he had coached Matrix executives on how to write their export applications so as to disguise their military use by Iraq. Britain's Iraqgate had unraveled right there in the Old Bailey courtroom. A few days later, the government dropped the case and Judge Smedley directed the jury to acquit Henderson and his fellow defendants. They proceeded to uncork bottles of champagne in the street outside the Old Bailey.

The House of Commons responded to the collapse of the Matrix trial the way Democratic members of the Congress had responded when it was learned the CIA had withheld crucial documents in the Atlanta case. In Britain, members of all parties, including the ruling Conservative party, were furious to learn about the Public Interest Immunity Certificates aimed at suppressing British documents. The ministers who had signed them were accused of being willing to sacrifice the businessmen from Matrix, who could have faced long prison terms, in order to protect some rather dubious national security interests. What the documents showed most of all was that the government had maintained a secret and extremely flexible approach to selling militarily useful equipment to Baghdad, right up to the weeks before the Iraqi invasion of Kuwait.

Within twenty-four hours of the collapse of the trial, Prime Minister Major faced an uproar in Parliament. He did his best to fight back against the unrelenting criticism. John Smith, the opposition Labour party leader, asked how Major could reconcile the sale of machine tools for Iraqi artillery shells in July 1990 with Major's own statement six months later that "for some considerable time we have not supplied arms to Iraq." Major didn't answer directly. He insisted that there had been firm guidelines from 1985 onward and a full embargo since August 1990.

What the prime minister did do was try to quell the mounting furor by ordering an independent judicial inquiry into allegations that government ministers had broken their own agreed guidelines on the export of arms to Iraq. Soon the prime minister was having to issue denials that he himself had been directly involved in the Matrix Churchill affair. While he denied that he knew of any breach in Britain's arms export guidelines, Major did admit that as foreign secretary in September 1989 he had been given background information about Matrix Churchill before meeting with Tariq Aziz. He claimed the information had to do only with media interest in Iraq's procurement network. Major, now facing mounting allegations that included the charge he had misled Parliament, responded by denying everything and telling Parliament over and over again that the entire issue of Iraqgate was now in the hands of Lord Justice Scott, the man chosen to head an independent inquiry. It would be some time before Scott undertook his proceedings, and many in London who were watching the unfolding Iraqgate scandal feared that given the British penchant for secrecy, a truly independent investigation was something of an oxymoron.

Geoffrey Robertson, the lawyer who exposed the government's deception during the Matrix trial, was concerned that bringing the charges "insured that Iraqgate never became an issue in the U.K. elections of April 1992." Robertson noted that since the Matrix charges had been pending, and sub judice under British law, the media were cowed into accepting that the *government* had been deceived by Henderson. Robertson revealed later that "as early as January 1988 Henderson was told by a minister of the government that its secret encouragement of machine tools trade with Iraq was contingent on continuing approval from the White House."

BACK IN WASHINGTON, that startling information was not available to congressional investigators, who were nonetheless coming to the conclusion that the Bush administration had no intention of allowing a full probe of Iraqgate. In mid-November, a week after the collapse of the Matrix Churchill trial in Britain, Barr informed the House Judiciary Committee he would decide whether to name an independent prosecutor in December. Brooks and others in Congress noted the timing; the post-Watergate law on special prosecutors was set to expire on December 15. The attorney general was "attempting to run out the clock" on the law, said Brooks. "I will not be buffaloed," remarked Barr a week later, adding that "frankly, I don't think prosecutors should be independent."

On December 9, Judge Lacey called a press conference to announce his findings on BNL and Iraqgate. His probe had lasted just seven weeks, and his message was clear within the first five minutes. His initial determination just before the presidential election that "credible allegations" warranted further investigation had gone out the window. "All of this stuff about there being a cover-up," said Barr's investigator, "is arrant nonsense." More to the point, he added, turning to the reporters seated before him, "you, in this room, have been taken in by it."

Eyes widened as Lacey continued, first when he proclaimed the work of BNL prosecutors "virtually perfect" and then when he boasted that "at this point I know more about this case than anyone else in the United States." The real problem, said Lacey, was the media. "It's you people who cover this city and accept and repeat the protected words and unbridled attacks of a legislator. . . . Why should anyone want to serve in a country, and perhaps more specifically in a city like this where irresponsibility like that prevails?"

The press conference became increasingly combative after that, even more so when Lacey revealed that half of his investigation report would not be made public. "There's some things in that report that I wish I could tell you about. I can't," he explained, referring to the voluminous section that dealt with the CIA and was classified "Top Secret-Codeword." This is one of the highest classifications in the U.S. government, generally used for nuclear matters and other state secrets.

What Lacey *could* say about the CIA, which had admitted less than two months before to having deliberately concealed some of the more important BNL documents, was that there had been some "blundering." It was all the result of "a series of mistakes by well-meaning and well-intentioned persons." Did Lacey look at the question of whether the CIA knew about the Iraqi loans before the FBI raid in August 1989? "No, sir, I did not." Did he examine illegal arms exports to Iraq? "No, sir, I did not." Did he find out if the intelligence information Matrix Churchill gathered in Britain was shared with the CIA? Lacey said he could not answer the question.

When asked about the Italian government's attempts to persuade Dick Thornburgh and other officials not to indict BNL, Lacey said he had spoken personally to Thornburgh, who could not remember any such meetings. Thornburgh had never put any pressure on anyone within the Justice Department, "except he said, 'Look, let's get this thing moving.' " Lacey disclosed that he had traveled to Rome, but he had not interviewed the former BNL chairman or director-general. Instead he had talked with Giampiero Cantoni, the chairman who had been named to the post only after the Atlanta loans were discovered.

At the end of his press conference, when a reporter insisted that further investigation was needed, Lacey had a ready reply. "Fine. Go investigate it. I'm not investigating. Thank you very much. It's been great. I've enjoyed it. I hope you have. Thank you." And with that he left the room, later billing the Justice Department $372,392 for his work.

William Barr took only a few hours to absorb the two-volume Lacey report before formally rejecting the idea of an independent prosecutor. Inevitably, he and Lacey soon found themselves under attack from congressional Democrats and from President-elect Bill Clinton as well. Clinton said he was not satisfied that all the facts had come to light. He pledged that he would ask his attorney general to reevaluate the entire BNL affair and advise him on whether to go ahead anyway with the naming of a special prosecutor. "I certainly think we need to know more about it than we now know," said Clinton.

In Atlanta, Judge Shoob, whose own conclusions about government wrongdoing had been savaged by Lacey, said Lacey "pretty much accepted the Justice Department's version of what has taken place"; in private he called it "a whitewash." Shoob later recalled that early in his inquiry, Lacey had come to Atlanta to talk about the Iraqi loans case. "We spent about one and a half hours together, but he devoted only five minutes to the BNL case and spent the rest of the time talking mostly about himself," remembered Shoob.

By now, there were few people in Washington who believed Lacey's version of Iraqgate; those who did were mostly staunch Republicans and members of the outgoing Bush administration. There were certainly believers in Italy, given that Lacey had concluded he was "certain" that no one at BNL Rome headquarters ever knew of the Iraqi loans that were made in Atlanta.

In Rome, BNL's top management heard this news and was delighted, no one more so than Chairman Cantoni. He was hoping the whole Iraqi loans scandal would be forgotten so he could get on with rebuilding the bank's shattered morale, and finances. And six days after Lacey reported and Barr shut down the whole affair, BNL filed a little-noticed lawsuit in a federal claims court in Washington. The Italian bank was demanding that the U.S. government pay it $340 million, plus interest, since the Atlanta loans to Iraq were in default. BNL justified the move on the grounds that since Baghdad had not paid back the loans, the U.S. should make good on the CCC guarantees that backed them.

BNL thus acted against the U.S. government, but only after the Bush administration had apparently laid questions about the Atlanta affair to rest. As it sued in Washington, the bank also took action in Rome. There, BNL quietly informed three of its midlevel executives that they were being fired. All three had been leaders of the bank's internal investigation of the Iraqi loans saga. In effect, it seemed that anyone at BNL who had come near the Atlanta affair was now a liability.

When senior officials at the Federal Reserve Board got word of the dismissals, they scratched their heads in amazement. Why was the Italian bank firing three of its investigators? More important, why was BNL still refusing to cooperate with the Federal Reserve's own investigation of BNL Atlanta, and at this late date? "Frankly, we were furious with BNL. They weren't playing ball, and we couldn't understand why," said a senior lawyer at the Federal Reserve. Then the Fed saw BNL's own demand for U.S. government compensation, which was filed on December 15. One week later, BNL's American lawyers received a sharply worded letter from the Federal Reserve—and with it a subpoena for documents. (See Appendix B, page 355.)

The Fed was asking BNL for information on Rome's dealings with both Atlanta and Iraq in October 1992, but two months later, BNL had still not complied with the requests. It was the firing of the three BNL bankers, said a lawyer for the Fed, that had proved the last straw. Why had the bank waited more than three years after the FBI raid in Atlanta to dismiss them? And why had the bank dismissed the very people who were investigating the wrongdoing in Atlanta? It made little sense in Washington.

In Rome, where BNL had been under pressure from Italian Senate investigators for nearly two years to do something to show it was serious about getting to the bottom of the Iraqi scandal, the firings fit a peculiarly Italian logic. In Italy it is often the form that counts as much as the substance, so the firing of three BNL executives—it didn't matter if they had previously investigated Drogoul—demonstrated to the outside world that *something* was being done.

In fact, BNL's handling of the Iraqi loans affair had been bizarre from the beginning. Executives inside the bank recalled that Giampiero Cantoni was under pressure from Italian politicians to resolve the Atlanta matter without embarrassing the government, and as the head of a state bank he had had little choice; the government was calling the shots. When he finally did take action—to fire three midlevel executives—it was at best a token gesture and at worst an unfair scapegoating of three rather minor players.

"We were under pressure from the senior management of the bank right from the start to go slowly on Atlanta," said a former BNL executive who formed part of the bank's original investigation of the Iraqi loans affair. The problem, as no fewer than four of the managers at BNL's Rome office recalled, was that the Iraqi loans, legal or illegal, were considered affairs of state and not merely banking transactions. Proof of this was to be found in the flurry of cable traffic between the Italian ambassador to

Baghdad and BNL officials in Rome, all of it indicating a frenzied effort to maintain good relations between Italy and Iraq after exposure of the Atlanta affair.

"Some of us in the Atlanta task force were trying to block the Iraqi loans from Rome, but even after Drogoul had been removed from his job in Atlanta, the new manager there was still making good on the transactions. It was very frustrating," recalled Gianmaria Sartoretti, who spent months poring through more than thirty thousand Atlanta telexes, faxes, and other Iraq-related documents. BNL bankers like Sartoretti who tried to get tough with Iraq in order to block payments to it on some of Drogoul's loans found themselves in conflict with other top executives. Sartoretti, an outspoken and devoted BNL banker, only made matters worse for himself when he went before the Italian Senate commission that was probing the Atlanta affair and revealed that Drogoul had also extended hundreds of millions of dollars of improper credits for exports to countries other than Iraq. These included some that an American intelligence officer later identified as having financed the purchase of arms by *Iran*.

In December 1992, Sartoretti was among the three BNL executives who were fired by the bank. Louis Messere, the hapless auditor who had originally discovered irregularities at the Atlanta branch back in the autumn of 1988, was another who was fired. The third was Teodoro Monaco, who met Drogoul on his first trip to Baghdad and reported this to headquarters, and had later channeled business for Iraq from Rome to Atlanta. None of these three were senior enough to be of great consequence, but out of the bank they went.

Even a more senior executive named Pierdomenico Gallo, who had been a deputy general manager at the bank, found life difficult after he fought a battle with Cantoni and the BNL board of directors over the issue of Atlanta. Gallo had written a long letter of protest to Cantoni in April 1991; he was particularly upset that an internal BNL report did not make clear the circumstances of the infamous $50 million Iraqi loan proposed by Drogoul in Atlanta and ultimately signed in Rome. Within days of Gallo's complaint, the bank's executive committee ordered the author of the flawed report to investigate Gallo's staff.

Gallo was now clearly identified as a dissident inside the BNL board. During a board meeting in June 1991, after Cantoni had fumed about media coverage and outside criticism of the bank, Gallo read his complaints out to the entire board. Two months later he left the bank, claiming it was for reasons of health.

These internal incidents received little attention in Italy and none in the United States. But they showed quite clearly that the bank's new management, reflecting government sentiment and its own impatience, wanted to wash its hands of the Iraqi scandal. After April 1992, when the Italian Senate commission on BNL concluded that the bank's Rome headquarters had been both aware of the Iraqi loans made from Atlanta and deeply involved in them, Cantoni continued to deny the charges. The Senate commission no longer accepted Cantoni's frequent denials, which grew more strident each time an allegation was made in the United States or in Italy.

"Atlanta was a deplorable incident," said one member of the Senate commission, "but what is far more serious is this insistent cover-up."

In effect, Rome's efforts to protect itself from charges that BNL was involved in the Iraqgate scandal were being set back more in the United States than in Italy. In early 1993 the Senate Intelligence Committee issued a 163-page report on the BNL affair. The report shed little new light on precisely what Rome knew and when, but it did break new ground. It announced that several intelligence reports that were widely disseminated inside the Bush administration had suggested that BNL's Rome headquarters knew of the billions of dollars of Iraqi loans made by Atlanta.

Over at CIA headquarters, another report was released, this one the Agency's internal investigation of itself. Robert Gates, the outgoing director, acknowledged that "mistakes clearly were made and there was carelessness" over the BNL affair. The entire matter, said Gates, was a "train wreck." It was the same old line that many Bush administration officials had used in trying to explain U.S. policy toward Iraq: Mistakes had been made.

FIFTEEN

The Fate of the Foot Soldiers

As the cover-up unraveled, it claimed some human victims. Frank Lemay watched the unfolding events in Washington with a mixture of fascination and anguish. Until the spring of 1992 he had been a hardworking bureaucrat as anonymous as any of the thousands like him who worked at the State Department. But the thirty-five-year-old Lemay's life changed radically in April 1992, after Henry Gonzalez revealed in a speech the contents of a memorandum the young Foreign Service officer had written back in the autumn of 1989, the one in which he reported his suspicions that Iraq had used U.S. loan guarantees to purchase equipment for its nuclear weapons.

In June 1992, the House Judiciary Committee began discussing the need for an independent prosecutor, and it called him to testify. Lemay soon found himself isolated inside the State Department, so much so that he was told to get his own lawyer to accompany him to Congress. Before the Brooks committee, Lemay did little more than confirm the accuracy of his reporting, but within weeks his professional life deteriorated. *He* was the "State Department employee" whose memo was disparaged by an angry President George Bush during a morning television show. After that, Lemay felt like a pariah in the State Department's office of legislative affairs, where he now worked.

"I was a career person, and after this memo came out, I was just frozen out," he recalled. "For a while my boss at legislative affairs wouldn't even talk to me. How do you work for somebody who won't talk to you? Other colleagues at the department would sneak up and tell me they were not supposed to talk to me, but they wanted me to know I had done the right thing."

"Frank became persona non grata at State," said a friend. "He had only been trying to do his job, but they made sure he was punished."

In November 1992, Lemay had another problem. The lawyer who had accompanied him to the House Judiciary Committee presented him with a bill for three thousand dollars. He asked the State Department to pay the bill and was told it was his personal responsibility. Yet his testimony had concerned official State Department business, and government officials had advised him to retain the lawyer. Now Frank Lemay became angry. In December 1992 he informed a personal assistant to Lawrence Eagleburger that he would go public with the story if State refused to pay, maybe telephone William Safire at *The New York Times*. "They didn't want anything written about this. The Bush administration wanted to muzzle this whole thing right up to the end. So in the last week of December 1992, they finally agreed to pay the lawyer," Lemay recalled.

The more he learned about the BNL affair and Iraqgate, the more Frank Lemay came to understand what had happened to him. He was bitter at the experience. "It was a shitty way for politicians to handle a career civil servant. They were pretty small-minded," he observed.

THE PROBLEMS Fred Haobsh faced extended well beyond legal fees and isolation in the workplace. Unlike Lemay, Haobsh did not even make the news; he was just a former foot soldier for the CIA whose life was ruined by the decade of deceitful relations between Washington and Baghdad. On a rainy evening in April 1993, Fred Haobsh stepped out of his rented house in suburban Atlanta to make his regular call to New York from a pay phone. As he had done for the past month, he reported on whether there had been any harassment that day.

For a couple of years now, Haobsh had been following the gradually unfolding tale of what the media had come to call Iraqgate. He had seen fragments emerging of a story he had lived for a while in the early 1980s, during his travels to and from Baghdad, and then again in the early 1990s, when he worked for the CIA.

Fred Haobsh was not the only operative who had played a role in America's secret policy to arm Saddam; there were dozens around the United States who, like Haobsh, had walked across the boundaries of the law on countless occasions in the name of national security. Yet he never read about the others in print or saw them on television, and he did not know if they too were suffering as a result of their actions.

The trail that had finally brought Haobsh to Atlanta was a long and rough one. For Haobsh, everything that had happened could be traced back to his meeting in New York with Hussein Kamel, disguised at the time as Lieutenant Abu Ali. He thought often, too often, about that first meeting, and about the brief encounter he had subsequently had with Saddam Hussein. In a way it was entirely appropriate that Haobsh would retain the gold watch that Saddam had given him in thanks for a mission that would ultimately wreck his life. With Haobsh it was always hard to tell whether the watch belonged closer to his heart than to his curio collection. It was a talisman, a symbol of a previous existence that kept intruding ever more menacingly into the present.

Haobsh admitted that back in 1981, when the opportunity had first presented itself, he had taken a perverse liking to the risks and rewards of the covert life. The watch, with its portrait of Saddam Hussein on its enameled face, represented both. Although Haobsh made various attempts during the 1980s to stay out of the world of intelligence, his interest in the Middle East as a place to do business would combine with his love of adventure to lead him to the Central Intelligence Agency. The truth was, he liked being an operative. He liked the buzz, and he liked the risks that challenged his ingenuity and self-sufficiency. What he found impossible to accept was the assumption that low-level government intelligence assets like himself should be utterly expendable. They were there to be used. They should serve their country without asking questions, accept whatever treatment came their way, and keep quiet about it. Haobsh's rejection of these fundamentals would ultimately be his undoing.

It was a lesson he had failed to grasp back in 1983, when he and Robert Johnson had parted ways after trying and failing to iron out the details of covert shipments to Iraq. Ultimately, trying to make ends meet as a salesman in New York became so tough for Haobsh that in 1985 he decided to move his family to the West Coast and start over in the only business he knew—trading with the Middle East. Using money he borrowed from family members, he set up an import-export operation in San Diego, with Saudi Arabia as its main market focus. He dealt in clothing, cosmetics, and medical equipment—the same sorts of products he had initially handled for American Steel, though no Maytag washing machines this time. Life for the Haobsh family began to look up once more, so much so that he was able to indulge his taste for old cars. He bought two antique Mercedes cars cheaply in Saudi Arabia, one black and one silver gray, and shipped them home to San Diego. Being a meticulous man, he kept them in perfect shape.

Haobsh could never really explain the reason why he had answered a discreet CIA recruiting advertisement in *The Los Angeles Times* in 1986. At the time he had a small but reasonably successful one-man business going, and prospects looked bright. Nevertheless he drove north from San Diego to Los Angeles one afternoon and met an Agency man in a hotel room. The interview was inconclusive, and Haobsh was not recruited. But the CIA representative learned a lot about Haobsh, in particular his interests and contacts in the Middle East, and his name was kept on file. Haobsh was not completely surprised to get a call two years later from a CIA officer, asking if he could help make an introduction to a Saudi prince living in Los Angeles. Nothing beyond that was called for, said the Agency man, and Haobsh obliged since he had done business with the prince before. It was a decision that Haobsh would look back on with dismay ever afterward: "I will always regret the moment I lifted a finger for the CIA," he said later.

Haobsh had encountered some dangerous people during his dealings with Iraq in the early 1980s, and he was haunted by the recollections. In 1988 he realized that it was one thing to have bad memories and quite another to face a more palpable danger. In September of that year a bomb exploded in the mailbox outside his home in the San Diego suburb of Rancho Bernardo, blowing a hole in the yard three feet wide. It took the local police eight hours to respond to his emergency call. When an officer finally arrived, he was apologetic. There was a lot of crime in San Diego, he explained, and it had taken that long to get around to Haobsh's emergency. "He said I should get myself a gun, as long as I was prepared to use it," recalled Haobsh. "He recommended a shotgun because there was no waiting period, and I could take it home from the store with me. He even told me where to buy it." Haobsh, who had not fired a gun since he was in army training in Jordan, got in his car and drove to the gun shop.

A week later, Haobsh's eight-year-old daughter Nadine crept into her parents' bedroom in the middle of the night and whispered between sobs that a man was breaking through the glass sliding doors into her bedroom downstairs. Haobsh grabbed his new shotgun from beside the bed and bounded down the stairs and into the yard to see a figure disappearing into the night. It was pointless to fire a shot. "Right then and there, we decided to move," said Haobsh. "So we picked Dallas because my parents had moved there when my father retired."

For a short while, Haobsh tried selling carpets and floor coverings in Dallas, but the business floundered. Although he managed to hold on to his two old Mercedeses, he lost a lot of money. Once again he was drawn

to the Middle East to make a living: He set up an import-export operation, just as he had done before. Once again the CIA would enter his life,
though not before the watchers—whoever they were—delivered another
message.

Christmas in Dallas in 1989, Haobsh decided, would be celebrated
in style, regardless of his family's economic situation. He had reasons to be
cheerful. Not only were his parents now within a few miles, there was a
new addition to the family, a son he had named Pierre. It was shop-till-
you-drop time, and that was what Haobsh did. On the afternoon of
December 20 he climbed into the black Mercedes and headed to the local
mall for a few last-minute items. With one thing and another, it was almost
two hours before he wheeled an overloaded shopping cart out to the
parking lot and headed for the car. It was gone. The security people drove
him all around the enormous lot, but there was no sign of the Mercedes.

He filed a report with the local police. This wasn't just any car, he
explained to the officer. It was a 1971 Mercedes 600 series limousine, one
of the last off the production line. It was black, very long, and it weighed
around four tons. Even in Dallas, the car turned heads. Once, while fixing
one of the headlights, a Mercedes dealer had commented admiringly that
there weren't likely to be more than a dozen of these in the country. Now
someone had stolen it from a shopping mall. Thankfully, it shouldn't be
that hard to find.

For twenty-four hours Haobsh sat by the phone. Eventually a police
lieutenant called from Texarkana, 166 miles away on the state line with
Arkansas. It was impossible to tell whether this was Haobsh's car, he said
apologetically. He ought to come and take a look.

Haobsh literally wept when he saw it. The fire had been so intense
that it had melted the interior into a tangled mass of shapeless metal,
punctuated by an occasional seat spring. Much of the window glass
seemed to have melted. Fires had been set in the trunk and the engine
compartment. Blistered and peeled to the bare metal in places, the doors
and even the roof had buckled into misshapen curves. The intensity of the
heat had popped one of the Mercedes emblems off a hubcap. Haobsh
bent down, picked up the twisted silver star, and put it in his pocket. This
was not the work of a joy-rider.

He drove back to Dallas in a state of terror. Inevitably, he reflected
once again on his involvement with Saddam Hussein. As far as Haobsh
was concerned, he was a patriot who had acted in the service of his
country. Yet he had been driven to move twice now, first to San Diego,
then to Dallas. His fear began to turn to anger. He was not going to be

intimidated anymore, except that he had no idea who was behind the intimidation or why.

It was not until 1991, when he parted company with the CIA in the wake of his missions to Amman and Tunis during Operation Desert Storm to meet Anas Dohan, that Haobsh began to feel apprehensive once more. America was celebrating the defeat of Saddam Hussein, but Haobsh had walked out on the CIA confused, afraid, and ultimately questioning the nature of the work he had done. He had taken risks but had never been told enough to understand why CIA officers had wanted him to sell weapons to Baghdad in the middle of the Gulf war.

The Agency had been displeased when Haobsh said he wanted to leave. But Haobsh didn't understand why anybody would expect him to be willing to sell weapons to Saddam in the middle of Desert Storm. "I had always heard that you are never ex-CIA. They always keep an eye on you," he said later. "I had put myself on the line in a very dangerous area. I did my bit for the United States just as the men in Desert Storm did. I provided all kinds of information to the Agency. But there was no way I was going to sell SAM missiles to the Iraqis, which is what they asked me to do. That is the reason why I stopped working for them."

Things went wrong for Haobsh almost immediately. His trading company, which he had used as a front for CIA intelligence-gathering, shrank to nothing. The CIA's promises that his import-export company would be favorably mentioned to U.S. embassies in the Middle East seemed never to have been kept. He wrote to his senators, Lloyd Bentsen and Phil Gramm, that during the Gulf war "I was working with our government in their effort to fight Iraq and the Iraqi regime" and that he had been promised business from Kuwait and Saudi Arabia after the war. Yet not being able to disclose that the government agency he had worked with was the CIA proved an insurmountable handicap. Senator Gramm put Haobsh in touch with David Jensen, a deputy assistant secretary at the Commerce Department's international trade division. Jensen tried to help, but in August 1991 he wrote to Senator Gramm that since Haobsh could not name the government agency he had worked with, "we cannot be of much more assistance to him."

In the spring of 1992, betrayed, angry, and on the verge of bankruptcy, he contacted a journalist he had seen interviewed on television about the Iraqgate scandal. The journalist initiated a lengthy series of meetings and debriefings with Haobsh. Going to the press had been a last resort; clearly it was another risky move, but Haobsh wanted help and protection. The problem was that somebody seemed to know he was talking. Thereafter, he and his family, already weary from past harassment, would suffer an escalating pattern of more of the same.

On the morning after Labor Day, September 8, 1992, Haobsh and his family were in Dallas, spending the weekend at his parents' home. In the driveway stood the family's single largest asset: the remaining silver Mercedes 600 limousine. Haobsh came outside to find that every window had been broken, every tire slashed. The dark blue velour interior had been cut to ribbons with a knife. Buried in the walnut dash, the wrecked clock was stopped at 3:10 A.M. On the roof, etched into the paintwork in crude letters twelve inches wide, was the word KILL. On the trunk lid, similarly etched, was the word YOU. It turned out that the neighbors had heard dogs barking during the night, but the Haobsh family had heard nothing. "We didn't stay in Texas after that," said Haobsh.

Moving to Atlanta did not solve his problems. Although Haobsh had given nobody his telephone number, not even his own lawyer, there was often only one night a week when the phone did not ring in the small hours of the morning. Mostly these would be hang-up calls. Then there were the cars, cruising at times and occasionally stopping in front of the rented house in Atlanta.

In early April 1993, a law enforcement friend ran a license plate check on a red Pontiac that had cruised up and down outside Haobsh's house and traced the owner's address. The address turned out to be at the Fort McPherson military base in Atlanta, the headquarters of FOR-SCOM, which was the military command responsible for maintaining the readiness of more than a million soldiers in the continental United States. FORSCOM hosted the U.S. Army, the Army Reserve, and the National Guard—and the Defense Intelligence Agency.

The harassment of Fred Haobsh sounded "like classic psy-ops," said a U.S. intelligence officer when asked to interpret what Haobsh was enduring. "It's the kind of thing the Special Operations people teach you at Fort Bragg. It's cheap to carry out because it doesn't take many people, it has very little chance of being traced to anywhere unless somebody really screws up, and it works. It is extremely tough to deal with. The guy may have been a patriot, but it sounds as if he is being hung out to dry."

By now, not surprisingly, Haobsh was living in a state of chronic fear, almost waiting at home for the telephone to ring. After his family was in bed, he would go over and over his life since his trips to Baghdad ten years earlier on behalf of the covert operatives who made things happen for the White House. He would relive the days of Desert Storm, when on behalf of the CIA he had sat with Saddam's chief military procurement officer in Tunis. He had played a tiny role in a larger sequence of events involving Washington and Baghdad, but now he had become a prisoner of a Kafkaesque nightmare. He could think of nothing else. Whether by design or accident, Saddam and the CIA had taken over his mind.

IN JUNE 1993, almost thirty-five hundred miles from Atlanta, Frank Machon was sitting, similarly despondent, in the cramped office of his empty warehouse in Glasgow. To pay outstanding debts, he had put his storage business into liquidation, and by now most of his customers had arrived with their trucks and moved their equipment out before he closed the doors for good. There were still some industrial engines and other bulky items left, but they would be out of there shortly. Years of hard work were being undone before his eyes, yet there was something within him that would not let him physically leave the place. The cavernous spaces were never really silent, not even during the depths of the night. The sound of the summer rain on the metal roof and the skylights would be amplified into a roar. Then would come a succession of creaks and sighs as the metal latticework supporting the roof moved slightly in the face of the breeze picking up off the river Clyde. There were no security guards patrolling anymore. Machon was alone here for most of the day and all of the night.

Machon was tough, but he had been shafted so badly these last few years that he now ran on rage and cigarettes. He was suffering, although he wouldn't willingly admit it. His wife, Marion, was as angry and disillusioned as he was. She was angry at the price in loneliness and fatigue and tears that she and her daughters had paid as a result of her husband's obsessive pursuit of his cause. She was disillusioned by the lack of results, the lack of interest on the part of the House of Commons, the lack of an honest and clear-cut resolution.

Marion had built this business with him and helped him run it. A week ago she had signed on at the government's local Jobs Centre, hoping to find some work, but Glasgow's economy was far from booming and almost no money was coming in. She would drop in to see him as often as she could because he wouldn't go back to their house from this place, and the kids rarely got to see him. The warehouse was his fortress, it had become his home, and the way he saw it, it was now under siege in an obsessive battle he saw himself waging against Her Majesty's government.

This was his life as the summer approached in 1993. Frank Machon was starting to crack under the strain.

He had briefly made the news when it was revealed that back in 1988 he had communicated what he had thought he knew about the covert arming of Iraq by British companies to Prime Minister Margaret Thatcher. It had not been a good move. Perhaps he had been naive, or too stubborn. Whatever the case, he had rebelled against what he saw as a growing cover-up of the British government's role in the arming of Iraq. Still, there was no getting away from the fact that for much of the past five years, nobody had wanted to listen. Machon had developed a slow-burning anger and a quick temper during that time, largely because of Allivane International Limited, the covert vehicle for arms shipments to both Iran and Iraq that had hired him as its trucker in 1988. On December 23, 1988, Machon wrote to Thatcher of his suspicion that "either Britain or America is funnelling war equipment through Allivane which is certainly destined for Iraq." (See Appendix B, page 358.)

He had become bitter, first at the government's reneging on a promise to repay him money he had advanced to Allivane on behalf of the Ministry of Defence, and then, as his obsession overtook him, at the blood he perceived to be on the hands of leading politicians. After years of his own investigation, he had concluded that ministers in the Thatcher government had talked a fancy line about an arms embargo and quietly approved a flood of weapons to the Middle East to keep the war going. Now this was no longer even news; it was virtually accepted after the revelations that had emerged in the Matrix Churchill trial.

Machon, however, had written to Margaret Thatcher about his suspicions before the government's policies became publicly known. And through the myriad ways in which the government responds to such challenges, he had been punished, most conspicuously by the customs people, who had demanded a tax payment on money from Allivane that he had never received. There would be court battles ahead, and more legal bills. He could see it all coming.

He walked out to a cold water faucet in the men's room, filled a battered electric kettle, and prepared to make more instant coffee. "You know," he said, "I never wanted to damage my country or my prime minister. I just thought she should know what had been going on. Then I get these threats, and these wee men telling me I'm trying to bring down the government. Me?" He gave a tired smile and mixed the coffee and heated water with a plastic spoon. It was cold in here, even in summer. "I'll not give up," he said, almost to himself.

An awful long time ago, said Machon, he had begun to perceive the shadowy outlines of an international political scandal in the machinations of Allivane. But he had lacked the political sophistication to see it as anything more than an act of moral betrayal, and while he had collected many important pieces of the puzzle, he had ultimately become a man who was easy to ignore. Machon was a sitting duck for those seeking to discredit him; journalists who met him came away thinking this was a man obsessed and prone to overkill. It was almost impossible to take him at his word without a detailed understanding of the deliberately complex nature of covert arms shipments to Iraq in the 1980s, the front companies, the arms-length relations between government and foot soldiers, and the banking channels that were employed. Machon started out as a patriot and ended up as a victim of both the government he had worked for and, ultimately, his own blind rage.

There had been a single moment at the beginning of May 1993, when Lord Justice Scott had begun his inquiry into British exports of defense equipment to Iraq, that Machon thought he saw the possibility of vindication. It had brought him a sudden uplift, as a tiny band of friends and allies in his cause jammed into his dingy Glasgow office to share the exciting sense of possibility that the full story might be laid bare.

Machon had drafted a letter to Lord Justice Scott, sending him a copy of the one he had sent to Margaret Thatcher back in December 1988, and hinting at further dark areas that could be explored as a result of his evidence. He put his lawyer in London on alert in case he was called to testify. Scott's office had politely acknowledged receipt of his letter, but Machon had not been called. His spirits sank once more. If there was a future ahead for him that did not involve his continuing crusade to expose the British role in arming Iraq, he couldn't see it. All that Frank Machon had left was a burning sense of betrayal, an empty warehouse, and a story to tell that hardly anybody wanted to hear.

THE SAME COULD not be said about Christopher Drogoul; there were many people who wanted to hear his story. Yet Drogoul shared one characteristic with Machon, Haobsh, and Lemay, although on a vastly different scale: He too was a fall guy.

During the Bush administration both the Justice Department and

Frederick Lacey had portrayed Drogoul as a kind of evil genius, the biggest fraudster since Lucky Luciano and Al Capone. By the summer of 1993, the only thing Drogoul had in common with Al Capone was his housing; he had spent fifteen months stuck in an isolation cell in the hospital ward of a maximum-security federal penitentiary in Atlanta. It was the same prison that was Capone's permanent home after he was sentenced to jail for his misdeeds in 1931.

Once Drogoul had been a high-flying banker. In the middle of 1993 he was a pasty-faced forty-four-year-old known as Prisoner Number 41701019. He was surrounded by 1,999 other inmates at the Atlanta pen, and his peer group consisted of murderers, rapists, and drug dealers. Drogoul was the only one of the two thousand prisoners who was not allowed out in the courtyard. He had not seen the sun for more than a year. He looked it. Pale and bedraggled in a khaki uniform, he ate very little of the food on offer—mostly a steady diet of beans, grits, hamburgers, hot dogs, and watery soup. As a gourmet treat, when visitors came, he was allowed a paper bag of microwave popcorn from the prison's vending machine.

Visitors to the penitentiary would come away with a sense of the contradictions of this fundamentally unremarkable man who had been thrust into the limelight of an international political scandal. His was now an exceedingly passive view of the world, almost resigned. Legal bills of half a million dollars had forced him to file for bankruptcy protection, and his home had been sold off by the bankruptcy court. His wife and children were now on welfare, and he got to see them only on Tuesday and Thursday afternoons, when they filed into the prison on visits. It was hard to conceive of him as the man who had flown to London aboard the Concorde to visit Matrix Churchill, who had dined with Iraqi procurement agents in Baghdad and discussed U.S. government loan guarantees with government officials in Washington. "I was a tool of both the Italians and the Americans," complained Drogoul, laying out brown paper napkins in a neat square on a Formica table and sharing his popcorn.

There was neither remorse nor self-pity as he recalled the years when he had handed out billions of dollars of loans to Baghdad. Above all, there seemed very little comprehension, even now, of what had actually transpired. He yearned for news of the outside world, seemed embarrassed by the way his friends talked of selling the film rights to his story, and approached the endless debriefings with his lawyers with a stoic, weary determination. In the meantime, he awaited his fate and joked about the prison food and anything else that came into his head. His sister had once remarked that "Chris is certainly no rocket scientist." He seemed more like an overgrown college sophomore who had flunked all his exams yet was curiously serene. As he prepared for his trial, scheduled to begin in September 1993, Drogoul said many times that he realized he was but a bit player in the broader story of BNL and Iraqgate. Yet he had handled real money, great sums of it, and the money had financed real arms.

SIXTEEN

Endgame

G eorge Bush was obsessed with Saddam Hussein until the bitter
end. Three days before he was due to vacate the White House,
the president launched one more missile attack against Iraq.

On the evening of Sunday, January 17, 1993, more than forty Toma-
hawk cruise missiles went streaking into the sky from U.S. Navy ships
stationed in the Persian Gulf and the Red Sea. The missiles, flying less
than a hundred feet above the ground as they sped over distances of up to
seven hundred miles, exploded into the sides of a dozen buildings in a
sprawling industrial park just eight miles south of downtown Baghdad.

The White House announced that the industrial complex was part of
Iraq's nuclear weapons program. But at that moment Washington's attention was focused on another event—the jubilant arrival in the nation's
capital of a bus cavalcade bearing President-elect Bill Clinton. Few people
knew or cared that the site of the cruise missile attack, known as the
Zaafaraniya plant, was stuffed with sophisticated machine tools that were
used to make components for Iraq's uranium enrichment program. Fewer
still knew that the machine tools at Zaafaraniya, located just north of the
River Tigris, came from a company named Matrix Churchill.

Those who paid attention to the American attack—the first to come
near the Iraqi capital since the end of Operation Desert Storm—learned
that civilians had died when one of the cruise missiles went off course and
slammed into the famous Al-Rasheed Hotel. Pentagon officials grudg-
ingly admitted that they might have blundered by routing the low-flying
missiles over the Iraqi capital en route to their target; meanwhile, the
civilian casualties proved an embarrassment to Washington and triggered
criticism in the Arab world and in Europe.

The White House justified the missile barrage as a response to
Saddam's restrictions on UN weapons inspectors. David Kay, the former
chief nuclear weapons inspector for the United Nations, who was in
London when the attack occurred, found a grim irony in this. Kay had
himself suffered Iraqi harassment, and he had personally visited
Zaafaraniya three times. He later recalled the paradox of "Western
technology going to destroy Western technology. You had to use very
advanced cruise missiles to destroy equally advanced Western products."

Kay's last visit to the complex had been in July 1991. "We rolled up to
the metal link gates of the facility on a challenge inspection," Kay recalled.
"It was a very modern industrial park, with about twenty-five buildings,
laid out like a California campus plant, and very well landscaped as well. I
split my team and took one group up to the third floor of a four-story
building, to the former office of the defector who had tipped us off. When
we got there, all of the offices were locked except for his, and it was clean.
The Iraqi security people just stood around laughing. They knew what we
were looking for."

The UN team had had better luck in a large production building,
where they found British-made Matrix Churchill equipment. "I think
everyone came away impressed by the quality of the facility. It was without
doubt the best industrial tooling facility we had seen, although the uranium enrichment method they were using there was primitive." During
the course of the inspection, recalled Kay, "we joked about one member of
the team, who came from British intelligence. We knew why he had such
good information on the total number of Matrix Churchill machines that
would be there." In January 1993, when Kay and his former colleagues
discussed the Bush administration's destruction of Zaafaraniya, they told
one another a new joke: "We said that this was the ultimate cover-up—to
bomb the place."

Saddam reacted to the bombing in his usual manipulative way—he
took one careful step backward. On January 19, two days after the cruise
missile attack and just twenty-four hours before the Clinton inauguration,
Saddam announced a new cease-fire, backed by a pledge not to harass
U.S. planes patrolling over Kurdish and Shi'ite Muslim enclaves in Iraqi
territory. Ever a wily politician, he also promised to guarantee the safety of
UN inspectors, terming it a gesture of goodwill toward Bill Clinton. His
welcome to the former governor of Arkansas had little effect; within hours
of the inauguration, two American warplanes locked on to a radar site that
appeared to pose a threat and fired. Thus did the new president have his

first opportunity to tell the Butcher of Baghdad that American policy on Iraq had not changed.

It was clear from the first day of the Clinton administration, therefore, that the problem of Iraq would not disappear as long as Saddam Hussein remained in power. Former White House officials from the Bush administration, now looking for new jobs, had another reason to worry about the tangled history of U.S. relations with Iraq: Clinton had pledged during the campaign to get to the bottom of Iraqgate. Whenever the Bush crowd made any remarks at all about the scandal, they would mouth the familiar Washington refrain that it was best to "put it behind us and move on."

Not everyone was prepared to do this. The Federal Reserve, unhappy at BNL's lack of cooperation, formally reopened its own probe and in early 1993 dispatched a team of investigators to Rome. Judge Shoob issued a new court order on February 1, instructing the CIA to turn over more classified documents that might shed light on the degree of Italian involvement in the case. And on Capitol Hill the iconoclastic Henry Gonzalez, still smarting from the treatment he had received during his previous work on Iraqgate, vowed to widen his inquiry, this time to examine the suspected *joint* involvement of the British and American governments in the illegal supply of money and arms. Gonzalez said he would investigate the degree to which London had shared intelligence information with the Bush administration concerning Matrix Churchill's exports to Iraq and their funding by BNL's Atlanta branch.

THE IDEA THAT Western politicians and intelligence services had been involved in some of the dirtier transactions that provided arms and money to Iraq was gaining currency in London as well. Word spread that Paul Henderson, the man at the center of the Matrix Churchill affair, had decided to write his memoirs about life as a reluctant spy for Her Majesty's government. The government of Prime Minister John Major was asked in Parliament to reveal the extent of its knowledge of illegal arms-dealing with both Iran and Iraq. In reply to almost all questions put to the government, Major's answer was always conveniently the same: It would be inappropriate to respond while a judicial inquiry was being conducted.

In early May 1993, nearly six months after Major had named him to probe Britain's Iraqgate scandal, Lord Justice Scott quietly called his judicial hearings to order. Unlike Frederick Lacey, Scott was prepared to let his investigation take as long as was needed. He proceeded at a deliberate and almost leisurely pace.

A fifty-eight-year-old judge with a reputation for speaking his mind, Scott had spent the winter sifting through nearly thirty thousand documents that had been transported in triple-locked security bags from government offices in Whitehall to a building just across from the Queen's Picture Gallery that adjoins Buckingham Palace. Scott was an unpretentious figure who loved cycling to his office when it was not raining, and he conducted the arms-to-Iraq hearings with the air of a quizzical schoolmaster. He would occasionally pose a question, but for the most part he leaned back in his chair and let his chief deputy—a no-nonsense barrister named Miss Presiley Baxendale—take the lead.

Scott's intentions seemed reassuring to the prime minister; he said he did not see himself "holding a gun pointing at the heart of government." But lacking subpoena power, he soon found himself facing some uncooperative witnesses, including some less-than-civil servants. In fact, the Scott inquiry, an unusual probe by British standards, was making dozens of government ministers and bureaucrats squirm. The discomfort was summed up by one former minister who had personally tried to withhold documents from the Matrix Churchill trial by signing one of the notorious Public Interest Immunity Certificates. "I'm a firm believer in the absolute secrecy of the government process," said the Conservative politician, insisting his name not be cited. As for the Scott inquiry, that was just "politics." It would all blow over. Parliament, he said wearily, would go through the ritual witch hunt that follows a failed policy and then things would get back to normal.

Another former minister, this one having served closely with Margaret Thatcher when she headed the government, was even more dismissive of Scott. "A lawyer always sees the pathology," he remarked, adding that "the Lord Justice Scott inquiry is a post-mortem on a death that didn't happen. . . . What Lord Scott is looking at is the consequence of a non-conspiracy, not a conspiracy." When asked about British arms sales to Baghdad during the Iran-Iraq war, the minister then allowed somewhat sheepishly: "Of course we wanted both sides to exhaust each other."

These ministers were underestimating Scott, a genuine believer in the concept of open government, who engendered resentment in the British political establishment precisely because he was not prepared to go easy on his peers. Despite his seemingly mild manner, Scott was unafraid of confrontation. In one of the comparatively few heated exchanges, he was accused by Sir David Miers, the former head of the Foreign Office's Middle East department, of failing to understand how government worked. "It did not really matter," Miers suggested, if the government's guidelines banning the export of arms to Iraq had been broken. Commercial considerations were more important. "Real people were being thrown out of work when everything turned on a semantic exercise about how the guidelines should be interpreted," said Miers. Lord Scott, in answer, declared that Foreign Office officials had taken a "cynical approach" to the arms export guidelines, which Sir Geoffrey Howe, the foreign secretary, had laid down in December 1984 and that banned the approval of orders from Iran or Iraq for defense equipment that "would significantly enhance the capability of either side to prolong or exacerbate the conflict."

As the Scott hearings went forward, a very senior aide to former Prime Minister Thatcher was asked in private about the British cabinet's previous attitude to Iraq. His reply was frighteningly nonchalant: "Yes, of course there was a degree of cynicism in the tilt toward Iraq. We were very concerned about Khomeini and the expansion of fundamentalism. Nobody was upset that these two nations wanted to fight themselves to a standstill." But how much did Britain actually do to help Saddam? "We did have information that British companies were building hardened shelters for Saddam and providing him with communications equipment, that kind of thing. British companies were involved in building Saddam's personal bunker. We used to encourage our businessmen to go over to Baghdad trade fairs and sell everything they could, within the guidelines."

When it came to selling to Iraq, the government's guidelines were supposed to have been sacrosanct; in truth, they were not sacrosanct at all. After Iran and Iraq ended their long war in 1988, British government ministers decided secretly to relax the rules on exports to Baghdad. Confidential documents show that on November 4, 1988, Alan Clark, the Department of Trade minister who later became the surprise star of the Matrix Churchill trial, wrote to William Waldegrave, a Foreign Office junior minister, arguing in favor of the relaxation of export controls toward Iraq. He sent a copy of the letter to Prime Minister Thatcher. In April 1989, Waldegrave confirmed in a letter back to Clark that he and Lord Trefgarne, a junior defense minister, had agreed "to interpret the guidelines more flexibly in respect of Iraq, as we have done in practice since the end of last year." But, noted Waldegrave, it was "preferable not to have to announce publicly any change."

When it was Waldegrave's turn to appear before Scott, he admitted that approving Matrix exports to Iraq in 1989 had been "the wrong judgment." Yet his testimony was by and large marked by circular arguments, denials, and contorted logic. Waldegrave, who by 1993 was John

Major's so-called "minister for open government," admitted that in 1988, in consultation with Prime Minister Thatcher, Foreign Minister Sir Geoffrey Howe had authorized "a little increased flexibility" in export controls toward Iraq. He insisted, however, that the changes were so marginal that there had been no need to tell Parliament. Scott was not impressed: "Isn't it a healthy factor of a democratic society that this kind of subject should be debated?"

Many in Britain thought so. Indeed, the explicit willingness on the part of government ministers to deceive the public was confirmed in detail before Scott by a whistle-blower from the Foreign Office, Mark Higson, the former Iraq desk officer. Higson told the Scott inquiry that the policy change had been treated within the government like a state secret, on a "need to know" basis. He said that when members of Parliament or the public asked about the policy on Iraq, they were given "dishonest" answers from Sir Geoffrey Howe. Like Waldegrave, Howe was opposed to a public announcement of the more relaxed attitude toward selling militarily useful equipment to Iraq because he in fact did fear that it would look "very cynical" so soon after the world had seen Saddam gassing the Kurds. "We were being economical with the truth," Higson confessed. "I did my job. Regardless of whether I thought it was a sham. I did my duty."

Another British official who did his duty was Sir Stephen Egerton, the former British ambassador to Saudi Arabia. It was his testimony before Scott in June 1993 that brought into the open, for the first time, the same fears that Frank Machon had had about Allivane being used as a covert channel for arms sales to Iraq. When Egerton was asked about suspicions that artillery shells that Allivane had sent were actually intended for Iraq, he demurred at first, then said, "this is coming back to me now, yes." He revealed that when he asked London about the mysterious company, "they told me it was not Her Majesty's government's responsibility to question Saudi's intention of using this firm instead of normal channels." Egerton added one final thought on the subject, which he said came up in a conversation he had had with a Saudi prince: "I did not like the smell of it." It was easier to stay away from matters such as Allivane, the ambassador seemed to be saying.

An army officer at the defense ministry took on a more activist role than the ambassador. Lieutenant Colonel Richard Glazebrook's father had been gassed during World War I, and he had no qualms about telling Scott that Her Majesty's government had been aware that Jordan passed British chemical warfare equipment on to Iraq. He also revealed that in 1988 and 1989 the government approved contracts with Jordan for artillery shells that used Space Research Corporation, the Gerald Bull company involved in Iraq's supergun project, as the main contractor. Glazebrook explained not only how Jordan had been used as a conduit for arms exports to Iraq, but how frustrated he had felt that he could do little to stop this. "I had an uncomfortable feeling that things were going on behind my back," he told Scott. Glazebrook found that some of the deals through Jordan had even been brokered by a British government company called International Military Services. A former director of that company later said it "did nothing without the full knowledge and approval of the government." Glazebrook was more explicit; he told Scott he had learned that details of the sales had been sent directly to Prime Minister Thatcher in one of the defense intelligence reports she received every three months about British arms sales.

Thatcher, who is scheduled to appear at the Scott inquiry toward the end of 1993, was allegedly well aware of the way her government had connived at feeding choice items to the Iraqi military machine. Mark Gutteridge, a former Matrix Churchill executive who had worked for MI5, said he was told by his handler that his own intelligence reports would be seen by the prime minister. "She knew what was going on," claimed Gutteridge.

Gutteridge's claim of Thatcher's personal involvement was later buttressed by the revelation during the Scott hearings of a Ministry of Defence document that described how intelligence sources had reported that Matrix Churchill lathes "were to be used for making shells and missiles." The memorandum suggested strongly that Thatcher had personally approved Matrix Churchill exports to Iraq in order to protect an intelligence source inside the company, believed to be Gutteridge himself. Written in December 1988 by Alan Barrett, a defence ministry official who was a member of a government committee privy to intelligence data on exports, the document stated: "The Prime Minister agreed that in order to protect the intelligence source, the licenses already granted should not be revoked."

Thatcher's personal involvement was underscored by the additional notation that "this case needs to go back to the Prime Minister before we could recommend approving the current application." In a later section of the same document there was a reference to why Thatcher should be consulted: "Press for a separate submission to go to the Prime Minister as she was involved last time."

Geoffrey Robertson, the lawyer who had defended the Matrix Churchill executives and originally laid bare much of the government's duplicity, said the Defence Ministry document was "the missing link which appears to take the chain of approval as far as the Prime Minister herself."

Scott's hearings were painting an ugly picture of ministerial deceit and repeated violations of both policies and guidelines on military exports to Iraq. Prime Minister Major was also to be called to testify, and aside from being questioned about allegations that he and others had misled Parliament, he was expected to be asked about government loan guarantees for Iraqi arms purchases. This was because part of his brief as chief secretary to the Treasury until July 1989 had included responsibility for the loan-guarantee program for Iraq, which in 1989 allocated a 20 percent portion for the sale of defense items to Baghdad. But Major was not scheduled to appear until January, as one of the last witnesses the Scott investigation would hear from.

Britain's Iraqgate was thus very much alive in 1993. And whatever happened in Washington, there were some very knowledgeable friends of Margaret Thatcher's who feared the ultimate result could be a political disaster. During Thatcher's tenure as prime minister until late 1990 and later under John Major, the government had allowed its ministers systematically to suppress information about militarily useful sales to Iraq and documents that could have acquitted innocent men, said one senior business executive from the defense sector who had dealt with Thatcher for many years. In a private conversation this businessman, who had personal knowledge of sales to Iraq, predicted the Scott inquiry would raise fundamental questions about government morality as it came to a close. "I think this could well bring down the government. The question of whether Parliament was misled is very serious," he said in May 1993, more in sadness than anger. And Parliament, he added, *had* been misled.

THERE WAS MORE than a little irony, given London's reputation for closed government, that by May 1993 the British investigation of Iraqgate seemed, improbably, to be overtaking efforts in the United States. In fact, largely out of the public view, it was dawning on officials at Bill Clinton's Department of Justice that they had inherited more legal debris in the form of pending cases than might have been imaginable, as a result of the Bush administration's handling of Iraqgate. It did not matter whether a particular case concerned Carlos Cardoen, James Guerin, Christopher Drogoul, or anyone else. As the British government had discovered in the Matrix Churchill trial, former foot soldiers were simply not willing to stay silent and take the blame for activities that politicians had previously encouraged.

In April, not long after Janet Reno became the new attorney general, the Department of Justice had launched a remarkable legal argument against BNL. In a Washington court, the new administration seemed to imply it was less convinced than its predecessor by the claim made by Dick Thornburgh and others in the Bush administration that Drogoul had been a lone wolf and BNL Rome an innocent victim of the fraud in Atlanta.

The Justice Department was responding to the Italian bank's lawsuit demanding that the United States hand over $340 million for unpaid Iraqi loans that BNL Atlanta had made with government guarantees. Contesting BNL's claim, the Justice Department now disclosed that the bank itself was still under investigation. More to the point, it said the focus of the upcoming Drogoul trial would be the question of whether Rome knew of the illegal loans. "It is evident," argued the attorney general's deputies, "that there is more than idle speculation that evidence might evolve in Mr. Drogoul's trial further implicating BNL and raising obvious conflicts."

Soon after the Justice Department filing, news from Italy raised more questions about BNL. Giacomo Pedde, the former director-general of the bank, was on the verge of being convicted and sentenced to four years in prison in a separate scandal, this one involving the bank's illegal financing of weapons sales in the mid-1980s to *Iran*. Months before, Judge Shoob had asked that Pedde come to Atlanta and testify in open court about the Iraqi loans case, but he never showed up. In the Iran arms case, the Italian prosecutor had implicated not only Pedde but also members of the Italian secret services. The entire affair, he complained, was bathed in "the stink" of intelligence agencies.

"That's a fair statement when it comes to Atlanta too," said an official at the Bank of Italy in Rome. "I can tell you first-hand that when we looked at the Atlanta case, we found that various intelligence services were involved in the Iraqi loans. The whole story is really about spies more than bankers."

Spies also featured in the long-standing investigation of Carlos Cardoen, which had landed on the Justice Department like one of the Chilean's cluster bombs. The main problem was the CIA, which since the summer of 1991 had been giving repeated assurances to the U.S. attorney's office in Miami that it had never known about or had any involvement in Cardoen's allegedly illegal export of American military technology to Chile for bombs that went to Iraq. The assurances turned out to be false.

"I was furious," recalled one U.S. law enforcement official, "when in February 1993 the CIA suddenly contacted a prosecutor in Miami to say they had just found a misplaced report from early 1984 that showed they *did* have detailed knowledge of U.S. exports to Cardoen in Chile for military purposes." As a result of the newly "found" CIA report, which had been sent in 1984 to the White House and to several government agencies, the pending indictment of Cardoen might now be in jeopardy. If the CIA knew of improper exports, it was hard to see how Cardoen could be charged.

The case was put on hold in Miami, while in Santiago the Chilean arms-maker decided to go public. "American officials patted me on the back," said Cardoen, finally revealing that the Reagan and Bush administrations had received detailed briefings throughout the 1980s of his use of U.S. equipment to provide cluster bombs and factories to Iraq.

In May 1993, it was decided that Cardoen could be indicted anyway, and he was, along with Teledyne, a Los Angeles defense contractor. The two were charged with the illegal export of zirconium, the metal used in the manufacture of cluster bombs for Iraq. Teledyne denied doing anything wrong and threatened to make public documents showing that the Reagan and Bush administrations had known exactly what it had been sending to Cardoen from 1982 to 1989. Cardoen reacted to the charges by announcing that over the years literally dozens of U.S. and British officials, diplomats, and intelligence officials had visited his factories and encouraged his work. "The Bush administration tried to produce some scapegoats. They were deeply involved in the supply of weapons to Iraq, and they tried to deny any involvement," said Cardoen, who began making available photographs of himself in the company of senior U.S. officials. As for the British, Cardoen said they also knew full well that the equipment Matrix Churchill sent to Chile was being used to make weapons for Iraq.

In Washington, Cardoen's lawyer summed up the paradox facing his client in stark terms: "The very government that now charges Mr. Cardoen as a criminal was supplying weaponry to Iraq. [It] knew of, approved of, and even solicited the conduct it now deems illegal."

A similarly telling disclosure was made in June by Robert Simels, a criminal lawyer who was the newest head of Drogoul's defense team. Simels had talked in London with Paul Henderson, and he now revealed in a court filing the details of a rather significant conversation back in 1989 between Henderson and Safa Al-Habobi, the Iraqi who masterminded Saddam's clandestine procurement network and who was indicted in the BNL case. Al-Habobi had told Henderson, reported Simels, not only that Rome was fully aware of the Atlanta loans but that these were an extension of a *government-to-government* agreement between Italy and Iraq. As if to underscore Habobi's importance, Saddam named him Iraq's oil minister in the summer of 1993.

At this stage Janet Reno, who came to Washington with a reputation as ethical, forceful, and unafraid to make tough calls and was soon more popular than any other Clinton cabinet member, began taking a personal interest in the BNL case. In early July she named John Hogan, who since 1984 had been her chief assistant at the Dade County state attorney's office in Miami, to supervise the BNL task force. Hogan had a tough time at first, since he joined the investigation only ten weeks before the case was set to go to trial. Within days of taking over, he also had to contend with some high-profile legal maneuvers by Drogoul's lawyer.

In mid-July, Simels dragged the name of George Bush into the BNL case by issuing a subpoena that demanded thirty-seven documents plus the former president's testimony for the Atlanta trial. The aim of the subpoena, explained Simels, was to compel Bush to appear and to discuss his knowledge of U.S. foreign policy toward Iraq in the 1980s, coupled with his alleged efforts to assist Iraqi purchases backed by loan guarantees from the U.S. government. Simels added: "We also want to show Mr. Bush's communications with Prime Minister Andreotti and the Italian government on this matter." Bush's lawyers moved to quash the subpoena almost immediately, but even as they did, Simels hit back with a new set of demands for testimony, this time leading off with James Baker and Lawrence Eagleburger. Simels said the reason he issued the new subpoenas was "to further corroborate U.S. awareness of BNL's role in the financing of exports to Iraq."

For many who had followed Iraqgate, the question of what James Baker knew and when he knew it seemed a central issue. The former secretary of state had been a primary architect of Bush's secret presidential directive on Iraq, and he had personally pressed the hardest to implement it. Very few people, however, were willing to speak about Baker on the record. Half of Washington respected him; the other half feared him.

Alexander Haig is an exception. He had known Baker for many years, had worked alongside him in the Reagan administration. When he looked back at the way Baker pushed U.S. support for Saddam during the

1980s, he became surprisingly blunt. The tilt policy Baker had supported during those years "brought Saddam to the belief that he would not be challenged in Kuwait," argued Haig. "And the consequences were a Gulf war and the outcome that the threat of Saddam is still there."

This view was harsh, although not nearly as harsh as the views of congressional investigators who still wanted a special prosecutor to investigate Baker along with other former top officials of the Bush administration. As for Baker himself, he went back to his family law firm after leaving office, laid plans to write a book of memoirs, and signed on at the Carlyle Group, a Washington investment bank full of Bush- and Reagan-era politicians such as Richard Darman, the former director of the Office of Management and Budget, and Frank Carlucci, the former secretary of defense.

In the spring of 1993 the Carlyle Group was busy seeking contracts in Saudi Arabia, although Baker was not directly involved in those efforts. He did, however, try to drum up some business in Kuwait on behalf of a big U.S. energy company. Baker traveled there in April together with George Bush, who was being feted as the liberator of the sheikdom. After Bush collected his plaudits, Baker stayed on, according to investigative journalist Seymour Hersh, writing in *The New Yorker*. Baker acted as a consultant to Enron, the Houston-based natural-gas pipeline company that was seeking contracts to rebuild bomb-damaged Kuwait power plants. Margaret Tutwiler, the master of spin-doctoring who had served as Baker's spokesperson at State and who now represents him through her public relations firm, claimed to Hersh that Baker's work in Kuwait was really in the interest of America. "He believes that to fairly make the case for American companies against foreign competition is a positive, not a negative, and that Kuwait—or any other country, for that matter—should make its decision based on the merits and its own economic interests, and he would not suggest otherwise." In the summer of 1993, when asked to discuss his role in the decade-long U.S. embrace of Saddam Hussein, Baker was absolutely unwilling to speak about the tilt years or the BNL affair or any other subject related to Iraq.

Boyden Gray, the former presidential counsel who next to Baker was Bush's closest confidant, had had no such qualms. Gray, who in the summer of 1993 was practicing law in Washington and organizing a politically conservative cable television venture, offered a different perspective. On two separate occasions he made the point that if the Bush administration had made a mistake, it was to exert *too much* pressure on

Saddam Hussein in the months leading up to the August 1990 invasion of Kuwait.

"If there was anything we did wrong, it was that we squeezed Saddam too much," said Gray, when asked about the $1 billion in government credits that the White House had promised Saddam despite signs of Baghdad's complicity in the BNL affair. Gray stressed that the second half of the $1 billion was eventually stopped after it became clear that Baghdad was abusing the U.S. program. But he displayed remarkable understanding for the man Bush had compared to Hitler: "God, this guy had real money problems. No wonder he went marching into Kuwait."

Saddam's money problems, of course, worsened in 1990 for two reasons—the collapse of the price of oil and the fact that his biggest Western bank source of funds, BNL, had largely dried up after the Atlanta operation was shut down. By August 1993, Atlanta was also the place where, finally, it seemed that the mysteries of the Iraqgate scandal would be revealed in public. Christopher Drogoul was awaiting the start of his trial on September 8, and five of his former subordinates, including Paul Von Wedel, were to be sentenced on August 23 by Judge Marvin Shoob.

Although Shoob had withdrawn from the Drogoul trial, he now had one last chance to make a BNL ruling from the bench as he sentenced the five lesser figures. Earlier that month he had made his views plain in conversation: "I think the government entered into an effort early on to support Iraq as a matter of national policy. They used the CIA and Italy to effectuate that purpose. Many of the things that were done were in violation of acts of Congress and U.S. arms export laws. They were aware of the law, and they skirted it. It was an effort to arm Iraq, and then, when things got out of hand, they didn't want that information to come out."

When Von Wedel and four other junior employees of BNL Atlanta came before him on August 23, Shoob acted on his best instincts and refused to send any of them to prison. Instead, he put them on probation, saying it would be "the height of hypocrisy to sentence these defendants as if this were a simple case of wrongdoing by a branch bank's employees."

When Hogan argued that evidence had not been found to implicate BNL's Rome headquarters in the Iraqi loans affair, Shoob shot back that "only in never-never land would a combination of circumstances such as I have seen indicate that all this happened by chance." Then a junior prosecutor dared to quote Frederick Lacey's conclusion that BNL Rome was an innocent victim, and Shoob erupted: "If Judge Lacey had investigated the Teapot Dome scandal, he would have awarded medals rather than jail terms."

That day, placing his signature on what would be his last court order on the subject, Shoob wrote that based on overwhelming evidence, it was now clear that the employees of BNL Atlanta had been "pawns or bit players in a far larger and wider-ranging sophisticated conspiracy that involved BNL Rome and possibly large American and foreign corporations, and the governments of the United States, England, Italy, and Iraq."*

All that remained now was for Drogoul finally to go to trial and, as promised, to name names in order to lay bare once and for all the degree to which Saddam's billions had been part of the covert policies designed to assist the Iraqi leader by the U.S. and Italian governments. Drogoul's defense team was ready to argue the case in court, but on September 2, just six days before the trial was to begin, Hogan and the other federal prosecutors stopped the clock. Janet Reno, it transpired, had approved an unexpected plea bargain that threw out all but three minor charges against Drogoul, these being two counts of bank regulatory violations and one count of wire fraud. No longer was the government insisting that Drogoul had defrauded either the U.S. government or BNL; indeed, the agreement would permit him to discuss who in Rome was involved, if he wished, at his sentencing hearing later in 1993. Now, instead of facing life imprisonment, Drogoul might face a five-year term.

What had happened? A Justice Department official explained that "it was our estimate that Mr. Drogoul would not have received a heavier sentence, so it was pointless to commit the government to a four-to-six-month-long trial." Simels was jubilant, revealing that he had planned to introduce evidence at the trial showing how U.S. intelligence agencies had intercepted telexes between BNL Atlanta and Baghdad for years. But the judge had ruled out the introduction of such evidence, so a deal was agreed to instead.

In the wake of that stunning development in Atlanta, it looked at first as though the Clinton administration were walking away from the Iraqgate scandal, despite Bill Clinton's campaign pledge to see that every lead would be followed. Henry Gonzalez called the Drogoul deal another whitewash and said he would call again for a special prosecutor once the Congress renewed the independent counsel law that had expired in December 1992.

Then, just when it seemed that all hopes of getting to the bottom of the story had vanished, Hogan revealed what was really going on behind

---

* The full text of this order will be found in Appendix A.

the scenes in Washington. No decision had been made about a special prosecutor for Iraqgate, he said, adding that the Clinton administration had decided to press on with a broader investigation into whether laws were broken by American companies and government officials in the arming of Iraq. "From the very beginning my task was to look at the Iraqi procurement network, both in terms of arms and financing, and to see if crimes were committed. Of necessity we had to look at Drogoul first because a trial date had been set, but now we can go forward. Obviously, part of the inquiry deals with people inside or outside the government." Did that mean that the Justice Department was finally prepared to examine the Iraqgate allegations made against former Bush administration officials? "Absolutely," replied Hogan. "Janet Reno has asked me to do this, and there have been no limits placed on me as to where the investigation might lead, no matter how senior the officials were, no matter who it hurts, and no matter who it makes happy."

In effect, in September 1993 Hogan was trying to understand the suspected links between banks and companies, covert operators and Reagan and Bush era officials, involved in Washington's decade-long danse macabre with the Iraqi dictator. He was studying the strange case of Carlos Cardoen, and the allegations that Robert Gates and others from the CIA had countenanced Cardoen's arms sales to Iraq. He was looking at the still unsettled investigation of Rexon, the New Jersey company whose fuses went to Allivane of Britain. And he was grappling with the manner in which the CIA had turned a blind eye to James Guerin's illegal arms shipments from Lancaster, Pennsylvania.

There is more than enough here to keep Reno's deputy busy for a long time, just as Lord Scott has a crowded agenda as he tries to unravel the tale of Britain's deception in its dealings with Saddam. In Italy, despite much ado about the continuing Senate investigation, there appears no serious effort to probe much further. In September 1993 officials from Italy's Guardia di Finanza and from Britain's Home Office admitted in private conversations that they were now convinced that the BNL affair was part of an American-driven covert operation, but as one Italian investigator put it, "I doubt this will ever come out in a formal report for political reasons." These comments, however, raise a fundamental question about the future of investigations in all three countries involved in this, the world's first global political scandal.

There is an urgent need for serious, open debate about the sordid tale of relations between Baghdad and Washington, London, and Rome. In the 1980s, at times in the name of anti-Soviet containment, and because

of the obsessive drive to guarantee access to Persian Gulf oil, the Reagan
and Bush administrations, with people like George Bush and James Baker
in positions of primary responsibility, did virtually anything they wanted.
The government's lack of accountability, either to Congress or to the
public, was so egregious as to pose a silent threat to the principles of
American democracy.

Still more insidiously, low-level American, British, and Italian foot
soldiers in government, in banking, in the military, and in the world of
espionage ended up taking the fall for the U.S.-driven embrace of Saddam
Hussein. In the end these individuals were punished for decisions that
were really made at the policy level and in government-to-government
understandings, whether these were between the United States and Iraq,
Britain and Iraq, Italy and Iraq, or among the United States, Britain, and
Italy.

The motivations behind this sorry chapter in international affairs
differed from country to country. For London, it was the mercantile
tradition that mattered most. For Rome, it was both that and a desire to
maintain good relations in the Arab world while seeking American goodwill, even if that meant behaving like a client of the United States. For
Washington, it was the arrogant decision of a few top government officials, George Bush among them, that they and they alone knew what was
best for America and for the world. There is no evidence to suggest that
while in government Bush or the others who fell victim to a fatal attraction
with Saddam profited personally from their actions. There is plenty of
evidence, however, that in the first half of the 1980s the White House
illegally armed Iraq and that in the latter period, running up through
1990, the tilt veered so far out of control, and so beyond reason, that it led
to the willful abuse of taxpayer-funded programs and, after Operation
Desert Storm, to efforts to hide the truth about U.S. policies toward
Baghdad.

These actions were not the result of a conspiracy. Bush, Baker, and
their advisers didn't think they were engaged in a cover-up, any more than
did Thatcher and her ministers, or Italy's Guido Carli—and that makes it
all the more outrageous. These politicians perceived their actions as
reasonable damage control, or as the legitimate desire to protect state
secrets. But the absence of malice is no excuse. The result *was* cover-up,
and the cavalier manipulation of the truth at the highest levels of government.

In fact, Iraqgate is not like other scandals that the Western world has
experienced over the past twenty years. It embodies a broader, more

systematic abuse of power, one that contributed to the prolonging of the Iran-Iraq war, in which one million people died, and to Operation Desert Storm, which cost the lives of tens of thousands of innocent Iraqis who were already living in the hardship of Saddam's tyranny. For these reasons the secret history behind these events demands a much fuller examination than has occurred to date.

There is a tendency today in politics and the media to shrug off government malfeasance on the grounds that we are so inured to such behavior that it almost doesn't matter. This is a dangerous way to think. If so telling a chapter of twentieth-century history is swept under the rug— and cynics may argue that it will be—then it will not be only historians of the future who suffer as a result. Policy-makers, the public, and all those who believed in honesty in government will be the real victims.

There is peril in store if the watchdogs of Western democracy abdicate their responsibilities as did those government officials who should now be placed under investigation. The issue far transcends Iraqgate or even the particular circumstances described in these pages. It is therefore now up to Congress, the Clinton administration, the Scott inquiry, and Parliament to pursue allegations wherever they lead, regardless of how politically awkward that might be. It is a grave responsibility. What is at stake is nothing less than the truth.

APPENDIX A

Judicial Order in the BNL Case Issued by Judge Marvin Shoob on October 5, 1992.

UNITED STATES DISTRICT COURT
NORTHERN DISTRICT OF GEORGIA
ATLANTA DIVISION

UNITED STATES OF AMERICA, Plaintiff, v. CHRISTOPHER P. DROGOUL, Defendant	CRIMINAL ACTION 1:91-cr-078-MHS

ORDER

This case involves billions of dollars raised and loaned in international finance. It involves allegations of an international bank fraud that may have helped pay for Iraq's military build-up. But the more important issue before this Court involves a man's liberty and serious questions about the integrity of our justice system and the almost unreviewable powers of prosecutorial discretion. The Court's judgment and decisions throughout the hearings and motions before it have been guided by its belief that there is a moral component to the Court's involvement in this case—the responsibility to do the right thing.

This order will set forth the reasons the Court will grant the Government's motion to recuse and why the Court, on October 1, 1992, orally granted defendant Christopher P. Drogoul's renewed motion to withdraw his guilty plea.

I. BACKGROUND OF THE CASE

For almost three weeks, the Court has heard evidence relating to the sentencing of Mr. Drogoul who entered a guilty plea to 60 counts of a 347-count indictment on June 2, 1992, and faced a life sentence. The indictment centers on charges that Mr. Drogoul, the manager of the Atlanta branch of one of Italy's largest banks, defrauded the parent bank ("BNL") by making some $2 billion in unauthorized loans to Iraq and other countries. A number of these loans were backed by the Department of Agriculture's Commodity Credit Corporation ("CCC"). The indictment also includes charges of tax evasion, making false reports to government agencies and money laundering. Mr. Drogoul is the highest ranking BNL official indicted and the focus of the Government's prosecution.

Mr. Drogoul entered his guilty plea during a three-hour hearing before this Court, following an unusual sequence of events. In the week or so before the plea hearing, Mr. Drogoul announced his intention to plead guilty to all 347 counts of the indictment and to make a full statement about the case. Several days before the plea hearing, however, he agreed to a surprising offer from the Government to plead to only 60 counts and delayed making any meaningful statement. His sentencing hearing began September 14, 1992.

The Government has said that this hearing was highly unusual, more of a mini-trial than a sentencing hearing. The Court agrees that this hearing was unusual, but this has been an unusual case. The Government initially sought the "mini-trial;" at one point before the plea bargain, prosecutors requested three weeks to present evidence rebutting defendant's anticipated statement at the plea hearing. Following the plea bargain, which was initiated by the Government, the Government sought three days to present witnesses. During the sentencing hearing, the Government proceeded to present detailed evidence as to how the money flowed from one account to another, how much money defendant had promised to Iraq and other nations, and how defendant and alleged co-conspirators covered up these transactions.

The Court has never intended to "put the Government on trial," as suggested by the prosecution but only to determine what transpired and Mr. Drogoul's involvement. The Court also points out that a sentencing hearing is not a trial, and the rules of evidence do not apply. Courts are permitted to rely on hearsay and even on the testimony of confidential informants without knowing their identity. In a sense, evidence at a sentencing hearing is not subject to the same testing as that put on at a trial; the Court simply must satisfy itself that the information is "sufficiently reliable."

II. PLEA WITHDRAWAL

On September 21, 1992, after one week of evidence in the hearing, the Court denied defendant's motion to withdraw his plea of guilty. The Court held that defendant had not shown that there was a "fair and just reason" to permit the withdrawal of his guilty plea. September 21, 1992, Order. However, after daily revelations undermining the Government's case, the prosecution announced on October 1 that it no longer opposed defendant's motion to withdraw his guilty plea. Defendant renewed his motion to withdraw the plea.

In the two weeks of testimony following defendant's first attempt to withdraw his plea, defendant presented credible evidence suggesting that the Government had not fully investigated whether defendant's superiors in the bank approved of and were aware of his activities. The Government also furnished to the Court classified documents from the Central Intelligence Agency ("CIA") suggesting that BNL-Rome was aware of Mr. Drogoul's activities and was not a victim of the alleged fraud. Furthermore, defendant named several BNL superiors who knew of his activities and described their involvement. Defendant did not resolve the questions about why he, a clearly intelligent person represented by counsel, entered his plea of guilty on June 2, 1992, and during a three-hour hearing before this Court testified only that his superiors should have known. However, other evidence presented at the sentencing hearing as outlined below raised such serious questions that the Court concluded that these issues could not appropriately be taken up on a motion for downward departure but should be heard at trial. In light of these conclusions and the Government's and defendant's request for a trial, the Court granted the motion to withdraw the plea.

III. RECUSAL

The Government has filed a written motion requesting recusal, and the Court will grant the motion. A judge should disqualify himself from "any proceeding in which his impartiality might reasonably be questioned." 28 U.S.C. § 455(a). Although the Court believes that it would be able to hear the evidence with an open mind, the Government's concerns that it would not act impartially counsel against this Court remaining on the case. From the evidence presented during the hearing, this Court has reached and voiced certain preliminary conclusions and concerns about this case and the Government's conduct in investigating and prosecuting defendant that may, from the prosecution's viewpoint, interfere with this Court's ability to hear evidence with an open and impartial mind. Furthermore, while some of the concerns raised by this Court may have legitimate explanations, the sheer number of unusual circumstances led this Court to reach these tentative conclusions. Accordingly, the Court will set forth some of the tentative conclusions it has reached in hearing this matter and its reasoning in arriving at those conclusions. Set forth below are the bases for the granting of the motions to withdraw the plea and to recuse.

A. *The knowledge of officials at BNL-Rome*

The Court concludes that officials at BNL-Rome were aware of and approved Mr. Drogoul's activities. At the very least, BNL-Rome chose to ignore what were obvious signs of Mr. Drogoul's extraordinary relationship with Iraq and his unusual lending practices. In support of this conclusion, the Court notes:

1) Classified reports from the CIA conclude, in part, that a number of high-level BNL-Rome officials supported Mr. Drogoul's activities.[1]

2) A senior BNL official, Mr. Monaco, referred an Italian company seeking financing for a major construction project in Iraq to BNL-Atlanta.

3) The former head of BNL's North American operations, Dr. Luigi Sardelli, provided credible testimony showing that senior officials in Rome approved or had knowledge of Mr. Drogoul's activities.

* Sardelli's letter criticizing defendant's activities was never delivered by the auditor to officials in Rome.

* Instead of auditing or investigating BNL-Atlanta, BNL-Rome officials elected to investigate Dr. Sardelli who appears to be the only "straight shooter" in the organization.

* BNL-Rome was an extremely political organization operating more as an agency of the Italian government than as a bank.

* Dr. Sardelli voiced his frustration with BNL-Rome in testifying that the BNL-Rome officials sent to the United States to investigate the Atlanta branch after the raid were the officials who should have been investigated.

* Dr. Sardelli testified that he believes officials at BNL-Rome knew of Mr. Drogoul's activities.

4) There is evidence that documents may have been shredded by BNL officials shortly after the raid and that some files and documents are missing.

5) BNL branches in Germany, England and Canada were aware of BNL-Atlanta's substantial financing of Iraqi purchases and projects.

6) The Government's witnesses from Morgan Guaranty and the Bank of New York and confidential CIA reports concluded that it was well-known in international banking circles that BNL-Atlanta provided substantial financing for Iraq's purchase of agricultural, military and non-military products.

7) The Italian parliament's extensive report on the "BNL scandal" concludes that Mr. Drogoul was not a "lone wolf" and that BNL-Rome's failure to adequately supervise the Atlanta branch permitted the continued illegal activity.

8) Mr. Drogoul's co-defendant Paul Von Wedel and Jean Ivey, a BNL-Atlanta employee who was granted immunity, testified that they believed that

---

[1] The Court will not reveal the contents of these documents because they remain classified. However, as the Court will discuss below, the Court is unable to see how they relate to national security and why they should remain secret from defense counsel and the public.

officials in Rome were aware of BNL-Atlanta's involvement with Iraq—testimony the Court found credible. Mr. Von Wedel also testified that Mr. Drogoul had regular access to Dr. Giacomo Pedde, the director general of BNL, that Mr. Drogoul met with Mr. Monaco, a senior BNL official, in Baghdad, and that Mr. Florio, another senior BNL official, verbally approved early CCC loans to Iraq.

9) Mr. Drogoul's first attorney, Theodore Lackland, testified credibly that several individuals involved with the allegedly fraudulent transactions told him that officials in Rome were aware of the transaction and in fact had in their possession one of the allegedly fraudulent loan agreements (MTL-4).

10) As the "victim" in this matter, BNL-Rome may be able to recover $1–2 billion in unpaid CCC-backed loans to the Iraqis.

11) When notified of the August 4, 1990, raid, Mr. Drogoul returned immediately to the United States, leaving his family in France. He met with BNL officials in New York, was furnished an attorney who was to be paid by the bank, and continued as manager of the Atlanta branch for a week.

12) Mr. Drogoul's chief mentor at BNL in 1986–87 retired from BNL in 1987 and became a consultant at Entrade, a defendant in this case and a participant in the scheme.

B. *The Investigation and Prosecution of Mr. Drogoul*

The Court has also come to a number of preliminary conclusions about the Government's investigation of this case. Primarily, the Court concludes that prosecutors failed to investigate seriously whether BNL-Rome knew of defendant Drogoul's activities. This failure, coupled with or provoked by the involvement of other departments of the United States Government, indicates an effort to absolve BNL-Rome of complicity in the Atlanta branch loans to Iraq. The Court notes:

1) High-level officials in the Justice Department and the State Department met with the Italian ambassador to discuss the case. They appeared to help steer this case and gave support to BNL-Rome's position that it was a victim in this matter, assuring the ambassador that there "would be no surprises" for the Italians.

2) The Justice Department cancelled investigators' necessary trip to Italy and Turkey, where they intended to interview bank officials and others with knowledge of the transactions and scheme.

3) The Italian ambassador met with then-Attorney General Richard Thornburgh in Spring 1990 and told him that incriminating BNL-Rome in these transactions would be tantamount to "a slap in the face" of the Italians and would not be understood by the government of Italy.

4) The local prosecutor in this matter received one or more highly unusual and inappropriate telephone calls from the White House Office of Legal Counsel about this case, indicating the potential embarrassment level of the case.

5) The draft indictment was delayed by the Justice Department from early 1990 until the end of the Gulf War, February 1991—almost one year. Also, the plea bargain in which Mr. Drogoul agreed to plead guilty to only 60 counts rather than 347 and initiated by an assistant prosecutor when the chief prosecutor was out of the city effectively silenced Mr. Drogoul who had announced his intention to make a full disclosure at the plea hearing.

6) The Government failed to produce and, apparently, made no effort to bring in any knowledgeable bank officials from Rome—including Pedde, Guadagnini, Monaco, Florio—for the sentencing hearing.

7) The Government failed to interview Wafai Dajani, despite evidence of his substantial involvement with the scheme, when he was in Atlanta and had agreed to meet with the prosecution. Mr. Dajani, who has ties to the King of Jordan, was not indicted.

8) Investigators were blocked by the Department of Agriculture from interviewing Iraqi officials who were in the United States negotiating CCC guaranties and later were prohibited from travelling to Iraq to interview potential co-conspirators and witnesses.

9) In early 1990, Atlanta prosecutors met with BNL-Rome lawyers, discussing the bank's position as a victim.

10) The American Ambassador to Italy notified the Secretary of State, Justice Department and others in the Fall 1989 that BNL's management was worried about the prosecution of the case and wanted it raised "to a political level" and to achieve "damage control."

11) Matrix Churchill, an Iraqi front company that was a clearinghouse for weapons procurement, was not indicted, although one of its officers was.

12) The Government has provided no credible explanation for its failure to indict Wafai Dajani, Matrix Churchill, Enka, and the Central Bank of Iraq.

C. *Intelligence agencies*

The Court also tentatively concluded during the course of the hearings that it is likely that the United States intelligence agencies were aware of BNL-Atlanta's relationship with Iraq. For example:

1) The Central Intelligence Agency did not respond to repeated requests from the Court concerning CIA knowledge of and involvement in the activities of the Atlanta branch. The agency's earlier response to the carefully crafted September 1, 1992, request from the Acting United States Attorney was evasive and concerned only knowledge of and involvement in *unauthorized* funding. The CIA continues to be uncooperative in attempts to discover information about its knowledge of or involvement in the funding of Iraq by BNL-Atlanta.

2) The raw intelligence reports indicate an awareness of extensive funding of Iraq by BNL-Atlanta.

3) There was no explanation as to the intelligence community's awareness or

lack of awareness of BNL-Atlanta's role in funding the Iraqi military build-up despite extensive cable traffic between Baghdad and Atlanta and several trips to Baghdad by Drogoul, including one to an Iraqi military fair attended by U.S. officials, such as the U.S. Ambassador.

D. *Classified Information*

The Court is also concerned that the local prosecutors lacked access to classified information which may have provided evidence on important elements of this case. The September 17, 1992, letter from the CIA to the local prosecutors shows that the CIA was not forthcoming with information it may have about the transactions at issue in this case—the one area of classified information made available to the Court supports Mr. Drogoul's contention that his superiors approved of his activities. While the Court is well aware that there may be classified information in support of the Government's theory of this case, the Court is concerned that the prosecutors may have been blocked by agencies with political agendas from developing a full picture of this affair. This is particularly troubling in light of the fact that this information no longer seems relevant to national security and that, even if it is, there are procedures through which the CIA, and other agencies, can make classified information available without revealing sources and methods.

IV. CONCLUSION

These are grave questions as to how the prosecutors made their decisions in this case—both as to the nature of the charges and whom to prosecute. It is apparent that decisions were made at the top levels of the United States Justice Department, State Department, Agriculture Department and within the intelligence community to shape this case and that information may have been withheld from local prosecutors seeking to investigate the case or used to steer the prosecution. Furthermore, the Attorney General's exceptional refusal to grant the Congressional request for an independent counsel in itself raises concerns for the Court about the Government's impartiality in handling this case.

Accordingly, this Court again strongly recommends that an independent prosecutor be named to investigate this matter. The Court also recommends that the trial of Mr. Drogoul and the sentencing of the other defendants in this case be postponed to enable the United States Government to employ its full resources to obtain all the facts rather than to continue with the prosecution's acceptance of BNL-Rome's version that BNL is a victim to avoid embarrassing a foreign government or to contain criticism of a failed foreign policy. The naming of an independent prosecutor in this matter would be an appropriate response to the 1990 Federal Reserve memorandum, commenting that the Iraqis are willing to sacrifice one individual to the vagaries of the United States criminal justice system.

The Court GRANTS defendant's motion to withdraw his plea of guilty and GRANTS the Government's motion to recuse.

IT IS SO ORDERED, this 5th day of October, 1992.

_____

Marvin H. Shoob, Senior Judge
United States District Court
Northern District of Georgia

Judicial Order in the BNL Case Issued by Judge Marvin Shoob on August 23, 1993.

UNITED STATES DISTRICT COURT
NORTHERN DISTRICT OF GEORGIA
ATLANTA DIVISION

UNITED STATES OF AMERICA, Plaintiff, v. AMEDEO DeCAROLIS and THERESE MARCELLE BARDEN, Defendants	CRIMINAL ACTION 1:91-cr-78-MHS
UNITED STATES OF AMERICA, Plaintiff, v. LEIGH ANN NEW, Defendant	CRIMINAL ACTION 1:91-cr-88-MHS
UNITED STATES OF AMERICA, Plaintiff, v. PAUL VON WEDEL, Defendant	CRIMINAL ACTION 1:91-cr-89-MHS
UNITED STATES OF AMERICA, Plaintiff, v. THOMAS MOBLEY FIEBELKORN, Defendant	CRIMINAL ACTION 1:91-cr-126-MHS

ORDER

This matter is before the Court on the motions of each of the defendants for a downward departure from the sentencing guidelines. Earlier the Court considered and ruled on the various objections to the presentence reports and determined the appropriate offense level for each defendant. Because of the absence of any prior criminal record, each defendant is in Criminal History Category I.

On August 19, 1993, the government in a sentencing memorandum advised the Court that it will move for a downward departure pursuant to § 5K1.1 of the Sentencing Guidelines for defendants Von Wedel, New, and DeCarolis, and reserved the decision whether to make a similar motion on behalf of defendants Fiebelkorn and Barden. The government also advised the Court that it does not oppose a downward departure for defendant Barden based on her extraordinary family situation.

While the government's new position makes this Court's task of imposing a fair and appropriate sentence far less burdensome, the extent of any downward departure is governed by considerations which go beyond defendants' cooperation or individual family circumstances.

The Court has reviewed considerable material, including National Security Agency reports; CIA documents prepared by the Directorate of Information and the Directorate of Operations; the book of 29, which includes 29 documents from these agencies determined by the government to be discoverable by defense; the so-called black book, which consists of a series of State Department memoranda, National Security Council reports and memoranda, and Defense Intelligence Agency confidential and unclassified cables and information (the black book was not furnished to defense counsel as the information is substantially a duplicate of that furnished in the form of summaries and the book of 29); the several reports of the Italian Senate Commission involving this matter; the diary of P. Di Vito, an official at BNL; the CIA report of the investigation of its handling of BNL-related matters; the Senate Select Committee on Intelligence staff report on the involvement of United States intelligence agencies in the BNL affair; the summaries of classified information prepared by the government and furnished to defense counsel;[1] the testimony during the three-week sentencing hearing of defendant Christopher Drogoul; and the various exhibits introduced during that proceeding.

The preponderance of the evidence well supports this Court's conclusion that BNL-Rome was not a victim in this case. The evidence of CIA knowledge of

---

[1] These summaries represent information from the NSA and CIA documents that the Court determined to be discoverable by the defense.

the activities of BNL-Rome and BNL-Atlanta prior to the August 1989 raid of BNL-Atlanta is less persuasive but clearly troublesome. Either the CIA knew of the activities or the CIA failed to detect a five-year international deception and large-scale illegal financing of arms for Iraq through a small branch bank in Atlanta, Georgia. That determination is not necessary or appropriate for this Court. The Court does conclude that this is an appropriate case for a downward departure as to each defendant and will grant defendants' motions in part and will also grant the government's motions for a downward departure for substantial assistance and will consider defendant Barden's extraordinary family situation.

Background

This case arises out of a loan scheme stretching across continents and cultures, involving weapons merchants and multi-national banks, and implicating governments. In February 1991, Christopher Drogoul, the branch manager of BNL-Atlanta and the alleged mastermind of the scheme, was named, along with an Iraqi Bank, some foreign nationals, and several of the above-named defendants, in a 347-count indictment. The indictment centered on charges that Mr. Drogoul, the branch manager, defrauded BNL over the course of several years by engineering billions of dollars in unauthorized loans to Iraq and other nations. A number of these loans were backed by the U.S. Department of Agriculture's Commodity Credit Corporation ("CCC").

Since the raid on BNL's Atlanta office in 1989, the scandal has sparked investigations across the Western world. Several committees of the United States Congress opened investigations into this matter, commissions of the Italian Parliament have explored the scandal, and aspects of this case were raised at a trial in England.

In September 1992, this Court presided over Mr. Drogoul's three-week sentencing hearing, which followed his guilty plea to sixty counts of the indictment. The Court heard detailed testimony on the loan scheme, international money markets, and the organization of BNL. The hearing ended during Mr. Drogoul's testimony when the Government announced that it did not oppose Drogoul's motion to withdraw his plea. The Court granted Drogoul's motion and later granted the Government's motion that the Court recuse itself. Mr. Drogoul is scheduled to go to trial before The Honorable G. Ernest Tidwell on September 8, 1993. These defendants, each of whom has pleaded guilty, have been awaiting a resolution of their involvement since the summer of 1989—four years.

Evidence and Standard

While the information and evidence reviewed by the Court are of uneven reliability and occasionally recount the hearsay statements of unknown informants, the Court has sifted through the information to make reliability findings and has considered only that information which it has found to contain "sufficient indicia of reliability to support its probable accuracy." U.S.S.G. § 6A1.3(a). In sentencing, the Court is permitted to rely on information that would not be admissible under the rules of evidence in a trial. "Reliable hearsay evidence may be considered. Out-of-court declarations by an unidentified informant may be considered: 'where there is good cause for the nondisclosure of his identity and there is sufficient corroboration by other means.' " *Id.*, Policy Statement (quoting *United States v. Fatico*, 579 F.2d 707, 713 (2d Cir. 1978)).

The Court also notes that while no single piece of information or evidence standing on its own would support the Court's conclusions, when taken as a whole, even in light of the Government's conflicting information and argument, the information more than adequately and credibly supports the Court's conclusion that the defendant employees of BNL-Atlanta with their personal agendas and paltry rewards were pawns or bit players in a far larger and wider-ranging sophisticated conspiracy that involved BNL-Rome and possibly large American and foreign corporations, and the governments of the United States, England, Italy, and Iraq.

It would be the height of hypocrisy to sentence these defendants as if this were a simple case of wrongdoing by a branch bank's employees, the sort of fraud contemplated by the sentencing guidelines. The Court's conclusions are supported by the following credible evidence:[2]

Evidence supporting Court's conclusion that BNL was aware of the activities of the Atlanta branch

1. BNL's relationship with Iraq
   * BNL is one of the largest banks in Italy, and the bank has a longstanding relationship with Iraq.
   * In the early 1980's, BNL financed a number of Italian exports to Iraq, and Iraq helped BNL during a liquidity crisis in the 1970's.
   * In late 1987, BNL-Rome helped finance a transaction for construction of a sewage plant in Iraq.
   * BNL was well-known, as were many Italian institutions, for its political

---

[2] At request of the Government agencies that produced this information, the Court, for security reasons, has not identified the specific document and source of the information from which it has drawn the facts set out below. The Court will provide the appropriate authority under seal at the request of the parties.

Also, defendant Von Wedel filed motion under the Classified Information Procedures Act ("CIPA") § 6(e) (2) (B) requesting a finding against the Government as to the truth of certain information in the classified materials because the Government has refused to produce the name of the sources. For the purposes of the downward departure, the Court is finding that this information is credible and accordingly DENIES AS MOOT defendant Von Wedel's motion.

spoils system. Members of the Italian parliament believed that U.S., Italian, and Iraqi officials received kickbacks from these deals. At the bank, commissions sometimes amounted to five percent of any deal. Other sources said that BNL officials received eight percent kickbacks.

2. BNL continued to do business with Iraq after the Iraqis were implicated in the scandal.

* BNL-Rome honored several letters of credit issued by the Atlanta branch to companies for carbide cutting tools (often used in the manufacture of weapons), and BNL-Rome participated in the financing of an Iraqi petrochemical plant.

* It remained Iraq's correspondent bank for Italy.

* Intelligence sources stated that the BNL-Atlanta loan scheme was only a continuation of this long-term relationship.

3. Evidence of BNL's knowledge.

* A branch of BNL in Udine, Italy referred an Italian steel company to BNL-Atlanta for financing of an Iraqi project. An official from the Rome office of BNL had personally handled the matter, advising the company to use BNL-Atlanta, because that branch handled the bank's Iraqi business.

* In 1989, General Motors sought financing for an automobile deal with Iraq from BNL in Rome and Toronto. BNL-Atlanta extended credit for $154 million to finance the transaction. *The financed automobiles were sold at almost double the unit price.* No explanation is available as to the $75 million overcharge or who benefitted from it.

* In January 1990, a CIA employee concluded, based on general intelligence reports and publicly available material, that managers at BNL-Rome were involved in the scandal.

* A source from the legal department at the bank is quoted as saying that the transactions from BNL-Atlanta were authorized and directed by the Italian government and under instructions to make it appear that the transactions were controlled exclusively by BNL-Atlanta.

* Others speculated that the loans could not have been made without the tacit approval of the BNL Rome office, and Western bankers assumed that BNL's headquarters knew of the loan scheme under way in Atlanta.[3]

* The BNL affair was considered by some sources to be part of an acknowledged cooperative strategy to support Iraq to ensure its victory in the Iran-Iraq war.

---

[3] A U.S. intelligence source found that this information *confirmed* press reports about BNL knowledge of the scandal.

* Italian treasury secretary Carli reported to the Italian Senate Commission that three BNL-Rome employees may have known about the unauthorized lending in Atlanta. He also said that the information of BNL-Atlanta's activities should not have slipped through the bank's controls.

* Senior BNL officials were indicted and later convicted for their involvement in arms sales to Iran.

* The Italian embassy in Iraq was under suspicion of complicity in the BNL matter. The military attache committed suicide shortly after the raid, and he was rumored to be related to the scandal.

* An Italian parliamentary commission member stated that the investigation showed that Drogoul was "no lone wolf."

* The former head of BNL's North American operations, Dr. Luigi Sardelli, provided credible testimony that senior officials in Rome approved or had knowledge of Mr. Drogoul's activities.

* Sardelli's letter criticizing defendant's activities was never delivered by the auditor to officials in Rome.

* Instead of auditing or investigating BNL-Atlanta, BNL-Rome officials elected to investigate Dr. Sardelli, who appears to this Court to be the only "straight shooter" in the organization.

* BNL-Rome was an extremely political organization, operating more as an agency of the Italian government than as a bank.

* Dr. Sardelli voiced his frustration with BNL-Rome in testifying that the BNL-Rome officials sent to the United States to investigate the Atlanta branch after the raid were the officials who should have been investigated.

* Co-defendant Paul Von Wedel and Jean Ivey, a BNL-Atlanta employee who was granted immunity, testified at Drogoul's hearing that they believed that officials in Rome were aware of BNL-Atlanta's involvement with Iraq—testimony the Court found credible. Mr. Von Wedel also testified that Mr. Drogoul had regular access to Dr. Giacomo Pedde, the director general of BNL, that Mr. Drogoul met with Mr. Monaco, a senior BNL official, in Baghdad, and that Mr. Florio, another senior BNL official, orally approved early CCC loans to Iraq.

* Senior officials in Rome signed onto some of the loans made by BNL-Atlanta to Iraq, at the request of the Iraqis.

* From early in the investigation, BNL's lawyers and Italian officials urged that this case be raised to a political level.

Connections with the weapons network

Matrix-Churchill, an Iraqi front company and a major component of the arms procurement network, was a major participant in the BNL-Atlanta scheme. The CIA became aware that Matrix-Churchill was an Iraqi front company in 1987. No CIA reports indicated a relationship with BNL-Atlanta. Later, in a criminal proceeding in Great Britain, it was confirmed that two employees of

Matrix-Churchill, one of whom was a director, Paul Henderson, were sources for British intelligence. The charges against the two men were dropped.

BNL-Atlanta was reported to have provided financing for major parts of the Iraqi procurement network, involving such companies as Space Research Corporation, Lear Fan, the Italian Endeco Barazuol, and Matrix-Churchill. BNL-Atlanta was reported to have helped finance large parts of the Condor II missile program, a joint program of Iraq, Egypt, and Argentina.

Awareness of U.S. Intelligence community

The CIA had non-public information from various sources[4] about BNL and BNL-Atlanta lending activities, though not information that they were unauthorized.

Miscellaneous Government Information

In the fall of 1989, shortly after the raid on BNL-Atlanta, there were a number of contacts between the prosecutors in the case and the federal agencies involved in the decision to approve new agricultural loan guarantees for Iraq. The Atlanta prosecutors met directly with representatives of the Agriculture Department. There were at least two telephone calls from a junior attorney in the White House counsel's office to the chief prosecutor in this case; the calls sought information concerning the case in connection with the decision to approve loan guarantees. In the spring of 1990, the prosecutors and investigators were invited to Washington on at least one occasion to discuss the case with National Security Council staff members and other administration officials concerned about the approval of a second tranche of loan guarantees. Later, in September 1990, the chief prosecutor and chief investigator on the case were part of a Justice Department delegation which met with the Italian ambassador to the United States, who argued that BNL was the victim of a "terrible fraud."

During a November 1989 meeting of the National Advisory Deputies Committee, certain officials reported that Iraq had not been implicated and that the scandal appeared to involve internal BNL matters. Some high-level members of the Executive Branch wanted to continue the CCC program with Iraq, arguing it was essential to the U.S. relationship with Iraq.

 * Following the execution of the search warrant and the implication of the Iraqis, the United States Government, particularly its foreign policy branches, continued to push for granting agricultural credits to Iraq.

 * A generally reliable source believed that BNL-Atlanta could not have operated without the knowledge and acquiescence of the Federal Reserve Board, the Department of Agriculture, and the Commodity Credit Corporation.

 * After 1985, the Exim bank maintained a rotating, short-term

---

4 At the request of the Government intelligence agencies, the Court does not identify these sources.

$200,000,000 facility for Iraq; it was the only listed country receiving Exim coverage. In January 1990, President Bush signed a waiver of sanctions to permit the Exim program for Iraq to continue through 1990. The United States also determined to release $500 million in CCC guarantees with the possibility that another $500 million would be released later.

* A U.S. Government memorandum prepared for the Executive Branch urged continued approval of the CCC program for Iraq, but acknowledged the improbability that Iraqi bank officials were unaware of kickbacks, deeply discounted interest rates, and other gross irregularities in the program. The U.S. Government was also aware that there were allegations of double and triple overpricing of some commodities, diversion and transshipment of commodities, and that CCC financing had been used for goods that did not originate in the United States.

Di Vito Diary

Attorney General Richard Thornburgh met with the Italian ambassador at a White House dinner. The ambassador pushed the idea that BNL was a victim and said incriminating BNL would be seen as an insult to Italy.

Overruns by BNL-Atlanta from 1986 were signaled to the North American office of BNL by the foreign credit office of the bank.

A number of new transactions, after the raid, between BNL-Rome and Iraq totalled more than $228,000,000 as outlined in the July 31, 1990 confirmations.

Specific Findings

These factual findings support the Court's downward departure for the following reasons.

One, the Court finds that there is substantially reliable evidence that the alleged victim in this case, BNL-Rome, encouraged defendants to act as they did and superiors at the bank were in fact complicit in the scheme. The defendants saw their superior, Mr. Drogoul, rewarded for his acts, and could reasonably conclude that the bank approved of their acts or was deliberately ignorant of their activities.

Section 5K2.10 of the Sentencing Guidelines provides:

> If the victim's wrongful conduct contributed significantly to provoking the offense behavior, the Court may reduce the sentence below the guideline range to reflect the nature and circumstance of the offense.

U.S.S.G. § 5K2.10. Downward departures relying on this section usually involve cases of a physical assault and the policy statement provides that the section is usually not "relevant in the context of non-violent offenses." *Id.* Neither the guideline nor the commentary, however, prohibits the section's application to a fraud case, and the fraud guideline clearly contemplates that the victim of the fraud was not complicit with the alleged fraud. *See* § 2F1.1.

The Court has considered the Government's argument that § 5K2.11 applies only to victim conduct that *provoked* a defendant's offenses. The Court finds, however, that it is within this Court's discretion to consider the victim's conduct throughout the course of this scheme in departing downward, and the Court concludes that this conduct permitted and encouraged the scheme. This conduct does not fit neatly in the category set out in § 5K2.11, but clearly this was not a pattern of conduct considered by the Commission in formulating the guidelines.

The evidence of BNL officials' knowledge of these loans and of the loans' role in international finance suggests that these defendants were merely functionaries in a scheme that benefitted the management of BNL and furthered the foreign policy of the United States and Italy. CCC loans to Iraq continued to be approved at the highest levels of the United States Government long after the scheme was uncovered, and BNL-Rome continued to do business with the Iraqis and other entities who had participated in the scheme "to defraud" the bank. The Di Vito diary lists in detail a total of $ 228 million in new loans by BNL-Rome to Iraq following a July 26, 1990 conversation. (Di Vito diary, July 31, 1990.)

Two, departure is proper because the offense level is exaggerated by the dollar value involved in the scheme. There is little evidence that defendants' activities were the factual or proximate cause of the loss.[5] As recounted above, defendants' roles were a minuscule part of the offense, and the offense level "bears little relation to" defendants' role in the offense. *United States v. Restrepo*, 936 F.2d 661 (2d Cir. 1991). Indeed, it is difficult to pinpoint the cause of the "loss" in this action. Until the Gulf War intervened, Iraq had continued to make payments on many of the loans extended. On other loans, however, Iraq had defaulted. The amount of loss caused by these defendants, then, "is complicated by considerations of multiple causation." *United States v. Gregorio*, 956 F.2d 341 (1st Cir. 1992) (permitting a downward departure for "multiple causation"); *United States v. Schneider*, 930 F.2d 555 (7th Cir. 1991); *United States v. Kopp*, 951 F.2d 521 (3d Cir. 1991). More important, the role [of] these defendants was trivial in relation to the scope of this scheme. Also, as recounted above, the victims'

---

[5] The Court notes that several of the defendants objected to the amount of the loss as stated in presentence reports. Others, inexplicably, did not.

conduct likely led to an increase in the amount loaned and the amount lost. This combination of causes takes the defendants outside the "heartland" of the fraud guideline and makes these cases appropriate for a downward departure.

Finally, the Court concludes that a downward departure is appropriate because there is simply no way the Sentencing Commission could have considered the vast range of conduct that is relevant to this case, dwarfing these individuals' involvement. Neither this Court nor the public is likely to know the underlying motivations and purposes of the scheme that touched the branch bank, but it is clear that this case and all its permutations are unlike any set of facts covered by the mathematical formulas of the sentencing guidelines. Accordingly, a downward departure in this case is appropriate.

The Court GRANTS the motions for downward departure.

IT IS SO ORDERED, this 23d day of August, 1993.

Marvin H. Shoob, Senior Judge
United States District Court
Northern District of Georgia

APPENDIX B

*Selected Documents Referred to
Throughout the Text*

THE UNDER SECRETARY OF DEFENSE

WASHINGTON, D.C. 20301

POLICY

MEMORANDUM FOR THE ASSISTANT CHIEF OF STAFF FOR INTELLIGENCE
                DEPARTMENT OF THE ARMY

SUBJECT: Possible Acquisition Opportunity (U)

    (TS/NF) While I fully recognize the value to the USA of
obtaining an MI-24 HIND, I recommend against pursuing this
particular deal because of the intermediary to be used. Based
on the recent fraud charges brought against the intermediary for
this very same type of transaction as well as his previous
record, I believe the potential for causing embarrassment to the
U.S. Government is too great — even if the exchange were to
occur successfully — if it became known that the U.S. had used
the services of such a notorious individual to arrange an arms
deal with Iraq.

                                Richard G. Stilwell
                                General, USA (Ret.)
                                Deputy

Memorandum from General Richard Stilwell, deputy undersecretary of defense,
advising against the proposed sale by Sarkis Soghanalian of U.S. helicopters to
Iraq in exchange for a Soviet helicopter, 1983.

Department of State

SECRET

SECRET

AN: N860007-0382

PAGE 01   STATE 234618
ORIGIN NOOS-00

INFO LOG-00   ADS-00   /000 R

------------------------040307 2604502 /11
O 2604482 JUL 86 ZFF6
FM SECSTATE WASHDC
TO AMEMBASSY BAGHDAD IMMEDIATE

S E C R E T STATE 234618

NOOIS
FOR AMBASSADOR FROM NEA MURPHY

E.O. 12356:   DECL: OADR
TAGS: PREL, MOPS, US, IZ
SUBJECT: USG SUPPORT FOR IRAQ DURING THE WAR

REF: BAGHDAD 2925

1. SECRET - ENTIRE TEXT.

State Department cable to the American ambassador in Baghdad, reporting that Vice President Bush had been encouraged to ask Jordanian and Egyptian leaders to urge Saddam Hussein to step up air force attacks on Iran, July 1986.

4. AS FOR THE POSSIBILITY OF IRAQ'S "BORROWING"
U.S.-SUPPLIED JORDANIAN EQUIPMENT, THERE ARE LEGAL
RESTRICTIONS ON ANY ACTION OF THAT SORT, BESIDES THE
DIFFICULT POLICY QUESTIONS WHICH YOU HAVE POINTED OUT.
THEN, TOO, ANY SUCH TRANSFER HAS TO BE NOTIFIED TO THE
CONGRESS AND THUS MADE PUBLIC. IN ADDITION, THE EXPERTS
HERE BELIEVE THAT THE EQUIPMENT IN QUESTION WOULD NOT
HAVE A SIGNIFICANT IMPACT ON THE WAR EFFORT.

5. WE IN NEA ARE IN ESSENTIAL AGREEMENT WITH YOUR
REACTION TO THE PROPOSAL TO SEND A SENIOR U.S. EMISSARY
TO TALK WITH SADDAM HUSSEIN. THE IDEA STILL HAS AN
ACTIVE BUREAUCRATIC LIFE, HOWEVER. WE HAVE ENCOURAGED
THE VICE PRESIDENT TO SUGGEST TO BOTH KING HUSSEIN AND
PRESIDENT MUBARAK THAT THEY SUSTAIN THEIR EFFORTS TO
CONVEY OUR SHARED VIEWS TO SADDAM REGARDING IRAQ'S USE OF
ITS AIR RESOURCES. THE VERY RECENT REPORT (AMMAN 7439)
FROM AMMAN ON THAT SUBJECT LEADS US TO CONCLUDE THAT
SADDAM MAY NOT BE OPEN TO SUGGESTION. ON THE OTHER HAND,
IF SADDAM DOES WHAT HE SAYS HE WOULD DO WITH THE AIR
FORCE, THAT WOULD BE A MAJOR PLUS. ARMACOST
SECRET
SECRET

```
2572 - 11 3 ).
300495 FMMFTI I
CCI RS39374
7CZC 29 OCT 85

TLX NR:  CCI/657/85

ATTN:  DR P TORSELLO

REF OUR TELCONVERSATION.  I ENCLOSE MESSAGE FROM BNL SINGAPORE:

''QUOTE''

FM: BANCA NAZIONALE DEL LAVORO - SINGAPORE

DOCUMENTARY CREDIT N. 85/1/387 FOR USDLR3,396,435 OPENED IN YOUR
FAVOUR BY CENTRAL BANK OF IRAO - BAGHDAD O/C D.G. OF MILITARY
ACCOUNTS BAGHDAD
------------------------------------------------------------------

FURTHER TO OUR RECENT CONVERSATION WE PEEPEY CONFIRM THAT WE ARE
PREPARED TO CONFIRM THE ABOVE MENTIONED DOCUMENTARY CREDIT, PROVIDED
WE ARE SO REQUESTED BY THE OPENING BANK, AT THE FOLLOWING CONDITIONS:

+ CONFIRMATION COMMISSION : 0.50 PERCENT PER QUARTER OR FRACTION
  THEREOF
- ACCEPTANCE COMMISSION   : 2 PERCENT FLAT

WE ARE FURTHERMORE PREPARED TO SUBSEQUENTLY DISCOUNT OUR ACCEPTANCES
AT THE BEST PREVAILING MARKET CONDITIONS.

ASSURING YOU OUR BEST ATTENTION AT ALL TIMES, WE REMAIN

YOURS FAITHFULLY
B.N.L. SINGAPORE BRANCH
GIROTTI / MATTEI

 'UNQUOTE''

2   I HAVE FURTHER REQUESTED THAT THEY REMOVE CONDITION
    ''PROVIDED WE ARE SO REQUESTED BY OPENING BANK

BEST REGARDS
CHAN CHOONG+
300495 FMMFTI I
CCI RS39374
VVVV
```

Above: Telex from the Singapore branch of Banca Nazionale del Lavoro, discussing the opening of a BNL credit by the Central Bank of Iraq to facilitate mines shipments to Iraq, October 1985.

Opposite: A middleman in the Italian-Iraqi mines deal confirms that BNL Singapore opened the letter of credit, that mines were delivered, and that payment is due from Baghdad, February 1986.

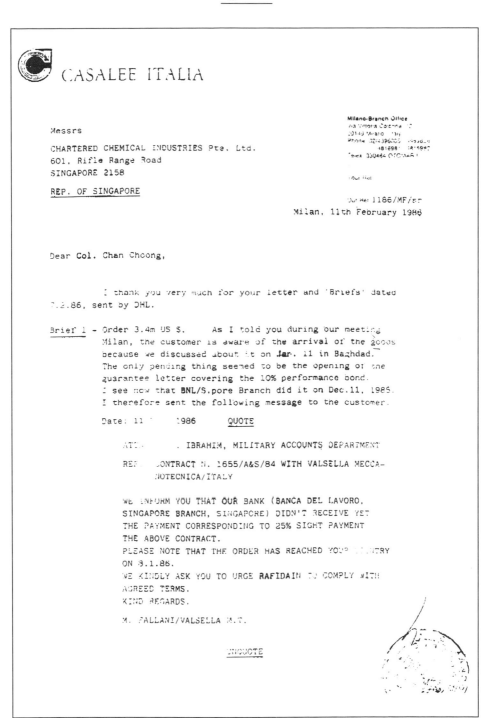

CASALEE ITALIA

Messrs

CHARTERED CHEMICAL INDUSTRIES Pte. Ltd.
601, Rifle Range Road
SINGAPORE 2158

REP. OF SINGAPORE

Milano-Branch Office
Via Vittoria Colonna 7
20149 Milano Italy
Phone 02/4396005 4396019
481698 481699
Telex 330464 CASIMIL I

Our Ref

Our Ref 1166/MF/sr
Milan, 11th February 1986

Dear Col. Chan Choong,

     I thank you very much for your letter and 'Briefs' dated
7.2.86, sent by DHL.

Brief 1 - Order 3.4m US $.   As I told you during our meeting
     Milan, the customer is aware of the arrival of the goods
     because we discussed about it on Jan. 11 in Baghdad.
     The only pending thing seemed to be the opening of the
     guarantee letter covering the 10% performance bond.
     I see now that BNL/S.pore Branch did it on Dec.11, 1985.
     I therefore sent the following message to the customer.

     Date: 11   1986   QUOTE

        ATTN   . IBRAHIM, MILITARY ACCOUNTS DEPARTMENT

        REF   CONTRACT N. 1655/A&S/84 WITH VALSELLA MECCA-
           NOTECNICA/ITALY

        WE INFORM YOU THAT OUR BANK (BANCA DEL LAVORO,
        SINGAPORE BRANCH, SINGAPORE) DIDN'T RECEIVE YET
        THE PAYMENT CORRESPONDING TO 25% SIGHT PAYMENT
        THE ABOVE CONTRACT.
        PLEASE NOTE THAT THE ORDER HAS REACHED YOUR COUNTRY
        ON 8.1.86.
        WE KINDLY ASK YOU TO URGE RAFIDAIN TO COMPLY WITH
        AGREED TERMS.
        KIND REGARDS.

        M. FALLANI/VALSELLA M.T.

            UNQUOTE

8705004

United States Department of State

Washington, D.C. 20520

February 26, 1987

'87 FEB 26 P 2 :39

DIST:
P
S/S
S/S-S
TMB
NEA
EB
RF:rw

CONFIDENTIAL

MEMORANDUM FOR MR. DONALD P. GREGG
THE WHITE HOUSE

SUBJECT: The Vice President's March 2 Meeting with Iraqi
            Ambassador Nizar Hamdoon

The Department forwards herewith additional background
material which may be useful for the Vice President's March 2
meeting with Iraqi Ambassador Hamdoon. This material,
supplementing the memorandum of February 14 on the same
subject, covers issues which Hamdoon may raise during the
meeting.

Since Hamdoon is planning to introduce the issue of Exim
credit insurance for Iraq, the Department strongly recommends
that, before meeting with Hamdoon, the Vice President telephone
Exim Chairman Bohn to discuss the issue. We believe the Vice
President should emphasize to Bohn the advantages for U.S.
regional policy of resuming short-term credit insurance for
Iraq. Recommended talking points for that call to Chairman
Bohn are attached.

Melvyn Levitsky
Executive Secretary

Attachments:

    Tab 1. Additional Issues to Be Raised
    Tab 2. Talking Points for Hamdoon Meeting: Licensing
    Tab 3. Talking Points for Call to Exim Chairman Bohn.

CONFIDENTIAL
DECL: OADR

CONFIDENTIAL

TALKING POINTS FOR THE VICE PRESIDENT'S CALL TO JOHN BOHN
(EXIM CREDIT INSURANCE FOR IRAQ)

EXIM CREDITS FOR IRAQ

-- Iraqi Ambassador Hamdoon is calling on me soon, and I
expect him to raise the issue of short-term Exim credit
'insurance for Iraq. I would like to be as responsive as
possible.

-- I understand that the Iraqis have resolved some
outstanding arrearages to Exim, and that the Exim Board
will decide soon whether to resume short-term credit
insurance for Iraq. I urge you and your colleagues on the
Board to give that favorable consideration.

-- As you know, there are major U.S. policy considerations
at work in this issue. Iraq has apparently contained the
latest Iranian offensive, and we are taking advantage of
that to try to put some life into peace efforts. Exim's
support for continued trade with Iraq would be a powerful,
timely signal -- both to Iraq and to the Gulf Arab states
-- of U.S. interest in stability in the Gulf.

-- Although in the near term Iraq will continue to face
financial stress because of the war, Iraq's prospects for
the medium- to long-term are good, considering the
country's vast oil reserves. Now is the time to begin
building a solid trade relationship with Iraq for the
future.

CONFIDENTIAL

Opposite: State Department memorandum to Vice President Bush's national security adviser, Donald Gregg, urging that Bush lobby the chairman of the Export-Import Bank to resume credits for Iraq, February 1987.

Above: Talking points prepared for the vice president's telephone call to John Bohn, the Eximbank chairman, in order to lobby for credits for Iraq, February 1987.

FERRANTI / INTERNATIONAL SIGNAL & CONTROL

REPORT TO BOARD

8 September 1987

4.6   **Summary of political risks**

4.6.1 Arising from the current business and as an ongoing feature of the
       very nature of ISC's market area political risks exist on a scale
       unusual in Ferranti markets.

4.6.2 These arise from the political or financial instability of the
       customer and then on the other hand the vagaries of US and UK
       governments in the overt and covert embargoes and strategic licensing
       systems. ISC insist they operate strictly within the laws of every
       country they work in. Whilst it appears that ISC keep very close
       relations with Washington one must recognise that some of this is in
       the covert policy areas and ISC could be left on a limb. In the UK
       ISC has only limited 'clearance' from MoD which could be because ISC
       is not a high profile UK company like Ferranti. A decision has to be
       taken as to what specific market areas and suppliers need to be

Report to the board of Ferranti discussing "covert policy" activities of International Signal and Control, September 8, 1987.

```
RX-DD2 0610 EST 04/08/89
4979333 BNL UI

APR 08 1989 0716
4979333 BNL UI
-214374 RSHBK IK
BAGHDAD  APRIL  08  1989
FM RASHEED BANK BAGHDAD
TO BANCA NAZIONALE DEL LAVORO ATLANTA -GEORGIA -U.S.A.
TEST 341490 ON 8.4.1989
FROM  BAGHDAD BRANCH 106
=============================
PLS NOTIFY  MESSRS. ENTRADE INTERNATIONAL LTD 630 FIFTH AVENUE NEW
YORK N.Y-10111 USA.    WE ESTABLISH OUR IRREVOCABLE LETTER OF
CREDIT NO 292/8/89 IN THEIR   FAVOUR FOR ACCOUNT OF IRAQ ATOMIC
ENERGY  COMMISSION  BAGHDAD  UPTO  THE  AGGREGATE  AMOUNT  OF  USD
5400000/- USDOLLARS FIVE MILLIONFOUR HUNDRED THOUSAND ONLY)
AVAILABLE FOR PAYMENT (IN U.S.A.) VALID UNTIL  4.9.89
AGAINST THEIR RECEIPT OR SIGHT DRAFT DRAWN ON US
ACCOMPANIED BY DOCUMENTS  BENEFICIARY'S  SIGNED COMMERCIAL
INVOICES IN ORIGINAL AND(10) COPIES   IN THE NAME OF THE BUYER
STATING THE MERCHANDISE DESCRIPTION QUANTITY PRICE VALUE NET AND
GROSS WEIGHTFREIGHT CHARGES SHIPPING(IF ANY) AND CERTIFYING ITS
CORRECTNESS AND THAT THE GOODS ARE OF TURKEY ORIGIN IF THE
GOO GOODS ARE INVOICED ON INCLUSIVE CANDF DETAILS  OF CHARGES AND
EXPENSES ARE NOT NECESSARY PROVIDED THEY ARE STATED TO BE
INCLUDED.    CERTIFICATE OF ORIGIN AND PACKING LIST.
PARCELS  AND RECEIPTS SHOULD BEAR BUYER'S NAME AND LETTER OF
CREDIT NUMBER EVIDENCING ONE SHIPMENT OFTHE FOLLOWING GOODS:
300 TONS WORSTEN YARN NM 40/2 45 PERCENT WOOL ON  CONES (AS
DETAILED)  IN THE SUPPLIER'S TELEX OFFER NO 1060/89 OF 14.3.89 AND
TELEXES NO T955/89 AND T 962/89 OF  21 AND 22/3/89     PACKING
```

Telex from Baghdad asking BNL Atlanta to open $5.4 million credit to finance "yarn" and "wool" shipments to the Iraq Atomic Energy Commission, April 8, 1989.

FROM CENTRAL BANK OF IRAQ BAGHDAD

DATE: 23.5.89

TO: BANCO NAZIONALE DE LAVORO - ATLANTA- U.S.A.
ORRECT TEST
TEST: RCZO7

PLEASE FIND BELOW FULL DETAILS OF OUR IRREVOCABLE LETTER
CREDIT NO 89/3/609....
AFTER ADDING YOUR CONFIRMATION PLEASE NOTIFY M/S MATRIX
CHURCHILL LTD P.O. BOX 88 FLETCHAMSTEAD HIGHWAY ,COVENTRY
COVENTRY
XXXXXXXXX CV4 9DA- ENGLAND....
WE ESTABLISH OUR IRREVOCABLE LETTER OF CREDIT NO 89/3/609 IN THEIR
FAVOUR. FOR ACCOUNT OF NASSR ENTERPRISE FOR MECHANICAL
INDUSTRIES BAGHDAD
UP TO THE AGGREGATE AMOUNT OF DM 81,000,000/- (SAY EIGHTY ONE
MILLION DM ONLY).
AVAILABLE FOR PAYMENT (IN U.S.A.) VALID UNTIL 28.2.1992...
AGAINST THEIR RECEIPT OR SIGHTDRAFT DRAWN ON US ACCOMPANIED BY
DOCUMENTS SPECIFIED HERE - BELOW MARKED WITH THIS CREDIT NUMBER
1. DOCUMENTS REQUIRED
A.   BENEFICIARYS SIGNED COMMERCIAL INVOICES IN ORIGINAL AND(5)
COPIES IN THE NAME OF THE   BUYER STATING THE MERCHANDISE
DESCRIPTION QUANTITY PRICE VALUE NET AND GROSS WEIGHT FREIGHT
CHARGES SHIPPING   MARKS COUNTRY OF ORIGIN COUNTRY OF MANUFACTURERS
TRADE DISCOUNT IF ANY) ANDCERTIFYING ITS CORRECTNESS AND
THAT THEGOODS ARE OF EUROPEAN
ORIGIN.IF THE GOODSARE
INVOICED ON INCLUSIVE C AND F DETAILS OF CHARGES AND EXPENSES
ARE NOT NECESSARY PROVIDED THEY ARE STATED TO BE INCLUDED

B. CERTIFICATE OF ORIGIN IN 5 COPIES.

(ATTESTATION AND LEGALIZATION-OF COMMERCIAL INVOICES AND
CERTIFICATE OF ORIGIN REFER TO RELATIVE ATTESTATION INSTRUCTIONS
PARA(11)
C.FULL   SET OF SHIPPING COMPANY CLEAN (ON BOARD) BILL OF
LADING MARKED FREIGHT PREPAID MADE OUT TO THE ORDER OF OUR BANK
MARKED (NOTIFY BUYERS)
D. PACKING LISTS IN 5 COPIES.
2-EVIDENCING ONE OR MORE SHIPMENTS OF THE FOLLOWING GOODS

HOT FORGING DIES PROJECT......
3. FROM EUROPE TO C AND F BAGHDAD BY SEA VIA AQABA
NOT LATER THAN 28.2.1992.
4- 'INSURANCE COVERED IN IRAQ.
5- TRANSHIPMENT NOT ALLOWED
6-   THIS CREDIT REPRESENT 100PCT VALUE OF THE GOODS.
C. AND F BAGHDAD.
7- ALL BANK CHARGES ARE ON THE BENEFICIARY'S ACCOUNT.
EXCEPT CONFIRMATION CHARGES.
8- IN REIMBURSEMENT OF YOUR PAYMENT AGAINST DOCUMENTS IN
CONFORMITY WITH THE TERMS OF THIS LETTER OF CREDIT:-
PAYMENT SHOULD BE EFFECTED ACCORDING TO AGREEMENT DATED

Telex from Baghdad asking BNL Atlanta to finance shipment of goods to Iraq by
Matrix Churchill of England, May 23, 1989.

OFFICE   MEMORANDUM

DATE___August 22, 1989___

TO___Legal Files___   SUBJECT___Call to Mr. Preston___

FROM___Bradley K. Sabel___

S T R I C T L Y   C O N F I D E N T I A L

COPY

At 9:15 a.m. on Tuesday, August 8, 1989, Mr. Corrigan placed a telephone call to Lewis T. Preston, Chairman of Morgan Guaranty Trust Company of New York ("Morgan"), to request his assistance in obtaining information regarding an account on Morgan's books in the name of the Atlanta, Georgia Agency ("Agency") of Banca Nazionale del Lavoro ("Lavoro"), which is under investigation by the United States Attorney in Atlanta for an off-books lending and funding operation. My verbatim notes of Mr. Corrigan's side of the conversation, which took place in the presence of Messrs. Patrikis and O'Sullivan and myself, are as follows:

> We have a tricky little problem that we need help
> with. We recently became aware of some irregular
> activities at the Atlanta Agency of Lavoro. I'll
> call it off-book stuff. They were undertaken largely
> if not exclusively through an account at Morgan and
> were being facilitated by your dedicated wire
> transfer system, MorCom. This is part of a criminal
> investigation. The Lavoro people here and in Rome
> and Atlanta are cooperating fully. We're involved,
> as is the Bank of Italy and the Italian government,
> and all are aware of the situation. The Agency is
> open. However, we've reached a point in the
> investigation where we feel we must try to come full
> circle on the reconciliation of transactions, for

Federal Reserve Bank of New York memorandum detailing telephone conversation of August 8, 1989, between Gerald Corrigan, president, and Lewis Preston, chairman of Morgan Guaranty Trust Company, concerning Morgan's clearing of BNL Atlanta funds.

UNCLASSIFIED

COVER SHEET FOR NSD 26

ADDRESSEES

```
TO:   THE VICE PRESIDENT
      THE SECRETARY OF STATE
      THE SECRETARY OF THE TREASURY
      THE SECRETARY OF DEFENSE
      THE ATTORNEY GENERAL
      THE SECRETARY OF ENERGY
      THE DIRECTOR OF THE OFFICE OF MANAGEMENT AND
          BUDGET
      THE ASSISTANT TO THE PRESIDENT FOR NATIONAL
          SECURITY AFFAIRS
      THE DIRECTOR OF CENTRAL INTELLIGENCE
      THE CHAIRMAN OF THE JOINT CHIEFS OF STAFF
      THE DIRECTOR, UNITED STATES ARMS CONTROL AND
          DISARMAMENT AGENCY
      THE DIRECTOR, UNITED STATES INFORMATION AGENCY
```

UNCLASSIFIED

Redacted version of National Security Directive 26, signed by President George Bush on October 2, 1989, outlining secret U.S. policies toward Iraq.

October 2, 1989   **UNCLASSIFIED**

U.S. Policy Toward the Persian Gulf

Access to Persian Gulf oil and the security of key friendly
states in the area are vital to U.S. national security. The
United States remains committed to defend its vital interests in
the region, if necessary and appropriate through the use of U.S.
military force, against the Soviet Union or any other regional
power with interests inimical to our own. The United States also
remains committed to support the individual and collective
self-defense of friendly countries in the area to enable them to
play a more active role in their own defense and thereby reduce
the necessity for unilateral U.S. military intervention. The
United States also will encourage the effective support and
participation of our western allies and Japan to promote our
mutual interests in the Persian Gulf region.

UNCLASSIFIED

Released
Partial Text of
NSD 26

Iraq

Normal relations between the United States and Iraq would serve
our longer-term interests and promote stability in both the Gulf
and the Middle East. The United States Government should propose
economic and political incentives for Iraq to moderate its
behavior and to increase our influence with Iraq. At the same
time, the Iraqi leadership must understand that any illegal use
of chemical and/or biological weapons will lead to economic and
political sanctions, for which we would seek the broadest
possible support from our allies and friends. Any breach by Iraq
of IAEA safeguards in its nuclear program will result in a
similar response. Human rights considerations should continue to
be an important element in our policy toward Iraq. In addition,
Iraq should be urged to cease its meddling in external affairs,
such as in Lebanon, and be encouraged to play a constructive role
in negotiating a settlement with Iran and cooperating in the
Middle East peace process.

We should pursue, and seek to facilitate, opportunities for U.S.
firms to participate in the reconstruction of the Iraqi economy,
particularly in the energy area, where they do not conflict with
our non-proliferation and other significant objectives. Also, as
a means of developing access to and influence with the Iraqi
defense establishment, the United States should consider sales of
non-lethal forms of military assistance, e.g., training courses
and medical exchanges, on a case by case basis.

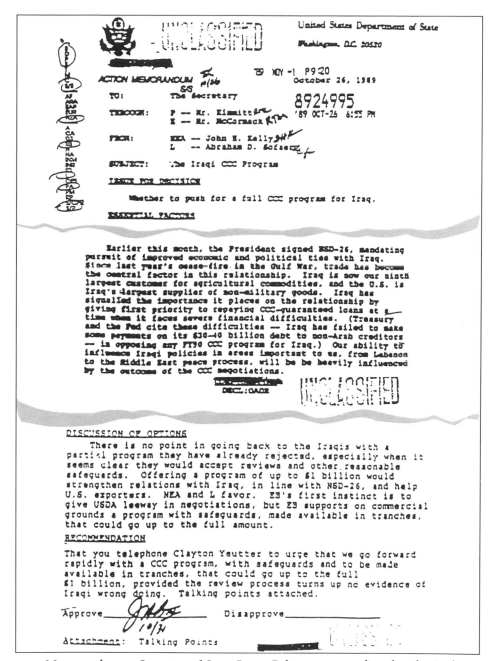

United States Department of State

Washington, D.C. 20520

ACTION MEMORANDUM

'89 NOV -1 P9 20

October 26, 1989

8924995

'89 OCT-26 6:55 PM

TO: The Secretary

THROUGH: P — Mr. Kimmitt
E — Mr. McCormack

FROM: NEA — John H. Kelly
L — Abraham D. Sofaer

SUBJECT: The Iraqi CCC Program

ISSUE FOR DECISION

Whether to push for a full CCC program for Iraq.

ESSENTIAL FACTORS

Earlier this month, the President signed NSD-26, mandating pursuit of improved economic and political ties with Iraq. Since last year's cease-fire in the Gulf War, trade has become the central factor in this relationship. Iraq is now our ninth largest customer for agricultural commodities, and the U.S. is Iraq's largest supplier of non-military goods. Iraq has signalled the importance it places on the relationship by giving first priority to repaying CCC-guaranteed loans at a time when it faces severe financial difficulties. (Treasury and the Fed cite these difficulties — Iraq has failed to make some payments on its $30-40 billion debt to non-Arab creditors — in opposing any FY90 CCC program for Iraq.) Our ability to influence Iraqi policies in areas important to us, from Lebanon to the Middle East peace process, will be be heavily influenced by the outcome of the CCC negotiations.

DECL:OADR

DISCUSSION OF OPTIONS

There is no point in going back to the Iraqis with a partial program they have already rejected, especially when it seems clear they would accept reviews and other reasonable safeguards. Offering a program of up to $1 billion would strengthen relations with Iraq, in line with NSD-26, and help U.S. exporters. NEA and L favor. E3's first instinct is to give USDA leeway in negotiations, but E3 supports on commercial grounds a program with safeguards, made available in tranches, that could go up to the full amount.

RECOMMENDATION

That you telephone Clayton Yeutter to urge that we go forward rapidly with a CCC program, with safeguards and to be made available in tranches, that could go up to the full $1 billion, provided the review process turns up no evidence of Iraqi wrong doing. Talking points attached.

Approve _____ Disapprove _____

10/31

Attachment: Talking Points

Memorandum to Secretary of State James Baker recommending that the Bush administration commit a full $1 billion of CCC loan guarantees for Iraq, October 26, 1989.

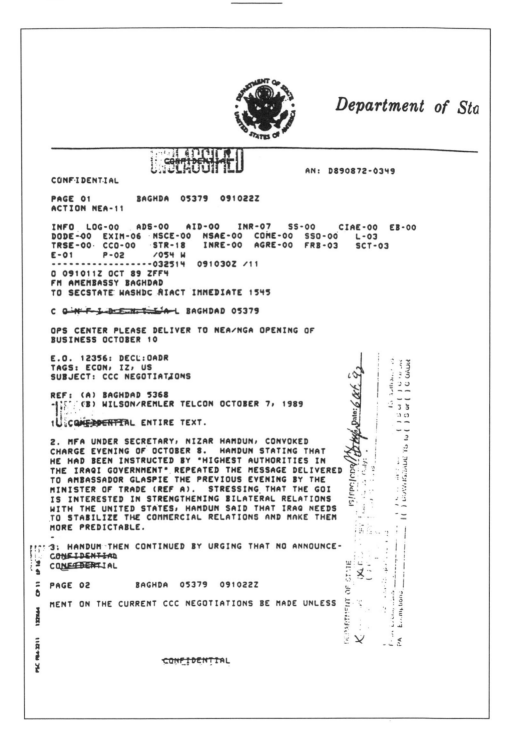

Department of Sta

CONFIDENTIAL

AN: D890872-0349

CONFIDENTIAL

PAGE 01   BAGHDA 05379 091022Z
ACTION NEA-11

INFO LOG-00   ADS-00   AID-00   INR-07   SS-00   CIAE-00   EB-00
DODE-00 EXIM-06 NSCE-00 NSAE-00 COME-00 SSO-00   L-03
TRSE-00 CCO-00   STR-18   INRE-00 AGRE-00 FRB-03   SCT-03
E-01   P-02   /054 W
------------------032514   091030Z /11
O 091011Z OCT 89 ZFF4
FM AMEMBASSY BAGHDAD
TO SECSTATE WASHDC RIACT IMMEDIATE 1545

C O N F I D E N T I A L BAGHDAD 05379

OPS CENTER PLEASE DELIVER TO NEA/NGA OPENING OF
BUSINESS OCTOBER 10

E.O. 12356: DECL:OADR
TAGS: ECON, IZ, US
SUBJECT: CCC NEGOTIATIONS

REF: (A) BAGHDAD 5368
     (B) WILSON/REMLER TELCON OCTOBER 7, 1989

1. CONFIDENTIAL ENTIRE TEXT.

2. MFA UNDER SECRETARY, NIZAR HAMDUN, CONVOKED
CHARGE EVENING OF OCTOBER 8. HAMDUN STATING THAT
HE HAD BEEN INSTRUCTED BY "HIGHEST AUTHORITIES IN
THE IRAQI GOVERNMENT" REPEATED THE MESSAGE DELIVERED
TO AMBASSADOR GLASPIE THE PREVIOUS EVENING BY THE
MINISTER OF TRADE (REF A). STRESSING THAT THE GOI
IS INTERESTED IN STRENGTHENING BILATERAL RELATIONS
WITH THE UNITED STATES, HAMDUN SAID THAT IRAQ NEEDS
TO STABILIZE THE COMMERCIAL RELATIONS AND MAKE THEM
MORE PREDICTABLE.

3. HAMDUN THEN CONTINUED BY URGING THAT NO ANNOUNCE-
CONFIDENTIAL
CONFIDENTIAL

PAGE 02   BAGHDA 05379 091022Z

MENT ON THE CURRENT CCC NEGOTIATIONS BE MADE UNLESS

CONFIDENTIAL

UNCLASSIFIED
CONFIDENTIAL

AN AGREEMENT ON THE FULL PROGRAM HAS BEEN REACHED.
HE EMPHASIZED THAT IRAQ WAS CONCERNED THAT THE
ANNOUNCEMENT OF A POTENTIAL PROGRAM MIGHT BE VIEWED
IN INTERNATIONAL FINANCIAL CIRCLES AS A JUDGMENT ON
THE PART OF THE USG THAT THE GOI WAS SOMEHOW IMPLI-
CATED IN THE BNL SCANDAL. ACCORDINGLY, IRAQ'S REPU-
TATION IN THESE FINANCIAL CIRCLES WOULD BE DAMAGED.
-

4. WITH HIS MAILED FIST STILL IN HIS VELVET GLOVE,
HAMDUN THEN POINTED OUT THAT IRAQ DOES HAVE ALTERNA-
TIVE SOURCES OF SUPPLY TO WHICH IT COULD TURN IF
THE U.S. WERE UNWILLING TO COMMIT ITSELF TO A PRO-
GRAM. THESE SOURCES WHICH HE SAID NEED NOT BE NAMED,
OFTEN COMPLAIN TO THE GOI THAT THE U.S. RECEIVES
PREFERENTIAL TREATMENT IN AGRICULTURAL TRADE. THESE
SAME SOURCES ALSO ACCUSE IRAQ OF FAVORING THE U.S.
WHEN IT COMES TO REPAYING ITS DEBTS. COMMENT: IM-
PLICIT IN HAMDUN'S REMARKS WAS THE SUGGESTION THAT
SHOULD WE BE UNABLE TO AGREE TO A PROGRAM, IRAQ
WOULD HAVE TO RETHINK BOTH ITS DEPENDENCE ON U.S.
SUPPLIERS OF AGRICULTURE PRODUCTS, AND THE PRIORITY
TREATMENT IT ACCORDS TO U.S. CREDITORS IN THE REPAY-
MENT OF ITS DEBTS. END COMMENT.

5. AT A LATER ENCOUNTER WITH HAMDUN AT A RECEPTION,
CHARGE ADVISED THAT HE HAD INFORMED WASHINGTON OF
THE GOI CONCERNS (AS HAD THE AMBASSADOR IN REF A)
AND THAT THE DEPARTMENT HAD CONFIRMED OUR INTEREST
IN SEEING THAT ISSUE RESOLVED AS EXPEDITIOUSLY
AS POSSIBLE (PER REF TELCON B). CHARGE EXPLAINED
THAT IT MIGHT NOT BE POSSIBLE TO REACH A SOLUTION
BY TUESDAY, OCTOBER 10, GIVEN THE LONG WEEKEND AND
CONFIDENTIAL
CONFIDENTIAL

PAGE 03   BAGHDA 05379 091022Z

THE TRIP TO MOSCOW BY FED CHAIRMAN GREENSPAN.
HAMDUN THEN REPEATED HIS URGING THAT IN THE ABSENCE
OF A FULL AGREEMENT, NO PUBLIC ANNOUNCEMENT SHOULD
BE MADE.
-

6. COMMENT: IT IS ABUNDANTLY CLEAR THAT THE IRAQIS
ARE CONCERNED AT THE HIGHEST LEVELS OF THE GOVERNMENT
ABOUT THE POSSIBLE ADVERSE AFFECT THAT A PUBLIC
ANNOUNCEMENT COULD HAVE ON ITS REPUTATION UNLESS
THAT ANNOUNCEMENT IS FOR A FULL 1990 PROGRAM. IN

CONFIDENTIAL

Report from the American embassy in Baghdad of Nizar Hamdoon's message
from Saddam Hussein regarding U.S. farm credits for Iraq, October 1989.

CONFIDENTIAL

MEMORANDUM OF CONVERSATION

DATE: October 13, 1989

SUBJECT: USDA Comments on Investigations of Iraq and the
           Banco Nazionale del Lavoro, Atlanta Branch, Scandal

DISTRIBUTION:

E: Richard T. McCormack, Under Secretary of State for
          Economic Affairs.
          Sam Hoskinson, Executive Assistant to the Under
          Secretary of State for Economic Affairs

L: Abraham D. Sofaer, Legal Adviser

NEA: Jock Covey, Acting Assistant Secretary

EB: Eugene McAllister, Assistant Secretary
          Robert Downes, Office of Development Finance

PARTICIPANTS: State: Frank Lemay, Special Assistant to the
                Under Secretary for Economic Affairs

                USDA: Tom Conway, Associate General Counsel
                       Kevin Brosch, Attorney, Office of the
                       General Counsel, FAS
                       Peter Bonner, Attorney, Office of the
                       General Counsel, FAS
                       Larry McElvain, Director of Export
                       Credits, CCC

LOCATION: Department of Agriculture, Office of the General
            Counsel, Room 2307,   Building

Summary:

There are currently 10 separate investigations of Banco
Nazionale del Lavoro, Atlanta Branch (BDLA), lending activity
to Iraq. As investigators dig further into the paper morass,
more and more indications of significant wrong-doing on the
part of BDLA and Iraq are surfacing. It now appears that at a
minimum elements of the Government of Iraq (GOI) knew of the
illegal dealings of the BDLA but found it convenient to
continue using its good offices. Indications are that in

CONFIDENTIAL

After Sales Services:

The GOI reportedly required exporters participating in CCC guaranteed exports to Iraq to provide "After Sales Services". These services required exporters to provide, free of charge, various types of equipment and spare parts to Iraq. The GOI was told by USDA about 18 months ago that these practices were illegal but they continued. The problem with these services, as with the payments, is that exporters figure the cost of the services into the declared value of the commodity sale. The upshot is that CCC is again guaranteeing financing of both commodities and non-commodity goods.

In both the required fee payments and the after sales services it is the exporter who is liable under US law for falsifying documents given to the USG. If they can show that Iraqi officials were involved, conspiracy charges could be brought against all those involved. The GOI has admitted to using both practices and sees both as "good business practice".

Conclusion and Comment:

Taken together the points discussed during the meeting indicate we should proceed carefully in urging the immediate provision of CCC guarantees to Iraq. If smoke indicates fire, we may be facing a four alarm blaze in the near future. This is particularly true given the intense scrutiny the CCC program has been under during the last year. McElvain indicated that there were 19 investigations of CCC this year and the "integrity of the program is now in question." USDA attorneys will be going to Atlanta for discussions with the US attorney during the coming week. Additional information on the various investigations will be available upon their return.

State Department memorandum written by Frank Lemay, warning of Iraqi abuse of the CCC program and describing allegations of wrongdoing uncovered in BNL investigation, October 1989.

PAGE 02 OF 04 STATE 338562   C12/25 009007   NOD191
ORIGIN NODS-00

INFO LOG-00   ADS-00   /000 R

------------------156337   212054Z /70
O 212051Z OCT 89 ZFF6
FM SECSTATE WASHDC
TO AMEMBASSY BAGHDAD IMMEDIATE

S E C R E T STATE 338562

NODIS
E.O. 12356: DECL: OADR
TAGS: PREL. IZ
SUBJECT: MESSAGE FROM THE SECRETARY TO TARIQ AZIZ

1.   SECRET - ENTIRE TEXT.

2.   PLEASE DELIVER THE FOLLOWING MESSAGE FROM SECRETARY
BAKER TO FOREIGN MINISTER AZIZ. THERE WILL BE NO SIGNED
ORIGINAL.

3.   BEGIN TEXT:

DEAR MR. MINISTER:

I APPRECIATED THE OPPORTUNITY TO MEET YOU. AND I FOUND OUR
MEETING EXTREMELY USEFUL., MY HOPE IS THAT IT HAS LAID THE
BASIS FOR A FRANK AND DIRECT RELATIONSHIP BETWEEN US. IN
THAT SPIRIT. I WANT TO RESPOND TO THE CONCERNS YOU RAISED
WITH ME.

SECRET \
Department of State

PAGE 03 OF 04   STATE   338562   C12/25 009007   NOD191

AS I SAID IN OUR MEETING. THE UNITED STATES SEEKS A
BROADENED AND DEEPENED RELATIONSHIP WITH IRAQ ON THE BASIS
OF MUTUAL RESPECT.   THAT IS THE POLICY OF THE PRESIDENT.

IN THIS REGARD. THE PRESIDENT HAS ASKED ME TO SAY TO YOU
AND THROUGH YOU TO PRESIDENT SADDAM HUSSEIN. IN THE MOST
DIRECT WAY POSSIBLE. THAT THE UNITED STATES IS NOT
INVOLVED IN ANY EFFORT TO WEAKEN OR DESTABILIZE IRAQ.
HAVING LOOKED INTO THE MATTER. AND DISCUSSED IT WITH THE
PRESIDENT. I CAN TELL YOU THIS WITH THE HIGHEST
AUTHORITY.   SUCH AN ACTION WOULD BE COMPLETELY CONTRARY TO
THE PRESIDENT'S POLICY. WHICH IS TO WORK TO STRENGTHEN THE
RELATIONSHIP BETWEEN THE UNITED STATES AND IRAQ WHENEVER
POSSIBLE.   IF YOU ARE IN A POSITION TO PROVIDE MORE
DETAILED INFORMATION I HOPE YOU WILL DO SO. I WANT TO BE
VERY SURE THAT THERE IS NO DOUBT ABOUT THIS IN THE MIND OF
THE IRAQI LEADERSHIP.

MR. MINISTER. YOU ALSO ASKED ME TO LOOK INTO THE ISSUE OF
CCC CREDIT GUARANTEES. I AM DOING SO ON AN URGENT BASIS
AND WILL GIVE YOU A FINAL RESPONSE AS SOON AS I CAN. AN
INVESTIGATION IS UNDERWAY. AND IN ALL CANDOR THERE ARE
SOME SERIOUS ALLEGATIONS THAT NEED TO BE EXAMINED
FURTHER. I CAN ASSURE YOU THAT OUR ACTIONS IN CONNECTION
WITH THE CCC PROGRAM ARE NOT IN ANY WAY MOTIVATED BY
POLITICAL CONSIDERATIONS. THE GOVERNMENT OF IRAQ HAS SET
A HIGH STANDARD ON ISSUES OF INTEGRITY OF PUBLIC OFFICIALS
AND CORRUPTION AND I AM SURE YOU WILL UNDERSTAND THE
DETERMINATION OF MY GOVERNMENT TO BE THOROUGH. AT THE
SAME TIME. I VERY MUCH HOPE THAT IT WILL BE POSSIBLE TO
RESOLVE THE PROBLEMS WHICH HAVE ARISEN QUICKLY AND TO
CONTINUE WITH THIS IMPORTANT PROGRAM. AS YOU REQUESTED

WILL CONTINUE TO GIVE THIS MATTER MY PERSONAL ATTENTION.

Message from Secretary of State James Baker to Foreign Minister Tariq Aziz, with
reference to President Bush's reassurance for Saddam Hussein, and promise of
Baker's personal interest in CCC credits for Iraq, October 1989.

Central Intelligence Agency

Washington D.C. 20505

DIRECTORATE OF INTELLIGENCE

6 November 1989

Iraq-Italy: Repercussions of the BNL-Atlanta Scandal

Summary

The revelation that a US branch of an Italian bank, Banca Nazionale del Lavoro (BNL), granted more than $3 billion in unauthorized letters of credit to Iraq has had wide-ranging repercussions for Iraq and Italy. For Iraq, public disclosure that it used some of the credits to acquire military-related technology has impeded procurement efforts, and the suspension of BNL credits has slowed civilian reconstruction and development projects. For Italy, the BNL scandal has cast at least a temporary shadow on Prime Minister Andreotti's new government, raised questions about public-sector enterprises, and reopened the issue of privatization.

The affair is unlikely to have a major impact on Iraqi military procurement efforts, but cash-short Baghdad probably will have to postpone plans for some civilian projects. The loss of BNL financing and, more important, any reduction in US agricultural credit guarantees because of negative publicity about the scandal probably would damage US-Iraqi commercial ties. For Iraq's part, however, the strain in political relations is likely to be short-lived, particularly if Baghdad believes US credit guarantees will be forthcoming. Iraq is eager to maintain good ties to the United States, an attitude intensified by improved relations between Iran and the USSR.

This memorandum was prepared by [   ] Office of Near Eastern and South Asian Analysis, and [   ] Office of European Analysis.

CIA report on the BNL-Iraqi loans affair, November 6, 1989.

BNL-Atlanta Financing for Iraq

The Atlanta, Georgia branch of the state-owned Banca Nazionale del Lavoro (BNL)—Italy's largest bank—extended $3.2 billion in 2,500 unauthorized letters of credit for Iraq between February 1988 and July 1989. US and Italian authorities have been investigating the scandal since July for violations of banking regulations and tax and customs laws.

Fragmentary reporting indicates BNL-Atlanta disbursed $1.85 billion of the $3.2 billion, including at least $800 million in letters of credit guaranteed by the US Commodity Credit Corporation (CCC). BNL headquarters agreed to release another $550 million in early October, [   ] after Iraq threatened to suspend payment to Italian firms if the bank failed to honor its commitments.

BNL-Atlanta's unusual activities included:

-- Exceeding the branch's allowable debt of $500,000 per customer.

-- Charging Baghdad an average 0.2-percent commission instead of the usual 15 percent for a poor credit risk.

-- Financing the letters of credit by borrowing from other banks for 90 to 180 days but allowing Iraq up to five years to repay.

BNL's North American headquarters in New York and the bank's directors in Rome publicly denied knowing about the letters of credit, although a BNL official in Chicago claims he notified New York and Rome several times about the unusual activity in Atlanta, according to press reports. Press reports also indicate a BNL branch in Udine, Italy referred customers exporting to Iraq to the Atlanta branch. Iraqi officials have generally denied knowledge of any wrongdoing, arguing that Baghdad is a victim in the scandal.

Iraq used some BNL credits--at least $600 million, according to British press--to buy military and dual-use technology through various front companies and legitimate firms in Western Europe. [

British press says that BNL-Atlanta also financed Iraqi military purchases from Kintex, the Bulgarian armament company.

Impact on Iraq

The suspension of credits from BNL—by far Baghdad's largest source of credits--and disclosure in the British press that Iraq used the credits to acquire military-related technology has almost certainly complicated Baghdad's procurement efforts. We believe that increased Western scrutiny of these activities has at least temporarily impaired Baghdad's ability to acquire such technology. Press coverage and London's opposition to Iraq's control of a company possessing sensitive technology, for example, led SRC Composites to divest its advanced composites factory, according to press reports. Some other firms in the networks have gone out of business.

The loss of BNL financing has almost certainly slowed civilian reconstruction and development in Iraq. Many US and West European firms supplying goods and services to projects in Iraq were being paid through BNL[ ]Many of these firms have probably suspended business with Iraq until alternate methods of payment--cash, other loans, or barter--are arranged. Financially strapped Baghdad, however, is unable to meet demands by some of these firms for payment in cash, especially for expensive purchases.[   ]reporting indicates Iraq has nearly exhausted available credit lines and barter opportunities.

Iraqi Procurement Networks

Baghdad has created complex procurement networks of holding companies in Western Europe to acquire technology for its chemical, biological, nuclear, and ballistic missile development programs. According to British press[

]one such network begins in Baghdad with the Al-Arabi Trading Company, which controls the London-based Technology and Development Group, Ltd. (TDG) and another UK firm, TMG Engineering. TDG and its Brussels-based partner, Space Research Corporation, own the Ulster-registered firm Canira Technical Corporation, Ltd. Canira in March established SRC Composites, which acquired access to advanced composite and carbon fiber technology used in aircraft and missile production. In 1987 TMG gained control of Matrix-Churchill, Ltd., the United Kingdom's leading producer of computer-controlled machine tools that can be used in the production of sophisticated armaments.

We believe Iraqi intelligence is directly involved in the activities of many holding companies funnelling technology to Iraq.[

]

Effect on US-Iraqi Relations

For Iraq, any reduction in bilateral commercial ties because of the BNL scandal takes on political significance, which Baghdad--ever paranoid--tends to exaggerate. The fallout from the scandal has strained US-Iraqi relations. Baghdad is seriously concerned that the affair is adversely affecting its economic ties to the United States-- the backbone of the bilateral relationship. Iraq is particularly upset that the CCC offered significantly less credit guarantees for FY1990 than Baghdad requested because of negative publicity about the scandal. Iraq fears that any large reduction in CCC credit guarantees would make it more costly and difficult to import agricultural goods and damage its international credit rating.

Several US firms have already been affected by the scandal.[   ] press reporting indicate BNL was financing at least $1 billion in sales to Iraq by US firms, including agricultural goods, an automobile plant, an ethylene plant, industrial machinery, construction materials, and irrigation equipment. Some US suppliers are worried that they will not receive payment on letters of credit that they have not yet submitted to BNL-Atlanta. Many US firms are trying to arrange other means of payment to avoid losing lucrative contracts.

The scandal has contributed to Iraq's perception that the United States is trying to hamstring Baghdad's efforts to promote better political ties. A senior Iraqi official told his US counterpart in early October that Baghdad was unhappy that Washington's decision on CCC credits is linked to the scandal, with which he maintained Iraq had no part. The official indicated this was not a sign that the United States wants to improve relations.

Baghdad is eager to resolve the BNL crisis because harmonious bilateral relations are important to its strategic planning. Iraq believes that the Iranians have not abandoned plans to oust the regime in Baghdad and wants to assure that the superpowers would back Iraq or at least remain neutral during any future hostilities. The Iraqis seek to prevent Washington from favoring Iran so much that Baghdad's interests are threatened. In Iraq's view, the superpowers regard Iran to be of greater importance in the region, and Baghdad is therefore trying to enhance Iraq's political and economic importance to the United States.

Impact on Italy

The BNL affair--in combination with other scandals--has cast a shadow on Prime Minister Andreotti's three-month-old government. Partly to divert attention from the BNL affair, the Socialists and some Christian Democrats are playing up other scandals, including renewed allegations that the Italian military covered up evidence concerning the 1980 crash of an Italian airliner north of Sicily. None of the governing political parties or their factions, however, appears now to believe it can strengthen its relative positions by exploiting the issue.

The scandal has also spotlighted the cost of Italy's longstanding and entrenched spoils system in the state-owned enterprises. Traditionally, appointments to key positions in public-sector companies have been allocated as a measure of party and even factional influence. Under this system, the president and several directors of BNL are members of the Italian Socialist Party, while the executive director usually comes from the Christian Democratic Party. Several backbenchers in parliament quickly denounced the spoils system for not allowing the most competent people to fill public-sector jobs. The attacks, however, have been discounted as political sour grapes, and the system shows no signs of collapse.

In light of the BNL affair, Treasury Minister Carli has renewed his efforts-- against admittedly long odds--to enlist support for privatizing state-owned banks and other public-sector corporations. Carli believes the breakdown in supervision at BNL is all too typical of the quality of Italian public-sector banking. In his opinion, privatization would force Italian banks to narrow the current 6-percentage-point spread between interest paid to depositors and that charged to borrowers--a prerequisite if Italian banks are to do well after the EC dismantles capital controls next year.

The discovery of BNL's exposure in Iraq forced the bank to seek funds to boost its capital, which the Bank of Italy already considered too low. If Iraq defaulted, BNL technically would have been bankrupt because the amount of its loans to Iraq exceeded the bank's capital. In that event, the Bank of Italy and the Treasury Ministry would have been compelled to bail out the bank. Rome was stymied in finding a Socialist-controlled institution to recapitalize the bank by itself, and the government in October finally cobbled together a $1.7 billion package from the Treasury, a state-owned insurance company, and the Social Security Fund, thus maintaining a Socialist majority on the BNL board of directors.

We believe the revelations of BNL's dealings with Iraq—along with other recent scandals—stand in counterpoint to growing Italian self-confidence on the international stage in recent years. After more than three decades of international diffidence, we believe Italian leaders have been pursuing a diplomatic profile more commensurate with their country's international economic role. Italians have felt particular pride because:

- Italian troops in the Beirut peacekeeping forces had fulfilled their mission as defined by Rome.

- The Italian decision to accept US cruise missiles played a decisive role in swinging West Germany behind deployment.

- Their country's GDP had surpassed that of the United Kingdom and possibly France.

In the opinion of almost all Italian press commentators, the BNL affair had a negative impact on Italy's credibility throughout the West. We believe, however, that the setback to Rome's international standing has been substantially less than that portrayed in the Italian press, and we expect the scandal will gradually fade from public view within Italy and will have little lasting impact on the country's perception of its international role.

Outlook

We believe Iraq will work hard to establish new military procurement networks to replace those disclosed by the press and by the US and Italian investigations as part of the fallout from the BNL affair. Baghdad highly values these networks to obtain technology that might otherwise be denied to it if the end user or purpose were revealed. Because of renewed Iraqi efforts and the likely existence of other networks that remain undetected, we do not believe that Iraq's covert procurement efforts will be set back seriously.

The drying up of this major financial source—at least for the next several years—will probably force Iraq to scale back ambitious civilian reconstruction and development plans. Baghdad probably formulated some economic plans under the assumption that BNL-Atlanta would continue to issue letters of credit on its behalf. Iraq will be unable, however, to replace BNL financing any time soon. Most commercial banks and foreign governments are likely to remain unwilling to grant or guarantee significant new credits to Baghdad until it repays more of its $45 billion non-Arab foreign debt—a low priority to Iraq. Furthermore, Iraq has overextended its barter commitments and will probably be reluctant to engage in many more such deals.

The BNL affair will probably have only a minimal impact on Italian-Iraqi relations. The scandal is unlikely to cause more than short-term political friction unless BNL fails to disburse the remaining letters of credit. Even then, Baghdad would probably employ economic--not political--means to punish Rome. Continued Iraqi threats to suspend payment to Italian firms if Rome fails to release the promised BNL credits will almost certainly be effective against the Italians, who have already agreed to release some of the undisbursed credits and have backed down in the past in the face of threats from other countries.

We have detected no sign of flagging Italian interest in Iraq, although we expect that Italian banks will scrutinize export financing and other credits for Baghdad more carefully. The Italians are maintaining existing levels of oil imports from Iraq while still trying to boost exports. Italian-Iraqi relations will continue to be strained, however, by the dispute over the delivery of Italian warships to Iraq, which is unlikely to be resolved any time soon because of Iraqi demands for additional financing for the ships and Iranian threats of retaliation against Italy if the ships are delivered.

Implications for the United States

The BNL scandal is likely to lead to a reduction in US-Iraqi commercial relations, particularly if CCC credit guarantees are decreased. Any loss of CCC credits probably would reduce Iraq's food imports from the United States because Baghdad prefers to buy on credit. Iraq probably would turn to Australia and EC countries-- which lost sales when the United States became Iraq's top Western agricultural supplier in 1983--as well as traditional suppliers Turkey and Brazil. Many of these suppliers are already trying to profit from the BNL scandal by boosting agricultural sales to Iraq at US expense. Furthermore, the bank's continued refusal to disburse remaining credits probably would prevent some US firms from implementing contracts with Iraq.

The strain in US-Iraqi political relations caused by the BNL scandal will probably be short-lived, particularly if Baghdad believes additional US credits will be forthcoming after the dust of the investigation settles. Iraq is eager to maintain good ties to the United States, an attitude intensified by improved relations between Iran and the USSR that make Baghdad uneasy. Iraq probably also believes that strained political relations would complicate its efforts to acquire US technology and credits in the future. We anticipate that Iraq will work hard to overcome the current frictions by offering commercial opportunities to the United States and lobbying US business and government officials.

Although the BNL affair embarrassed the Italian Government and banking sector, we do not believe it will not have a major impact on Italian relations with the United States. Rome appears satisfied to date with the cooperation of the US investigating agencies and appreciates the low-key manner in which Washington has reacted. BNL will probably close its Atlanta office and may suffer a loss of business in financing exports for US companies.

BUREAU OF OCEANS AND INTERNATIONAL
ENVIRONMENTAL AND SCIENTIFIC AFFAIRS

November 21, 1989

UNCLASSIFIED

~~SECRET~~

MEMORANDUM

TO: OES/N -   S/NP -
       T -   NEA/NGA -

FROM: OES/NEC -

SUBJECT: SNEC Cases of Interest

Background

The November 12 meeting of the SNEC and the November 20, briefing on Iraq's nuclear program and the activities of state enterprises provided a thorough presentation of available information and Intelligence Community views on these matters. However, we are still left with no clear indication of how to proceed on the majority of cases currently before the SNEC.

POLICY

The problem is not that we lack a policy on Iraq; we have a policy. However the policy has proven very hard to implement when considering proposed exports of dual-use commodities to ostensibly non-nuclear end users, particularly state enterprises.

SNEC policy for some years has been not to approve exports for Iraq's nuclear program, except for very insignificant items for clearly benign purposes such nuclear medicine. However, at the same time, U.S. policy, as confirmed in NSD 26, has been to improve relations with Iraq, including trade, which means that exports of non-sensitive commodities to "clean" end users in Iraq should be encouraged. According to NEA/NGA, although U.S. policy precludes approval of Munitions Control Licenses for Iraq, exports of dual use commodities for conventional military use may be approved.

Complicating factors in decision making include:

1. A presumption by the Intelligence Community and others that the Iraqi Government is interested in acquiring a nuclear explosive capability;

2. Evidence that Iraq is acquiring nuclear related equipment and materials without regard for immediate need;

3. The fact the state enterprises which are ordering substantial quantities of dual use equipment needed for post war reconstruction, such as, computers and machine tools, are involved in both military and civil projects;

4. Indications of at least some use of fronts for nuclear-related procurement.

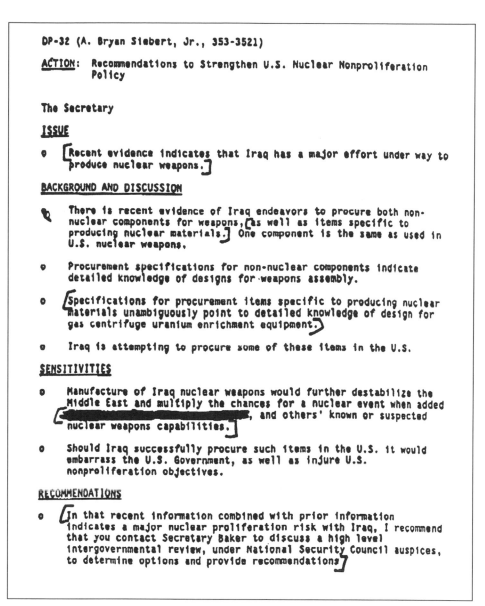

DP-32 (A. Bryan Siebert, Jr., 353-3521)

ACTION: Recommendations to Strengthen U.S. Nuclear Nonproliferation Policy

The Secretary

ISSUE

o [Recent evidence indicates that Iraq has a major effort under way to produce nuclear weapons.]

BACKGROUND AND DISCUSSION

There is recent evidence of Iraq endeavors to procure both non-nuclear components for weapons, [as well as items specific to producing nuclear materials.] One component is the same as used in U.S. nuclear weapons.

o Procurement specifications for non-nuclear components indicate detailed knowledge of designs for weapons assembly.

o [Specifications for procurement items specific to producing nuclear materials unambiguously point to detailed knowledge of design for gas centrifuge uranium enrichment equipment.]

o Iraq is attempting to procure some of these items in the U.S.

SENSITIVITIES

o Manufacture of Iraq nuclear weapons would further destabilize the Middle East and multiply the chances for a nuclear event when added [███████████████████████], and others' known or suspected nuclear weapons capabilities.]

o Should Iraq successfully procure such items in the U.S. it would embarrass the U.S. Government, as well as injure U.S. nonproliferation objectives.

RECOMMENDATIONS

o [In that recent information combined with prior information indicates a major nuclear proliferation risk with Iraq, I recommend that you contact Secretary Baker to discuss a high level intergovernmental review, under National Security Council auspices, to determine options and provide recommendations]

Opposite: State Department memorandum discussing the November 12, 1989, meeting of the interagency group on U.S. exports that could assist Iraq's nuclear program.

Above: Memorandum warning of Iraqi efforts to procure U.S. goods for its nuclear weapons program, April 1989.

OF NEW YORK

OFFICE MEMORANDUM

DATE April 5, 1990

TO Mr. Corrigan

SUBJECT Lavoro

FROM Thomas C. Baxter, Jr.

       I followed up on your suggestion about a possible connection between Banca Nazionale del Lavoro ("BNL") and the nuclear triggers that were seized in London. As you suspected, there is a connection. Apparently, Von Wedel (a former officer of BNL who is now cooperating with the government) says that one of the transactions done with Rafidain Bank at some point referenced nuclear detonators. According to Von Wedel, this reference scared BNL away from this particular transaction, but it is possible that the lesson the Iraqis learned was to be generic in preparing the credit documentation. Thus, it is entirely possible that BNL financed some of this material.

       At any rate, I have been assured that those conducting the criminal investigation in Atlanta are looking into these connections, with a view to developing additional criminal charges. The resignation of the United States Attorney in Atlanta has led to a number of difficulties in that investigation. These difficulties have been compounded by what is perceived as interference from the Justice Department in Washington.

       The press has also made a connection between BNL and the detonators. Attached you will find copies of two Financial Times articles doing just that.

TCB/sw

Attachments

cc: Messrs. Oltman
       Patrikis

Memorandum to Gerald Corrigan, president of the Federal Reserve Bank of New York, discussing suspected BNL financing of nuclear triggers destined for Iraq, April 5, 1990.

THE WHITE HOUSE
WASHINGTON

August 8, 1990

MEMORANDUM FOR THE ATTORNEY GENERAL

FROM: THE PRESIDENT

SUBJECT: Conflict-of-Interest Waiver

I am writing to notify you of a conflict-of-interest
determination I have reached under 18 U.S.C. 208(b)(1) in
connection with the current Middle East crisis.

As you know, vital United States and world interests are at stake
in the Middle East as a result of the Iraqi invasion of Kuwait.
As Commander in Chief and the Nation's Chief Executive, I am
confronting decisions of immense import with lasting consequences
for the nation and the world. The United States, along with
other world powers, has strongly condemned the Iraqi invasion,
and we have instituted a range of measures, including a freeze on
Iraqi and Kuwaiti assets in this country among other economic
sanctions.

We now face a series of decisions, large and small, about
policies and military measures required to defend United States
interests and counter this act of blatant aggression. I expect
that these decisions will be among the most difficult that I ever
face as President. As I confront the demanding choices ahead, it
is essential that I be able to call freely upon my advisors for
counsel and assistance.

I am aware that under Federal conflict-of-interest law (18 U.S.C.
208), an Executive branch employee cannot participate personally
and substantially in a particular matter, in which, to the
employee's knowledge, he has or is deemed to have a financial
interest. I understand that the Department of Justice has
historically interpreted this statute to mean that an individual
cannot personally and substantially participate in a particular
matter if the resolution of the matter would have a direct and
predictable effect on such financial interests. An individual's
appointing official is authorized to waive this prohibition based
upon a determination that the individual's financial interests
are "not so substantial as to be deemed likely to affect the
integrity of the services which the Government may expect" from
the employee.

It is not clear which, if any, of the decisions ahead would
constitute "particular matters" that would have a "direct and

predictable effect" on the financial interests of advisors on
whom I will need to rely. Based on the consultations between our
staffs over the past week, I have been advised that most of the
high-level decisions and actions ahead will be at a level of
generality so broad as not to implicate Federal conflict-of-
interest law.

Nonetheless, in the interest of caution and prudence, I believe
that under current circumstances, Cabinet members and other key
foreign policy advisors should not be needlessly restricted in
assisting me in shaping the United States response to the Iraqi
offensive or be left in doubt about when they can and cannot
assist me. I have therefore directed my Counsel, C. Boyden Gray,
to review the financial interests of those of my foreign policy
advisors for whom I have not delegated the waiver authority
vested in me under 18 U.S.C. 208(b). In particular, I have had
him conduct a special review of the financial interests held
by --

> The Assistant to the President for National Security;
> The Assistant to the President and Deputy for National
>   Security;
> The Attorney General;
> The Chief of Staff to the President;
> The Director of Central Intelligence;
> The Secretary of Commerce;
> The Secretary of Defense;
> The Secretary of Energy;
> The Secretary of State; and
> The Secretary of Treasury.

I have also had the Department of Justice review the financial
interests of the Counsel to the President.

I have now been briefed on the financial interests of these
individuals. Some of the individuals in question hold only
interests such as mutual funds that under no foreseeable
circumstances could be construed to implicate any prohibition
under conflict-of-interest law. In other instances, individuals
have quite substantial financial interests in industries that may
be affected (though not necessarily in a "direct" or
"predictable" way) by the resolution of situations that may
arise.

In light of current world events and the significance of our
response to the nation's security, it is my judgment that none of
these individuals' financial interests are "so substantial as to
be deemed likely to affect the integrity of the services which
the Government may expect" from him in all aspects of the current
effort to develop and implement a United States and international
response to Iraq's occupation of Kuwait. I have been counseled

that the Department of Justice, in interpreting conflict-of-
interest waiver authority, has said that the appointing official
should consider the size of the financial interest(s) and the
nature of the services the individual is called upon to provide.

In my judgment, the nature of the current crisis and the gravity
of the measures under consideration by the United States are such
that even vast financial interests could not be deemed likely to
affect the integrity of the services the Government may expect
from its chief foreign policy officers. Maintaining the highest
standards of integrity in the Government has been a paramount
priority for me throughout the Administration. In my view,
national security considerations at stake in the current
situation are so great as to diminish to insignificance the
likelihood that individual employees could be swayed by their
private interests.

On this basis, I hereby determine that the financial interests
held by the individuals indicated above are not so substantial as
to be deemed likely to affect the integrity of the services that
the Government may expect from them in the course of current
United States policy-making, discussion, decisions, and actions,
in response to the Iraqi invasion of Kuwait. This waiver shall
remain in effect until further notice.

[signature: G. Bush]

Memorandum from President George Bush to Attorney General Dick Thornburgh, announcing the signing by Bush of conflict-of-interest waivers for James
Baker and ten other cabinet officers and government officials involved in U.S.
policy discussions concerning Iraq, August 8, 1990.

```
HOLDINGS OF JAMES A. BAKER, III, AND HIS IMMEDIATE FAMILY
                    JANUARY 25, 1989
```

Corporations, Including Affiliates and Subsidiaries

```
Amoco
Chemical New York Corporation and National Loan Bank
Commonwealth Edison
Exxon Corporation
Houston Industries, Inc.
MCorp
Salomon, Inc.
Schlumberger, Ltd.
Texaco, Inc.
Texas American Bancshares, Inc.
Time, Inc.
United Technologies Corp.
Wainoco
```

Limited Partnerships, Closely Held Corporations, Other Entities

```
Frio County Ranch
Garrett Ranch, Inc.
Property Capital Trust SBI
Residential Resources Mortgage Investments Corp.
Trinity Petroleum Trust
Sublette County Ranch
Wilson Industries
```

```
Bonnie Sue (Texas and Louisiana Limited Partnership)
Lady Thelma (Texas and Louisiana Limited Partnership)
Alice Jean (Texas and Louisiana Limited Partnership)
Hollywood 1004-7, 3009-14, 3003-6, 3007-8, 1008-14 and
   3015 (Texas and Louisiana Limited Partnerships)
Hollywood Chem. 107 and 108 (Texas and Louisiana Limited
   Partnerships)
Hollywood LPG No. 2 (Texas and Louisiana Limited Partnership)
Lana Louise (Texas and Louisiana Limited Partnership)
Petro-Quest Associates 1980-1 (Pennsylvania Limited Partnership)
Hope # 1, 2, 3 and 4 wells, Lewis County, West Virginia
Claude Owens lease, Pecos County, Texas
```

Disclosure by Secretary of State James Baker of his family holdings in oil and other industries, January 1989.

OFFICE MEMORANDUM

FEDERAL RESERVE BANK
OF NEW YORK

DATE___February 6, 1990___

TO___Legal Files_____

FROM___Ernest T. Patrikis_____

SUBJECT___Recent Developments_____
Regarding Banca Nazionale
del Lavoro

On February 6, I spoke with Ed Willingham, General Counsel of the Atlanta Reserve Bank, and among the topics we discussed was current developments regarding BNL. Obviously, the indictments that were expected to come down in January did not materialize. A planned trip to Italy by criminal investigators was put off because of BNL asserted concerns regarding the Italian press.

A trip to Istanbul was put off at the request of Attorney General Thornburg. The criticism of the BCCI criminal settlement has motivated the Attorney General to have the BNL matter reviewed by main Justice in Washington before any settlement is agreed to by the United States Attorney.

Ed reported that Entrade is willing to pay a $1 million penalty provided no individual from that firm is convicted. The Iraqis are willing to sacrifice one individual to the vagaries of the United States criminal judicial system. Mr. Dragoul has retained high-powered defense counsel. All in all, Ed believes that we will hear little about this matter until some time late in March.

cc: Messrs. Corrigan
Oltman
Schadrack
Baxter
O'Sullivan
Zunic

Federal Reserve Bank of New York memorandum, discussing why planned trips to Italy and Turkey by BNL investigators from Atlanta had been put off by the Justice Department, February 6, 1990.

UNCLASSIFIED   OUTGOING

Department of State

PAGE 02 OF 05   STATE 208057   C12/25 787546   MOD329
ORIGIN ████-00

INFO LOG-00   ADS-00   /000 R

DECLASSIFIED BY: Frank Machak
        Director, Office of FOI,
        Privacy and Classification
        Review

        June 1, 1992

O 2701082 JUN 90 ZFF6
FM SECSTATE WASHDC
TO AMEMBASSY BAGHDAD IMMEDIATE
INFO AMEMBASSY TEL AVIV IMMEDIATE
AMEMBASSY DAMASCUS
AMEMBASSY AMMAN
AMEMBASSY CAIRO
AMEMBASSY RIYADH
AMEMBASSY TUNIS
AMEMBASSY KUWAIT

████████ T STATE 208057

████

E.O. 12356: DECL: OADR
TAGS: PTER, PREL, IZ
SUBJECT: IRAQ AND TERRORISM

1. ████ - ENTIRE TEXT.

2. WE ARE VERY CONCERNED ABOUT RISING TENSIONS IN THE REGION AND
THE PROSPECT FOR FURTHER TERRORISM. WE ARE ESPECIALLY CONCERNED
ABOUT RECENT REPORTING YOU HAVE SEEN THAT IRAQ MAY BE RENEWING ITS
TIES TO TERRORIST GROUPS, SUCH AS THE ANO AND AT LEAST ONE OTHER
ANTI-ARAFAT GROUP. IRAQ ALSO MAY BE ENCOURAGING OTHER HARDLINE
GROUPS AND FACTIONS TO UNDERTAKE NEW TERRORIST OPERATIONS AGAINST

UNCLASSIFIED

Department of State

PAGE 04 OF 05 STATE 208057   C12/26 007546   NUD349

THAT IN OUR VIEW THERE WAS NO DISCERNIBLE MILITARY
TARGET FOR THAT GROUP'S MAY 30 SEABORNE ATTACK ON
ISRAEL; IT COULD ONLY HAVE RESULTED IN SIGNIFICANT
NON-COMBATANT CASUALTIES.

-- SINCE THAT ATTACK, ABU ABBAS HAS BRAGGED THAT
FURTHER OPERATIONS ARE IN THE OFFING. WE HAVE REASON TO
BELIEVE THAT IS CORRECT. AND WE WANT TO MAKE CLEAR THAT
ANY STATE THAT PROVIDES SUPPORT FOR TERRORIST ACTIVITIES
IS IMPLICATED IN THEM AND MUST SHARE RESPONSIBILITY FOR
THEM. INDEED WITHOUT STATE SUPPORT IT IS DOUBTFUL THAT
THE MAY 30 ATTACK COULD HAVE COME AS CLOSE AS IT DID TO
SUCCEEDING.

- WE HAVE ALSO RAISED WITH YOU DISTURBING REPORTS
THAT IRAQI OFFICIALS HAVE BEEN IN CONTACT WITH MEMBERS
OF THE NOTORIOUS ABU NIDAL ORGANIZATION. WE UNDERSTAND
FORM YOU THAT IT IS IRAQI POLICY NOT TO ALLOW ABU NIDAL
TO COME TO IRAQ. IT IS TROUBLING THEREFORE, THAT WE
CONTINUE TO HEAR REPORTS THAT THE ANO HAS BEEN ALLOWED
TO OPEN A NEW OFFICE IN IRAQ. AS YOU WELL KNOW, IN OUR
VIEW THE ANO IS AMONG THE MOST DANGEROUS TERRORIST
ORGANIZATIONS IN EXISTENCE. IT WAS ONLY AFTER YOUR
GOVERNMENT EXPELLED THE ANO THAT WE WERE ABLE TO REMOVE
IRAQ FROM OUR LIST OF STATES THAT SUPPORT TERRORISM

-- IN ADDITION TO THESE TWO GROUPS, WE ARE VERY
CONCERNED WITH THE ACTIVITY OF A NUMBER OF OTHER,
PALESTINIAN GROUPS AND FACTIONS WHICH WE BELIEVE HAVE
REPRESENTATIVES IN IRAQ AND WITH WHICH YOU HAVE
INFLUENCE.

Message from Secretary of State James Baker to Ambassador April Glaspie in
Baghdad, discussing reports of Iraqi government contacts with members of the
Abu Nidal terrorist group, June 27, 1990.

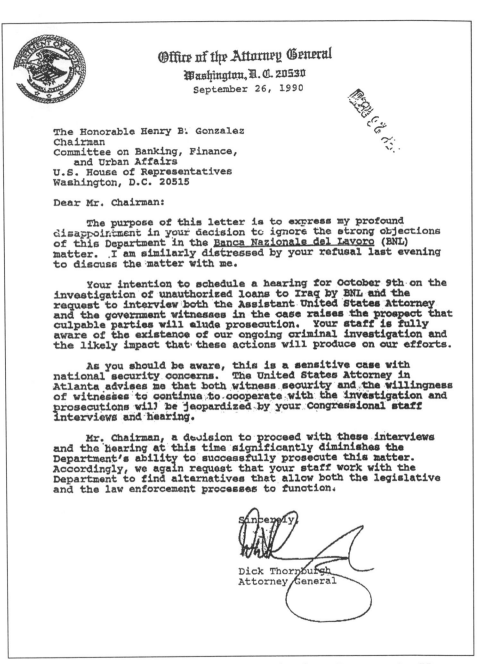

Office of the Attorney General

Washington, D. C. 20530

September 26, 1990

The Honorable Henry B. Gonzalez
Chairman
Committee on Banking, Finance,
    and Urban Affairs
U.S. House of Representatives
Washington, D.C. 20515

Dear Mr. Chairman:

The purpose of this letter is to express my profound disappointment in your decision to ignore the strong objections of this Department in the <u>Banca Nazionale del Lavoro</u> (BNL) matter. I am similarly distressed by your refusal last evening to discuss the matter with me.

Your intention to schedule a hearing for October 9th on the investigation of unauthorized loans to Iraq by BNL and the request to interview both the Assistant United States Attorney and the government witnesses in the case raises the prospect that culpable parties will elude prosecution. Your staff is fully aware of the existence of our ongoing criminal investigation and the likely impact that these actions will produce on our efforts.

As you should be aware, this is a sensitive case with national security concerns. The United States Attorney in Atlanta advises me that both witness security and the willingness of witnesses to continue to cooperate with the investigation and prosecutions will be jeopardized by your Congressional staff interviews and hearing.

Mr. Chairman, a decision to proceed with these interviews and the hearing at this time significantly diminishes the Department's ability to successfully prosecute this matter. Accordingly, we again request that your staff work with the Department to find alternatives that allow both the legislative and the law enforcement processes to function.

Sincerely,

Dick Thornburgh
Attorney General

Letter from Attorney General Dick Thornburgh to Representative Henry Gonzalez protesting the congressman's plan to hold a BNL hearing, September 26, 1990.

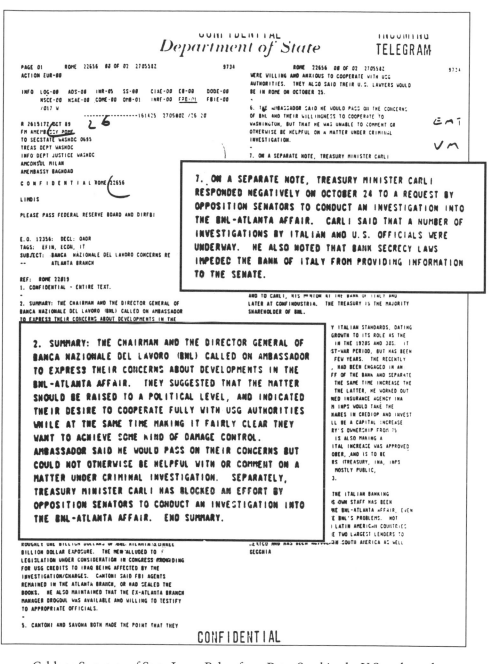

Department of State
INCOMING
TELEGRAM

PAGE 01   ROME 22656 01 OF 02 270558Z   9734
ACTION EUR-00

INFO LOG-00 ADS-00 INR-05 SS-00 CIAE-00 EB-00 DODE-00
      NSCE-00 NSAE-00 COME-00 OMB-01 INRE-00 FPB-01 FBIE-00
      /017 V
                    ------161425 270580Z /26 20

R 261517Z OCT 89
FM AMEMBASSY ROME
TO SECSTATE WASHDC 0695
TREAS DEPT WASHDC
INFO DEPT JUSTICE WASHDC
AMCONSUL MILAN
AMEMBASSY BAGHDAD

C O N F I D E N T I A L ROME 22656

LIMDIS

PLEASE PASS FEDERAL RESERVE BOARD AND DIRFBI

E.O. 12356: DECL: OADR
TAGS: EFIN, ECON, IT
SUBJECT: BANCA NAZIONALE DEL LAVORO CONCERNS RE
--   ATLANTA BRANCH

REF: ROME 22019
1. CONFIDENTIAL - ENTIRE TEXT.

2. SUMMARY: THE CHAIRMAN AND THE DIRECTOR GENERAL OF
BANCA NAZIONALE DEL LAVORO (BNL) CALLED ON AMBASSADOR
TO EXPRESS THEIR CONCERNS ABOUT DEVELOPMENTS IN THE

PAGE 02   ROME 22656 01 OF 02 270558Z   9734
WERE WILLING AND ANXIOUS TO COOPERATE WITH USG
AUTHORITIES. THEY ALSO SAID THEIR U.S. LAWYERS WOULD
BE IN ROME ON OCTOBER 25.

6. THE AMBASSADOR SAID HE WOULD PASS ON THE CONCERNS
OF BNL AND THEIR WILLINGNESS TO COOPERATE TO
WASHINGTON, BUT THAT HE WAS UNABLE TO COMMENT OR
OTHERWISE BE HELPFUL ON A MATTER UNDER CRIMINAL
INVESTIGATION.

7. ON A SEPARATE NOTE, TREASURY MINISTER CARLI

---

7. ON A SEPARATE NOTE, TREASURY MINISTER CARLI
RESPONDED NEGATIVELY ON OCTOBER 24 TO A REQUEST BY
OPPOSITION SENATORS TO CONDUCT AN INVESTIGATION INTO
THE BNL-ATLANTA AFFAIR. CARLI SAID THAT A NUMBER OF
INVESTIGATIONS BY ITALIAN AND U.S. OFFICIALS WERE
UNDERWAY. HE ALSO NOTED THAT BANK SECRECY LAWS
IMPEDED THE BANK OF ITALY FROM PROVIDING INFORMATION
TO THE SENATE.

AND TO CARLI, HIS MENTOR AT THE BANK OF ITALY AND
LATER AT CONFINDUSTRIA. THE TREASURY IS THE MAJORITY
SHAREHOLDER OF BNL.

---

2. SUMMARY: THE CHAIRMAN AND THE DIRECTOR GENERAL OF
BANCA NAZIONALE DEL LAVORO (BNL) CALLED ON AMBASSADOR
TO EXPRESS THEIR CONCERNS ABOUT DEVELOPMENTS IN THE
BNL-ATLANTA AFFAIR. THEY SUGGESTED THAT THE MATTER
SHOULD BE RAISED TO A POLITICAL LEVEL, AND INDICATED
THEIR DESIRE TO COOPERATE FULLY WITH USG AUTHORITIES
WHILE AT THE SAME TIME MAKING IT FAIRLY CLEAR THEY
WANT TO ACHIEVE SOME KIND OF DAMAGE CONTROL.
AMBASSADOR SAID HE WOULD PASS ON THEIR CONCERNS BUT
COULD NOT OTHERWISE BE HELPFUL WITH OR COMMENT ON A
MATTER UNDER CRIMINAL INVESTIGATION. SEPARATELY,
TREASURY MINISTER CARLI HAS BLOCKED AN EFFORT BY
OPPOSITION SENATORS TO CONDUCT AN INVESTIGATION INTO
THE BNL-ATLANTA AFFAIR. END SUMMARY.

Y ITALIAN STANDARDS, DATING
GROWTH TO ITS ROLE AS THE
IN THE 1920S AND 30S. IT
ST-WAR PERIOD, BUT HAS BEEN
FEW YEARS. THE RECENTLY
, HAD BEEN ENGAGED IN AN
FF OF THE BANK AND SEPARATE
THE SAME TIME INCREASE THE
THE LATTER, HE WORKED OUT
WED INSURANCE AGENCY INA
N INPS WOULD TAKE THE
NAMES IN CREDIOP AND INVEST
LL BE A CAPITAL INCREASE
RY'S OWNERSHIP FROM 75
IS ALSO MAKING A
ITAL INCREASE WAS APPROVED
OBER, AND IS TO BE
RS (TREASURY, INA, INPS
MOSTLY PUBLIC,
3.

THE ITALIAN BANKING
S OWN STAFF HAS BEEN
NE BNL-ATLANTA AFFAIR, EVEN
E BNL'S PROBLEMS. NOT
I LATIN AMERICAN COUNTRIES
E TWO LARGEST LENDERS TO

ROUGHLY ONE BILLION DOLLARS OF BNL-ATLANTA'S THREE
BILLION DOLLAR EXPOSURE. THE MEN ALLUDED TO
LEGISLATION UNDER CONSIDERATION IN CONGRESS PROVIDING
FOR USG CREDITS TO IRAQ BEING AFFECTED BY THE
INVESTIGATION/CHARGES. CANTONI SAID FBI AGENTS
REMAINED IN THE ATLANTA BRANCH, OR HAD SEALED THE
BOOKS. HE ALSO MAINTAINED THAT THE EX-ATLANTA BRANCH
MANAGER DROGOUL WAS AVAILABLE AND WILLING TO TESTIFY
TO APPROPRIATE OFFICIALS.

5. CANTONI AND SAVONA BOTH MADE THE POINT THAT THEY

RIED AND HAS BEEN ACTIVE IN SOUTH AMERICA AS WELL
SECCHIA

CONFIDENTIAL

Cable to Secretary of State James Baker from Peter Secchia, the U.S. ambassador
to Rome, reporting that the chairman of BNL suggested the Iraqi loans affair be
"raised to a political level," October 19, 1989.

→ make sure NSC makes
   acc'able progress
      (if not, o no ext →
      → subp requires Sec to
         appear

            made of line unless
               fully ripe controv —
            find way out

   → NSC has long-standing policy
      on these docs — I have
      been very firm on not
      letting copies go to Hill
      ⌐subpoena → got access
      by all staff.

¯P²
   → Sec wld have to appear
      → or run risk of contemp.
   → On app up docs →
      — still run risk of contemp

Handwritten notes from a meeting of the Rostow group in 1991.

— able to say Pres directed her
to withold
↳ no <u>crim</u> liab.
(Burford)
(U.S. Atty will not prose when
official witholds at dir
of Pres a EP grds)↑

— then cld go thru
Hse, vote citation of
contempt

↓
Then try to enf
crim — out here

NATIONAL SECURITY COUNCIL
WASHINGTON, D.C. 20506

"Iraq"
cc: Orosch
Coulter
Truman
Ficker
Dickerson
Gene Bailey
David Hauermale
Blumenthal
E'Connor

April 8, 1991

MEMORANDUM FOR JEANNE S. ARCHIBALD — Treasury
C. BOYDEN GRAY — White House
FRED GREEN
MICHAEL LUTTIG — Justice
TERRENCE O'DONNELL — DOD
ALAN RAUL — USDA
ELIZABETH RINDSKOPF
EDWIN WILLIAMSON — State
WENDELL WILLKIE — Commerce

SUBJECT: Meeting on Congressional Requests for Information
                and Documents

First of all, I apologize to Treasury and Agriculture for not
inviting them to the meeting today on responding to congressional
requests for information and documents pertaining to U.S.-Iraq
policy prior to August 2, 1990. At the meeting, it became
apparent that these departments should have been present. I
shall schedule a meeting for tomorrow on requests pertaining to
the BNL/CCC matters to which Agriculture and Treasury will be
invited.

After reviewing the requests thus far received for information,
today's meeting concluded that:

--   Department General Counsels should review and inventory all
        requests to determine which, if any, raise issues of
        executive privilege (deliberative process, foreign
        relations, national security, etc.);

--   Alternatives to providing documents should be explored
        (e.g., briefings);

--   When access to documents may be recommended, such
        recommendation should be circulated to this group for
        clearance;

--   A recommendation to provide access should be restricted to
        members only subject to these conditions: no document may
        be retained; notes may be taken but should be marked for
        classification by the department or agency in question.
        (FYI: our legislative affairs office recommends against
        insisting that members come to departments to read
        documents.); and

Memorandum from Nicholas Rostow to government lawyers setting out the initial
strategy for dealing with congressional requests for Iraq-related documents, April
8, 1991.

The Under Secretary for Export Administr
Washington, D.C. 20230

February 26, 1991

MEMORANDUM FOR WENDELL WILLKIE
              General Counsel

FROM: Dennis Kloske *DK*

SUBJECT: Iraq Printout

At your request, I have asked the Office of Export Licensing
staff to prepare a report on the preparation of the printout for
Chairman Barnard. A copy of this report titled "Iraq Data Base
Assessment" is attached, along with Qs & As and a case-by-case
summary of any corrections made to the printout. I believe this
fully responds to your memorandum to me of February 8. The first
printout provided to the Committee is a summary reference document which is responsive to the Chairman's request concerning the
history of exports to Iraq. The document also reflects Fifth
Floor and White House guidance not to provide information that
was not directly responsive to the Chairman's request. Please

> The document also reflects Fifth
> Floor and White House guidance not to provide information that
> was not directly responsive to the Chairman's request. Please

briefing sessions. I have given instructions that the list be
given to the Committee.

I would be happy to brief you on the report in greater detail.

Attachments

Memorandum from Dennis Kloske, undersecretary of commerce, to Wendell
Willkie, general counsel to the Commerce Department, concerning a congressional request for Iraq-related documents, February 26, 1991.

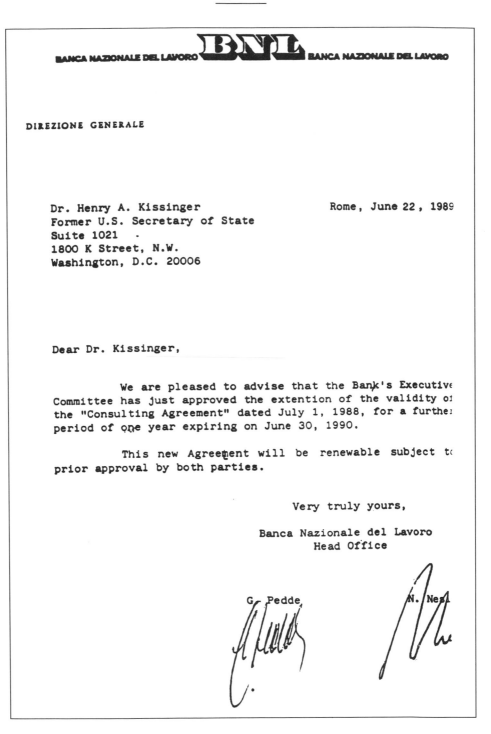

BNL

BANCA NAZIONALE DEL LAVORO   BANCA NAZIONALE DEL LAVORO

DIREZIONE GENERALE

Dr. Henry A. Kissinger   Rome, June 22, 1989
Former U.S. Secretary of State
Suite 1021   ·
1800 K Street, N.W.
Washington, D.C. 20006

Dear Dr. Kissinger,

        We are pleased to advise that the Bank's Executive
Committee has just approved the extention of the validity of
the "Consulting Agreement" dated July 1, 1988, for a further
period of one year expiring on June 30, 1990.

        This new Agreement will be renewable subject to
prior approval by both parties.

                            Very truly yours,

                            Banca Nazionale del Lavoro
                                  Head Office

            G. Pedde,   N. Nesi

BNL

BANCA NAZIONALE DEL LAVORO   BANCA NAZIONALE DEL LAVORO

Rome, June 26, 1990

Dear Dr. Kissinger,

      I am pleased to advise that the Bank's Executive Committee recently approved the extention of the validity of the "Consulting Agreement" dated July 1, 1988, for a further period of one year expiring on June 30, 1991.

      Kindly return the enclosed copy of this letter signed for acceptance.

      Warm personal regards.

(Giampiero Cantoni)

Dr. HENRY A. KISSINGER
Suite 1021
1800 K Street, N.W.
Washington, D.C. 20006

Letters from top BNL executives to Dr. Henry Kissinger, extending the Italian bank's "consulting agreement" with the former secretary of state, June 1989 and June 1990.

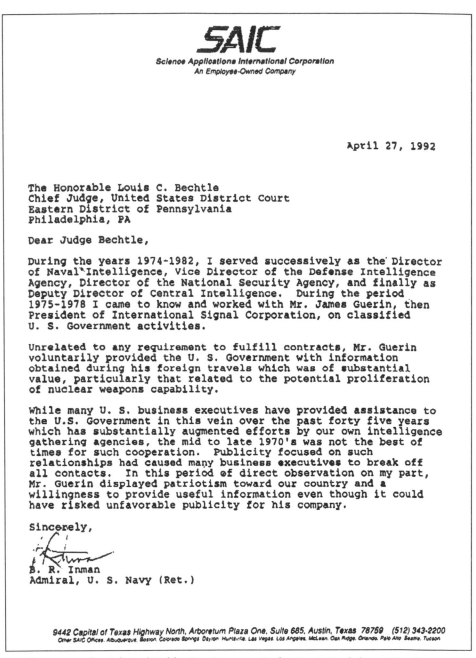

SAIC

Science Applications International Corporation
An Employee-Owned Company

April 27, 1992

The Honorable Louis C. Bechtle
Chief Judge, United States District Court
Eastern District of Pennsylvania
Philadelphia, PA

Dear Judge Bechtle,

During the years 1974-1982, I served successively as the Director
of Naval Intelligence, Vice Director of the Defense Intelligence
Agency, Director of the National Security Agency, and finally as
Deputy Director of Central Intelligence. During the period
1975-1978 I came to know and worked with Mr. James Guerin, then
President of International Signal Corporation, on classified
U. S. Government activities.

Unrelated to any requirement to fulfill contracts, Mr. Guerin
voluntarily provided the U. S. Government with information
obtained during his foreign travels which was of substantial
value, particularly that related to the potential proliferation
of nuclear weapons capability.

While many U. S. business executives have provided assistance to
the U.S. Government in this vein over the past forty five years
which has substantially augmented efforts by our own intelligence
gathering agencies, the mid to late 1970's was not the best of
times for such cooperation. Publicity focused on such
relationships had caused many business executives to break off
all contacts. In this period of direct observation on my part,
Mr. Guerin displayed patriotism toward our country and a
willingness to provide useful information even though it could
have risked unfavorable publicity for his company.

Sincerely,

B. R. Inman
Admiral, U. S. Navy (Ret.)

9442 Capital of Texas Highway North, Arboretum Plaza One, Suite 685, Austin, Texas 78759 (512) 343-2200
Other SAIC Offices. Albuquerque. Boston. Colorado Springs. Dayton. Huntsville. Las Vegas. Los Angeles. McLean. Oak Ridge. Orlando. Palo Alto. Seattle. Tucson

Letter sent by Admiral Bobby Ray Inman to Judge Louis Bechtle praising James Guerin, convicted former head of International Signal and Control, April 27, 1992.

BOARD OF GOVERNORS
OF THE
FEDERAL RESERVE SYSTEM
WASHINGTON, D. C. 20551

ADDRESS OFFICIAL CORRESPONDENCE
TO THE BOARD

December 22, 1992

BY FEDERAL EXPRESS

Walter W. Driver, Jr., Esq.
King and Spalding
191 Peachtree Street, N.E.
Atlanta, Georgia   30303

      Re: <u>Production of Banca Nazionale del Lavoro (BNL)</u>
              <u>Documents</u>

Dear Mr. Driver:

      By letter dated October 20, 1992, I requested production of various BNL documents to facilitate the Federal Reserve's ongoing investigation of the activities of BNL's Atlanta agency. Even though my letter requested production within ten days, now, more than two months later, production remains incomplete; in fact, as to some requested items, nonexistent. It is clear based upon BNL's refusal to produce documents in a timely and complete manner, and other recent events, that BNL does not intend to fully and voluntarily cooperate with the Federal Reserve's investigation. I am, therefore, serving upon you, in your capacity as BNL's attorney, and agent, the enclosed subpoena, which I expect BNL to comply within a timely and complete manner.

      If you have any questions regarding this matter, please contact me at (202) 452-3789.

              Sincerely,

              John L. Kuray
              Senior Attorney

Enclosure (2 pages)

cc: A.E. Martin
     Michael Nelson

Letter from Federal Reserve lawyer in Washington to BNL attorney in Atlanta, serving a subpoena on the bank to force production of various BNL Atlanta documents, December 22, 1992.

SECRET
Covering SECRET UK EYES A

FROM : S Lillie (MED)

DATE : 1 February 1989

cc : PUSD

Defence Department

SEND

MOD, DESS 2A

DTI

RECEIVED IN REGISTRY
-7 FEB 1989

Mr Lamport
Mr Gore-Booth
PS/Mr Waldegrave

MATRIX CHURCHILL : EXPORT OF LATHE EQUIPMENT TO IRAQ

Problem
1.   Matrix Churchill have three applications before the IDC for the
export of lathe equipment to Iraq. Should we be prepared to approve
these applications?

Recommendation
2.   I recommend that all three applications be approved. MOD and
DTI officials are submitting similar recommendations to their
Ministers. SEND and PUSD concur.

Background and Argument
3.   Matrix Churchill is a company which produces general purpose
industrial lathe equipment, suitable for use in any branch of
industry. We have had to consider various applications from the
company to export equipment to Iraq since 1987. Some of these have
been approved and not all the equipment the company wishes to export

SECRET
Covering SECRET UK EYES A

7.   There is good reason to be sceptical about allowing any export
which might help in the achievement of Iraq's nuclear objectives.
However, officials from interested departments have agreed that
there is no reason to believe that Matrix Churchill lathe equipment
is of specific interest to the Iraqi nuclear programme. We know of
course that machine tools capable of contouring in two axes, as is
the case with these machines, are essential for the production of
nuclear weapons. But they also have many other legitimate
industrial uses. Consequently, no international agreements are in
place to prevent the export of such machines to potential
proliferators. Therefore, unless we had convincing evidence which
we ~~would wish~~ to disclose to show that the Iraqis were developing a
nuclear weapon, we should not be in a position to persuade our
partners in the non-proliferation regime to apply equal restraint in
the export of machine tools. Simply withholding the Matrix
Churchill lathes would not therefore be an effective obstacle to the
Iraqis' objectives. Neither would it absolve Britain morally from
any involvement in this network, since all non-licensable Matrix
Churchill equipment would remain freely available to Iraq.

8.   There remains one more important factor. We have reason to
believe that the refusal of these export licences could force Matrix
Churchill to close down. If this happened, we would lose our
intelligence access to Habobi's procurement network. By keeping

Secret memorandum to officials at the British Foreign Office discussing Matrix
Churchill requests to export equipment to Iraq and recommending they be
approved, February 1989.

MACHON GROUP OF COMPANIES LTD.

Main Works:
63/89 Jessie Street,
Polmadie,
Glasgow G42 0PG,
Scotland,
Great Britain.

Reg. Office:
90 Mitchell Street,
Glasgow G1 3NQ.

Tel: 041-423 3023 (6 lines)
Fax: 041-423 2719

23/12/1988
FM/PF2

The Right Honourable Margaret Thatcher
The Prime Minister
10 Downing Street
London.

STRICTLY PRIVATE AND CONFIDENTIAL.

Dear Prime Minister,
                              I find myself writing to you regarding the
treatment levelled at us by the Custom & Ecxise Investigation
Unit in Glasgow,the Department of Trade & Industry Explosive
Export licence division,and the activities of the Crown overseeing a simple commercial dispute.

Having spoken with the British Embassy in Saudia Arabia only
last month regarding the exportof the Allivane/Saudi contract
for 15000 155mm full rounds andthe origin thereof,some doubt

Having spoken with the British Embassy in Saudia Arabia only
last month regarding the exportof the Allivane/Saudi contract
for 15000 155mm full rounds andthe origin thereof,some doubt
was voiced as to the legality of this contract by the embassy
with regard to the true END USER,indeed the legitimacy of the
production areas,the Export Licences being three times the
contract size,and the commissions being paid to a certain
Major General in Saudi all point to onegeneral view under these
circumstances and that does strongly suggest that the Ministerial
meeting of April 88 on issuing Allivane additional Saudi Export
licences is nothing short of,either Britain or America is funnelling war equipmentthrough Allivane which is certainly destined for
Iraq.

I look forward to hearing from you by return.

Yours Faithfully

Francis Machon.

Encl.Europe newspaper cutting of early 88.Heading Irangate.

By fax,orig to post.

Letter from Frank Machon to Prime Minister Margaret Thatcher, reporting his
suspicion that Allivane, a British company, was being used to ship "war equipment" to Iraq, December 23, 1988.

APPENDIX C

Public Interest Immunity Certificate Signed by Tristan Garel-Jones of the Foreign Office, Autumn 1992

IN THE MATTER OF:

COMMISSIONERS OF CUSTOMS & EXCISE

– v –

HENDERSON, ABRAHAM AND ALLEN

CERTIFICATE OF
MR TRISTAN GAREL-JONES MP

1. I am the Minister of State at the Foreign and Commonwealth Office ("FCO"). I make this Certificate on behalf of the Crown. I make this Certificate in the place of the Secretary of State for Foreign and Commonwealth Affairs who is absent abroad.

2. I am advised that Counsel instructed by H.M. Customs and Excise who are prosecuting this case has examined FCO papers and advised that under the Attorney General's Guidelines certain of such papers are disclosable to the defence. The purpose of this Certificate is to explain to the Court why for reasons of public interest, such documents should not be so disclosed.

3. The documents identified by Counsel fall into three categories:—
   a) Category A consists of two documents; a document from a confidential

informant who is a member of the public and whose personal security and livelihood may be jeopardised if his or her identity is disclosed and a second document which is also in Category B described below which discussed the first document and identified the informant.

b) Category B consists of minutes, notes and letters passing between Ministers and Ministers, Ministers and Officials and Officials and other Officials either within the FCO or inter departmentally with the Ministry of Defence ("MOD") and Department of Trade and Industry ("DTI"). It also includes notes or records of meetings between such persons. All these documents relate to the formation of the policy of HM Government in particular, with regard to relations with and the export of military and quasi military equipment to foreign countries.

c) Category C consists of documents as described in Category B and which either include material relating to secret intelligence emanating from the Security and Intelligence Services primarily relating to Iraq and other Middle Eastern countries or which discuss such intelligence information.

4. I have read all the documents in Categories A, B and C and have satisfied myself that they are of the nature described.

5. With regard to the Documents in Category A it is undoubtedly in the public interest that the identity of a person carrying out his duty to inform the authorities of suspected wrong doing and thereby jeopardising himself and his livelihood should as far as possible be kept confidential.

6. With regard to the documents in Categories B and C I have formed the opinion that, for the reasons hereinafter set out, the production of such documents or any requirement of witnesses to give oral evidence as to the meetings, discussions and deliberations would be injurious to the public interest and that it is necessary for the proper functioning of the public service that the documents should be withheld from production. All these documents fall into a class of documents which relate to the formulation of Government policy and the internal dealings of Government departments. Such policy was decided at a high level, for the most part by Ministers of the FCO, MOD and DTI although the documents include documents preparatory to advice given for the benefit of Ministers in office during the relevant period. Decisions made by Ministers are frequently preceded by detailed discussions within and between Government departments and by consideration of the various possibilities open to Ministers. It is out of such discussion and consideration that the advice to be tendered to Ministers is often formulated (frequently, initially in the form of drafts of documents intended for the consideration and approval of Ministers). This is true of the present case. It would, in my view, be against the public interest that documents or oral

evidence revealing the process of providing for Ministers' honest and candid advice on matters of high level policy should be subject to disclosure or compulsion. Similarly records of discussions between Ministers within or between Departments should not be disclosed. In this connection, I would respectfully pray in aid the reasoning of Lord Reid in *Conway v Rimmer* 1968 AC910, to whose remarks (at page 952 of that report) my attention has been drawn, as regards the effect on the inner workings of the government machine of the public disclosure of documents concerned with policy.

7. With regard to documents in Category C there are additional reasons why disclosure thereof would be contrary to the public interest. The very nature of the work of the security and intelligence services of the Crown requires secrecy if it is to be effective. It has for this reason been the consistent policy of successive Governments of the United Kingdom not to disclose information about the operations of the security and intelligence services and neither to confirm nor deny matters relating to their work. Evidence about the identity of members of the security and intelligence services could put their lives at risk and would substantially impair their capability to perform the tasks assigned to them. Any evidence about the organisation of the security and intelligence services, their theatre of operations or their methods could substantially impair their operational efficiency. In particular any disclosure of these matters would substantially impair the work of the security and intelligence services in protecting the United Kingdom and its allies from threats from hostile or potentially hostile foreign powers.

8. The disclosure of any sources or alleged sources of intelligence information, and any aspects of the means by which it was gathered (including dates and times and associated transactions) would cause unquantifiable damage to the functions of the security and intelligence services in relation to their role both in the United Kingdom and abroad. Any evidence, whether documentary or otherwise, relating to such matters would tend to reveal aspects of the *modus operandi* of those services which would necessarily render them less effective in the future, and in particular would make it more difficult to gather such information hereafter. Where the resources upon which those services rely to gather information are human, the information is provided in the knowledge that what is imparted will be treated as having been imparted in confidence and any breach of confidentiality by the Crown in revealing the identities of those supplying the information would cause unquantifiable damage. If this position is not maintained, there would be a real and serious danger that the supply of such information would be less readily forthcoming and could result in grave danger to those who have supplied or might in the future supply it.

9. In the case of certain of the documents only part thereof has any relevance whatever to this case. The rest of such documents discuss secret or highly

confidential matters relating to proposed exports of military or quasi military equipment by companies not in any way associated with the defendants to this prosecution. While I should make it clear that the disclosure of any part of any of the documents in the categories I have described would be objectionable, if the Court should, contrary to this objection and in the exercise of its discretion contemplate ordering the disclosure of any document I would ask that only the parts of the document strictly relevant to these proceedings should be disclosed.

10. If oral evidence were sought to be given by any person as to the contents of the documents in Categories A, B and C, I would object to such evidence being given or adduced on the grounds which I have set out.

11. I should explain that some of the documents identified by Counsel as mentioned in Paragraph 2 above are copies of documents originating either from the MOD or the DTI. I have not considered such documents for the purposes of this certificate. It has been arranged that where a document has originated from a department it will be for a Minister of that Department to consider whether a claim for public interest immunity should be made for such document. I understand that Ministers from the MOD and DTI will be making certificates in respect of documents originating from their respective departments where public interest immunity ought to be claimed.

NOTES

ONE: The Tilt Takes Off

page

3 The roof collapsed instantly . . . a crude nuclear weapon.: "Attack and Fallout," *Time,* June 22, 1981; "After the Israeli Shocker," *U.S. News & World Report,* June 22, 1981.

3 Few in Washington wanted to hear about it.: Interview with former White House official, Washington, D.C., May 27, 1993.

3 Most of Reagan's aides . . . dictator's progress.: Interview with former White House official, Washington, D.C., May 27, 1993.

3 "The first concrete step toward the production of the Arab atomic weapon.": Quoted in Kenneth Timmerman, *The Death Lobby: How the West Armed Iraq* (Boston: Houghton Mifflin, 1991), p. 30.

4 he had begun cultivating the Europeans, especially the French: Timmerman, *Death Lobby,* p. xvii.

4 "O'Chirac.": Timmerman, *Death Lobby,* p. 30.

4 "Mr. Iraq.": Timmerman, *Death Lobby,* p. 34.

4 America's KH-11 "Big Bird" . . . to assess the damage.: Joseph Persico, *Casey* (New York: Viking, 1990), pp. 253–54.

4 what should be said in public about the Israeli action . . . "My position was thank God they did it.": Interview with Alexander Haig, Washington, D.C., June 7, 1993.

4 Weinberger . . . wanted to punish Israel.: Howard Teicher and Gayle Radley Teicher, *Twin Pillars to Desert Storm: America's Flawed Vision in the Middle East from Nixon to Bush* (New York: William Morrow, 1993), p. 124.

4 he persuaded President Reagan to delay . . . Haig was not even informed of the decision: Interview with Haig, June 7, 1993.

5 "Reagan was sleeping through it all.": Interview with Howard Teicher, former National Security Council official, Washington, D.C., May 27, 1993.

5 U.S. ambassador to the United Nations, was secretly cooperating . . . "not from some flack in the White House.": Interview with Haig, June 7, 1993.

6 a de facto American ambassador: Dilip Hiro, *The Longest War* (London: Paladin Grafton Books, 1989), p. 75.

6 During the week of September 17 . . . Ambassador Saleh at the United Nations.: Interviews with Ambassador Saleh al-Ali, London, December 15, 1992, and June 5, 1993.

6 State Department's files on him painted quite another picture.: Conversation with Dr. Laurie Mylroie, Washington Institute for Near East Policy, Washington, D.C., May 26, 1993.

6 To assist Iraq in its war against Iran. . . . The most prominent target was the newly elected vice president: Interview with Ambassador Saleh, December 15, 1992.

6 Both men represented their countries at the United Nations.: Interview with Ambassador Saleh, December 15, 1992; *Facts on File Yearbook* (New York: Facts on File, September 25, 1981), p. 684.

6 buried his friend George Bush in flowers.: Interview with Ambassador Saleh, December 15, 1992.

7 informal requests for military aid: Interview with U.S. intelligence officer, New York, March 22, 1983; interview with Fred Haobsh, Dallas, April 6, 1992.

7 Kittani had been elected president of the General Assembly: *Facts on File Yearbook,* p. 684.

7 Did Haig have any good news? . . . the answer had been in the affirmative.: Interview with Ambassador Saleh, December 15, 1992.

7 American military observers had been sent to Iraq: Interview with Ambassador Saleh, December 15, 1992. Saleh recalled that he was "not officially supposed to know" about the presence of U.S. military personnel in Iraq at the time but had received the information from government colleagues in Baghdad.

7 the threat Baghdad was facing from the Khomeini regime . . . Appropriate measures would be taken: Interview with Ambassador Saleh, December 15, 1992.

7 "the Iraqis didn't get any help from me." . . . extensive clandestine help that had been provided to Iraq: Interview with Haig, June 7, 1993.

7 He conveyed the news to a friend at American Steel: Interview with Haobsh, April 6, 1992.

8 Home was an apartment on Sutton Place . . . a decent bunch: Interview with Haobsh, April 6, 1992.

8 Lieutenant Abu Ali had arrived at American Steel with an introduction: Interview with Haobsh, April 6, 1992.

8 Since 1979 . . . identified as sponsors of terrorism.: "U.S. Links Four Nations to Terrorists," *Facts on File World News Digest,* May 21, 1977.

9 A special group . . . where Lieutenant Abu Ali was staying. . . . Madame Saddam Hussein . . . had arrived in New York on a private Iraqi

page

government–owned Boeing 747.: Interview with Ambassador Saleh, December 15, 1992.

9 Half a dozen bombproof cars . . . Lieutenant Abu Ali was Hussein Kamel: Interview with Haobsh, April 6, 1992.

9 his true role as head of Saddam's weapons-procurement program.: Interview with Ambassador Saleh, December 15, 1992.

10 Haobsh took no part in the discussions beyond pleasantries . . . a phone call came in from the New York–based Iraqi: Interview with Haobsh, April 6, 1992.

10 signed by the ambassador "upon the instructions of Lieutenant Abu Ali.": Interview with Haobsh, April 7, 1992.

11 Why was he doing this when he wasn't even sure what the mission was about?: Haobsh detailed his progressive involvement in Saddam Hussein's efforts to procure American weapons over the course of a series of interviews with the author. These interviews took place on April 6–7, 1992, in Dallas; January 10, 1993, in New York; March 1–2, 1993, in Atlanta; March 30, 1993, in New York; May 10–11, 1993, in Cairo; and May 23, 1993, in New York.

11 Fred Haobsh was now a guest of the Iraqi government. . . . to fill this wish list would be one hundred percent illegal: Interview series with Haobsh.

12 American exports with military potential: Arms Export Control Act, June 30, 1976, as amended.

12 President Jimmy Carter had imposed a ban on arms sales: "Terrorism—Iraq," United Press International, February 27, 1982.

12 Morris Draper . . . had been visiting Saadun Hamadi: Hiro, *Longest War,* p. 75; Elaine Sciolino, *The Outlaw State* (New York: John Wiley and Sons, 1991), p. 163.

13 U.S. allies such as Jordan and Saudi Arabia were advising the administration to get closer to Saddam.: Hiro, *Longest War,* p. 75; interview with former White House official, Washington, D.C., May 27, 1993.

13 how could Hickey have responded to Hussein Kamel that, in essence, he would see what he could do? . . . he was assigned back to his normal task: Interview with Haobsh, April 7, 1992.

13 a deal was made with a factory in Rio de Janeiro: Interview series with Haobsh.

13 It made him nervous—he didn't relish the idea of going to jail: Interview with Haobsh, March 1, 1993.

15 the White House seemed quietly to let it be known: Interview with former CIA operative, Washington, D.C., April–June 1991; interviews with White House officials, Washington, D.C., May and August 1993; interview with U.S. intelligence officer, Washington, D.C., May 17, 1993.

15 On December 2, 1981, . . . Fred Haobsh: Haobsh personal records.

16 Johnson was also on very friendly terms . . . rising steadily at Langley

as William Casey's protégé: Interview with a former CIA operative, Lexington, Kentucky, March 30, 1991; interviews with Department of Defense officials, Washington, D.C., April–July 1991 and February–April 1993; interview with U.S. intelligence officer, New York, July 1, 1993.

16   Haobsh was unprepared for this meeting in Virginia.: Interview series with Haobsh.

16   few paid attention to the unanimous resolutions . . . a further escalation of the conflict: The UN Security Council passed several resolutions that had the effect of requesting an embargo on arms sales to Iraq and Iran, but they proved difficult to implement in practice. See "U.N. Text on Iran-Iraq Cease-Fire Call," The Associated Press, September 28, 1980; "Text of a Resolution on the Iran-Iraq Conflict," The Associated Press, July 12, 1982.

17   No problem, said Johnson: Interview series with Haobsh.

17   "after a few meetings, they loosened up a bit,": Interview with Haobsh, March 1, 1993.

17   The word *Jordan* should be substituted: Interview with Haobsh, March 1, 1993.

17   "they kept asking me to put pressure on anyone I could in Jordan to try and move things along.": Interview series with Haobsh.

17   "That 1981–82 period was pretty grim . . . in the war with Iran,": Telephone interview with former cabinet member, June 30, 1993.

17   By 1982, the Jordanian military was diverting U.S.-made helicopters . . . approval from Washington.: "U.S. Secretly Gave Aid to Iraq Early in Its War Against Iran," The New York Times, January 26, 1992; Arms Export Control Act, June 30, 1976, as amended.

17   the Reagan administration . . . looked the other way: Interview with former White House official, Washington, D.C., May 27, 1993.

17   By chance, . . . walking across the office parking lot.: Interview with Haobsh, April 6, 1992.

17   The Jordanian diplomat was soon befriended by Johnson: Interview with Haobsh, April 6, 1992.

18   the Jordanian air force . . . had to settle for a less-advanced model.: "Bell Helicopter Sales Set," The New York Times, September 27, 1982.

18   He learned from Jweiber . . . the American government.: Interview series with Haobsh.

18   "That is what really convinced me . . . the way normal arms dealers work.": Interview with Haobsh, March 1, 1993.

18   He had left the staff of American Steel . . . he was better off than most people he knew.: Interview with Haobsh, April 6, 1992.

18   Iraq had spent a billion dollars a month on the war.: "Fact Sheet on Military Expenditure and Iraqi Arms Imports," Stockholm International Peace Research Institute (Stockholm, 1990), p. 1.

page

19 military officers were awaiting their turn at bat.: Interview with Haobsh, April 6, 1992.

19 On February 26, 1982 . . . acts of international terrorism.: "U.S. Said to Favor Sale of F-16 Jets to the Jordanians," *The New York Times,* February 27, 1982.

19 The State Department had made it clear . . . its ban on arms shipments to Iraq.: "U.S. Adds Cuba, Drops Iraq from Terrorism List," The Associated Press, February 26, 1982.

19 they now had political cover to go ahead with their plans: Interview with Robert Johnson, Washington, D.C., July 11, 1991.

19 Haobsh was bothered by a more pedestrian concern . . . The audience was over within three minutes: Interview series with Haobsh.

20 there were no more difficulties with customs.: Details and documentation, including copies of sample airline tickets and stamped passport pages, provided by Fred Haobsh.

21 "a lot of such activity and some hurry-up requests for arms from Casey.": Telephone interview with a former Reagan administration cabinet member, June 30, 1993.

21 Gates has repeatedly denied he was involved in any covert operations to arm Iraq: Statements to this effect were provided by the CIA to ABC News, *Nightline,* on June 17 and July 15, 1991.

21 Clark has said he has "no recollection": Telephone interview with William Clark, August 26, 1993.

21 his marching orders came "directly from the White House.": Interview with Johnson, July 11, 1991.

Two: The Covert Ethic

22 embarrassing scandal: "Allen's Travels," *The New York Times,* September 30, 1982.

22 "political liability.": "Allen Exonerated by Justice Department on Gifts and Financial Disclosure," *The New York Times,* December 24, 1981.

22 "Baker was angling . . . Allen bite the dust.": Interview with Alexander Haig, Washington, D.C., June 7, 1993.

23 to his pleading guilty to four criminal misdemeanor charges: McFarlane pleaded guilty in 1988, was sentenced a year later, and was pardoned by President George Bush in December 1992. "McFarlane Enters Guilty Plea Arising from Iran-Contra Affair," *The Washington Post,* March 12, 1988; "McFarlane Is Fined $20,000 for Role in Iran-Contra Affair; Former NSC Aide Put on Two Years' Probation," *The Washington Post,* March 4, 1989.

23 Teicher al-Tikriti: Howard Teicher and Gayle Radley Teicher, *Twin Pillars to Desert Storm: America's Flawed Vision in the Middle East from Nixon to Bush* (New York: William Morrow, 1993), p. 59.

page

23   "I disagree. . . . moderated its behavior.": Brown quoted in Teicher and
      Teicher, *Twin Pillars,* p. 70.

25   when monitoring arms transactions in the Middle East . . . they would get
      it.": Interview with Howard Teicher, May 27, 1993.

25   "Casey was very fearful . . . active neutrality.": Interview with Haig, June 7,
      1993.

26   "I was not consulted,": Interview with Haig, June 7, 1993.

26   "We knew very well . . . was Casey's, and Clark's": Interview with Teicher,
      May 27, 1993.

26   "could very well be": Telephone interview with William Clark, August 26,
      1993.

26   willing middleman for arms shipments to Iraq.: Interview with U.S. intel-
      ligence officer, New York, April 28, 1993.

26   King Hussein had been advocating assistance: Interview with former U.S.
      military officer, New York, April 29, 1993.

27   share some of its more sensitive intelligence photography with Saddam.:
      Teicher and Teicher, *Twin Pillars,* p. 207.

27   persuaded the president to make it happen.: Interview with former White
      House official, May 27, 1993.

27   it wasn't lost or stolen.: Interview with former U.S. military officer, April 29,
      1993.

27   even built an expensive high-tech annex in Baghdad: Interview with U.S.
      intelligence officer, New York, July 1, 1993.

28   could be as reliable a partner in the Persian Gulf: Elaine Sciolino, *The
      Outlaw State* (New York: John Wiley and Sons, 1991), p. 165.

28   "selectively lift restrictions . . . military equipment to Iraq.": "Saudi Arms
      Link to Iraq Allowed," *The Los Angeles Times,* April 18, 1992; "What We
      Gave Saddam for Christmas," *The Village Voice,* December 18, 1990;
      interview with U.S. intelligence officer, New York, July 1, 1993.

28   "under present circumstances . . . regional stability.": Declassified SECRET
      State Department cable, from Secretary George Shultz to U.S. interests
      section in Baghdad, "Proposal to Provide Arms to Iraq," June 1984.

28   covert shipments of U.S. arms: Interview with U.S. intelligence officer, July
      1, 1993.

28   "Here was the U.S. government . . . 'Let us help you' ": Interview with
      Teicher, May 27, 1993.

29   a U.S.-brokered political guarantee: Teicher and Teicher, *Twin Pillars,*
      p. 276.

29   "just forget it.": Declassified SECRET State Department cable reporting on
      Murphy-Aziz meeting of February 2, 1984, "Middle East Mission: Febru-
      ary 2 Meeting with Foreign Minister Aziz: Pipeline Follow-Up."

30   to urge financing for the project.: Declassified CONFIDENTIAL State De-

page

partment memorandum, from Charles Hill, executive secretary to Secretary George Shultz, to Donald Gregg, "Eximbank Financing for Iraqi Export Pipeline," June 12, 1984.

30 The background paper ... the Administration's support": Declassified CONFIDENTIAL State Department background paper, "Status of Iraqi Export Pipelines," June 12, 1984.

30 "means to bolster" ... "destabilizing effect on the region.": Declassified CONFIDENTIAL State Department talking points, "Exim Financing for Iraqi Pipelines," June 12, 1984.

30 a lavish banquet at ... Iraqi ambassador.: Sciolino, *Outlaw State,* p. 158.

30 relations with Iraq were good: ITT Corporation, internal memorandum, "Sensitive Countries: U.S. Relations with Iraq," May 6, 1985.

30 to discuss American support for Iraq.: Declassified SECRET State Department cable, to U.S. embassy in Baghdad, "USG Support for Iraq During the War," July 26, 1986.

31 move U.S. weaponry from Jordan to Iraq: Interview with former White House official, Washington, D.C., June 4, 1993.

31 "As for the possibility ... would not have a significant impact on the war effort.": Declassified SECRET State Department cable, July 26, 1986.

31 The CIA was worried: Interview with former White House official, June 4, 1993.

31 "reviewed the military ... looked at U.S.-Iraq relations.": Declassified SECRET State Department cable, July 26, 1986.

32 "We have encouraged ... that would be a major plus.": Declassified SECRET State Department cable, July 26, 1986.

32 "nothing but politics.": "Bush Departs on Mideast Image-Building Trip," *The Washington Post,* July 26, 1986.

32 According to a member ... against Iranian troops.: Interview with former White House official, June 4, 1993.

33 "We knew ... He was actually our covert agent.": Interview with Teicher, May 27, 1993.

33 The Iraqi air force suddenly intensified its raids against Iran: Anthony H. Cordesman, *The Iran-Iraq War and Western Security* (London: Jane's Publishing, 1987), p. 112.

33 Shultz, who did not share ... "report promptly repeat promptly to Congress": Declassified SECRET State Department cable, to American embassy in Riyadh, "Saudi Arms Transfer to Iraq," August 5, 1986.

34 had informally blessed: Interview with U.S. intelligence officer, New York, April 28, 1993.

34 "no way in the world ... without getting U.S. government approval.": "U.S. Admits Saudis Gave Military Gear to Three Countries," *The Los Angeles Times,* April 21, 1992.

THREE: The Secret War

page

35   His contacts in the intelligence community . . . handling the shipments fell to operatives like Johnson: Telephone interview with Robert Johnson, August 24, 1993.

36   "I didn't like . . . We were supposed to keep the entire operation to ourselves.": Interview with Robert Johnson, Washington, D.C., July 11, 1991.

36   This kind of work . . . he had had enough: Telephone interview with Johnson, August 24, 1993.

36   "liaison officers" or "observers.": Interview with Howard Teicher, Washington, D.C., May 27, 1993.

36   reporting many of his transactions to officials in Washington.: Interview with Sarkis Soghanalian, Miami, June 10, 1991.

36   a key conduit for CIA and other U.S. government operations.: Interview with former White House official, Washington, D.C., June 4, 1993; interview with U.S. intelligence officer, New York, July 1, 1993.

37   a nongovernment carrier in Miami: Interview with Soghanalian, June 10, 1991; "Questions on Aides Shadow Bush," *The Miami Herald,* September 10, 1988.

37   a "friend of the U.S. government.": telephone interview with Joseph Trento, June 29, 1993. Trento spent several weeks accompanying Sarkis Soghanalian through Iraq and Europe during 1984.

37   "I believe the potential . . . arrange an arms deal with Iraq.": Memorandum from General Richard G. Stilwell, deputy undersecretary of defense, to the assistant chief of staff for intelligence department of the army, "Possible Acquisition Opportunity," 1983.

37   probably be used by the Iraqi military.: "Iraqi Officers Trained in Texas," *Armsfax,* July 1992; "Miami Arms Dealer Indicted," *The Miami Herald,* December 3, 1987.

37   transmit U.S. satellite photographs to the Iraqis . . . "you have to do what you have to do.": Telephone interview with Trento, June 29, 1993.

38   "by 1987 . . . alongside Iraqi troops.": Interview with former White House official, Washington, D.C., June 4, 1993.

38   "Access to the battlefield . . . inside Iranian territory": Interview with retired military officer, Washington, D.C., March 22, 1993.

38   some White House officials . . . another off-the-books operation.: Interview with former White House official, June 4, 1993.

38   NATO stockpiles in Europe were the source . . . European airlift requirements.: Interview with former White House official, June 4, 1993. Shipments from Rhein-Main were also confirmed by former Iraqi ambassador to the United Nations Saleh Omar Al-Ali, during an interview in London in December 1992.

39   "The chain of command was secret . . . sensitive bits and pieces.": Inter-

page

view with retired U.S. military officer, Washington, D.C., April 18, 1993.

39 Washington was either ambivalent or duplicitous.: Interview with former U.S. diplomat, Washington, D.C., July 19, 1993.

39 Casey led the drive . . . more attacks on Iranian economic targets.: "C.I.A. Aiding Iraq in Gulf War; Target Data from U.S. Satellites Supplied for Nearly Two Years," *The Washington Post,* December 15, 1986.

40 so that the U.S. Navy could escort them: George P. Shultz, *Turmoil and Triumph* (New York: Charles Scribner's Sons, 1993), p. 925.

40 War Powers Act ought to be invoked.: "Murphy," United Press International, May 21, 1987.

40 U.S. involvement in the war in the Gulf.: "Senate Demands Assurance on Navy in Gulf," *The New York Times,* May 22, 1987.

40 American clandestine operations in the Persian Gulf.: Interviews with Lt. Col. Roger Charles, Washington, D.C., April–June 1992, and by telephone, August 27, 1993.

41 "low to moderate.": "President Minimizes War Risk," *The Washington Post,* May 28, 1987; "The Reagan Vows to Keep Persian Gulf Open; Big Military Operation Seen," The Associated Press, May 29, 1987.

41 sharing strategic information with Iraq: Telephone interview with Lt. Col. Charles, August 27, 1993.

41 "What happened . . . helping the Iraqis to choose their targets.": Interview with retired U.S. military officer, April 18, 1993.

41 bounced up into the air: Admiral William J. Crowe, Jr., *The Line of Fire* (New York: Simon and Schuster, 1993), p. 192.

41 to comply with the War Powers Act: "Pentagon Lashes Back at Congressional Critics of Gulf Policy," The Associated Press, July 31, 1987.

41 The lawsuit was ultimately dismissed: "Judge Throws Out Democrats' Suit over War Powers," *The Los Angeles Times,* December 19, 1987.

41 "There is no support . . . draw attention away from the reflagging idea.": Shultz, *Turmoil,* p. 930.

41 a resolution calling for a cease-fire.: "Iraq, Iran Signal They May Honor Gulf Truce," *The Los Angeles Times,* July 22, 1987.

42 over Iranian bases starting in July 1987.: "Sea of Lies," *Newsweek,* July 13, 1992; "The USS *Vincennes;* Public War/Secret War," ABC News, *Nightline,* July 1, 1992.

42 blew up a warehouse full of mines.: Interview with retired U.S. military officer, April 18, 1993; interview with U.S. intelligence officer, New York, July 1, 1993.

42 *Iran Ajr,* a minelaying ship; . . . four who were wounded.: "Twenty-six Iranians Seized with Mine Vessel; More U.S. Shooting," *The New York Times,* September 23, 1987; "Iranian Ship Gashed and Riddled in U.S. Attack," Reuters, September 22, 1987.

page
42   authorized by law: "Twenty-six Iranians Seized," *New York Times.*
42   many of the military actions . . . deny any awareness of the details.: Tele-
     phone interview with Lt. Col. Charles, August 27, 1993.
43   "These things looked extremely sinister, . . . staring at you before you die.":
     Interview with Special Operations officer, Fayetteville, N.C., May 1992.
43   "A Marine buddy of mine . . . killed in a car crash.": Telephone interview
     with former Pentagon official, August 2, 1993.
43   "They took off at night . . . designed to provoke the Iranians.": Telephone
     interview with Lt. Col. Charles, August 27, 1993.
43   "The argument . . . we were sticking to it": Crowe, *Line of Fire,* p. 198.
44   "Oh, yes, I don't think there's any question . . . it was a conflict.": ABC
     News, *Nightline,* July 1, 1992.

FOUR: The Chilean Connection

45   empty Iraqi cargo aircraft: Conversation with Jay Weiss, June 28, 1993. Mr.
     Weiss worked with the author in 1991, conducting a number of interviews
     with former employees and associates of Carlos Cardoen in the United
     States and Chile.
45   "social sin" . . . "and now they have been turned on our brethren.": "Trou-
     ble Ahead for Chile's Cardoen," *Latin America Regional Reports,* April 18,
     1986; "Gulf War Ties Appear in Feud Between Chilean Firms," United
     Press International, May 21, 1987.
46   ninety dollars a month, often for a twelve-hour day: "Trouble Ahead," *Latin
     America Regional Reports.*
46   output of the factory was one thousand bombs a month.: "Chile's Defense
     Industry Booms to Supply Persian Gulf War," Reuters, March 8, 1986.
46   Cardoen was able to price . . . less than his competitors in Europe: Nasser
     Beydoun *v.* Carlos Cardoen et al., U.S. District Court, Southern District of
     Florida, case number 90-43689, 1990, complaint and amended complaint;
     United States *v.* Carlos Cardoen et al., U.S. District Court, Southern Dis-
     trict of Florida, case number 93-241, 1993, exhibit; "From Chile to Miami,
     Miami to Baghdad," *Newsweek,* April 8, 1991.
46   In February 1976 the United States had imposed an arms embargo: The
     legislation, known as the International Security Assistance and Arms Export
     Control Act, was drafted by Senator Hubert H. Humphrey of Minnesota
     and approved 60–30 by the Senate on February 18, 1976. It incorporated
     the so-called Kennedy amendment, which barred any U.S. company from
     selling military goods to Chile. On the same day, the House International
     Relations Committee approved a similar version of the bill. "Senate Votes
     Overhaul of Military Aid," *The New York Times,* February 19, 1976.
47   a sample fashioned by his engineers.: "Chilean Arms Maker Helps Fill a
     World Demand," *The New York Times,* July 22, 1987.
47   "If it hadn't been . . . we would never have invested in arms production

page

here.": "Chile Becoming Arms Merchant," United Press International, August 25, 1984.

47 The financing . . . was kept a mystery.: "From Chile to Miami," *Newsweek.*

48 Nasser Beydoun . . . exporting food and other goods to the Middle East: Beydoun *v.* Cardoen et al., complaint.

48 about five hundred dollars for every cluster bomb he could sell.: United States *v.* Cardoen et al., exhibit.

48 "The sky was the limit . . . He called me his golden key. Rightfully really.": Interview with Nasser Beydoun, Miami, January 23 1991.

48 a trial order of three thousand cluster bombs.: Beydoun *v.* Cardoen et al., complaint.

48 "We are pleased to inform you . . . cluster bombs at the lowest possible price.": Beydoun *v.* Cardoen et al., exhibit.

48 "iron out the bugs" in the bomb's mechanism.: Beydoun *v.* Cardoen et al., complaint.

48 export revenues of $100 million a year.: "Arms Maker Putting Chile in Thick of Things in International Market," *The Los Angeles Times,* December 6, 1987.

49 "a great deal of trouble with U.S. Customs": "How U.S. Arms and Technology Were Transferred to Iraq," ABC News, *Nightline,* September 13, 1991.

49 they had come from the United States.: . . . "identified them.": Interview with Lt. Col. Carlos Rickertson, Washington, D.C., July 12, 1991.

49 General Henry D. Canterbury: Photographs of Cardoen and General Canterbury at the Feria Internacional del Aire, Santiago, March 1986.

49 General Robert Reed . . . "Technology Transfer." Photographs of Cardoen and Reed, Santiago, March 1986; of Cardoen and Vega, Santiago, March 1986; of Cardoen and U.S. ambassador Charles Gillespie, Santiago, March 1990.

50 white-painted cylindrical objects . . . with the help of colored brochures.: Video archive, ABC News, *Nightline,* 1991.

50 "I knew Cardoen quite well." . . . "drawings in a suitcase.": Interview with Robert Johnson, Washington, D.C., April 24, 1991.

50 the Chilean model was "almost a duplicate.": Interview with Lt. Col. Rickertson, July 12, 1991.

50 "I remember seeing cable traffic . . . he kept saying the Iraqis were undermanned.": Interview with Howard Teicher, Washington, D.C., May 27, 1993.

51 the 1982 incident was viewed as a breach of that agreement.: "78 Pact Said to Limit Israeli Use of Cluster Bombs," *The New York Times,* June 30, 1982; "Use of Cluster Bombs Is Confirmed by Israel," *The New York Times,* June 28, 1982.

51 "He was an all-purpose asset, . . . Cardoen became extremely useful": Interview with former CIA contract employee, Miami, June 2, 1991.

page
51   Robert Gates . . . was taking a personal interest: Interview with Robert Johnson, Washington, D.C., July 12, 1991.

51   went beyond the scope of the White House guidelines.: U.S. Senate, Select Committee on Intelligence, report, "Nomination of Robert Gates to be Director of Central Intelligence," October 24, 1991.

51   "I believed . . . significant intelligence activity": Senate Select Committee on Intelligence, "Nomination of Gates," pp. 180–81.

52   bend the rules when necessary.: Robert Woodward, *Veil* (New York: Simon & Schuster, 1987), p. 103.

52   "There was no reason . . . He just liked it.": Interview with U.S. intelligence officer, July 1, 1993.

52   "Gates got things done . . . without micromanaging, if you see what I mean.": Interview with U.S. intelligence officer, July 1, 1993.

53   who supplied arms to Baghdad.: Interview with U.S. intelligence officer, July 1, 1993; interview with Johnson, July 12, 1991.

53   "One of the less . . . sitting behind the desk all the time.": Interview with U.S. intelligence officer, July 1, 1993.

53   "Sure. . . . those who helped get things done.": Interview with Teicher, May 27, 1993.

53   The CIA has denied in blunt terms: "Allegations that Robert Gates facilitated illegal shipments to Iraq during the 1980s are totally without basis," statement by the CIA to ABC News, *Nightline,* June 17, 1991.

53   "Gates is a great patriot, . . . He didn't have to get into details.": Interview with Robert Johnson, Washington, D.C., July 11, 1991; telephone interview with Johnson, August 24, 1993.

54   denied that the two men had met: A series of statements was issued by the CIA to ABC News, *Nightline,* during the summer of 1991. The most comprehensive statement, dated July 15, 1991, reads as follows: "Allegations by Nightline in its July 12 broadcast that the Central Intelligence Agency provided military equipment or technology to Iraq, with or without authorization, are totally false. There has never been a covert action program authorizing such action. Reports suggesting the contrary are totally without basis. Moreover, the C.I.A. has never had a relationship with Carlos Cardoen." The White House statement was issued to ABC News, *Nightline,* on July 12, 1991.

54   encounter between the two in Florida: Interview with U.S. intelligence officer, July 1, 1993.

54   "First, Cardoen knew . . . we wanted Saddam to have.": Interview with U.S. intelligence officer, July 1, 1993.

54   "If I start to make trouble . . . meetings in the States and in Europe.": Interview with former Cardoen executive, Santiago, September 23, 1991.

54   "I received the information . . . even though I was ambassador," he said

page

with a smile.: Interview with Ambassador Saleh Omar al-Ali, London, December 15, 1992.

54 James Theberge, would be willing to help.: Interview with Commerce Department official, Dallas, July 2, 1991.

55 his civilian mining activities.: Interview with Commerce Department official, July 2, 1991.

55 "Cardoen is best known . . . a responsible recipient of U.S. products.": Cable, "Additional information on extrancheck for Cardoen Industries contained in reftel," from American embassy, Santiago, to U.S. Department of Commerce, April 23, 1987.

55 Cardoen offering a handshake to Saddam Hussein.: Interview with former Cardoen executive, September 23, 1991.

55 subsidiary of Cardoen's armaments company.: Senate Select Committee on Intelligence, "Nomination of Gates," p. 186.

FIVE: **The Tools of the Trade**

56 The conversation was intense . . . bespectacled man named James Guerin.: Interview with Tom Jasin, former ISC executive, Lancaster, Pennsylvania, October 24, 1992; telephone interview with former ISC executive, September 1, 1993.

57 "He had nothing but accolades . . . it's international business, the world.": Interview with Tom Jasin, October 24, 1992.

57 A former personnel . . . "not very impressive.": Interview with former Hamilton Watch human relations executive, Lancaster, Pennsylvania, April 17, 1991.

58 Its beginnings were inauspicious . . . "production control manager.": "American Arms Dealer Was Amazing Success, or So Ferranti Believed," *The Wall Street Journal,* January 23, 1990.

58 such as video games, computers, electric insect killers, and radio parts: "How a Small Bug-Killer Company Helped Guerin Obtain Millions in Loans," *Lancaster New Era,* January 15, 1990.

58 "He was hanging on by his teeth . . . Lockheed and Hamilton days.": Telephone interview with former ISC executive, September 1, 1993.

58 shipment to South Africa.: Interview with former ISC executive, Lancaster, Pennsylvania, May 8, 1991.

58 covert operator for the Ford administration.: Letter from Admiral Bobby Ray Inman to Judge Louis C. Bechtle, chief judge, U.S. District Court, Eastern District of Pennsylvania, Philadelphia, April 27, 1992; interviews with former ISC executives, May and June 1991; "Saddam's Secret South African Connection," *Financial Times,* May 24, 1991; "A Lancaster Firm, the C.I.A. and Illegal Arms Deals," *The Philadelphia Inquirer,* September

page

13, 1991; *"Nightline/Financial Times* Arms Sales Report," ABC News, *Nightline,* May 23, 1991.

59 which was code-named Project X.: Letter from Admiral Inman to Judge Bechtle; "A Lancaster Firm," *Philadelphia Inquirer.*

59 Inman later confirmed.: "A Lancaster Firm," *Philadelphia Inquirer.*

59 aboard airliners bound for South Africa.: "Saddam's Secret South African Connection," *Financial Times.*

59 a special code into a lock on the door.: Telephone interview with former ISC executive, September 1, 1993.

59 Former colleagues . . . sales to South Africa.: Interviews with former ISC executives, May 1991 and August 1993.

60 the cancellation of Project X.: "A Lancaster Firm," *Philadelphia Inquirer.*

60 "I get bored . . . he later observed: "At the Helm of Another Ship; Adm. Inman Pursues Speedy, Efficient Use of High Tech," *Industry Week,* June 1, 1987.

60 sold $56 million worth of stock in a matter of weeks.: "International Signal's Offering of Shares Sells Well in U.K., Despite Scant Information," *The Wall Street Journal,* October 22, 1982.

60 "The London financial community . . . the need for more confidentiality.": "International Signal's Offering of Shares," *Wall Street Journal.*

61 The board was responsible . . . cluster bombs for the Department of Defense.: "Ferranti/I.S.C. Deal Throws Role of Proxy Boards into Question," *Financial Times,* September 21, 1989.

61 the Rockeye cluster bomb.: "International Signal and Control Is Planning to Purchase C.C.I. Aerospace Unit for $43.5 Million Plus Stock," *The Wall Street Journal,* July 14, 1983.

61 on a navy weapons depot site: Interviews with former ISC executives, Lancaster, Pennsylvania, May 1991.

61 that detonated explosives used by the Chilean air force.: Interview with former ISC executive, Lancaster, Pennsylvania, August 28, 1991; telephone interview with former ISC executive, September 1, 1993; "I.S.C. technology linked to building of Iraqi bomb factory," *Financial Times,* November 19, 1990.

61 for use in Eastern Bloc artillery rounds.: United States *v.* James H. Guerin, U.S. District Court, Eastern District of Pennsylvania, indictment of James Guerin, October 31, 1991.

61 transfer of ISC cluster bomb technology.: "I.S.C. Technology Linked," *Financial Times.*

61 a front company indirectly owned by the CIA.: "I.S.C. Technology Linked," *Financial Times.* On various occasions, Guerin and Cardoen have both denied that ISC sold cluster bomb technology to Chile, but the transfer of technology by CIA operatives has been confirmed by a senior U.S. Customs agent in interviews in June 1991 and April 1993.

page

62 "The Carter administration . . . with the cooperation of the CIA.": Telephone interview with former ISC executive, September 1, 1993.

62 "Despite that ban . . . lied to me about what they were doing": "A Lancaster Firm," *Philadelphia Inquirer.*

62 a new rapport with Guerin and his fellow ISC executives.: Interview with former ISC executive, Lancaster, Pennsylvania, May 10, 1991.

62 nuclear weapons programs in South Africa.: Interview with former ISC executive, Lancaster, Pennsylvania, May 10, 1991.

63 established during Project X: Robert Clyde Ivy *v.* Ferranti International Inc., U.S. District Court, Eastern District of Pennsylvania, case number EC90-2535, fifth affidavit of Robert Clyde Ivy, August 30, 1991.

63 load up a South African Airways 747 cargo jet.: Interviews with U.S. prosecutors, Philadelphia, May and June 1991.

63 more than $15 million a year.: "C.I.A. Didn't Report I.S.C. Arms Sales to South Africa." *Lancaster Intelligencer Journal,* May 24, 1991.

63 "I discussed some . . . relationship and contacts with South Africa.": Ivy *v.* Ferranti, fifth affidavit.

63 "let all that shit go and did nothing to stop it." . . . didn't trust some of his fellow government employees.: Interview with U.S. Customs agent, Washington, D.C., July 11, 1991.

63 "longstanding contacts . . . those kinds of arrangements.": "A Lancaster Firm," *Philadelphia Inquirer.*

64 "Robert Gates . . . of these things.": Telephone interview with staff member of the Senate Select Committee on Intelligence, Washington, D.C., October 28, 1991.

64 shipping them on to Baghdad.: United States *v.* Armaments Corporation of South Africa Ltd., et al., U.S. District Court, Eastern District of Pennsylvania, indictment counts 28–48, October 31, 1991.

64 sending the power supplies to Iraq.: Telephone interview with former ISC executive, September 2, 1993.

64 that would be fired from Iraqi guns.: "U.S. Troops Found I.S.C. Gear in Iraq," *Lancaster Intelligencer Journal,* November 1, 1991.

64 "We keep it quiet . . . one new recruit.: Interview with Tom Jasin, Lancaster, Pennsylvania, October 24, 1992.

65 new international markets for the company: Memorandum to Alexander Haig, "Worldwide's Association with I.S.C.," December 11, 1986.

65 "I always thought Jim Guerin was a weirdo,": Interview with Alexander Haig, Washington, D.C., June 7, 1993.

65 recycling the same cash from account to account.: United States *v.* Guerin, indictment.

65 a polite no thank you.: United States *v.* Guerin, indictment.

66 The directors were told . . . South Africa, and others: Ferranti/International Signal and Control, report to board, September 8, 1987.

page

66 "significant drain" on Ferranti's cash resources.: "Lazard Brothers' Comments," October 15, 1987.

66 prior to its takeover by Ferranti.: Chronology, *The Lancaster Intelligencer,* September 4, 1990.

67 he misled banks . . . in Santiago: United States *v.* Guerin, indictment.

67 for auditors in Santiago.: United States *v.* Guerin, indictment.

SIX: On Her Majesty's Secret Service

68 or as had happened before . . . you and the West: Interview with Frank Machon, Glasgow, April 16, 1993. A series of interviews with Machon was conducted between April and July 1993.

69 they'd learn to live with it: Interview series with Machon.

69 "Outside Basra . . . Nobody shot at us.": Interview series with Machon.

71 Machon lit a cigarette and told his story.: Interview with Machon, April 16, 1993.

72 At a quarter to midnight . . . nothing had happened: Copy of receipt from Strathclyde police, Andrew Sloan, chief constable.

73 The police officer hung up.: Interview with Machon, April 16, 1993.

73 figured he might be intelligence . . . had had it with Her Majesty's government: Interview with Machon, April 18, 1993. As a result of the incident, Machon wrote to H.M. Customs Investigation Unit, Glasgow, on November 9, 1989, stating that "no further discussions should take place between us at all." A handwritten postscript refers to "the threats issued on my family's safety" during the visit by customs, and a warning from Machon that "if further threats are issued I will certainly take legal action."

74 ammunition rounds to Saudi Arabia.: Documentation of the deal between Allivane International Limited and the Saudi Ministry of Defense and Aviation, including letter of credit from the Saudi International Bank, London, British export license from the Department of Trade and Industry, and details of commission on the deal.

74 Byrne had founded Allivane with Guerin's encouragement.: Interviews with former Allivane executives, Glasgow and London, May and June 1993; interview with former ISC executive, Pennsylvania, June 16, 1993; "Scots Arm Inquiry Firm Linked to Ferranti Affair," *The Scotsman,* October 2, 1989.

74 the first two years of Allivane's existence.: Interviews with former Allivane executives, May and June 1993; interview with former ISC executive, May 1993.

74 the London arm of Guerin's group.: Curriculum vitae of Allivane executives, forming part of an overview of the company's history, prepared in June 1988.

75 having trouble paying its bills.: Interviews with former Allivane executives,

page

May and June 1993; "Company Relied on Foreign Assistance," *The Independent,* September 7, 1992.

75 missile plastered on a wall.: Interview with Machon, May 14, 1993.

75 executive later admitted.: Interview with former Allivane executive, Glasgow, June 3, 1993.

75 arms shipments to Iraq in the 1980s.: Interview with former Allivane executive, June 3, 1993; interviews with U.S. Department of Defense officials, Washington, D.C., May 27, 1993.

75 "Allivane was a facilitator" . . . an American intelligence officer.: Interview with U.S. intelligence officer, New York, July 1, 1993.

75 "all the time . . . shipments to Iran.": Interview with former Allivane executive, June 3, 1993.

75 selling the popular 155-mm. shell to Iran.: Report of Jean-François Barba, comptroller-general of the French Armed Forces, June 6, 1986; interviews with former Allivane executives, May and June 1993.

76 actually destined for Baghdad.: Interview series with Machon; interviews with former Allivane executives, May and June 1993.

76 government-provided grants.: "How the U.K. Fed a War Machine," *The Independent,* August 30, 1992.

76 in order to collect the insurance.: Interview with Machon, April 16, 1993.

76 The explosives onboard . . . Department of Trade and Industry.: Copies of documents from the Departments of Trade and Industry, and Health and Safety Executive, explosives division.

76 arms to Saudi Arabia were shipped on time: Interview with Machon, April 18, 1993; "Leading British Firms Flouted Iran Arms Ban," *The Independent,* August 30, 1992.

76 "I may well . . . It probably is," he said, embarrassed.: "Leading British Firms Flouted," *Independent.*

76 "Secretary of State's Crime Prevention Committee . . . secretary of state for Scotland.: Photograph of certificate signed by George Younger.

78 An eighteen-page copy of the plan . . . artillery projectiles.: Interviews with former Allivane and Space Research Corporation executives, Glasgow and London, May 1993; telefax, "Proposal and Offer for Fuzes M739A1 and M131 in 15 Pages," with cover letter from Stuart Blackledge, Space Research Corporation, Brussels, to Terrence C. Byrne, Jr., Allivane International Limited, August 3, 1987.

78 "exploit . . . defence equipment.": "Inquiry into Exports of Defence Equipment and Dual Use Goods to Iraq" before the Right Honourable Lord Justice Scott (the Scott Inquiry), London, May 10, 1993; "Ministry Withholds Iraq Arms Papers," *The Guardian,* May 11, 1993.

78 "lethal items . . . as flexibly as possible.": The Scott Inquiry, May 10, 1993.

78 "We never had any problems . . . Allivane manager recalled.: Interview with former Allivane executive, Glasgow, May 14, 1993.

page

78 "We learned about Allivane . . . and began coordinating.": Interview with U.S. intelligence officer, July 1, 1993.

78 For a small company . . . use in artillery shells.: Interview with former Allivane executive, May 14, 1993; interview with senior U.S. Customs investigator, Washington, D.C., June 2, 1993.

78 to get things moving.: Interview with former Allivane executives, May 14, 1993.

78 "Allivane bought the fuse parts . . . It was like clockwork." Interview with former Allivane executive, June 3, 1993.

79 transferred through the Space Research Corporation to Rexon.: Letter from Lloyds Bank, Paradise Street, Birmingham, to Rexon Technologies Corporation, Wayne, New Jersey, advising a $2.9 million transfer from S.R.C. Engineering S.A. in favor of Rexon, February 6, 1990. The letter continues: "This credit is available by payment of your draft(s) at sight on Central Bank of Iraq, Baghdad, Iraq, bearing the clause 'Drawn under Documentary Credit number 89/3/1146 dated 3 January 1990 of Central Bank of Iraq, Baghdad' accompanied by the following documents." The Lloyds Bank letter then listed the paperwork required from Rexon before payment would be made, including certification that "the goods are of UK or USA origin." In response to reports that the company was under investigation by a U.S. law enforcement agency, Rexon president Gary Kauf told the *Bergen Record* on February 26, 1991, "the company has never sold anything to Iraq. Rexon has done nothing wrong." In October 1992, the U.S. Senate Select Committee on Intelligence conducted its own inquiries into Rexon's alleged links with the CIA: "Panel Questions C.I.A. on Iraqi Arms," *The New York Times,* October 20, 1992.

79 with approval from the State Department.: State Department memorandum, "Alleged Attempt to Export to Iraq," from Office of Defense Trade Controls, Compliance Analysis Division, to Bureau of Politico-Military Affairs, October 3, 1990.

79 "the Al-Fao State Establishment, c/o Jordan Armed Forces.": State Department memorandum, "Al-Fao State Establishment," from Office of Defense Trade Controls, Compliance Analysis Division, to Near East and South Asia Bureau, March 6, 1991.

79 "We suspect . . . possibly including nonconventional weapons—for many years.": State Department memorandum, "Al-Fao State Establishment," from Near East and South Asia Bureau to Office of Defense Trade Controls, Compliance Analysis Division, March 25, 1991.

79 "I have followed . . . without government approval.": Interview with senior U.S. Customs investigator, Washington, D.C., June 2, 1993.

79 that really went to Iraq.: "Haulier Tells of Threats over Embargo Affair," *The Scotsman,* November 14, 1992; "Papers 'Prove Sanctions-Busting to Iraq,' " *The Scotsman,* November 24, 1992.

page

80   "I read of Mark Thatcher's involvement . . . in Europe and Saudi Arabia.":
     "Mark Thatcher Linked to Arms Sales," *The Guardian,* November 25,
     1992.

80   was also swiftly denied.: "Payments to Mark Thatcher Denied in Saudi
     Arabian Arms Deal," *The Sunday Times,* May 10, 1992.

80   "highly sensitive" situation: "Watchdog Suppresses its Saudi Arms Deal
     Report," *The Independent,* March 12, 1992.

SEVEN: From Rome to Atlanta

82   Washington's willingness to offer some contracts to its European allies.:
     Details of the White House discussions were described to the author by
     two Italian participants and one American participant; "Star Wars Will
     Trigger Arms Build-up, Soviet Warns," *The Washington Post,* March 6,
     1985; "Craxi and Reagan Discuss Arms Plan," *The New York Times,* March
     6, 1985.

82   against terrorism, drug-trafficking, and organized crime.: Handwritten
     memo to the author, May 22, 1993, referring to notes from the White
     House meeting with Ronald Reagan on March 5, 1985.

82   more than twenty thousand deaths in a single battle.: Anthony H. Cordes-
     man, *The Iran-Iraq War and Western Security* (London: Jane's Publishing,
     1987), pp. 71–74.

82   "Craxi, Andreotti, . . . clear in saying they must do something.": Interview
     with former Italian diplomat, Washington, D.C., March 29, 1993; interview
     with former American diplomat, New York, July 19, 1993.

82   "Yes, that is true," . . . the Italian capital.: Two participants at the White
     House meeting, one American and the other Italian, confirmed that Presi-
     dent Reagan made a request for Italian assistance in supplying arms to Iraq.
     During a two-hour tape-recorded interview with the author in Rome on May
     21, 1993, Giulio Andreotti himself confirmed that Reagan had made the
     request. However, in a subsequent handwritten note to the author on May
     22, 1993, Andreotti stated that the official Italian government record of the
     White House meeting made no mention of Iraq having been discussed.

83   "I gave it to Reagan . . ." he recollected with relish.: Interview with An-
     dreotti, May 21, 1993.

83   "My position with them . . . push them too much in one direction and
     they'll go in the other.": Interview with Andreotti, May 21, 1993.

84   The Italians had even contributed . . . Osirak.: A list of Italian companies
     involved in the arming of Iraq was provided to the author in May 1993 by
     Gary Milhollin of the Wisconsin Project on Nuclear Arms Control. See also
     Howard Teicher and Gayle Radley Teicher, *Twin Pillars to Desert Storm:
     America's Flawed Vision in the Middle East from Nixon to Bush* (New York:
     William Morrow, 1993), p. 67.

page

84 A year later the Italians trained . . . on the atomic project.: Rachel Schmidt, *Global Arms Exports to Iraq 1960–1990* (Santa Monica: RAND, 1991), p. 62.

84 "a symbol of peace and stability.": Cited in documents pertaining to relations with Iraq, prepared by Banca Nazionale del Lavoro.

85 "being the chairman . . . life is almost impossible.": Nerio Nesi, *Banchiere di complemento* (Milan: Sperling & Kupfer Edition, 1993), p. 125.

85 Dubbed "the bank of the P-2,": *La Repubblica* (Rome), June 3, 1981, and June 6, 1981.

85 arms to Iran through Luchaire: The Civil and Criminal Court of Venice, Office of Investigation, court documents.

85 fitted out for antisubmarine warfare.: Kenneth Timmerman, *The Death Lobby: How the West Armed Iraq* (Boston: Houghton Mifflin, 1991), p. 175.

85 "Certainly the policy . . ." said Andreotti.: Interview with Andreotti, May 21, 1993.

86 "that while we do not sell . . . limit weapon sales to Iraq.": State Department cable, "Italian Frigates for Iraq," from Ambassador David Newton to Secretary of State George Shultz, June 21, 1987.

86 "I met with Andreotti six or seven times . . . official at the time.": Interview with Howard Teicher, Washington, D.C., May 27, 1993.

86 As for BNL and Iraq, . . . between the Italian bank and Saddam's minions.: Interview with U.S. intelligence officer, New York, July 1, 1993.

86 had warm relations with the bank's executives.: Interview with former U.S. diplomat, New York, July 19, 1993.

86 "the Italian intelligence . . . the American embassy.": Conversation with senior aide to former Prime Minister Bettino Craxi, Rome, March 24, 1993.

86 user-friendly place as far as the CIA was concerned.: Interview with former U.S. Army intelligence officer, New York, February 25, 1993.

86 antipersonnel mines worth a total of $225 million.: Defense Intelligence Agency report on Valsella sale of mines to Iraq by way of Singapore intermediary, with financing from BNL, February 15, 1991. BNL has consistently denied any involvement in the financing of these mines.

86 the mines and the financing.: Interview with U.S. intelligence official, as quoted in "Iraq Appealed for BNL Help Ten Years Ago," *Financial Times,* October 19, 1992.

86 just like the frigates deal.: Letter from Mario Fallani to Valsella, May 29, 1984.

87 blown apart as they trod on them.: "I curdi decimati dalle mine italiane," *L'Indipendente,* May 20, 1993.

87 Mines that were shipped to Iraq: Contract between the Iraqi Defense Ministry and Valsella Meccanotecnica for the supply of land mines.

87 Condor II nuclear missile project: For a detailed description of the origins of the Condor project and the role of employees at a Fiat subsidiary, see

page

      Alan Friedman, *Agnelli: Fiat and the Network of Italian Power* (New York: New American Library, 1989), chap. 15.

87   "management control" over the company.: This was Fiat's standard line on the Valsella affair. See "Italian Arms Charges Denied," *Financial Times,* September 8, 1987.

87   declined to respond further.: "Italian Arms Charges Denied," *Financial Times.*

87   the paper trail . . . Andreotti himself: Foreign Trade Ministry, "Documentazione relativa alla ditta Valsella di Castenedolo di Montichiari (Brescia)," Rome, August 31, 1987.

87   The mine sales required ministerial approval.: Foreign Trade Ministry, August 31, 1987.

88   as the fake end-user certificates claimed.: Interview with Italian government official, Brescia, November 14, 1992.

88   interministerial committee approved the shipments to Singapore.: Foreign Trade Ministry, August 31, 1987.

88   "On this Valsella matter, . . . in these matters.": Interview with Andreotti, May 21, 1993.

88   BNL had never financed any mine sales to Iraq.: "Iraq Appealed for BNL Help," *Financial Times.*

88   of which the Iraqi mines deal was only one.: Casalee has been accused of arms deals in the Swiss, French, and Italian press. For an overview, see "Trading Company Is at the Center of Furor in Congress over Bush's Ties to Iraq," *The Wall Street Journal,* June 1, 1992.

88   Western intelligence officials . . . worked with U.S. and British agencies.: The Brussels Gendarmerie, report on Casalee, October 24, 1984 (provided by P-Network); interview with U.S. intelligence officer, Washington, D.C., May 23, 1993.

88   "He flew in and out of Baghdad, . . . a real-life James Bond," claimed one admiring Swiss investigator.: Interview with Ferruccio Petracco, P-network journalistic investigator, Milan, November 14, 1992.

89   consulted with the Italian embassy in Baghdad.: Letter from Mario Fallani to Valsella, May 29, 1984 (provided by P-network).

89   delays in the shipments were causing "grave difficulties": Letter from Mario Fallani to Valsella, September 10, 1985 (provided by P-network).

89   to a middleman involved in the mines deal.: Telex from Chan Choong, Singapore, to Valsella, containing message from Mario Girotti of BNL Singapore, October 29, 1985 (provided by P-network).

89   "opened in your favor . . . military accounts.": Telex from Chan Choong to Valsella, October 29, 1985 (provided by P-network).

89   a bit slow when it came to paying.: Letter from Casalee Italia to Chartered Chemical Industries of Singapore, containing Fallani telex, February 11, 1986 (provided by P-network).

page

89   introduced him to an Italian banker named Giuseppe Vincenzino.: Interview with Christopher Drogoul, Atlanta, April 1, 1993.

90   "I know you don't like lawyers . . . write your own ticket.": Quoted in Mary Fisher, "The Fall Guy," *GQ,* May 1993.

90   sent off to Dallas for a one-week training course: Interview with Drogoul, April 1, 1993; telephone interview with Christopher Drogoul, July 19, 1993.

90   a job at a salary of $42,000.: Christopher Drogoul, internal employee evaluation form, Banca Nazionale del Lavoro (BNL), Atlanta branch, 1981.

91   acquaintances included Andrew Young, the mayor of Atlanta: *Proceedings of the Italian Senate,* testimony of Renato Guadagnini to the committee investigating BNL Atlanta (Rome 1992), vol. 18, p. 439; interview with Christopher Drogoul, Atlanta, May 13, 1993.

92   anywhere in its sprawling network.: Christopher Drogoul, internal employee evaluation form, BNL Atlanta. 1982.

92   wanted a replacement.: *Proceedings of the Italian Senate,* testimony of Giuseppe Vincenzino to the committee investigating BNL Atlanta (Rome 1992), vol. 18, p. 587.

92   "A lackey, like a bag-carrier . . . on those Italian espresso machines.": Telephone interview with Priscilla Rabb, July 25, 1993.

93   At a time like that $1 billion in deposits was a lot to lose.: *Proceedings of the Italian Senate,* final report of the committee investigating BNL Atlanta (Rome 1992), p. 18.

93   had dropped to only a third the level of 1980: Eximbank report, "Iraq Country Appendix," May 13, 1985, p. 7.

93   tumbled from $28 billion a year in 1980 to what would be only $8 billion in 1983.: Eximbank report, "Iraq," p. 7.

93   success of the ground attacks Iran had launched.: Eximbank report, "Iraq," p. 7.

93   a shortfall of as much as ten billion dollars for the year.: Declassified SECRET State Department action memorandum, "U.S. Credit Possibilities for Iraq," from Richard McCormack to Secretary of State George Shultz, March 16, 1983.

93   the law governing the bank required "a reasonable reassurance of payment,": Declassified SECRET State Department action memorandum, March 16, 1983.

94   "the question of whether Iraq was harboring terrorists would have to be decided.": Declassified SECRET State Department action memorandum, March 16, 1983.

94   said Shultz's advisers: Declassified SECRET State Department action memorandum, March 16, 1983.

94   an obscure U.S. government loan-guarantee program: In November 1990, the General Accounting Office (GAO) summarized the role of the Commodity Credit Corporation as follows: "The CCC guarantees that U.S.

exporters or their assignees will be repaid for a credit sale made to a foreign buyer in an eligible country. If the buyer defaults, the exporter can file a claim with the CCC for the loss." The ability to assign the account receivable and the repayment guarantee to a bank participating in the CCC program would normally mean that an exporter could obtain immediate payment from the bank on a credit sale.

94 the first $230 million of CCC guarantees: National Advisory Council memorandum, "CCC—Proposed $230 Million Blended Credit Program—Iraq," February 1, 1983.

94 the senior U.S. diplomat in Baghdad, William Eagleton, to tell Saddam's aides the good news.: State Department cable, "U.S. Possibilities with Iraq: Follow Up to February 14, 1983 Secretary-Hamadi Meeting," from Secretary of State George Shultz to U.S. embassy, Baghdad, March 16, 1983.

95 to lend a hand to other banks in times of weakness.: In December 1990, the New York Federal Reserve contacted Morgan and asked it to consider assisting in covering commercial paper obligations of a large U.S. bank that was suffering from a short-term liquidity squeeze because of the slump in U.S. banking at the time. Executives of both that bank and Morgan have confirmed to the author that this was one of various occasions when federal authorities informally asked Morgan to "lend a hand" in the interest of maintaining systemic stability in the financial markets. Morgan had played a role at the very inception of the Federal Reserve System, early in the twentieth century, when J. P. Morgan strongarmed other banks into providing "lifeboat" facilities to those institutions facing solvency problems.

95 initially providing CCC-backed loans: Telephone interview with senior Morgan executive, July 23, 1993.

95 unwilling to support any further increases in the program: Treasury Department memorandum, "CCC Export Credit Sales Guarantees to Iraq," October 17, 1984.

95 "was popular at the time. . . . We were suspicious of Saddam, but we didn't hate him.": Interview with Maxwell Rabb, New York, July 19, 1993.

95 £300 million of guaranteed financing available to Saddam.: Eximbank report, "Iraq," p. 13.

95 used poison gas against the Kurds in the north: BNL chronology, prepared by the U.S. Senate Select Committee on Intelligence, 1984–1992.

95 concerned that Saddam would almost certainly make military use of them: Interviews with Department of Defense officials, Washington, D.C., April 1991; BNL chronology, 1984–1992.

95 made plain in a memo sent to Shultz: Declassified SECRET State Department memorandum, "Easing Restrictions on Exports to Iraq," from David Schneider, through Lawrence Eagleburger, to Secretary of State George Shultz, January 30, 1984.

96 briefing the CIA on their Iraqi activities.: Information provided to the

page

author by a Cargill executive, April 1992, and confirmed in interview with
U.S. intelligence officer, New York, July 1, 1993.

97   "They said 'Iraq? No problem. Go ahead.' So we did.": Telephone inter-
      view with Christopher Drogoul, July 19, 1993.

97   Taha was trusted, and he enjoyed having that trust.: Telephone interview
      with Drogoul, July 19, 1993; interviews with former BNL executives,
      Rome, May 22, 1993.

98    $100 million BNL Atlanta line of credit was agreed.: Telephone interview
      with Drogoul, July 19, 1993.

98   he was the man to see for CCC-backed loans to Iraq: Interviews with two
      former BNL executives and one current BNL executive, Rome, February
      1993.

98   "that it was very important . . . They relied on it.": Fisher, "The Fall Guy."

98   bought gifts of solid gold Parker pens: Unpublished manuscript by Paul
      Von Wedel, "From the Gates of Babylon to the Gates of Hell." The
      information in the manuscript was confirmed in interviews with Christo-
      pher Drogoul in Atlanta in April and May 1993. Mr. Von Wedel first
      provided a copy of the manuscript to the author in 1990, and in a telephone
      interview on July 21, 1993, gave his permission to quote small fragments
      from it provided any quotations were credited to him.

99   took them to a lavish dinner at Trader Vic's: Telephone interview with
      Drogoul, July 19, 1993; telephone interview with Paul Von Wedel, July 21,
      1993.

99   had never authorized him to lend sums beyond $100 million: Documents
      pertaining to relations with Iraq prepared by BNL Rome.

99   The answer, three days later, was no.: Frederick B. Lacey, *Report of the
      Independent Counsel: The Banca Nazionale Del Lavoro Investigation,* part 1,
      December 8, 1992, p. 31.

99   not making any new loans to Iraq.: Interviews with Bank of Italy officials
      and former BNL executives, Rome, May 20–22, 1993.

99   they would hide them again.: Telephone interview with Drogoul, July 19,
      1993.

100   The report . . . failed to show a total of more than $406 million worth of
      CCC-backed loans.: Confidential BNL memo, concerning the activities of
      U.S. branches, Rome, June 17, 1986.

100   "We were in a state of near anarchy . . . a host of sins.": Interview with
      former BNL executive, Rome, April 5, 1993.

100   a blistering attack: Documents pertaining to relations with Iraq prepared
      by BNL Rome.

100   BNL Atlanta's results . . . were described as brilliant.: Documents pertain-
      ing to relations with Iraq prepared by BNL Rome.

100   "Atlanta . . . That's how Drogoul came to be loved so well in Rome.": Inter-
      view with former deputy general manager of BNL, Rome, May 22, 1993.

page

100 like a mantra.: Interview with former BNL executive, Rome, April 5, 1993.

101 "Iraq had a special relationship with Italy and the United States.": Interview with Drogoul, April 1, 1993. Pedde's shock has been described by former BNL executives and is also reported in Nerio Nesi, *Banchiere di complemento* (Milan: Sperling & Kupfer Edition, 1993), pp. 1–5; telephone interview with Giacomo Pedde, September 24, 1993.

EIGHT: The Money Machine

102 "I recognized . . . people had to know what we were doing,": Telephone interview with Christopher Drogoul, July 19, 1993.

102 "There were people in Rome who knew . . .": Telephone interview with Paul Von Wedel, September 8, 1993.

102 "There was . . . Larry Panasuk,": Interview with Christopher Drogoul, Atlanta, April 1, 1993.

103 "I tried . . . to reach him.": Telephone interview with Larry Panasuk, July 21, 1993.

103 a thousand bodies on the bloodiest days: Information on this stage of the war can be found in Anthony H. Cordesman, *The Iran-Iraq War and Western Security* (London: Jane's Publishing, 1987), pp. 127–30.

103 $25 million of unsecured loans: United States *v.* Christopher P. Drogoul et al., U.S. District Court, Northern District of Georgia, Atlanta Division, criminal indictment number 1:91-CR-078, February 28, 1991.

103 "It was unprecedented . . . had pulled out.": Interview with Paul Von Wedel, Atlanta, April 30, 1991.

103 "We went from not showing . . . showing them on any day,": Telephone interview with Drogoul, July 19, 1993.

104 to remove the records of gray book transactions from the branch: New York Federal Reserve, strictly confidential memorandum, "Banca Nazionale Del Lavoro Atlanta Agency Operations," from Kathleen D. Tyson to Gerald Corrigan et al., July 31, 1989.

104 a total of $5 billion of the loan guarantees for Iraq: General Accounting Office (GAO) Report, *International Trade: Iraq's Participation in U.S. Agricultural Export Programs,* November 1990.

104 reported, filed, and stored at the Department of Agriculture.: U.S. Department of Agriculture records of CCC credit-guarantee transactions, in which BNL figured among the banks providing finance.

104 the Agriculture Department didn't always know: U.S. House of Representatives, statement of Congressman Charles Schumer to the House Banking Committee, October 16, 1990. See also GAO, *International Trade.*

104 The information might have caused a halt in the CCC program for Iraq: According to a U.S. intelligence officer, the information was reported back to Washington, but once there it was filtered through a series of policy

prisms that rendered it almost moot. The reasons for this were several: Different intelligence services, such as the CIA and the DIA, were competitors and sometimes wasted their energies virtually spying on each other; some pieces of information were considered "raw" or unevaluated intelligence, no matter how accurate they might have been to agents in the field; even more problematic, some senior officials of intelligence agencies, such as William Casey, had political agendas that caused them to deliberately ignore reports of covert grain-for-arms swaps that they actually approved of.

104 "It was done through places . . . They were watching us.": Interview with former BNL executive, Rome, August 1992.

105 "no doubt about the swap.": Interview with former Defense Department assistant secretary, Washington, D.C., January 31, 1991.

105 more than double the normal market price.: GAO, *International Trade.*

105 able to skim large sums: Interview with U.S. intelligence officer, Washington, D.C., May 17, 1993; "Waiting for the Last Word on Iraqgate," *U.S. News & World Report,* December 21, 1992.

105 "There is no doubt . . . not as a single instrument.": "Iraqgate," *U.S. News & World Report,* May 18, 1992.

105 "money is fungible . . . more on defense.": Telephone interview with Paul Dickerson, July 20, 1993.

105 met then-ambassador David Newton: Interview with Christopher Drogoul, Atlanta, April 1, 1993.

105 had been suspended in March 1986: Eximbank memorandum to the board of directors, "Interagency Review of Iraq," April 17, 1987.

105 "from zero to not much,": Quoted in "Bush Aid to Iraq," *The Los Angeles Times,* February 24, 1992.

106 It told Bush . . . "your conversation with Hamdoon.": Declassified CONFIDENTIAL State Department memorandum for the White House, "The Vice President's March 2 Meeting with Iraqi Ambassador Nizar Hamdoon," February 26, 1987.

107 He had personally telephoned the chairman of Eximbank: Declassified CONFIDENTIAL State Department memo for the White House, February 26, 1987; "Bush Aid to Iraq," *Los Angeles Times.*

107 had just been approved by the government.: "Bush Aid to Iraq," *Los Angeles Times.*

107 process $47 million of Eximbank-backed loans for Iraq.: Telephone conversation with staff members of the House Banking Committee, May 16, 1993.

108 Fiat . . . demanding that BNL "find a solution.": Letter from Fiat to Banca Nazionale del Lavoro, "Iraq—linea di credito Rafidain Bank a 24 mesi," with handwritten note by BNL banker dated September 1986.

108 the Rome government promised to Iraq.: Internal memorandum on Iraq from Teodoro Monaco, Banca Nazionale del Lavoro, December 9, 1986.

page

108 Baghdad could take another couple of years: Ministry of Foreign Trade, minutes of Italo-Iraqi meeting, Rome, March 17–19, 1987.

108 flew to Baghdad: U.S. Senate, Select Committee on Intelligence, BNL chronology, 1984–1992; interview with Drogoul, April 1, 1993.

109 a performance by dancing girls: Paul Von Wedel, unpublished manuscript.

109 series of loans that Iraq would use: Interview with Drogoul, April 1, 1993.

109 dwarfed BNL Atlanta's authorized limit: New York Federal Reserve memorandum, July 31, 1989.

109 "and he had every reason" . . . visiting Baghdad to restructure a $50 million Iraqi debt: *Proceedings of the Italian Senate,* testimony of Teodoro Monaco to the committee investigating BNL Atlanta (Rome 1992), vol. 7, p. 26.

109 "I told him . . . keep him advised.": Interview with Drogoul, April 1, 1993.

110 introduce Monaco to a senior Iraqi Central Bank official: *Proceedings of the Italian Senate,* testimony of Monaco.

110 "running a bank in the closet.": New York Federal Reserve memorandum, July 31, 1989.

110 The NSA . . . was monitoring: Interview with Norman Bailey, former NSC official, Washington, D.C., September 30, 1989.

110 acknowledged to Drogoul that he was a former NSA official.: Interview with Drogoul, April 1, 1993.

110 It was, Bailey said . . . the Bush administration: Interview with Norman Bailey, Washington, D.C., July 27, 1993.

110 "The only explanation . . . the financing of certain activities": "Fatal Attraction," *Financial Times,* May 3, 1991.

111 "voluminous" information: "Cover-Up," *U.S. News & World Report,* October 26, 1992.

111 "The U.S. government . . . to which U.S. suppliers they should go.": Interview with U.S. intelligence officer, New York, July 1, 1993.

111 "The other thing . . . intelligence services": Interview with BNL executive, Rome, September 8, 1989.

111 knew of the $200 million Iraqi loan that he signed: Telephone interview with Drogoul, July 19, 1993.

111 Monaco had told several colleagues, including Pedde: *Proceedings of the Italian Senate,* testimony of Monaco.

111 "I inherited Drogoul . . . disorganized bank.": Telephone interview with Giacomo Pedde, September 24, 1993.

111 "There was only one bank . . . through its branch in Atlanta.": "The Flight of the Condor," *Financial Times,* November 21, 1989.

112 he and his partners exercised effective control over the Jordanian port of Aqaba: Interview with U.S. intelligence officer, Washington, D.C., May 17, 1993; *Congressional Record,* House of Representatives, floor statement of Congressman Henry Gonzalez, March 30, 1992, H2010.

page

112 Drogoul provided the loan finance.: *Congressional Record,* floor statement of Congressman Gonzalez, March 30, 1992.

112 a fifty-fifty partnership with a big Norwegian shipping concern called Gearbulk.: Telephone interview with Drogoul, July 19, 1993; "Iraqgate," *U.S. News & World Report;* "Federal Investigators Turning Their Attention to Jordanian in the Middle of BNL Mystery," *The Wall Street Journal,* December 31, 1992.

112 then loaded onto a fleet of eighteen hundred trucks: Telephone interview with Drogoul, July 19, 1993.

112 thanks to Dajani's connections, it ended up being funded: "Iraqgate: Now the Scrutiny Intensifies," *U.S. News & World Report,* June 22, 1992.

113 one of King Hussein's closest personal friends.: State Department action memorandum, to Robert Kimmitt, "Proposed Indictments in the BNL Case," February 25, 1991.

113 studied under a State Department scholarship: "Federal Investigators Turning Their Attention to Jordanian," *The Wall Street Journal.*

113 By the 1980s, Dajani was operating . . . Georgetown section of Washington: Interview with Drogoul, April 1, 1993.

113 "Please excuse me . . . Thanks again, Chris,": Banca Nazionale del Lavoro, Atlanta, fax from Christopher Drogoul to Wafai Dajani, London, December 12, 1988, with attached draft telex to Subhi Frankool, acting governor, Central Bank of Iraq; amended version of telex from Christopher Drogoul to Subhi Frankool, December 13, 1988.

113 alleged to have acted as a broker: *Congressional Record,* floor statement of Congressman Gonzalez, March 30, 1992.

113 "I couldn't be involved in arms, I am too big and easy to watch,": *Congressional Record,* floor statement of Congressman Gonzalez, March 30, 1992; "Iraqgate," *U.S. News & World Report,* May 18, 1992.

113 "If you wanted the business . . . no business.": "Iraqgate," *U.S. News & World Report.*

113 Dajani denied each allegation that came from Congress: *Congressional Record,* floor statement of Congressman Gonzalez, March 30, 1992; "Federal Investigators Turning Their Attention to Jordanian," *The Wall Street Journal.*

113 his firms were not involved in Iraqi weapons programs.: *Congressional Record,* floor statement of Congressman Gonzalez, March 30, 1992.

114 "the intermediary for German . . . he dealt with everybody.": Interview with U.S. intelligence officer, May 17, 1993.

114 "We knew that Dajani was doing work for the CIA . . . one of his visits.": Telephone interview with Paul Von Wedel, July 21, 1993.

114 "Well, Dajani . . . He would have been used by the Agency.": Interview with U.S. intelligence officer, New York, July 1, 1993.

114 "Yes, it does. . . . was involved in the CCC program.": Interview with Howard Teicher, Washington, D.C., May 27, 1993.

page

114 "I don't work for anybody. I work for myself.": "Federal Investigators Turning Their Attention to Jordanian," *The Wall Street Journal.*

114 The goods . . . were not the kind that would be eligible for purchase with CCC loan guarantees.: New York Federal Reserve, strictly confidential memorandum, "Banca Nazionale Del Lavoro Atlanta agency operations," from Kathleen D. Tyson to Corrigan et al., July 31, 1989.

114 "It doesn't matter . . . an arms linkage,": British government official quoted in "Flight of the Condor," *Financial Times.*

114 nuclear, and chemical weapons projects: United States *v.* Christopher P. Drogoul, chart number 3, sentencing hearings, Atlanta, September 14, 1992.

114 welcomed Chris Drogoul to Baghdad: Telephone interview with Drogoul, July 19, 1993.

115 "We have been tracking . . . It is not a pretty picture.": Interview with British government nuclear policy adviser, London, October 1989.

115 processing more than twenty-five hundred separate letters of credit: United States *v.* Christopher P. Drogoul et al., indictment, February 28, 1991.

115 and technologies to Baghdad for the Condor II missile project: Interview with BNL executive, Rome, September 5, 1989; telephone interview with Drogoul, July 19, 1993.

115 top of the State Department's list: "Flight of the Condor," *Financial Times.*

115 an Iraqi entity called Project 395.: Letters of credit from BNL Atlanta for export of goods to Iraq's Project 395.

115 ran the Condor II and other missile projects: Letters of credit from BNL Atlanta for exports of goods to Iraq's Technical Corps for Special Projects.

115 listed clearly on a telex sent to Drogoul from Baghdad: Rasheed Bank, Baghdad, telex to Banca Nazionale del Lavoro, Atlanta, April 8, 1989, describing shipment to the Iraqi Atomic Energy Commission.

116 financed purchases for Bull thanks to loans from BNL Atlanta.: Kenneth R. Timmerman, *The BNL Blunder* (Los Angeles: The Simon Wiesenthal Center, 1991), a special report commissioned from *Middle East Defense News,* p. 30; "Washington Link to Iraqi Supergun," *Financial Times,* October 27, 1992.

116 in the company of Sadik Taha in London in October 1988.: Interview with Drogoul, April 1, 1993.

116 "hot forging dies project.": Central Bank of Iraq, telex to Banca Nazionale del Lavoro, Atlanta, May 23, 1989.

116 funded genuinely dangerous projects . . . allow Iraqi troops to see their enemy in the dark.: *Congressional Record,* House of Representatives floor statement of Congressman Gonzalez, February 3, 1992.

116 was shipped by a Belgian company: Frederick B. Lacey, *Report of the Independent Counsel: The Banca Nazionale Del Lavoro Investigation,* part 1, December 8, 1992, pp. 34–35.

116   what Baghdad was doing with the Atlanta loans.: Timmerman, *BNL Blunder*, pp. 31–32.

117   "There is nothing to worry about. . . . working together for years with the Americans.": Telephone interview with Drogoul, July 19, 1993.

117   head of Saddam's ballistic missile and chemical weapons programs: Timmerman, *BNL Blunder*, p. 20.

117   encouraged Bechtel to go ahead.: "Warning Forced Bechtel out of Iraq Chemical Project," *Financial Times*, February 21, 1991.

118   "something is going to go very wrong . . . get blown up too.": "Warning Forced Bechtel," *Financial Times*.

118   "I cannot categorically state . . . converted to such.": Eximbank memorandum, "Proposed Dow Chemical Sale of Pesticides to Iraq," December 6, 1988.

118   did not get Eximbank's blessing, but it did obtain loans from BNL Atlanta: Telephone interview with former BNL executive, July 21, 1993; BNL Atlanta letters of credit for Dow Chemical exports to Iraq.

119   to use BNL Atlanta in order to finance the Sidewinder component shipments.: Handwritten notes on Sidewinder components and other military orders for the Italian Defense Ministry, financed by BNL 1986–1988, furnished by Christopher Drogoul; interview with Drogoul, April 1, 1993; "U.S.-Italy Arms Deal via BNL Is Probed," *The Atlanta Constitution*, August 4, 1993; *Proceedings of the Italian Senate*, hearings of the committee investigating BNL Atlanta, September 15, 1993.

119   transhipped to Iraq rather than remain: Memorandum, "BNL Investigation," from Gale McKenzie, assistant U.S. attorney, Atlanta, to Ray Rukstele, chief of criminal division, Department of Justice, Washington, D.C., July 2, 1990.

119   and Morgan processed a total of $1.7 billion worth of Drogoul's Iraqi business in just seventeen months.: "Fatal Attraction," *Financial Times*.

119   cleared sums many times larger than this each day.: Interviews with Morgan executives, New York, September 30, 1989.

119   to take a piece of Iraq's CCC business.: Interview with Drogoul, April 1, 1993; letter from Christopher Drogoul to J. Chap Chandler, Continental Concepts, recommending various banks, including the Bank for Cooperatives, January 12, 1989.

120   "If some bank starts . . . other banks would hear about it?": "Flight of the Condor," *Financial Times*.

120   "highly exposed to Iraqi risk.": "Iraq Has Radically Overhauled Its Financial Arrangements," *Middle East Economic Digest*, February 20, 1988.

120   "the situation is really very bad.": *Proceedings of the Italian Senate*, hearings of the committee investigating BNL Atlanta (Rome 1992), vol. 18, p. 23.

120   a summary of the draft report was handed to a visitor from BNL's Rome

page

headquarters in October 1988.: *Proceedings of the Italian Senate,* hearings of the committee investigating BNL Atlanta (Rome 1992), vol. 18, p. 24; report on Atlanta branch by BNL internal auditors, New York, December 22, 1988; interview with BNL North American regional manager Luigi Sardelli, New York, April 1992.

120 Drogoul seemed untouchable.: "The BNL Case: How Much Did the Bank Know?" *The Atlanta Constitution,* February 28, 1993.

120 Pedde was protecting Drogoul: *Proceedings of the Italian Senate,* hearings of the committee investigating BNL Atlanta (Rome 1992), vol. 18, p. 31; interview with Giacomo Pedde, September 24, 1993.

121 "the Democrats will cut you off.": Telephone interview with Drogoul, July 19, 1993.

121 Atlanta would handle the transaction: *Proceedings of the Italian Senate,* final report of the committee investigating BNL Atlanta (Rome 1992), pp. 82–88; "The BNL Case," *The Atlanta Constitution.*

121 He provided all the details: BNL Atlanta, telex from Christopher Drogoul to BNL Rome, December 20, 1988.

121 ". . . not what you would call the greatest.": Interview with former deputy general manager of BNL, Rome, May 22, 1993.

122 Croff and his colleagues signed the approval form: BNL Rome, final approval of $50 million line of credit to Iraq, July 14, 1989.

122 "It was strange, real strange,": Telephone interview with William Hinshaw II, former special agent in charge, FBI Atlanta, September 8, 1993.

122 what they and Drogoul had been up to for the past five years.: Federal Reserve Bank of New York, strictly confidential memorandum, Atlanta agency operations, July 31, 1989.

123 it was a hot and humid Friday: Federal Reserve Bank of Atlanta, confidential memorandum, "Information on Banca Nazionale Del Lavoro, Atlanta Agency," from Madeline Marsden to Zane R. Kelley, vice-president, September 25, 1989.

123 two dozen federal agents fanned out: Interviews with former BNL employees, Rome and Atlanta, September 1989; Giuseppe Mennella and Massimo Riva, *Atlanta Connection* (Bari: Laterza, 1993), pp. 19–20.

123 The document seizure took hours . . . meticulously recorded: Federal Reserve Bank of Atlanta, confidential memorandum, September 25, 1989.

125 An hour later Pedde told Nesi: Conversations with BNL executive, Rome, September 1989.

125 a female colleague whom the FBI had just released: Interview with Drogoul, April 1, 1993.

125 In London he conferred with a handful of Iraqi contacts: Interview with Drogoul, April 1, 1993.

126 Instead, he was told not to worry: United States *v.* Drogoul, sentencing

page

hearing, September 14, 1992; Lacey, *Report of the Independent Counsel,* part 1, December 8, 1992, p. 39; interview with Drogoul, April 1, 1993.

126 built up to a "pretty goddamn" good size.: Federal Reserve Bank of New York, strictly confidential memorandum to the files, "Call to Mr. Preston," from Bradley K. Sabel, August 22, 1989.

126 BNL asked U.S. officials to avoid making any public statements.: Interviews with BNL executives, Rome, April–May 1993.

127 in fact, BNL categorically denied that arms sales were involved.: "Big Italian Bank in Iraq Export Inquiry," *Financial Times,* August 18, 1989.

NINE: BushBaker and Saddam

131 noted in her daily logs that Baker was "most interested" in BNL: Justice Department memorandum, "BNL Investigation," October 10, 1989.

131 "had firmly decided to establish . . . made government agencies nervous.": Telephone interview with staff member, House Banking Committee, September 9, 1993.

132 "what knowledge and role, if any . . . a decision to prosecute.": Memorandum, "Banca Nazionale Del Lavoro (BNL) Investigation," from Joe Whitley and Rimantas Rukstele, Office of U.S. Attorney, Atlanta, to Mark Richard, deputy assistant attorney general, Department of Justice, July 3, 1990.

132 It had first reported on BNL's role: U.S. Senate, Select Committee on Intelligence, report on BNL, February 5, 1993, p. 56; interview with U.S. intelligence officer, Washington, D.C., May 17, 1993.

132 "BNL's work with the Iraqis . . . so did the Defense Intelligence Agency.": Interview with U.S. intelligence officer, May 17, 1993.

132 CIA obtained information clearly linking BNL Atlanta: Senate Select Committee on Intelligence, report on BNL, pp. 58–60.

132 describing Saddam's efforts: Interviews with Senate staff members, Washington, D.C., April and May 1991; "CIA told White House of Iraqi Arms Efforts," *The Los Angeles Times,* August 6, 1992.

132 U.S. Customs Service reported its suspicion: U.S. Customs Service, letter to Robert L. Barr, U.S. Attorney for the Northern District of Georgia, from resident agent in charge, Atlanta, Georgia, September 21, 1989.

132 The Pentagon, the Federal Reserve, and prosecutors in Atlanta were also communicating their fears: Federal Reserve memorandum, September 28, 1989, which states "The Department of Defense is investigating allegations that BNL's funding was used at least in part to finance arms shipments to Iraq in violation of U.S. law." Cited in the hearing on "The BNL Scandal and the Department of Agriculture's CCC Program for Iraq" before the Banking, Finance, and Urban Affairs Committee of the House of Representatives, May 21, 1992.

page

132   how hard Iraq was working to develop its missiles: Declassified SECRET
       State Department briefing memorandum, "Meeting with Iraqi Under-
       Secretary Nizar Hamdun," from Paul J. Hare to Secretary of State James
       Baker, March 23, 1989; interviews with former White House officials,
       Washington, D.C., June 7, 1993.

133   "to decide whether to treat Iraq as a distasteful dictatorship . . . the latter
       view.": Bush administration transition papers, "Guidelines for U.S.-Iraq
       Policy."

134   "vast oil reserves promising a lucrative market for U.S. goods.": Bush
       administration transition papers, "Guidelines for U.S.-Iraq Policy."

134   "to embrace Saddam in a cocoon of moderation.": "Iraqgate," *U.S. News &
       World Report,* May 18, 1992.

134   "When you look at NSD 26 . . . and he was waving the sellers on.":
       "Officials Investigating Whether U.S. Loans Helped Buy Iraqi Arms," *The
       Los Angeles Times,* May 30, 1992.

134   NSD 26 stated the BushBaker policy in unequivocal terms.: National
       Security Directive 26 (NSD 26), "U.S. Policy Toward the Persian Gulf,"
       October 2, 1989.

135   April Glaspie recommended such steps: Department of Defense telex,
       "Proposed U.S.-Iraq Military Initiatives," from U.S. Central Command,
       Florida, to Joint Chiefs of Staff, Washington, D.C., November 29, 1989.

135   officials at the Treasury Department, were fearful of giving Iraq more
       financial aid: Treasury Department memorandum, "CCC Credit Guaran-
       tees for Iraq," from William E. Barreda to Assistant Secretary Dallara,
       October 1989.

135   CCC guarantees for Iraq "should not go forward at this time.": Treasury
       Department, note from W. L. McCamey, director, Office of Trade Finance,
       October 2, 1989.

135   reports that summer stating that Baghdad was not creditworthy: *Congres-
       sional Record,* House of Representatives, statement of Congressman Henry
       Gonzalez, July 27, 1992, H6699.

136   Baghdad was desperate for cash: National Advisory Council, minutes of
       meeting, October 3, 1989.

136   Treasury officials in Washington had learned: Treasury Department mem-
       orandum, "Proposed CCC Program for Iraq in FY 1990 and Proposed
       Additional Guarantees in FY 1989," to Assistant Secretary Dallara, Sep-
       tember 25, 1989.

136   "overspending its resources . . . ever-increasing amounts of credit.": Declas-
       sified SECRET State Department cable, "Under Secretary Kimmitt Meeting
       with Eximbank Acting Chairman Ryan, June 15, 1989," from Secretary of
       State James Baker to American ambassador, Baghdad, June 22, 1989.

136   a "Ponzi-type" scheme: National Advisory Council, minutes of meeting,
       October 3, 1989.

136 reluctant to do any more for Saddam: Declassified SECRET State Department cable, June 22, 1989.

136 "courting disaster": National Advisory Council, minutes of meeting, October 3, 1989.

137 break the news to a visiting Iraqi delegation: House of Representatives, Committee on Banking, Finance, and Urban Affairs, "Cover-up Chronology: October 2–November 9, 1989."

137 a normal Iraqi business practice.: Department of Agriculture memo of conference, "Subject: Banca Nazionale Del Lavoro, Atlanta, Ga.," October 5, 1989.

137 Baker had been told by his briefers: Declassified SECRET State Department briefing memorandum, "Meeting with Iraqi Foreign Minister Tariq Aziz," from John Kelly to Secretary of State James Baker, October 4, 1989.

137 the Henry Clay Room: Background information on the Henry Clay Room was provided by the State Department, Office of the Curator, July 30, 1993.

138 warned him that Aziz liked to lecture: State Department briefing memorandum, October 4, 1989.

138 "some American agencies" . . . "very unhappy": Declassified SECRET State Department cable, "Secretary's October 6 meeting with Iraqi Foreign Minister Tariq Aziz," from Secretary of State James Baker to the American ambassador in Baghdad, October 13, 1989.

139 no U.S. intention "to infer Iraqi involvement in the BNL issue.": State Department cable, "CCC Negotiations," from April Glaspie, American embassy, Baghdad, to Secretary of State James Baker, October 8, 1989.

140 "With his mailed fist still in his velvet glove . . . the repayment of its debts.: State Department cable, "CCC Negotiations," from Joseph Wilson, American embassy, Baghdad, to Secretary of State James Baker, October 9, 1989.

140 "The unfolding BNL scandal . . . separated from it.": State Department memorandum, "CCC Credits for Iraq," from Richard McCormack to Secretary of State James Baker, October 11, 1989.

141 McKenzie was a junior prosecutor: Interviews with Atlanta attorneys, September 14 and 17, 1992.

141 McKenzie was visited in Atlanta: Justice Department memorandum to file, "Briefing of USDA-OGC by NDGA re: Criminal Investigation of BNL Atlanta," from Assistant U.S. Attorney Gale McKenzie, June 16, 1992.

141 that exceeded the needs of the entire country.: Federal Reserve System, Board of Governors memorandum, "CCC Credits at BNL," September 29, 1989.

141 Secretary of Agriculture was briefed by his people: Department of Agriculture informational memorandum, "Iraq GSM-102/103 program," from R. E. Anderson, Jr., to Secretary Clayton Yeutter, October 1989.

141 "step in the wrong direction . . . Get it back onto the table!" he instructed his aides: A note of James Baker's instructions at the staff briefing was taken

page

by a senior State Department official and published as part of the record during the hearing before the Banking, Finance and Urban Affairs Committee of the House of Representatives, "The BNL Scandal and the Department of Agriculture's CCC Program for Iraq," May 21, 1992; interviews with congressional investigators, Washington, D.C., June 1993.

142 The investigations had reached "the explosion state" . . . "blow the roof off the CCC.": State Department memorandum of conversation, "USDA Comments on Investigations of Iraq and the Banca Nazionale Del Lavoro, Atlanta Branch, Scandal," prepared by Frank Lemay, October 13, 1989.

142 the unmistakable signature of "James A. Baker, III": "Bush Administration Knew about Arms Network," *Financial Times,* November 11, 1992.

142 "we may be facing a four-alarm blaze in the near future.": State Department memorandum of conversation, October 13, 1989.

142 "I guess I'm the guy who did the wrong thing at the wrong time": Telephone interview with Frank Lemay, July 23, 1993.

142 "We knew Saddam wasn't a saint . . . hunches and assertions.": "Iraq Loans Put What's-His-Name in a Public Role," *The New York Times,* July 13, 1992.

143 "The President has asked me to say . . . my personal attention.": SECRET State Department cable, "Message from the Secretary to Tariq Aziz," from Secretary James Baker to the American embassy, Baghdad, October 21, 1989.

143 reported back from Baghdad . . . in Washington's court.": State Department cable, "Tariq Aziz' Reply to Secretary's Letter," from Ambassador April Glaspie to Secretary of State James Baker, October 24, 1989.

144 "We had a CCC policy . . . the president had signed.": Interview with Abraham Sofaer, Rome, May 22, 1993.

144 "Iraq is now our ninth largest . . . provided there was no further evidence of Iraqi wrongdoing.: State Department action memorandum, from Abraham Sofaer to Robert Kimmitt, May 19, 1990.

144 Baker was then handed talking points . . . "you guys are.": Attachment to State Department action memorandum, "Whether to Push for a Full CCC Program for Iraq," from John Kelly and Abraham Sofaer to Secretary of State James Baker, October 26, 1989.

145 had moved formally to block the decision.: State Department action memorandum, "How to Expedite Approval of a Full CCC Program for Iraq," from John H. Kelly to Lawrence Eagleburger, acting secretary of state, November 6, 1989; State Department, letter from Lawrence Eagleburger to John Robson, deputy secretary of the treasury, urging support for a "full billion dollar program" of export credit guarantees for Iraq during fiscal 1990, November 8, 1989.

145 "We had a lot on BNL . . . We knew all about that one.": Interview with Stephen Danzansky, Washington, D.C., April 30, 1991.

page

146   a string of meetings and conversations: Telephone interview with Stephen
       Danzansky, July 28, 1993.

146   The six-page report . . . the CIA explained.: "Iraq-Italy: Repercussions of
       the BNL Atlanta Scandal," CIA, directorate of intelligence, November 6,
       1989.

146   Jay Bybee, a lawyer in the office of C. Boyden Gray: An indication of
       Bybee's active interest in following the BNL investigation is found in the
       "list of Iraq dates" in the calendar of Alan Raul of the Agriculture Depart-
       ment, cited in the hearing on "The BNL Scandal and the Department of
       Agriculture's CCC Program for Iraq," before the Banking, Finance, and
       Urban Affairs Committee of the House of Representatives, May 21, 1992.

146   Bybee breached normal procedure: Handwritten fax note from Gale
       McKenzie to Jay Bybee, November 9, 1989; "Bush Staff Lawyer's Call on
       Iraq Case Is Reported," *The New York Times,* July 9, 1992.

146   "got the impression they were concerned about embarrassment level.":
       Congressional Record, House of Representatives, statement of Congress-
       man Henry Gonzalez, July 7, 1992, p. 9.

147   "He shouldn't have called Atlanta . . . had them check.": Interview with
       C. Boyden Gray, Washington, D.C., May 27, 1993.

147   "clearly run counter to the President's intention . . . with the Iraqis.":
       National Advisory Council, minutes of deputies meeting, November 8,
       1989.

147   "there was State doing its thing.": Interview with Danzansky, April 30,
       1991.

147   suggested "that you break the news to the Foreign Minister Tariq Aziz.":
       State Department memorandum, "Message to Iraqi Foreign Minister on
       CCC Credits," from Robert Kimmitt to Secretary of State James Baker,
       November 9, 1989.

147   "this decision . . . relationship with Iraq.": State Department cable, "Mes-
       sage to Iraqi Foreign Minister Tariq Aziz," from Secretary of State James
       Baker to American embassy, Baghdad, November 1989.

TEN: See No Evil

148   goods, including computers . . . almost all military establishments: Declas-
       sified SECRET State Department memorandum, Bureau of Oceans and
       International Environmental and Scientific Affairs, "SNEC Cases of Inter-
       est," November 21, 1989.

149   "SNEC policy" . . . go into military projects: Declassified SECRET State
       Department memorandum, November 21, 1989.

150   A similar warning . . . terminal ballistics.": Department of Commerce,
       computer printout of export-license approval, March 22, 1990.

page

150 "State had the policy responsibility ... "We sent a lot.": Telephone interview with Bryan Siebert, July 26, 1993.

150 a $140,000 shipment ... "is involved in military matters.": Department of Commerce, computer printout of export-license approval, November 1, 1989; "Report Says U.S. Exports to Iraq Aided Military," *Financial Times,* June 20, 1991.

150 the Bush administration knew ... an Iraqi surveillance radar system: Telephone interview with Gary Milhollin, director, Wisconsin Project on Nuclear Arms Control, August 9, 1993.

151 "our licensing procedures have been a drag on trade with Iraq.": Declassified CONFIDENTIAL State Department action memorandum, "Licensing for Iraq," from John Kelly to Robert Kimmitt, 1990.

151 concerns by SNEC needed to be balanced "by other considerations ... the overall relationship.": Confidential State Department draft letter, from Robert Kimmitt to Stan Sienkiewicz, Department of Commerce, Washington, D.C., 1990.

151 "If we were selling nuclear equipment ... We did not have a close relationship.": Interview with Abraham Sofaer, Rome, May 22, 1993.

151 "The U.S. granted scores ... 'See no evil, hear no evil, and speak no evil.' ": Telephone interview with Gary Milhollin, July 27, 1993.

151 cleared to supply nuclear-grade vacuum pump oil: Department of Commerce, computer printout of export-license approval, February 17, 1989.

151 "was used or intended for use in Iraqi efforts to establish ... operation capability.": Telephone interview with Gary Milhollin, August 9, 1993.

152 received SNEC approval to buy $661,000 worth: Telephone interview with Milhollin, August 9, 1993; Department of Commerce, computer printout of export-license approval, December 12, 1988.

152 on the morning of December 5, 1989, as a three-stage, eighty-foot-long rocket: Memorandum, "Zeitgeschichtliches Panorama," Bonn, January 4, 1990; translated from the German by the Congressional Research Service, Washington, D.C.

152 a bundle of modified Scud missiles: "Iraqgate," *U.S. News & World Report,* May 18, 1992.

152 "When Saddam sent up his Roman candle ... with this country,": Interview with Dennis Kloske, Washington, D.C., April 10, 1991.

153 "We were being left in a situation ... we were met with indifference.": Interview with Commerce Department official, Washington, D.C., April 11, 1991.

153 Saddam was not ten years away from building an atomic bomb: Interview with Bryan Siebert, Washington, D.C., May 26, 1993.

153 His strategy was to have Admiral James Watkins, the energy secretary: Interview with Siebert, May 26, 1993; Department of Energy draft memorandum, "Recommendations to Strengthen U.S. Nuclear Non-

page

proliferation Policy," from Bryan Siebert, director, Office of Classification and Technology Policy, to Secretary of Energy Admiral James D. Watkins, April 1989.

153 In preparation for a March 24 meeting . . . Iraq's military capabilities: Declassified SECRET State Department briefing memorandum, "Meeting with Iraqi Under-Secretary Nizar Hamdun," from Paul J. Hare to Secretary of State James Baker, March 23, 1990.

154 "At White House meetings . . . complicated questions,": Interview with Siebert, May 26, 1993.

154 "Recent evidence," he wrote . . . "nonproliferation objectives.": Department of Energy draft memorandum, Siebert to Watkins, April 1989.

154 George Bush had proclaimed: President George Bush, State of the Union message, February 9, 1989.

154 He felt relieved . . . dismissed as overly alarmist by Robert Walsh: Interview with Siebert, May 26, 1993.

154 "uncomfortable with a Secretarial level initiative. . . . premature.": Department of Energy draft memorandum, "Comments on Export Control Initiative," from Robert J. Walsh, deputy assistant secretary for intelligence, defense programs, April 1989.

155 "I would bet my job . . . stop it is now.": U.S. House of Representatives, the Committee on Energy and Commerce, Subcommittee on Oversight and Investigations, hearing, "Failed Efforts to Curtail Iraq's Nuclear Weapons Program," April 24, 1991, p. 67.

155 left with lesser responsibilities: Subcommittee on Oversight and Investigations hearing, p. 71.

155 had invited two Iraqi nuclear scientists to visit Portland, Oregon: Subcommittee on Oversight and Investigations hearing, pp. 367–400.

155 "In a nutshell . . . weapon proliferant.": Department of Energy, memorandum, from Richard A. Claytor, assistant secretary for defense programs, to Steve May, December 5, 1990.

155 "On two occasions he accompanied Admiral Watkins . . . unable or unwilling to see the big picture.": Telephone interview with Siebert, July 26, 1993.

156 "Siebert's goal . . . weren't even sure what had happened.": Telephone interview with Siebert, August 8, 1993.

156 "During the Reagan administration . . . he wanted to help Iraq.": Interview with former White House official, Washington, D.C., May 27, 1993.

157 "It was policy. . . . didn't really care.": Interview with U.S. intelligence officer, Washington, D.C., May 17, 1993.

157 a waiver . . . "not in the national interest of the United States.": "Application of Export-Import Bank Restrictions in Connection with Iraq," Presidential Determination number 90-07, January 17, 1990.

157 Saddam was once again eligible . . . some $200 million worth.: Declassified

page

SECRET State Department memorandum, "NSC Deputies Committee Meeting on Iraq," from John Kelly to Robert Kimmitt, April 16, 1990.

157 "If Arabs are not careful, they will see the Gulf governed by U.S. will,": Elaine Sciolino, *The Outlaw State* (New York: John Wiley, 1991), pp. 196–97.

158 called to account when their newspapers published articles: Banca Nazionale del Lavoro, report of Paolo Di Vito, November 24, 1989.

158 "considerable adverse Congressional reaction . . . the Condor missile.": Department of Agriculture, Foreign Agriculture Service memorandum, "Pros and Cons for Announcing Additional Coverage under Iraq's GSM-102/103 Export Credit Guarantee Program," from F. Paul Dickerson, associate administrator, to R. E. Anderson, administrator, February 23, 1990.

158 intercepted a shipment of nuclear detonators: "Iraqi bid to Acquire N-arms Parts Foiled at Heathrow," *Financial Times,* March 29, 1990.

158 "As you suspected . . . some of this material.": Federal Reserve Bank of New York memorandum, "Lavoro," from Thomas C. Baxter, Jr., to Gerald Corrigan, April 5, 1990.

159 "We can make these in our own factories,": ABC News, *A Line in the Sand,* broadcast September 11, 1990, transcript p. 4.

159 Wearing a general's insignia, Saddam delivered a chilling speech: Pierre Salinger with Eric Laurent, *Secret Dossier: The Hidden Agenda Behind the Gulf War* (New York: Viking Penguin, 1991), p. 21.

159 "We don't need an atomic bomb . . .": "Saddam Threatens Israel with Chemical Weapons," United Press International, April 2, 1990.

159 ". . . let our fire eat half of Israel": "Iraq Threatens to Attack Israel with Chemical Weapons," Reuters, April 2, 1990.

159 "I think these statements . . . chemical or biological weapons be forgotten.": Salinger with Laurent, *Secret Dossier,* p. 22.

160 "He indicated . . . image of his government and his country,": "Hussein Tells Dole Iraq Ready to Destroy Weapons," United Press International, April 12, 1990.

160 "I believe that your problems . . . political geniuses.": Salinger with Laurent, *Secret Dossier,* p. 25; Sciolino, *Outlaw State,* p. 175.

160 prepared to destroy all of Iraq's weapons of mass destruction: "Hussein tells Dole," United Press International.

160 "assured me . . . better relations with Iraq.": Salinger with Laurent, *Secret Dossier,* p. 25.

161 a secret cable to the U.S. embassy . . . "telling Israel so.": Declassified SECRET State Department cable, "Tensions in U.S.-Iraqi Relations Demarche," from Secretary of State James Baker to Ambassador April Glaspie, April 12, 1990.

161 Bush told him he hoped that ties between the United States and Iraq: Salinger with Laurent, *Secret Dossier,* p. 27.

page

161 Kelly laid out the problem . . . Iraq's nuclear or missile programs.: Declassified SECRET State Department memorandum, "NSC Deputies Committee Meeting on Iraq," April 16, 1990.

162 "We had already labeled" . . . measures "that singled out Iraq.": Interview with Commerce Department official, Washington, D.C., April 11, 1991.

162 "State effectively told him to get out of our face.": Interview with senior Commerce Department official, Washington, D.C., April 11, 1991.

162 a House Foreign Affairs subcommittee . . . actively pursuing a nuclear weapons capability.": House of Representatives, Middle East Subcommittee of the House Foreign Affairs Committee, hearing, "U.S.-Iraq relations," witness, John Kelly, April 26, 1990.

163 a list of policy options: Declassified SECRET National Security Council memorandum, "Iraq: Options Paper," May 16, 1990.

163 "oil provides the wherewithal . . . production capacity.": "Iraq: Options Paper," May 16, 1990.

163 The CIA calculated . . . a quarter of Iraq's total oil exports.: "Iraq: No End in Sight to Debt Burden," CIA, directorate of intelligence, April 12, 1990, p. 5.

163 exceeding agreed-upon quotas on oil production: Mohamed Heikal, *Illusions of Triumph* (London: HarperCollins, 1992), p. 170.

164 "needed to return to its economic situation of 1980.": Excerpted from personal minutes of the closed sessions of the Baghdad Arab summit meeting, prepared by one of the participants, May 28, 1990.

164 "If we believe that the agreement . . . protect our national interests,": Heikal, *Illusions,* p. 163.

ELEVEN: And So to War . . .

165 "We are not ruling any options in, . . . It has stood me very well in Parliament.": Lawrence Freedman and Efraim Karsh, *The Gulf Conflict* (London: Faber and Faber, 1993), p. 74.; "Thatcher to Cut Short Aspen Visit," *Denver Post,* August 5, 1990.

165 The list of policy options . . . soft on Saddam.": Declassified SECRET National Security Council memorandum, "Iraq: Options Paper," May 16, 1990.

166 intelligence photographs that showed Iraqi troops transporting ammunition . . . travel long distances.: Mark Perry, *Eclipse* (New York: William Morrow, 1992), p. 354.

166 "Let me reassure you . . . "another busted signal.": "Bush Policy Toward Iraq Emerging as Possible Achilles Heel," *The Los Angeles Times,* October 13, 1992; "Without a Compass," *Foreign Service Journal,* January 1991.

page

166 "We were already seeing troops moving . . . much more threatening,":
"Pentagon Objected to Bush's Message to Iraq," *The New York Times,*
October 25, 1992.

167 Waldegrave, a senior Foreign Office official, . . . drum up business.: "The
Scott Inquiry: MPs Misled by Ministers," *The Daily Telegraph,* July 16,
1993.

167 "the big prize": "MPs Were Misled by Foreign Office," *Financial Times,*
July 16, 1993.

167 "I doubt if there is any future market . . . would make this more difficult,":
"MPs Were Misled," *Financial Times.*

167 Iraq had been secretly provided with details . . . while they were airborne.:
ABC News, *Nightline,* July 1, 1992; "Sea of Lies," *Newsweek,* July 13, 1992.

167 the man who held direct responsibility . . . White House strategy toward
Iraq.: *Congressional Record,* House of Representatives, statement of Congressman Henry Gonzalez, March 9, 1992, H1109; interview with U.S.
intelligence officer, New York, March 22, 1993.

168 An options paper that was prepared that May . . . latter view that prevailed.:
National Security Council memorandum, May 16, 1990; interview with
U.S. intelligence officer, March 22, 1993.

168 There were those . . . U.S. surveillance.: "U.S. Gave Data to Iraq Three
Months Before Invasion," *The Los Angeles Times,* March 10, 1992; interview with U.S. intelligence officer, March 22, 1993.

168 in the company of Soviet foreign minister Eduard Shevardnadze: "U.S.,
Soviets Cut Deal, Make History," Associated Press, August 4, 1990.

169 UN Security Council voted overwhelmingly on August 6: Elaine Sciolino,
The Outlaw State (New York: John Wiley, 1991), p. 222.

169 most of the hard work was done by Thomas Pickering: Interview with State
Department official, Washington, D.C., April 1991.

169 calls for Baker's resignation appeared in the media: "U.S. Policy Failure in
the Middle East—James Baker Should Resign," *The New Republic,* November 5, 1990.

169 "During most of the post-Cold War period . . . Scowcroft, Cheney, and
their staffs.": "The Scrambling Vicar," *National Journal,* April 20, 1991.

169 The idea was dismissed as "ludicrous". . . take a break.: "Baker Back in the
Saddle at the State Department," *The Washington Post,* August 29, 1990.

170 a financial conflict-of-interest waiver . . . the Iraqi invasion of Kuwait.":
White House memorandum, "Conflict-of-Interest Waiver," from the president to the attorney general, August 8, 1990.

170 "I insisted we couldn't afford to take any chances, . . . get it so goddamn
wrong.": Interview with Boyden Gray, Washington, D.C., May 5, 1993.

170 "As you know . . . the resolution of situations that may arise.": Memorandum, "Conflict-of-Interest Waiver," August 8, 1990.

170 not even Baker himself was to be given a copy . . . directly involving oil

page

production and prices.": State Department memorandum, from the Office of Legal Counsel to Robert Kimmitt, August 8, 1990.

170   the holdings of Baker and his immediate family . . . in oil wells or leases.: State Department memorandum, "Recusal from Participation," from Secretary James Baker to undersecretary for political affairs et al., January 25, 1989, with attachment "Holdings of James A Baker III, and his immediate family, January 25, 1989."

171   Weeks before the invasion . . . arms shipments to Iraq that were transiting through Jordan.: Interview with U.S. intelligence officer, Washington, D.C., May 17, 1993; telephone interview with Yossef Bodansky, July 17, 1993.

171   Jordan had refused to join Saudi Arabia, Kuwait, and Egypt . . . the king's stance.: "Jordan Gave Iraq Broad Assistance, Papers Show," *The Los Angeles Times,* November 29, 1992.

171   television pictures showed trucks . . . destined for Iraq.: "King Hussein Leaves Road to Baghdad Open," ABC News, *World News Tonight,* August 13, 1990.

172   officials from Baker's State Department . . . new arms exports to Jordan.: General Accounting Office (GAO), report, "Jordan: Suspension of U.S. Military Assistance During Gulf Crisis," September 1992.

172   intelligence briefings . . . on to Baghdad.: "U.S. Ignored Alert on Arms to Baghdad," *Financial Times,* April 17, 1991.

172   the flow of weapons from the United States to Jordan in fact continued: GAO report, "Jordan," p. 5.

172   that Jordan was fronting as an arms buyer for Iraq . . . "Jorq.": Interview with former Department of Trade and Industry official, London, July 9, 1993.

172   "We'd had a forty-year relationship . . . let them have it.": Interview with former British cabinet minister, London, July 8, 1993.

172   On August 31 . . . "quite far apart.": "Crisis in the Gulf: King Hussein's Hopes Dashed at Downing Street," *The Independent,* September 1, 1990.

172   "We did appreciate the difficulties . . . very frosty indeed.": Interview with former senior government official, London, July 9, 1993.

173   business-as-usual approach . . . liable to be diverted to Iraq.: "Sale Cleared after Check on Kuwait," *Financial Times,* June 23, 1993; "Guns and Ruses," *The Guardian,* July 5, 1993.

173   "Hitler revisited": "Hussein Is a Hitler," *Newsday,* October 16, 1990.

173   "The economic lifeline of the industrial world" . . . something of a stretch.: "U.S. Jobs at Stake in Gulf, Baker Says," *The New York Times,* November 14, 1990; "Not Oil nor Jobs," *The New York Times,* November 19, 1990; "On the Job Priorities," *The Washington Post,* November 22, 1990.

174   "Those who would measure the timetable . . . a real sense of urgency.": *Facts on File,* November 22, 1990.

page

174   local office of the CIA on the line . . . Jordan on an assignment.: Interview with Fred Haobsh, Dallas, April 6, 1992. A series of tape-recorded and videotaped interviews with Haobsh was conducted in various locations between April 1992 and May 1993. Haobsh made available to the author his complete travel diaries, passports, airline tickets, and expense reports for the periods covered. In addition, he provided copies of the business cards of his contacts and copies of the reports he filed with the CIA.

175   Anas Dohan, a man who ranked: Interview with Haobsh, New York, March 30, 1993; interview with U.S. intelligence officer, New York, July 1, 1993.

175   Haobsh and Dohan talked over a period of twenty-four hours . . . to Jordan, for transshipment to Iraq.: Interview series with Haobsh.

176   Twenty-four hours later, in a safe house across the Potomac . . . as soon as possible.: Interview with Haobsh, March 1, 1993.

176   "get in touch with Union Carbide . . . It did not seem to bother them.": Interview with Haobsh, March 1, 1993.

177   Hurd had just announced . . . "within a few days.": "Hurd Against UN Veto on Use of Force in the Gulf," *The Times,* September 8, 1990.

177   Despite the jittery times . . . "was to sell weapons to Iraq.": Interview with Haobsh, March 1, 1993.

178   "disturbing reports . . . most dangerous terrorist organizations in existence.": Declassified SECRET State Department cable, "Iraq and Terrorism," from Secretary of State James Baker to Ambassador April Glaspie, Baghdad, June 27, 1990.

178   "Sometimes, . . . you have to get your hands dirty.": Interview with U.S. intelligence officer, March 22, 1993.

178   an extraordinary deal was implemented . . . They didn't really want to know,": Interview with U.S. intelligence officer, Washington, D.C., May 17, 1993.

179   Washington had learned of Saddam's links to Abu Abbas: Declassified SECRET/SENSITIVE State Department information memorandum, "Iraq's Retreat from International Terrorism," from Frank McNeil to Secretary Shultz, July 1, 1986.

179   State Department knew that shortly thereafter, Abu Abbas had been permitted to take refuge in Iraq.: State Department information memorandum, July 1, 1986.

179   Judge William Clark undertook a secret mission to Baghdad . . . flew to Saddam in the Iran-Iraq war.: Conversation with a former senior Reagan administration official, August 2, 1993.

179   "a letter addressed to Saddam Hussein . . . will pay a terrible price.": Micah Sifry and Christopher Cerf, *The Gulf War Reader* (New York: Times Books, 1991), pp. 178–79.

page
179   Aziz responded to Baker . . . we will not yield to threats.": Sifry and Cerf,
      Reader, pp. 173–75.
180   "I realized this was it: we were going to war," he thought to himself.:
      Norman Schwarzkopf, *It Doesn't Take a Hero* (New York: Bantam Books,
      1992), p. 408.
180   The cluster bomb factories that Carlos Cardoen had supplied and built
      were among the very first targets.: "How U.S. Arms and Technology Were
      Transferred to Iraq," ABC News, *Nightline,* September 13, 1991.
180   All the paperwork covering Dohan's order of graphite . . . the price quota-
      tions.: Copies of specifications and price details, and Union Carbide corre-
      spondence with Haobsh.
181   Another CIA agent who would be . . . from Marietta, Georgia.: Interview
      with Haobsh, March 1, 1993.
181   "He explained that Iraq had at least 150 Scud missiles . . . there were only
      thirty-six,": Interview with Haobsh, March 1, 1993.
181   "The technical specifications and prices . . . and I became frightened.":
      Interview with Haobsh, April 6, 1992.
181   for their Agency debriefing . . . " 'Great,' she said, 'now we're going to sell
      Saddam some missiles,' " recalled Haobsh.: Interview with Haobsh, March
      1, 1993.
182   offering him twenty-five SAM 7 and twenty-five SAM 16 shoulder-fired
      missiles: Fax letter on his company letterhead, from Fred Haobsh to office
      of Anas Dohan, February 4, 1991.
182   had already shot down some U.S. Marines' Harrier jump-jets: "Stinger-style
      SAM Detailed," *Jane's Defence Weekly,* July 20, 1991.
182   "Dear Fred . . . when the matter is solved.": Fax message to Fred Haobsh,
      timed at 12:36 P.M., May 18, 1991.
182   "on February 28, the day after Desert Storm was over . . . with the CIA.":
      Interview with Haobsh, Dallas, April 7, 1992.

TWELVE: Justice Delayed

184   "Here it is folks, the Mother of all Indictments.": Justice Department press
      conference with Attorney General Richard Thornburgh and Bob Mueller,
      assistant attorney general, Criminal Division, Washington, D.C., February
      28, 1991.
186   "Reading from a prepared text . . . may cause some exposure to the U.S.":
      Justice Department press conference, February 28, 1991, transcript.
186   "As he listened to the next questioner . . . and we always get our man, one
      way or the other!": Justice Department press conference, February 28,
      1991, transcript.
188   the first time indictments . . . autumn of 1989.: Frederick B. Lacey, *Report*

of the Independent Counsel, the Banca Nazionale Del Lavoro Investigation, December 8, 1992, p. 37.

188 the rather unusual practice . . . Drogoul's statements.: Federal Reserve Bank of Atlanta confidential memorandum, "Information on Banca Nazionale Del Lavoro Atlanta Agency," from Madeline Marsden to Zane R. Kelley, vice-president, September 25, 1989.

188 A memorandum reflecting that meeting . . . "things could be different.": Federal Reserve Bank of New York office memorandum, "Banca Nazionale Del Lavoro," from Thomas C. Baxter to Corrigan, Oltman, Patrikis et al., September 12, 1989.

189 Mueller of the Justice Department . . . overtones of the situation.: Lacey, *Report of the Independent Counsel,* p. 37.

189 a senior lawyer at the New York Federal Reserve . . . "reviewed by main Justice.": Federal Reserve Bank of New York office memorandum to legal files, "Recent Developments Regarding Banca Nazionale Del Lavoro," from Ernest T. Patrikis, February 6, 1990.

189 "willing to sacrifice one individual": Federal Reserve Bank memorandum, February 6, 1990.

190 When her superiors asked her . . . "assume anything of that nature.": U.S. Senate, Select Committee on Intelligence, *The Intelligence Community's Involvement in the Banca Nazionale Del Lavoro (BNL) Affair,* 103rd Cong., 1st sess., February 1993, p. 67.

190 McKenzie and Bob Mueller discussed . . . abuses in the CCC program.: Senate Select Committee on Intelligence, *Intelligence Community's Involvement,* p. 67.

190 Baker's legal advisers told Agriculture . . . to Baghdad in advance.: State Department memorandum, "Seeking Iraq's Cooperation Regarding Certain Allegations," from State Department deputy legal adviser to Allan Charles Raul, general counsel, Department of Agriculture, February 14, 1990.

190 She balked . . . with a list of questions in advance.: Lacey, *Report of the Independent Counsel,* p. 136.

190 Instead of going to Baghdad . . . to the United States for questioning.: Senate Select Committee on Intelligence, *Intelligence Community's Involvement,* p. 67.

190 a lengthy prosecution memorandum . . . the first half of her probe.: Lacey, *Report of the Independent Counsel,* p. 53.

191 Robert Kimmitt . . . area of nuclear proliferation.: State Department memorandum, "Meeting on Iraq," from Robert Kimmitt to Secretary of State James Baker, April 17, 1990.

191 They returned bubbling with enthusiasm . . . promised to end the practice.: Select Committee on Intelligence, *Intelligence Community's Involvement,* p. 68; State Department cable, "USDA Team Meetings with GOI Min-

trade," from Ambassador April Glaspie, Baghdad, to Secretary of State James Baker, April 22, 1990.

191 It was passed on . . . and was traveling overseas.: Lacey, *Report of the Independent Counsel,* p. 97.

191 dashed off a memorandum . . ."violations" that she had found.: Senate Select Committee on Intelligence, *Intelligence Community's Involvement,* p. 68.

191 other BNL investigators, . . . "Justice Department in Washington.": Federal Reserve Bank of New York office memorandum, "Lavoro," from Thomas C. Baxter to Gerald Corrigan, April 5, 1990.

192 McKenzie fired a second shot . . . it would put the Justice Department "in a position of misleading Congress.": Justice Department memorandum, "Northern District of Georgia, Recommendation to Decline DOJ Clearance of USDA Report of Administrative Review of Iraq GSM-102 Program," from Gale McKenzie, assistant U.S. attorney, to Larry Urgenson, chief of Fraud Section, Justice Department, May 21, 1990.

192 On May 18, 1990, Scowcroft telephoned Clayton Yeutter, . . . "saying we are terminating the program.": Handwritten notes taken by Treasury Department staff lawyer.

192 a special review would have to be held at the White House . . . he told Yeutter.: Declassified SECRET State Department memorandum, "Weekly Report," to legal adviser Abraham D. Sofaer, May 18, 1990.

192 "We would be shooting ourselves in the foot," . . . and policy options.: State Department briefing memorandum, "NSC Deputies Committee Meeting on Iraq, May 29, 1990: White House Situation Room 4.30 pm," from John H. Kelly to Robert Kimmitt, May 26, 1990.

192 McKenzie met with officials from State . . . until the investigation in Atlanta was completed.: Senate Select Committee on Intelligence, *Intelligence Community's Involvement,* p. 69.

193 admitted later . . . "complex both legally and because of foreign policy concerns.": "Investigators Say U.S. Shielded Iraqis from Bank Inquiry," *The New York Times,* March 20, 1992.

193 in the spring of 1990, . . . "I still have no idea why.": Telephone interview with William Hinshaw II, September 8, 1993.

193 Yet when the Treasury official . . . "That's classified information.": Interview with senior official in the Treasury Department, Office of Foreign Assets Control, Washington, D.C., October 1990.

193 one prominent exception . . . "illegally acquiring critical weapons technology.": "U.S. Knew Firm Was Iraq's a Year Before It Was Closed," *The Los Angeles Times,* July 24, 1992.

194 "was brokering a whole host . . . their missile development sites."; "U.S. Officials Ignored Objections to 'Dual Use' Export to Iraq," *Financial Times,* September 19, 1990.

page

194 "our best attempt . . . contact Chairman Gonzalez directly.": Justice Department memorandum, "Talking Points for Telephone Call to Chairman Gonzalez," from Lee Rawls, acting assistant attorney general, to Richard Thornburgh, attorney general, September 1990.

194 "The purpose of this letter . . . case with national security concerns,": Letter from Richard Thornburgh, attorney general, to Henry B. Gonzalez, chairman of the House Banking, Finance and Urban Affairs Committee, September 26, 1990.

194 A memo was hastily drafted . . . "now that Joe Whitley is in place?": Justice Department memorandum, "BNL," from Peter Clark, September 21, 1990.

195 the more the Atlanta team examined the BNL case, . . . at CIA headquarters: Justice Department memorandum, Northern District of Georgia, "Banca Nazionale Del Lavoro (BNL) Investigation," from Joe Whitley and Rimantas Rukstele, Atlanta, to Mark Richard, deputy assistant attorney general, Department of Justice, July 3, 1990.

195 By December 1989, Whitley had written . . . promises of credit to Matrix Churchill.: Telephone interview with Kenneth Milwood, former partner with Smith, Gambrell, August 3, 1993.

196 "although it could be argued . . . as the case progresses.": Justice Department memorandum, Northern District of Georgia, "Banca Nazionale Del Lavoro," from Joe D. Whitley to Gale McKenzie, June 8, 1990.

196 "Whitley's Recusal . . . it was disappointing.": "The Crimes of Iraqgate, II," *The New York Times,* May 25, 1992.

196 Justice Department officials . . . might have to be "readdressed via Joe Whitley.": Justice Department memorandum, "Banca Nazionale Del Lavoro," from Peter B. Clark to Laurence A. Urgenson, chief, Fraud Section, Department of Justice, February 25, 1991.

197 "One guy was dead . . . work with them after the war.": Interview with former legal adviser to the State Department, Washington, D.C., June 7, 1993.

197 Prepared by State Department aides . . . is willing to carry the argument with Representative Gonzalez.": Declassified SECRET State Department action memorandum, "Proposed Indictments in the BNL Case," to Robert Kimmitt, February 25, 1991.

197 "Don't indict them, just destroy them.": Interview with former U.S. government official who participated in the White House deliberations, Washington, D.C., June 7, 1993.

197 they did single out one man . . . His indictment would be seen as a further U.S. attempt to 'punish' Jordan.": State Department action memorandum, February 25, 1991.

198 State implied that the indictment would be a personal affront to the king of Jordan: *Congressional Record,* House of Representatives, "BNL indictment

page

delayed and Thornburgh misled Congress," Statement of Congressman
Henry Gonzalez, March 30, 1992.

198   a 516-count indictment against twelve defendants . . . against eleven defendants.": "Prosecutors Surmised Early That Case Was More Than a Bank
Scandal," *The Washington Post,* October 20, 1992.

198   "the really important question to ask is who in the bank knew.": Interview
with Giulio Andreotti, Rome, May 21, 1993.

198   "The folks representing BNL did a very good job of directing the U.S.
government, and the prosecutors fell for it.": Telephone interview with
former law partner of Joe Whitley, August 3, 1993.

199   a disturbing report from Joseph Wilson . . . "strong suspicion of complicity
in the BNL financial scandal.": CONFIDENTIAL State Department cable,
"BNL Bank Scandal," from American embassy, Baghdad, to Secretary of
State James Baker, September 13, 1989.

199   at least six U.S. intelligence reports that were widely disseminated inside
the Bush administration: Senate Select Committee on Intelligence, *Intelligence Community's Involvement,* pp. 60, 63.

199   Cantoni expressed his concerns . . . "they want to achieve some kind of
damage control.": CONFIDENTIAL State Department cable, "Banca
Nazionale Del Lavoro Concerns re Atlanta Branch," from Ambassador
Peter Secchia, Rome, to Secretary of State James Baker, October 26, 1989.

200   Rome "appears pleased at the low-key manner in which Washington has
reacted.": CIA, "Iraq-Italy: Repercussions of the BNL-Atlanta Scandal,"
November 6, 1989.

200   ". . . the orders were to keep paying and keep quiet,": Interview with former
BNL executive, Rome, April 5, 1993.

200   ". . . even though the loans were bogus and the end-users were Iraqi
military installations. It was terrible,": Interview with former BNL executive, Rome, May 22, 1993.

201   Andreotti called in his treasury minister for a talk.: Italian Treasury Ministry
memorandum, from Treasury Minister Guido Carli to BNL chairman
Giampero Cantoni, December 7, 1989.

201   a top secret report from SISMI: TOP SECRET report from SISMI, the Italian
Military Intelligence Service, to Prime Minister Giulio Andreotti, September 14, 1989.

201   That same evening Carli sat down with the Iraqi minister: Memorandum
from Carli to Cantoni, December 7, 1989.

201   Carli went before the Italian parliament . . . on behalf of Iraq.: "Carli Says
BNL's Rome Headquarters Involved in Scandal," *Financial Times,* December 15, 1989.

201   In Langley, . . . filed a classified report confirming Carli's conclusion.:
Senate Select Committee on Intelligence, *Intelligence Community's Involvement,* p. 63.

page

201 "We were obligated, in banking and legal terms,": Interview with Andreotti, May 21, 1993.

201 "The meeting lasted two days . . . little aside from details to negotiate.": Interview with BNL executive who participated in the negotiations, Rome, April 5, 1993.

201 "The most important element . . . the complex Italo-Iraqi relationship.": Paolo Di Vito, daily diary, January 3, 1990. Di Vito's diaries describe his frenetic and itinerant life. Among other things, he was responsible for keeping in touch with dozens of company officials, other bankers, diplomats, politicians, and lawyers.

202 Drogoul planned to charge that BNL management had been aware: Di Vito, daily diary, January 4, 1990.

202 "with the principal aim of solidifying BNL's role as victim . . . from Drogoul's defenders.": Di Vito, daily diary, February 8, 1990.

202 "the situation seems to be sliding . . . to a more markedly political one.": Di Vito, daily diary, March 6, 1990.

202 his briefing papers had included a review of the status of the BNL investigation.: Lacey, *Report of the Independent Counsel,* p. 51.

203 steps would need to be taken: Di Vito, daily diary, March 14, 1990.

203 "What worries us is that the bank might be indicted.": Interview with former Italian government official, New York, March 29, 1993.

203 "The foreign minister is personally concerned,": Interview with senior Italian government official, Rome, May 21, 1993.

203 "This is a bank that belongs to the Treasury ministry,": Interview with Andreotti, May 21, 1993.

204 "Why worry now? There won't be any surprises,": Di Vito, daily diary, March 21, 1990.

204 "taking advantage of access at political levels appears more promising,": Di Vito, daily diary, March 23, 1990.

204 "The Attorney General promised to treat the issue with absolute fairness,": "Court Is Told BNL Attempted to Limit Inquiry," *The Wall Street Journal,* October 1, 1992; "Envoy Pressed U.S., Loan Case Document Shows," *The Los Angeles Times,* October 1, 1992.

204 BNL's lawyers should go directly to the Department of Justice: Di Vito, daily diary, April 4, 1990.

204 "serious government of Italy concern over the possible federal indictment of the state-owned BNL.": "Italian Pressure Cited in Iraq Fraud Case," *The Los Angeles Times,* September 29, 1992.

204 Cantoni asked for help in finding some high-powered Washington lawyers: Interviews with former Italian government official and former BNL executive, Rome, April 6, 1993.

205 legal counsel to *both* BNL and the Italian government.: Di Vito, daily diary, April 5, 1990.

page
205   Di Vito received a call from Atlanta . . . target of indictment.: Di Vito, daily
         diary, May 30, 1990.
205   "We were all much more tranquil at that point,": Interview with former
         Italian government official, New York, March 29, 1993.
205   Cantoni "expressed once more . . . go slowly before making indictments.":
         CONFIDENTIAL State Department cable, "BNL Atlanta Concerns re At-
         lanta and a Partner," from Ambassador Peter Secchia to Secretary of State
         James Baker, July 25, 1990.
205   When asked later if Rome had exerted . . . made at the Department of
         Justice.": Interview with Boyden Gray, Washington, D.C., May 27, 1993.
206   "substantial and formidable obstruction" . . . Justice Department.: "Wash-
         ington Accused of Iraq Loans Cover-up," *Financial Times,* February 1, 1991.
206   "our boys" could face death . . . the American taxpayer.: *Congressional
         Record,* House of Representatives, Committee on Banking, Finance and
         Urban Affairs, Investigation of Banca Nazionale Del Lavoro, statement of
         Congressman Henry Gonzalez, February 21, 1991, H1111.
206   "We are obstructed blatantly, premeditatedly and coldly,": *Congressional
         Record,* statement of Congressman Gonzalez, February 21, 1991, H1114.
206   "Legitimate objections were made and clear-cut national security informa-
         tion provided, . . ." Senate Select Committee on Intelligence, *Intelligence
         Community's Involvement,* chronology 1984–1992.
207   one official, . . . "going to be more careful in the future,": "Washington
         Gave Green Light to Iraq Sales," *Financial Times,* March 12, 1991.
207   Embarrassing revelations . . . companies were BNL-funded.: "U.S. Will
         Reveal Alleged Iraqi Front Companies," *Financial Times,* March 30, 1991.
207   Dan Pettus, . . . "everybody in the U.S. government has known since 1988
         that we were hired by Mr. Cardoen.": "Prototype of Helicopter Seized in
         Texas," *Financial Times,* March 28, 1991.
207   "the BushBaker policy was appeasement of the dictator.": William Safire,
         "I'll Remember April," *The New York Times,* March 25, 1991.
208   "wanted to let the documents go and hope it would look like we had
         nothing to hide.": Interview with former White House official who partici-
         pated in the Rostow group meetings, Washington, D.C., June 7, 1993.

THIRTEEN: The White House Steers the Cover-Up

209   seated around a long table, they listened to Nicholas Rostow: Interview
         with former White House official, Washington, D.C., June 7, 1993.
209   the first of a dozen "fairly straightforward meetings": Interview with
         C. Boyden Gray, Washington, D.C., May 27, 1993.
209   a letter to Brent Scowcroft seeking a copy of National Security Directive
         26.: House of Representatives, letter from John Dingell, chairman, Sub-
         committee on Oversight and Investigations, Committee on Energy and
         Commerce, to National Security Adviser Brent Scowcroft, March 21, 1991.

page

209 "Stiff-arming," a State Department official who was present ... "won't work.": Handwritten notes taken by State Department participant at White House meeting of Rostow group, April 8, 1991.

209 Rostow wrote a memorandum ... requests pertaining to "the BNL/CCC matters.": National Security Council memorandum, "Meeting on Congressional Requests for Information and Documents," from Nicholas Rostow, special assistant to the president and legal adviser, to C. Boyden Gray, White House counsel, and lawyers from State, Commerce, Treasury, Agriculture, Defense departments and the Central Intelligence Agency, April 8, 1991.

210 The Commerce Department's top export official ... opposition to halting the sales to Iraq.: "Official Reported to Face Ouster After His Dissent on Iraq Exports," *The New York Times,* April 10, 1991.

211 when asked if Sununu had fired him, Fitzwater ... "I don't know.": "Mosbacher Says Export Official Will Stay Until Resignation Date," Associated Press, April 11, 1991.

211 "Firing a government official ... the way our government is supposed to work.": "U.S. Accused of Iraq Exports Cover-Up," *Financial Times,* April 11, 1991.

211 "It was a really scary thing, ... would all point the finger.": Interview with Stephen Rademaker, former White House official, Washington, D.C., June 7, 1993.

211 "It is normal ... over a period of several months,": Interview with former U.S. government official, Washington, D.C., June 6, 1993.

211 "a bunker mentality.": Interview with former State Department official, Washington, D.C., June 7, 1993.

211 "there was really a high level of discomfort ... just kept scheduling more meetings.": Interview with former White House official, Washington, D.C., June 7, 1993.

212 He ended up as one of the principal writers of the commission's report.: "Washington Talk: The Tower Commission; Those Who Labored on the Report," *The New York Times,* March 3, 1987.

212 "important statutory and constitutional issues": "The White House Won't Give Up Documents on Noriega Drug Info," The Associated Press, August 19, 1988.

213 "that Tower is the President's nominee.": "NSC Aide Plays Down Warning to Secretary," *The Washington Post,* February 25, 1989.

213 "Political vulnerability" was the heading ... "largely, we were feeding the Iraqi army.": Handwritten notes taken by State Department participant at White House meeting of Rostow group, April 9, 1991.

213 a Justice Department official ... "to control the process.": Handwritten notes taken by State Department participant at White House meeting of Rostow group, April 15, 1991.

page

214 "The Secretary would have to appear ... then try to enforce crime.":
Handwritten notes taken at White House meeting of Rostow group concerning Commerce secretary Robert Mosbacher, spring 1991.

214 Gray lectured the Rostow group ... executive privilege where appropriate.: House of Representatives, Committee on Banking, Finance and Urban Affairs, statement of Michael Cifrino, senior attorney, Office of the Deputy General Counsel, International Affairs and Intelligence, Department of Defense, May 29, 1992.

214 "He suggested bringing in ... agencies are making the same cut.": Handwritten notes taken by State Department participant at meeting of the Rostow group, June 5, 1991. The notes refer to remarks by Boyden Gray.

214 "Doesn't it look bad ... this is the Executive Branch.": Interview with former government official who participated in Rostow group meetings, Washington, D.C., June 7, 1992.

214 Wendell Willkie ... "issues raised by the request" for Iraq-related documents.: Commerce Department, information memorandum, "Gejdenson request for Iraq information," by Wendell L. Willkie II, June 6, 1991.

214 "I remember one of the meetings ... Boyden got up and walked out.": Interview with former White House official who participated in Rostow group meetings, Washington, D.C., June 7, 1993.

215 Handwritten notes taken at Rostow group meetings by government lawyer, spring 1991. During interviews in Washington in June 1993, the notes in question were shown to three other participants at the meetings, who confirmed their authenticity and the accuracy of the events described. According to these three participants, the personal involvement of President Bush in the Rostow group process was the result of his being consulted by Brent Scowcroft and James Baker.

215 "Baker did not want to get into a shoot-out with Congress. . . . had a set-to about it.": Interview with former U.S. government official, Washington, D.C., June 6, 1993.

215 "involved personally in one decision.": Interview with C. Boyden Gray, Washington, D.C., May 27, 1993.

215 "I don't want to be the on-the-record source ... talked with Brent extensively about it.": Interview with former White House official, Washington, D.C., June 7, 1993.

216 "The President ... was worried about it.": Interview with former U.S. government official, Washington, D.C., June 6, 1993.

216 "When you're a lawyer at the White House ... a potential hand grenade.": Interview with Stephen Rademaker, Washington, D.C., June 7, 1993.

216 christened them "the Rostow gang" ... "the machinery of this administration.": *Congressional Record,* House of Representatives, Committee on Banking, Finance and Urban Affairs, statement of Congressman Henry Gonzalez, March 16, 1992, H1276.

page
216 On June 4, 1991, the inspector general . . . were "unjustified and mislead-
     ing.": House of Representatives, Committee on the Judiciary, testimony of
     Congressman Doug Barnard, Jr., chairman, Subcommittee on Commerce
     and Monetary Affairs, House Committee on Government Operations, June
     2, 1992.

217 Commerce had prepared . . . "White House guidance not to provide infor-
     mation . . .": Commerce Department memorandum, "Iraq Printout," from
     Dennis Kloske to Wendell L. Willkie II, February 26, 1991.

217 an intelligence report . . . during allied bombings.: Interview with U.S.
     intelligence officer, Washington, D.C., June 12, 1991.

217 both photographic evidence . . . turning himself in.: "U.S. Finds Iraq Still
     Has N-capacity," *Financial Times,* June 13, 1991.

217 in specially hollowed-out oil tanker trucks.: Interview with Department of
     Defense official, Washington, D.C., April 29, 1991.

217 "Wafai Dajani and others . . . They just started up the old network again.":
     "A Fatal Attraction," *Financial Times,* May 3, 1991; interview with U.S.
     intelligence officer, Washington, D.C., May 17, 1993.

218 the name of Robert Gates featured prominently . . . holding back from
     Congress: The documents in question were minutes and memos describing
     a series of senior-level meetings, held in the White House Situation Room in
     April and May 1990, that Gates chaired.

218 new allegations . . . had then gone on to Baghdad.: "Saddam's Secret South
     African Connection," *Financial Times,* May 24, 1991; "*Nightline/Financial
     Times* Arms Sales Report," ABC News, *Nightline,* May 23, 1991.

219 The Agency had been warned . . . later shipped to Iraq.: "CIA Knew of
     Cyanide Exports to Iraq," *Financial Times,* July 3, 1991.

219 The White House was livid . . . to the network.: In the summer of 1991 both
     the White House and the CIA contacted ABC management and the senior
     journalists involved.

219 a former CIA operative and friend of Gates . . . "You might get them in
     trouble,": Interview with former CIA operative involved in the transfer of
     cluster bomb technology from the United States to Chile, Washington,
     D.C., May 16, 1991.

219 "They ought not to accept a rumor. . . . by rumor and insinuation.": "Bush
     Demands Fair Play for Gates Nomination," United Press International,
     July 12, 1991.

220 it brought shivers to those in law enforcement agencies: Telephone inter-
     view with U.S. Customs agent, February 24, 1993.

220 Martinez had a quick solution . . . promised to avoid any conflict of inter-
     est.: "Link to Iraqis Makes Nominee Less Than Best Choice for U.S.
     Attorney," *Miami Sun-Sentinel,* May 13, 1992.

220 an Italian Senate investigation . . . an "international political operation" to
     support Iraq.: "BNL Report Hints at Government Links to Loan Scandal,"

page

Financial Times, February 19, 1992; "Higher-ups Gave OK to Iraqi Loans? Report May Snarl BNL-Atlanta Case," *The Atlanta Constitution,* April 24, 1992.

221 Brent Scowcroft had failed in his efforts to impose the argument of executive privilege.: Interview with former White House officials, Washington, D.C., June 6–7, 1993.

221 Dennis Kane . . . "or any of those documents.": "Loner Gonzalez Toils to Expose White House Role in Years Leading Up to Gulf War," *The Wall Street Journal,* July 31, 1992.

221 it was not really Gonzalez . . . as much frequency as Gonzalez's floor statements.: Private conversations with former State Department official, July 1993. Baker, Eagleburger, and others at State, according to this official, continued to regard Gonzalez as a "flake" who need not be taken seriously. It was the extended campaign of op-ed articles on Iraqgate by William Safire in *The New York Times* that riled Baker and his colleagues the most.

221 an article entitled "Crimes of Iraqgate,": William Safire, "Crimes of Iraqgate," *The New York Times,* May 18, 1992.

221 informed Gonzalez he was damaging "national security" . . . with *any* classified documents.: Telephone interview with congressional staff member, July 2, 1993.

221 told Gonzalez that if more . . . no longer disclose any of the documents.: Safire, "Crimes of Iraqgate," May 18, 1992; telephone interview with congressional staff member, July 2, 1993.

222 Gonzalez retorted . . . "to obstruct a proper and legitimate investigation.": *Congressional Record,* House of Representatives, statement of Congressman Henry Gonzalez, May 18, 1992, H3366–3376.

222 "In the first few months of 1992 . . . Baker's stance allowed us to become a punching bag.": Interview with former White House official, June 6, 1993.

222 "the long-standing practice of the Executive Branch": Letter from Nicholas E. Calio, assistant to the president for legislative affairs, to Henry B. Gonzalez, May 26, 1992.

222 "They just won't testify. They won't go public on Iraqgate,": Interview with aide to Congressman Henry Gonzalez, Washington, D.C., May 27, 1992.

223 "several interesting links" . . . and companies involved with Iraq.: *Congressional Record,* House of Representatives, statements of Congressman Henry Gonzalez, April 25 and May 2, 1991, H2547, H2762.

223 Gonzalez quoted from a Federal Reserve inspection report . . . LBS's business in New York.: *Congressional Record,* Gonzalez statement, May 2, 1991.

223 In 1987, LBS hired Renato Guadagnini: *Proceedings of the Italian Senate,* testimony of Renato Guadagnini to the committee investigating BNL Atlanta (Rome 1992), vol. 18, pp. 456–57.

223 "because I don't want to be asked about this sort of question.": "Kissinger Had BNL Links," *Financial Times,* April 26, 1991.

page

224 "I would like to report . . . the President's personal staff.": House of Representatives, hearing before the Committee on Banking, Finance and Urban Affairs, statement of Chairman Henry Gonzalez, May 21, 1992.

224 Charles Schumer . . . termed Saddam Hussein "President Bush's Frankenstein" . . . "programs, banks, and private companies.": Banking Committee hearing, statement of Congressman Charles Schumer, May 21, 1992.

224 Joe Kennedy, Jr., . . . "to provide embarrassment.": Banking Committee hearing, statement of Congressman Joe Kennedy, Jr., May 21, 1992.

224 Eagleburger . . . finally replied . . . "storage and protection of such materials.": Banking Committee hearing, testimony of Lawrence Eagleburger, May 21, 1992.

225 "Although the records at Kissinger Associates . . . with anyone from BNL.": Banking Committee hearing, testimony of Eagleburger, May 21, 1992.

225 "That statement, I respectfully submit, is patently untrue." . . . influence Saddam to some moderation.": Banking Committee hearing, statement of Congressman Gonzalez, May 21, 1992.

225 Bernie Sanders . . . "let me get you an answer in writing that is accurate.": Banking Committee hearing, testimony of Eagleburger, May 21, 1992.

225 Allen Mendelowitz, a senior official . . . "clearly was a White House initiative.": Banking Committee hearing, testimony of Allan Mendelowitz, May 29, 1992.

226 when the GAO asked the CIA for a briefing . . . some of those minutes were classified.: Banking Committee hearing, testimony of Mendelowitz, May 29, 1992.

FOURTEEN: The Cover-Up Unravels

228 Shoob had been growing more and more suspicious . . . he be jailed.: Telephone interview with Judge Marvin Shoob, August 11, 1993.

228 investigators in the Italian parliament . . . than where he is, on the outside.": "Banker May Help Answer Questions on Iraqi Loans," *The Atlanta Constitution*, June 2, 1992.

229 Sheila Tyler, . . . "says the government is afraid to go to trial.": Telephone interview with Shoob, August 11, 1993.

229 that Drogoul had changed his mind . . . received covert U.S. government approval.: Telephone interview with Sheila Tyler, May 27, 1992; "Guilty Plea May Lead to BNL Trial Cancellation," *Financial Times,* May 28, 1992.

230 A second strange occurrence . . . to the Russell Building.: Telephone interview with Shoob, August 11, 1993.

230 Attorney General Ed Meese wanted the Cubans detained or deported . . . parachutes.": Telephone interview with Shoob, August 11, 1993. For further details, see *Almanac of Federal Judiciary* (Englewood Cliffs, N.J.: Prentice-Hall Law and Business, 1993), vol. 1, pp. 59–60.

page
231 "I do not want to be in a position . . . presented to me at the time of sentence.": United States *vs.* Christopher P. Drogoul, U.S. District Court for the Northern District of Georgia, Atlanta division, case number 1:91-CR-078, statement of Marvin Shoob, June 2, 1992.

231 Shoob went back to his chambers . . . knowledge and involvement in the Iraqi scandal.: Interviews with aides to Marvin Shoob, Atlanta, June 2, 1992.

231 BNL, said congressional investigators . . . under the table.: Interviews with staff of the House Banking Committee, Senate Intelligence Committee, House Agriculture Committee, and House Foreign Affairs Committee, May to October 1992.

232 "Wrongdoing has taken place,": House of Representatives, Committee on the Judiciary, testimony of Congressman Doug Barnard, Jr., chairman, Subcommittee on Commerce and Monetary Affairs, House Committee on Government Operations, June 2, 1992; "Judge Wants Special Prosecutor in Iraq-loan Case," *The Atlanta Constitution,* June 3, 1992.

232 Leahy . . . accused the Bush administration of misleading Congress . . . U.S. policy toward Iraq.: House of Representatives, Committee on the Judiciary, testimony of Senator Patrick Leahy, chairman, Senate Agriculture Committee, June 2, 1992.

232 "The stop in Rome is necessary . . . subjects of our criminal investigation.": Justice Department, Northern District of Georgia, letter from Robert L. Barr, U.S. attorney, to Zane Kelley, Federal Reserve Bank of Atlanta, January 9, 1990.

233 Inman . . . revealed in the letter to the judge . . . including the CIA.: Letter from Admiral Bobby Ray Inman to the Honorable Louis C. Bechtel, chief judge, U.S. District Court, Eastern District of Pennsylvania, April 27, 1992.

233 The fact that an intelligence official . . . raised further concern among Iraqgate investigators.: Interviews with law enforcement officials and congressional staff, June 1992.

233 The General Accounting Office had already told . . . by the Rostow group: House of Representatives, Committee on Banking, Finance and Urban Affairs, statement of Alan Mendelowitz, General Accounting Office, May 29, 1992.

233 In Rio de Janeiro . . . "That policy was not successful.": Administration of George Bush, official records, 1992, June 13, 1992, p. 1052.

234 Frank Lemay . . . no regrets about sounding the alarm.: House of Representatives, Committee on the Judiciary, testimony of Frank Lemay, June 23, 1992.

234 "Obstruction of Congress, false statements, and perjury . . . and prosecutorial discretion.": House of Representatives, Committee on the Judiciary, statement of Congressman Jack Brooks, chairman, July 9, 1992.

234 In testimony before the Judiciary Committee . . . Dennis Kloske as the man

page

responsible for the changes.: House of Representatives, Committee on the Judiciary, testimony of Frank DeGeorge, inspector general, Department of Commerce, June 23, 1992.

234 But Kloske . . . the altered records before they were submitted to Congress.: "Testimony on Iraq Export List Is Contradicted," *The Los Angeles Times,* June 24, 1992.

234 Richard Crowder . . . "Mr. Wade said no.": House of Representatives, Committee on Banking, Finance and Urban Affairs, testimony of Richard Crowder, undersecretary of agriculture, May 21, 1992.

234 Wade told Senate Agriculture Committee investigators . . . "I never have.": Interview by U.S. Senate Agriculture Committee with Art Wade, June 30, 1992.

235 Elliot Richardson . . . probably government wrongdoing in the Iraqgate saga.: Conversation with Elliot Richardson, July 1992.

235 The president was finding . . . chemical weapons capabilities.: "Digging Deeper in Iraqgate," *The New York Times,* July 6, 1992.

235 "This is not an attempt to second-guess . . . may have broken the law.": House of Representatives, Committee on the Judiciary, statement of Congressman Jack Brooks, chairman, July 9, 1992.

236 the conspiracy allegations were based . . . involved in Iraqi policy.: Interviews with staff of the House Judiciary and Banking committees, July 1992.

237 This was Jay Bybee . . . "was indicting Iraqi officials.": "House Panel Urges Special Counsel for Iraq Inquiry," *The New York Times,* July 10, 1992.

237 Jack Brooks, fuming . . . "stonewalling, plain and simple.": "Justice Dept. Rebuffs Democrats on Special Prosecutor on Iraqi Aid," *The New York Times,* August 11, 1992.

237 The Senate Intelligence Committee . . . Robert Gates, the CIA director.: Interviews with State Department officials, Washington, D.C., July 1992.

238 his sister contacted Bobby Lee Cooke, a prominent Southern trial lawyer: Interview with Bobby Lee Cooke, Atlanta, September 14, 1992.

238 Brill sought almost immediately . . . When it was Cooke's turn to respond . . .: United States *v.* Christopher P. Drogoul, U.S. District Court for the Northern District of Georgia, Atlanta Division, case # 1:91-CR-078, hearing, September 14, 1992. The author was present at the hearing.

239 "This case is the mother of all cover-ups," . . . to provide U.S.-backed loans.: "White House Accused of Iraqi Loan Cover-Up," *Financial Times,* September 15, 1992.

239 questioning of Art Wade, . . . a single member of the BNL board.: "Investigator of BNL Admits Inexperience," *The Wall Street Journal,* September 17, 1992.

239 questioned a previous lawyer for Drogoul . . . Paul Von Wedel . . . to U.S. intelligence.: "BNL Judge Rejects Government Claim That Manager Acted Alone in Fraud," *The Wall Street Journal,* September 23, 1992; "Former

BNL Aide Says Rome Officials Knew of Branch's Loans to Iraq," *The Wall Street Journal,* September 24, 1992.

239 Gonzalez took the unusual step . . . "had been witting of BNL-Atlanta's activities.": Press release from the House Banking, Finance and Urban Affairs Committee, September 14, 1992.

239 CIA simply prepared a three-page document . . . publicly available sources.: U.S. Senate, Select Committee on Intelligence, *The Intelligence Community's Involvement in the Banca Nazionale Del Lavoro (BNL) Affair,* 103rd Cong., 1st sess., February 1993, p. 4.

240 three CIA reports . . . "a lone wolf type operation.": "Rome Aware of BNL Iraqi Loans," *Financial Times,* September 30, 1992.

240 two former BNL executives . . . "political cover in Rome for the bank,": Interview with BNL executives, Milan, August 30 and September 20, 1992; "Head Office of Italian Bank May Have Approved Iraq Loans," *Financial Times,* September 28, 1992.

240 BNL documents in court . . . that the bank not be indicted.: "Italy Pressured U.S. over Iraqi Loan Affair," *Financial Times,* October 1, 1992.

241 a fifteen-page court order . . . "The court concludes" . . . an independent prosecutor be named to investigate this matter.": United States *v.* Drogoul, order of Judge Marvin Shoob, October 5, 1992.

241 remove himself from the trial . . . strong views about the case.: "U.S. Backs Trial in Bank-Loan Case," *The Wall Street Journal,* October 2, 1992; "Judge Orders Full Trial in BNL Loans Case," *Financial Times,* October 2, 1992.

242 Senator Boren soon learned . . . Judge Shoob, the Atlanta prosecutors and Congress.: Senate Select Committee on Intelligence, *Intelligence Community's Involvement,* p. 6.; interviews with staff of Senate Select Committee on Intelligence, Washington, D.C., October 8, 1992.

242 Gates came up with a solution . . . "an honest mistake.": Conversation with Mike Mansfield, CIA spokesman, October 7, 1992; "CIA Chief Orders Investigation of Statements in Iraq Bank Case," *The New York Times,* October 8, 1992.

242 Elizabeth Rindskopf . . . "We did not handle ourselves well.": "Justice Department Role Cited in Deception on Iraq Loan Date," *The New York Times,* October 10, 1992.

243 The FBI was asked . . . the FBI was merely a participant.: "Justice Dept. Now Clashes with FBI over Inquiry into Bank Loans to Iraq," *The New York Times,* October 12, 1992.

243 The FBI director was himself facing . . . conduct an independent investigation.": "Justice Department Criminal Unit Is Investigating FBI Chief," *The New York Times,* October 14, 1992.

243 Sessions himself was suspicious about the timing . . . "a warning shot across the bow.": Telephone interview with William Sessions, July 30, 1993.

244 Senator Howard Metzenbaum . . . Boren wrote to Barr demanding "a truly

page

independent investigation.": "Administration Is Again Asked to Begin Independent Inquiry into BNL Scandal," *The Wall Street Journal,* October 14, 1992; letter from Senator Howard Metzenbaum to Attorney General William Barr, October 13, 1992.

244   Standing at Lacey's side . . . "media sensationalism.": "Counsel Named to Probe BNL Loans Scandal," *Financial Times,* October 17, 1992.

244   Barr did let slip . . . Boyden Gray to tell him of his plans.: Remarks by Attorney General William Barr at Department of Justice press conference, October 16, 1992, as reported by George Graham, Washington correspondent, *Financial Times.*

245   Jack Brooks said . . . "and not to the American public.": "Barr Appoints Special Counsel in BNL Inquiry," *The Wall Street Journal,* October 19, 1992.

245   "George Bush is presiding over . . . to manage this cover-up.": "Gore Likens Iraq Issue to Watergate Coverup," *The Los Angeles Times,* October 16, 1992.

245   "We were making agricultural loans. . . . wiped out in the war.": "An Interview with President George Bush," CNN, *Larry King Live,* October 4, 1992.

245   "To allege that we were building up his arms . . . is simply fallacious.": "Bush on Iraqgate," *The New York Times,* October 8, 1992.

245   helped Brent Scowcroft draft an op-ed article . . . "low-level computers and heavy-duty trucks.": "We didn't coddle Saddam," *The Washington Post,* October 10, 1992.

245   Almost the same words were used by Lawrence Eagleburger: Lawrence Eagleburger, letter to the editor, *The New York Times,* October 15, 1992.

245   "If you create Saddam Hussein . . . the family of nations.": "President Comes Out Slugging in Final Debate: Clinton and Perot Accuse Bush of Mishandling Iraq," *The Washington Post,* October 20, 1992.

246   "There hasn't been one single scintilla of evidence": "Bush Dealings with Saddam Questioned; Evidence Does Not Support Perot's Assertions on Iraq," *The Washington Post,* October 20, 1992.

246   David Kay . . . "used in Iraq's nuclear program.": "Arms Experts Challenge Bush Claim on U.S. Aid to Iraq," *The Los Angeles Times,* October 22, 1992.

246   In a television interview the following week . . . Let him make the determination,": Interview with President George Bush, ABC News, *Prime Time Live,* October 29, 1992.

246   a preliminary determination . . . "sufficiently specific and credible": "US Closer to Special Prosecutor," *Financial Times,* November 14, 1992.

247   a member of former Prime Minister Margaret Thatcher's government stepped up to the witness box: Richard Donkin, a London-based research associate of the author, was present at the Old Bailey trial on November 4, 1992.

247   a secret offer of immunity . . . in the United States.: Letter to Kenneth

page

Millwood from Rimantas Rukstele and Gale McKenzie, U.S. attorney's office, Atlanta, January 22, 1991.

247   In November 1989, the CIA had reported . . . ballistic missile development programs.": Directorate of Intelligence, "Repercussions of the BNL-Atlanta Scandal," CIA, November 6, 1989.

247   the U.S. Treasury . . . frozen its assets.: "Bush Administration Knew About Arms Network," *Financial Times,* November 11, 1992.

247   Matrix Churchill had shipped special lathes . . . development of nuclear weapons.: David Leigh, *Betrayed* (London: Bloomsbury, 1993), p. xii; *Congressional Record,* House of Representatives, "More Details on Matrix Churchill Corporation," statement of Congressman Henry Gonzalez, September 21, 1992.

248   four ministers in John Major's government . . . to be released during the trial.: Commissioners of Customs and Excise *vs.* Henderson, Abraham and Allen: Public Interest Immunity Certificates, signed by Kenneth Clarke, Tristan Garel-Jones, Michael Heseltine, and Malcolm Rifkind, September 1992.

248   Such was the secrecy surrounding these agencies: Leigh, *Betrayed,* p. 81.

248   Henderson's own dealings with Cardoen . . . known in detail to British intelligence.: Leigh, *Betrayed,* p. 144; "DTI knew of Iraqi Deal, Court Told," *Financial Times,* October 14, 1992.

248   Matrix received British government loan guarantees . . . "involved in chemical weapons manufacture.": London, Export Credit Guarantee Department documentation.

249   Evidence of the Matrix Churchill shipments . . . "to protect sources.": Paul Henderson, *The Unlikely Spy* (London: Bloomsbury, 1993), p. 188.

249   a Matrix executive had worked for MI6 . . . selling to Iraq.: "MI6 Link with Toolmaker Alleged," *Financial Times,* October 15, 1992.

249   An August 1989 British intelligence telegram . . . other British and European companies involved in procurement.: London, SECRET British intelligence (MI6) memorandum, August 23, 1989, describing the reaction of Paul Henderson of Matrix to reports in the *Financial Times* that BNL was under investigation. The telegram described dealings between BNL and Matrix Churchill.

249   damage Henderson's cover . . . "That was one of the considerations,": "DTI Admits Company Chief Worked for MI6," *Financial Times,* October 27, 1992.

249   a secret February 1989 report . . . "would remain freely available to Iraq.": London, SECRET memorandum, Foreign Office, Middle East Department, "Matrix Churchill: Export of Lathe Equipment to Iraq," from Stephen Lillie to Department of Trade and Industry and Ministry of Defence, February 1, 1989.

250   Geoffrey Robertson . . . about Bull and his supergun in May 1988: Leigh,

page

Betrayed, p. 137; "MI5 told of plan for Iraqi gun in 1988," *Financial Times*, November 3, 1992.

250 Secret documents . . . machine tools for the supergun a year later: London, SECRET British intelligence memorandum, "Iraqi Long Range Projectile," October 30, 1989.

250 Bush administration was approving . . . technology to Iraq's supergun project.: "Washington Link to Iraqi Supergun," *Financial Times*, October 26, 1992.

250 The information provided by Gutteridge . . . passed straight to the CIA.: Henderson, *Unlikely Spy*, p. 171.

250 "There are very few people . . . sent to a "very high ministerial level.".: "MI6 Praises Iraq Exports Case Defendant," *Financial Times*, November 4, 1992.

251 one memo, marked "Advice to Prime Minister,": London, confidential summary record of the Inter-Departmental Committee on Defence Sales to Iran and Iraq, February 24, 1988.

251 "Alan is a charming fellow, but not a natural team player.": Interview with former British cabinet minister, London, July 8, 1993.

251 "tiresome and intrusive": Leigh, *Betrayed*, p. 215.

251 "to emphasize their peaceful" rather than military aspects.: "Tory Ex-Minister Knew Exports Could Make Arms," *Financial Times*, November 5, 1993.

251 "I do not think it was principally . . . a matter for Whitehall cosmetics.": Leigh, *Betrayed*, p. 252.

252 asked how Major could reconcile the sale of machine tools . . . a full embargo since August 1990.: "Judicial Inquiry Ordered into Iraqi Defense Contracts," *Financial Times*, November 21, 1992.

252 Soon the prime minister . . . denials that he himself had been directly involved: "Major Rejects Matrix Claims," *Financial Times*, November 21, 1992.

252 Major did admit that as foreign secretary . . . media interest in Iraq's procurement network.: "Major Faces New Questions on Arms for Iraq," *The Times*, November 16, 1992.

253 accused of having misled Parliament . . . supplied arms to Iraq.: "Don't Tell the Public," *The Independent*, November 15, 1992.

253 Geoffrey Robertson, the lawyer . . . "approval from the White House.": Telephone interview with Geoffrey Robertson, September 23, 1993.

253 The attorney general was "attempting to run out . . . I don't think prosecutors should be independent.": "House Judiciary Chairman Accuses Barr of Foot-Dragging in Probe of Iraqgate," *The Wall Street Journal*, November 16, 1992; "Facing His Term's End, Barr Defends His Record," *The New York Times*, November 23, 1992.

253 On December 9, Judge Lacey called a press conference . . . "Thank you.":

page

Comments made by Judge Frederick Lacey, independent counsel, at his press conference, Washington, D.C., December 9, 1992.

254 billing the Justice Department $372,392 for his work.: Justice Department, "Summary of Expenses for Investigation by Special Counsel Frederick Lacey in the BNL Scandal," April 6, 1993.

255 He pledged that he would ask his attorney general: "Clinton Says He'll Consider Inquiry into Bank Case Involving Iraq," *The New York Times,* December 11, 1992.

255 "pretty much accepted the Justice Department's version" . . . "a whitewash.": "Prosecutors Were Split on BNL Probe," *The Atlanta Constitution,* December 13, 1992.

255 "We spent about one and a half hours . . . talking mostly about himself": Telephone interview with Shoob, August 11, 1993.

255 he was "certain" that no one at BNL Rome headquarters ever knew: Lacey press conference, December 9, 1992, transcript.

255 In Rome, BNL's top management heard this news: Interview with former BNL executives, Rome, February 1993.

255 BNL filed a little-noticed lawsuit . . . make good on the CCC guarantees that backed them.: Banca Nazionale del Lavoro (BNL) *v.* the United States of America, U.S. Court of Federal Claims, Washington, D.C., December 15, 1992.

255 BNL quietly informed three of its midlevel executives . . . investigation of the Iraqi loans saga.: Interviews with former BNL executives, Rome, April–May 1993.

256 "Frankly, we were furious . . . we couldn't understand why.": Conversation with senior attorney, Federal Reserve System, Washington, D.C., March 8, 1993.

256 a sharply worded letter from the Federal Reserve: Board of Governors of the Federal Reserve System, letter from John Kuray, senior attorney, to Walter Driver, Jr., BNL attorney, Atlanta, December 22, 1992.

256 Giampiero Cantoni was under pressure . . . the government was calling the shots.: Interview with former BNL executives, Rome, May 22, 1993.

256 "We were under pressure . . . go slowly on Atlanta,": Interview with former deputy general manager of BNL, Rome, May 22, 1993.

256 The problem . . . considered affairs of state and not merely banking transactions.: Interview with three former BNL executives and one current BNL executive, Rome, February and April 1993.

256 flurry of cable traffic: BNL Atlanta, copies of telex traffic, 1988–89.

257 "Some of us in the Atlanta task force . . . It was very frustrating,": Interview with Gianmaria Sartoretti, Rome, April 5, 1993.

257 he went before the Italian Senate commission . . . having financed the purchase of arms by *Iran.: Proceedings of the Italian Senate,* memorandum

from Gianmaria Sartoretti to the committee investigating BNL Atlanta, Rome, September 1991.

257   Sartoretti was among the three BNL executives . . . from Rome to Atlanta.: Interviews with former BNL executives, Rome, April 6, 1993.

257   a long letter of protest to Cantoni in April 1991 . . . ultimately signed in Rome.: BNL Rome, letter from Pierdomenico Gallo, member of the board, to Giampiero Cantoni, chairman, April 17, 1991.

257   Within days of Gallo's complaint . . . to investigate Gallo's staff.: BNL, Rome, executive committee minutes, June 1991; copy of letter from Francesco Petti to Gianmaria Sartoretti with list of questions, April 29, 1991.

257   During a board meeting . . . Gallo read his complaints out to the entire board.: BNL executive committee minutes, June 12, 1991.

258   no longer accepted Cantoni's frequent denials: *Proceedings of the Italian Senate,* final report of the Italian Senate committee investigating BNL Atlanta, Rome, 1992, p. 7.

258   "Atlanta was a deplorable . . . but what is far more serious is this insistent cover-up.": Final report of the committee investigating BNL Atlanta, p. 32.

258   a 163-page report on the BNL affair . . . the billions of dollars of Iraqi loans made by Atlanta.: "BNL HQ Knew of Iraq Scandal," *Financial Times,* February 7, 1993.

258   another report was released . . . The entire matter, said Gates, was a "train wreck.": CIA, Office of the Inspector General, "CIA's Handling of BNL-Related Matters" (unclassified summary), January 14, 1993; "Reports Attack CIA for Its Role in BNL Case," *The Wall Street Journal,* February 8, 1993.

FIFTEEN: The Fate of the Foot Soldiers

259   "I was a career person, . . . they wanted me to know I had done the right thing.": Telephone interviews with Frank Lemay, July 23, 1993, and August 17, 1993.

260   "Frank became persona non grata at State . . . he was punished.": Telephone interview with a close friend of Frank Lemay, July 23, 1993.

260   "It was a shitty way for politicians to handle a career civil servant.": Interview with Lemay, August 17, 1993.

260   his regular call to New York from a pay phone.: The regular call Haobsh made was to the author, who had been in continuous contact with him since March 1992. During a meeting with Haobsh on March 1, 1993, Haobsh reported a growing pattern of harassment. It was arranged that Haobsh and the author would make daily contact wherever possible, and details of any harassment would be logged. Over the following weeks, a list of vehicles cruising Haobsh's house was developed and provided to law enforcement authorities. Between March 1 and May 22, Haobsh reported eight vehicles

surveilling his home, as part of a pattern of harassment that included hang-up telephone and fax calls and an unauthorized entry into his house. Local law enforcement authorities in Atlanta assisted in attempting to trace the vehicles.

260   had walked across the boundaries of the law: Interview with Fred Haobsh, Dallas, April 6, 1992.

261   traced back to his meeting in New York with Hussein Kamel: Interview with Fred Haobsh, New York, March 30, 1993.

261   he had taken a perverse liking to the risks: Conversation with Fred Haobsh, Cairo, May 11, 1993.

261   It was a lesson he failed to grasp back in 1983: Interview with Fred Haobsh, Atlanta, March 1, 1993.

262   met an Agency man in a hotel room: Interview with Haobsh, April 6, 1992.

262   "I will always regret the moment I lifted a finger for the CIA,": Interview with Haobsh, March 30, 1993.

262   "He said I should get myself a gun . . . told me where to buy it.": Interview with Haobsh, March 1, 1993.

262   Haobsh tried selling carpets and floor coverings in Dallas: Interview with Fred and Nancy Haobsh, Atlanta, March 1, 1993.

263   Haobsh literally wept when he saw it.: Interview with Haobsh, April 6, 1992.

264   questioning the nature of the work he had done.: Interview with Fred Haobsh, New York, March 13, 1993.

264   "I had always heard . . . I stopped working for them.": Interview with Haobsh, April 6, 1992.

264   The CIA's promises: Interview with Haobsh, March 1, 1993.

264   "we cannot be of much more assistance to him.": Correspondence between Fred Haobsh and Senator Lloyd Bentsen, July 8, 1991, et seq., and Senator Phil Gramm, July 5, 1991, et seq.

264   he contacted a journalist: In March 1992, Fred Haobsh made contact with the author. He had seen him a number of times on ABC News, *Nightline,* during 1991, in the course of a joint *Nightline/Financial Times* investigation into U.S. policy toward Iraq.

265   in crude letters twelve inches high, was the word KILL: Videotape of the damaged car was shot by a colleague of the author.

265   only one night a week when the phone did not ring: Interview with Haobsh, March 1, 1993.

265   ran a license plate check on the red Pontiac: Information on the registration and ownership of the car was provided to Haobsh and the author by law enforcement authorities.

265   "It's the kind of thing . . . he is being hung out to dry.": Interview with U.S. intelligence officer, Washington, D.C., May 17, 1993.

page

265 he would go over and over his life since his trips to Baghdad ten years earlier: Interview with Haobsh, March 1, 1993.

266 He had become the prisoner of a Kafkaesque nightmare: This is the impression gained by the author as a result of five formal interviews and dozens of telephone conversations and personal communications between Haobsh and himself over a fifteen-month period.

266 Frank Machon was sitting, similarly despondent, in the cramped office of his empty warehouse in Glasgow.: Interviews with Frank Machon, Glasgow, June 3–4, 1993.

266 He was suffering, although he wouldn't willingly admit it.: Interviews with Frank Machon, Glasgow, May 6–7 and June 3–4, 1993.

266 His wife, Marion, was as angry and disillusioned as he was.: Interviews with Marion Machon, Glasgow, April 16 and May 6, 1993.

266 The warehouse was his fortress: Interviews with Machon, June 3–4, 1993.

267 He had briefly made the news: "Papers Prove Sanctions-Busting to Iraq," *The Scotsman,* November 24, 1992; "Parliament and Politics: Move to End Arms Trade," *The Scotsman,* June 16, 1993; "Thatcher Told of Arms for Iraq," *The Guardian,* June 16, 1993.

267 Allivane International Limited, the covert vehicle: Interview with former executive of Allivane International Limited, Glasgow, June 3, 1993.

267 On December 23, 1988, Machon wrote to Thatcher: "Strictly private and confidential" letter from Frank Machon to Prime Minister Margaret Thatcher, December 23, 1988.

267 "I never wanted to damage my country or my prime minister . . . I'll not give up,": Interview with Machon, June 3, 1993.

268 He put his lawyer in London on alert: Interview with Machon, Glasgow, May 13, 1993.

268 Machon had not been called.: Interview with Machon, June 4, 1993.

269 Pale and bedraggled in a khaki uniform: Interview with Christopher Drogoul, Atlanta, April 1, 1993.

269 Visitors to the penitentiary: The author visited Christopher Drogoul on two occasions in the spring of 1993, spending more than eight hours with him in the visitors' room of the Atlanta penitentiary.

269 file for bankruptcy protection: Conversations with Robert Simels, attorney for Christopher Drogoul, New York, August 1993.

269 "I was a tool of both the Italians and the Americans,": Interview with Christopher Drogoul, April 1, 1993.

269 approached the endless debriefings with his lawyers with a stoic, weary determination.: The author observed Drogoul in conversation with his chief defense lawyer in April 1993.

270 "Chris is certainly no rocket scientist.": Conversation with Christopher Drogoul's sister, Atlanta, September 17, 1992.

page
270   a bit player in the broader story: Telephone interview with Christopher
      Drogoul, July 19, 1993.

      SIXTEEN: **Endgame**

271   The missiles . . . a dozen buildings: "Bush Launches Missile Attack on a
      Baghdad Industrial Park as Washington Greets Clinton," *The New York
      Times*, January 18, 1993.
271   the machine tools at Zaafaraniya . . . a company called Matrix Churchill.:
      Telephone interview with David Kay, former chief UN nuclear weapons
      inspector in Iraq, August 18, 1993.
271   the civilian casualties proved an embarrassment to Washington . . . and in
      Europe.: "U.S. Leads Further Attacks on Iraqi Antiaircraft Sites; Admits Its
      Missile Hit Hotel," *The New York Times,* January 19, 1993.
272   The White House justified the missile barrage. . . . UN weapons inspec-
      tors.: "Bush Launches Missile Attack," *The New York Times.*
272   David Kay, the former chief nuclear weapons inspector . . . "We said that
      this was the ultimate cover-up—to bomb the place.": Telephone interview
      with David Kay, August 18, 1993.
272   he also promised to guarantee . . . a gesture of goodwill toward Bill Clinton:
      Facts on File World News Digest, January 21, 1993, p. 29.
273   American policy on Iraq had not changed: "Understanding Orders, U.S.
      Jets Hit Iraqi Radar Seen as a Threat," *The New York Times,* January 22,
      1993.
273   they would mouth . . . "put it behind us and move on.": Conversations with
      congressional staff in the House and Senate, January–February 1993.
273   The Federal Reserve . . . dispatched a team of investigators to Rome.: "Fed
      Reopens Inquiry into BNL Loans," *Financial Times,* March 9, 1993.
273   he would investigate the degree to which London had shared . . . and their
      funding by BNL's Atlanta branch.: "Wider Probe into BNL Affair
      Pledged," *Financial Times,* January 22, 1993.
273   John Major was asked in Parliament to reveal the extent of its knowledge of
      illegal arms-dealing with both Iran and Iraq.: "Government Questioned
      over Illegal Arms Trade," *The Independent,* March 17, 1993.
274   Scott had spent the winter sifting through nearly thirty thousand docu-
      ments: "Sceptics Fear Iraq Arms Inquiry May Be Lost in Whitehall Sands,"
      Daily Telegraph, February 5, 1993.
274   he leaned back in his chair . . . take the lead.: These and other observations
      from the Scott inquiry were based on the presence at a number of Scott's
      hearings of Richard Donkin, a London-based research associate of the
      author.
274   "holding a gun pointing at the heart of government.": "Major Sets Date to
      Testify at Iraq Arms Probe," *Financial Times,* August 1, 1992.

page

274 one former minister who had personally tried . . . go through the ritual witch hunt that follows a failed policy: Interview with former British government minister, London, June 7, 1993.

274 "A lawyer always sees the pathology . . . both sides to exhaust each other.": Interview with former British cabinet minister, London, July 8, 1993.

274 Sir David Miers . . . "how the guidelines should be interpreted,": "Arms Sales Did Not Matter," *The Guardian,* July 21, 1993.

275 Lord Scott, in answer . . . "to prolong or exacerbate the conflict.": "Scott Inquiry," *Daily Telegraph,* July 29, 1993; "U.K. Designed Missile Site for Iraq: Concrete Bunker Deal May Have Contravened British Foreign Policy," *Financial Times,* July 2, 1991.

275 A very senior aide to former Prime Minister Thatcher . . . We used to encourage our businessmen to go over to Baghdad trade fairs and sell everything they could, within the guidelines,": Interview with a former Downing Street official, London, July 9, 1993.

275 Confidential documents show that . . . it was "preferable not to have to announce publicly any change.": London, Department of Trade and Industry, confidential letter "End of the Gulf War: Defence Sales Guidelines," from Alan Clark, minister for trade, to William Waldegrave, minister of state, Foreign Office, November 4, 1988; confidential letter from William Waldegrave to Alan Clark, April 27, 1989.

275 When it was Waldegrave's turn . . . "the wrong judgment": "UK Minister Blames Intelligence Lapse for Iraqi Exports 'Error,' " *Financial Times,* October 3, 1993.

276 . . . Waldegrave, who by 1993 . . . "this kind of subject should be debated?": "Waldegrave on Defensive in Iraq case," *Financial Times,* September 24, 1993; "I Did Not Mislead MPs Says Waldegrave," Press Association, September 22, 1993.

276 Mark Higson, the former Iraq desk officer . . . "dishonest" answers from Sir Geoffrey Howe.: "Howe Urged Silence on Iraq Arms," *The Guardian,* July 28, 1993.

276 fear that it would look "very cynical" . . . I did my duty.": "Howe urged silence," *The Guardian.*

276 when Egerton was asked . . . "I did not like the smell of it.": "Iraq Arms Inquiry Told of Saudi Deals," *Financial Times,* June 16, 1993; "Interference in Iraq Trial a Disgrace," *Daily Telegraph,* June 16, 1993.

276 telling Scott that Her Majesty's government had been aware . . . chemical warfare equipment to Iraq.: The Right Honourable Lord Justice Scott, Inquiry into Exports of Defence Equipment and Dual Use Goods to Iraq (The Scott Inquiry), June 22, 1993; "Soldiers at the Heart of Arms Sales Control," *The Independent,* June 23, 1993.

277 Glazebrook explained not only how Jordan . . . "that things were going on behind my back,": The Scott Inquiry, June 21, 1993; "Chemical Warfare

page

　　　Equipment Sold by MoD Likely to Have Gone to Iraq," *The Guardian,*
　　　June 22, 1993.

277　International Military Services . . . "did nothing without the full knowledge
　　　and approval of the government.": Interview with former director of Inter-
　　　national Military Services, London, May 21, 1993.

277　he told Scott . . . details of the sales had been sent directly to Prime Minister
　　　Thatcher: The Scott Inquiry, June 22, 1993.

277　Mark Gutteridge . . . "She knew what was going on,": Interview with Mark
　　　Gutteridge, London, November 1992.

277　"were to be used for making shells" . . . "as she was involved last time":
　　　"The Scott Inquiry: Thatcher Approved Exports of Lathes to Iraq, Says
　　　Memo," *The Daily Telegraph,* October 8, 1993; "Scott Inquiry: Thatcher
　　　'Directly Implicated' in Approving Exports for Arming Iraq," *The Guard-
　　　ian,* October 8, 1993.

278　"the missing link": Telephone interview with Geoffrey Robertson, October
　　　9, 1993.

278　until July 1989 had included responsibility for the loan-guarantee program
　　　for Iraq: Commissioners of Customs and Excise *v.* Henderson, Abraham
　　　and Allen (the Matrix Churchill trial), court documents.

278　the government had allowed its ministers . . . And Parliament . . . *had* been
　　　misled: Interview with former board member of U.K. company and confi-
　　　dant of Margaret Thatcher, London, May 22, 1993.

278　it was dawning on officials . . . handling of Iraqgate.: Interview with a senior
　　　U.S. prosecutor, New York, June 3, 1993.

279　The Justice Department was responding . . . "and raising obvious con-
　　　flicts.": Banca Nazionale del Lavoro (BNL) *v.* the United States of America,
　　　U.S. Court of Federal Claims, Washington, D.C., "Defendant's motion to
　　　dismiss for Lack of Jurisdiction, or in the Alternative, for a Stay," April 23,
　　　1993.

279　Giacomo Pedde was convicted . . . weapons sales in the mid-1980s to *Iran.*:
　　　"BNL Convictions in Italy Raise Questions about Atlanta Case," *The At-
　　　lanta Constitution,* May 14, 1993; "Chiesta la condanna dell'ex presidente
　　　della BNL. Il ruolo de servizi," *La Repubblica,* Rome, April 17, 1993.

279　months before, . . . but he never showed up.: The author was present
　　　in court when Judge Shoob made the request of the BNL attorneys that
　　　they ask Pedde to come and testify in the September 1992 Drogoul hear-
　　　ings.

279　the Italian prosecutor . . . in "the stink" of intelligence agencies.: "Chiesta la
　　　condanna dell'ex presidente della BNL. Il ruolo dei servizi," *La Repubblica*,
　　　April 17, 1993.

279　"That's a fair statement . . . The whole story is really about spies more
　　　than bankers.": Conversation with Italian central bank official, Rome, May
　　　21, 1993.

page

279 the CIA . . . for bombs that went to Iraq.: Conversations with U.S. law enforcement officials, Miami, July 1991, February 1993, May 1993.

280 "I was furious . . . for military purposes.": Interview with U.S. law enforcement official, New York, April 15, 1993; CIA, Office of General Counsel, letter by secure telefax, "Re: Cardoen Export Investigation," from John Greer, assistant general counsel, to Eduardo Palmer, assistant U.S. attorney, Miami, February 12, 1993. The report referred to was a confidential CIA report, "Chilean zirconium pellet purchase," dated January 1984.

280 "American officials patted me on the back," . . . to provide cluster bombs and factories to Iraq.: "Is He Merchant of Death or Scapegoat for U.S.?," *The New York Times,* May 15, 1993; "U.S. Weighs Action Against Chilean over Arms for Iraq," *Financial Times,* May 17, 1993.

280 The two were charged with the illegal export of zirconium: "Two Accused of Selling Arms Material to Iraq," *The Los Angeles Times,* May 27, 1993.

280 "The Bush administration tried to produce some scapegoats." . . . was being used to make weapons for Iraq.: London, BBC Television, Interview with Carlos Cardoen, June 2, 1993.

280 "The very government . . . knew of, approved of, and solicited the conduct it now deems illegal.": "Companies May Face Charges on Iraq Sales," *Financial Times,* May 28, 1993.

280 a rather significant conversation . . . an extension of a *government-to-government* agreement between Italy and Iraq.: United States *v.* Christopher P. Drogoul, U.S. District Court, Northern District of Georgia, Atlanta Division, "Motion to Disqualify the Department of Justice," June 25, 1993.

281 "The aim of the subpoena," explained Simels . . . "the Italian government on this matter.": Interview with Robert Simels, New York, July 13, 1993; "Subpoena for Bush in BNL Affair," *Financial Times,* July 14, 1993.

281 the question of what James Baker knew and when he knew it: This was the view of numerous members of Congress, their staffs, and law enforcement officials with whom the author discussed the matter between 1991 and 1993.

282 "brought Saddam to the belief . . . the threat of Saddam is still there.": Interview with Alexander Haig, Washington, D.C., June 7, 1993.

282 "He believes that to fairly make the case . . . he would not suggest otherwise.": "The Spoils of the Gulf War," *The New Yorker,* September 6, 1993.

282 Baker was absolutely unwilling to speak about the tilt years or the BNL affair or any other subject related to Iraq.: The author requested comments from James Baker through Mr. Baker's public relations spokesperson, Margaret Tutwiler. Ms. Tutwiler informed the author on August 19, 1993, that "Secretary Baker has no comment for your book."

282 on two separate occasions . . . it was to exert *too much* pressure on Saddam Hussein: Interviews with Boyden Gray, Washington, D.C., May 5, 1993, and May 27, 1993.

page

283   "If there was anything we did wrong, . . . No wonder he went marching into
       Kuwait.": Interview with Boyden Gray, May 27, 1993.

283   "I think the government entered . . . didn't want that information to come
       out.: Telephone interview with Judge Marvin Shoob, August 11, 1993.

283   he put them on probation . . . "wrongdoing by a branch bank's em-
       ployees.": "Bit Players Sentenced to Probation in BNL Case: Judge Con-
       cludes Atlanta Branch Did Not Act Alone," *The Atlanta Constitution,*
       August 24, 1993.

283   "If Judge Lacey . . . medals instead of jail terms.": "Judge Scoffs at Defense
       of Bush on Iraq," *The New York Times,* August 24, 1993.

284   "pawns or bit players in a far larger and wider-ranging sophisticated con-
       spiracy . . . the governments of the United States, England, Italy, and Iraq.":
       United States *v.* Christopher P. Drogoul, U.S. District Court, Northern
       District of Georgia, Atlanta Division, order of Judge Marvin Shoob, August
       23, 1993.

284   "it was our estimate . . . it was pointless to commit the government to a four-
       to-six-month-long trial.": Telephone interview with Justice Department
       official, September 2, 1993.

284   Hogan revealed what was really going on . . . "no matter who it makes
       happy.": Telephone interview with John Hogan, special assistant to Attor-
       ney General Janet Reno, September 14, 1993.

285   "I doubt this will ever come out . . . for political reasons.": Conversation
       with officials from the Guardia di Finanza and the British Home Office,
       September 15, 1993.

INDEX